Approaches to

Childhood Education

Approaches to Early Childhood Education

Fifth Edition

Jaipaul L. Roopnarine
Syracuse University

James E. Johnson
The Pennsylvania State University

Merrill
is an imprint of

Upper Saddle River, New Jersey
Columbus, Ohio

Library of Congress Cataloging-in-Publication Data
Approaches to early childhood education / [ed. by] Jaipaul L. Roopnarine, James E. Johnson.—5th ed.
p. cm.
Includes bibliographical references and index.
ISBN-13: 879-0-13-512628-8
ISBN-10: 0-13-512628-2
1. Early childhood education—United States. 2. Educational innovations—United States. 3. Early childhood educators—Training of—United States. 4. Inclusive education—United States. 5. Multicultural education—United States. I. Roopnarine, Jaipaul L. II. Johnson, James E. (James Ewald)
LB1139.25.A66 2009
372.21—dc22

2008021776

Vice President and Executive Publisher: Jeffery W. Johnston
Acquisitions Editor: Julie Peters
Editorial Assistant: Tiffany Bitzel
Senior Managing Editor: Pamela D. Bennett
Senior Project Manager: Linda Hillis Bayma
Production Coordinator: Shelley Creager, Aptara, Inc.
Design Coordinator: Diane C. Lorenzo
Photo Coordinator: Valerie Schultz
Cover Designer: Candace Rowley
Cover image: PhotoDisc
Operations Specialist: Laura Messerly
Director of Marketing: Quinn Perkson
Marketing Manager: Erica DeLuca
Marketing Coordinator: Brian Mounts

This book was set in Galliard by Aptara, Inc. It was printed and bound by R.R. Donnelley & Sons Company. The cover was printed by R.R. Donnelley & Sons Company.

Pearson Education, Ltd., London
Pearson Education Singapore Pte. Ltd.
Pearson Education Canada, Inc.
Pearson Education—Japan
Pearson Education Australia PTY, Limited
Pearson Education North Asia Ltd., Hong Kong
Pearson Educación de Mexico, S.A. de C.V.
Pearson Education Malaysia, Pte. Ltd.
Pearson Education Upper Saddle River, New Jersey

Merrill
is an imprint of

10 9 8 7 6 5 4 3 2 1
ISBN-13: 978-0-13-512628-8
ISBN-10: 0-13-512628-2

We dedicate this book to the memory of Irving Sigel, Patricia Monighan-Nourot, and Edna Shapiro.

Jaipaul L. Roopnarine
James E. Johnson

Preface

We are proud to introduce this volume as a very timely and important book in the field of early childhood education (ECE). ECE has undergone a great deal of change in a few short years since the publication of the fourth edition of *Approaches to Early Childhood Education* in 2005. While ECE remains devoted to excellence and equity and inclusiveness, the field has become more publicized and politicized, with greater attention, higher expectations, and more scrutiny attached to it than ever before. Research, including studies from molecular genetics and neuroscience, has bolstered the status of ECE in the public eye and has drawn increased attention. Pressures for quantity and quality in early childhood programs affect teacher education programs, as much as they put pressure on basic children's programs, which are themselves very diverse: community child development programs, family child care, early intervention programs, Head Start, the new and increasing trend toward pre-kindergarten programs in public schools, and more.

This fifth edition of *Approaches to Early Childhood Education* addresses current tensions in the field, as well as new developments in curricula, assessment strategies, and teaching methods. Teachers who aspire to become leaders in ECE must be kept abreast of new directions in research and application so they can build flexible conceptual frameworks and working models for practices and policies that can fit a range of community contexts and specific concrete circumstances. This text focuses on enhancing readers' ECE knowledge base and skill set so they can meet current needs and challenges that face our profession, very notably in the area of inclusive education and the needs of diverse learners. We believe a fluid transactional model can be derived by assimilating the content from this text's chapters, including an understanding of the interactions between research and theory and practice and policy, as well as across content and context variables found within ECE programs.

With respect to prevailing and contrasting ideologies, ECE is again at a crossroads. Should the field move more in the direction of an emphasis on academic learning and achievement or on development and care? Many approaches to instruction, learning, and intentional teaching in ECE are presented in this volume. This book should assist us all as we grapple with clearer definitions of our field, our identities, our functions, and our boundaries.

FEATURES OF THE FIFTH EDITION

While this textbook remains an authoritative resource for teacher educators, researchers, and students in early childhood development and education, this new edition reflects the latest intellectual history of the field and new innovations in educating young children in diverse contexts. This edition contains new foci that highlight the importance of considering the history of ECE from perspectives of multiculturalism, developmental science, and prevention research in early education practice and policy in infancy and the toddler years, as well as the preschool, kindergarten, and primary school years. This is represented by Chapter 1, *History of Early Childhood Education in Multicultural Perspective* by Blythe F. Hinitz; Chapter 2, *The Program for Infant/Toddler Care* by J. Ronald Lally and Peter L. Mangione; and Chapter 7, *Early Prevention Initiatives* by Karen L. Bierman, Celene Domitrovich, and Harriet Darling.

Another new emphasis links the relationships of curricular activities to the goals and standards of ECE today and provides coverage of the movement toward an aligned and coordinated pre-kindergarten to 3rd grade (PK–3) system as a major idea in educational reform. A new Chapter 8 by James E. Johnson and Jennifer L. Chestnut discusses the PK–3 initiative and ECE in relation to the institution of public schooling. In this vein, all chapters that can do so include coverage of their model, approach, or focus in relation to the PK–3 initiative: that is, the education of children in the primary grades, in addition to younger children.

How can we best integrate ECE into the public schools? How can we best prepare new teachers for working within a PK–3 system? Very helpful in this regard is a new Chapter 11, *From Spectrum to Bridging: Approaches to Integrating Assessment with Curriculum and Instruction in Early Childhood Classrooms* by Jie-Qi Chen and Gillian McNamee. Another outstanding feature of this fifth edition is a new Chapter 10, *Tools of the Mind: The Vygotskian Approach to Early Childhood Education* by Elena Bodrova and Deborah J. Leong.

Acknowledgments

We are very grateful for the continued understanding and support of our families during the production of the fifth edition of this text: Nancy, Beth, Miles, Maya, India, Karen, and Clayton. We are very grateful to Diana Janice Biro of the College of Human Ecology at Syracuse University for her editorial assistance with the chapters in this volume, and to Kara Kaufman of the Department of Curriculum and Instruction at The Pennsylvania State University for organizing the manuscript and managing communications for us. We also thank Mei-Fang Cheng who assisted in obtaining permissions, selecting photographs, and proofreading. Megan Lape and Prarthana Pant assisted with verifying the citations.

We further appreciate the reviewers' comments and suggestions on both the content and organization of the book. Our thanks to reviewers Deborah A. Ceglowski, University of North Carolina, Charlotte; Angie Cranor, University of North Carolina, Greensboro; Mary Hanrahan, Northern Virginia Community College; and Regina Miller, University of Hartford.

Brief Contents

Contents

Note: Every effort has been made to provide accurate and current Internet information in this book. However, the Internet and information posted on it are constantly changing, so it is inevitable that some of the Internet addresses lised in this textbook will change.

Part I
Introduction

Chapter 1
History of Early Childhood Education in Multicultural Perspective

Blythe F. Hinitz ❧ *College of New Jersey*

INTRODUCTION

In the beginning, in the Americas, lived indigenous peoples—hundreds of tribes speaking approximately 600 languages.[1] They were erroneously called "Indians" by the explorers and colonists who originally thought they had reached Asia. The Native Americans had a strong tribal and family system and codified methods of preparing, educating, and inducting young children into the skills, knowledge, and rituals they needed to become functioning members of society. Many of the original tribes have disappeared as a result of warfare, disease, or assimilation (see Chapters 14 and 18 in Lascarides & Hinitz, 2000; and the maps throughout the September 1992 issue of *Young Children*).

The history of early childhood education in the United States usually begins with its European roots; however, it is important to note that Native Americans had a viable system of early childhood education with many aspects similar to the ancient Greeks (Lascarides & Hinitz, 2000). The European colonizers from England, France, Spain, and Portugal brought with them aspects of the education system for children utilized in their home countries: for example, those originated by Robert Owen and Samuel Wilderspin. Later they imported the kindergarten from Germany, the nursery school from England, and the Montessori Method from Italy. This early history led to a two-tiered system of care and education for young children: (1) child care (day care) for families in lower socioeconomic levels and (2) kindergartens and nursery schools for middle- and upper-income families. In many of the colonies, a religious group was responsible for setting up the educational system. These groups attempted to assimilate the Native Americans into their European system, often with disastrous results. Another group, Black indentured servants who came to Jamestown as early as 1619, was gradually enslaved in what has been called the United States' "peculiar institution" (Yetman, in Lascarides & Hinitz, 2000). Most slaves were not permitted to read and write, and their care from birth on was left to older women or children too young to work in the fields. Those slaves who learned to read and write often escaped from the plantation or fomented rebellions.

The population of the United States includes the descendants of the indigenous peoples, the colonists, the slaves, and the immigrants, each of whom have contributed their languages and cultures to the diversity that exists in the country today. The history of early childhood care and education from the 1600s through the 1850s forms the basis for what is recorded

[1] In 1990, the U.S. Census Bureau identified 136 different Native American languages, of which approximately 70 are spoken by fewer than 200 persons.

about early childhood education up to the present time. We will see that the history of early childhood care and education in the United States is wonderfully diverse. It encompasses numerous cultures, philosophies, and beliefs. It is based on the traditions of Europe, Asia, Africa, and the American Indian nations. By participating in a child development program in their early years, the members of many underrepresented groups have evolved and continue to progress on their way to personal and academic success. Historically, early childhood care and education have supported the development of women's administrative and leadership skills. They also constitute a major economic factor in many parts of the United States.

This chapter explores the origins, histories, and current status of selected early education programs for young children aged birth to 8 years. The chapter addresses the development of three streams of early childhood education: kindergarten, nursery school, and child-care programs for children of diverse personal, cultural, and linguistic backgrounds. It includes some of the historical trends that are observable in present time and those that can reasonably be expected to extend into the future. The work and lives of selected early childhood education leaders and workers are incorporated where relevant to the understanding of historical developments.

NATIVE AMERICAN EARLY CHILDHOOD EDUCATION

Native Americans ("Indians") were the only indigenous groups living in North America prior to the arrival of European colonists. The heterogeneous tribes included nomadic hunters, farmers living in agricultural communities, and fishermen. The members of existing tribes have maintained their specific group identity and culture to the present day, in spite of all attempts to assimilate them into other religious and secular cultures from the 1600s on. Although they were native to the land that became the United States, the majority of Native Americans were not granted full citizenship until the passage of a 1924 act of Congress. Some became citizens by virtue of specific treaties as early as 1817, while others earned citizenship by receiving a land allotment through the Dawes Severalty Act of 1887. The Fourteenth Amendment to the U.S. Constitution, ratified in 1868, provided that all citizens of the United States were also citizens of the state in which they resided.

Adults in tribes gained social standing and became eligible to participate in the functioning of the group by having children. Married people had to have children to be considered fully adult. The French and Spanish missionaries of the 1600s and 1700s attempted to convert children and adults to Christianity, but they made little attempt to educate them. The Puritans, on the other hand, established schools for boys and girls, formed Native American "praying towns," and printed the Bible and several other books in tribal languages or bilingual versions. An 1819 act of Congress provided for a "civilization fund" to teach agriculture and trades to Indians and to teach the children reading, writing, and arithmetic (Lascarides & Hinitz, 2000). Some tribes, in particular the Cherokee and Choctaw, developed well-defined school systems that existed until the Curtis Act of 1898 ended tribal governments in Indian territory. The original schools were established in the Southeast, and when the Removal Act of 1830 was promulgated by President Andrew Jackson, they were closed and reopened after the forced move on western reservations.

Three types of government-funded schools were open for American Indian children during the 1800s and early 1900s: reservation boarding schools, reservation day schools, and off-reservation boarding schools. Each type of school had its own problems; however, the off-reservation boarding schools had the most difficulties connected with them. Although some parents responded to enticements to send their children to off-site boarding schools, the majority went to great lengths to hide their children from the police and government agents. This was done because the boarding school personnel attempted to assimilate Native American children (some as young as 6 years of age) into society by extinguishing their name, their language, and their culture while forcing them to dress as Euro-Americans and to speak only English. Harsh punishments, including beatings, sticking their heads in the toilet bowl, and jailing, were meted out to children who disobeyed or ran away. The lack of hygiene and nutritious food in most of these schools led to epidemics of illness, and even death. In *First Peoples,* Calloway (2006) presents another aspect: the ways in which the students were able to band together to keep their culture alive. This was more prevalent in the reservation boarding and day schools but also occurred to a certain extent in the off-reservation boarding schools. Some of the students who survived the experience returned to the boarding schools as teachers in the hope of providing their students with a better academic and experiential education. Two of the better-known boarding schools were the Carlisle Indian School and Hampton Institute, which were originally founded to educate former slaves and became controversial for mixing African Americans and American Indians. Hampton was one of the few schools that permitted Native American students to speak their tribal languages and engage in traditional religious and cultural practices.

William Hailmann was appointed the Superintendent of Indian Schools for the Bureau of Indian Affairs (BIA) in 1894 by President Grover Cleveland (Beatty, 1995). Hailmann was a Froebelian kindergarten movement leader, who had been a school principal and superintendent, as well as an active participant in and speaker for the National Education Association (NEA) and the International Kindergartens Union (IKU) prior to his undertaking this position. According to Hewes (2001), "Hailmann's involvement with Indian education came at a time when the federal government's attitude and public opinion toward Native Americans was changing from a demand for military enforcement of reservation confinement to an emphasis on education for citizenship and assimilation" (p. 209). He was expected to administer all the schools on and off the reservations, select employees, prepare courses of study, select textbooks, and maintain the schools. He was also directed to visit and inspect all the schools, either personally or through his agents and to report to the Commissioner of Indian Affairs concerning the conditions and requirements of the schools. Hailmann attempted to foster interdependence and to support the web of interpersonal relationships among boarding school students by suggesting communal entertainments and partitioning of the dormitories into small-group living areas. For educational reasons, he favored day schools over boarding schools, and he opened a number of day schools during his tenure in office. Froebelian kindergartens, staffed by trained teachers, were successfully introduced into the reservation schools during his administration. The kindergarten teachers received pay equal to that of the elementary teachers, who introduced elements of Froebel's system into the primary grades. Three normal schools were opened to train Indian students in Froebelian methods, preparing them for professional life off as well as on the reservation. When Hailmann left office in 1898, he was praised by the Indian Rights Association as "a fine example of the merit principle," for his "honest and sensible administration" and his successes "in spite of the fact that partisan politics . . . sought to thwart his efforts at every turn" (Hewes, 2001, p. 232).

The Board of Indian Commissioners contracted with the Institute of Government Research, an independent unit of the Brookings Institution, to study Indian life and education. The report, entitled *The Problem of Indian Administration* and financed by John D. Rockefeller, was released in 1928. Better-known as the *Meriam Report* for its lead investigator Louis Meriam, the report criticized the funding of "Indian Affairs" and Indian schools and was particularly critical of conditions in the boarding schools. Its release resulted in major shifts in Indian education. The BIA was to keep children in their home communities, which meant providing day schools as opposed to boarding schools. Progressive pedagogical methods utilized stories, songs, mathematics, and science from the life of the children and the tribe. Curriculum was grounded in local conditions, history, and culture.

Several pieces of federal reform legislation affecting Indian education were passed before and after World War II. The Johnson O'Malley Act of 1934 provided for federal–state contracts issued through the BIA to improve education. The 1972 Indian Education Act provided federal assistance designed to help close the achievement gap. The Office of Indian Education (OIE) and the National Advisory Council for Indian Education (NACIE) were established. The Indian Self-Determination and Education Assistance Act of 1975 granted American Indians local school control and self-determination for what happened in the Indian education system, provided for development of human resources and teacher training, and created a youth intern program.

According to Hewes (2001), the compensatory education programs of the 1960s and 1970s stimulated examination of the educational needs of American Indians. Hewes stated that analysis of methods to cope with these needs had brought Froebelian principles to bear. She cited Milton Akers' 1968 National Association for the Education of Young Children (NAEYC) proposal, *Training Program for Kindergarten Teachers of American Indian Children,* as an example of the appropriateness of this approach. The proposal states that special attention would be given to fostering pride and cultural identification, effective utilization of materials from the natural environment, and designing a working partnership with the family, the tribal community, and the school (Hewes, 2001). All these ideas demonstrate sensitivity to the needs of the children and their prospective teachers. A 1983 NAEYC publication provides another example, detailing "The Use of American-Indian Oral Tradition with Young Children" (Tafoya, 1983). Pedagogy designed to incorporate aspects of the tradition supports traditional values, particularly the involvement of tribal elders, who are the safekeepers of stories and songs to be passed on to each new generation.

The past 20 years have seen further developments that impact the educational lives of young American Indian children. The 1987 publication *Developmentally Appropriate Practice in Early Childhood Programs Serving Children from Birth Through Age 8* was designed to provide a guidance framework for the early childhood profession. The volume emphasizes individuality and the "perfection of individual capability across domains of development" (Williams, 1994, p. 159). It values independent construction of knowledge over teacher models and guidance, as well as oral language and direct practice over thoughtful language usage. According to Williams, there is a clash between developmentally appropriate practices (DAP) and the cultural tendencies and dispositions nurtured in many Native American communities. For American Indians, group activity, collaborative effort, and cooperation are valued above individual attainment and praise. Observation of a respected adult model is valued for its assistance in the social rather than individual construction of knowledge. Therefore, in a Native American classroom a child's ability to observe carefully and follow directions in carrying out an assignment would be valued, rather than deemphasized. Although many Native American communities have an elaborate oral tradition, silence is also greatly valued. The extended family is responsible for overseeing a Native American child's education. Therefore, exchanges of information about school may take place with individuals who are not the child's parents.

The family may also expect provision of clear standards, leading to interdependent actions. American Indian children and adults may be reluctant to display verbal facility, even though they have the ability to present powerful arguments orally. These few examples point to ways in which DAP and traditional values diverge. Williams suggests that the time has come for rethinking the DAP guidelines in light of cultural diversity.

The dawn of the twenty-first century saw the passage of No Child Left Behind (NCLB) legislation by the U.S. Congress and its endorsement by President George W. Bush. The legislation promised to "have every child reading by the end of third grade," but it also prevented Native American students from studying and using their heritage languages. It is difficult to pass on rituals, legends, ancestral ties, and other cultural aspects without the assistance of tribal languages. During the boarding school movement, authorities attempted to stamp out Native American culture and language, but they were unsuccessful. Over a century later, the United States government may unintentionally be succeeding with No Child Left Behind. In 2004, the National Indian Education Association (NIEA) was successful in petitioning President Bush to sign Executive Order 13336, which gives American Indians self-determination based on "their own needs and precedence." It assists "American Indian and Alaska Native students in meeting the challenging student academic standards of the No Child Left Behind Act of 2001 (Public Law 107-110) in a manner that is consistent with tribal traditions, languages, and cultures." The order also mentions preserving students' culture in the process of doing so. The executive order is being implemented through a multiyear study researching successful curriculum practices and the progress of American Indian students. NCLB supports English language usage over heritage language usage. Therefore, the only schools that have avoided the language-related pitfalls of NCLB are the bilingual American Indian schools.

The NIEA, founded in 1969, is the largest and oldest organization for the improvement of American Indian education in the United States. The organization embraces all native peoples in its paid membership. It has a board of 12 directors who are American Indian, Alaskan Native, or Native Hawaiian. Its goal is American Indian self-determination. Its purpose is to contribute to society to protect indigenous values and cultural heritage while improving educational resources. The NIEA has influenced a variety of federal decisions since its creation.

In 2007, after consultation with a member of the Indian Education Office in the U.S. Department of Education and the College Institutional Review Board, a research questionnaire (Besser, 2006) was sent to a group of American Indian schools for young children. Among its purposes were to determine (1) whether the school believed it had sufficient resources and funding, (2) whether particular state or federal laws supported or hindered the program, and (3) the relative value placed upon American Indian culture in that program. Administrators were asked about the current degree of success their program was experiencing, in addition to their complaints about the current state of the American Indian early childhood education system. The results highlighted problems relating to state and federal legislation, particularly NCLB, and funding. For example, the law requires classroom assistants to have achieved a certain level of education. Individuals of American Indian descent who do have the required academic background often seek better paying jobs for which they are qualified. BIA schools continue to receive a lower level of funding than public schools. Preschool and kindergarten attendance is not mandatory in all states; therefore, primary level teachers are unable to assume that children entering elementary school have learned the content and skills presented at those educational levels. Some schools highlighted successful new programs, curricula, and support from standards designed specifically to guide American

Indian education. Other administrators felt that the greater emphasis on meeting "data driven" goals and improving test scores was impeding the development and implementation of culturally appropriate curriculum and practice. The research results demonstrate that progress is being made in Native American early childhood education. However, work remains to be done.

BLACK EARLY CHILDHOOD EDUCATION

The story of early childhood education for Black Americans begins in the 1600s when Black indentured servants arrived on the shores of North America. Although the three-way shipping trade from New England to Africa to the Caribbean involved slave sales in the northeastern United States, the great majority of "slave states" were found in the southeastern part of the country. In all those states, with the exception of Kentucky, the law forbade anyone from teaching slaves to read and write. However, an exception was made for reading the Bible. Therefore, most of the early efforts to educate Black children and adults were initiated by religious authorities, beginning with the Church of England, followed by the Quakers, the Baptists, and the Methodists. What little formal education young slave children were given took place sporadically in ramshackle buildings. Because they wanted to Christianize them, French and Spanish colonists were more active in educating their slaves than were the English.

Black beginnings in North America were marked by cultural discontinuity as they lost the political, economic, and social institutions that had organized their lives, attitudes, and values in West Africa. Slavery was a system of forced dependency, and therefore, unlike immigrant parents, slave parents could not prepare their children for greater opportunities in the new culture. In addition, the slaves were not a single, cohesive ethnic group, so they did not share a unifying set of customs and traditions. On some of the larger plantations, a respected central figure was able to unify the group.

During the 1700s separate schools for Blacks were opened in Massachusetts, New York, Pennsylvania, and New Jersey. The Emancipation Proclamation that officially ended slavery also had the effect of ending the legacy of Blacks having their own schools by choice. The Bureau of Refugees, Freedmen, and Abandoned Lands (Freedmen's Bureau) had responsibility for assembling the framework of an education system for African Americans during the reconstruction period (Ashelman, 2003). The impermanence of the bureau prevented it from equalizing public school systems; however, it did introduce into the South the idea of free elementary education for all children. Blacks had been closed out of mainstream political, economic, and social power. For the most part, they were unable to circumvent the denial of opportunities or the disparity in educational expenditures (Comer, 1989). Public school systems in many parts of the country, particularly in the South, maintained segregated schools for the next century, until the U.S. Supreme Court decision of *Brown vs. Board of Education* (1954) and beyond.

At the end of Reconstruction, Black women organized clubs to meet urgent social needs. They trained in churches and in "secret orders" to take up "club work" (Cahan, 1989). These local organizations in cities around the country united into the National Association of Colored Women (NACW) in 1896. The National Council of Women (a White women's group) pledged in 1902 to assist the NACW with its day nursery and kindergarten work. In northern cities, the creation of separate day nurseries for Black children in the early 1900s resulted from prevailing racial prejudice. The Hope Day Nursery in New York City, one of the first, was founded by a committee of Black women.

Through local clubs in most southern states, the NACW provided kindergartens, nursery schools, and day nurseries for working mothers. Mary Church Terrell and Josephine Silone Yates were instrumental in the founding and implementation of these kindergartens. While most of the kindergartens for Black children were private, educators such as Anna Murray advocated for public kindergartens. Ashelman writes that it took 70 years, and the support of several national organizations, including the NEA and the National Kindergarten Association, to bring this hope to fruition in Virginia.

Patty Smith Hill became the Director of the Louisville Free Kindergarten Association (LFKA) in 1893 and began 12 years of supervisory leadership. Her philosophy was one of inclusion. Under the influence of the Northern Presbyterian Church, Hill inaugurated a kindergarten for Black children in which Finnie Burton and other teachers from the demonstration kindergarten were involved. As was true of many kindergartens during that time, the LFKA kindergartens served as learning spaces for children, as well as for prospective teachers. The LFKA kindergarten program was aimed at children from different environmental conditions; races; and physical, social, and intellectual status, especially those from "wretched and degraded homes on the other side of the tracks" (Snyder, 1972). The Louisville Education Association "invited the Louisville Colored Kindergarten Association (LCKA) to become a branch of the Association," something unheard of up to that time (Fowlkes, 1987).

The first "public Kindergarten for Colored Children" was opened in 1879 (Whitney & Ridgeway, 1938). The public schools in Louisville began providing classroom space for both Black and White kindergartens in the same building. Mildred Hill (Patty's sister) was a kindergarten teacher in the school, and Francis Ingram, who was trained by Colonel Francis Wayland Parker in Chicago, taught first grade. By 1938 there were 31 "Kindergartens for Colored Children," successfully directed by women of color, graduates of the St. Louis Kindergarten Normal School (Fowlkes, 1987).

A number of private Black day nurseries were opened between 1900 and World War II. Oneida Cockrell, holder of degrees from the University of Chicago and Columbia University, founded Chicago's Rosenwald Child Nursery in 1930. Her purpose was "to redefine early childhood education so that it would not be merely custodial care, but educational par excellence" (Simpson, 1981). This was in keeping with the trend of the times toward incorporating an educational program based on work in the kindergarten and nursery school into the day nursery. After his wartime navy service, Ira August Calhoun realized that many of the children cared for by his wife and daughters in family child care came from struggling one-parent homes. He and his family took early childhood development courses to meet the State of California requirements for operation of a nursery school. In 1965 they opened Blue Bird Day Nursery to serve neighborhood children and families (Simpson, 1981).

The parallel and independent child development movement among Blacks led historically Black colleges and universities (HBCUs), such as Hampton Institute (1929), Spelman College (1930), and Bennett College (1931), to found laboratory nursery schools. Two illustrious graduates of Hampton's home economics program, Dr. Flemmie P. Kittrell and Dr. Evangeline Howlette Ward, went on to promote the formation of day nurseries and nursery schools around the country and the world in their roles as university professors and professional organization executives. Dr. Kittrell, the first Black recipient of a doctorate in home economics/early childhood education, carried her work to India. In 1964 she opened "a nursery school program within day care hours for culturally deprived children and parents" at Howard University (Cahan, 1989; Kittrell, 1970, vita 2 & 3; Kittrell, 1966). This 2-year research project became part of the foundation for Project Head Start. Dr. Ward, the first Black president of the NAEYC, was a member of the World Executive

Council of the World Organization for Early Childhood Education (OMEP) at the time of her death in 1985.

The term *culturally deprived* was used extensively in the early education research literature of the 1960s. It referred primarily to poor, urban, mostly Black children and families. In actuality, the children usually were not deprived of their family culture, and often they resided in communities that contained numerous cultural institutions, though not necessarily those of the Euro-American culture. Comer (1989) said that the parents of Black children are members of a social network that may not be part of the social mainstream. He stated that race-related social conditions of the past and present have put a disproportionate number of minority parents under stress. Therefore, many are not able to provide their children with the kind of developmental experiences that will prepare them for school. He advocated more supports for the family and better teacher preparation to help ameliorate this condition.

Comer (1989) reminded us that gaining access to higher education for Black students over the past two centuries has been challenging. But many twenty-first-century Black leaders in early childhood education and teacher education overcame these difficulties and received higher degrees from prestigious universities. For example, Barbara Bowman, Alice M. Reffels, and Drs. Carol Brunson Day, Ed Greene, Marjorie W. Lee, and Thomas Moore graduated from such prestigious universities as University of Chicago, University of Illinois, National College of Education [now National Louis University], Indiana University, Erikson Institute, Howard University, and Teachers College of Columbia University.

The following quote from a magnet-school kindergarten teacher in Topeka, Kansas, that was opened as a result of the *Brown III* decision can serve as a summary of decades of working toward the ideals of equal and integrated education for young children. She said, "You have children from three different backgrounds, like I teach and others in the school teach. [They learn] to love one another, to do the right thing, and to be an asset to their communities, so I think the magnet schools provide an opportunity to mold children to change things . . . or if they [the magnet schools] weren't there things would remain the way they used to be in the past" (McConnell, Hinitz, & Dye, 2005, Interview with Mrs. Johnnie Sanders). Let us hope that teachers like these will continue to foster change and divergent thinking in their students, to put an end to the "the peculiar institution" (enslavement) of the mind just as the Emancipation Proclamation ended the physical enslavement of Black people.

EARLY CHILDHOOD EDUCATION FOR IMMIGRANTS

Scenario A

You are 5 years old. You are sitting in the classroom at a low table with four other children. Each of you has a worksheet, a box of crayons, and a pencil. The fair-skinned, brown-haired young teacher gives some directions orally in English. The other four children open their crayon boxes, and begin to make marks with the pencil and to color in certain pictures on the page. You look with frustration at the paper and wait, eyes downcast, for the teacher to come and help you.

Scenario B

You are 5 years old. You are sitting in the classroom at a low table with an adult and three other children. Each child has a worksheet, a box of crayons, and a pencil. The fair-skinned, brown-haired young teacher gives a few directions in English. The adult at the table repeats them in another language. You and your tablemates open your crayon boxes. You take your pencil and make a mark on one of pictures in the first box. The other children are doing the same thing. You take out your crayons and color in some of the other pictures according to what the adults tell you to do. You complete the paper and give it to the adult at your table. You take your symbol card and go to the block area.

Think about these two scenarios for a moment. They both depict the same immigrant child, coming from the same family. However, there is a world of difference between the views of immigrant and bilingual young students that these scenarios represent.

A look back in history will reveal that all of the colonial and immigrant populations that came to what is now the United States of America sought institutions that provided education and care in the language of the local population. This was readily available to members of the middle and upper classes because they had the funds to support the institutions to which they wanted to send their children. The German-speaking kindergartens, and later the accompanying training schools, founded by Margarethe Schurz, Caroline Luise Frankenberg, Maria Krause Boelte, and Eudora and William Hailmann, were available to those who could pay the fees. However, as Cahan (1989) tells us in *Past Caring*, there was and is a two-tiered system of early care and education in the United States. The poorer members of numerous waves of immigration to U.S. shores could ill afford the tuition for private schools. The free day nurseries and kindergartens, and the majority of schools that their children attended, used the English language and attempted to assimilate both children and families into the prevalent culture. As with the American Indians before them, these immigrant children were stripped of their language and culture and were forced to use English and study and practice "citizenship" from an "American" point of view.

One example is the situation that occurred following the Civil War and the Depression of 1873. The welfare systems that had been in place collapsed under the pressure of increased immigration and high birth rates. This led charity workers to seek new ways of working with young children and their families. Free or charity kindergartens were organized in many urban areas throughout the United States. Some of the kindergartens were supported by "patrons" from upper-income families, and others were supported by subscriptions. Gradually the free kindergarten associations expanded their services to the community to include home visits and classes for parents (Lascarides & Hinitz, 2000). Eventually some free kindergarten associations redefined their role and merged with other social agencies to form social settlements. Among the most famous of these are Hull House in Chicago and the Henry Street Settlement in New York City. In similar fashion, the constituents of the International Institute movement engaged in collaborative practices. Edith Terry Bremer of the Young Women's Christian Association (YWCA) began the International Institute movement in New York City in 1910. Its purposes included assisting newly arrived and second-generation immigrant girls and women by providing English classes, recreational and club activities, and assistance in dealing with housing, employment, naturalization, and other problems (Bhavnagri, Krolikowski, & Vaswani, 2006). The International Institute of Metropolitan Detroit, one of the first institutes, continues its work to the present day.

During the late 1800s, as the numbers of people utilizing the free kindergartens expanded exponentially, the free kindergarten associates began to have difficulties supporting and managing the organizations. This led the reformers to campaign for public school kindergartens. The pattern began with the exposure of corruption and inefficiency in the public school system by the press. Then the free kindergarten associates, along with municipal reformers, would demonstrate the contrast between the realities of the public schools and the ideals of the free kindergarten. The publicity generated often led to the incorporation of philanthropic kindergartens into the public school system. A major purpose of the public school kindergartens continued to be

"Americanization" of immigrant children and their families. This included building the health, English language skills, and morality of the children, and socializing them toward the ideal of U.S. citizenship (Lascarides & Hinitz, 2000).

Let us turn our thoughts back to the 1800s, when Hispanic and Asian laborers and immigrants came to the United States. Members of these groups also were initially treated poorly. However, while some of the Asians were soon able to purchase land of their own, the Hispanic immigrants, for the most part, remained members of the poor laboring class. The stories of these groups diverge from each other in several ways. First we will examine aspects of the history of Hispanic/Latina/Latino early childhood education. Then we will look at the multifaceted early education history of several Asian American groups.

HISPANIC/LATINA/LATINO EARLY CHILDHOOD EDUCATION

Two Spanish-speaking cultural groups make up the greater percentage of the Hispanic population of the United States: (1) Mexicans and Mexican Americans and (2) Puerto Ricans. Cubans and others from Central America and South America are a third segment of this population. Mexicans immigrated to the United States in the late 1800s and early 1900s as agricultural laborers. When jobs became scarce, immigration was discouraged; however, Mexicans were excluded from the National Origins Quota Act of 1924, as non-quota immigrants. Puerto Ricans became U.S. citizens in 1917 and were then able to take advantage of free public education on the island. There was continual migration between the island and the mainland by political exiles, those who sought higher education, and families that wanted to escape poverty.

Immigrants currently represent a major component of the labor force of the future at a time when the baby boom generation is reaching retirement age. One in four poor children has at least one foreign-born parent. The overwhelming majority of immigrants are Hispanic, and they are underserved by child care and early education programs. Census data demonstrate that Hispanics are the fastest growing racial/ethnic "minority" group in the United States, representing one out of every eight persons in the population. Approximately two-thirds of first-generation poor children are Hispanics, and they are the most likely of all the immigrant groups to live in poverty. The number of Hispanic children as a proportion of all children has been increasing more rapidly than the number of non-Hispanic White and Black children, for all age groups.

Research studies published over the past 30 years arrived at the same conclusions about the conditions of child care and early education for, and the needs of, young Latina/Latino children and their families in the United States. Hispanic families confront lower quality, and a lower supply of, available child care in relation to the general public. They struggle to find child care that is linguistically and culturally compatible. Some of the workforce issues that Hispanic families encounter, along with other families demonstrating comparable socioeconomic characteristics and a high incidence of poverty, include low-wage jobs and jobs with inflexible work schedules and nontraditional hours, including nights and weekends. In several studies Hispanic families expressed a strong preference for "informal" child-care arrangements in contrast to organized care (child-care centers, nurseries or preschools, federal Head Start programs, and kindergartens). Care by relatives, friends, and neighbors is strongly preferred. The spouse or parent may stay at home with the child. Some parents who avoid group care have available forms of social support that have traditionally provided child care, such as extended family networks, or they perceive considerable cultural dissonance between informal arrangements and formal preschools. Latina/Latino demand for center-based care may also be constrained by limited purchasing power or by weaker community

Anne Vega/Merrill

Early childhood educators increasing is serving diverse populations.

organizations than those found within other ethnic communities. Household-level forces probably interact with the political and economic ones found that shape the organization of early childhood services within neighborhoods. One study found that few Latinos use child-care centers because affordable center-based care is not available in their neighborhoods (Collins & Ribeiro, 2004; Fuller, Eggers-Pierola, Holloway, & Liang, 1996).

Many factors influence Latina mothers' choice of child-care organizations, shared language being one of the most important. Some mothers want their children to continue developing language skills in both Spanish and English, and they search for child-care staff members who can support that desire. Shared values about child rearing, socialization, and education are important. Latina mothers talk about a *compromiso*—the parent shares a commitment with the teacher or care provider as to the child's socialization, which must be manifested through warm personal relationships. When Latina mothers feel that providers are not expressing this mix of warmth, openness, and discipline, conflicts may arise. Latina mothers' concept of *educación* encompasses a broad agenda emphasizing learning to get along with other children, developing respect for adult authorities, understanding rules, and "learning the ropes" of a formal school setting. This is part of the maturation process of learning how to be competent and personally effective within the rules of a given situation. Latina mothers have a real concern with the early socialization and schooling of their young children (Collins & Ribeiro, 2004; Fuller et al., 1996).

Several challenges to early educators of Latina/Latino children have been reported in the literature. Hispanic children were less likely to be read to or to visit a library. Their scores on the National Assessment of Educational Progress (NAEP) reading test were lower than those of other groups, and the gap did not decrease over testing periods between 1975 and 1999. Latino students have higher rates than non-Hispanics of being retained in a grade level and of suspension/expulsion. However, the literature does report gains made by children who participated in center-based group early education programs. RAND researchers found that Head Start participation had large, positive effects on test scores, including language and literacy, and on the school attainment of Hispanic children. They estimated that attending Head Start closes at least one-quarter of the gap in test scores between Hispanic children and others, and two-thirds of the gap in the possibility of grade repetition. Children of Mexican origin appeared to reap the largest gains. A Head Start benefit for children of foreign-born mothers is to provide "compensatory exposure" for limited exposure to English during early childhood. The presence of teacher education and training, and some academic activities in classrooms, were associated with greater satisfaction and program involvement by Hispanic Head Start parents (Collins & Ribeiro, 2004; Fuller et al., 1996).

According to a recent study (Collins & Ribeiro, 2004), about one-fourth of the enrollees in public pre-kindergarten classes were Hispanic. In those schools with the highest concentration of economic poverty and minority enrollment, Hispanic and Black children were equally represented. Many of this study's findings have relevance for future planning for all immigrant and minority populations. The researchers found differences in the length of the school day and in the number of days per week that pre-kindergarten classes met. Only 32% of the pre-kindergarten classes studied were a full day in length. The majority of those met 5 days per week. Public schools with higher poverty concentrations and a higher percentage of minority enrollments were more likely to provide full-day classes (Barnett, Hustedt, Hawkinson, & Robin, 2007; Collins & Ribeiro, 2004; Fuller et al., 1996; Frede, Jung, Barnett, Lamy, & Figueras, 2007).

ASIAN EARLY CHILDHOOD EDUCATION

Asian immigrant groups came to the United States under a variety of circumstances, depending on the era in which they arrived. Each group brought with it distinct characteristics. However, there were similarities among the groups. Three of the major countries from which Asians and Asian Americans came to the United States are China, Japan, and India. Other cultures represented among the Asian population are Filipino, Urdu-speaking Mirpuris from Pakistan, and Bengali-speaking Sylhetis from Bangladesh. The majority of these people emigrated to the United States for such reasons as religious freedom, job opportunities, or education. The largest group of émigrés from Southeast Asia included the Vietnamese, Cambodian, Hmong, Iu Mien, and Laotian refugees who came in five waves between 1972 and 1989, during the Vietnam War and after the collapse of South Vietnam.

Historical Background

Chinese Immigration. Among the first Chinese to arrive in the United States were merchants and traders. However, the majority of those who came from the mid-1800s on were laborers. Because of the strict immigration laws, the men were forced to leave their wives and families behind. Their wives became increasingly self-sufficient. They became familiar with preschool and kindergarten education because the ideas of Froebel, Pestalozzi, and other European philosophers and educators were brought to China in the early 1900s. Chinese parents were comfortable with the idea of early and formal education of young children. Preschools and public and private kindergartens appeared all over China. The private kindergartens were often run by Christian missionaries. The public normal schools and junior normal schools trained child-care nurses and preschool teachers. When the families were finally permitted to enter the United States, they sought education for their young children. However, beginning in 1879, exclusion laws abridged the Chinese workers' opportunities, and they were forbidden to send their children to "White" schools or to own land.

Frank Siteman

Early childhood educators need flexible approaches when working in settings that are multicultural.

Anti-Chinese bias in San Francisco and other communities was particularly evident in public education. Between 1871 and 1884 the San Francisco Board of School Trustees refused to acknowledge the right of children of Chinese descent to attend public schools. In response to the California Supreme Court ruling that children of all ethnic groups had the right to attend schools in the state, San Francisco initiated a "separate but equal" ordinance that forced children of Chinese ancestry to attend segregated Chinese schools. So, in the afternoons and evenings and on weekends, they attended ethnic schools, where they learned the history, literature, language, and sometimes the religion of their ancient homeland. The ethnic curriculum was less successful in homes where the Chinese language was not spoken. However, it did give the children hope because they learned that their collective past extended beyond the squalid urban tenements in which they were living.

Many Chinese mothers were forced to work long hours in garment and other factories. In New York City, a few child-care centers were set up to meet their needs after discovery of the horrible conditions in which children existed. Sung (1967) and her staff discovered that children were left alone in apartments, tied up, set in front of televisions on a daily basis, or forced to take care of themselves. By 1978 only three group programs had a specific focus on Chinese children: the Chinatown Day Care Center, the Hamilton Madison House Day Care, and The Educational Alliance. Together the centers accommodated approximately 250 children.

Japanese Immigration

The Japanese men who settled the California Wakamatsu Colony near Sacramento in the 1870s were young, relatively wealthy, and well educated. They were the product of a smoothly functioning system of Japanese early childhood and primary education. The *Japanese Fundamental Code of Education* of 1872, a Japanese law, created an educational system of elementary and middle schools, normal schools, and universities. As a result of the work of Shinzo Seki, a government-sponsored kindergarten was opened in 1876. The early kindergartens were influenced by Froebel and the American kindergarten movement; however, these influences were modified to fit the Japanese culture. Kindergarten regulations were established by the ministry of education as early as 1899. They became the foundation of the Kindergarten Act of 1926, which covered school age, hours of operation, number of children, facilities, purposes, and curriculum. This act remained in effect until 1947. The most recent updates to the Japanese education standards occurred in 2001 and 2006. The National Curriculum Standards for Kindergartens was updated in April 2001. The revised standards include ideals and goals, as well as curricula in the areas of health, human relationships, environment, language, and expression. The *Fundamentals Code of Education* was revised for the first time in 60 years in December 2006. Important parts of the revision include college education, improvement of teacher quality, and family and early childhood education (Perry, 2007).

In the early 1900s, the Japanese had preschools (*yochien*) that primarily served the children of upper income families. There were child-care centers (*hoikuen*) to serve the children of the poor, including poor workers. As time passed, many *hoikuen* were founded by social reformers in response to the industrialization and urbanization of the country. Family changes and the improvement of children's health and welfare were the impetus for the spread of these centers. It can thus be seen that the Japanese were familiar with early childhood and primary education. However, as the Japanese immigration to the United States increased, they were placed in the same inferior position as the Chinese, working as agricultural day laborers. Some Japanese men had money and were able to buy their own land and farms, but that did not prevent San Francisco from passing school laws that forced Japanese students to attend the segregated Chinese schools. These laws were broadened in 1905 to include "all Orientals." However, the cultural assimilation of the Japanese into U.S. society, particularly in the western states and Hawaii, made the later anti-Japanese movement and exclusionary legislation especially troubling to the Issei.[2] The signing of the Japanese Exclusion Act of 1924 ended Japanese immigration to the United States until after World War II.

The resentment against the Japanese people was magnified with the bombing of Pearl Harbor, and on February 19, 1942, President Franklin Delano Roosevelt signed Executive Order 9066. Although this order applied to the aliens of Germany, Italy, and other nations, it was primarily used to justify the incarceration of Japanese and Japanese Americans. All persons of Japanese ancestry were included. It was not limited to suspected Japanese informants and collaborators.

Little is known about the "enemy alien internment camps," which housed the pre-war Issei leadership of some Japanese American communities, as well as those deemed "disloyal" on the basis of an administered loyalty questionnaire. Descriptions of the Manzanar, Camp Harmony, Tule Lake, and other relocation centers are available in the literature and on the Internet. The following description applies to most of the relocation centers.

The presidential order was particularly shocking to the Nisei. According to Hewes (1988), in 1941 young adults who had been "educated in American schools, and surrounded by American culture . . . were just reaching adulthood and becoming parents of the third generation, the Sansei." At first, assembly centers were set up at race tracks, fairgrounds, or livestock pavilions. Detainees were housed in windowless shacks or livestock stalls before being deported. Schools were omitted from the Wartime Civilian Control Administration (WCCA) plan for the assembly centers and relocation camps. However, the Japanese Americans within the camps soon saw a need for the creation of an educational structure for children and adults. At Camp Harmony, in the State of Washington, classes were offered for Grades 1 to 8. The instructional staff consisted of internees who had been employed as teachers prior to the evacuation and their assistants.

At the Manzanar Relocation Camp in California, the Civilian War Relocation Authority (WRA) allocated funds for both K–12 and nursery school classes during the summer of 1942. The purpose of the nursery schools was to help preschool children overcome language difficulties and prepare for entrance into the elementary grades. The availability of Nisei teachers, as well as college students and graduates with training in child development or related fields, was a key factor in the development of high-quality preschool programs in the camp. Trained evacuee preschool teachers worked in order to survive the misery, discomfort, and frustration

---

[2] The Issei were the first-generation Japanese immigrants. The Nisei were their Japanese-American children born in the United States, who held automatic U.S. citizenship. The Sansei are the third generation and the Yonsei are the fourth.

of internment life. Some teachers were recruited and received training at Manzanar. About half of them were mothers of young children in the programs. Preference was given to women 21 to 35 years of age. Professional development continued with a program of in-service readings and staff meetings on such topics as the objectives of preschool programs, a job analysis of the teacher's work, child development, health and safety, developing creativity, and guiding children's growth. Kindergarten teachers had additional training regarding informal experiences with reading, writing, spelling, and math. Parents had a policy-making role through the nursery school Parent Teacher Association (P.T.A.). The English language was used in all classrooms. Religious books were the only Japanese language books permitted in the camp; therefore, all storybooks were in English. The result was that all the Manzanar children entering first grade in 1943 and 1944 had competent English abilities because of their preschool programs.

Although the nursery school program was equivalent to any other 1940s preschool, several problems were unique to the situation in the relocation camp. The communal toilets, which served both living units and nursery school classrooms, were inconveniently located, so children had to be escorted for their use. They got so much usage that they could not be kept sterile, and the floors were often flooded, presenting a danger to the children. Crowding in the apartments made it difficult for children to get a good night's sleep. Therefore, six of the seven units were designated for afternoon sleep sessions. Regulations required that juice and milk stay in the communal mess halls, so they were unavailable for snacks. Children were taught to wash and cup their hands to get a drink of water (Hewes, 2000).

The last camps were closed in 1946, leaving the victims to deal with the aftermath and the memories. Many of the members of the nursery school staffs obtained teaching positions on the "outside" based on the recommendations of the Caucasian supervisors who worked with them closely in the camps. Reparations were passed by Congress in 1988 and paid to the families under the administration of President Bill Clinton. (President Clinton's October 1993 Letter of Apology may be viewed on the Internet at www.pbs.org.) The relocation and internment serve as a current source of study for several Sansei graduate students who are using their work as a method of attempting to deal with the ramifications of the internment for themselves and their families. They have presented aspects of their research to the American Educational Research Association and the History of Education Society (Lascarides & Hinitz, 2000).

Asian Indian Immigration

Asian Indians constitute the third-largest Asian population in the United States. According to the 2000 U.S. Census (the most recent data available as of this writing), nearly 1.7 million Asian Indians, many of whom speak English, were living in the country. They are unique among Asian immigrants because the majority of the adults have a college degree and approximately 60% are employed in management, professional, or related occupations. Indian society is diverse in terms of caste, subculture, socioeconomic status, geography, and education. However, Asian Indian families do share a common culture and set of values with each other and with other Southeast Asian immigrants.

Southeast Asian Immigration. Vietnamese, Cambodian, Hmong, Iu Mien, and Laotian refugees came to the United States as a result of the Vietnam War. According to the Refugee Act of 1980, a refugee is any person who is outside his or her country of nationality and is unable or unwilling to return to that country because of persecution or a well-founded fear of persecution (University of California-Irvine, 2007 p. 1–2). The waves of immigration included the families of military personnel and those close to the South Vietnamese or U.S. administrations, in 1975; the "boat people" who arrived between 1975 and 1989; the "Amerasians" (children fathered by U.S. servicemen), during the 1980s; and "political prisoners" who were released from Vietnamese "reeducation" camps during the 1980s and allowed to emigrate to the United States with their families.

The first wave of refugees was unique, because the U.S. government assumed the responsibility of transporting them to their new home. They were a well-educated group, and were more conversant with Western culture than later waves of immigrants. The people in the second and third waves had between five and nine years of education. Many of them had spent a great deal of time in refugee camps located throughout the Far East. The "Amerasians" had a very limited education. The Cambodians, who came mainly from a rural agricultural background, had only two or three years of elementary education; they and the Laotians also spent many years in refugee camps before being allowed to emigrate. When all five groups arrived on the U.S. mainland, they faced racial prejudice and poor economic conditions. Initially, they were unable to form concentrated communities as previous Asian immigrants had done. However, a number of communities and social service, educational, and religious entities provided them with assistance. The provision of specialized Head Start and public-school programs aided the refugees' integration into several communities (see discussion of refugee families in Lascarides & Hinitz, 2000).

There are striking similarities among the educational philosophies and cultural values held by all of the Asian and Asian American groups, whether they emigrated to the United States during the twentieth or twenty-first century. They share these values with many other immigrant groups. Among the most important of these values are respect for education, the importance of the teacher, and a preference for academic work over messy play. Parents tend to grant total responsibility for their children's education to teachers. They view too much parental involvement as interference and prefer to limit themselves to such activities as monitoring and supervising homework. Many parents request that even young children be given homework. If none is sent from the school, they will review writing and mathematical concepts with the child on a daily basis. Children are expected to learn correct conduct and habits. They are trained to answer only when specifically asked to respond. Therefore, questioning adults and spontaneous expression of thoughts are considered impolite. Children are taught to display deference toward all adults, including teachers. Schooling is considered extremely important, and in some cases it is a status symbol. The literature suggests that teachers of all young children should be aware of the cultural and family milieu of their students, as described. Teachers should regularly communicate child development and other information to parents and significant adults. Asian parents, in particular, want to know about the intellectual, affective, and physical value of play and the timing of specific kinds of messy or unusually creative activities (Joshi, 2005; West, 1992).

BILINGUAL EARLY CHILDHOOD EDUCATION

Bilingualism and many of its related problems have been present since before the founding of the United States. (See the previous discussion of indigenous peoples in this chapter.) The physical and mental abuse inflicted on the First Americans has been meted out in various forms to all the immigrant populations that followed into schools and child-care centers. It is for this reason that bilingualism must be part of the discussion of the experiences of young immigrant children and their families in early education programs in the United States. The discussion of the history of Hispanic and Asian early childhood education in the United States is linked to a discussion of bilingual education for young children because these two populations are often bilingual.

A search of the history of the United States shows that the country has often been intentionally isolationist and monolingual. Remnants of these thought and action patterns are still present today. They place the country at a distinct disadvantage in world society. At a time when 50% or more of U.S. jobs are related to the global economy, it is important for children (and adults) to have fluency in multiple languages. The parents who want their children to develop linguistically in two languages have not only their children's best interests, but also those of the country, at heart.

Garcia (1999), in his discussion of the distinction between the sociocultural approach and ethnic studies, makes the point that it is almost impossible for educators to acquire complete ethnological knowledge of the student groups with whom they work. Therefore, the ethnic studies approach could lead to stereotyping and assumptions of cultural deprivation. (That is the reason why the researchers of the 1960s and 1970s who used the term *culturally deprived* were referring to ethnicities and cultures that were different as *deviant.*) Garcia stresses that educators should focus on understanding the intersection of the school context with the student's family, home, and community. He describes the "culturally bound and socially mediated process of language development" through which children construct mental frameworks (schema) for perceiving the world around them.

Culturally diverse and language minority students face far greater challenges than their classmates. The child creates mechanisms for functioning in and perceiving the world through his or her first language. If the classroom culture negates that language, and the accompanying representations of the child's world, it negates the tools the child has used to construct the basic cognitive framework. As language skills develop, the child's cognitive processes become more independent from the directly perceived environment. Language development allows the child to act reflectively according to a plan, rather than on impulse. From the perspective of sociocultural theory, cognitive development is reflected by the increasing ability to use language in abstract ways. If the relationship between language and cognitive development operates as theorists claim, educational practices that ignore or negatively regard a student's native language and culture could possibly have adverse effects on the student's cognitive development (Garcia, 1999). The research literature contains examples of bilingual early education programs that have motivated their participants toward academic success. One example is the Carpenteria Preschool Project. It demonstrated a direct correlation between progress in school and attending to the social and cultural context of learning for language minority Latino students (Campos, 1995).

The current interest of the federal government in immigration issues has shone a spotlight on early childhood education, in conjunction with other factors. The presence of young, often bilingual, children from immigrant families in publicly funded child development centers and primary schools has often been the cause of heated debate. Historically, the majority of controversy has occurred in the areas of the country with the greatest percentage of Hispanic population. Today however, immigrants from all over the world, speaking numerous Hispanic, Asian, and other languages, have settled throughout the entire United States. This factor has placed the discussion of immigration and related educational issues on blogs and television programs, and in newspapers, from coast to coast (Garcia & McLaughlin, 1995).

WOMEN IN EARLY CHILDHOOD EDUCATION

A discussion of diversity in early childhood education would be incomplete without examining the role of women. Early childhood education has been a proving ground for female leadership. From cooperative nursery schools (Hewes, 1998) to program management, women have demonstrated through the decades that they have the intellectual capacity, skills, and knowledge to be both "caring and businesslike" (Hewes, 2000). Early childhood education has provided the venue for women to demonstrate their creativity, resourcefulness, and administrative and supervisory skills. A majority of the directors of early childhood education programs are women. They usually are promoted from the operations or educational arena, with little or no preparation or training for their new responsibilities. In the early history of programs for young children in the United States, there were no schools of educational administration or textbooks, and therefore prospective managers would apprentice themselves to the directors of existing kindergartens or day nurseries. The knowledge base for contemporary managers has changed from a focus on program information to a broad range of fiscal, regulatory, personnel-related, team-building, assessment, and organizational knowledge (Hinitz, 1998). As foreshadowed by Hewes (2000), many states have recently added criteria for directors to state licensing regulations. Several states (for example, Illinois) have initiated director credentialing procedures and standards, and the current NAEYC Accreditation Standards include this topic.

Three "founding mothers" (Sadovnik & Semel, 2002)—Elisabeth Irwin, Margaret Naumburg, and Caroline Pratt—were leaders of the Progressive Movement, and their work in the public and private sectors helped to create a new era of education reform beginning in the 1920s. Let us examine some of the parameters of their work in light of the social milieu and the evolving definitions of progressivism in their lifetimes.

The Progressive Movement was a reform movement that addressed pressing social issues of the time. It was a response to the oppression of Puritan restraint; rapid increases in urbanization, industrialization, and immigration; and the great disparity between wealth and poverty in the nation. Progressive schools were designed to be pluralistic and to provide the environment necessary for the development of a democratic society. A number of them were founded in response to dissatisfaction with the conditions of crumbling buildings, overcrowded classrooms, outdated materials, and teaching in the public schools that relied on drill and rote memorization. Common characteristics of progressive schools were child-centered curricula; teachers as guides in the learning process and creators of environments; long, flexible time periods; fostering originality in the expressive arts; learning through exploration and experimentation; "projects" and "jobs"; and the importance of a sense of community.

Many of the leaders in the Progressive Movement were feminists who resented the restraints imposed by the Victorian era. They wanted to overcome the deeply rooted societal views that women were inferior intellectually and physically. They resented the fact that women's education was channeled into the areas of homemaking and nurturing, which was designed to prepare them for marriage and child rearing rather than the working world (Beatty, 2005). They wanted citizenship, autonomy, sexual liberation, and equal wages for equal work (Hauser, 2006). These women found a home in New York City's Greenwich Village during the first half of the twentieth century. At the dawn of the twentieth century, Greenwich Village was an area of Manhattan that attracted bohemian and intellectual residents. Artists, writers, businesspeople, bankers, and immigrants lived in adjoining neighborhoods. The Dinner Club at Patchin Place, followed by the Heterodoxy Club, provided havens from 1912 through 1940 for the pioneers who were forming a new feminist theory and practice. Elisabeth Irwin was a member of both clubs, and Caroline Pratt attended many meals and meetings there.

Irwin, Naumburg, and Pratt were all college educated, with a burning desire to help those in need. Among the commonalities these women shared were their initial work in settlement houses, as well as their extensive review of existing educational theories and philosophies, including those of Montessori, Dewey, Kilpatrick, Thorndike, and the Gary Plan. The founders of Little Red Schoolhouse (Irwin) and Walden School (Naumburg) did not originally envision themselves as educators of young children, while Pratt, founder of City and Country School, began her career in a kindergarten teacher preparation program (from which she withdrew in favor of manual training). All three found fault with aspects of the early childhood teacher education programs of their day. Each in her own way was able to foster changes in teacher preparation curriculum and practice, particularly through their participation in the work of the Cooperative School for Student Teachers (which became the Bank Street College of Education) and the Bureau of Educational Experiments and its nursery school (which became the Harriet Johnson Nursery School). Although each of the private schools founded by these leaders charged a high tuition in order to remain open, scholarship students were enrolled each year.

Irwin, Naumburg, and Pratt each had experiences in working with the public school system in New York City, and each returned happily to the private school setting. Naumburg taught a Montessori-based kindergarten class at Public School 4 in the Bronx from April 1915 through February 1916. She faced many obstacles, including lack of heat in the winter and a paucity of appropriate supplies, materials, and furnishings. But it was the lack of support from the Board of Education hierarchy that eventually caused her to resign. Little Red Schoolhouse, founded in 1921, was originally a public school experiment in Progressive education.

According to O'Han (2005), Irwin was a central figure in the effort to transform public education. She was one of the first educators to introduce mental hygiene into the New York City Public Schools. Her activity-based curriculum challenged existing primary school practices. That fact, and her disagreements with board of education supervisors and administrators, eventually led to the closing of the program. Committed parents supported the 1931 reopening of the school as a private enterprise, and its metamorphosis into the educational institution (Little Red Schoolhouse and Elisabeth Irwin High School) that exists today.

Caroline Pratt worked only as a consultant in the public schools. Beginning with one play program and one program on service jobs in Putnam Valley Central School in 1935, she and her staff integrated aspects of the City and Country School program into public education. Pratt was involved in the formation of the All Day Neighborhood Schools, a demonstration program in the New York City schools, funded by the Progressive Education Association and other community agencies.

As was demonstrated in previous sections of this chapter, early childhood education leaders come from many cultural and ethnic backgrounds. Like women, persons of color have found that the pathway to leadership and success involves a necessary journey through early childhood education programs, their sponsoring government or nongovernmental agencies, or courses in higher education institutions. Drs. Josué Cruz, Olivia Saracho, Eugene Garcia, Elsie Gee, Deborah Leong, Karen Liu, Celia Genishi, and Meiko and Constance Kamii are among the prominent child development and early childhood education leaders who have represented both their personal cultural heritages and their chosen profession admirably.

CONCLUSION

In reviewing and writing the history of early childhood education, a few major aspects stand out. When the European colonists came to America, they tried to eradicate the native culture and the cultures of those who followed them.

Fortunately, they were unsuccessful in these endeavors. Each culture has retained its individuality and language, often in the face of hostility and great adversity. The intermingling of these cultures makes our early education programs and our country as a whole much more robust, vigorous, and resilient. Early childhood education is richer due to the diversity represented in our society. The foremothers and forefathers of early childhood education in the United States are different in many ways, but they share an abiding love for children and the strong desire to provide the most motivational and beneficial programs possible for them. We are enriched by their work and I am honored to be able to share it with you. I have confidence that we will continue to use the lessons of history to make a difference in the lives of children and families.

WEB SITES

Asian American Media. Exploring the Japanese American internment through film and the Internet. Retrieved March 25, 2008, at http://www.asianamericanmedia.org/jainternment

49th Congress of the United States. (1887). *Dawes Act (1887)*. Retrieved October 2, 2006, at http://www.historicaldocuments.com/DawesAct.htm

N. P. Bhavnagri, S. Krolikowski, & T. G. Vaswani, "A Historical Case Study on Interagency Collaboration for Culturally Diverse Immigrant Children and Families." Proceedings of the Lilian Katz Symposium, November 5–7, 2000. Clearinghouse on Early Education and Parenting, Early Childhood and Parenting (ECAP) Collaborative, University of Illinois at Urbana-Champaign. Retrieved online March 25, 2008, at ceep.crc.uiuc.edu/pubs/katzsym/bhavnagri.html and ceep.crc.uiuc.edu/pubs/katzsym/bhavnagri.pdf

Indian Nations at Risk Task Force. (1991). *Final report of the Indian Nations at Risk: An Educational Strategy for Action.* Retrieved September 20, 2006, at http://www.tedna.org/pubs/nationsatrisk.pdf

Public Broadcasting System. Children of the camps: Internment history. Retrieved March 25, 2008, at http://www.pbs.org/childofcamp/history

Southern Poverty Law Center, http://www.splcenter.org/index.jsp

Teaching Tolerance magazine, http://www.tolerance.org/teach/magazine/index.jsp

REFERENCES

Ashelman, P. (2003). *The southern workman: A resource for documenting the development of early care and education in Virginia*. Unpublished manuscript.

Barnett, W. S., Hustedt, J. T., Hawkinson, L. E., & Robin, K. B. (2007). *The state of preschool: 2006* State Preschool Yearbook. New Brunswick, NJ: National Institute for Early Education Research. Retrieved May 7, 2008, at http://nieer.org

Beatty, B. (1995). *Preschool education in America: The culture of young children from the Colonial Era to the present.* New Haven, CT: Yale University Press.

Beatty, B. (2005). The rise of the American nursery school: Laboratory for a science of child development. In D. B. Pillemer & S. H. White (Eds.), *Developmental psychology and social change* (pp. 264–287). New York: Cambridge University Press.

Besser, D. (2007, April/2006, November). A history and current analysis of issues in early childhood education affecting American Indian children. Research paper and literature review submitted in partial fulfillment of the requirements for ECE 390 Research Seminar at The College of New Jersey.

Bhavnagri, N. P., Krolikowski, S., & Vaswani, T. G. (2000). A historical case study on interagency collaboration for culturally diverse immigrant children and families. Proceedings of the Lilian Katz Symposium, Issues in Early Childhood Education: Curriculum, Teacher Education and Dissemination of Information. November 5–7, 2000 Urbana–Champaign, IL.

Cahan, E. D. (1989). *Past caring: A history of U.S. preschool care and education for the poor, 1820–1965.* New York: National Center for Children in Poverty, Columbia University.

Calloway, C. G. (2006). *First peoples: A documentary survey of American Indian history.* Boston, MA: Bedford/St. Martin's.

Collins R., & Ribeiro, R. (2004, Fall). Toward an early care and education agenda for Hispanic children. *Early Childhood Research and Practice, 6*(2), 2. Retrieved online March 25, 2008, at http://ecrp.uiuc.edu

Campos, J. (1995). The Carpenteria Preschool Program: A long-term effects study. In. E. Garcia & B. McLaughlin (Eds.), *Meeting the challenge of linguistic and cultural diversity in early childhood education* (pp. 34–48). New York: Teachers College Press.

Comer, J. P. (1989). Racism and the education of young children. *Teachers College Record, 90*(3), 352–361. Retrieved March 24, 2008, from http://www.tcrecord.org/Content.asp?Contentid=478

Fowlkes, M. A. (1987, November 13). *Patty Smith Hill of Louisville: Her role in the Americanization of the kindergarten.* Paper presented at the annual meeting of the National Association for the Education of Young Children, Chicago, Illinois.

Frede, E., Jung, K., Barnett, W. S., Lamy, C. E., & Figueras, A. (2007, June). *The Abbott preschool program longitudinal effects study (APPLES).* New Brunswick, NJ: National Institute for Early Education Research.

Fuller, B., Eggers-Pierola, C., Holloway, S. D., & Liang, X. (1996, Spring). Rich culture, poor markets: Why do Latino parents forgo preschooling? *Teachers College Record, 97*(3), 400–418.

García, E. (1999). *Student cultural diversity: Understanding and meeting the challenge* (2nd ed.). Boston: Houghton Mifflin Company.

García, E., & McLaughlin, B. (Eds.) [with Spodek, B., & Saracho, O. N]. (1995). *Meeting the challenge of linguistic and cultural diversity in early childhood education.* New York: Teachers College Press.

Hauser, M. (2006). *Learning from children: The life and legacy of Caroline Pratt.* New York: Peter Lang.

Hewes, D. W. (1988, November 18). Nisei nursery: Preschool at Manzanar Relocation Camp 1942–1945. Discussion paper presented at the History Seminar of the Annual Conference of the National Association for the Education of Young Children, Anaheim, California.

Hewes, D. W. (1998). *"It's the camaraderie": A history of parent cooperative preschools.* Davis, CA: Center for Cooperatives, University of California.

Hewes, D. W. (2000). Looking back: How the role of director has been understood, studied, and utilized in ECE programs, policy, and practice. In M. L. Culkin (Ed.), *Managing quality in young children's programs: The leader's role* (pp. 23–39). New York: Teachers College Press.

Hewes, D. W. (2001). *W. N. Hailmann: Defender of Froebel.* Including *The personalized sequel.* Grand Rapids, MI: The Froebel Foundation.

Hinitz, B. F. (1998). Early childhood education managers. In L. Eisenman (Ed.), *Historical dictionary of women's education in the United States* (pp. 139–141). Westport, CT: Greenwood Press.

Hinitz, B. F. (2003, October 30). *Chicago: Crucible of Early Childhood Teacher Education for the Midwest.* Paper presented at the Annual Meeting of the History of Education Society-U.S., Evanston, IL.

Hinitz, B. F. (2004). Margaret Naumburg. In S. Ware (Ed.), *Notable American women: A biographical dictionary: Completing the twentieth century,* vol. V. Cambridge, MA: Harvard University Press.

Hinitz, B. F. (2006). Historical research in early childhood education. In B. Spodek, & O. N. Saracho, *Handbook of research on the education of young children.* (2nd ed., pp. 573–594). Mahwah, NJ: Lawrence Erlbaum Associates, Publishers.

Joshi, A. (2005, May). Understanding Asian Indian families: Facilitating meaningful home-school relations. *Young Children, 60*(3), 75–78.

Kittrell, F. P. (1966, December). *A nursery school program within day care hours for culturally deprived children and parents.* Washington, DC: Department of Home Economics, Howard University. [Reproduced by Division of Home Economics, Federal Extension Service, U.S. Department of Agriculture.]

Kittrell, F. P. (1970). *Curriculum vita.* Archives of Howard University per J. Simpson.

Lascarides, V. C., & Hinitz, B. F. (2000). *History of early childhood education.* New York: Falmer Press.

O'Han, N. (2005). *Elisabeth Irwin and the founding of the Little Red School House.* Paper presented at the History of Education Society–U.S. Annual Meeting. Baltimore, MD.

Perry, E. I. (2007, June 25). *The significance of the revision of* The Fundamentals Law of Education *in Japan.* Paper presented at The Fifth International Conference: Teacher Education at a crossroad. Mofet Institute, Tel Aviv, Israel.

Sadovnik, A. R., & Semel, S. F. (Eds.). (2002). *Founding mothers and others: Women educational leaders during the Progressive Era.* New York: Palgrave.

Simpson, W. J. (1981). *A biographical study of Black educators in early childhood education.* Ph.D. diss., The Fielding Institute.

Snyder, A. (1972). *Dauntless Women in Childhood Education, 1856–1931.* Washington, DC: Association for Childhood Education International.

Sung, B. L. (1967). *The Story of the Chinese in America.* New York: Collier Books. Southeast Asia Archive. Retrieved March 25, 2008, at http://www.lib.uci.edu/libraries/collections/sea/seaexhibit/firstpage.html

Tafoya, T. (1983). Coyote in the classroom: The use of American-Indian oral tradition with young children. In O. Saracho & B. Spodek (Eds.), *Understanding the Multicultural Experience in Early Childhood Education* (pp. 35–44). Washington, DC: National Association for the Education of Young Children.

University of California–Irvine. Documenting the Southeast Asian refugee experience. Southeast Asia Archive. Retrieved May 7, 2008, at http://www.lib.uci.edu/libraries/collections/sea/seaexhibit/firstpage.html

West, B. (1992). Children are caught—Between home and school, culture and school. In B. Neugebauer (Ed.), *Alike and different: Exploring our humanity with young children* (pp. 131–132). Washington, DC: National Association for the Education of Young Children.

Whitney, E., & Ridgeway, K. (1938, April). The kindergarten movement in Kansas City. In *Association for Childhood Education, history of the kindergarten movement in the Mid-Western States and in New York.* Washington, DC: Author.

Williams, L. R. (1994). Developmentally appropriate practice and cultural values: A case in point. In B. L. Mallory & R. S. New (Eds.), *Diversity & developmentally appropriate practices: Challenges for early childhood education* (pp. 155–165). New York: Teachers College Press.

Yetman, N. R. (1970). *Life under the "Peculiar Institution": Selections from the slave narrative collection.* New York: Holt, Rinehart & Winston.

Young Children (1992, September). Entire Issue. *Young Children, 47*(6).

Chapter 2
The Program for Infant/Toddler Care

J. Ronald Lally and Peter L. Mangione ↝ *WestEd, San Francisco, California*

MISSION

The Program for Infant/Toddler Care (PITC) seeks to ensure that America's infants get a safe, healthy, emotionally secure, and intellectually rich start in life. Its five-pronged mission is to: (1) increase the quality and availability of child care for all children under age 3; (2) increase the number of knowledgeable trainers focused on the 0 to 3 age period through making available high-quality video and print training materials and promoting effective training strategies; (3) disseminate information that increases the practice of responsive, respectful, and relationship-based infant toddler care; (4) promote a curriculum planning process that honors each infant's unique curriculum; and (5) inform national, regional, and local policies and practices so that curriculum development and program activity are centered around the needs and interests of infants, toddlers, and their families.

INTRODUCTION

PITC took on its mission in 1985 in response to the low quality of infant/toddler child care found in the United States, the increased use of and demand for infant/toddler care, and the paucity of trainers and training materials available for the age period. With regard to quality, what we observed then and what subsequent research confirmed was frightening. Less than 10% of care for children under age 3 was rated as developmentally appropriate, and 40% was rated as damaging (Cost, Quality, and Child Outcomes Study Team, 1995). With regard to demand, requests for infant care slots far outnumbered slots available (California Child Care Resource and Referral Network, 2007). With regard to available training and training materials, most of the training at the time was conducted by trainers knowledgeable in preschool care but little experience with infants. In a search for audio and video training materials targeted to group care for infants, Honig and Wittmer (1986), who were commissioned by PITC to develop an annotated guide on that topic, found little.

As of this writing, little has changed concerning the availability and quality of care. Only the number of trainers and availability of training materials have changed. As reported in *America's Babies* (Oser & Cohen, 2003), each day 6 million American children under age 3 spend some or all of their day being cared for by someone other than their parents, and 61% percent of mothers with children under age 3 are employed. The California Child Care Resource and Referral Network reports a lack of availability of infant care similar to what they reported in 1985 (Whitebrook et. al., 2003). As for quality, an important indicator—turnover rate—is 75% every 4 years (Oser & Cohen, 2003). Moreover, the infant/toddler care field has yet to be recognized as a profession worthy of appropriate compensation. The average hourly wage for a child-care center worker is $8.91 (Oser & Cohen). These factors have seriously dampened the effect of training efforts in the field.

Yet quality clearly matters, as a growing body of research shows. The National Institute of Child Health and Human Development (NICHD) (1997, 1998, 2002a, 2002b, 2007) study of early child care found that higher quality care was related to better mother–child relationships, lower probability of insecure attachment in infants of mothers with low sensitivity, fewer reports of children's problem behaviors during the early childhood years, higher cognitive performance of children in child care, higher children's language ability, and higher levels of school readiness. Conversely, lower quality care predicted less harmonious mother–child relationships, a higher probability of insecure mother–child attachment with mothers who were already low in sensitivity to their children, more problem behaviors, lower cognitive and language ability, and lower school readiness scores.

It was also found that children benefit most from higher quality child care under certain circumstances. Consistently reported was the impact of the family on development. Family characteristics and the quality of the mother's relationship with the child were found to be stronger predictors of children's development than child-care factors. Yet there appears to be an interactive effect between home conditions and conditions in care: The more children are in need of support at home, the greater the effect on them of high-quality or low-quality care. For example, in the NICHD study quality child care modestly predicted greater involvement and sensitivity by the mother (at 15 and 36 months) and greater positive engagement of the child with the mother (36 months). But infants who received either poor-quality care for more than 10 hours per week of care, or were in more than one child-care setting in the first 15 months of life, were more likely to be insecurely attached *only if their mothers were lower in sensitivity.*

Overall, however, children in care who received more sensitive and responsive attention had fewer caregiver-reported problems at ages 2 and 3. Instability of care, as measured by the number of entries into new care arrangements, was found to be associated with higher probability of insecure attachment in infancy if mothers were not providing sensitive and responsive care. Only 45% of children with both mothers and child-care providers in the bottom 25% of the sample on the sensitivity dimension were found to be securely attached, whereas 62% of those with more sensitive mothers and caregivers were securely attached. Conditions of poverty also had an important interactive effect with conditions of care. A difference was found in the quality of care available to infants from families who were consistently poor and received public assistance, as compared with children from families in near poverty who did not receive assistance. Families that met poverty criteria for subsidized care were found to receive a higher level of care than the children from near-poverty situations whose families had to pay for care out of their budget. Families more dependent on the mother's income placed their infants in child care at earlier ages and used more hours of care than did families less dependent on the mother's income. Families who moved in and out of poverty—known as *transitory poverty*—were most likely to place their infants in child care very early, before 3 months of age.

Given these and many other confounding issues related to the impact of quality of care on children's development, PITC developed a set of program policies that were aimed at creating a climate with a high probability of ensuring quality regardless of family and child circumstances. Although excellent programs may be developed without one or more of the PITC program policies, the entire set of policies was conceived to maximize the chances for the actualization of accessible high-quality infant/toddler care.

Together, the six PITC program policies establish stable child-care experiences for all infants and toddlers and their families. Emphasis is placed on achieving relationship stability and emotional connection for each child and family. The underlying purpose of these policies is to help each child become emotionally secure in care, which serves as the foundation for enhancing the child's learning, development, and well-being.

PITC-RECOMMENDED PROGRAM POLICIES

- *Primary Care. The assignment of a primary infant care teacher to each child and family.* In a primary-care system, each child is assigned to one teacher who is principally responsible for that child's care (Bernhardt, 2000). When children spend a longer day in care than their primary teacher does, a second teacher is assigned to be the primary relationship. Each child should have a special person assigned to him or her at all times during the child-care day. Teaming is also important. Primary care works best when teachers team up and support each other and provide a backup base for security for each other's primary-care children. Primary care does not mean exclusive care. It means, however, that all parties know who has primary responsibility for each child.
- *Small Groups. The creation of small groups of children and caregivers.* Every major research study on infant and toddler care has shown that small group size *and* good ratios are key components of quality care. PITC recommends primary-care ratios of 1:3 or 1:4 in groups of 6 to 12 children, depending on the children's ages. The guiding principle is this: the younger the child, the smaller the group. Small groups facilitate the provision of personalized care that infants and toddlers need, supporting peaceful exchanges, freedom and safety to move and explore, and development of intimate relationships.
- *Continuity. Continuity of teacher assignments and groups over time.* Continuity of care is the third key to providing the deep connections that infants and toddlers need for quality child care. Programs that incorporate the concept of continuity of care keep primary teachers and children together throughout the 3 years of infancy or the time period that covers the child's enrollment in care.
- *Personalized Care. Responsiveness to individual needs, abilities, and schedules.* Following children's unique rhythms and temperaments promotes well-being and a healthy sense of self. It is important to help a child feel good about himself or herself, even if his or her biological rhythms or needs are different from those of other children. Responding promptly to children's individual needs supports children's growing ability to self-regulate—that is, to modulate their behavior and emotional responses in personal and social contexts. The program adapts to the child, rather than vice versa, and the child receives the message that he or she is important, that her or his needs will be met, and that his or her choices, preferences, and impulses are respected.
- *Cultural Continuity. Cultural continuity between home and program through dialogue and collaboration with families.* Children develop a sense of who they are and what is important within the context of culture. Traditionally, it has been the child's family and cultural community that have transmitted values, expectations, and ways of doing things, especially during the early years of life. As more children enter child care during the tender years of infancy, questions of their cultural identity and sense of belonging in their own families are raised. Consistency of care between

home and child care, always important for the very young, becomes even more so when the infant or toddler is cared for in the context of cultural practices different from those of the child's family. Because of the important role of culture in development, teachers who serve families from diverse backgrounds can support cultural continuity by:

1. heightening their understanding of the importance of culture in the lives of infants,
2. developing cultural competencies,
3. acknowledging and respecting cultural differences, and
4. learning to be open and responsive to families and willing to negotiate with them about child-rearing practices. In this way, families and infant-care teachers, working together, can facilitate the optimal development of each child.

- *Inclusion of Children with Special Needs. Appropriate accommodations and support for children with disabilities or other special needs. Inclusion* means making the benefits of high-quality care available to all infants through appropriate accommodations and support so each child may participate fully and actively in a program. Issues already embraced by PITC—a relationship-based approach to the provision of care that is individualized and responsive to the child's cues and impulse to learn—are important for all children, including those with disabilities or other special needs. Infants who have responsive, enduring relationships develop emotional security, which gives them the foundation for becoming socially competent and resilient. Infants who have individualized care are allowed to learn and grow in their own way and at their own pace.

These policies are rooted in work that dates back to the 1960s. By the time PITC's development began in 1985, the need for policies that support the implementation of responsive, relationship-based care for infants and toddlers was abundantly clear.

HISTORY OF PITC

The beginnings of PITC originate with work at the Syracuse University Children's Center, the first federally funded infant/toddler center in the United States. In 1964, this program opened its doors to study the effect of center-based care on infant development. Created jointly by Bettye Caldwell and Julius Richmond, with the assistance of Alice Honig, it combined strategies from the fields of developmental psychology, child development, early childhood education, and pediatrics to create and provide a child and family enrichment program designed around center-based child care. In 1969, J. Ronald Lally succeeded Bettye Caldwell as director of the center and initiated the Syracuse University Family Development Research program, a longitudinal intervention for 108 children from low-income families beginning in the third trimester of pregnancy and continuing through the fifth birthday of each target child. Throughout the period from 1964 through 1977, continuous improvement efforts were conducted based on classroom and child observations and assessments. One of the results of these efforts was the book *Infant Caregiving: A Design for Training* (Honig & Lally, 1981), which disseminated many of the lessons learned about the provision of infant/toddler care at the Syracuse University Children's Center and formed the foundation for PITC. As the longitudinal follow-up study report states, the approach toward care used in the center program was designed to achieve the following:

> [So] that children could expect to be treated fairly and with loving kindness by adults and other children in a secure and consistent

> setting, that they would come to expect daily educational experiences, and that they would see the resources of their childcare community as available for their use and to meet their needs. The staff functioned under the agreed upon assumptions that these children were capable of: 1) learning something about anything in which they showed interest; 2) learning to understand that their actions and choices had an impact on others; 3) learning that cooperation and concern for the rights of others would ultimately allow them to express their own creativity, excitement, curiosity, and individuality more fully; 4) learning that wonder and exploration were encouraged by adults; and 5) imitating the actions of staff to other children and other adults. Additional assumptions were that these children were to be treated as special creations, each with particular skills and specialties that would be appreciated by and useful to the larger society; these special powers were protected and allowed to rise to ascendance by the adults who spent their daytime hours with them. In summary, the context that was fostered set a daily tone of freedom of choice and awareness of responsibility, an expectation of success in each child; confidence in the fairness and consistency of the environment; an emphasis on creativity, excitement and exploration in learning; expectation of internal rather than external motivation; and the safe, cheerful place to spend the day. (Lally, Mangione, & Honig, 1987)

During the same time period, Glen Nimnicht and his team were creating the Responsive Education Program (Thoms & Lewis, 1975) at Far West Laboratory for Educational Research and Development (now called WestEd). This federally funded and carefully evaluated early childhood education program (pre-K to Grade 2) had three goals: (1) to support children's cognitive development by promoting the development of problem-solving abilities, (2) to support a healthy self-concept by supporting learners in using their own ideas, values, and learning styles productively, and (3) to support cultural pluralism by promoting the development of attitudes and behaviors that enable learners to understand and value ethnic and cultural diversity and to interact equitably in a pluralistic society. Evaluation findings showed significant positive growth movement as compared with controls on all three goals. When Lally moved from Syracuse University to Far West Laboratory and was later joined by Peter Mangione, they worked to blend these two well-thought-out and carefully studied approaches. By 1985, when the opportunity arose to help the California Department of Education (CDE) with concerns about the quality of care infants and toddlers were receiving in subsidized programs, the PITC approach was already well on its way to being formulated. Half the nation's infants and toddlers were spending long hours in child-care programs in which their care and education were often relegated to underappreciated, poorly compensated, and inadequately trained providers. California trends mirrored national trends. CDE, through the leadership of Robert Cervantes and Janet Poole (the latter who had visited the Syracuse Children's Center in the late 1970s), entered into a historic and long-lasting collaboration with Far West Laboratory for Educational Research and Development to develop and operate the Program for Infant Toddler Care (PITC).

As work began, PITC's developers soon found, although both research and experience pointed to the significance of the first 3 years of life and a good deal was known about individual infant development, that little information was available to child-care professionals about how to provide optimal care for infants and toddlers in group-care settings. Poole and others—in particular, Mary Smithberger of CDE's Child Development Division (CDD), and Lally, and Mangione of WestEd's Center for Child and Family Studies—started by gathering a team of child and family researchers, child-care experts, and media specialists. Together, they began to develop a comprehensive multimedia training system centered on user-friendly broadcast-quality videos that would bring directly to infant-care teachers theoretical and practical knowledge about infant development and care. Partnerships were forged with private foundations, including Carnegie Corporation, The Ford Foundation, Smith Richardson Foundation, and the Harris Foundation, to support video and print material development.

Since PITC's beginning, it has focused on assisting center and family child-care providers to implement high-quality infant/toddler care. It has developed strategies aimed to help caregivers read and respond to the emotional, social, and intellectual messages of infants in their care and to recommend policies that enable programs to focus on the importance of the relationships between the caregiver and child, and the caregiver and family, as the foundation of good-quality care. PITC materials and approach have been used to train many trainers throughout the country, who, in turn, have trained thousands of caregivers.

From its inception, PITC has included the perspectives of a wide range of stakeholders. In the project's first year, 3,000 parents, caregivers, and trainers participated in an assessment of training needs in California. A panel of nationally recognized experts in the field of infant/toddler care and development was enlisted to be the project's advisors and reviewers. In addition, a state panel of child-care experts was formed. Special consultants, noted experts, and theorists on early learning, environment, culture, and language, as well as trainers, caregivers, children, and parents, have made significant contributions to PITC, including the conceptualization, review and piloting of training materials, writing articles for PITC curriculum guides, and appearing in PITC videos.

A pilot study early in the development of PITC (Mangione, 1987) suggested that trainers needed more than high-quality videos and guides to be able to use the materials effectively in training. Trainer's manuals were developed to offer lesson plans based on PITC materials. In addition, CDE and WestEd took a major step toward far-reaching dissemination of the PITC philosophy and materials with the creation of a series of Trainer Institutes. The first of these Trainer Institutes were presented in 1990, taking the form of training by module in three-and-a-half-day segments, with faculty including notable figures in the field of infant care and development, as well as the CDD and WestEd creators of PITC. The Trainer Institutes offer a deep understanding of PITC content and philosophy—as well as guidance in effective adult learning techniques—to college teachers, program managers, resource and referral agency staff, and others responsible for training caregivers in home-based and center settings. Since 1992, CDE/CDD has provided fellowships for eligible California residents, significantly increasing the accessibility of the trainings to diverse communities in all regions of California. The Institutes are also open to trainers from out of state, a decision that provided the impetus for national dissemination of PITC.

In 1994, Carnegie Corporation issued the report titled "Starting Points: Meeting the Needs of Our Youngest Children"(Carnegie Task Force on Meeting the Needs of Young Children, 1994), which resulted in a significant increase in awareness and will on the part of public and private groups to address infant/toddler care needs. Two years later, national welfare reform legislation placed additional demands on child-care systems and raised concerns about the quality of care, particularly for children under 3 years of age. It became more imperative than ever to expand and support training efforts, and federal and state agencies and private foundations looked to California for guidance and training materials. Representatives of the departments of education, departments of health, and departments of social services in several states contracted with WestEd to present PITC Trainer Institutes and to provide technical assistance in the creation of statewide

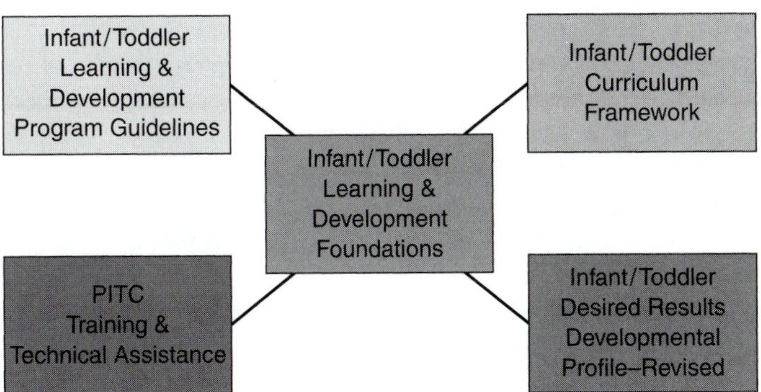

FIGURE 2–1 California Department of Education Systems Chart

training networks. To date, PITC has conducted Trainer Institutes, along with graduate conferences and satellite trainings, in 16 states. In addition, between 1996 and 2003, PITC played a major role in providing training and technical assistance to the 700 Early Head Start (EHS) and Migrant Head Start programs serving infants and toddlers. In fact, all grantees in the first four waves of EHS participated in PITC training.

In 1998, California's CDE/CDD expanded the partnership with WestEd in a wide-ranging plan to increase the quality of care for infants and toddlers with disabilities, as well as typically developing children. PITC became the heart of a system of training and technical assistance designed to reach every region of California. New PITC activities included the following:

- Partners for Quality (regional training network)
- PITC demonstration programs
- *Beginning Together* Trainer Institute, focusing on the inclusion and care of children with disabilities or other special needs
- Expanded PITC Trainer Institutes
- An evaluation of PITC training efficacy
- Outreach to community colleges and local planning councils

As of 2007, the PITC training system has reached more than 100,000 caregivers nationwide. Collaboration with the California Department of Education continues. In 2008, CDE's comprehensive Infant/Toddler Learning & Development System was made available to state practitioners to link PITC training and technical assistance with newly created program guidelines, child development foundations, a curriculum framework, and an assessment instrument, all based on PITC philosophy (Figure 2–1).

THEORETICAL AND RESEARCH FOUNDATIONS OF PITC

The PITC approach is constructed to help programs and infant-care teachers provide infants and toddlers with close and responsive relationships; safe, interesting, and developmentally appropriate environments; uninterrupted time to explore; and interactions with adults that both emotionally and intellectually support and expand their learning. These emphases reflect the research-based understanding that developing infants and toddlers exhibit both great competency and great vulnerability (Shonkoff & Phillips, 2000). Both of these attributes need to be addressed by parents and teachers. On one hand, the infant has been found to be vulnerable and in great need of adults. Human infants operate in a state of what David Hamburg, past president of Carnegie Corporation, calls "prolonged helplessness" (Hamburg & Takanishi, 1997). The infant needs adults for survival, protection, and early nurturance. Without this protection and nurturance, they will die. The infant also relies on the adult for social, emotional, and intellectual survival. Young children seek out adults not only for protection but also for guidance on successful ways to function in the particular society and culture into which they are born. They depend on adults to share with them society's "rules of the road." On the other hand, it has been found that, in addition to their vulnerability, infants are also quite competent. Infants have their own agenda, they are born ready to learn, they move toward organizing their experience, and they create order. Their brains are structured to make sense of things, to find meaning, and to explore possibilities. They actively explore and experiment. They are genetically predisposed to learn language. They are inclined to watch and learn from others. Through imitation and incorporation of their perceptual experiences, they develop ways of thinking, feeling, and acting. PITC has created strategies to assist program leaders and infant-care teachers with understanding and simultaneously addressing these two attributes. With regard to attention to the child's vulnerability, the PITC approach emphasizes that, through the infant-care teacher's prompt, appropriate, and contingent responses, the child learns that her or his actions are acknowledged and addressed and begins to understand that these actions can produce a desirable result. Yet the child's vulnerability is never addressed without simultaneous attention to the child's competence. Therefore, PITC recommends that infant-care teachers watch and wait as a child struggles with a problem until the child gives a signal for help, rather than either rushing in to do things for the child or not helping when the signal is given. This simultaneous responsiveness to both the child's vulnerability and competence is at the heart of the PITC approach. The supportive presence of the infant-care teacher allows the child to learn to persist in the face of a challenge and yet feel that help is available if needed. This type of learning is fundamental in a child's cognitive growth (Hauser-Cram, Warfield, Shonkoff, & Krauss, 2001).

Being attentive to secure base behavior is also emphasized in the PITC approach. As an infant grows, the child becomes a more willing and confident explorer if he or she has a "secure base," in the form of a supportive and trusted caregiver, from which to explore (Bowlby, 1969). Again the presence of both vulnerability and competence is addressed. As the young child exhibits new and sophisticated exploration skills—such as crawling and hand-to-hand transfer of objects—these competencies are both recognized and supported as the infant-care teacher attends to the child's vulnerability through being a secure base for exploration and continuing to strengthen the child's feeling of security and well-being.

With this vision of the infant or toddler as an exhibitor of both vulnerability and competence at the center of PITC philosophy, our approach is further based on 10 additional attributes of infancy that have been identified in the research literature.

Ten Attributes of Infant/Toddler Development upon Which the PITC Approach Is Based

1. Relationships are essential for development. The infant is dependent on close, caring, ongoing relationships for positive physical, social, emotional, and intellectual growth. Infants develop best when they are sure of having trusted caregivers who can read their cues and respond to their needs. The impact on the infant's development of the quality of the relationship between caregiver and infant, parent and infant, or home visitor and parent cannot

Holding baby on the caregiver's lap, hugging, and stroking the baby help in the development of a trusting parent–child relationship.

be emphasized enough. PITC recommends infant/toddler care policies to increase the probability that these relationships are formed and have a chance to deepen over time.

2. Infants learn holistically. Parents and caregivers need to relate to infant learning by being conscious of the impact of their actions on all developmental domains, not just the one upon which they focus at any given time. Infants do not experience social, emotional, intellectual, language, and physical learning separately. Infant learning is best fostered in very young children through attending to the "whole child" rather than through giving focused attention to one developmental domain at a time (Bornstein & Bornstein, 1999; Shonkoff & Phillips, 2000). For this reason, adults are most helpful to young children when they interact in ways that reflect an understanding that the child is learning from the whole experience, not just the part of the experience to which the adult gives attention. PITC recommends that teachers adopt this "whole child" approach to facilitating young children's development and learning. Within its holistic approach, PITC trains teachers and parents to see the component parts of early learning experiences by focusing on each developmental domain and identifying the various learning interests of infants and toddlers. Teachers and parents using this approach become much more likely to match what they do with children to the children's needs and interests. This approach to early learning can have tremendous impact on a child's development and learning because it focuses on issues that are of interest and meaningful to the child.

3. Infancy consists of three broadly defined stages. Between birth and age 3, a child goes through three distinct developmental stages: young infant, mobile infant, and older infant. At each of these stages, infants organize their thoughts and actions differently. Adults need to be able to adjust the way they attend to an infant depending on what the child presents developmentally. If a teacher, for example, expects the young infant to have the same level of impulse control as an older infant, that teacher might employ discipline techniques that are damaging to the child. PITC recommends that teachers always look at the "developmental equipment" (Fraiberg, 1955) a child possesses as a key variable in how the adult should act. In doing so, the adult comes to see that there is no one approach to issues such as biting, fighting, and crying but that each time one's approach has to take into account what the child brings to the issue—in particular, the child's developmental level. PITC advises that the type of care provided and experiences introduced should be in harmony with the child's developmental stage and should change as the child moves from one stage to another.

4. Infants are active, self-motivated learners. Each infant is born curious and motivated to learn and actively participates in learning each day. Environments and activities that keep motivation, experimentation, and curiosity alive must be constructed to facilitate the infant learning process. Environmental design, toys and equipment, activities, and facilitation of play and exploration must reflect awareness of infants' self-motivation. If, for example, the caregiver selects all the lessons that are to be learned or provides an environment that is neither challenging nor interesting, the child will push to do what he or she is interested in or to create his or her own stimulation. In an adult-directed world, infants and toddlers often will be told "No," "Stop," or "Bad" when they are either passionately following their own learning agenda or searching for experiences of interest. In contrast, PITC tries to help teachers see that, when engaged in self-directed learning, children should not be made to feel "This is wrong" or "I am bad" or "I should not take the initiative in learning." Awareness of a child's self-motivation actually frees parent and caregivers. Rather than assuming that they have to supply all the learning motivation and create every learning experience, they can look for ways to take advantage of the child's natural desire to learn and then expand, adapt, and encourage what they observe. This approach not only helps the child learn but also encourages the child to feel good about himself or herself as a learner.

Anne Vega/Merrill

Sensory experences such as touching are the building blocks of early exploration and peer play.

5. Infants differ from one another. They are individuals with unique temperaments and unique relationship experiences. Each child is born an individual with an individual temperament, a different rate of development, and different ways of relating to others. It is essential for caregivers to acknowledge the effect of temperament on individual children's development and to respect these temperamental differences. Doing so requires professionals working with young children to know the different temperamental traits and to be knowledgeable of the dynamic quality of development. Awareness and allowance for temperamental differences in children comprise a first step toward individualizing care. Temperament is a window through which adults can view their relationship with each child. Understanding that the active child, slow-to-warm-up child, and child who is not intense or is easily overstimulated all need a slightly different approach is crucial to individualization.

6. Infants develop their first sense of self through contact with others. An infant or toddler learns most of how he or she thinks and feels by imitating and incorporating the behaviors of those who care for her or him. How infants first see themselves, how they think they should function, and how they expect others to respond to them all come from and through their relationships.

7. Home culture and family are a fundamental part of a child's developing identity. Because an infant's sense of self is such a crucial part of a child's development and learning, early care programs must, in addition to carefully selecting and training caregivers, ensure that links with family, home culture, and home language are a central part of program policy. PITC consciously strives both to respect and incorporate the cultural values of the families served and to seek out from family members information about how they would like their child to be treated. Making connections with young children requires that caregivers and home visitors make connections with families. To serve a child well, program staff need to know his or her family. Thus, teachers and program administrators need to be skilled observers and respectful interviewers with a commitment to engage families. PITC advises teachers that much of the information needed to better serve children would either be incomplete or not learned at all without family connections.

8. Language skills and habits develop early. The development of language is particularly crucial during the infant/toddler period. PITC supports teachers to provide various opportunities for infants to engage in meaningful, experience-based communication with trusted adults who acknowledge and encourage their communications. Creating a verbally rich environment enhances language development, but it also promotes cognitive development. Singing, talking, asking questions, waiting for a response, and verbally labeling objects directly affect the formation of neural pathways (Shore, 1997). For infants learning more than one language, the same principles apply. In addition, teachers need to focus on enhancing babies' comfort with a second language by creating continuity between the home and the child-care setting. Whether supporting a child learning one or more languages, infant/toddler care should emphasize warm, nurturing conversation that is responsive to the child's attempts to communicate (Pearson & Mangione, 2006).

9. Environments are powerful. "What young children learn, how they react to events and people around them, and what they expect from themselves and others are deeply affected by their relationships with parents, the behavior of parents, and the environment of the homes in which they live" (Shonkoff & Phillips, 2000, p. 226). Infants and toddlers are strongly influenced by the environments they experience each day. This is particularly true for very young infants who cannot move themselves from one environment to another. PITC shares information with infant-care teachers about the importance of creating safe, healthy, and interesting environments that are not cluttered, confusing, noisy, or chaotic. Careful attention is paid to the impact on child functioning of materials, equipment, size of groups, and stability of environments.

10. Caregiving routines are prime avenues for infant/toddler learning. Some of infants' most important learning experiences occur during caregiving routines. When carried out in a consistent manner and at a pace the infants can follow, infants can learn to anticipate what will happen next in a routine. This experience allows infants to participate and eventually cooperate in caregiving routines. They learn how their needs are met and how to begin regulating themselves. Routines also offer opportunities for the teacher to talk about the steps in the routine and engage in conversations with infants and toddlers, thereby fostering language development. Through routines, families transmit culturally based practices. Because caregiving practices are culturally meaningful, it is important for teachers to create links between the child's experiences with routines at home and those in the childcare program.

PITC APPROACH TO CURRICULUM

Good infant/toddler care is not like babysitting or preschool. It is a special kind of care that looks like no other. Because infants and toddlers have unique developmental needs and interests, their care must be constructed specifically to meet those needs. For care to be designed well and carried out appropriately, decisions about environments, routines, staffing, group size, relationships with families, supervision, and training must have as their starting point the individual infants in care. The PITC approach to curriculum therefore includes the infant as an active partner in the process of curriculum creation. In a curriculum following the PITC philosophy, a good portion of lesson planning has to do with altering teacher behavior and environments in ways that adapt to the lessons that infants choose to learn. PITC curriculum planning explores ways to help infant-care teachers attune themselves to each infant they serve and learn from the infant what he or she needs, thinks, and feels. Once in tune with individual children, teachers draw on their knowledge base (child development, environments, developmentally appropriate materials, awareness of their own personal characteristics—to facilitate the next step of those children's development. This two-part process) putting oneself in the child's position and then using one's own knowledge and experience to inform the next interaction with the child—is the essence of the PITC approach to curriculum. In this approach the most critical curriculum components are often not planned lessons but planned settings. Thus, this approach respects the active role of infants in their learning and development, as well as the manner in which they learn, which often changes from moment to moment in unpredictable ways. In essence, PITC curriculum planning looks to the infant for direction. Understanding who the individual infants and toddlers are, what their needs and interests are, and how they learn drives decisions about what kind of care best supports their development, learning, and well-being. This approach requires ongoing cycles of observation and documentation of children, discussion, contemplation, reflection, planning, and implementation. Figure 2–2 illustrates the curriculum process.

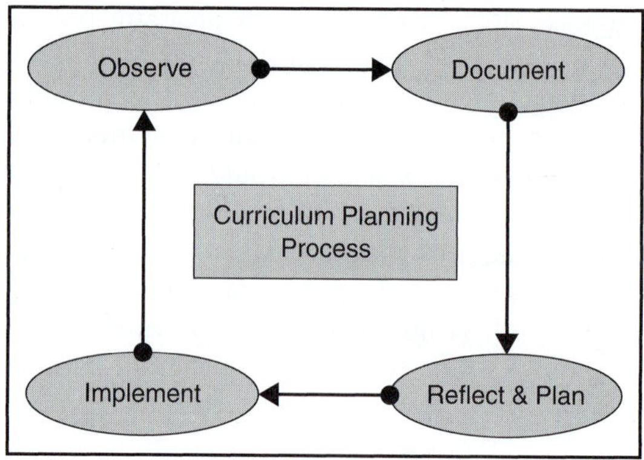

FIGURE 2–2 PITC Curriculum Process

Observe Each Child. To facilitate learning and development effectively, infant-care teachers need to observe what children do. In the PITC approach, teachers participate actively with the children while observing, take notes on the fly, selectively record what they think will be meaningful at a later time to them, to the child, and to the child's family. PITC encourages teachers to use their knowledge to interpret behavior as they focus on dynamics that arise in the child's relationships. These observational strategies place value on teachers' active role in identifying and then recording what they think has meaning.

Document Observations. Infant care teachers record their observations in three different ways: (1) immediately taking notes or photos, or videotaping or audiotaping the children; (2) setting aside time for note taking; or (3) collecting what older children create. Teachers often work together to document their observations in ways that do not interfere with time spent with the children or with the flow of the day.

Reflect and Plan. PITC encourages infant-care teachers to study their observation records and documentation information both by themselves and with colleagues and family members. Taking time to slow down, review, and think about each child's behavior, temperament, learning interests, developmental profile, and needs helps teachers deepen their understanding and appreciation of each child; these also give them ideas on how to continue to support that child's learning and development. This process can be exciting and invigorating for teachers as they come up with ideas and think about how they might adapt the environment or routines, or introduce a new routine or material based on observations, notes, reflection, and discussion. Part of the reflection and planning process includes narrowing down the list of ideas to one or two that relate directly to the interests and abilities of a child or a small group of children. Once teachers have a plan for the next step in supporting a child's learning and development, they then introduce the adaptation or change in a way that allows the child to make choices and to interact with the new material or environmental set-up, and to experience freely and creatively.

Implement Plans. Teachers using the PITC curriculum process try out their plans by making changes in the environment, introducing materials, relating and interacting in new ways, and highlighting objects or concepts for selective focus. As teachers test their plans with children, the process begins again with observation. Through observation, followed by documentation, assessment, and reflection, teachers learn how each child responds to the changes made. This dynamic process of ongoing study of children's learning and development leads to new curriculum ideas to plan and implement. Through this curriculum process, teachers deepen their understanding of each child. They become more sensitive in adapting the environment and more responsive to each child's evolving interests and abilities.

PITC COURSE OF STUDY

Infant/Toddler Development

PITC focuses on four developmental domains: social-emotional, cognitive, language, and motor and perceptual.[1] As PITC is aligned with the California Department of Education's *Infant/Toddler Learning and Development Foundations,* the specific competencies and learning interests identified in each of these domains correspond to the foundation's. As stated previously in this chapter, infant learning and development are understood to be holistic in PITC's perspective. Although the division of competencies and learning interests into domains is artificial, it helps teachers understand and attend to the breadth and depth of early learning and development. In some cases, the division of competencies into domains is arbitrary. For example, only four specific competencies or interests appear under the language development domain, yet interactions, relationships, expression of emotion, and imitation directly relate to children's developing abilities to communicate and use language. PITC training works to help teachers focus on specific competencies within domains, while always maintaining a focus on the interrelated nature of learning and development. Within this approach, the specific competencies and interests of infants and toddlers are as follows:

Social-Emotional Development

- Interactions with adults
- Relationships with adults
- Interactions with peers
- Relationships with peers
- Identity of self in relation to others
- Recognition of ability
- Expression of emotion
- Empathy
- Emotion regulation
- Impulse control
- Social understanding

[1] These areas are described in detail in the California Department of Education *Infant/Toddler Learning and Development Foundations* and illustrated in accompanying DVDs developed by PITC in collaboration with CDE. Sacramento, CA: CDE Publications, 2008.

Cognitive Development

- Cause and effect
- Spatial relationships
- Problem solving
- Imitation
- Memory
- Number sense
- Classification
- Symbolic play
- Attention maintenance
- Understanding of personal care routines

Language Development

- Receptive language
- Expressive language
- Communication skills and knowledge
- Interest in print

Motor and Perceptual Development

- Gross motor
- Fine motor
- Perceptual

The Practice of Group Care

PITC integrates the information about the developmental domains with information on group care practice by organizing both sets of information into five training modules: (1) Social-Emotional Growth and Socialization, (2) Group Care, (3) Learning and Development, (4) Culture, Family, and Providers, and (5) Beginning Together—Caring for Infants and Toddlers with Disabilities or Other Special Needs in Inclusive Settings.

Module I: Social-Emotional Growth and Socialization. This module is based on the belief that all children need physically and emotionally secure care that simultaneously supports their developing self-knowledge, self-control, and self-esteem while encouraging respect for the feelings and rights of others. Healthy social-emotional development in infancy underlies all other learning and is, to a great extent, dependent upon the child's close relationships with respectful, caring adults. Infant-care teachers can support an infant's growing sense of self by providing security, warm acceptance, and appreciation for the child's growing independence. A teacher's ability to promote social-emotional development in children is influenced by the teacher's own feelings and experiences, and so training also focuses on self-awareness. Training topics include infant temperament, stages of emotional development, responsive caregiving, and guidance and discipline. The following are the specific training sessions:

- Social-Emotional Milestones
- Responsive Caregiving
- Temperament and Individual Differences in Group Care
- Meeting Children's Emotional Needs
- Guidance and Discipline with Infants and Toddlers in Group Care

Module II: Group Care. Module II focuses on the implementation of the PITC philosophy through program policies that support close relationships among children, families, and child-care providers. These policies are the creation of small groups, primary caregiver assignments, and continuity of care that keeps children and caregivers together over time. In addition, this module addresses the basics of daily care, the development and maintenance of an environment that supports the child's health and safety, and social-emotional development and learning. Training topics in this module include creating intimacy in infant/toddler groups, caregiving routines, creating safe and interesting environments, and respectful caregiving. The following are the specific training sessions:

- Primary Care and Continuity of Care
- Group Size and Individualization of Care
- Setting Up Environments for Infants and Toddlers
- Daily Routines in Group Care Settings

Module III: Learning and Development. This module emphasizes the approach to infant learning taken by PITC, an approach that focuses on facilitating infants' natural interests and urges to learn rather than teaching them specific lessons. This facilitation is done by providing children with close and responsive relationships with caregivers; designing safe, interesting, and developmentally appropriate environments; giving infants uninterrupted time to explore; and interacting with infants in ways that emotionally and intellectually support their discovery and learning. Such practices are consistent with the attitude of respect toward infants and toddlers that is the hallmark of PITC. Training topics include cognitive development; the development of language and communication skills; the relationship between language, learning, and culture; and including children with special needs in infant/toddler care groups. The following are the specific training sessions:

- Cognitive Development and Learning
- Language Development and Communication
- Special Needs
- Culture, Language, and Cognition
- Brain Development in Infancy

Module IV: Culture, Family, and Providers. The family is the single most important influence in a young child's life, and child-care providers need to include the family in important decisions about the child's care. Creating a strong partnership between the child-care program and families strengthens infants' feelings that who they are and where they come from are valued. Communicating in an infant's home language is also important. Module IV's recommendations include becoming aware of one's own cultural perspective and negotiating differences respectfully with families. The module offers support to caregivers in easing parents' concerns about using infant care, as well as in exploring, accepting, and dealing with their own feelings. Topics include culture and identity formation, dealing with cultural differences, program policies for culturally sensitive care, and creating partnerships with parents. The following are the specific training sessions:

- Self-Awareness and Cultural Perceptions
- Culturally Responsive Care
- Using the Process of Acknowledge, Ask, and Adapt
- Culture and Early Identity Formation
- Creating Partnerships with Parents

Module V: Beginning Together—Caring for Infants and Toddlers with Disabilities or Other Special Needs in Inclusive Settings. *Beginning Together:* Caring for infants and toddlers with disabilities or other special needs in inclusive settings provides regional outreach and supports the inclusion of children with disabilities or other special needs in all PITC activities. PITC implements this as a 5-day trainer institute open only to certified PITC graduates who have completed the first four modules. The institute's goal is to ensure that the training and technical assistance provided by PITC trainers incorporate issues related to children with special needs and promote appropriate inclusive practices.

THE PITC MODULE TRAINING PROCESS

PITC training institutes are provided for both professional trainers and infant-care teachers. Each training module focuses on both the content and strategies for training adults in that module. The presenters, comprised of PITC developers and adjunct faculty experts in specific topic areas, model the PITC training philosophy of responsiveness to different adult learning styles with a variety of strategies: lecture, video, readings, large group and small group discussions, experiential learning, reflection, and collaborative problem solving. After attendance at each module institute, participants may become certified PITC trainers in that module through the successful completion of a certification paper describing their training plans for each of the module's topics. An integral part of PITC's training philosophy is the concept of "Creating a Community of Learners," which focuses attention on the variety of learning styles, knowledge, and experiences of adult learners and emphasizes the value of supportive, cooperative learning. At these institutes the PITC content experts use video and print materials as the core of the curriculum.

PITC Regional Caregiver Training Systems

PITC has worked with a number of states to develop training and technical assistance for child-care providers at their sites. The Partners for Quality (PQ) system in California is the most comprehensive of the systems created and is used here to illustrate regional training efforts.

PQ brings PITC training to both high-density population centers and underserved rural areas of California. PITC-certified Regional Infant/Toddler Specialists organize capacity-building efforts in their respective regions and coordinate training by PITC-certified PQ trainers. Regional Infant/Toddler Specialists and PQ trainers provide training, coaching, and mentoring to centers, and family child-care homes in their region. This mentoring process happens on site and it usually takes place over a period of 18 months and includes 64 hours of training and up to 80 contact hours of program observation and reflective practice exchanges with providers and program directors. Since the inception of PQ, more than 38,000 California child-care providers have received mentoring. An evaluation of PQ has shown a strong positive impact on programs that complete the mentoring activity (*see* Impact Evidence) similar to that found by Fiene (2005, 2007) and by Korkus-Ruiz, Dettore, Baghato, and Ho (2007) in their studies of mentoring. The Regional Infant Toddler Specialists also work with various local community-based organizations: child-care resource and referral agencies, child-care planning councils, county First Five commissions, early intervention programs, and other groups to publicize and disseminate PITC training. In addition, an Infant/Toddler Specialist is assigned to coordinate and support each of four PITC demonstration programs located at community college campuses in various regions of California.

Demonstration Programs

In collaboration with the Community College Chancellor's office, PITC has developed four community college–based PITC demonstration programs in California. These programs, at Cabrillo College near Santa Cruz, Grossmont College near San Diego, Chabot College in Hayward, and Santa Rosa Junior College, offer observers the opportunity to see PITC policies and practices in action. Trainer-institute and regional-training participants, early childhood education students, program managers, policy makers, teachers, and other visitors are invited to observe relationship-based care, responsive teaching and nurturing, and safe and interesting environments using one-way-vision observation rooms or electronic audio and video monitoring. Each demonstration site is unique, offering visitors to more than one site the experience of viewing programs that differ in size, physical environment, location, history, and culture. The programs have been available for observation as PITC demonstration programs since 2002 and can be seen by arrangement with the local Infant Toddler Support (ITS).

Home Visiting the PITC Way

PITC is also a key element in early intervention efforts with low-income children and families. In 2002, PITC developers embarked on the creation of a curriculum for home visitors, addressing ways that home visitors can be more effective in their work with parents, blending the philosophy of PITC with best practices in home visiting. *Home Visiting the PITC Way* is a training curriculum that prepares home visitors to support parents in understanding, promoting, and delighting in their children's healthy development. Home visitors learn how to establish trust with parents, how to communicate with parents about child development stages, and how to model positive parenting practices. Participants practice with scenarios of teaching opportunities and problem-solving situations with parents, watch and analyze videotaped examples of young children's developmental needs and capacities, and create personal professional development agendas.

The core institute, facilitated by PITC faculty and a *Home Visiting the PITC Way* trainer's manual, requires at least 5 days, either in a block or spaced over time. It is customized for trainers or supervisors with the option of additional days, based upon the needs of the participants.

THE PITC MEDIA-BASED TRAINING APPROACH

The philosophy and content presented in the previous sections are disseminated in various ways, with the centerpiece being a series of 15 training DVDs supplemented by various written materials, most notably guides and manuals on infant and toddler care. Several considerations influenced the decision by PITC's developers to make videotaped materials central in the training system. Above all, becoming a sensitive observer of young children is an essential part of learning about how to care for them appropriately and effectively. Without guidance, an untrained observer can miss many subtle aspects of an infant's behavior. Videotaped materials can be highlighted with both visual effects and narration to draw the attention of viewers to subtleties of infant behavior and to help them become more sensitive observers.

Another consideration underlying the choice of video is that high-quality training materials can be made available to larger numbers of child-care providers. Videotaped programs are easily transportable and can be broadcast over public and private networks. Also, if made well, videos can both inform and inspire the viewer. A video that shows quality care being provided to young children can both engage the interest of caregivers and present positive role models to them.

As stated previously, Honig and Wittmer (1989) compiled information from a review of 91 media training materials for infant/toddler caregivers in an annotated guide. At the time PITC development commenced, most of the materials identified by Honig and Wittmer in their search were either for parents or for college-level students of human development. These materials rarely addressed questions related to caring for infants in groups. Thus, such topics as designing environments for groups of infants, group size, age mixture of infants in groups, individual variations within a group, and dealing with parental concerns and needs receive little treatment in currently available media training materials.

Against this background, the number of training videos being made on topics related to group care has recently increased. PITC is part of the growing recognition of the need to support the training of center-based and family child-care providers. It represents an attempt to provide a comprehensive series of training videos in English, Spanish, and Chinese, with each video/DVD covering a specific topic grounded in a coherent approach to caring for young children.

NEEDS ASSESSMENT

In the first phase of developing PITC, survey data were gathered from 405 child-care providers in the State of California (278 center based, 127 family child-care providers) to document their perceived needs for training. Over 50% of the questionnaire respondents ranked the topic "Setting Up a Safe and Interesting Environment" among their top-five choices of videos they would find useful to view. Other topics that frequently received high rankings were in the domain of social-emotional growth and socialization. These findings were used to establish priorities in the development of the PITC videos and related written guides.

Caregivers were also asked to rank the effectiveness of different means of learning about early development and care. The option that was most often ranked among the top five was "Observing a Master Caregiver in Action." This result strengthened the view that observation is an important mode of learning for students of early development and care.

Finally, respondents ranked the desirability of various contexts or settings for viewing a training video on infant care. They were found to favor settings in which a trainer and peers are present. Opportunities to ask questions of a specialist, as well as to discuss video content in a group, were identified as vital to their learning. The general interest of caregivers in opportunities for discussion with a trainer or specialist indicated that presenting information via video should be integrated into a comprehensive training system.

Information derived for the review of media materials, the needs assessment, and the articulation of guidelines for quality infant care provided a framework for the development of the training videos. Advice and recommendations to the project team from PITC's national state advisors, video production experts, caregiver trainers, and practitioners helped shape such characteristics as the length of the videos, the extent to which theory is covered versus practical suggestions, the breadth of material presented, and the type of visual effects used.

For several reasons, a length of 25 to 30 minutes was considered to be optimal for the videos. Advisors representing public television systems recommended this length because it would make the videos suitable for programming in half-hour time slots.

Experts in video production advised that each video should be narrow in scope, covering only a limited number of concepts. Since as a series the videos were intended to constitute a comprehensive package, each could focus on a specific topic. However, to be handled adequately, a narrowly defined video topic must be treated in considerable detail.

In light of these competing concerns, the approach adopted was to give ample coverage to a small number of concepts, while trying not to overdo the presentation of any given concept. In effect, the concepts themselves organized the information presented in a video.

Another consideration in making the videos was striking a balance between developmental theory/research and practical guidelines/suggestions. The advisory groups strongly recommended creating videos that are practical in nature. Following this advice, the videos introduce background material on early development and then spell out practical tips and recommendations based on theory and practice. Much of the theory and research on the development of young children and related practical advice refers to caregiving by parents in the child's home. This material has been adapted to the context of group care and supplemented by knowledge derived form group-care practice.

One of the challenges in making videos on infant care is finding ways to convey the subtle aspects of quality caregiving. Critically analyzing each scene before deciding what to communicate about it has become an essential part of the process of creating each video. The analysis stage often consists of repeated viewing of a sequence and discussion among the project team on how to interpret the behavior of both the caregiver and the children. A thorough analysis results in the development of simple, direct language to draw attention to the key aspects of the scene and gives insight into the kinds of editing techniques and visual effects that would effectively highlight the points made in the narration. To engage the interest of caregivers, the videos emphasize the rewarding aspects of infant caregiving and also acknowledge

Module I: Media Training Materials

- *In Our Hands*
- *The Ages of Infancy: Caring for Young, Mobile and Older Infants*
- *Getting In Tune: Creating Nurturing Relationships with Infants and Toddlers*
- *First Moves: Welcoming a Child to a New Caregiving Setting*
- *Flexible, Fearful, or Feisty: The Different Temperaments of Infants and Toddlers*
- *Getting In Tune: Creating Nurturing Relationships with Infants and Toddlers*

Module II: Media Training Materials

- *Respectfully Yours: Magda Gerber's Approach to Professional Infant/Toddler Care*
- *Space to Grow: Creating a Child Care Environment for Infants and Toddlers (2nd edition)*
- *It's Not Just Routine: Feeding, Diapering and Napping Infants and Toddlers (2nd edition)*
- *Together in Care: Meeting the Intimacy Needs of Infants and Toddlers in Groups*

Module III: Media Training Materials

- *Discoveries of Infancy: Cognitive Development and Learning*
- *Early Messages: Facilitating Language Development and Communication*
- *The Next Step: Including the Infant in the Curriculum*

Module IV: Media Training Materials

- *Protective Urges: Working with the Feelings of Parents and Caregivers*
- *Essential Connections: Ten Keys to Culturally Sensitive Child Care*
- *Talking Points for Essential Connections: Video Clips for Group Discussion*
- *Talking Points for Protective Urges: Video Clips for Group Discussion*

Module V: Media Training Materials

DVDs from the other four modules are used in this module's sessions.

FIGURE 2–3 Needs Assessment Videos (Aviailable on DVD)

its challenges and difficulties. The videos visually and verbally communicate young children's need for warm and trusting relationships with their caregivers. Examples of the natural enjoyment of the relationship shared by caregiver and child are shown throughout the series of videos. Humor is used in the videos to convey the light and playful side of infant caregiving. A respectful tone is conveyed in the videos, and the importance of responsive caregiving to young children is underscored. In other words, the style of presentation in the videos is intended to recognize and honor the profession of infant/toddler caregiving. And in light of increasing numbers of infant/toddler caregivers in the United States who are non-English speakers, it was decided that the materials should be created in Chinese and Spanish, in addition to English. The videos are also available in Phase Alternating Line (PAL) format for international distribution and are closed captioned. (See Figure 2–3.)

IMPACT EVIDENCE

Several field-based evaluation studies have demonstrated the efficacy of PITC. In a 1996–1997 study, PITC training was found to have a positive effect on 18 participating family child-care providers. After completing training, 89% of the caregivers were rated as providing high-quality care (a mean of 5.93), 2 points higher on the 7-point Family Day Care Rating Scale (FDCRS) than that provided by a national sample of caregivers (Carollee Howes, personal communication, 1997).

In 1999, a team at Nova Southeastern University used the PITC materials to prepare infant/toddler-care program administrators in Broward County, Florida, to train caregivers in centers. Prior to training, the centers received an overall mean rating of 3.7 (minimal quality) on the Infant/Toddler Environment Rating Scale (ITERS); observed quality increased to a mean of 5.0 (good quality) following training (Masai, 1999).

The Child Development Division of the California State Department of Education has supported statewide training and technical assistance based on the PITC for the past 5 years. Child-care programs and groups of at least five family child-care providers can apply to receive 60 hours of training and technical assistance from a certified PITC trainer. In 2002, 436 programs received this PITC training and technical assistance. WestEd conducted two evaluations to assess the change in the quality of child care under this initiative. In a statewide study, the difference between overall pre-training ($\bar{X}$ = 4.00) and overall post-training ($\bar{X}$ = 4.38) ITERS score for classrooms with children under 24 months was statistically significant, and the difference between the overall pre-training ($\bar{X}$ = 4.00) and overall post-training ($\bar{X}$ = 4.48) ECERS score for classrooms of 2-year-old children was statistically significant (WestEd, 2003). In a San Diego study, all post-training ITERS subscale scores were significantly higher than the corresponding pre-training ITERS subscale scores. Similarly, all post-training ECERS subscale scores were significantly higher than the corresponding pre-training ECERS subscale scores (WestEd, 2002). In the evaluation of family child-care homes, all FDCRS subscale means increased significantly between the pre- and post-assessments. Before training they ranged from to 2.34 to 4.38. Most of the subscales showed that programs were providing care in the "minimal" range or worse at pre-assessment. Post-assessment means ranged from 3.76 to 5.50 (WestEd, 2003).

In summary, studies have demonstrated statistically significant improvements in overall quality of three samples of programs (two center-based and one family child-care sample) that completed PITC training and technical assistance. The quality of the caregivers' interaction with infants and toddlers was the area in which the most consistent positive change was found. The mean ratings were clearly in the "minimal" range on the Infant/Toddler Environment Scale, Early Childhood Environment Scale, and Family Day Care Rating Scale (ITERS/ECERS/FDCRS) before training began and moved upward within that range or up to the "good" range following the services. These results are promising and warrant further study. A randomized study of PITC was launched in 2008. When completed, this evaluation study will provide additional insights into the impact of PITC training and technical assistance.

CONCLUSION

As stated in the introduction to this chapter, today there are 6 million infants and toddlers in child care in the United States. Most are experiencing a level of quality care that is either inadequate or harmful. At PITC we believe that 50 years from now people will look back at the current treatment of infants and toddlers in the United States as we now look back at the child labor conditions of the early 1900s—with horror. Most centers currently do not meet "children's needs for health, safety, warm relationships, and learning." In addition, when infants are in poor-quality settings they "are more vulnerable to illness because basic sanitary conditions are not met for diapering and feeding; are endangered because of safety problems that exist in the room; miss warm, supportive relationships with adults; and lose out on learning because they lack the books and toys required for physical and intellectual growth" (Cost, Quality, and Child Outcomes Study, 1995, p. 2).

Conditions for infants in family child-care settings have been found to be similar to those described in this chapter for centers. In a study of family-based care in California, North Carolina, and Texas, Galinsky, Howes, Kontos, and Shinn (1994) rated only 9% of 226 settings as good quality and 35% "as inadequate (growth-harming)" (p. 4). Only half of the children were rated as securely attached to their child-care providers. It is noteworthy that 65% of the parents in the study believed they had no alternative to the family child-care setting they were using. Children from low-income homes were found to be in lower-quality family child care than those from higher-income homes. Galinsky et al. (1994) reported that several factors affected the quality of family child care. Quality appeared to be higher in settings in which the providers were trained. Another factor is that an extremely high percentage of settings (81%) were not regulated and were operating illegally. These researchers also identified *intentionality* as an important factor, with intentionality referring to the group of family child-care providers in the sample "who are committed to caring for children, who seek out opportunities to learn more about child care and education, and who seek out the company of other providers to learn from them" (p. 5).

What Can Be Done About Inadequate, Damaging Care?

Recommendations that stem from the research on infant-care quality and PITC's 20 years of experience include all of the following:

- Training based on child-development knowledge and sound practice must be mandated. Federal, state, and local agencies must work together to create training systems that reach all infant/toddler caregivers, including family child-care providers.
- The regulation of infant care is essential. Regulations should ensure that care settings meet infants' fundamental needs for (1) close, caring relationships, (2) health and safety, (3) connection to family, and (4) knowledgeable, responsive caregivers.
- Attention must be paid to the selection of infant/toddler caregivers. Not just anyone is appropriate to care for infants. Individuals who are committed to providing good care will take advantage of opportunities to learn about child care and early development and are likely to be warm, responsive caregivers.
- Caregiver training must be comprehensive, with a dual focus on content and delivery strategies. For the content of training to be sound, it should be based on current knowledge of child development research and practice. The training curriculum should help caregivers understand the social-emotional foundation of early development, the infant's inborn motivation to learn and explore, the impact of the child's language and culture, the critical role of the child's family, and the child's individuality and special needs. It should also include information about setting up group care environments, individualizing child-care routines, and structuring care to promote the development of close caregiver–infant relationships.

Babies are born with an amazing capacity to learn and develop. By age 3 roughly 85% of the brain's core structures are formed. It has become clear that the quality of the child's experiences during the early years contributes to cognitive and language development, relationships with adults, and the ability to engage in positive interactions with adults and peers. Making sure that young children have these positive early experiences starts with attention to the type of care that they receive each day. Both the structure of services and the system of professional development need to drastically improve if infants are to grow and prosper. We at PITC hope that in the near future not only will the infant/toddler period be given the serious attention it deserves but also that those who care for them will be afforded the training and professional status appropriate to their essential work.

RECOMMENDED WEB SITES

http://www.pitc.org

The Program for Infant/Toddler Care seeks to ensure that America's infants get a safe, healthy, emotionally secure, and intellectually rich start in life. The PITC approach equates good care with trained caregivers who are preparing themselves and the environment so that infants can learn. For care to be good, it must explore ways to help caregivers get attuned to each infant they serve and learn from the individual infant what he or she needs, thinks, and feels.

http://www.wested.org

A nonprofit research, development, and service agency, WestEd enhances and increases education and human development within schools, families, and communities. Among its specialties are education assessment and accountability, early childhood and youth development, program evaluation, community building, and policy analysis.

http://www.zerotothree.org

The mission of ZERO TO THREE: National Center for Infants, Toddlers and Families is to support the healthy development and well-being of infants, toddlers, and their families. It is a national nonprofit multidisciplinary organization that advances its mission by informing, educating, and supporting adults who influence the lives of infants and toddlers.

REFERENCES

Bernhardt, J. L. (2000). A primary caregiving system for infants and toddlers: Best for everyone involved. *Young Children, 55*(2), 74–80.

Bornstein, M., & Bornstein, H. (1999). Caregiver's responsiveness and cognitive development. In *Infants and toddlers: Theory and research, infant toddler caregiving: A guide to cognitive development and learning,* Sacramento: California Department of Education.

Bowlby, J. (1969). *Attachment and loss: Vol. 1. Attachment.* London: Hogarth Press. New York: Basic Books.

California Child Care Resource and Referral Network. (2007) *Child Care Portfolio.* San Francisco, CA: Author.

Carnegie Task Force on Meeting the Needs of Young Children. (1994). *Starting points: Meeting the needs of our youngest children.* New York: Carnegie Corporation of New York.

Cost, Quality, & Child Outcomes Study Team. (1995, January). *Cost, Quality, and Child Outcomes in Child Care Centers: Executive Summary.* Denver: University of Colorado at Denver.

Fiene, R. (2005, April). *The effectiveness of an infant caregiver mentoring program: Multidimensional interventions utilizing random clinical trials.* Paper presented at the Society for Research in Child Development Biennial Meeting. Atlanta, GA.

Fiene, R. (2007). Using child care programs as a portal to changing the eating behaviors of young children. In L. Birch and W. Dietz (Eds.), *Eating behaviors of the young child* (pp. 247–261). Princeton, NJ: Johnson & Johnson Pediatric Institute and the American Academy of Pediatrics.

Fraiberg, S. H. (1955). *The magic years: Understanding and handling the problems of early childhood.* New York: Fireside.

Galinsky, E., Howes, C., Kontos, S., & Shin, M. (1994). The study of children in family child care and relative care—Key findings and policy recommendations. *Young Children, 50*(1), 58–61.

Hamburg, D., & Takanishi, R. (Eds.). (1997). Meeting essential requirements for healthy adolescent development in a transforming world. Preparing adolescents for the 21st century: Challenges facing Europe and the United States. Cambridge, England: Cambridge University Press.

Hauser-Cram, P., Warfield, M. E., Shonkoff, J. P., & Krauss, M. W. (2001). Children with disabilities. A longitudinal study of child development and parent well-being. *Monographs of the Society for Research in Child Development, 66*(3), Serial No. 266.

Honig, A. S., & Lally, J. R. (1981). *Infant caregiving: A design for training*. Syracuse, NY: Syracuse University Press.

Honig, A. S., & Wittmer, D. (1989). Recent infant/toddler researches: A helpful guide for caregivers. Paper presented at the Annual Meeting of the National Association for the Education of Young Children, Atlanta, GA.

Korkus-Ruiz, S., Dettore, E., Bagnato, S., & Ho, H. Y. (2007). Improving the quality of early childhood education programs: Evaluation of a mentoring process for staff and administrators. Early Child Services: An Interdisciplinary Journal of Effectiveness, *1*(1), 33–38.

Lally, J. R. (1987). Long range impact of an early intervention with low-income children & their families. The Syracuse University Family Development Research Program. San Francisco: WestEd.

Mangione, P. (1987). Program for infant toddler caregivers: Year-end report to California Department of Education, Sacramento, CA.

Masai, W. (1999). "Making connections: Enhancing the quality of infant toddler child care through training of center directors." *Zero to Three, 19*(6).

National Institute of Child Health and Human Development Early Child Care Research Network (1997). "Poverty and Patterns of Child Care." In G. J. Duncan and J. Brooks-Gunn, Eds., *Consequences of growing up poor.* New York: Russell Sage Foundation.

National Institute of Child Health and Human Development Early Child Care Research Network (1998). Early child care and self-control, compliance, and problem behaviors at twenty-four and thirty-six months. *Child Development, 69,* 1145–1170.

National Institute of Child Health and Human Development Early Child Care Research Network (2002a). Early child care and children's development prior to school entry. *American Educational Research Journal, 39,* 133–164.

National Institute of Child Health and Human Development Early Child Care Research Network (2002b). Structure>process> outcome: Direct and indirect effects of caregiving quality on young children's development. *Psychological Science, 13,* 199–206.

National Institute of Child Health and Human Development Early Child Care Research Network (2007). The interaction of child care and family risk in relation to child development at 24 and 36 months. *Journal of Applied Developmental Science.*

Oser, C., & Cohen, J. (2003) *America's babies: The zero to three policy center data book.* Washington, DC: Zero to Three Press.

Pearson, B. Z., with Mangione, P. (2006). Nurturing very young children who experience more than one language. In J. R. Lally, P. L. Mangione, & D. Greenwald (Eds.), *Concepts for care: 20 essays on infant/toddler development and learning* (pp. 31–39). San Francisco: WestEd.

Shonkoff, J. A., & Phillips, D. (Eds.). (2000). *From neurons to neighborhoods. The science of early childhood development.* Washington, DC: National Academies Press.

Shore, R. (1997). *Rethinking the brain: New insights into early development.* New York: Families and Work Institute. [Full report and executive summary available. Volume discounts available. (212) 465-2044.]

Thoms, D., & Lewis, F. (1975). *The responsive education program for children and adult learners: Summary.* San Francisco, CA: Far West Lab. for Educational Research and Development.

WestEd. (2002). San Diego *Children and families commission final report:* Grant Award #37979. Sausalito, CA: WestEd.

WestEd. (2003). *Preparing the way for California's infants and toddlers: The Program for Infant/Toddler Caregivers. 2002 Year End Report.* Sausalito, CA: WestEd.

Whitebrook, M., Almaraz, M., Jo-Yung, J., Sakai, L., Boots, S., Voisin, T., et al. (2003). *California Child Care Workforce Study: Family child care providers and assistants in Alameda County, Kern County, Monterey County, San Benito County, San Francisco County, San Mateo County, Santa Cruz County, and Santa Clara County.* Washington, DC: Center for the Child Care Workforce.

Chapter 3
The Head Start Program

Douglas R. Powell ~ *Purdue University*

Head Start is the largest federal early childhood program in the United States. By 2006, Head Start had served more than 24 million children since its beginnings in 1965, enrolling more than 909,000 children nationwide in 2006. The program has evolved from its original form as a summer program to a comprehensive set of services for economically disadvantaged young children and their families. Head Start has served as the nation's laboratory for experimenting in the field with quality programs for children birth through 5 years of age. The program has been a pioneer in methods of working with parents and in the development of innovative demonstration programs focused on families with very young children. It also has been at the forefront of approaches to the inclusion of children with disabilities, as well as responsiveness to culturally and linguistically diverse populations. Remarkably, Head Start has gained widespread support from policy makers of contrasting political orientations. It has been called "the most important social and educational experiment of the second half of the twentieth century" (Zigler & Muenchow, 1992, p. 2).

This chapter provides an overview of the Head Start program. It is divided into four sections: the history of Head Start, including its goals and current scope; program services, staffing arrangements, and evaluation results regarding program effectiveness; innovative demonstration projects developed by Head Start; and issues regarding the future of Head Start.

THE EVOLUTION OF HEAD START

Origins of the War on Poverty

Head Start was conceived in 1964 as a key part of the nation's War on Poverty during a highly optimistic time in U.S. history. Its origins are based in the social and political struggles of the Civil Rights era, renewed scientific interest in environmental influences on the course of human development, and the promising results of educational intervention programs for children from economically disadvantaged backgrounds (Zigler & Anderson, 1979).

The Civil Rights Movement of the 1960s drew attention to the widespread nature of poverty and its threats to the economic and social well-being of the nation. The movement also highlighted inequitable treatment of racial and ethnic minorities, as well as poor people, in accessing quality education, jobs, housing, health care, and social services. The War on Poverty programs advanced by Presidents John F. Kennedy and Lyndon B. Johnson adhered to a basic belief in education as the solution to poverty. Job training and education were core features of the Economic Opportunity Act of 1964, which led to the creation of programs aimed at eradicating poverty. There also was a belief that individuals in disadvantaged circumstances should help plan and administer programs aimed at compensating for inequalities in social and economic conditions. The concept of *maximum feasible participation* was incorporated into the Economic Opportunity Act and subsequently into policies of War on Poverty programs such as Head Start.

During this era, social policies affecting young children were shaped by research evidence demonstrating the lasting power of environmental influences on human development. This environmental view was in marked contrast with the hereditarian perspective that prevailed in the 1950s and early 1960s. Noted scholar J. McVicker Hunt's 1961 book *Intelligence and Experience* was particularly instrumental in challenging the widespread view of intelligence and abilities as fixed by heredity. Hunt argued that intellectual development was determined largely by the quality of environmental inputs, particularly from the mother.

Benjamin Bloom, also an eminent scholar, reached a similar conclusion in an exhaustive review of a large body of research in his 1964 book *Stability and Change in Human Characteristics*. Bloom's work pointed to the first 4 or 5 years of life as the period of the most rapid change in intellectual growth. He concluded that the preschool years were the best time to have long-lasting impact on cognitive functioning. This conclusion gave rise to the popularity of the "critical period" of development in the early years and to claims that about half of learning takes place before the age of 5 years.

Later research clearly pointed to the extreme nature of a view of human development that disregards heredity and the significance of experiences that occur beyond 5 years of age. Eventually there was recognition of the need for elementary school experiences to be designed in a way that sustains the benefits of early childhood education. Nonetheless, the environmental perspective dominated the mid-1960s period in which Head Start was launched. The early years were seen as analogous to the importance of the foundation of a building: "If the foundation is shaky, the structure is doomed. . . . The public hailed the construction of a solid foundation for learning in preschool children as the solution to poverty and ignorance" (Zigler & Anderson, 1979, pp. 7–8).

Promising evaluation results from several early intervention programs also contributed to the decision to establish the Head Start program. Although preschool programs focused on the education of children from economically disadvantaged backgrounds were rare in the 1950s and early 1960s, a handful of innovative programs were established in this era to serve children from poor families. The Early Training Program directed by Susan Gray at Peabody College in Nashville, Tennessee, was among these prominent forerunners of Head Start. The project's focus on achievement motivation and aptitudes for learning resonated with the environmental view and had commonsense appeal among the general public. Of importance, the positive impact of this early education program on IQ and verbal abilities (Gray & Klaus, 1965) offered hope of what might be achieved on a broader scale.

Naïve Assumptions and Political Realities

Head Start was offered in the summer of 1965 to far more communities and children than recommended by experts. One point of view was that the program should begin as a small, closely monitored pilot effort. Proponents of this view were concerned about the logistics of successfully launching a major new effort in a short period of time, and they also reasoned that information from experience and research was insufficient for making informed decisions about how best to provide a preschool program for children from poor families. However, a large-scale effort initially involving 500,000 children in some 2,000 centers was envisioned by the time of President Johnson's May 18, 1965, Rose Garden speech announcing plans for Head Start. The goal was to reach as many children as possible, even if the summer program for some children entailed nothing more than modest interventions, such as immunizations and badly needed health services (Richmond, Stipek, & Zigler, 1979). There were high hopes of boosting children's IQ and intellectual competence through preschool education. Sweeping claims were made in the 1960s about the ability of a preschool program for children from disadvantaged backgrounds to eventually reduce the prevalence of poverty in the United States.

Soon after Head Start was launched, the great expectation of achieving significant improvements in children's intellectual functioning through a relatively small dose of environmental enrichment (initially a summer program) proved to be naïve and overly optimistic. Serious questions were raised about the prevailing view of children as clay that could be molded easily and permanently through approximately stimulating environments. The lack of attention to biological factors in the environmentalism of the mid-1960s prompted the pendulum to swing toward a more reasonable middle ground by the late 1960s. Interactions between genetic factors and the environment were increasingly recognized as key developmental processes, a trend that continues today (Bronfenbrenner & Morris, 2006).

The early years of Head Start also were marked by simplistic assumptions about the nature of poverty and the characteristics of children and families living in economic disadvantage. A common stereotype was that low-income mothers were generally incompetent and incapable of providing appropriate guidance and affection to their children (Baratz & Baratz, 1970). Life in poor families was seen as either overstimulating (e.g., too much noise) or understimulating (e.g., too few toys). As noted by Zigler and Anderson (1979), "verbal activity in the poor household was supposed to consist of body language, monosyllables, shouts, and grunts" (p. 9). The anthropologist Oscar Lewis's studies of poverty were interpreted by many to indicate that there was a uniform "culture of poverty" and that children growing up in poor families were "culturally deprived." Deviations from the norms of mainstream middle-class family life often were viewed as forms of pathology or dysfunction.

By the late 1960s there were clear challenges to stereotypical views of poor families and children. Studies heightened professionals' sensitivity to the biases of tests developed on middle-class samples of children and of testing situations that were unfamiliar to lower-income and minority children. For example, research indicated that the verbal performance of African American children was significantly better when tested by an African American tester in a nonacademic setting (Labov, 1970). Studies, program experiences, and media reports also demonstrated the diverse manifestations of poverty across regions, communities, and populations, thereby casting doubt on research and programs that assumed all people are alike in needs, characteristics, and aspirations. Further, the influence of community and societal contexts on individual and family functioning was emphasized in policy analyses (e.g., Keniston & Carnegie Council on Children, 1977); families and individuals were not to be viewed as self-sufficient units to be blamed when things go wrong (Ryan, 1971). Eventually a backlash against the concept of "cultural deprivation" led to calls for educational and human service programs to celebrate cultural diversity, respect individual differences, and build on family strengths rather than weaknesses.

Over time, then, simplistic views were modified regarding the magnitude of environmental influences, the early years as a highly malleable period of development, and poor families as uniformly incompetent. Still, the original expectation that a short-term preschool program could achieve dramatic and lasting improvements in the IQ and general competence of children from economically disadvantaged families has long persisted as a powerful, albeit flawed, framework for Head Start and other early childhood programs. This expectation supports a view of an early childhood program as an inoculation against future effects of poverty. As demonstrated in this chapter, the inoculation model has shaped what policy makers and the general public often expect of Head Start.

Program Goals

Head Start has long embraced a broad set of objectives focused on the development and learning outcomes of children in low-income families. The major domains of child development—social, emotional, cognitive, and physical—are viewed as interrelated. Accordingly, Head Start deals with the "whole child."

Significant attention has been given to Head Start's role in preparing children for school success. School readiness is a strong theme in the 1998 federal legislation that reauthorizes funding for the Head Start program. The purpose of Head Start was revised by the 105th Congress to indicate that Head Start promotes "school readiness by enhancing the social and cognitive development of children through the provision of educational, health, nutritional, social and other services that are determined to be necessary, based on family needs assessments" (Public Law 105-285). Performance standards also were added to ensure that children enrolled in Head Start meet the following minimum expectations: develop phonemic, print, and numeracy awareness; understand and use oral language to communicate needs, wants, and thoughts; understand and use increasingly complex and varied vocabulary; develop and demonstrate an appreciation of books; and, in the case of children for whom English is a second language, progress toward acquisition of the English language.

In 2000, the Head Start Bureau issued a Child Outcomes Framework of building blocks deemed important for school success. The framework is intended to guide programs in their ongoing assessment of progress and accomplishments of children and in program efforts to use child outcomes data for program self-assessment and continuing improvement. The framework, which was revised in 2003, is composed of 8 general domains, 27 domain elements, and 100 examples of more specific indicators of children's skills, abilities, knowledge, and behaviors, all aimed at 3- to 5-year-old children. The framework includes the outcomes legislatively mandated in 1998 (U.S. Department of Health & Human Services, 2003). The 8 domains and their respective elements are these:

- *Language development:* listening and understanding, speaking and communicating
- *Literacy:* phonological awareness, book knowledge and appreciation, print awareness and concepts, early writing, alphabet knowledge
- *Mathematics:* number and operations, geometry and spatial sense, patterns, and measurement
- *Science:* scientific skills and methods, scientific knowledge
- *Creative arts:* music, art, movement, dramatic play
- *Social and emotional development:* self-concept, self-control, cooperation, social relationships, knowledge of families and communities
- *Approaches to learning:* initiative and curiosity, engagement and persistence, reasoning and problem solving
- *Physical health and development:* fine motor skills, gross motor skills, health status and practices

The 2007 reauthorization of Head Start (Public Law 110-134) continued the emphasis on school readiness goals, including the mandated literacy and language skills specified by the Head Start Child Outcomes Framework.

From the beginning, Head Start has viewed the family in general and parents and primary caregivers in particular as essential partners in achieving improved outcomes for children. It is understood that children develop in the context of their family and culture and that "parents are respected as the primary educators and nurturers of their children" (Head Start Bureau, 1997, p. 1). The program provides numerous opportunities for parents to be involved in program decisions and activities and to develop their own strengths and interests in a variety of adult roles, including child rearing. A premise of these provisions is the realization that no 1- or 2-year program is likely to make lasting improvements in a child's development unless the program helps parents become the "agents of change, reinforcing positive changes in the child long after the formal program's conclusion" (Zigler & Muenchow, 1992, p. 101).

Head Start's approach to working with parents has consistently been at the forefront of methods of parent participation. For example, a Head Start requirement is that parents constitute more than one half of the local policy council for a program. This policy provision for a parent role in local program governance reflects a family empowerment perspective wherein parents are to be viewed as active, respected participants rather than passive recipients of professionally determined services. The provision stems from Head Start's War on Poverty roots and the "maximum feasible participation" language of the Economic Opportunity Act. It has "*always* been designed to be more than preschool education" (Washington & Oyemade Bailey, 1995, p. 8).

Confusion about Head Start's goals has been noted for many years. One area of misunderstanding has been Head Start's role in eradicating poverty. As described previously, Head Start was established during an era of great optimism about the power of social and educational programs to successfully address numerous societal ills. President Johnson spoke to the goal of combating poverty in his May 18, 1965 speech on Head Start: "Five- and six-year-old children are inheritors of poverty's curse and not its creators. Unless we act these children will pass it on to the next generation, like a family birthmark. This program this year means that 30 million man-years—the combined lifespan of these youngsters—will be spent productively and rewardingly, rather than wasted in tax-supported institutions and in welfare-supported lethargy" (cited in Zigler & Valentine, 1979, p. 68).

The idea that an early childhood program could reduce welfare costs and crime in adult life was given a major boost in 1984. An influential study of the Perry Preschool Project in Ypsilanti, Michigan, indicated that at age 19 years, participants in the Perry Preschool Project had better high-school completion rates and less adolescent pregnancy and juvenile delinquency than youth who had not participated in the preschool program (Berrueta-Clement, Schweinhart, Barnett, Epstein, & Weikart, 1984). In 1993, results of follow-up studies of the Perry Preschool Project participants at 27 years of age (Schweinhart, Barnes, & Weikart, 1993) and again at 40 years of age (Schweinhart, Montie, Xiang, Barnett, Belfield, & Nores, 2005) showed that preschool participants had fewer criminal arrests, higher earnings and property wealth, and higher levels of employment than their counterparts who did not attend preschool.

Many policy makers and children's advocates erroneously assumed the Perry Preschool findings were applicable to Head Start and ambitiously promoted Head Start as a proven strategy for reducing welfare. Some analysts believe this inappropriate generalization to Head Start of evaluation data from the Perry Preschool Project ran into serious trouble when informed citizens realized the Perry Preschool Project is not

Head Start. This realization is thought to have contributed to a period of reduced political support for the program and limited progress in allocating funds for Head Start expansion and quality improvements (Zigler, 1998).

Another point of confusion in Head Start's goals has been whether the program is primarily focused on improving children's IQ and intellectual competence. Programmatic attention to all aspects of children's development has been in place from the beginning. The original goals for Head Start set forth in 1965 by the program's planning committee emphasize physical health, social and emotional development, mental processes and skills, and self-confidence in future learning efforts. Children's IQ became an early focus in policy makers' and general public understanding of Head Start, however, partly because IQ is a well-known (yet poorly understood) construct in U.S. society. It is important to note that IQ tests were readily available for use by program evaluators and, in contrast, reliable, valid, and efficient tests of most other aspects of children's functioning were not available. Thus, early program evaluations held Head Start accountable for achieving gains in IQ and cognitive abilities mostly or exclusively.

Current Scope and Organization

Some key numbers offer an impressive profile of Head Start's current status. In 2006, the program served 909,201 children in all 50 states plus the District of Columbia, Puerto Rico, and the Virgin Islands. There were 18,875 Head Start centers and 50,030 classrooms. The paid staff numbered 218,000, and volunteers numbered more than 1.3 million. The 2006 budget was more than $6.7 billion, and the average cost per child was $7,209 per year.

The racial background of children enrolled in Head Start in 2006 was as follows: white, 39.8%; African American, 30.7%; American Indian/Alaska Native, 4.2%; Asian, 1.8%; Hawaiian/Pacific Islander, less than 1%; biracial/multiracial, 6.4%; and unspecified or other, 16.2%. Thirty-four percent of children were Hispanic/Latino. In 2006, 12% of enrolled children had one or more disabilities, defined to include mental retardation, health impairments, visual handicaps, hearing impairments, emotional disturbance, speech and language impairments, orthopedic handicaps, and learning disabilities. Head Start has long required that children with disabilities represent at least 10% of enrolled children in a local program.

The vast majority of children are 4 years (51%) or 3 years (35%) of age. Most Head Start programs operate a part-day program, although a growing number provide full-day services. A minimum of two home visits annually is expected of all centerbased Head Start programs. A relatively small number of programs provide home-based services in a significant way. In 2006, nearly 48,000 children participated in home-based Head Start program services.

Since 1995 the program has been serving infants and toddlers through the Early Head Start program. Early Head Start programs tailor their services to meet the needs of low-income pregnant women and families with children 3 years of age or younger through home-based, center-based, or a combination of home- and center-based options. In 2006, more than 650 programs were given funds to provide Early Head Start child development and family support services to some 62,000 children under the age of 3 years.

Head Start is administered federally by the Head Start Bureau, located in the Administration for Children and Families office of the U.S. Department of Health and Human Services. Local programs are operated through grants to public agencies, private nonprofit organizations, faith-based organizations, and school systems. Grants are awarded by regional offices of the Department of Health and Human Services and by the Head Start Bureau's Native American and Migrant and Seasonal Program Branches. In 2006, there were 1,604 local grantees. Federal funds are limited to 80% of total program costs;

A child enrolled in Early Head Start spends some time with his mother during a field trip into the community.

Anne Vega/Merrill

there is a matching requirement of 20% from nonfederal sources. Federal law prohibits Head Start programs from charging fees of parents.

PROGRAM SERVICES AND EFFECTIVENESS

A core tenet of Head Start is that local programs need flexibility in order to meet the particular needs of their communities. The intent is to provide a range of individualized services that are responsive and appropriate to each child and family within a community context. Flexibility occurs within firm parameters set forth in program performance standards by the federal Head Start Bureau (also published in the *Federal Register*). The performance standards define the services that Head Start programs are to provide to children and families and constitute the best statement of Head Start's expectations of high quality.

The standards are organized into three major areas: Early Childhood Development and Health Services, Family and Community Partnerships, and Program Design and Management. Each area contains a set of standards, which in essence are mandated regulations for all Head Start programs, plus a rationale for the standards and guidance in the form of examples of how a standard could be implemented. A detailed section on standards of working with children with disabilities and their families is also provided. To provide maximum flexibility in implementation, the performance standards do not prescribe *how* the services defined in the standards are to be carried out. Head Start seeks to provide a coordinated set of services, not separate components in early childhood, health, and parent involvement. To this end, the standards include a number of cross-references to other standards and examples, in an attempt to support an integrated approach to service delivery.

Early Childhood Development and Health Services

A common misconception of Head Start is that a standard curriculum is implemented in all classrooms. In reality, local programs are given a good deal of flexibility to select or design and implement a curriculum based on developmentally and linguistically appropriate practices with young children. Program standards recognize that children have individual rates of development, as well as individual interests, temperaments, languages, cultural backgrounds, and learning styles. Head Start programs are to be inclusive of children with disabilities, as noted, and to foster an environment of acceptance that respects differences in gender, culture, language, ethnicity, and family composition. The need for Head Start to support the home language, culture, and family composition is emphasized repeatedly in descriptions of program standards.

Head Start standards follow closely the developmentally appropriate practices in early childhood programs recommended by the National Association for the Education of Young Children (Bredekamp & Copple, 1997). The daily program is to contain a balance of child-initiated and adult-directed activities, including individual and small group activities. Social and emotional development is to be supported by building trust; fostering independence; encouraging self-control by setting clear, consistent limits and having realistic expectations; encouraging respect for the feelings and rights of others; and providing timely, predictable, and unrushed routines and transitions. Each child's learning is to be supported through experimentation, inquiry, observation, play, exploration, and related strategies. Art, music, movement, and dialogue are viewed as key opportunities for creative self-expression, and language use among children and between children and adults is promoted. Developmentally appropriate activities and materials are to be provided for support of children's emerging literacy and numeracy development. Center-based programs are to provide sufficient time, space, equipment, materials, and adult guidance for active play and movement that support fine and gross motor development. Home-based programs are to encourage parents to appreciate the value of physical development and to provide opportunities for safe and active play.

Program standards for education and early childhood development include separate sections on infants/toddlers and preschool-age children. Services for infants and toddlers emphasize the development of secure relationships (e.g., limited number of consistent teachers over an extended period of time), emerging communication skills, fine and gross motor development, and opportunities for each child to explore a variety of sensory and motor experiences. The curriculum for preschool-age children is to foster skills that form a foundation for school readiness and later school success, including opportunities for each child to organize experiences, understand concepts, and develop age-appropriate literacy, numeracy, reasoning, problem-solving and decision-making skills. The curriculum also is intended to help children develop emotional security and facility in social relationships, self-awareness, and feelings of competence, self-esteem, and positive attitudes toward learning.

As noted, emphasis on school readiness and especially literacy outcomes is growing in Head Start. To support local programs in promoting children's literacy development, the Head Start Bureau provided a professional development program known as Strategic Teacher Education Program (STEP) in 2002 to ensure that every Head Start program and classroom teacher has a fundamental knowledge of early literacy and state-of-the-art early literacy teaching techniques. Another nationally disseminated professional development program is the *HeadsUp! Reading* initiative developed by the National Head Start Association. A study of this program offered as a 15-week satellite broadcast training series found positive effects on children's literacy skills compared to a control group (Jackson, Larzelere, St. Clair, Corr, Ficther, & Egertson, 2006).

Parents are to be an integral part of the development of the local program's curriculum and approach to child development and education. Also, opportunities are to be provided for parents to strengthen their child observation skills and to share assessments with staff that inform program planning for each child. Parent-staff discussion of each child's development and education is to occur in conferences and home visits. One of the purposes of home visits is to support parents in their role as their child's first teacher and to assist families in the development and attainment of family goals. Services to children with disabilities are to be consistent with each child's Individualized Family Service Plan (IFSP) or Individualized Education Program (IEP).

Head Start has had a strong commitment to improving children's health outcomes since its inception. The first director of the national Head Start program was a physician, Dr. Robert Cooke, chair of the Department of Pediatrics at Johns Hopkins University. Careful attention to children's health care needs was a central part of Head Start's original purpose.

This tradition continues today with detailed attention to child health and safety, child nutrition, and child mental health in the performance standards. Within 90 days of a child's entry into a Head Start program, the staff is to collaborate with parents in determining the health status of each child. This entails an assessment of whether each child has an ongoing source of continuous, accessible health care. If ongoing health care is not accessible to a child, the program must assist parents in accessing a source of care. The child's health status review also includes a determination as to whether the child is up to date on a schedule of preventive and primary health care, including medical, dental, and mental health. Again, the program is to assist the family in making arrangements to bring the child up to date if necessary. The Head Start program also is to ensure that children continue with the recommended schedule of well-child care and to track the provision of health care services. When a child has a known or suspected health or developmental problem, the Head Start program is to obtain or arrange for further diagnostic testing, examination, and treatment by a licensed or certified professional.

Within 45 days of each child's entry into Head Start, the program is to perform or obtain developmental, sensory, and behavioral screenings of motor, language, social, cognitive, perceptual, and emotional skills. The screenings must be sensitive to the child's cultural background and home language, and multiple sources of information on all aspects of each child's development and behavior are to be obtained, including input from family members, teachers, and other relevant staff. A follow-up plan for children with identified health needs is to be established and monitored with parents. Dental follow-up and treatment must include fluoride supplements and topical fluoride treatments for every child with moderate to severe tooth decay and in communities where there is a lack of adequate fluoride levels. Further, Head Start programs are to develop and implement procedures that enable staff to identify any new or recurring medical, dental, or developmental concerns so as to permit prompt and appropriate referrals. Parents are to be fully informed and involved in this process.

Program provisions for mental health services include collaborations with families to solicit parental information and concerns about their child's mental health and to enable staff to provide information to parents about staff observations of the child and anticipated changes in the child's behavior and development, especially separation and attachment issues. There also is to be parent-staff discussion of how to strengthen nurturing, supportive environments and relationships at home and in the program. Programs are to help parents better understand mental health issues and to support parents' participation in needed mental health interventions. Staff and/or family concerns about a child's mental health are to be addressed in a timely manner through the services of a mental health professional secured by the program. A regular schedule of mental health consultation with program staff and parents is also provided to address individual children's needs and ways to promote mental wellness.

Head Start performance standards also call for staff and families to work together to identify each child's nutritional needs, with consideration of a family's eating patterns, including cultural preferences and special dietary requirements. Local programs are to design and implement a nutrition program that meets the nutritional needs and feeding requirements of each child. Children in center-based programs are served a meal on a daily basis; each child receives a nutritious snack plus breakfast and/or lunch, depending on morning, afternoon, or full-day enrollment. A variety of foods—responsive to cultural and ethnic preferences, as well as for the broadening of a child's food experience—are to be served. Food is not to be used as a reward or punishment. Each child is to be encouraged, but not forced, to eat or taste the food. At least one third of a child's daily nutritional needs are to be met through meals and snacks in a part-day center-based program, and one half to two thirds of a child's daily nutritional needs are to be met in a full-day center-based program. Dental hygiene is to be promoted in conjunction with meals at programs. Parents are to be involved in planning, implementing, and evaluating a program's nutritional services, and parent education activities must include opportunities for families to learn about food preparation and strengthen nutritional skills.

Last, Head Start standards include health emergency procedures; a description of conditions for short-term exclusion from the program due to a health-related matter; and provisions for medication administration, injury prevention, hygiene, and first-aid kits.

Family and Community Partnerships

Among model early childhood programs in this country, Head Start has perhaps the most comprehensive and detailed set of provisions for working with families. Scholars have long pointed to parent involvement as a cornerstone of Head Start's success.

Head Start seeks to establish a collaborative partnership with parents that is built on mutual trust and an understanding of family goals, strengths, and necessary services and other supports. To this end, programs are to offer parents an opportunity to develop and implement an individualized Family Partnership Agreement that sets forth family goals, responsibilities, timetables, and strategies for achieving the goals and for monitoring progress. The agreement is to take into account and coordinate with preexisting family plans developed with other programs or agencies. The services here pertain to emergency assistance with basic needs such as housing, food, clothing, and transportation; education and counseling programs focused on such mental health issues as substance abuse, child abuse and neglect, and domestic violence; and continuing education and employment training.

Head Start's concept of parent involvement is broad based and emphasizes two parental roles: parents as active contributors to program policies and practices, and parents as competent supporters of their child's healthy growth and development. Parent participation in any program activity, including home visits, is voluntary and must not be required as a condition of a child's enrollment.

Probably the best-known Head Start provision for parent participation is the shared governance requirement that 51% of the members of the local program policy group must be parents of currently enrolled children. Also, parents of formerly enrolled children may serve as community representatives on the policy group. The policy group is charged with working collaboratively with key management staff and the governing body responsible for legal and fiscal administration of the local program to determine policies and procedures in many areas, including the following:

- Program philosophy and long- and short-term goals and objectives
- Criteria for determining recruitment, selection, and enrollment priorities
- Decisions to hire or terminate the Head Start director and any person who works primarily for the program

The policy group also advises staff in developing and implementing local program policies, activities, and services.

Many other provisions address parent participation. One is for parents to serve as employers or volunteers. Nearly 925,000 parents volunteered in their local Head Start program during the 2005–2006 program year, and 27% of Head Start staff members were parents of current or former Head Start children. As noted, local programs are to provide opportunities for parents to help select or develop the program's curriculum. Parents must be welcomed as visitors and encouraged to observe and participate with children in group activities. Facilities must be open to parents during all program hours.

Head Start addresses numerous parenting tasks faced by adult participants in the program. Opportunities are provided for parents to enhance their parenting skills, knowledge, and understanding of the educational and developmental needs and activities of their children. Parents also are encouraged to share concerns about their children with program staff (as described in the previous section). In addition to two home visits per year, teachers in center-based programs are to hold at least two staff-parent conferences per program year. The goal of the conferences is to enhance the knowledge and understanding of both staff and parents of each child's educational and developmental progress in the program.

A wide range of content areas is addressed in parenting education and support services. Parents have opportunities to be involved in health, nutrition, and mental health education. Another content area is community and child advocacy. The program is to support and encourage parents to influence the nature and goals of community services in a way that makes services more responsive to their needs and interests. Programs also are to help parents become advocates for their children as they transition from home to Head Start or another early childhood program and from Head Start to elementary school. Further, support for the child advocate role focuses on parents' continued involvement in their child's education in school, including education and training for parents to exercise their rights and responsibilities regarding the education of their child in the school setting, as well as communication with teachers and other school personnel so parents can participate in decisions related to their child's education. In addition to the health and advocacy content areas, the revised program standards call for local Head Start programs to support family literacy development directly or through referrals to other local programs. An aim here is to assist parents as adult learners in recognizing their own literacy goals.

No one program can meet all the needs of a child and family. An intent of Head Start's community partnerships is to improve the delivery of services to children and families and to ensure that a local Head Start program responds to community needs. Strong communication, cooperation, and sharing of information are to occur between Head Start and the following types of community organizations:

- Health care providers such as clinics, physicians, and dentists
- Mental health providers

- Nutritional service providers
- Individuals and agencies that provide services to children with disabilities and their families
- Family preservation and support services
- Child protective services
- Local elementary schools and other educational and cultural institutions, such as libraries and museums
- Providers of child-care services
- Other organizations or businesses that may provide support and resources to families

Each Head Start program is to establish and maintain a Health Services Advisory Committee comprised of professionals and volunteers from the community.

The program gives considerable attention to children's transitions into Head Start and from Head Start to elementary schools or other child-care settings. Local Head Start programs are to ensure that children's relevant records are transferred to the school or the child's next setting. In addition, each Head Start program is to take an active role in encouraging communication between the program staff and their counterparts in the schools and other child-care settings, including principals, teachers, social workers, and health-care staff. The aim of these communications is to facilitate continuity of programming for each child. Meetings are to be initiated for Head Start staff, parents, and kindergarten or elementary school teachers to discuss developmental progress and abilities of each child. In the Early Head Start programs, transition planning is to begin for each child and family at least 6 months prior to the child's third birthday.

Program Planning and Staffing

Planning is an integral part of the management of local Head Start programs. Specifically, each program is to develop and implement a systematic, ongoing process of program planning that includes consultation with the program's governing body, policy groups, and program staff, as well as with other community organizations that serve Head Start or other low-income families with young children. The program planning is to include an assessment of community strengths, needs, and resources; the development of both short- and long-range program goals and objectives; written plans for implementing services; and a review of progress in meeting goals at least annually. A self-assessment of program effectiveness and progress in meeting program goals and objectives is to be conducted at least once each program year. Communication with parents, governing bodies, and policy groups and among staff is to be carried out on a regular basis. Records are to be maintained on all children, families, and staff, with appropriate provisions for confidentiality.

The staffing structure for a local Head Start program entails a director, classroom teachers, and home visitors, plus content experts in each of the following areas: education and child development services, health services, nutrition services, family and community partnership services, parent involvement services, and disabilities services. The content experts are staff or regular consultants, depending on the size of the local program. Staffing patterns and staff organizational structures are determined by local programs.

All staff working as classroom teachers are required to obtain a Child Development Associate (CDA) or equivalent credential. The CDA credential, administered nationally, is a competency-based certificate in early childhood education. The federal reauthorization of Head Start in 1998 required that by September 2003, at least one half of all Head Start teachers in center-based programs must have an associate, baccalaureate, or advanced degree in early childhood education or a related field, with preschool teaching experience. In addition, teachers of infants and toddlers must have training and experience necessary to develop consistent, stable, and supportive relationships with very young children and must develop knowledge of infant/toddler development, safety issues in infant/toddler care (e.g., reducing the risk of sudden infant death syndrome), and methods for communicating effectively with infants and toddlers and their parents. In 2005–2006, 72% of Head Start teachers had an associate's degree or higher in early childhood education. The 2007 reauthorization of Head Start stipulates that at least 50% of Head Start teachers nationwide in center-based programs should have a bachelor's or advanced degree in early childhood education or related field by the year 2013.

Qualifications of staff or consultants serving as content experts are specific to the content area. For example, the content expert responsible for the education and child development services must have training and experiences in areas that include theories and principles of child growth and development, early childhood education, and family support.

Sensitivity to cultural and linguistic differences is a staff qualification. Staff and program consultants must be familiar with the ethnic background and heritage of families in the local program and, to the extent feasible, must be able to communicate effectively with children and families with no or limited English proficiency. When a majority of children speak the same language in a Head Start program, at least one classroom staff member or home visitor interacting regularly with the children must speak their language.

Program Effectiveness

An extensive research literature on Head Start has accumulated since the program's inception in 1965. Results indicate that the program provides immediate benefits for children. In short, "Head Start participants can begin kindergarten on a stronger footing than they would without the program" (Love, Tarullo, Raikes, & Chazan-Cohen, 2006, p. 569).

The first several decades of Head Start research were summarized in a 1985 synthesis of 210 published and unpublished reports on Head Start research (McKey, Condelli, Ganson, Barrett, McConkey, & Plantz, 1985). The synthesis found immediate gains in children's cognitive abilities, achievement motivation, self-esteem, social behavior, and health indicators. There also were some indications of improvements in mothers' well-being and in community services, although it is not clear Head Start played a causal role in these changes. The synthesis review also found that cognitive test score gains achieved during Head Start did not persist over the long term (generally 2 years after participation in Head Start). Similarly, the gains in socioemotional functioning also did not persist long term (generally 3 years after participation). Not all of the 210 research reports included in the 1985 synthesis examined each aspect of Head Start. For example, the report's findings on cognitive gains were based on 72 studies, and the findings on socioemotional development were based on 17 studies (McKey et al., 1985).

Until 2000, rigorous experimental designs were used infrequently to assess Head Start effects. Limitations of much of the research on Head Start were highlighted in a 1997 U.S. Government Accounting Office (GAO) report on the impact of Head Start (GAO, 1997). From a review of some 200 reports on Head Start effects, the GAO identified only 16 studies that compared Head Start participants to an unserved comparison group, and only 1 of these 16 studies used random assignment to a Head Start group or to a non–Head Start comparison group. The GAO report also noted a pattern of studies focusing mostly on academic or cognitive outcomes rather than the broad range of child functioning addressed by Head Start, as well as a reliance on studies conducted in the 1960s and 1970s that may not be applicable to current-day programs and populations.

Partly in response to the GAO report, congressional reauthorization of Head Start in 1998 called for an experimental study of Head Start impact. To these ends, currently Head Start is supporting an ambitious research agenda that includes an experimental (random assignment), longitudinal study of Head Start and Early Head Start program effects, plus a range of other research projects designed to inform improvements in program effectiveness.

The Head Start Impact Study is the congressionally mandated investigation of Head Start. It is examining contributions to key outcomes of development and learning and the conditions under which Head Start works best and for which children. The Head Start Impact Study includes a nationally representative sample involving 84 agencies across 23 different states. Approximately 5,000 newly entering 3- and 4-year-old children applying for Head Start were randomly assigned to either a Head Start group or to a control group that could receive any other non–Head Start services chosen by their parents. Children are being followed through the spring of their first-grade and third-grade years (Puma et al., 2005).

Preliminary results of the first year of data collection involving approximately 9 months of program participation point to small to moderate positive effects favoring the 3-year-old children assigned to the Head Start program. Fewer positive impacts were found for 4-year-old children. In the cognitive domain, statistically significant positive impacts for both 3- and 4-year-old children were found on measures of children's pre-reading, pre-writing, vocabulary, and parent reports of children's literacy skills but not oral comprehension and phonological awareness or early mathematics skills. In the social-emotional domain, a small statistically significant Head Start impact on the problem behaviors (fewer) was noted among children who entered the study as 3-year-olds. There were no impacts on social skills, approaches to learning, or on social competencies for 3-year-olds. No significant impacts on social-emotional competence were found for children entering the program as 4-year-olds. In the health domain, impacts were statistically significant for 3-year-olds on parent reports of children's access to health care (higher) and health status (better). For children who entered the program as 4-year-olds, there were moderate significant impacts on access to health care (higher) but not on health status. In addition, the study found small impacts on parenting practices. Parents of children who entered the program as 3-year-olds exhibited a higher use of educational activities and lower use of physical discipline, and parents of children who entered the program as 4-year-olds exhibited higher use of educational activities (Puma et al., 2005). The magnitude of these effects is likely larger than indicated in the study because analyses focused on groups randomly assigned to Head Start or to the control group ("intent to treat") rather than children who actually enrolled in Head Start or remained out of Head Start. That is, some children who were offered the opportunity to participate in Head Start did not actually enroll in Head Start, and some children assigned to the control group eventually became Head Start participants (Ludwig & Phillips, 2007).

The outcome study of Early Head Start, initiated in 1995, involves a sample of 17 programs selected to represent diverse program approaches, geographic locations, and participant backgrounds. Results when children were 36 months of age showed positive program impacts on children's cognitive, language, and socioemotional development, as well as on parents' interactions with their children during play and support of language and learning at home (e.g., more likely to read daily to their children; Love et al., 2005). The study will again assess children in fifth grade with an anticipated sample of approximately 1,900 children in the 17 program sites.

In addition to these two national outcome studies, the Head Start Bureau sponsors the Head Start Family and Child Experiences Survey (FACES), designed to describe characteristics, experiences, and outcomes for children and families in Head Start and beyond. The first cohort consisted of a nationally representative sample of 3,200 children and their families, assessed in the fall and spring of the children's Head Start year, on entry into kindergarten and, for some children, first grade. Two more national cohorts of children and their families were comprised of approximately 2,800 children each. The FACES study is useful for answering questions about Head Start quality and effectiveness. For example, one recent analysis found that children entered the Head Start program with early literacy and numeracy skills that were less developed than those of most children of the same age, and that children in Head Start showed significant advances in some emergent literacy skills between the beginning and end of the program year but continued to lag behind national norms. Children who attended Head Start for 2 years showed greater progress than their peers who attended for 1 year (Zill & Resnick, 2006).

The Head Start research literature also includes numerous smaller-scale studies of program impact. For example, a study conducted in a metropolitan community in the Southeast examined school readiness outcomes for children eligible to enroll in Head Start. The children were randomly assigned to Head Start or to a wait-list control group. The children enrolled in Head Start achieved greater gains from fall to spring in receptive vocabulary and phonemic awareness than the control group children, but there were no group differences on measures of social skills and approaches to learning (Abbott-Shim, Lambert, & McCarty, 2003).

DEMONSTRATION PROJECTS

Child Care and Family Self-Sufficiency

Child care is a pressing need in the United States as growing numbers of parents enter school or the paid labor force when their children are young. For low-income families, welfare reform policies have escalated the need for child care due to job training and work requirements now imposed on parents who receive welfare benefits. The typical Head Start offering of part-day classrooms that typically do not operate during summer months does not accommodate the child-care needs of families with adults in school or the paid labor force during times Head Start is not provided.

Ways to combine Head Start and child care have been in development for some time (Poersch & Blank, 1996), and in 1997 Head Start launched an initiative aimed at building partnerships with child-care providers and, in some communities, to deliver full-day, full-year Head Start services. One model is for Head Start to connect with a child-care program that provides care before and/or after the Head Start day. The Head Start program generally provides transportation to the child-care program in this arrangement. Another approach is a "wraparound care" model wherein Head Start provides child care before and after the Head Start day and on days when Head Start is not in session. The program may use the same staff or other part-time staff to provide extended-day care. A third model is a collaborative "wrap-in care partnership" that involves Head Start contracting with a child-care program to provide full-day care and education services for Head Start–eligible children. The child-care program is expected to meet pertinent Head Start performance standards, with Head Start providing ("wrapping in") its usual comprehensive services and parent involvement opportunities (Blank & Poersch, 2004).

The "wrap-in" model is growing in popularity and provides a number of potential benefits. These include increasing family access to health and social services, maximizing facility space and resources, improving quality in early childhood settings, and providing more flexible hours of service. Preliminary evaluation findings from one partnership program in Kansas City,

Missouri, point to positive impacts on teacher behavior, teacher-child attachment, and classroom quality (Blank & Poersch, 2004).

Head Start also has experimented with supports for family child-care homes. Eighteen Head Start family child-care demonstration projects were launched in 1992 to determine whether Head Start performance standards could be met in family child-care homes through additional training and support services. An experimental study was undertaken to compare the impact on children and families in family child care with those participating in center-based classroom programs. Participating families had a 4-year-old child, and the parent was required to be working, in job training, or in school. Results indicated no significant differences between Head Start family child-care homes and centers overall on the total number of quality indicators implemented, except the centers slightly surpassed the family child-care homes in indicators of parent involvement. The children assigned to family child care performed at least as well as children in centers on measures of cognitive, socioemotional, and physical development. A follow-up study in kindergarten found that children from the two Head Start settings performed equally well on measures of cognitive, social-emotional, and physical outcomes and were equally likely to be recommended for promotion to first grade. Also, about equal percentages of parents from the two Head Start settings participated in parent-teacher conferences or kindergarten activities (Faddis, Ahrens-Gray, & Klein, 2000).

Among families who needed full-day, full-year child care outside the Head Start program in 2005, a majority (57%) used family, friend, and neighbor caregivers (Center for Law & Social Policy, 2006). These informal caregivers (also known as kith and kin caregivers) typically are not licensed or regulated and do not participate in formal child-care training programs. In 2004, the Head Start Bureau provided funds to 24 Early Head Start programs to implement an Enhanced Home Visiting Pilot Project designed to support the quality of care that family, friend, and neighbor caregivers provide to infants and toddlers enrolled in home-based Early Head Start programs. The initiative includes home visits to caregivers, group training and support group events, and the provision of materials (e.g., children's books) and equipment to be used in the home for promoting positive child outcomes. An outcome evaluation is currently underway (Paulsell, Mekos, Del Grosso, Banghart, & Nogales, 2006).

Comprehensive Approaches to Supporting Families

Head Start has built on its strong commitment to parent involvement by designing and implementing several demonstration programs aimed at testing innovative and comprehensive approaches to family support (Powell, 2006). These include the Parent-Child Centers, the Child and Family Resource Centers, and others.

The Parent-Child Centers began in 1967 as Head Start's first experimental effort to serve children from birth to age 3 years and their families. Lessons learned in the Parent-Child Centers provided one of the bases of the Early Head Start program launched in 1995. From the outset, the Parent-Child Centers were designed to meet the needs of individual communities; as a result, each of the 36 original demonstration programs was quite different from the others in program design and methods. At the time of their initial development in the late 1960s, the Parent-Child Centers were the first national effort to focus on families with children under 3 years of age. The goals included strengthening family organization and functioning in order to maximize young children's developmental potential (Lazar, Anchel, Beckman, Gethard, Lazar, & Sale, 1970). In 1970, three Parent-Child Centers became the focus of an experimental study aimed at investigating different approaches to early intervention with parents and very young children. These centers were known as the Parent and Child Development Centers and were based in Houston, New Orleans, and Birmingham, Alabama. Each implemented a different strategy of education and support for parenting during the early years of life. In the Houston model, for example, a year of home visits was followed by center-based activities for both mother and child. Careful evaluations found positive program effects on mothers' child-rearing skills and children's cognitive functioning (Andrews et al., 1982).

The Child and Family Resource Centers provided Head Start's "purest example of an early model family support program" (Zigler & Freedman, 1987, p. 64). Center staff developed an individualized plan for meeting the unique needs of each enrolled family through a needs assessment and goal-setting process. The age of the target child was birth to age 8 years. Home visiting was a central component, as was coordination with a range of community services to address pressing family issues such as alcohol abuse, poor health, inadequate housing and health care, and unemployment. An evaluation found improvements in family circumstances but no significant effect on child outcomes (Travers, Nauta, & Irwin, 1982). The centers were established in the 1970s and eventually phased out.

THE FUTURE OF HEAD START

Many challenges faced Head Start at the turn of the century. Two notable areas pertain to the need to strengthen attention to children's school readiness skills and to respond programmatically to changes in the needs of low-income families.

Throughout its history, questions have been raised periodically about the quality and focus on Head Start's preparation of children for school success. Results of recent outcome evaluations, summarized in this chapter, suggest that Head Start programs make a positive contribution to children's school readiness, including literacy skills. The gains are modest, however, with room for improvement. The growing emphasis on early reading skills has generated concern that Head Start's comprehensive focus, including dental care, immunizations, nutrition, and family support services, will erode in favor of attention to children's literacy and school readiness experiences in classrooms. Concern also focuses on the possibility that outcome assessments will drive curriculum emphases through "teaching to the test" practices. Head Start's challenge is to embrace literacy and school readiness goals in an approach that fully recognizes that positive growth in all developmental domains coupled with a range of appropriately focused support services contribute to early success in school.

Head Start also must grapple with the changing needs of families in poverty. The contemporary social landscape differs substantially from the days when Head Start was founded. Today's low-income families seeking to move off welfare generally need the following: full-day child care; services for infants and toddlers; and systematic assistance with employment readiness and perhaps other family needs (Parker, Piotrkowski, Horn, & Greene, 1995). Clearly, Head Start has developed high-quality services in each of these areas. As described, Head Start is responding to the realities of welfare reform policies by strengthening its ability to provide or arrange for full-day child care for families. These efforts are not widespread or universally available to families. The services are lodged in a relatively small number of programs. Head Start remains primarily a part-day program for 3- and 4-year-old children. In addition to collaborations with child care programs, coordination with programs that target the same population could expand resources and improve benefits for children and their families. One option here is the welfare reform program Temporary Assistance to Needy Families (TANF; Horn, 2004). Nineteen percent of Head Start families received TANF benefits in 2005 (Center for Law and Social Policy, 2006). Another option for collaborative ties is the growing number of state-funded preschool programs, which often are aimed at children from lower-income families (Stebbins & Scott, 2007).

Creative responses to these challenges will require Head Start to capitalize on its status as the "birthplace of comprehensive services in a family setting" (Zigler & Muenchow, 1992, p. 243) and its tradition of adaptation and improvement (Bowman, 2004). Head Start needs to retain and strengthen its role as a national laboratory for developing new models of innovative programs for children and their families. Strong partnerships with other institutions and resources in local communities are essential in these efforts. No matter how comprehensive or well administered, Head Start can only do so much to combat the poor prenatal care and nutrition, inadequate housing, crime-ridden neighborhoods, and racial and gender discrimination that affect the lives of many families living in poverty . Head Start is not a "panacea for poverty" (Washington & Oyemade Bailey, 1995, p. 141). It is, however, a demonstrated leader in mobilizing the energies of diverse institutions in communities on behalf of young children. Improvements in children's development and learning outcomes require not only stimulating classrooms and supportive parent-child relationships but also communities that genuinely care about children, families, and their environments.

REFERENCES

Abbott-Shim, M., Lambert, R., & McCarty, F. (2003). A comparison of school readiness outcomes for children randomly assigned to a Head Start program and the program's wait list. *Journal of Education for Students Placed at Risk, 8,* 191–214.

Andrews, S. R., Blumenthal, J. B., Johnson, D. L., Kahn, A. J., Ferguson, C. J., Lasater, R. M., Malone, P. E., & Wallace, D. B. (1982). The skills of mothering: A study of Parent Child Development Centers. *Monographs of the Society for Research in Child Development, 47* (6, Serial No. 198).

Baratz, S. S., & Baratz, J. C. (1970). Early childhood intervention: The social science base of institutional racism. *Harvard Educational Review, 48,* 161–170.

Berrueta-Clement, J. R., Schweinhart, L. J., Barnett, W. S., Epstein, A. S., & Weikart, D. P. (1984). Changed lives: The effects of the Perry Preschool Program on youths through age 19. *Monographs of High/Scope Educational Research Foundation Number 8.* Ypsilanti, MI: High/Scope Press.

Blank, H., & Poersch, N. O. (2004). Head Start and child care: Programs adapt to meet the needs of working families. In E. Zigler & S. J. Styfco (Eds.), *The Head Start debates* (pp. 339–349). Baltimore, MD: Brookes.

Bloom, B. S. (1964). *Stability and change in human characteristics.* New York: Wiley.

Bowman, B. T. (2004). The future of Head Start. In E. Zigler & S. J. Styfco (Eds.), *The Head Start debates* (pp. 533–544). Baltimore, MD: Brookes.

Bredekamp, S., & Copple, C. (Eds.). (1997). *Developmentally appropriate practice in early childhood programs.* Rev. ed. Washington, DC: National Association for the Education of Young Children (NAEYC).

Bronfenbrenner, U., & Morris, P. A. (2006). The bioecological model of human development. In R. Lerner & W. Damon (Eds.), *Handbook of child psychology (6th ed.): Vol. 1. Theoretical models of human development* (pp. 793–828). Hoboken, NJ: Wiley.

Center for Law and Social Policy (2006, September). *Head Start participants, programs, families, and staff in 2005.* Washington, DC: Author.

Faddis, B., Ahrens-Gray, P., & Klein, E. L. (2000). *Evaluation of Head Start family child care demonstration.* Portland, OR: RMC Research Corp.

Government Accounting Office. (1997). *Head Start: Research provides little information on impact of current program.* Washington, DC: Author.

Gray, S. W., & Klaus, R. A. (1965). An experimental preschool program for culturally deprived children. *Child Development, 36,* 887–898.

Head Start Bureau. (1997). *Head Start program performance standards and other regulations.* Washington, DC: Head Start Bureau, Administration on Children, Youth and Families, U.S. Department of Health and Human Services.

Horn, W. F. (2004). Coordinating Head Start with the states. In E. Zigler & S. J. Styfco (Eds.), *The Head Start debates* (pp. 459–465). Baltimore, MD: Brookes.

Hunt, J. McV. (1961). *Intelligence and experience.* New York: Ronald Press.

Jackson, B., Larzelere, R., St. Clair, L., Corr, M., Fichter, C., & Egertson, H. (2006). The impact of *HeadsUp! Reading* on early childhood educators' literacy practices and preschool children's literacy skills. *Early Childhood Research Quarterly, 21,* 213–226.

Keniston, K., & Carnegie Council on Children. (1977). *All our children: The American family under pressure.* New York: Harcourt Brace Jovanovich.

Labov, W. (1970). The logic of nonstandard English. In F. Williams (Ed.), *Language and poverty* (pp. 153–189). Chicago: Markham.

Lazar, I., Anchel, G., Beckman, L., Gethard, E., Lazar, J., & Sale, J. (1970). *A national survey of the Parent-Child Center program.* Washington, DC: Kirschner.

Love, J. M., Kisker, E. E., Ross, C. M., Constantine, J., Boller, K., Chazan-Cohen, R., et al. (2005). The effectiveness of Early Head Start for 3-year-old children and their parents: Lessons for policy and programs. *Developmental Psychology, 41,* 885–901.

Love, J. M., Tarullo, L. B., Raikes, H., & Chazan-Cohen, R. (2006). Head Start: What do we know about its effectiveness? What do we need to know? In K. McCartney & D. Phillips (Eds.), *Blackwell handbook of early childhood development* (pp. 550–575). Malden, MA: Blackwell.

Ludwig, J., & Phillips, D. (2007). The benefits and costs of Head Start. In L. Sherrod (Ed.), *Social policy report* (pp. 3–18). Ann Arbor, MI: Society for Research in Child Development.

McKey, R. H., Condelli, L., Ganson, H., Barrett, B. J., McConkey, C., & Plantz, M. C. (1985, June). *The impact of Head Start on children, families, and communities. Final report of the Head Start Evaluation, Synthesis, and Utilization Project.* Washington, DC: Superintendent of Documents, U.S. Government Printing Office (ERIC document #ED395681).

Parker, F. L., Piotrkowski, C. S., Horn, W. F., & Greene, S. M. (1995). The challenge for Head Start: Realizing its vision as a two-generation program. In S. Smith (Vol. ed.) & I. Sigel (Series ed.), *Two generation programs for families in poverty: A new intervention strategy. Advances in Applied Developmental Psychology, Vol. 9* (pp. 135–159). Norwood, NJ: Ablex.

Paulsell, D., Mekos, D., Del Grosso, P., Banghart, P., & Nogales, R. (2006, January). *The Enhanced Home Visiting Pilot Project: How Early Head Start programs are reaching out to kith and kin caregivers.* Princeton, NJ: Mathematica Policy Research, Inc.

Poersch, N. O., & Blank, H. (1996). *Working together for children: Head Start and child care partnerships.* Washington, DC: Children's Defense Fund.

Powell, D. R. (2006). Families and early childhood interventions. In W. Damon & R. M. Lerner (Series Eds.) & K. A. Renninger & I. E. Sigel (Vol. Eds.), *Handbook of child psychology (6th ed.): Vol 4. Child psychology in practice* (pp. 548–591). Hoboken, NJ: Wiley.

Puma, M., Bell, S., Cook, R., Heid, C., Lopez, M., Zill, N., et al. (2005). *Head Start Impact Study: First year findings.* Washington, DC: U.S. Department of Health and Human Services.

Richmond, J. B., Stipek, D. J., & Zigler, E. (1979). A decade of Head Start. In E. Zigler & J. Valentine (Eds.), *Project Head Head Start: A legacy of the War on Poverty* (pp. 135–152). New York: Free Press.

Ryan, W. (1971). *Blaming the victim.* New York: Pantheon Books.

Schweinhart, L. J., Barnes, H. V., & Weikart, D. P. (1993). Significant benefits: The High/Scope Perry Preschool Study through age 27. *Monographs of the High/Scope Educational Research Foundation, 10.* Ypsilanti, MI: High/Scope Press.

Schweinhart, L. J., Montie, J., Xiang, Z., Barnett, W. S., Belfield, C. R., & Nores, M. (2005). Lifetime effects—High/Scope Perry Preschool study through age 40. *Monographs of the High/Scope Educational Research Foundation, 14.* Ypsilanti, MI: High/Scope Press.

Stebbins, H., & Scott, L. C. (2007, January). *Better outcomes for all: Promoting partnerships between Head Start and state pre-k.* Washington, DC: Center for Law and Social Policy.

Travers, J., Nauta, M., & Irwin, N. (1982). *The effects of a social program: Final report of the Child and Family Resource Program's infant-toddler component.* Cambridge, MA: Abt Associates.

U.S. Department of Health & Human Services. (2003). *The Head Start path to positive child outcomes.* Washington, DC: Administration of Children, Youth and Families/Head Start Bureau, U.S. Department of Health and Human Services.

Washington, V., & Oyemade Bailey, U. J. (1995). *Project Head Start: Models and strategies for the twenty-first century.* New York: Garland.

Zigler, E. (1998). By what goals should Head Start be assessed? *Children's services: Social Policy, Research, and Practice, 1,* 5–17.

Zigler, E., & Anderson, K. (1979). An idea whose time had come: The intellectual and political climate for Head Start. In E. Zigler & J. Valentine (Eds.), *Project Head Start: A legacy of the War on Poverty* (pp. 3–19). New York: Free Press.

Zigler, E. F., & Freedman, J. (1987). Head Start: A pioneer of family support. In S. L. Kagan, D. R. Powell, B. Weissbourd, & E. F. Zigler (Eds.), *America's family support program: Perspectives and prospects* (pp. 57–76). New Haven, CT: Yale University Press.

Zigler, E., & Muenchow, S. (1992). *Head Start: The inside story of America's most successful educational experiment.* New York: Basic Books.

Zigler, E., & Valentine, J. (1979). *Project Head Start: A legacy of the War on Poverty.* New York: Free Press.

Zill, N., & Resnick, G. (2006). Emergent literacy of low-income children in Head Start: Relationships with child and family characteristics, program factors, and classroom quality. In D. K. Dickinson & S. B. Neuman (Eds.), *Handbook of early literacy research, vol. 2* (pp. 347–371). New York: Guilford.

Chapter 4

The Portage Model

An International Home Approach to Early Intervention for Young Children and Their Families

David E. Shearer ↝ *President, The International Portage Association (IPA), Tampa, Florida*
Darlene L. Shearer ↝ *Lawton and Rhea Chiles Center for Healthy Mothers and Babies, University of South Florida*

INTRODUCTION

The past four decades have seen a dramatic increase in both the number of programs devoted to early intervention for young children and the amount of financial and human resources dedicated to such efforts. Early intervention services are mandated by the U.S. government for young children with developmental disabilities. State and local education systems have the option to also provide such services to young children who are at risk for developmental disabilities. These mandated services are very complex and continue to evolve into a comprehensive early intervention system. The system is currently regulated by Public Law 105-17 (the amendments to the Individuals with Disabilities Education Act, 1997). Such legislation has set the precedent that parents and families will be involved in all facets of services that are planned, implemented, and evaluated for their young children. In addition, it mandates that services be provided in the child's least restrictive or natural learning environment. There continues to be much discussion regarding what constitutes the least restrictive environment for older, school-age children with disabilities. However, for very young children, the general consensus is that the most natural learning environment is the home or a child-care setting.

The target population of early intervention includes young children under the age of 6 and their families. Providing an intervention program for young children with, or at risk of, a developmental delay or disability and directly involving their parents have become common practices in the United States and industrialized countries, particularly for very young children (Giudice et al., 2006; Johnson, 2001; Odom & Karnes, 1988). As early as 1978, the U.S. Department of Health and Human Services (HHS), the governmental body that has provided the resources and much of the impetus for the early childhood programs in the United States, recognized the importance of parent involvement when it announced greater steps would be taken in the future to ensure parental involvement in the education of children. These steps included a stronger role for parent–teacher projects, parent advisory bodies, and development of educational materials for use in the home. Today parent programs abound in the early intervention field. In the United States and internationally, the young child, the parent, and the intervention program designed to meet the needs of the child are recognized as interdependent elements in the development of the society in which they exist (Brorson, 2005; Ray, Bowman, & Robbins, 2006).

Two important principles in the study of early educational interventions for children at risk for delayed or retarded cognitive development are timing and intensity. The summative results concerning these principles are clear: high-quality, intensive educational efforts beginning early in life lead to greater cognitive gains among early intervention participants than do programs that are either less intensive or that begin later in life (Love, Kisker, Ross, et al., 2005; Ramey & Ramey, 1992). Results from a large, nationally representative, randomized intervention trial suggest that intellectual development of young children is associated with the additive effects of intervention components (in this case, the number of home visits, days attended at child centers, and the number of meetings parents attended) and not with children's background characteristics (i.e., maternal education, birth weight) (Blair, Ramey, & Hardin, 1995). The findings suggest a dose–response relation between intervention and outcome, that the quantity of child and parent participation is of major importance for the development of cognitive skills. In these examples, there is ample evidence that an intense home-intervention program that serves children in the early years of development and emphasizes direct parent participation helps to ensure successful outcomes.

The Portage Model, since its introduction in 1969, has emphasized the importance of a strong parental role and gives parents the opportunity to be their child's primary interventionist and teacher in partnership with an intervention program. The Portage Model has developed, implemented, and demonstrated a highly successful intervention strategy. The model is a home-based delivery system centering on the entire family and a home teacher who helps the caregivers become more effective teachers/nurturers of their children. (The term *hometeacher* will be used throughout this chapter and is intended as a generic description of a function rather than a reference to a professional discipline.)

The basic premises of the model as they relate to parents and families are these:

- Families care about and want their child to attain maximum potential, however great or limited that potential may be.
- With instruction, modeling, and reinforcement, families will become more effective teachers/nurturers of their child.
- The socioeconomic and educational or intellectual levels of families do not necessarily determine either their willingness to teach their child or the extent of gains the child will attain as a result of parental instruction.

Structured teaching methods provide important feedback daily to the family and weekly to the staff, thereby reinforcing both when goals are met. Moreover, the structured method provides a continual database for curriculum modification, thus maximizing the likelihood of success for families and children.

Rationale for Active Parent Participation

Developers of the model chose to emphasize direct involvement of parents in the intervention model for many important reasons, including these:

- Parents as nurturers/caretakers provide support and encouragement to their children, The dependence of very young children places them in a daily role where they watch, mimic, and learn from their parents.
- Parents are consumers. They pay, either directly or indirectly, for the program and the service their child receives. Most parents want a voice in what and how their

Teaching and modeling by the home teacher help parent and child to develop an effective instructional style.

Todd Yarrington/Merrill

child is taught, and they want to participate in the teaching of their child.

- Parents, if knowledgeable about the program their child is receiving, can be the best advocates for program continuation and expansion. School boards, advisory councils, and state legislatures throughout the United States have substantially changed policy and laws as a direct result of parental advocacy.
- Family support is a dynamic system that includes those interactions and interventions that strengthen the integrity of the family unit.
- Parents of a child with a disability usually have more responsibility for their child over a significantly longer period of time than parents of a typically developing child.
- Parents serve as a vital resource to the center- or home-based staff in the area of functional program objectives for the child that will be useful in the child's home environment.
- Transferring learning from the classroom to the home has been an acknowledged problem that occurs because of insufficient or ineffective communication between the family and the program staff. Thus, planned consistency between the educational program and the educational experiences provided by the family is vitally important.
- Parent involvement can greatly accelerate the child's rate of learning. The degree of parental participation is positively related to cognitive development.

Rationale for a Home-Based Approach

As mentioned previously, one of the key premises of an effective early intervention program is intensity (Blair et al., 1995; Ramey and Ramey, 1998). A home-based approach with active family participation provides the potential for daily and sometimes hourly teaching, maintenance, and generalization of intervention opportunities. Additional rationales for using a home-based approach include these:

- Learning occurs in the family's and child's natural environment; hence the need is eliminated for transfer of learned concepts from classroom or clinic to the home and daily routines.
- Home intervention allows for direct and constant access to behavior as it occurs naturally. This is more likely to result in curriculum goals that are functional for the child within the child's own unique environment. In fact, the differences in cultures, lifestyles, and value systems held by the family are incorporated into the curriculum planning because the family will make the final determination of what and how their child will be taught.
- Learned behaviors are more likely to generalize and be maintained if they have been learned in the child's home environment and have been taught by the child's natural reinforcing agents, the family.
- Instruction in the home offers more opportunity for full family participation in the teaching process. Father, mother, sibling, and extended family involvement becomes a realistic and obtainable goal.
- The home provides access to a fuller range of behaviors, many of which could not be targeted for modification within a classroom (e.g., having temper tantrums that only occur in the home or crawling into bed with parents each night).
- Training parents, who already are natural reinforcing agents, provides them with the skills necessary to deal with new child behaviors as they occur.
- Individualization of instructional goals for the parents and child is an operational reality because the home teacher is working on a one-to-one basis with both.

THE PORTAGE MODEL

The three principal ingredients that constitute the major content of the Portage model are (1) parental involvement, (2) home-based programming, and (3) use of the structured teaching method (see Figure 4–1). The effectiveness of the components of the model have been documented over the past 30 years (Bijou, 1983, 1991; Brinker & Lewis, 1982; Cameron, 1986, 1990; Jellnek, 1985; Miller, 1990; Muelen van der & Sipma, 1991; Shearer, 1991, 1995; Shearer & Shearer, 1972; Shearer & Shearer, 1976; Shearer & Snider, 1981; Thorburn, 1997; White, 1997). These components are now recognized as essential components by most of today's successful intervention programs and to some degree have been adapted or adopted as recommended practice (Blechman, 1984; Brorson, 2005; Dunst, Trivette, & Mott, 1994; Hoyson, Jamieson, & Strain, 1984; Johnson, 2001; Klein and Rye, 2004; Love, 2005; Robinson, Rosenberg, & Beckman, 1988; Rosenberg, Robinson, & Beckman, 1984; Shearer, 1993, 2004; Shearer and Loftin, 1984; Shelton & Stepanek, 1994; Sturmey et al., 1992; Thorburn, 1997; U.S. General Accounting Office, 1990; Wasik, Bryant, & Lyons, 1990).

Parents as Primary Teachers

From its inception, Portage has emphasized the parent's role as the child's primary teacher. The rationale for this emphasis is that parents are the child's first teacher, a concept well supported in the literature (Bijou, 1991; Cameron, 1990; Eiserman, Weber, & McCoun, 1995; Kohli, 1991; Shearer, 1993; Shearer & Loftin, 1984; Thorburn, 1992, 1997; Yamaguchi, 1988). Parents as teachers can motivate children, can reinforce newly acquired skills at home, and can provide valuable information for others working with the child (Bailey & Wolery, 1984; Cameron, 1990; White, 1997). The potential for larger

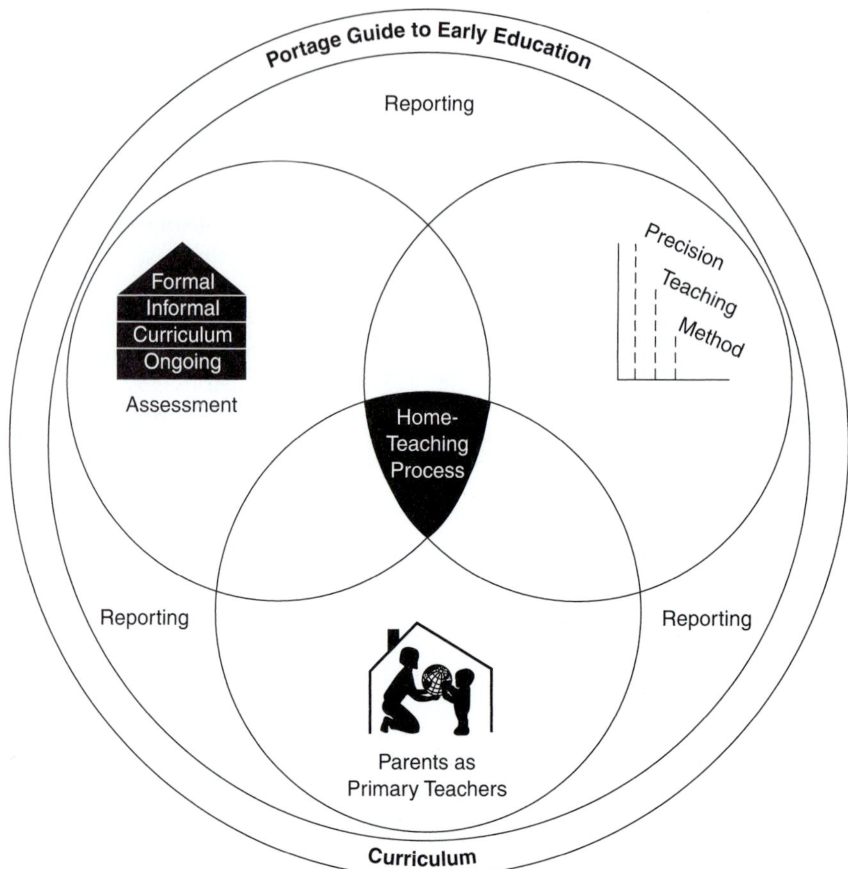

FIGURE 4–1 Components of the Portage Model

and longer-lasting effects on the child increases because of the amount of time spent with the parent and the amount of reinforcement opportunity. In other words, the intensity of the intervention increases when the parent serves as the child's primary teacher. Intensity is a critical element often missing in early intervention demonstrations that fail to show positive effects on intellectual, academic, or social performance of the child (Grantham-McGregor, Powell, Walker, et al., 1994; Hebbeler & Gerlach-Downie, 2002; Ramey, Ramey, Gaines, & Blair, 1995).

The question of whether all parents are capable of or want to serve as the child's primary teacher is a valid concern. However, empirical studies suggest that successful intervention gains in very young children are directly related to the level or degree of parent participation (Johnson et al., 2000; Ramey & Ramey, 1992; Wasik, Bryant, & Lyons, 1990). Involvement should be viewed as a continuum along which parents can progress based on their individual needs and circumstances and with the expectation that they do not wish to remain static at any given point.

Assessment Procedures

Systematic measurement of the child's developmental status is a critical component in Portage and occurs through four types of assessment procedures:

1. *Formal* (e.g., a standardized instrument that assesses major developmental domains such as the Hawaii Early Learning Profile [HELP]; Assessment, Evaluation and Programming System [AEPS]; Battelle Developmental Inventory, 2nd edition [BDI-2]; or the Alpern–Boll Developmental Profile II)
2. *Informal* (e.g., observation)
3. *Curriculum based* (e.g., The Portage Checklist)
4. *Ongoing assessment*

Information from these procedures provides the means by which a curriculum can be developed to meet the child's individual needs. During formal assessment, standardized instruments are used to assess strengths and needs of the individual child. A number of formal instruments are available. Some of the most popular instruments, however, do not yield information about the child's specific developmental domains. Deficiencies of this nature make it difficult to obtain before-and-after measures of progress or to evaluate a program's overall effectiveness. Some practitioners have confused curriculum assessment methods (e.g., the Portage Checklist) with formal assessment and have used the checklist to document developmental status rather than to develop teaching goals for the child. Distinction between formal and curriculum assessment is critical to understanding the intent of this component.

To facilitate planning for individual children, the *Portage Guide to Early Education* (Bluma, Shearer, Frohman, & Hilliard, 1976) was devised. This curriculum guide, for use with children functioning between birth and 6 years of age, consists of a manual of instructions, a sequential checklist of behaviors that includes five areas of development (cognitive, language, self-help, motor, and socialization), an infant stimulation section, and a set of curriculum cards to match each of the 580 behaviors stated on the checklist. The cards contain suggestions on materials and teaching procedures, along with task breakdowns to assist teachers in individualized programming.

The checklist is used to pinpoint the behaviors the child already exhibits in developmental areas. The behaviors on the checklist that indicate emerging skills (unlearned behaviors immediately following learned behaviors) are areas that the teacher may wish to target for learning. The user can then refer to the matching curriculum cards in the deck that state the goal in behavioral terms and suggest materials and methods for teaching the skill. These materials can only serve as a guide for the teacher and parent. Fully 50% of behaviors actually prescribed for children are not found on the checklist, but any may well be a behavior leading to a long-term goal that is listed on the checklist. Thus, many behaviors listed can be thought of as long-term goals that merit being divided into smaller behavioral segments. These can then be chained together to achieve the long-term goal. Consequently, the child, not the checklist, determines the curriculum.

It should be noted, however, that professionals and staff sometimes confuse the Portage home-based model with the Portage materials and curriculum. For clarification of this discussion, the Portage Model is not the *Portage Guide to Early Education*. The popularity of the Portage curriculum results from its simplicity and practicality—essential points for the many cultures and languages to which it has been adapted (see Shearer, 1991; Thorburn, 1997; Yamaguchi, 1988). The success in producing measurable change in a child's development, however, is largely based on the use of the *Portage Guide* within the entire Portage Model, specifically the benchmarks described in this chapter. The *Portage Guide* is an important part of the system but is not central to the model. In other words, the Portage Model is the entire home visitation model with all of the processes that are described in this chapter—not just curriculum materials that have been developed by the project.

Use and supplementation of other curricula with the *Portage Guide* have occurred because of the need to apply the model to populations with specific disabilities or needs and because of the urgent need to systematically revise and update the materials. It is our belief, in the context and presence of the other components of the Portage Model, that such substitutes and supplements expand the application of the model rather than hinder it.

An important change in early intervention assessment practice is the expansion of the focus of assessment beyond the individual child. The interrelatedness and impact of family support and the home environment upon the child's developmental outcome have been widely discussed (e.g., Bailey et al., 1988; Bradley & Caldwell, 1984; Bronfenbrenner, 1979; Dunst, Trivette, & Deal, 1988; Dunst, Trivette, & Mott, 1994; Ramey et al., 1992; Ramey & Shearer, 1999; Shonkoff & Phillips, 2000; Turnbull et al., 1993). Consequently, comprehensive assessment includes a survey of family concerns and available resources, as well as evaluation of key elements of the child's environment. The shift to a broader concept of assessment compels users of Portage to consider the additional training needs of their staff. Our experiences in training home teachers have shown that helping staff to develop accurate and unbiased observation skills requires significant time and effort.

Structured Teaching Method

The Structured Teaching Method used in the Portage intervention model includes a precision teaching approach This approach is an established paradigm based on behavioral principles and has been particularly successful with children with disabilities (Hallahan & Kauffman, 1976; Stephens, 1976). The method is based on the work of Lindsley (1968) and utilizes a set of simple but effective procedures that home teachers follow to identify, monitor, and make decisions about critical skills or behaviors a child needs to acquire. The procedure includes (1) precise operational definitions of the specific behaviors to teach, (2) task analysis to break down complex skills into smaller units or subskills, (3) direct teaching methods that require practice of the new skill many times, and (4) direct daily measurement to monitor progress and evaluate the intervention.

Development proceeds rapidly during the first years of a child's life. Intervention approaches that facilitate development are heavily based on theory and methodology and support a tendency toward trial and error. Infants and young children cannot afford to wait 3 to 6 months to see if a particular intervention is successful. Hence precision teaching reduces the use of trial and error. It emphasizes watching and recording behavior to identify the unique strengths or problems of the child and recording the responses to determine results of the intervention. The likelihood of success is greatly enhanced with this method of teaching. Precision teaching is particularly advantageous when using paraprofessional or less experienced staff. It allows supervisors to specify where problems occurred and to determine why a particular approach did or did not work.

Home-Teaching Process

The centrality of the home-teaching process to other components of the Portage intervention model (see Figure 4–1) is not an accident. It is the heart and soul of Portage, the point at which all the components converge and where successful intervention occurs (Shearer & Shearer, 1995). The home-teaching process has four critical steps, as demonstrated in Figure 4–2.

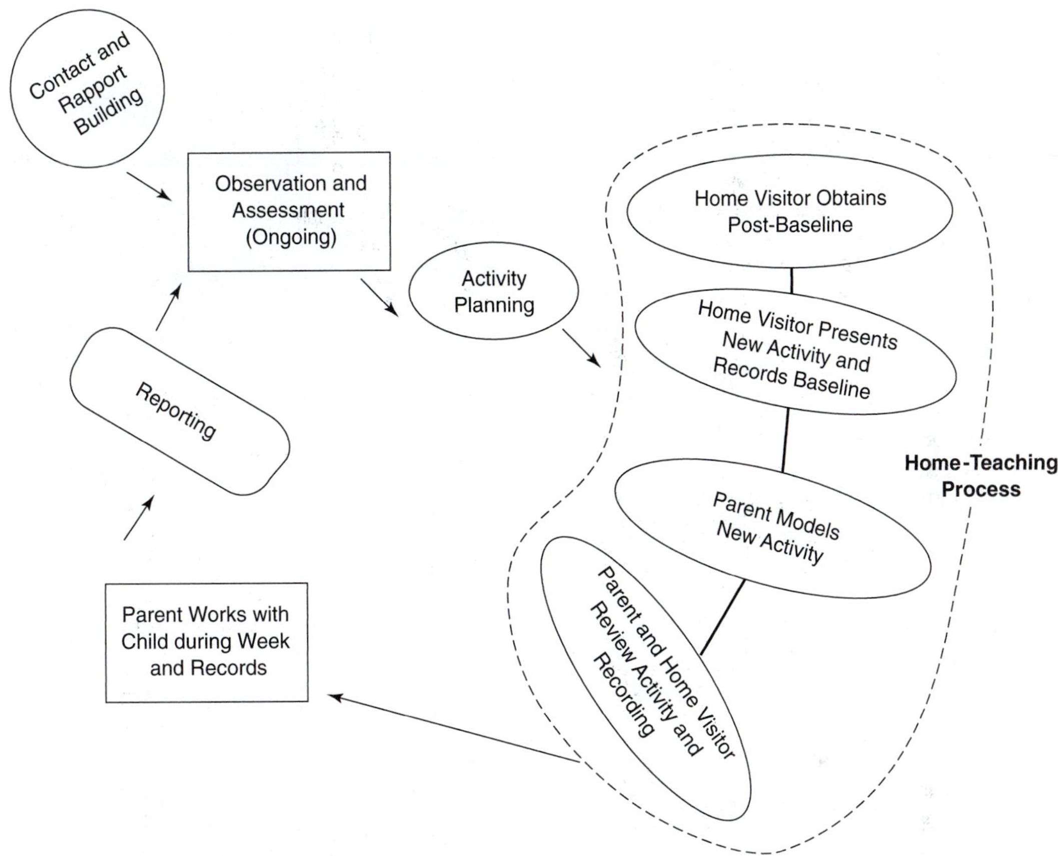

FIGURE 4–2 The Portage Home Visitation Model

Approximately two to three skill behaviors or tasks are targeted for learning each week. The behaviors and criteria for success are chosen with the goal that the child (and also the family) will achieve success in one week.

1. The home teacher enters the home and takes post-baseline data on the previous week's activities.
2. After discussion and planning with the family, the home teacher introduces the new tasks for the coming week. The home teacher models the teaching techniques for the parent and takes baseline data on the new tasks.
3. The parent then models back the teaching activity in the presence of the home teacher to ensure that there are no misunderstandings about the tasks or techniques to be used and to ensure that the parent feels comfortable conducting the tasks.
4. The home teacher supports the parent by addressing other concerns or problems the parent wishes to share. Key topics generally include (a) daily routines to use for the activities, (b) criteria for measuring the child's success with the activity, and (c) ways to reinforce the child.

Following both formal and informal assessment, the home teacher will suggest two or three skill behaviors that are emerging and could be prescribed. The parents also make suggestions of emerging behaviors they wish to see targeted. The home teacher, with the parents, writes the chosen goal(s) as a behavioral objective, together with directions, on an activity chart. Activities are written with the goal of ensuring that the parents and child will succeed on each activity within a week. As parents experience success and gain confidence in their ability to teach their child and record the child's progress, the number of activities are gradually increased to three or four per week. These activities are often in several areas of development. For instance, within the same week the parent might be working on reducing tantrums, buttoning, and counting.

The home teacher writes the activity chart incorporating the selection of targeted behaviors. Again, the most important point is for the home teacher to break down the tasks and prescribe only those that can be achieved within a week. This provides the parents with rapid reinforcement because what the child learns is a direct result of parental teaching. The directions are precisely written so that the parents will have no difficulty understanding them if they need to refer to them during the week. Recording is always uncomplicated and usually involves noting frequency of success.

After the activity is pinpointed, the home teacher introduces the activity to the child and records baseline data—the frequency of correct responses prior to instruction—on the activity chart. The home teacher then follows the directions written on the chart and begins the teaching process. The home teacher thus is modeling teaching techniques for the parents, showing them what to do and how to do it. After several opportunities, the parent takes over and works with the child, modeling for the home teacher. The home teacher then is able to offer suggestions and reinforcement that increases the likelihood that the parents will carry out the activities during the week.

Anne Vega/Merrill

Mother instructs her child at home, following the Portage model.

Throughout the visit, the home teacher stresses the importance of working with the child in naturally occuring household routines during the week. The home teacher leaves home and office phone numbers with the parents and encourages them to call if any questions or problems arise during the week. Every attempt is made to use materials available in the home. However, at times materials are brought to the home and left for the parents and child to use.

When the home teacher returns the following week, post-baseline data on the previous week's activities are collected. This helps the home teacher validate the accuracy of the parent's recording and provides feedback concerning the degree of success achieved by the child and the child's readiness for the next developmentally appropriate sequential step. Based on these data, the home teacher alters the previous prescriptions or introduces new activities, beginning with taking baseline data. And so the cycle is repeated, weekly.

This is the sequence of the home-visit process. It is the direct intervention phase of the entire home visit. However, in reality, in the beginning, intermediate or additional steps are sometimes necessary in the parent-teaching process. Parents are not all alike; thus it is important to individualize the teaching process for them. Even parents with cognitive limitations can successfully participate in the teaching process. In this case, activity charts are not used; however, parents still record using a specially adapted chart. Babysitters and other caregivers can also be effective teachers with this model. Parents, and even professionals, have said that they had almost given up hope for teaching children with severe disabilities, but with the help of task analysis and precision teaching, progress and learning become more tangible in a shorter period of time.

Data Collection and Accountability

Evaluation is an ongoing process in the Portage method. Activity charts left in the home are collected weekly. The home teacher reviews these charts and completes a weekly progress report. Prescribed behaviors from the previous week, determination of whether the child has attained the criteria needed for success, and prescriptions for the coming week are all recorded on the weekly progress report (usually found on the back of the activity chart). A behavior log is kept for each child and lists all activities that the developmental domain addressed, as well as the date they were prescribed. This log provides an ongoing record of every written skill behavior activity whether success was achieved, and the duration of each prescription. The log also provides a percentage of success achieved by parents, child, and home teacher. The continual input of data allows supervisory personnel and each home teacher to spot problems quickly, thus providing regular feedback for program monitoring and modification.

Portage Home Visits

Each Portage home visit includes three distinct phases: (1) *direct intervention,* focusing on the infant or child's developmental progress, review and demonstration of activities to be left in the home, practice and return demonstration by the parent, and discussion about the purpose and expected outcome of the tasks (referred to as the Home-Teaching Process); (2) *informal interaction and play,* which provide important curriculum assessment information to the home teacher for planning informal play activities and assisting the mother in helping the infant or child to generalize and maintain learned activities by incorporation into daily routines; and (3) *family support efforts,* in which the home teacher serves as a sounding board for the mother, provides information and assistance as it is appropriate and asked for by the family, and gains further trust and rapport with the family (see Figure 4–3).

RESEARCH AND EVALUATION OF THE PORTAGE MODEL

In the earlier implementations of the model, several types of evaluation were conducted to examine parents' ability to teach within the model and to determine what effect the teaching had on children's growth and development. In one study, activity charts were analyzed and pre- and post-testing were done on 75 children receiving Portage intervention. The overall rate of daily recording by families was 92%, and an average of 128 prescribed activities were written per child. The children themselves were successful on 91% of the activities. These children began the intervention with an average IQ of 75, as determined by the Cattell Infant Scale and the Stanford–Binet Intelligence Test. Their average cognitive gain was 13 months mental age in an 8-month period (Shearer & Shearer, 1972).

Another study compared Portage intervention children with randomly selected children in local Head Start programs. The Stanford–Binet Intelligence Scale, the Cattell Infant Scale, and the Alpern–Boll Developmental Profile were used as pre- and post-measures for both groups. Multivariate analysis of covariance indicated that children in the Portage service model made greater gains in IQ, language, academic, and social skills

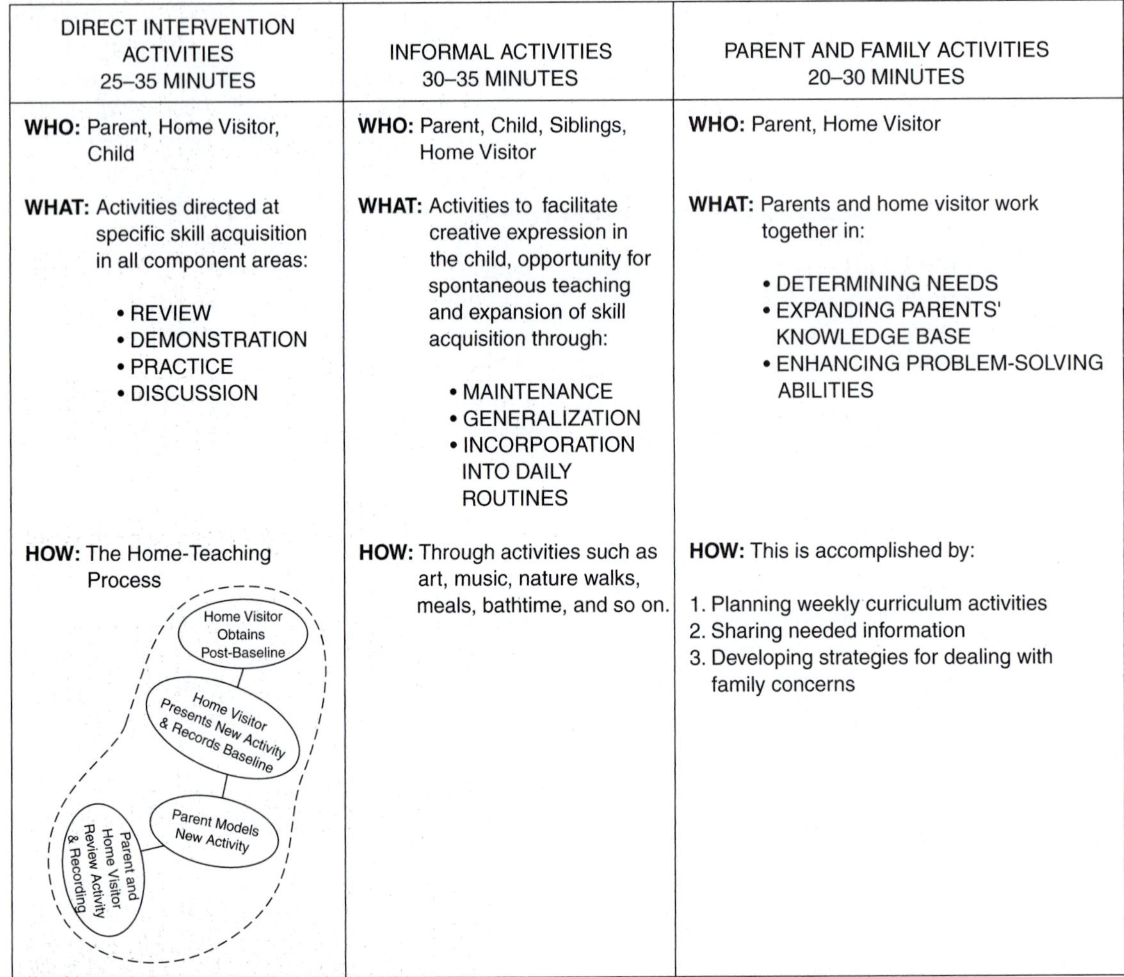

DIRECT INTERVENTION ACTIVITIES 25–35 MINUTES	INFORMAL ACTIVITIES 30–35 MINUTES	PARENT AND FAMILY ACTIVITIES 20–30 MINUTES
WHO: Parent, Home Visitor, Child **WHAT:** Activities directed at specific skill acquisition in all component areas: • REVIEW • DEMONSTRATION • PRACTICE • DISCUSSION **HOW:** The Home-Teaching Process	**WHO:** Parent, Child, Siblings, Home Visitor **WHAT:** Activities to facilitate creative expression in the child, opportunity for spontaneous teaching and expansion of skill acquisition through: • MAINTENANCE • GENERALIZATION • INCORPORATION INTO DAILY ROUTINES **HOW:** Through activities such as art, music, nature walks, meals, bathtime, and so on.	**WHO:** Parent, Home Visitor **WHAT:** Parents and home visitor work together in: • DETERMINING NEEDS • EXPANDING PARENTS' KNOWLEDGE BASE • ENHANCING PROBLEM-SOLVING ABILITIES **HOW:** This is accomplished by: 1. Planning weekly curriculum activities 2. Sharing needed information 3. Developing strategies for dealing with family concerns

FIGURE 4–3 Three Parts of a Portage Home Visit

compared with the group that received classroom instruction (Peniston, 1972).

The first replication evaluation involved 44 children with language impairments who had a mean language age of 36.9 months at pretest. Changes after 8 months of Portage intervention showed gains in Peabody Picture Vocabulary ages from 35.6 to 50.7 months and Alpern–Boll Communication subscale scores from 30.3 to 47.8 months. In 8 additional Portage replications, average Alpern–Boll IQ gains were 1.2- to 1.8-month mental age per month (Ghoca, 1972). Similar findings have been documented in Portage model replications in Finland (Arvio, Hautamaki, & Tilikka, 1993); the Gaza Strip (Oakland & Ghazaleh, 1995); India (Kohli, 1988, 1991; Kohli & Datta, 1986); Jamaica (Thorburn, Brown, & Bell, 1979); Japan (Yamaguchi, 1987, 1996); the Netherlands (Meulen & Sipma, 1991; Meulen van der & Bulsink, 1992); Pakistan (Shazadi, 2002); and the United Kingdom (Barna, Bidder, Gray,

Clements, & Gardner, 1980; Revill & Blendon, 1979; White, 1997).

Outcome studies are essential in demonstrating the efficacy of intervention models. However, numerous practical, ethical, and methodological difficulties surround the design of research in this arena, particularly as related to young children. Most of the early studies of Portage were conducted prior to today's current emphasis on methodological soundness and rigor. It must also be noted that, contrary to many recent intervention strategies, Portage was funded solely as a demonstration model and did not have research as a contingency or mission. In addition, the use of cognitive gain as the central measure of efficacy is no longer viewed as practical given our growing understanding of other family influences on children's development (i.e., parental attitudes, expectations, and parent–child interactions). In the case of Portage and its many adaptations, the authors support the continued need for stronger and more rigorous evaluation of the model.

ADAPTATIONS AND APPLICATIONS OF PORTAGE

Having discussed the Portage Model and the rationale behind its development, it is also important to demonstrate the model's utility and versatility by discussing varied adaptations and applications.

The Portage Parent Program

Early in its implementation stages, Portage model staff frequently expressed concern that a systematic procedure was needed to help parents to become gradually less dependent on the home teacher and eventually to assume full responsibility for determining the goals and nature of the child's early education. The parents often viewed the home teacher as the educational authority who visited once a week to tell them what to do for their child. Careful consideration was given to the best way to empower these parents to gradually become their child's best advocate and interventionist. As a result, the Portage Parent Program was developed, which includes a set of readings for parents, an instructor's manual, and a parent behavior inventory (Boyd, Stauber, & Bluma, 1977). The materials provide parents with more in-depth information about skills taught in the model.

To evaluate this approach, a group of children and their parents was designated to receive the systematic parent training program in addition to the basic Portage Model of home teaching. The parent program was specifically designed to encourage acquisition and generalization of parental teaching and management skills. The evaluation compared three groups of families: those receiving the supplemental parent training program, parents receiving the basic Portage Model, and a nontreatment control group of parents with preschool children without exceptional educational needs. The results of the evaluation showed that both treatment groups produced superior performance on certain child and parent measures compared with the nontreatment control group (Boyd et al., 1977). The efficacy of the evaluation findings were attributed to the Portage Model's use of precision teaching and modeling. The program's emphasis on more systematic parent training and parental involvement in the planning and implementation phases of the home-teaching process yielded modest but important gains above those noted for the Portage-only group. Furthermore, parents' acquisition and generalization of child management and teaching behaviors potentially benefited not only the child with a disability but also the child's siblings.

Urban Applications

The Portage Model was originally funded as an education program for preschool children in rural areas. Its initial success prompted additional federal funding in 1974 from the U.S. Bureau for the Education of the Handicapped (BEH) for replication of the model in a large urban area in the Midwest. The program, Operation Success, opened in Milwaukee, Wisconsin, and later served as the demonstration model for the Home Start Training Center to provide training and technical assistance to Head Start programs wishing to implement a home-based option. BEH funding also provided outreach training and technical assistance to programs throughout the United States to disseminate Portage Model information and materials. Through these efforts, components of the Portage Model were implemented by public schools, state institutions, and private facilities; in center-based and home-based settings; in major urban communities throughout the United States; and in programs serving a wide range of disability and need.

International Applications

Through continued dissemination, the Portage Model has become well-known internationally. The curriculum guide has been translated into 35 languages, and the model itself has been introduced into more than 90 countries. The model's family-centered orientation, clearly defined and structured curriculum, and simplistic nature have great appeal to people in countries and programs with limited resources or experience in serving young children. A strength of the Portage Model is that it can be tailored to individual needs. It offers a focus for action, and it can provide a counseling element for families who may feel that their life has been turned upside down and, as a result, feel de-skilled and inadequate (Russell, 1986).

United Kingdom. Portage was first introduced into the United Kingdom in 1976 as the subject of a research evaluation led by Albert Kushlick, director of the Wessex Health Care Evaluation Research Team (Smith, Kushlick, & Glossop, 1977). A significant research aim was the design of an effective replication model within the U.K. context. Following extensive dissemination during the late 1970s and early 1980s, Portage services were established in a number of areas of the country, culminating in a successful bid for central government funding in 1986. Services are now established throughout the United Kingdom, funded primarily by local education authorities and health trusts with some involvement from nongovernment organizations.

In 1983, the United Kingdom became the first country to establish a National Portage Association representing individual parents, professionals, and services working with the Portage Model. The association has taken a leading role in the campaign to establish Portage services throughout the United Kingdom. The association also supports standards of local service delivery through a program of training workshops linked to a code of practice agreed to by the membership. Over 150 local Portage services are presently registered with the U.K. National Portage Association (NPA). A register of accredited trainers, with current involvement in Portage service activities, is maintained by the association. The association conducts an annual conference attended by families and professionals, during which new ideas and developments within the Portage movement are shared. In 2005 NPA published findings from *Survey of Portage Provision in England*. The study identified gaps in access to Portage services. A program entitled *Developing Portage Services* soon followed the report and promoted the establishment of new Portage services in needed areas along with training initiatives responding to the changing needs of early-years practitioners working in these communities. Training is a central activity for NPA. The association recently developed the *Portage Curriculum for Further Professional Development* training modules. A major revision of the Basic Portage Workshop materials was completed and linked to ongoing accreditation of Portage trainers. This revision responds to the raised awareness of the dynamics of the individual family as the context for the support offered by Portage services. Other new training initiatives include the development of a toolkit—"Equally Different"—for service self-evalution of inclusive practice, and a course focusing on the use of active listening skills as an essential element of Portage service practice (White, 2006).

Portage services in the United Kingdom are playing an increasingly active role in the newly established local Early Years and Childcare Development Partnerships. The demand for quality training has put Portage trainers in great demand in programs such as the Sure Start initiatives, which promote a family-centered approach (Hassall, Weston, & Raine, 2001; Horne, 2006; Wolfendale, 2001).

Japan. The Portage Model was introduced in Japan in 1977 as an experimental study funded by the Japan Ministry of Welfare. During its introduction, the Portage Checklist was revised to include fewer items (562), suggested activities on the curriculum cards were modified, and illustrations of material and teaching situations were added—all to accommodate linguistic and cultural differences. In Japan, the instruction to mothers of the Portage program takes place at educational facilities because the Japanese culture and difficult conditions hinder instruction in the home. Intervention visits are conducted weekly or biweekly. Parents bring their child to consult with Portage teachers and return home with new activities to practice. Recently, families living great distances from Portage centers have been offered home-teaching services through telephone consultation and correspondence. Based on 20 years of experience in Japan, the model has been adapted into a group teaching curriculum for use in inclusive settings, such as kindergartens, nurseries, and day-care centers. Several modifications have been made to the curriculum, checklist, and activity cards to reflect changes in Japanese society.

Effectiveness of the Japanese Portage model has been studied since 1983, particularly at seven experimental centers around Tokyo. More than 1,000 children have received services in these centers; more than 60% of them with Down syndrome. A cohort of 200 children has been followed longitudinally, and results suggest significant long-term developmental and academic gains (Yamaguchi, 1996). More recent studies have focused on the adaptations for inclusive early education in kindergartens, nurseries, and day-care centers. Early findings show that the addition of multi-level teaching and play units and the use of prompts make the educational experience similar and comparable for children with and without disabilities. All children can finish their tasks in almost the same time. The Portage Model has been officially incorporated as an early intervention model throughout Japan (Yamaguchi, Shimizu, & Nishinaga, 2006). A Japan Portage Association was founded in 1985. Today 2,500 members are registered, representing parents and professionals, with 40 branches throughout the country.

India. Under the direction of Dr. Tehal Kohli, a major replication and adaptation of the Portage Model was implemented in India in 1980 (Kohli, 1991). After the curriculum was translated and home teachers were trained, an experimental program was offered to children with a developmental quotient (DQ) less than 75. A majority of these originally targeted children joined regular schools after early intervention, significant developmental gains were documented, as measured on the 20 Point Program of India, and the model was deemed suitable for families living in rural and slum areas and for families who are illiterate. With help from UNICEF, India was able to adapt the Portage materials in Hindi and to develop Portage training for professionals, paraprofessionals, and nonprofessionals. Using home advisors, Anganwadi (i.e., paraprofessionals who work with families in their communities and homes) functionaries, and parents, a low-cost affordable model was developed for the urban slums of Chandigarh. Several workshops have been conducted to promote use of the model in other major cities in India. Use of Anganwadi, or nursery teachers, is one of India's adaptations to the model, because families living in the slums have such complex child-care issues and needs. Children targeted for intervention are frequently left at home in the care of siblings, who are often younger than 8 years of age themselves (Kohli, 1990). The Anganwadi centers provide a variety of services besides child-care and parent instruction. In 1994 the India National Portage Association (INPA) was formed. Among this organization's main areas of emphasis are the training of preschool educators, research, a clearinghouse for dissemination of material, and night-working services through the country. As of 2007, INPA has sponsored programs that serve over 6,000 children and 8,000 mothers and has trained over 500 Anganwadi or nursery teachers, and over 700 preschool teachers, primarily in the Punjab region of India.

Portage colleagues in southeastern India developed the Udisha Portage Index for early inclusion, which assesses the development of learning and inclusion in Anganwadi centers and communities. It helps Anganwadi workers to assess the effectiveness of their centers and their early intervention programs. The Community-Based Rehabilitation (CBR) Network initiated the Udisha Portage Project in 2003 to include children with special needs into the India Child Development System (ICDS), a large network of early childhood services in 40,301 Angawadi centers reaching 6,826,168 children. Early childhood inclusive education is a new challenge in the rural areas of India. The Udisha project aims to reach all Anganwadi centers within the 27 districts of Karnataka State.

"Portage to Every Village" is supported by the Sir Dorabji Tata Trust and is a concept similar to Head Start in the United States. Translation of the Portage Checklist into Marati, Hindi, Telegu, Bengali, Tamil, and Konkani has been completed by the Udisha Portage Project. Translations into Urdu and Gujarathi are in process (Rao, 2007).

The Netherlands. The University of Groningen has been an active proponent of introducing and studying various applications of Portage in the Netherlands. This effort has been spearheaded by B. F. van der Meulen, D. E. Oenema-Mostert, A. T. Hoekstra, and S. A. J. Ruiter. A Portage Group Programme was created as a center-based version of the Portage Model to support the professionals working in specialized day-care and rehabilitation centers in The Netherlands. The Portage program aims to stimulate a child's development within a group of other children by offering them specific activities and games. It works on functional, individual targets within the child's daily group activities to help the child and to support the family and educators. The program is carried out at the individual child level and the group level. The program conducts in-service training to educators and health professionals. A number of studies have been published on outcomes of The Netherlands Portage Model. The first was with children and families with parent–child interaction problems rather than developmental delays. Child-development activities were used to introduce appropriate skills for behavior management to parents. Both the parents and children responded positively, with the children having significant gains in social and academic domains (Meulen & Bulsink, 1992). A second study conducted using Portage with children who had mental disabilities also documented cognitive gains (Meulen van der & Sipma, 1991). Between 2001 and 2006 a series of papers were published by Oenema-Mostert that focused on families of chronically ill young children and the effects of home-based intervention on the development of education of the children and on parental behavior. Using a recent quasi-experimental, time-series experiment, researchers examined the effects of the Portage Group Programme by measuring the probable changes in development of the child and changes in the sense of increased competence of parents (Meulen & Oenema-Mostert, 2006). During this same period the Groningen researchers conducted pilot research into the order of the items on the Portage Checklist and the revision of the original Dutch version materials. The revisions focused more on pedagogical and ecological variables to be more family-based and less focused on isolated child behavior. After pilot testing, the researchers concluded that the Portage Model should be introduced throughout the rest of the Netherlands (Hoestra, Muelen, & Jansen, 2007; Oenema-Mostert, 2007). The Netherlands hosted the 12th Biennial International Portage Conference in 2008.

Cyprus. Prior to 1996, few early intervention services were available in Cyprus. None were home based. The authors introduced Portage to professionals and government programs in March 1996. With the financial support of Mr. Dakis Ioannou and the Christos Stelios Ioannou Foundation, a pilot Portage project was implemented to test the applicability of the model in Cyprus. The pilot was completed in 1999 when the authors formally evaluated and validated the program as a Portage Model. It then began replication in other communities in 2003.

The Portage program in Cyprus is a legal foundation. A board of management is the policy-making body, while the program's administration is conducted through an advisory committee that has representation from governmental and private bodies such as the Ministry of Health, the Ministry of Education and Culture, the Ministry of Labor and Social Insurance, the Christos Stelios Ioannou Foundation, the Committee for the Protection of the Rights of Persons with Mental Handicap, and the Federation of Parents of Disabled Children.

The Cyprus Portage Foundation was registered as a nongovernmental organization, which enabled Portage to be a successful, self-sufficient program by bringing professionals and parents into a collective and coordinated effort to empower the families and offering them guidance in meeting the needs of children with disabilities in Cyprus (Samaria & Neophytou, 2005).

Currently, Portage in Cyprus is in the process of rapid development and expansion in other major cities in the country. With the cooperation and financial support of the European Union, the Cyprus Portage Foundation is working on a large bi-communal project, which will establish three new Portage programs in the areas of Limassol, Ayia Napa, and Paphos, as well as three in the northern part of the island.

Latvia. The Latvian Portage Association was established in June 1997 and is the first and only organization to offer early intervention services to preschool-age children with special needs in Latvia. Prior to the introduction of the Portage Model in Latvia, as in other post-Soviet states, the education system lacked a special education training program that could be used for preschool children with mental and physical impairments. This void has been filled by the Portage Model, which is based on the classical Portage system but is modified to suit national characteristics.

Currently the Latvian Portage Association is working with over 250 children and their families. Over 110 persons have attended Portage Basic Workshops in Latvia, and approximately 50% of them work as Portage Home Visitors, with the remainder working in other special needs institutions.

The Latvian Portage Model is characterized by the following components:

- It is a home-teaching model with the aim of preparing children for the earliest possible inclusion in the society of their peers.
- It is used with children with special needs who live at home with their families and whose parents follow the model within the home.
- It now has a Portage Specialist training program with a certification awarded after the specialists have completed a series of intense Portage workshops.

David Shearer visited Latvia and validated the model implementation in 2005. The Portage work in Latvia is managed by the Latvian Portage Association, which operates on a statutory basis as a nongovernmental organization. The association receives financing from the local government authorities when children and families receive Portage services (Kursiete & Kursiete, 2006).

The Latvian Portage Association has expanded and developed a common Portage early intervention network in Latvia by opening new regional centers in Liepaja, Daugavpils, and Gulbene, in addition to the existing centers in Riga, Valmiera, and Cesis. In addition, the Latvian Portage Association introduced the Portage Model in Georgia in 2005, which has resulted in a pilot program in home visitation services and the creation of the Georgian Portage Association (Tsintsadze, 2006).

The Latvian Portage Association hosted the 11th Biennial International Portage Association Conference in Riga in 2006.

Turkey. The Hacettepe University in Ankara became interested in the Portage Project in 1989 when advised about the model by two UNESCO representatives. In 1999, an informational workshop on early intervention was conducted by the authors, which gained the attention of many professionals working in special education programs in Turkey. The authors returned to Anakara to conduct an intensive Portage training in 2002. More than 20 teachers and interventionists completed the course. Currently, the Early Childhood Care Development Project is being developed to assess the home environment and child-care practices in Turkey. The *Portage Guide* is one tool that will be used in this process. Plans for extending the use of the Portage Model throughout Turkey are in progress.

The University of Hacettepe staff conducted a study to assess the applicability of the Portage Model in Turkey (Guven, Bal, & Tugrul, 1998). Over 800 normal children and children with disabilities were included in the study. It was determined that the model applied both to typically developing children and to children with disabilities. A follow-up study was conducted by the university to determine the applicability of the model throughout Turkey (Guven, Bal, Metin, & Atay, 2000). University researchers continue to study the applicability of the model with very-low-birth-weight premature infants (Karaaslan & Bal, 2002). The Portage Association of Turkey was established in July 2003 as a nongovernmental organization. One of its major goals will be the expansion of Portage throughout Turkey via a trainer's model. This training will be provided by the headquarters of the International Portage Association (Atay, 2004).

Gaza Strip. In 1984, the Sun Day Care Center, sponsored by the Society for the Care of the Handicapped in the Gaza Strip, brought David Shearer to Gaza to introduce a massive adaptation of the Portage Model. He returned to Gaza six times over the next 6 years to conduct intensive training of home teachers and to validate the implementation of the model in the Gaza Strip. Today the project serves over 500 families living in the villages and camps of the Gaza Strip. Portage materials were translated from English into Arabic, with only minor cultural adaptations. Portage services have endured in this region despite periods of severe economic hardships and civil disruption. Curfews have frequently been imposed, during which times all persons living in the Gaza Strip were required to remain in their homes, significantly altering normal working and living conditions. During curfews, teachers did not make home visits. However, in anticipation of curfew days, teachers provided mothers with additional new activities to use should they be needed. During strike days, teachers typically maintained their teaching schedules by innocuously moving from home to home. Teachers typically live in neighborhoods in which they work and thus were better able to move about under the protection of their neighbors (Ghazaleh, Ghazaleh, & Oakland, 1990; Oakland & Ghazaleh, 1995).

Saudi Arabia. Portage was introduced in Saudi Arabia in the late 1990s. The authors have visited Jeddah three times to train staff at the Help Center. Since this training, early intervention services have expanded to include a Portage home visitation program for children ages birth to 9 months who have been diagnosed as having a disability. Families, especially the mothers, become very active in their child's program. This continues as the children are brought into a "home/center" program at age 9 months and eventually enrolled full-time into a center-based program. The center's early intervention currently serves over 90 children. A great many more need services, because this is the only early intervention program in Jeddah for children with disabilities.

Caribbean. Portage in Jamaica has been established since 1975, beginning with the Jamaican Early Stimulation Project. The model was replicated with only relatively minor modifications. Differences include the use of Portage for all types of disabilities and for older children who are disabled, living in areas where there are few or no services. The total enrollment in 1990 was over 500 families, of which 80% received weekly home visits. Visits were conducted by non-professional community workers called "child development aides." The typical level of education of most community workers and home teachers is sixth to eighth grade, thus training requires intensive and ongoing effort. Over the years a comprehensive training program has been established to support these workers. Dr. Marigold Thorburn conducted numerous research activities related to the use of Portage and its application to young children with disabilities in Jamaica. She was also instrumental in introducing the model to nearly every country and island in the Caribbean (Thorburn, 1997).

Pakistan. Pakistan has been using Portage since the early 1990s. It was introduced by Dr. Shazadi and associates at the University of Karachi's Department of Special Education. They conducted a study to explore the role of parents of children with disabilities in promoting their child's education by using a Pakistani adaptation of the Portage Model. The study used an experimental design involving 20 children and families. Following 6 months of home visits, the researchers measured the impact of using the *Portage Guide to Early Education* (the Pakistani Model) on the social, cognitive, physical, and behavioral development of young children with disabilities. Children who received parental instruction with Portage activities made more developmental gains, and their parents were more likely to feel they could help their child than those in the control group. The conclusion was that the Portage Model can be used for guidance of parents of developmentally delayed children and that field workers in rural communities of Pakistan can be trained to use it in a short period of time. They also concluded that the model is cost effective (Shazadi, Anjum, & Siddqui, 2004). The model is popular with both governmental and private entities and with the Directorate General of Special Education. The Ministry of Education has endorsed the translation and adaptation of the model for use in Pakistan. There is now a Portage Parent Association and a National Portage Association of Pakistan, with provincial chapters. These organizational chapters conduct the Portage training in their respective regions. The authors visited Karachi and neighboring villages in 2006 and confirmed the successful adaptation of the Portage Model in Pakistan. Graduate students in the Department of Special Education at the University of Karachi fill an important gap in special education and other intervention services by using the *Portage Guide* and visiting homes of children who are not able to attend school or who require more intensive intervention.

Ireland. Theresa Ghalaieny worked for many years at the HELP Center in Jeddah, Saudi Arabia, and introduced the Portage Model at that center. Since returning to Ireland in 2000, she and Mollie White from the United Kingdom conducted ten 3-day "basic" Portage workshops in Ireland, with more scheduled. The majority of home visitors are community nurses who are using the Portage materials. A support group for Portage home visitors has been set up, and advanced training workshops have been conducted. Many centers for clients with an intellectual disability were using the Portage Checklist in spite of having received little or no training. At this time there is no government financial support for the use of the Portage Model. Mrs. Ghalaieny is a tireless worker for Portage and continues to build a training network and to seek support for research and evaluation of the model in Ireland.

NEW CHALLENGES FOR PORTAGE

As a model that is now approaching its 38th year, Portage faces new challenges in both its practicality and usefulness in a world of ever-increasing sophistication in technology and knowledge. There are those service providers who see themselves as "early adopters" and who reach out to every new gadget, curriculum, or procedure that comes their way. Other providers prefer to remain in the "mainstream" and wait until sufficient research and use determine the appropriateness and staying power of new ideas. Still others become so comfortable with what is familiar to them that it takes a great deal of persuasion, or even legislation, to get them to change or try new methods. As research moves closer toward addressing what works best with families and young children, the Portage Model, and indeed all intervention models, must be responsive to and must incorporate research findings to remain relevant (Shearer, 2006).

Applications with At-Risk Populations

Prevention of Mild Mental Retardation. Mild mental retardation accounts for approximately 70% of all developmental disabilities in the United States (Stoneman, 1990). This type of disability occurs almost exclusively in the context of psychosocial disadvantage and poverty and is transmitted intergenerationally. Early intervention is deemed essential to prevent mental retardation and poor intellectual development in children whose families do not provide adequate stimulation in the early years of life. The mounting evidence about the significance of early experience in brain development provides a stronger impetus for systematic efforts to enhance children's learning opportunities and development in the first three years of life (Ramey & Ramey, 1998). Whether development can be influenced directly by interventions designed specifically for the child versus indirectly by teaching parents how to provide these opportunities is an important issue and question for models such as Portage.

In this context a research prevention initiative was launched in 1995 to apply the Portage Model as a primary prevention strategy for young infants deemed at risk because of being born in low-resource families and communities. Forty adolescent mothers who had not yet completed high school and who were living in a poor urban community were recruited during their last trimester of pregnancy and were randomly assigned to a weekly home visitation group or to a control group. The study ran for 3 years and all children received at least 2 years of intervention, at which time families were tested on a variety of child and parenting measures. The intervention activities were primarily designed to address cognitive and language development in the children. Mothers in the home-visiting group were taught how to play and interact with their children using the Portage Model and materials described in this chapter. The study's findings showed no developmental differences between the home visitation and control groups. Problems with attrition limited our ability to interpret the effectiveness of the intervention.

However, several observations and experiences with this population are worth noting. Contrary to our previous experience working with families of children with identified disabilities or developmental delays, the children in the at-risk sample were, for all intents and purposes, "normal." The adolescent mothers were willing and eager to have weekly support and teaching during their child's first year of life when parenting experiences were relatively new and challenging. By the time their infants reached a year of age, it became more and more difficult to maintain the routine of weekly visits. Mothers returned to school or work and expressed more confidence about their roles as parents. With no outward physical or mental differences to be noted in their children, the mothers' priorities, unlike parents of children with disabilities, turned to pursuit of their own developmental needs. As the children became more independent during the second year of life, the mothers—in both the treatment and control groups—demonstrated less nurturing and greater use of discipline, thus ignoring or bypassing other important learning experiences for the children. These parent attitudes were much greater than seen in the general population yet appear to reflect the understanding and values of the culture in which these adolescent mothers live.

A second observation from working with this study sample is worth reporting. More than half the mothers in the study had cognitive scores in the mild mental retardation (MMR) range. This finding was not known during the intervention phase, and thus no adjustments were made to the home visitation protocol to accommodate the mothers' needs. Upon further analysis, the mothers in the MMR range—regardless of group assignment—had less understanding of basic infant and child development, and they tended to score lower on measures of nurturing skills and attitudes and higher on use of punitive behavior management techniques. Our feeling is that once again we have demonstrated and learned that merely initiating a home-based program does not ensure that parents will or can be active and effective, or that the children will automatically benefit from such efforts.

Preterm Infants. Preterm children have well-documented and poorer developmental outcomes—including cognitive, motor, and behavior—than children born at full term. Not all will have poor outcomes, but prematurity and perinatal insult increase the risk of developmental vulnerability. Studies of the efficacy of early intervention programs of developmental care and education for preterm children and their families have shown modest improvements in short-term cognitive and behavioral skills (Bao, Sun, & Wei, 1999; Resnick, Armstrong, & Carter, 1988). A group of U.K. researchers assessed the impact of a Portage home-based developmental education program on families with preterm children (Avon Premature Infant Project, 1998). To our knowledge this is one of the very few well-controlled randomized trials of the Portage Model to date. The study was conducted with infants born at less than 33 weeks gestation and living in the greater Bristol area. The infants were randomized into three groups: Portage (developmental intervention), parent adviser (nondirectional counseling support only), and preterm control. The Portage group received detailed precision teaching involving a task analysis approach as traditionally provided by Portage programs in the United Kingdom. After 2 years of home visits the study found benefit from Portage in preterm infants with birth weights below 1,250 grams and those with identified lesions on cerebral ultrasound scans. The findings led the investigators to speculate that the increased developmental risk in such children might be ameliorated by developmental interventions. Unfortunately the Portage advantage shown at 2 years of age was no longer detectable at 5 years (Johnson, Ring, Anderson, & Marlow, 2005). This is not the first major study that failed to find continued or new beneficial effect of an intervention 3 years after the period in which it was delivered. Investigators of the Infant Health and Development Program (IHDP) study found that intervention effects were not maintained past the period of intervention delivery either (Brooks-Gunn, Liaw, & Klebanov, 1992; McCormick et al., 1993; Ramey, Bryant, Wasik, et al., 1992). The Avon study investigators are conducting pilot work to further adapt the Portage Model for specific use with families with young very preterm babies. Some parents in the study expressed the opinion that the interventions were provided too late for real benefits to ensue (Johnson et al., 2005).

Infants with Birth Asphyxia. The authors are currently engaged in a collaborative effort with investigators in Birmingham, Alabama; Lusaka, Zambia; Belgaum, India; and Karachi, Pakistan, to develop and evaluate an approach to improve the health and development of infants in developing countries who are at risk for cognitive disability because of birth asphyxia. The research study is a randomized controlled evaluation of an innovative, cost-effective, home-based, parent-provided early intervention trial using a hybridization of the Portage Model with an educational curriculum that is concerned with 31 child development areas and is oriented toward adult–child transactions involving well-formed and conversational language about topics of everyday interest to young children. The study will also examine the contextual influences of parental responses and participation in home learning activities. Each of the three target countries is using paraprofessional-level members of the community with varying levels of education to deliver the hybrid home-based training to parents.

CONCLUSION

We do not believe that we have yet found the answers for parenting and parent education for all types of families and children. When viewed from a global perspective, however, the implementation of Portage services or variants of them across the world is a remarkable phenomenon. Central to its success is the inherent requirement that those implementing the model have a thorough understanding of the values and norms of the population or culture to which it is applied. Our research has raised more questions than it has provided answers, yet we remain anxious to share the information. We want to put the facts on the table, to specify what we have done and what we are doing so that others may replicate, adapt, or modify our work and have the opportunity to analyze objectively and critique what has occurred.

Although many questions concerning home-based parent-training programs remain unanswered, we have learned a great deal. The Portage Model has been in use since 1969.

Let us look at what we know from our 38 years of experiences:

Any successful home-based parent-teaching intervention must be developed in alliance with parents. They must want the alliance and see its benefit for their family.

Parents can and do teach their own child effectively when given structured sequential assistance, and if appropriately supported they can eventually plan, implement, and advocate an educational program for their child.

By using a behavioral, systematic, developmental approach, the child can achieve developmental gains in a home-based program.

Without direct and consistent parent involvement in any preschool setting, the child is not likely to maintain gains. Individualization of instruction is more likely to occur in the home rather than the classroom.

Father, sibling, and extended family member involvement in child teaching can be realistic and attainable.

Differences in cultures, lifestyles, and value systems of parents can be and should be incorporated into the curriculum because the parents share in the planning and are the final determiners of what and how their child will be taught.

Learning that occurs in the child's natural environment eliminates the problems of transferring learning from classroom to home.

The skills the child learns will more likely generalize to other areas and be maintained if they have been learned in the home environment and have been taught by the child's natural reinforcers—the parents and the family.

REFERENCES

Alpern, G., Boll, T., & Shearer, M. (1980). *Manual: Developmental profile.* Aspen, CO: Psychological Development Publications.

Arvio, M., Hautamaki, J., & Tilikka, P. (1993). Reliability and validity of the Portage assessment scale for clinical studies of mentally handicapped populations. *Child: Care, Health and Development, 19*(2), 89–98.

Atay, M. (2004). *The successful implemention and expansion of the Portage Model in Turkey.* The 10th International Portage Association Conference, Manila, Philippines.

Avon Premature Infant Project. (1998). Randomised trial of parental support for families wih very preterm children. *Archives of Disease in Childhood, 79,* 4F–11F.

Bailey, D. B., Simeonsson, R. J., Winton, P. J., Huntington, G. S., Comfort, M., Isbell, P., et al. (1988). Family-focused intervention: A functional model for planning, implementing, and evaluating individualized family services in early intervention. *Journal of the Division for Early Childhood, 10,* 156–171.

Bailey, D. B., & Wolery, M. (1984). *Teaching infants and preschoolers with handicaps.* Columbus, OH: Charles E. Merrill Publishing.

Bao, X., Sun, S., & Wei, S. (1999). Early intervention promotes intellectual development of premature infants—a preliminary report. *Chinese Medical Journal, 112,* 520–523.

Barna, S., Bidder, R. T., Gray, O. P., Clements, J., & Gardner, S. (1980). The progress of developmentally delayed preschool children in a home-training scheme. *Child: Care, Health and Development, 6,* 157–164.

Bijou, S. W. (1983). The prevention of mild and moderate retarded development. In *Curative aspects of mental retardation: Biomedical and behavioral advances* (pp. 223–239). Baltimore, MD: Paul Brookes.

Bijou, S. W. (1991). Overview of early childhood programs around the world. In J. Herwig & M. Stine (Eds.), *A symposium on family-focused intervention: Exploring national and international practices and perspectives* (pp. 63–71). Portage, WI: Cooperative Educational Service Agency 5.

Blair, C., Ramey, C. T., & Hardin, J. M. (1995). Early intervention for low birthweight, premature infants: Participation and intellectual development. *American Journal on Mental Retardation, 99*(5), 542–554.

Blechman, E. (1984). Competent parents, competent children: Behavioral objectives of parent training. In R. Dangel & R. Polster (Eds.), *Parent training* (pp. 15–27). New York: Guilford.

Bluma, S., Shearer, M., Frohman, A., & Hilliard, J. (1976). *Portage guide to early education* (rev. ed.). Portage, WI: Cooperative Educational Service Agency 5.

Boyd, R., Stauber, K., & Bluma, S. (1977). *Portage Parent Program.* Portage, WI: Cooperative Educational Service Agency 5.

Bradley, R., & Caldwell, B. (1984). 174 children: A study of the relationship between home environment and cognitive development during the first 5 years. In A. Gottfried (Ed.), *Home environment and early cognitive development* (pp. 5–57). Orlando, FL: Academic Press.

Brinker, R. P., & Lewis, M. (1982). Discovering the competent infant: A process approach to assessment and intervention. *Topics in Early Childhood Special Education, 2,* 1–16.

Bronfenbrenner, U. (1979). *The ecology of human development: Experiments by nature and design.* Cambridge, MA: Harvard University Press.

Brooks-Gunn, J., Liaw, F., & Klebanov, P. K. (1992). Effects of early intervention on cognitive function of low birth weight preterm infants. *Journal of Pediatrics, 120,* 350–359.

Brorson, K. (2005). The culture of a home visit in early intervention. *Journal of Early Childhood Research, 3*(1), 51–76

Cameron, R. J. (1986). Portage: Some directions for applied research. In R. J. Cameron (Ed.), *Portage: Preschoolers, parents and professionals* (pp. 101–109). Windsor, England: NFER-Nelson.

Cameron, R. J. (1990). *Parents, professionals and preschoolers with special educational needs: Towards a partnership model of problem solving.* Unpublished doctoral dissertation, University of Southampton.

Dunst, C., Trivette, C., & Deal, A. (1988). *Enabling and empowering families: Principles and guidelines for practice.* Cambridge, MA: Brookline.

Dunst, C. J., Trivette, C. M., & Mott, D. W. (1994). Strengths-based family-centered intervention practices. In C. J. Dunst, C. M. Trivette, & A. G. Deal (Eds.), *Supporting and strengthening families. Vol. 1. Methods, strategies, and practices* (pp. 115–131). Cambridge, MA: Brookline.

Eiserman, W., Weber, C., & McCoun, M. (1995). Parent and professional roles in early intervention. *Journal of Special Education, 29,* 20–44.

Ghazaleh, H., Ghazaleh, K., & Oakland, T. (1990). Primary and secondary prevention services provided to mentally handicapped infants, children, and youth in the Gaza Strip. *International Journal of Special Education, 5,* 21–27.

Ghoca, M. L. (1972*). The development of language in preschool multiply handicapped children.* Unpublished master's thesis, University of Wisconsin–Milwaukee.

Giudice, E. D., Titomanlio, L., Brogna, G., Bonaccorso, A., Romano, A., Manst, G., et al. (2006). Early intervention for children with Down syndrome in southern Italy. *Infants & Young Children, 19*(1), 50–58.

Grantham-McGregor, S., Powell C., Walker S., et al. (1994). The long term follow up of severely malnourished children who participated in an intervention program. *Child Development, 65,* 428–439.

Guven, N., Bal, S., Metin, N., & Atay, M. (2000). *Usage of the Portage Project in Turkey and extending its usage throughout Turkey.* The 8th International Portage Association Conference, Birmingham, Alabama.

Guven, N., Bal S., & Tugrul, B. (1998). *A contrastive study examining, on the basis of the Portage Early Education Programme Checklists, cognitive development in two groups of normal children aged 37 to 72 months, attending two different kindergartens, one which had classes in the same group whereas the other had mixed-aged classes.* The 7th International Portage Association Conference, Hiroshima, Japan.

Hallahan, D. P., & Kauffman, J. M. (1976). *Introduction to learning disabilities. A psychobehavioral approach.* Englewood Cliffs, NJ: Prentice Hall.

Hassall, L., Weston, B., & Raine, P. (2001). *Portage and Sure Start—Towards community development.* Annual Conference Proceedings, U.K. National Portage Association, Tampa, FL.

Hebbeler, K. M., & Gerlach-Downie, S. G. (2002). Inside the black box of home visiting: A qualitative analysis of why intended outcomes were not achieved. *Early Childhood Research Quarterly, 17,* 28–51.

Horne, J. (2006). *Parental empowerment and Portage.* The 11th International Portage Association Conference, Riga, Latvia.

Hoyson, M., Jamieson, B., & Strain, P. S. (1984). Individualized group instruction of normally developing and autistic-like children: The LEAP curriculum model. *Journal of the Division for Early Childhood, 8,* 157–172.

Individuals with Disabilities Education Act Amendments of 1997, Part C. 105th Cong., 1st Sess. 1 (1997).

Jellnek, J. A. (1985). Documentation of child progress revisited: An analysis method for outreach or local programs. *Journal of the Division for Early Childhood, 9,* 175–182.

Johnson, K. A. (2001). *No place like home: State home visiting policies and programs.* Summary report of survey of states regarding home visiting activities. New York: The Commonwealth Fund.

Johnson, S., Ring, W., Anderson, P., & Marlow, N. (2005). Randomised trial of parental support for families with very parental children: Outcome at 5 years. *Archives of Diseases in Childhood, 90,* 909–915.

Johnson, Z., Molloy, B., Scallan, E., Fitzpatrick, P., Rooney, B., Keegan, T., & Byrne, P. (2000). Community mothers programme—seven years follow-up of a randomized controlled trial of non-professional intervention in parenting. *Journal of Public Health Medicine, 22*(3), 337–342.

Karaaslan, B. T., & Bal, S. (2002). *Evaluation of the effect of home based early intervention programmes on the development of very low birth weight premature infants.* Ankara, Turkey: Hacettepe University, Health Sciences Institute. Master's degree thesis in Child Development and Education.

Klein, P. S., & Rye, H. (2004). Interaction-oriented early intervention in Ethiopia. *Infants and Young Children, 17*(4), 340–354.

Kohli, T. (1988). Effectiveness of Portage in India. In M. White & R. J. Cameron (Eds.), *Portage progress, problems and possibilities* (pp. 82–93). Windsor, England: NFER-Nelson.

Kohli, T. (1990). Impact of home centre based training programme in reducing developmental deficits of disadvantaged young children. *Indian Journal of Disability and Rehabilitation, 4*(2), 65–74.

Kohli, T. (1991). A decade of strides in Portage programs in India. In J. Herwig & M. Stine (Eds.), *A symposium on family-focused intervention: Exploring national and international practices and perspectives* (pp. 63–71). Portage, WI: Cooperative Educational Service Agency 5.

Kohli, T., & Datta, R. (1986). Portage training: An international program for pre-school mentally retarded children with motor handicaps. *Journal of Practical Approaches to Developmental Handicaps, 9.*

Kursiete, V., & Kursiete, I. (2006). *Portage in Eastern Europe.* 11th Biennial Conference of the International Portage Association, Riga, Latvia.

Lindsley, O. R. (1968). *Training parents and teachers to precisely manage children's behavior.* Paper presented at CS Mott Foundation—Children's Health Center, New York City.

Love, J. M., Kisker, E. E., Ross, C., Constantine, J., Boller, K., Schochet, P. Z., et al. (2005). The effectiveness of Early Head Start for 3-year-old children and their parents: Lessons for policy and programs. *Developmental Psychology, 41*(6), 885–901.

McCormick, M. C., McCarton C., Tonascia, J., et al. (1993). Early educational intervention for very low birthweight infants: Results from the Infant Health and Development Program, *Journal of Pediatrics, 123,* 527–533.

Meulen van der, B. F., & Bulsink, R. H. H. (1992). The Portage Project Groningen. In H. Nakken, G. H. van Gemert, & Tj. Zandberg (Eds.), *Research on intervention in special education* (pp. 239–254). Lewiston, ME: Mellen Press.

Meulen van der, B. F., & Oenema-Mostert, I. (2006). *Early childhood intervention for families with a young chronically ill child.* 11th Biennial Conference of the International Portage Association, Riga, Latvia.

Meulen van der, B. F., & Sipma, W. G. (1991). The Portage Project Groningen: Measurement procedures and results. In J. Herwig & M. Stine (Eds.), *A symposium on family-focused intervention: Exploring national and international practices and perspectives* (pp. 125–144). Portage, WI: Cooperative Educational Service Agency 5.

Miller, D. (1990). *The importance of home-based support in providing early intervention services.* Madison: University of Wisconsin, Department of Educational Administration.

Oakland, T., & Ghazaleh, H. (1995). *Primary prevention of handicapping conditions among Palestinian children in Gaza.* Unpublished manuscript.

Oenema-Mostert, I. (2007). *Early intervention for families with a young chronically ill child.* 2nd Conference of the International Society on Early Intervention, Zagreb, Croatia.

Odom, S., & Karnes, M. (Eds.). (1988). *Early intervention for infants and children with handicaps.* Baltimore, MD: Paul Brookes.

Peniston, E. (1972). *An evaluation of the Portage Project.* Unpublished manuscript.

Rao, I. (2007). *Udisha-Portage: Inclusive early childhood education.* Progress Report of Community Based Rehabilitation Network (South Asia), Bangalore. Submitted to Sir Dorabji Tata Trust, Mumbai, India.

Ramey, C., Bryant, D., Wasik, B., Sparling, J., Vendt, K., & LaVange, L. (1992). Infant health and development program for low birth weight, premature infants: Program elements, family participation, and child intelligence. *Pediatrics, 89,* 454–465.

Ramey, C. T., & Ramey, S. L. (1998). Early intervention and early experience. *American Psychologist, 53*(2), 109–120.

Ramey, C. T., Ramey, S. L., Gaines, K. R., & Blair, C. (1995). Two-generation early intervention programs: A child development perspective. In S. Smith (Ed.), *Two-generation programs for families in poverty: A new intervention strategy. Vol. 9. Advances in Applied Developmental Psychology.* Norwood, NJ: Ablex.

Ramey, C. T., & Shearer, D. L. (1999). A conceptual framework for interventions with low birth weight and premature children. In E. Goldson (Ed.), *Nurturing the premature infant: Developmental interventions in the neonatal intensive care nursery* (pp. 86–101). New York: Oxford University Press.

Ramey, S. L., & Ramey, C. T. (1992). Early educational intervention with disadvantaged children—To what effect? *Applied and Preventive Psychology, 1,* 131–140.

Ray, A., Bowman, B., & Robbins, J. (2006). *Preparing early childhood teachers to successfully educate all children: The contribution of four-year undergraduate teacher preparation programs.* The Foundation for Child Development. New York.

Resnick, M. B., Armstrong S., & Carter, R. L. (1988). Developmental intervention program for high-risk premature infants: Effects on development and parent-infant interactions, *Developmental and Behavioral Pediatrics, 9,* 73–78.

Revill, S., & Blendon, R. (1979). A home training service for pre-school developmentally handicapped children. *Behavior Research Therapy, 17,* 207–214.

Robinson, C. C., Rosenburg, S. A., & Beckman, P. J. (1988). Parent involvement in early childhood special education. In J. B. Jordan, J. J. Gallagher, P. S. Huttinger, & M. B. Karnes (Eds.), *Early childhood special education: Birth to three.* Reston, VA: Council for Exceptional Children.

Rosenberg, S. A., Robinson, C. C., & Beckman, P. J. (1984). Teaching skills inventory: A measure of parent performance. *Journal of the Division of Early Childhood, 8,* 107–113.

Russell, P. (1986). Parental involvement in the 1980s. In R. J. Cameron (Ed.), *Portage: Preschoolers, parents and professionals* (pp. 72–83). Windsor, England: NFER-Nelson.

Samaria, I., & Neophytou, D. (2005). *Portage in Cyprus,* Thirteenth International Portage Association Conference, Ireland.

Shazadi, S. (2002). Developing a home based programme for special needs children. *Journal of Education and Research,* Karachi Pak Organization of Workers in Educational Research, *1*(2).

Shazadi, S., Anjum, S., & Siddqui, N. (2004). *A study of parent guidance through the Portage Guide to Early Education: The Pakistani Model.*

10th International Portage Association Conference, Manila, Philippines.

Shearer, D. E. (1991). Portage makes a difference. In J. Herwig & M. Stine (Eds.), *A symposium on family-focused intervention: Exploring national and international practices and perspectives* (pp. 1–5). Portage, WI: Cooperative Educational Service Agency 5.

Shearer, D. E. (1993). The Portage Project: An international home approach to early intervention of young children and their families. In J. Roopnarine & J. Johnson (Eds.), *Approaches to early childhood education* (2nd ed.). New York: Merrill-Macmillan.

Shearer, D. E. (1995). The application of the Portage Model in developing countries [Letter to the editor]. *Actionaid Disability News, 6*(1), 33–34.

Shearer, D. E. (2004). *Current status of international Portage early intervention programs.* The 10th International Portage Association Conference, Manila, Philippines.

Shearer, D. E. (2006). *New challenges for the future of Portage.* 11th International Portage Association Conference, Riga, Latvia.

Shearer, D. E., & Loftin, C. (1984). The Portage Project: Teaching parents to teach their preschool child in the home. In R. Dangel & R. Polster (Eds.), *Parent training: Foundations of research and practice.* New York: Guilford Press.

Shearer, D. E., & Shearer, D. L. (1995, October). Has Portage experienced a paradigm shift? *International Portage Association News, 11,* 1–6.

Shearer, D. E., & Shearer, M. (1976). The Portage Project: A model for early childhood intervention. In T. Tjossem (Ed.), *Intervention strategies for high risk infants and young children* (pp. 338–350). Baltimore, MD: University Park Press.

Shearer, D. E., & Snider, R. A. (1981). On providing a practical approach to the early education of young children. *Child Behavior Therapy Review, 3,* 119–127.

Shearer, M., & Shearer, D. E. (1972). The Portage Project: A model for early childhood education. *Exceptional Children, 36,* 210–217.

Shelton, T. L., & Stepanek, S. S. (1994). *Family centered care for children meeting specialized health and developmental services* (3rd ed.). Bethesda, MD: Association for the Care of Children's Health.

Shonkoff, J. P., & Phillips, D. A. (Eds.). (2000). *From neurons to neighborhoods: The science of early child hood development.* Washington, DC: National Academy Press.

Smith, J., Kushlick, A., & Glossop, C. (1977). *The Wessex Portage Project research report 125.* Southampton, United Kingdom: University of Southampton.

Stephens, T. M. (1976). *Directive teaching of children with learning and behavioral handicaps.* Columbus, OH: Charles E. Merrill.

Stoneman, Z. (1990). Conceptual relationships between family research and mental retardation. In N. W. Bray (Ed.), *International review of research in mental retardation.* Vol. 16 (pp. 161–202). San Diego, CA: Academic Press.

Sturmey, P., Thorburn, M., Brown, J., Reed, J., Kaur, J., & King, G. (1992). Portage guide to early intervention: Cross-cultural aspects and intra-cultural variability. *Child: Care, Health, and Development, 18,* 377–394.

Thorburn, M. J. (1992). Parent evaluation of a community-based rehabilitation program in Jamaica. *International Journal of Rehabilitation Research, 15,* 170–176.

Thorburn, M. J. (1997). Raising children with disabilities in the Caribbean. In. J. L. Roopnarine & J. Brown (Eds.), *Caribbean families: Diversity among ethnic groups* (pp. 177–204). Greenwich, CT: Ablex.

Thorburn, M. J., Brown, J. M., & Bell, C. (1979). *Early stimulation of handicapped children using community workers.* Paper presented at the Fifth Congress of the International Association of the Scientific Study of Mental Deficiency, Jerusalem, Israel.

Tsintsadze, N. (2006). *The introduction of the Portage Model for special needs children in Georgia and future plans.* 11th International Portage Association Conference, Riga, Latvia.

Turnbull, A., Patterson, J., Behr, S., Murphy, D., Marquis, J., & Blue-Banning, M. (1993). *Cognitive coping, families and disability.* Baltimore, MD: Paul Brookes.

U.S. General Accounting Office (USGAO). (1990, July). *Home visiting: A promising early intervention strategy for at-risk families.* Report to the Chairman, Subcommittee on Labor, Health and Human Services, Education and Related Agencies, Committee on Appropriations, U.S. Senate.

Wasik, B. H., Bryant, D. M., & Lyons, C. M. (1990). *Home visiting: Procedures for helping families.* Newbury Park, CA: Sage.

White, M. (1997). A review of the influence and effects of Portage. In S. Wolfendale (Ed.), *Working with parents of special education needs children after the code of practice,* Chapter 2. London, England: Fulton.

White, M. (2006). *Update on Portage training and programs in the United Kingdom.* 11th International Portage Association Conference, Riga, Latvia.

Wolfendale, S. (2001). Portage in contemporary contexts, in National Portage Association (UK) *Proceedings of Annual Conference,* Yeovil, England.

Yamaguchi, K. (1987). *The Japan adaptation of the early intervention model and some results.* Tokyo: Tokyo Gakugei University, The Research Institute for the Education of Exceptional Children.

Yamaguchi, K. (1988). The Japanese adaptation of the Portage early intervention model and some results. In M. White & R. Cameron (Eds.), *Portage: Progress, problems, and possibilities.* Windsor, England: NFER-Nelson.

Yamaguchi, K. (1996). A follow-up study of Japanese children who received early intervention through a Portage programme. In S. Cameron & M. White (Eds.), *The Portage early intervention model: Making the difference for families across the world.* Somerset, England: UK National Portage Association.

Yamaguchi, K., Shimizu, N., & Nishinaga, K. (2006). *Recent Developments of Portage Activities in Japan.* 11th International Portage Association Conference, Riga, Latvia.

Part II
Integral Dimensions

Chapter 5

Including Everyone

A Model Preschool Program for Children With and Without Disabilities

Ellen Barnes ✣ *Jowonio School, Syracuse, New York*
David Smukler ✣ *State University of New York at Cortland*

Federal and state regulations and research support the education of children with disabilities in the least restrictive environment with their nondisabled peers. For over 30 years, Jowonio School in Syracuse, New York, has served as a program for a wide range of children, including those with differing physical, social, communication, and cognitive needs. The curriculum developed as an integration of the knowledge from special education and early childhood developmentally appropriate practice. Special education as a field developed in public schools in the early part of the 20th century (Sarason & Doris, 1959). In the last 40 or 50 years, as a result of both scientific knowledge about children and social changes in American society, interest has increased in early education (child care, preschool, etc.) that addresses the needs of diverse learners (Ramsey, 2006; Ray, Bowman, & Robbins, 2006). Notably, the 1960s saw a rebirth of scientific interest in the rapid normal cognitive, language, emotional, and physical development in the early childhood (preschool) years (Brown, 1973; Hunt, 1961; Piaget, 1963). Women were challenging traditional roles and entering the job market in increasing numbers, government social programs were being developed, and many social issues and customs (civil rights, sexual mores, war) were being debated. Parents of children with disabilities, unable to get services, organized together (e.g., Association for Retarded Children, United Cerebral Palsy) and started preschool programs. They also advocated for the development of federal and state funding for these programs. At the federal level with Head Start in 1964 (and amendments in 1972 requiring the inclusion of disabled children) and the Handicapped Children's Education Assistance Act (PL 90-538), an early intervention focus on children with disabilities was developed. The Americans with Disabilities Act (ADA, effective 1992), under its Public Accommodations Section (Title III), states that day-care centers may not discriminate on the basis of disability. Physical barriers to accessibility must be removed if readily achievable and, if not, alternative methods of providing service must be offered. Any new construction should be accessible to persons with disabilities.

The most important education act was PL 94-142, the Education for All Handicapped Children Act of 1975 (renamed in 1990 the Individuals with Disabilities Education Act), which set the standards for all of America's public schools for the education of children with disabilities from 3 to 21 years of age. This law included the most important ideas of what is called special education. The following are the ideas embedded in PL 94-142:

1. All children should go to school.
2. Children with disabilities should have an education appropriate to their individualized needs (an Individual Education Plan [IEP]).
3. This education should be based on fair assessment of the child.
4. Children with disabilites should be educated with nondisabled children to the fullest extent possible (the "least restrictive environment").
5. Parents should have an opportunity to be actively involved in meaningful ways in their child's education, including procedural due process appeals (Turnbull & Turnbull, 1982).

Subsequent legislation (PL 99-457) has resulted in these ideas being extended to children from birth to 3 years with special emphasis on the family unit as an important part of any early intervention program (Bailey, McWilliams, Buysse, & Wesley, 1998; Gallagher, Trohanis, & Clifford, 1989). The new law is called the Individuals with Disabilities Education Act (IDEA), and it was reauthorized by Congress in 1997 and 2003. The IDEA amendments place a strong emphasis on parent involvement in the initial evaluation process, in eligibility and placement decisions, and in the development and revision of the IEP. The IDEA has a new focus on ensuring that services be offered in natural environments. Part C encourages the provision of early intervention services for children under 3 years of age at risk for substantive developmental delay. In addition, there is incentive to establish collaborative efforts with community agencies to identify, evaluate, and serve infants and toddlers and to create a smooth transition to preschool services.

The language describing the least restrictive environment has changed over the years. Initially, *mainstreaming* referred to the placement

The early intervention teacher and a child who is typically developing aid a child with cerebral palsy, providing hand-over-hand instruction to paint with a toy car. The involvement of children without special needs is one of the benefits of inclusionary practice.

Susan Welteroth

of students with disabilities into regular classrooms, often without supports and often on a part-time basis. *Integration* has meant that children are temporally, socially, and instructionally integrated for a meaningful amount of time, but the assumption is still made that the mainstream environment is designed for typical students and that special needs students must fit in. An *inclusive school* is structured to serve a wide range of students; the environment is flexible and organized to meet the unique needs of all students. In an inclusive school everyone belongs, is accepted, supports, and is supported by all members of the community while having individual educational needs met (Biklen, 1992; Sapon-Shevin, 2000/2001; Stainback & Stainback, 1990). The Council for Exceptional Children, Division of Early Childhood Education's (DEC) position statement explicity "supports the rights of all children regardless of their diverse abilities to participate in natural settings in their communities" and "that young children and their families have full successful access to health, social, educational, and other support services that promote full participation in family and community life". This full inclusion is the vision of the future that is held by the people at the Jowonio School and modeled by their practice. Inclusive education models today frequently use the construct of *universal design for learning* (UDL). Universal design is a set of architectural principles related to the access of structures to the largest number of people possible. Many inclusive educators have adopted UDL as a framework for their practice (Rose & Meyer, 2002).

While it has been an important step for promoting greater participation by students with disabilities, the notion of "least restrictive environment" articulated in the IDEA is problematic to the inclusive educator because the descriptor "least restrictive" implies a continuum of services that also includes more restrictive options (Nisbet, 2004; Taylor, 1998). Table 5-1 illustrates a range of program models with regard to contact between children with and without disabilities. Such settings are all commonly employed to serve children with disabilities. However, it should be noted that educators with an inclusive perspective are critical of most of these models and do not assume that a student who needs more extensive support ought to have less contact with nondisabled peers. An inclusive education approach resists the notion that "inclusion" is just another program option on one end of a continuum of service that is calibrated to serve children with ever-increasing support needs. Indeed, students with significant disabilities and the same characteristics as those placed in residential schools (the "most restrictive" setting in Table 5-1) are often placed at Jowonio, where they are included in the same classroom groups as nondisabled children and are viewed as full members of the group with much to contribute.

With the exception of reverse mainstreaming, all the programming options listed in Table 5.1 are also employed once children are of school age. Some students with disabilities are full members of an inclusive education environment. Others may be placed in a general education room with consultant services, or they may have a special education classroom as their home base but be mainstreamed into general education settings for some part of their school day. Such students may also be placed full time in self-contained special education classrooms (housed either in a public school or special setting), provided with home-bound instruction, or sent to a residential facility. (There is considerable variation in how the term *inclusion* is applied, and it is often used to describe settings that do not meet our criteria for inclusive education, both at the early-childhood and school-age level. Sometimes *inclusion* is distinguished from *full inclusion*.)

TABLE 5–1
Programs for Children with Disabilities

Setting	Characteristics/Assumptions
Residential school	• No significant contact with nondisabled peers • Complete institutional control of daily life
Home-based	• Teachers and/or therapists make visits to the child at home to implement interventions • Parent "training" or support of a common component
Itinerant services outside the home	• Use of the community as a resource • Some contact with nondisabled peers possible in community settings
Early childhood special education	• Early childhood classroom designed exclusively to serve children with special needs • Needs and services "clustered" for efficient provision of services
Reverse mainstreaming	• Early childhood special education program that includes a handful of nondisabled peers • Possibility of incentives (e.g., free tuition) being offered to attract nondisabled students
Mixed day (part time in special education setting and part time in early childhood setting)	• "Visits" for children with disabilities to an early childhood education setting for a substantial part of the day, as well as "home" classroom designed solely for children with special needs
Early childhood setting with consultant services	• A typical early childhood class where specialists (special educators and therapists) visit to support staff and provide direct services to students with disabilities
Inclusive early childhood education	• Similar to the early childhood setting with consultant services, except the classroom environment is designed to respond to the needs of all students • Service providers, such as special educators and therapists, integrated into the team of professionals who plan for all students

HISTORY OF THE JOWONIO SCHOOL

Created in 1969 by a group of parents in Syracuse, New York, as an alternative to the public schools, the Jowonio School reflected the humanistic free-school movement of the 1960s. It was run as a community program in which decisions were made cooperatively, and it emphasized an individualized curriculum for the whole child, including emotional and social development, as well as academic achievement. Because of these values, focus, and structure, Jowonio always attracted children with special needs. In 1975, Jowonio cooperated with community agencies serving disabled people and with the local university to develop a proposal to create a planned and well-staffed program that integrated children with various disabilities. That fall at Jowonio School, one third of the students were classified as having special needs, including several students with the label of *autism,* a syndrome in which language and social skills are typically quite delayed or different (Kluth, 2003).

Since that time, the school has functioned as an inclusive program: students ages 2 to 5 are served in classrooms populated with students with and without identified special needs (Knoblock, 1982; Knoblock & Lehr, 1985). A number of powerful yet simple beliefs have guided the Jowonio program since its inception, and these are described next.

PHILOSOPHICAL BASE OF THE JOWONIO SCHOOL

All Children Can Learn

We approach the wide range of students we serve with the expectation that they can grow and change and that the impetus to do so is inherent in human nature. Children whom many might call developmentally delayed have enormous potential if adults can help them find ways to express what they know and participate in their environment effectively. We are finding, for instance, that a number of nonverbal preschool children can demonstrate age-appropriate academic skills with help from adults.

The Right to Participate

Just as the civil rights movement showed Americans that racial and ethnic minorities have a right to be part of American life, so it is with persons with disabilities. The segregated system of special education services arose out of a medical model, as well as out of discomfort with and prejudice against people perceived as different. In a democracy, not only should all citizens have access to the mainstream, but there is also a dire need to understand how children's characteristics, such as race, class, and differing physical or psychological characteristics, intersect with the characteristics of teachers and other professionals in different environments (Ramsey, 2006; Ray, Bowman, & Robbins, 2006). Not only those with special needs benefit from including everyone; the nondisabled students and teachers also grow from their contact and interaction (Odom & Diamond, 1998).

We also do not subscribe to the myth of readiness that children are included in the mainstream only when they are ready to be like their typical peers (Ladd, Herald, & Andrews, 2006). That belief assumes that children must change to fit the program. Our assumption is the opposite: The program should adapt to meet the needs of the children. Any child can be successfully included when school personnel exhibit a willing attitude and children and adults receive appropriate supports.

Learning Through Relationships

We become open to learning when we are in trusting situations with others. We are more likely to put ourselves in new situations and respond to requests or demands of others when we feel safe and cared about (Collins, Maccoby, Steinberg, Hetherington, & Bornstein, 2000; Denham, 2006). The position statement of the National Association for the Education of Young Children (NAEYC) regarding developmentally appropriate practice (Bredekamp & Copple, 1997) begins with the principle that all "domains of children's development—physical, social, emotional and cognitive—are closely related." Greenspan and Wieder (1998) also describe emotions as the basis of learning, and this informs their intervention approach aimed at children with developmental disabilities ("Floortime"). Greenspan and Wieder (1998) suggest that children are first motivated to engage and learn through relationships in which significant adults interact and follow a child's interests. During a playful period, an adult focuses on four goals: to encourage joint attention and connection; to participate as a partner in a circle of two-way communication; to express feelings and ideas through words and play; and to link ideas together into a logical understanding of the world (e.g., classification, cause and effect).

In addition, children learn as much from other children as they do from teachers (Guralnick,

Connor, Hammond, Gottman, & Kinnish, 1996; Ladd et al., 2006). They model how their peers move through routines, how they follow directions, and how they interact with one another. Often a child who has receptive language problems and does not understand the teacher's verbal instructions imitates other children to know what to do. Developing language and appropriate social skills requires both models and practice (Cavallaro & Haney, 1999; Grisham-Brown, Hemmeter, & Pretti-Frontczak, 2005; Guralnick, 1980; Jenkins, Odom, & Speltz, 1989). When children with special needs, particularly children with severe speech and language needs, are in segregated programs, how can they learn to talk and interact when their peers all have similar needs? Learning skills within the typical environment rather than in isolated artificial situations means that children will be more likely to demonstrate these skills in the home, school, or community. That is, they will be more likely to generalize. A good and inclusive early childhood classroom offers many opportunities for play and communication with a wide range of peers.

At Jowonio the emphasis is on cooperative rather than competitive activities (Johnson & Johnson, 1999; Johnson, Johnson, & Holubec, 1990; Sapon-Shevin, 1999; Sapon-Shevin, 2007). Nondisabled children need to have their questions about their peers answered and to have caring behavior modeled by adults. Teachers should explore the ways in which bias about disabilities affects their language and behavior and the classroom. Integrating nonstereotyped images of disabled and nondisabled persons in the curriculum and structuring activities for children to explore individual differences will facilitate an inclusive atmosphere (Barnes, Berrigan, & Biklen, 1978; Froschl, Colon, Rubin, & Sprung, 1984; Lieber et al., 1998).

Age-Appropriate Curriculum

Jowonio staff use the guidelines from the NAEYC on Developmentally Appropriate Practice (Bredekamp & Copple, 1997). Classrooms offer many opportunities for children to manipulate a wide variety of materials; to play alone and with others in sensory, constructive, and symbolic activities; to ask questions and develop concepts about themselves and the world; to be physically active; and to express themselves in words, art, and music. A stimulating early childhood environment is designed so that any student can succeed in it. This may require adaptations in terms of the physical environment, expectations of level of participation and amount of teacher support, size and nature of groupings during the day, schedule, and presentation of activities and materials used.

Communication-Based Classrooms

Just as social relationships are the basis for learning, communication is central to the establishment and maintenance of those relationships, to children's receptive understanding of the world around them, and to their ability to express that understanding to others and to have their needs and wants met. Speech and language are communicative, and our efforts with children must be geared toward enhancing their power to influence their environment through verbal or nonverbal communication. We also believe that for young children, language is learned primarily through play (Johnson, Christie, & Wardle, 2005; Musselwhite, 1986; Westby, 1980). Obviously, having peers with strong play and communication skills as stimuli and models is very important, as is the opportunity to learn and practice language in natural contexts.

Communication occurs all day long. Even a nonverbal person is constantly communicating if another individual is present. However, what one person intends and another understands may be different. As teachers, we must learn to read a child's behavior for its communicative intent and then learn to help a child develop appropriate ways to express those intents.

The same behavior may have different meanings in different contexts, and different behaviors may have the same meaning (Donnellan, Mirenda, Mesaras, & Fassbender, 1984). Children need opportunities to make real choices in their environment. We have used a number of alternative or augmentative systems for children to express themselves. These may include symbol systems, signing, and typing that occurs with adult facilitation.

Parent–Teacher Partnership

Despite an emphasis in the IDEA on the importance of parents to the special education process, parents are often viewed by some teachers as irrelevant to the decision-making process of education and, at worst, as adversaries. At Jowonio we view parents as partners in our efforts to create the best program for children. Teachers and parents share their respective types of expertise, and each brings an important perspective to a dialogue about children. As teachers we have access to information about available services, rights, procedures, and support networks for parents. We offer a view of a particular child from our experiences with a range of children and from seeing that child in the school setting. We are in a position to coordinate programming between home, school, and related service personnel and to communicate to other professionals about a child (e.g., when the child makes the transition to public school from preschool). Parents bring to the parent–teacher dialogue essential information about a child: historical developmental information; an understanding of a child's daily behaviors, needs, and emerging skills; and a repertoire of successful interventions. Parents will be the child's lifelong advocates, and their understanding of the child is critical in effective long-term programming (Bailey et al., 1998; Biklen, 1992; Kluth, Biklen, English-Sand, & Smukler, 2007).

Teachers have four major roles in relation to parents:

1. Facilitate a child's growth through parent contact
2. Support and empower parents in their parenting role
3. Provide resources
4. Facilitate the transition of parents and children to their next environment

Facilitating a child's growth through parent contact means listening to parent input and wishes and incorporating these into IEP goals that reflect the child's participation not only in school but also at home and in the community.

Teachers must establish ongoing communication with families so that expectations of the child at home and at school are known and coordinated and so that parents are aware of how their child is doing and progressing at school. At Jowonio this communication can occur in many ways, depending on the individual family's preferences and resources. Parents may observe in the classroom and communicate directly with other team members through conferences, home visits, telephone calls, e-mail, daily or intermittent exchange in a home–school notebook, and classroom social events (e.g., potluck suppers, awards ceremonies, grandparents' teas, birthdays). Teachers can help parents feel competent by listening and reinforcing them for their effective strategies, by focusing on the child's progress, and by helping them enjoy their child in the present.

Building positive and trusting relationships with parents begins with respecting their love and hopes for their child, soliciting and listening to their ideas and concerns, and sharing one's own questions. It also requires a realistic understanding of what parents can do given all the demands on their time and energy (e.g., a single parent of several children may not be able to do a toileting program when money, meals, and laundry have top priority).

Providing resources begins with developing an understanding of family strengths and needs and natural ways to help them meet their needs (Bailey et al., 1998; Dunst, Trivette, & Deal, 1988). This may include information (e.g., literature or workshops on legal rights, autism, toilet training), problem solving to access their own networks, and, if necessary, referrals to agencies and support groups (e.g., financial-aid programs, respite care, counseling, parent or sibling support groups).

The staff members of Jowonio's community-based ENRICH program provide special education and therapy services to children identified as having special needs from birth to age 5 years. After a comprehensive evaluation, youngsters receive itinerant services in their home or in nursery, day-care, or home child-care settings. The opportunity for intensive parent contact, as well as child contact, means that families can receive emotional and instrumental support and can model effective teaching strategies. In these early months after diagnosis, the contact between therapists, teachers, and parents gives many opportunities to process the nature and implications of the child's developmental and unique needs and to try out strategies to support the child toward growth. The transdisciplinary team approach (including the parent) is invaluable in providing a variety of perspectives on the child's needs. Collaborating with community day-care and nursery programs not only supports individual students with special needs but also enhances the clinical programming for all children in these settings. The special education staff learns to address the functional skills youngsters need to be successful in natural environments.

The transition to the next environment occurs more easily when a teacher can give parents information and a perspective on the process (e.g., school options, IEP procedures). Staff can help parents to express what they want and to work with the new school to create it, establish lines of communication between parents and the new school, and relate positive specific information about the child to the new teacher (we send a portfolio to the new school). Preschools are often the first place where parents have trusted others to be so important in their child's life; it can be hard to move on to what seems to be a bigger, more impersonal, and less supportive setting. Teachers can help this transition by fostering positive relationships with the new school.

Teaming Skills

Quality teaching is enhanced by working within a team; we all can benefit from the ideas of others and models of different ways of doing things (Bailey, 1996; Thousand & Villa, 1990). Good teaching is never a script; it takes an experimental attitude and the openness to try things in new ways. Our program is set up with teachers working in teams of three or four full-time staff and involving additional part-time and resource staff, including language, occupational, and physical therapists. We allocate specific time each week for teachers to plan together, to have clinical conferences about children, to participate in staff development activities, and to work on their roles and relationships with one another. Most people working with young children have not been taught teaming skills; this is often the most complex part of the job in our program because of the large number of adults with whom one has contact. As we learn to problem solve about programming for children, we can also do so about one another. We have built in a system of peer and administrative supports for all our teachers.

The conscious emphasis on how we are working together pays off in the quality of the programming for children, as well as in the job satisfaction of our staff. In addition, we look at adults developmentally, as we look at children, and we provide incentives for all staff to grow in their professional skill.

DEALING WITH DIFFICULT BEHAVIOR

Developing effective strategies for dealing with children's difficult behaviors can be one of the most challenging aspects of a teacher's job. In a classroom including children with special social, behavioral, and communication needs, a wider variety of behavior may occur, much of which will require specific planned approaches. What children do is the result of an interaction with or reaction to what is going on around them. You can never look at a particular behavior as only coming from within the child. The adults and what they are saying and doing, the space and sensory environment, the peer group, and the nature of the materials and tasks that are presented always have an important impact on the behavior. Once behavior is understood within its context, a variety of approaches can be implemented to support the child to get his or her needs met more effectively (Kaiser & Rasminsky, 2006). Such approaches might include a functional analysis of behavior, preventative environmental planning, and support for particular social skill sets, including sharing, taking turns, and problem solving. Combining approaches avoids a narrow focus that can cause adults to miss the point of children's behavior.

Behavior as Communication

What a child does must be looked at as an effort to communicate. To understand what the child is trying to tell you by a particular action (communicative intent), you must understand the context. The single behavior might have different meanings in different situations; a child might scream when hurt, frustrated, excited, angry, or to get an adult's attention. Several different behaviors might have the same meaning; grabbing, smiling, yelling, or pinching could all be efforts to avoid a task the child finds difficult (Carr & Durand, 1985; Donnellan et al., 1984).

Using a problem-solving process, teachers and others attempt to identify the communication content of the behavior by analyzing the relationship between the environment and the occurrence of the behavior. What happens before or after the behavior? What is the setting? Who is present? When did it occur? This process attempts to discover functional relationships between the behavior and elements in the environment that we can potentially change (see Dunlap, Kern-Dunlap, Clarke, & Robbins, 1991; O'Neill, Horner, Albin, Storey, & Sprague, 1990; Touchette, MacDonald, & Langer, 1985).

If such an analysis shows a predictable pattern of behavior, teachers will be more easily able to intervene effectively. Sometimes patterns are not obvious, but our assumption nevertheless is that all behavior occurs for a reason. Intervening respectfully entails considering the emotional, physical, and sensory context of the behavior. Interventions should be chosen that maintain everyone's well-being, consider the child's point of view, and attempt to increase (rather than limit) the social and behavioral repertoire of the child whose behavior is of concern.

Positive Programming

Planning to teach children appropriate behaviors is the most important approach to dealing with difficult behaviors (Dunlap, Johnson, & Robbins, 1990; Evans & Meyer, 1985; Kaiser & Rasminsky, 2006; Meyer & Evans, 1989). You need to teach children what you want them to do, not just tell them what not to do. This might mean teaching an alternative way to communicate (e.g., "If you want my attention, tap me on the shoulder and say my name"). Or you can teach an alternative response to a stressful situation (e.g., "If it is too noisy for you to work, put on headphones rather than flapping your hands and crying"). Many times teaching appropriate social skills or how to control emotions using role playing can effectively reduce problem behaviors (Goldstein & McGinnis, 1990). The use of *social stories* (Gray, 1996) can also help to reduce difficult behavior by generating insights for children with differing understandings about unstated social rules and conventions.

Reinforcing Positive Behaviors

Encouraging or rewarding someone for doing what is appropriate is always more effective than reacting to inappropriate behavior. This means that teachers need to create opportunities for children to exhibit positive behaviors and then to respond in a genuine and very reinforcing way when the positive behavior occurs.

Interventions Within Relationships

Implementing interventions around difficult behaviors is always more effective within the context of a positive relationship with the child. This means teachers need to plan time each day for enjoyable positive activities, supportive attention to the child's emotions, and warm and consistent contact (physical and social) with the child. If a strong relationship exists between the adult and the child, the teacher can deal with conflict and limits in a way that is meaningful for the child.

McGee and his colleagues (McGee, Menolascino, Hobbs, & Menousek, 1987) describe an approach to problem behavior called "gentle teaching," which generally reverses many notions about behavior problems. This point of view sees a child who throws a tantrum as a child who has not developed positive relationships ("bonded") with others. Teachers should have unconditional positive regard toward the student. Problem behaviors are prevented or ignored ("not valued"), and the child is redirected into other tasks that will develop mutual positive human relationships ("interdependence"). Because the goal is to develop human relationships, skill training or activities are used to foster these interdependent relationships. Any procedure that might interfere with the development of bonding (e.g., punishment) is excluded. If both the teacher and the learner are not having fun, then the activity is not building positive relationships.

Using Natural Consequences

As much as possible, interventions should be natural so that they will generalize to the environments in which we all function (e.g., home, school, community). If Jim dumps food on the floor, he should clean it up. In the long term, we want the normal environment to provide the control and consequences for the problem behavior. It may be necessary to be in the "real" environment to accomplish this, especially for children with more significant disabilities. Waiting in line at McDonald's can be simulated in the classroom, but nothing substitutes for the real thing.

Aversive Treatment Is Unacceptable

We exclude the use of aversive interventions, including seclusion, physical punishment, and prolonged physical restraint, on both ethical and pragmatic grounds. For example, we may use a time-out technique to allow students to leave a group so that they can calm down, but we never use exclusion from the group as a punishment. Teaching appropriate behaviors or positive programming is more effective and generalizable (Donnellan, LaVigna, Negri-Shoultz, & Fassbender, 1988; Dunlap et al., 1990; Evans & Meyer, 1985; LaVigna & Donnellan, 1986; McGee et al., 1987; Meyer & Evans, 1989). When using aversive methods, teachers often lose perspective, and punishment makes everyone feel bad. Focusing on positive experiences, building positive relationships, and not reinforcing (valuing) bad behaviors are more effective in the long run. Research reviews and studies point to the negative consequences of severe forms of punishment across cultural groups (Gershoff, 2002; Lynch et al., 2006; McLoyd, Kaplan, Hardaway, & Wood, 2007).

Behavioral Interventions in an Inclusive Setting

In any classroom, teachers must balance the needs of the individuals with the needs of the group. Often people opposed to inclusion talk about "the rights of the other students." The reality is that in any group setting teachers make decisions that balance the needs of the individual with the needs of the group, and all individuals must be considered in such decisions, not just those with disability labels. If a child screams to get attention, the appropriate strategy may be to ignore the screaming. However, the screaming may be so disruptive to the rest of the children that the teacher may feel a need to address it directly. Talking with other adults will help a teacher to analyze this and similar dilemmas and develop a richer repertoire of positive responses.

Problem-Solving Team Approach

Good teachers are those who seek as much help as necessary to deal with a problem. We hold meetings that may involve speech and language pathologists, occupational and physical therapists, other teachers, aides, parents, psychologists, graduate students, and any other people who know the student and might have good ideas. The diversity of the participants is important. Working with such a diverse set of creative people requires some direction and focus, and the teacher needs to have some skills to keep the group on task.

Teachers at Jowonio use a general problem-solving approach that involves as many people and their ideas as possible. The problem to be solved may be an educational, social, emotional, or behavioral problem. The solutions are to be found in changing the environment. The child is never the problem. A single teacher never has all the right answers.

Implementing an Individualized Education Program

Because it makes sense and because it is mandated by state and federal regulations, children with special needs must have an IEP, a planned description of their individual program. This IEP must include a statement of each child's current level of functioning, annual long-term goals, a breakdown of those goals into short-term behavioral objectives, and a time line and description of the means by which these goals will be measured and reached.

A typical early childhood curriculum and its themes and concepts are the framework within which specific goals are addressed for children with special needs. The scope and sequence of that curriculum must allow for diverse levels of achievement and diverse learning styles (Gardner & Hatch, 1989; Goodman, 1992; Ramsey, 2006; Ray et al., 2006). Lesson plans usually incorporate multiple objectives and multiple modes of instruction in keeping with a universal design for learning approach (Rose & Meyer, 2002). Adaptations for children with special needs may occur in a number of ways: targeted skill or skill sequence, space, groupings, level of participation expected, kinds of materials used, and nature of cues or support required (Janney & Snell, 2004; Udvari-Solner, 1996).

Technology, especially the use of computers, allows all children to participate in highly motivating activities that encourage independence, foster positive self-esteem and sense of mastery, and increase attention span and problem-solving skills. Students prefer open-ended interactive software, which often can be used independently after initial and intermittent adult assistance. Since children can play together at the computer, opportunities abound for taking turns, cooperation, and social interaction. Technology also offers options for students to communicate through keyboards and the increasingly sophisticated voice-output equipment. Anyone with a reliable movement can have access through a myriad of switches to computerized communication devices and enhanced learning opportunities. Nonverbal students can demonstrate their knowledge and in some cases can serve as models and teachers for their peers (Johnston, Beard, & Carpenter, 2006). As well as preparing children for the future, technology can enhance significantly the learning and social possibilities in the classroom.

SCHOOL AND CLASS COMPOSITION

The wide range of children served at Jowonio includes nondisabled students 2 to 5 years of age and peers with special needs. These include children who have been identified by professionals as having speech or language impairments, orthopedic disabilities, autism, other health impairments, and multiple handicaps. Each class has a 1- to 2-year age range and a balance of students with skills and needs. For instance, our toddler class has 10 children, 5 with disabilities and 5 typically developing peers. Our full-day 3-, 4-, and 5-year-old classrooms normally have 16 students, 6 of whom have been identified as having special educational needs. It is important that the tone of the classroom group be age appropriate and that each group has good models for social and language skills. A cross-age student population offers a greater range of possibilities for peer interactions and friendships.

Three adults are assigned to the toddler class of 10; in the 3- to 5-year-old rooms of 16 children, 4 full-time adults are assigned. Related services of speech and language therapy, physical therapy, and occupational therapy are available as needed. In every classroom, we try to have staff trained in both early childhood and special education. Background and experience with typically developing children lend awareness of the usual sequence of skills and developmental tasks to expect at each particular age. Then, for example, one can have a perspective that views issues in a 3-year-old's behavior as within normal developmental limits rather than as a symptom of a special need.

STRATEGIES FOR ACCOMPLISHING INCLUSION

To support maximum participation of a wide range of students in the classroom, we allow for flexibility in scheduling, in grouping, and in levels of support and expected participation (Stainback & Stainback, 1992). In addition, materials and activities that have multiple objectives

Inclusive classrooms will also help to sensitize children to the diverse abilities of individuals.

Frank Siteman

and several modes of instruction allow for the inclusion of students with different levels of skill.

Flexibility in Scheduling

The scheduling of the day serves to provide a predictable routine within which children can gain independence while having opportunities for open-ended exploration, spontaneity, and choice making. Adults make use of teachable moments to extend play and broaden learning. We try to minimize the number of transitions and the amount of waiting between events. Time is allowed for learning skills embedded in natural situations, such as cleanup and dressing. A balance must always be achieved between active gross motor activities and sitting activities, and children should have opportunities for movement throughout the building and neighborhood. A typical schedule might be as follows:

8:45–9:45	Open play/learning centers, choose and do
9:45–10:00	Meeting or circle time
10:00–10:15	Snack
10:15–10:30	Books and toileting
10:30–11:30	Special activities (movement, music, skill group, paired play, play choices, play group, acting, story stretchers, cooking)
11:30–12:00	Lunch
12:00–12:30	Rest and reading
12:30–1:00	Gym/outside
1:00–2:00	Special activities (as in the morning) or learning centers
2:00–2:30	Good-bye preparation (music/closing circle)

Classes take frequent field trips. Schedules are often planned around a theme of the week, and efforts are made to design activities, select books, and arrange experiences both inside and outside the classroom to reinforce the concepts of the theme. Therapists frequently work in the classroom and may be responsible for planning group activities designed to meet individual goals for target children. Classroom-based therapy maximizes the opportunities for generalization of skills, the modeling of therapeutic techniques for teachers, and the probability that therapy goals will be useful for the child in the classroom and at home. Janney and Snell (2004) refer to this practice as "pull in" therapy, turning the usual jargon ("push in" vs. "pull out" therapy) on its head.

Flexibility in Grouping

Flexibility in grouping children also facilitates inclusion. At Jowonio we use a variety of group formats to balance individualization and independence, as well as to allow for effective peer modeling and socialization. Groups vary in the level of support needed, complexity of planning, and degree of true integration. In one-to-one situations with adults, students may be working on their relationship with that adult; a one-to-one time may also be used for assessment, teaching a new skill, or rehearsing classroom content to facilitate group participation. Pairs or small groups offer opportunities for social interaction that can be structured by the teacher. Children also benefit from learning to handle large-group settings after their preschool years, so opportunities to experience larger groups are important.

Curriculum Adaptation

Typical curricula may need to be adapted so that students with special needs can participate successfully. This adaptation may involve changing the nature of the instruction in the classroom to use several modalities and to have multiple objectives. In addition, we allow for the partial participation of students, varying our expectations to meet their current capabilities (Baumgart et al., 1982). Adaptations occur in materials and cues, sequences and rules, and levels of support (Janney & Snell, 2004; Udvari-Solner, 1996).

Materials and Cues. Children may need visual and object cues to comprehend language; they also benefit from manipulating objects related to the content being taught. We label everything with the written word or with symbols. Labeling the classroom is an important tool for the development of emergent literacy (reading) in all children (Anderson, Moffat, & Shapiro, 2006; Hill & Nichols, 2006; Neuman & Roskos, 1993, 1994; Schickedanz, 1986). This has been a particular emphasis at Jowonio, since we realized that a number of our less verbal children can demonstrate relatively strong literacy skills if provided support to do so (Kliewer & Biklen, 2001). Of course, the use of many cues to communicate the same content is good general early childhood practice. An inventory of favorite topics and materials gained through observations and child and parent interviews suggests materials that will make an activity motivating. For example, if a child is interested in cars, you can easily develop seriation, classification, and counting activities using cars.

Sequences and Rules. For some students, we may change the number of steps in an activity or the rules of a game to allow all children to succeed. In addition, the number of choices may be limited, waiting time decreased, or the amount of time required to stay at an activity reduced. For example, a child who has a hard time sitting in the large-group circle may initially be expected to stay in the meeting for 5 minutes (even under protest!) and then may be allowed to get up and do something quietly in another part of the room. The goal is that by later in the year becoming comfortable in the routine will encourage the child to stay longer.

Flexibility in Levels of Support

An important strategy for successful participation is providing support from teachers and peers that eventually can be faded so the child functions as independently as possible. The support may include physical assistance, gestures, individualized verbal cues, teacher proximity, peer partners, and peer modeling. Some students with physical disabilities may need physical assistance from adults but may become independent with technological devices, such as computers.

To plan integrated activities, goals are developed around motor, social-emotional, language, behavioral, and cognitive skill areas. The general goals may be based on theme, content area, and skill level used for typically developing students. Then child-specific goals drawn from the IEPs of children with special needs are incorporated into particular activities. In structuring each activity, the general sequence of events, range of materials, and group composition should be planned. Also, necessary adaptations are made for individual children. The role of peers must be an important consideration.

The following individualized lesson plan (see Figure 5–1) is an example of how a cooking activity is adapted to include two students with special needs. Brad has severely delayed motor and cognitive skills. James, who is considered autistic, has a good deal of language, but it tends to be rote and scripted.

TRANSITIONING TO THE NEXT ENVIRONMENT

An important aspect of any preschool teacher's work is the preparation of children and families for their transition to their next environment, kindergarten (Donovan, 1987). A comparative study of preschool special education classrooms and regular kindergarten classrooms showed that the expectations in the two settings were very different (Vincent et al., 1980). For example, kindergarten teachers require children to respond to directions given once to a large group, while preschool special education teachers often give their students repeated individual directions in a small group or one to one. Conscious of the need to bridge early development and education

Lesson Plan

DATE: 4/24 Theme: Spring Week TEACHER: Rae

ACTIVITY: Cooking: "Grasshopper Shakes" Jowonio Cookbook p.12

LONG-TERM GOAL: To participate in a verbally directed sharing activity

MATERIALS NEEDED: blender, measuring spoons + cup, ice cream, scoop, milk, ice cream, vanilla, eggs, food coloring

Short Term Objectives	Method/Procedure	Materials	Evaluation
Group: 1. Passing materials to a peer 2. Counting, measuring concepts: whole vs. half 3. Following sequence of recipe 4. Completing a task 5. Beginning reading	small group * each child does a step in the recipe * label materials with signs		
Individualization: Brad 1. Explore ingredients - some tastes 2. Tool use - spoon for scooping pitcher for pouring blender - cause + effect 3. Follow simple commands - "put in" "give to" 4. Attend to peer	* hand over hand as needed - then fade support * encourage tasting by placing food in hand + bring to his mouth	* seat near blender * DLM pictures of milk, ice cream, eggs, blender	
Individualization: James 1. Use vocabulary in context 2. Attend to + respond to peer requests 3. Request needed item from peer 4. Comment on activity 5. Begin reading	* review chart before activity * encourage peer to request * model comments		
Individualization: Terry, Alicia + Mary — group activity			
Individualization:			
Individualization:			

Recipe Chart
Grasshopper Shakes
Mix in bowl:
½ cup milk
2 scoops ice cream
½ teaspoon vanilla
1 teaspoon green food coloring
1 egg
Pour contents of bowl into the blender
Blend briefly!
Enjoy!

FIGURE 5–1 Lesson Plan

(see Chapter 8, this volume), part of the responsibility of preschool teachers is to be conscious of the demands of the next environment and to help children acquire the task and social skills to succeed there.

A second responsibility of an early education teacher is to work with families to have a positive impact on the kindergarten placement of our students. We seek to find or create inclusive education programs that will meet the needs of the individual children. The students with special needs who attend Jowonio come from several local school districts. Consequently, when Jowonio staff members support the transition to school-age special education services for our "graduates," they work with all of these districts to support the continuity of an inclusive education approach. This often requires skills as an advocate and consultant for which teachers are not usually trained. It is important to describe the specific needs of the child in all areas to find an existing inclusive education program or to support the development of a new one (e.g., placement of a child in a regular kindergarten with a full-time aide and therapy services). Building positive relationships with the school district staff may begin by observing their classrooms and inviting their teachers and administrators to observe our classroom and the student in question.

Parents and their wishes are critical in this transition process. They need to know their rights under the law, to understand the process by which their child will be evaluated and placed in a classroom, to describe program components important to them, and to develop a working relationship with school district staff to achieve the most appropriate integrated kindergarten placement for their child. As preschool teachers and administrators, we work closely with parents to give them the information and support they need to be an advocate for their child. In addition, this transition is an extremely stressful time for parents. Teachers can ease this transition by their active planning and reassurance.

Many parents are increasingly convinced of the importance of their child with special needs attending their neighborhood school rather than being bused across town. The local school may not have served a child with similar needs before. A home-school placement maximizes the development of long-term social relationships for a child, allows a child to be with siblings and neighbors, increases the communication between parents and school staff, and supports the generalization of skills to the child's natural environment (see Brown et al., 1989).

Once a child has been formally assigned a kindergarten placement, the preschool teacher communicates in person and through paperwork about the child. We develop a portfolio for the new teacher that includes samples of the child's work, evaluation reports, and descriptions of favorite activities and effective approaches in behavior management and teaching. All of our efforts are geared toward a positive transition to regular kindergarten or first grade with sufficient supports to guarantee success.

IMPLICATIONS FOR TEACHER TRAINING

Teacher preparation is an integral part of the program at Jowonio. Based on the wide variety of activities expected of teachers, new teachers need practical experience in quality inclusive settings. The effective teacher is flexible and reflective in the planning, programming, and management of the classroom. While teachers clearly must relate well with children, they also must be able to work and interact with a variety of adults. New teachers are sometimes overwhelmed by dealing with the various adults involved in an inclusive classroom. Teachers must be able to work well with other teachers, therapists, parents, administrators, aides, and student teachers, all of whom may have different perspectives on the classroom, different values, and different skills. Because interactions with other adults can be very difficult, teacher training must include a focus on working cooperatively with other adults. Developing a problem-solving approach is essential. The best way to achieve this goal is for teacher training programs to require participation in a variety of cooperative, real-life, problem-solving experiences with adult peers.

ADDITIONAL INCLUSION EFFORTS

A variety of inclusive education models for young children are described by Berres and Knoblock (1987), Biklen (1985), Cavallaro and Haney (1999), and Grisham-Brown et al. (2005). Head Start programs have since their inception often considered it part of their mandate to include students with disabilities, although their ability to do so effectively was sometimes limited by funding constraints (Schwartz & Brand, 2001). Jowonio is one of the earliest models of its kind, and as such represents a mature program that may be of particular interest to the field. However, since 1975 when Jowonio first began its systematic approach to inclusive early childhood education, interest in such models has been increasing, and many other similar programs have evolved. As a consequence, once students with disabilities leave Jowonio, they will attend a great variety of program models, but at present virtually none of these are entirely self-contained special education programs. This is because over its history Jowonio has spawned so many inclusive education options in nearby communities. Parents of former Jowonio students are strong inclusion advocates, and several area programs are staffed in part by teachers who used to work at Jowonio. This process has been going on for years. Knoblock and Lehr (1985) wrote:

> Jowonio's "graduates" often continue in integrated settings because parents are convinced that this is an appropriate placement for their children. . . . Some children are integrated into regular classrooms with the assistance of an aide or by utilizing a resource room teacher. . . . As a result of [pilot programs developed in collaboration with Jowonio staff] Syracuse has designed kindergarten-through-grade-5 classes where severely handicapped [sic] children are integrated on a full-time basis. (pp. 300–301)

In the more than 20 years since Knoblock and Lehr described the way that Jowonio's high-quality preschool inclusive education model could stimulate similar efforts for school-age children with disabilities, the range of available programs has continued to expand. Currently, so-called "full inclusion" options exist for Syracuse students through age 21. (Some Syracuse city students aged 18 to 21 with significant disabilities are integrated into college classes and campus life at Syracuse University.) At the elementary-school level, the options vary in different neighboring districts. Some involve dividing the student's time between a special education classroom and a general education classroom. Many of the programs rely heavily on paraeducator support for the students with disabilities. The use of consultant special education teacher services to a regular education classroom has become very common. Among this variety of program designs, it is gratifying that many models follow Jowonio's lead and provide programs in which inclusive education practice infuses every aspect of the classroom.

Currently, an enormous variety of program designs in inclusive education exists. For example, in addition to the center-based program described in this chapter, Jowonio has also developed working relationships with different childcare and nursery programs in its community (e.g., Syracuse University Early Childhood Education programs), Jowonio provides a team of special education and resource staff to work with a small group of children with special needs. No matter what the design, inclusive education requires a great deal of creativity, energy, and dedication. Willing teachers and administrators and a commitment to teaming are central ingredients in the success of these programs. Different programs also stand to benefit greatly by learning from each other.

A majority of the research in this area has focused on the impact of inclusive early childhood education on both nondisabled children and children with special needs, as well as on parent and teacher attitudes (e.g., Blacker & Turnbull, 1982; Ostrosky, Laumann, & Hsieh, 2006), social interaction patterns (Strain, 1984, 1985), developmental and behavioral outcomes (Guralnick, 1980; Jenkins et al., 1989), and methods of intervention (Strain & Odom, 1986).

Odom and McEvoy (1988), in their review of the research on integration, conclude that there is "good evidence that children with handicaps can receive an appropriate education in mainstreamed . . . preschool programs" (p. 262) but that the quality of instruction, not simply the mainstreaming, is an important factor in the success of these programs. Social interactions between disabled and nondisabled children that are available in inclusive settings do not necessarily occur spontaneously but rather require direct, planned interventions. Although the effect of integration alone is hard to separate from other variables, the empirical literature seems clear in demonstrating that "normally developing children are not adversely affected by integrated classes, and in fact benefit developmentally from the curriculum and instructional strategies" (p. 259). Odom and Bailey (2001) had similar conclusions that inclusive preschool programs had generally favorable outcomes for students. But the outcomes depend on a variety of factors that go into the making of excellent early childhood programs more generally, including systematic planning and programming, support for adult collaboration, and type of preservice teacher training and level of educational attainment (Sandall, Hemmeter, Smith, & McLean, 2005).

Research findings suggest that peer interactions for children with disabilities occur more often in inclusive classrooms than in segregated classrooms (Guralnick et al., 1996; Odom & Bailey, 2001), and less unoccupied play and less inappropriate or self-abusive behavior occur in inclusive classrooms (Erwin, 1993). A natural proportion of children with and without disabilities has a positive effect on peer interactions (Hauser-Cram, Bronson, & Upshur, 1993); parents and teachers report that a majority of children in inclusive classrooms have at least one friend (Buysse, 1993). Nondisabled students in inclusive classrooms gave higher social acceptance scores in response to scenarios about children with disabilities than did their counterparts in noninclusive early childhood programs (Diamond & Hestenes, 1996); and mixed-age inclusive programs facilitated social conversations between children and led to more play mastery than same-age groupings (Blasco, Bailey, & Burchinal, 1993; Roberts, Burchinal, & Bailey, 1994).

Acknowledging the difficulties associated with defining and assessing belief systems, the data on teacher beliefs about inclusion are fairly consistent. Positive teacher attitudes toward inclusion were related to their competency in working with young children with disabilities (Gemmell-Crosby & Hanzlik, 1994). However, insufficient time for planning and collaboration (Marchant, 1995), lack of knowledge about teaching children with disabilities (Dinnebeil, McInerney, Roth, & Ramaswamy, 2001), the context within which inclusion takes place (Stoiber, Gettinger, & Goetz, 1998), and the perceived ability levels of children served (Eiserman, Shisler, & Healey, 1995) all affected community-level teachers' attitudes toward working with children in inclusive settings.

At base, committing to an inclusive education approach is a values-based decision. Certainly it is affirming when research validates particular inclusive practices. However, even when research is more ambiguous, the position that all students deserve full membership in a classroom community is an ethical and defensible perspective. What makes Jowonio (or any inclusive education program) a successful inclusive education program is its staff and families' commitment to these values. As Kluth and her fellow authors conclude (2007), inclusion cannot be characterized as a place: "Rather, it is an attitude or set of practices and policies that translate into an open-arms acceptance of their children as participants in the life of the classroom and school" (p. 54).

CONCLUSION

Accepted developmentally appropriate practice in early childhood (see Bredekamp & Copple, 1997) and accepted practice in special education are consistent. Both emphasize the unique pattern of development of each child. The chosen curriculum is responsive to the child's current level of skill and interests. Effective curriculum calls on an integration of all areas of development, including physical, social-emotional, language, and cognitive skills. Within a group of children, differences in ability and style are expected and valued. Each member of the community is enhanced by the diversity of the whole.

An inclusive preschool program that serves all children makes both philosophical and practical sense. In this chapter we have described one "full inclusion" early childhood setting, in which students with and without disabilities are all considered full members of their classroom communities. The Jowonio program is guided by beliefs that all children are valued; all children have a right to and can benefit from high-quality, age-appropriate early education; learning occurs through models and relationships; and problem-solving partnerships between teachers and parents and within the teaching team are central to a good program for children. The core activity in an inclusive program is the adaptation of the typical curriculum to ensure successful participation for all students. The goal is to create an inclusive community in which all children and adults can learn and feel valued.

REFERENCES

Anderson, J., Moffat, L., & Shapiro, J. (2006). Reconceptualizing language education in early childhood: Socio-cultural perspectives. In B. Spodek & O. Saracho (Eds.), *Handbook of research on the education of young children* (pp. 131–151). Mahwah, NJ: Erlbaum.

Bailey, D. (1996). An overview of interdisciplinary training. In D. Bricker & A. Widerstrom (Eds.), *Preparing personnel to work with infants and young children and their families: A team approach* (pp. 3–22). Baltimore, MD: Paul Brookes.

Bailey, D., McWilliam, R., Buysse, V., & Wesley, P. (1998). Inclusion in the context of competing values in early childhood education. *Early Childhood Research Quarterly, 13,* 27–47.

Barnes, E., Berrigan, C., & Biklen, D. (1978). *What's the difference: Teaching positive attitudes toward people with disabilities.* Syracuse, NY: Human Policy.

Berres, M., & Knoblock, P. (1987). *Program models for mainstreaming.* Rockville, MD: Aspen.

Biklen, D. (1985). *Achieving the complete school: Strategies for effective mainstreaming.* New York: Teachers College Press.

Biklen, D. (1992). *Schooling without labels.* Philadelphia: Temple University Press.

Blacker, J., & Turnbull, A. P. (1982). Teacher and parent perspectives on selected social aspects of preschool mainstreaming. *Exceptional Child, 29,* 191–199.

Blasco, P., Bailey, D., & Burchinal, M. (1993). Dimensions of mastery in same-age and mixed-age integrated classrooms. *Early Childhood Research Quarterly, 8,* 193–206.

Bredekamp, S., & Copple, C. (1997). *Developmentally appropriate practice in early childhood programs* (Rev. ed.). Washington, DC: National Association for the Education of Young Children.

Brown, R. (1973). *A first language: The early stages.* Cambridge, MA: Harvard University Press.

Buysse, V. (1993). Friendships of preschoolers with disabilities in community-based childcare setting. *Journal of Early Intervention, 17,* 380–395.

Carr, E. G., & Durand, V. M. (1985). Reducing behavior problems through functional communication training. *Journal of Applied Behavior Analysis, 18,* 111–126.

Cavallaro, C. C., & Haney, M. (1999). *Preschool inclusion.* Baltimore, MD: Paul Brookes.

Collins, W. A., Maccoby, G. E., Steinberg, L., Hetherington, E. M., & Bornstein, M. H. (2000). Contemporary research on parenting: Nature versus nurture. *American Psychologist, 55,* 218–232.

Denham, S. (2006). The emotional basis of learning and development in early childhood education. In B. Spodek & O. Saracho (Eds.), *Handbook of research on the education of young children* (pp. 85–103). Mahwah, NJ: Erlbaum.

Diamond, K., & Hestenes, L. (1996). Preschool children's conceptions of disabilities: The salience of disability in children's ideas about others. *Topics in Early Childhood Special Education, 16,* 458–475.

Dinnebeil, L. A., McInerney, W. F., Roth, J. & Ramaswamy, V. (2001) Itinerant early childhood special education services: Service delivery in one state. *Journal of Early Intervention, 24,* 35–44.

Donnellan, A. M., LaVigna, G. W., Negri-Shoultz, N., & Fassbender, L. L. (1988). *Progress without punishment: Effective approaches for learners with severe behavior problems.* New York: Teachers College Press.

Donnellan, A. M., Mirenda, P. L., Mesaros, R. A., & Fassbender, L. L. (1984). Analyzing the communicative functions of aberrant behavior. *Journal of the Association for Persons with Severe Handicaps, 9,* 201–212.

Donovan, E. (1987). *Preschool to public school: A teacher's guide to successful transition for children with special needs.* Syracuse, NY: Jowonio School.

Dunlap, G., Johnson, L. F., & Robbins, F. R. (1990). Preventing serious behavior problems through skill development and early intervention. In A. C. Repp & N. N. Singh (Eds.), *Perspectives on the use of nonaversive and aversive interventions for persons with developmental disabilities* (pp. 273–286). Sycamore, IL: Sycamore.

Dunlap, G., Kern-Dunlap, L., Clarke, S., & Robbins, F. R. (1991). Functional assessment, curricular revision, and severe behavior problems. *Journal of Applied Behavior Analysis, 24,* 387–397.

Dunst, C., Trivette, C., & Deal, A. (1988). *Enabling and empowering families.* Cambridge, MA: Brookline.

Eiserman, W. D., Shisler, L., & Healey, S. (1995) A community assessment of preschool providers' attitudes toward inclusion. *Journal of Early Intervention, 19,* 149–167.

Erwin, E. J. (1993). Social participation of children with visual impairment in specialized and integrated environments. *Journal of Visual Impairments and Blindness, 87,* 138–142.

Evans, I. M., & Meyer, L. H. (1985). *An educative approach to behavior problems.* Baltimore, MD: Paul Brookes.

Froschl, M., Colon, L., Rubin, E., & Sprung, B. (1984). *Including all of us: An early childhood curriculum about disabilities.* New York: Educational Equity Concepts.

Gallagher, J. J., Trohanis, P. L., & Clifford, R. M. (Eds.). (1989). *Policy implementation and PL 99-457.* Baltimore, MD: Paul Brookes.

Gardner, H., & Hatch, T. (1989). Multiple intelligences go to school. *Educational Researcher, 18,* 4–10.

Gemmell-Crosby, S., & Hanzlik, J. R. (1994). Preschool teachers' perceptions of including children with disabilities. *Education and Training in Mental Retardation and Developmental Disabilities, 29,* 279–290.

Gershoff, E. T. (2002). Corporal punishment by parents and associated child behaviors and experiences: A meta-analytic and theoretical review. *Psychological Bulletin, 128,* 539–579.

Goldstein, A., & McGinnis, E. (1990). *Skillstreaming the preschool child.* Champaign, IL: Research Press.

Goodman, J. F. (1992). *When slow is fast enough.* New York: Guilford Press.

Gray, C. (1996). Teaching children with autism to "read" social situations. In K. A. Quill (Ed.),

Teaching children with autism: Strategies to enhance communication and socialization (pp. 219–242). New York: Delmar.

Greenspan, S., & Wieder, S. (1998). *The child with special needs: Encouraging intellectual and emotional growth.* Cambridge, MA: Perseus Publishing.

Grisham-Brown, J., Hemmeter, M. L., & Pretti-Frontczak, K. (2005). *Blended Practices.* Baltimore: Paul Brookes.

Guralnick, M. (1980). The social behavior of preschool children at different developmental levels: Effects of group composition. *Journal of Experimental Child Psychology, 31,* 115–130.

Guralnick, M., Connor, R. T., Hammond, M., Gottman, J., & Kinnish, K. (1996). Immediate effects of mainstreamed settings on the social interactions and integration of preschool children. *American Journal of Mental Retardation, 100,* 359–377.

Hauser-Cram, P., Bronson, M. B., & Upshur, C. C. (1993). The effects of the classroom environment on the social and mastery behavior of preschool children with disabilities. *Early Childhood Research Quarterly, 8,* 479–498.

Hill, S. E., & Nichols, S. (2006). Emergent literacy: Symbols at work. In B. Spodek & O. Saracho (Eds.), *Handbook of research on the education of young children* (pp. 153–165). Mahwah, NJ: Erlbaum.

Hunt, J. M. (1961). *Intelligence and experience.* New York: Roland.

Janney, R., & Snell, M. (2004). *Modifying Schoolwork* (2nd edition). Baltimore, MD: Paul Brookes.

Jenkins, J. R., Odom, S. L., & Speltz, M. L. (1989). Effects of social integration on preschool children with handicaps. *Exceptional Children, 55,* 420–428.

Johnson, D., Johnson, R., & Holubec, E. J. (1990). *Circles of learning.* Edina, MN: Interaction.

Johnson, D. W., & Johnson, R. T. (1999). Making cooperative learning work. *Theory into Practice, 38,* 67—73.

Johnson, J., Christie, J., & Wardle, F. (2005). *Play, development and early education.* Boston: Allyn & Bacon.

Johnston, L., Beard, L., & Carpenter, L. B. (2006). *Assistive technology: Access for all students.* Upper Saddle River, NJ: Pearson/Prentice Hall.

Kaiser, B., & Rasminsky, J. S. (2006). *Challenging behavior in young children: Understanding, preventing, and responding effectively.* Boston: Allyn & Bacon.

Kliewer, C., & Biklen, D. (2001). "School's not really a place for reading": A research synthesis of the literate lives of students with severe disabilities. *The Association for Persons with Severe Handicaps, 26,* 1–12.

Kluth, P. (2003). "You're going to love this kid!": Teaching students with autism in the inclusive classroom. Baltimore, MD: Paul Brookes.

Kluth, P., Biklen, D., English-Sand, P., & Smukler, D. (2007). Going away to school: Stories of families who move to seek inclusive educational experiences for their children with disabilities. *Journal of Disability Policy Studies, 18,* 43–56.

Knoblock, P. (Ed.). (1982). *Teaching and mainstreaming autistic children.* Denver, CO: Love.

Knoblock, P., & Lehr, R. (1985). A model for mainstreaming autistic children: The Jowonio School. In E. Schopler & G. Mesibov (Eds.), *Social behavior in autism* (pp. 285–303). New York: Plenum.

Ladd, G., Herald, S. L., & Andrews, R. K. (2006). Young children's peer relations and social competence. In B. Spodek & O. Saracho (Eds.), *Handbook of research on the education of young children* (pp. 23–54). Mahwah, NJ: Erlbaum.

LaVigna, G. W., & Donnellan, A. M. (1986). *Alternatives to punishment: Solving behavior problems with non-aversive strategies.* New York: Irvington.

Lieber, J., Capell, K., Sandall, S., Wolfberg, P., Horn, E., & Beckman, P. (1998). Inclusive preschool programs: Teachers' beliefs and practices. *Early Childhood Research Quarterly, 13,* 87–105.

Lynch, S. K., Turkheimer, E., D'Onofrio, B. M., Mandle, J., Emery, R. E., Slutske, W. S., et al. (2006). A genetically informed study of the association between harsh punishment and offspring behavioral problems. *Journal of Family Psychology, 20,* 190–198.

Marchant, C. (1995). Teachers' views of integrated preschools. *Journal of Early Intervention, 19,* 61–67.

McGee, J. J., Menolascino, F. J., Hobbs, D. C., & Menousek, P. E. (1987). *Gentle teaching.* New York: Human Science.

McLoyd, V. C., Kaplan, R., Hardaway, C. R., & Wood, D. (2007). Does endorsement of physical discipline matter? Assessing moderating influences on the maternal and child psychological correlates of physical discipline in African American Families. *Journal of Family Psychology, 21,* 165–175.

Meyer, L. H., & Evans, I. M. (1989). *Nonaversive intervention for behavior problems: A manual for home and community.* Baltimore, MD: Paul Brookes.

Musselwhite, C. R. (1986). *Adaptive play for special needs children.* San Diego, CA: College Hill.

Neuman, S., & Roskos, K. (1993). Access to print for children of poverty: Differential effects of adult mediation and literacy-enriched play settings on environmental and functional print tasks. *American Educational Research Journal, 30,* 95–122.

Neuman, S., & Roskos, K. (1994). Bridging home and school with a culturally responsive approach. *Childhood Education, 70*(4), 210–214.

Nisbet, J. (2004). Commentary: "Caught in the continuum." *Research & Practice for Persons with Severe Disabilities, 29,* 231–236.

Odom, S., & Diamond, K. (1998). Inclusion of young children with special needs in early childhood education: The research base. *Early Childhood Research Quarterly, 13,* 3–25.

Odom, S. L., & Bailey, D. (2001). Inclusive preschool programs. In M. J. Guralnick (Ed.), *Early childhood inclusion: Focus on change.* Baltimore, MD: Paul Brookes.

Odom, S. L., & McEvoy, M. A. (1988). Integration of young children with handicaps and normally developing children. In S. L. Odom & M. B. Karnes (Eds.), *Early intervention for infants and children with handicaps* (pp. 241–267). Baltimore, MD: Paul Brookes.

O'Neill, R. E., Horner, R. H., Albin, R. W., Storey, K., & Sprague, J. R. (1990). *Functional analysis of problem behavior.* Sycamore, IL: Sycamore.

Ostrosky, M. M., Laumann, B. M., & Hsieh, W. Y. (2006). Early childhood teachers' beliefs and attitudes about inclusion: What does the research tell us? In B. Spodek & O. Saracho (Eds.), *Handbook of research on the education of young children* (pp. 411–422). Mahwah, NJ: Erlbaum.

Piaget, J. (1963). *The origins of intelligence in children.* New York: Norton.

Ramsey, P. (2006). Early childhood multicultural education. In B. Spodek & O. Saracho (Eds.), *Handbook of research on the education of young children* (pp. 279–301). Mahwah, NJ: Erlbaum.

Ray, A., Bowman, B., & Robbins, J. (2006). Preparing early childhood teachers to successfully educate all children: The contribution of four-year undergraduate teacher preparation programs. Report to the Foundation for Child Development, New York.

Roberts, J., Burchinal, M., & Bailey, D. (1994). Communication among preschoolers with and without disabilities in same-age and mixed-age classrooms. *American Journal of Mental Retardation, 99,* 231–249.

Rose, D. H., & Meyer, A. (2002). Teaching every student in the digital age: Universal design for learning. Alexandria, VA: Association for Supervision and Curriculum Development.

Sandall, S. R., Hemmeter, M. L., McLean, M. E., & Smith, B. J. (2005). *DEC recommended practices: A comprehensive guide for practical application in early intervention/early childhood special education.* Longmont, CO: Sophris West.

Sapon-Shevin, M. (1999). *Because we can change the world: A practical guide to building cooperative, inclusive classroom communities.* Needham Heights, MA: Allyn & Bacon.

Sapon-Shevin, M. (2000/2001). Schools fit for all. *Educational Leadership, 58,* 34–39.

Sapon-Shevin, M. (2007). *Widening the circle: The power of inclusive classrooms.* Boston: Beacon Press.

Sarason, S. B., & Doris, J. (1959). *Educational handicap, public policy and social history.* New York: Free Press.

Schickedanz, J. (1986). *More than the ABC's: The early stages of reading and writing.* Washington, DC: National Association for the Education of Young Children.

Schwartz, B., & Brand, M. E. (2001). Head Start and the inclusion of children with disabilities. In M. Guralnick (Ed.), *Early childhood inclusion: Focus on change.* Baltimore, MD: Paul Brookes.

Stainback, S., & Stainback, W. (1992). *Curriculum considerations in inclusive classrooms.* Baltimore, MD: Paul Brookes.

Stainback, W., & Stainback, S. (1990). *Support networks for inclusive schooling.* Baltimore, MD: Paul Brookes.

Stoiber, K. C., Gettinger, M., & Goetz, D. (1998). Exploring factors influencing parents' and early childhood practitioners' beliefs about inclusion. *Early Childhood Research Quarterly, 13,* 107–124.

Strain, P. S. (1984). Social behavior patterns of nonhandicapped and nonhandicapped-developmentally disabled friend pairs in mainstreamed preschoolers. *Analysis and Intervention in Development Disabilities, 4,* 15–58.

Strain, P. S. (1985). Social and nonsocial determinants of acceptability in handicapped preschool children. *Topics in Early Special Education, 4,* 47–58.

Strain, P. S., & Odom, S. L. (1986). Peer social initiations: Effective intervention for social skills development of exceptional children. *Exceptional Children, 43,* 526–530.

Taylor, S. J. (1998). Caught in the continuum: A critical analysis of the principle of the least restrictive environment. *Journal of the Association for Persons with Severe Disabilities, 13,* 41–53.

Thousand, J., & Villa, R. (1990). Sharing expertise and responsibilities through teaching teams. In W. Stainback & S. Stainback (Eds.), *Support networks in inclusive schooling* (pp. 201–218). Baltimore, MD: Paul Brookes.

Touchette, P. E., MacDonald, R. F., & Langer, S. N. (1985). A scatter plot for identifying stimulus control of problem behavior. *Journal of Applied Behavior Analysis, 18,* 343–351.

Turnbull, H. R., & Turnbull, A. P. (1982). Public policy and handicapped citizens. In N. G. Haring (Ed.), *Exceptional children and youth* (3rd ed.) (pp. 21–44). Upper Saddle River, NJ: Merrill/Prentice Hall.

Udvari-Solner, A. (1996). Examining teacher thinking: Constructing a process to design curricular adaptations. *Remedial and Special Education, 17,* 245–254.

Vincent, L., Salisbury, C., Walter, G., Brown, P., Gruenewald, L., & Powers, M. (1980). Program evaluation and curriculum development in early childhood special education: Criteria for the next environment. In W. Saylor, B. Wilcox, & L. Brown (Eds.), *Instructional design for the severely handicapped* (pp. 130–182). Baltimore, MD: Paul Brookes.

Westby, C. E. (1980). Assessment of cognitive and language abilities through play. *Language, Speech, and Hearing Services in Schools, 11,* 154–168.

Chapter 6

A Framework for Culturally Relevant, Multicultural, and Antibias Education in the Twenty-First Century

Louise Derman-Sparks ⁓ *Pacific Oaks College*
Patricia G. Ramsey ⁓ *Mount Holyoke College*

We are a nation of many peoples: many races, cultures, religions, classes, lifestyles, languages, and histories. We are also a nation where access to achieving the "inalienable right" to "life, liberty and the pursuit of happiness," for which the American Revolution was fought, has not been equal for all. From their first arrival and consequent takeover of the land, European settlers encountered people whose race, cultures, religions, and history were vastly different from their own. As they consolidated their power, the Europeans established institutions and laws that embodied a fundamental contradiction between their goals to establish a democratic, free republic for themselves and their practices that enslaved or subjugated other groups. This duality has shaped our nation's history as illustrated in the current legal and extra-legal efforts to exclude recent immigrants from Asia and Latin America and to roll back affirmative action as well as by the increasing economic disparities that often follow racial lines.

At the end of the first decade of the twenty-first century, these contradictions in both values and practices continue to pose an enormous challenge to all institutions, especially schools. First, the population of our country is becoming increasingly diverse. According to Ray, Bowman, and Robbins (2006), in 1998 28% of the population was people of color; by 2050 it will be 47%. These trends are particularly evident for children ages 3 to 9. Currently, 25% of children have parents born outside the United States, and one third are children of color. Second, the contradictions inherent in our society continue to manifest themselves in the pervasive and intransigent inequities in educational opportunities, resources, and outcomes that separate affluent and poor children. Because social class often overlaps with race and immigrant status, the increase in diversity potentially means that economic disparities will adversely affect larger numbers of children.

In the face of all these pressures, how do educators honor their mandate to foster every child's full potential and to prepare all children to function effectively as members of a democratic society, when many of these children are victims of racism and other forms of discrimination and/or live in poverty? How do educators respond to the diversity of the population in this country while developing a common foundation on which to build a unified nation?

Responses to these questions have evolved at different points in American educational history,

Anne Vega/Merrill

Educating children about diverse cultures will prepare them for life in the twenty-first century.

at the core of which are divergent philosophical and political positions, including differing demarcations of power between white European Americans and other racial/ethnic groups. Before discussing these responses, we first consider how young children develop their identities and their attitudes about their own groups and about those who are racially, culturally, and otherwise different from themselves. This research provides an essential framework in which to consider how different approaches to diversity might apply to early childhood education.

HOW YOUNG CHILDREN LEARN ABOUT DIVERSITY

Young children do not arrive in early childhood programs as blank slates on the subject of diversity. Rather, they bring a personalized data bank that includes observations of people's characteristics, experiences with adult responses to their questions that may reflect varying degrees of discomfort with these issues, exposure to common biases about specific groups, and self-constructed theories about the causes and implications of diversity (Derman-Sparks, 1992). Children are growing up in a world of contradictions, as described in the opening paragraph of this chapter. We teach our children about equality, freedom, and fairness, but every day they are witnesses to inequities and discrimination. Often their ideas about diversity reflect these inconsistencies and confusions.

Children absorb stereotypes and assumptions about a wide range of human dimensions, including race, social class, culture, gender, sexual orientation, and abilities/disabilities. (For reviews of research on how they develop their ideas and feelings about each of these categories, please see Derman-Sparks and Ramsey, 2006; Ramsey, 2004; Ramsey, 2006; Ramsey and Williams, 2003.) Preschoolers are aware of and curious about differences and similarities among people. However, because of their cognitive limitations, young children often misunderstand specific phenomena (Pfeifer, Brown, & Juvonen, 2007). They ask questions, organize the information, and construct theories about diversity, congruent with their general cognitive stages of development, as well as with their life experiences. In this process, they depend on concrete information and assimilate it into familiar schemas, often ignoring or misinterpreting relevant information. For example, they sometimes assume that individuals have different skin color because they have been exposed to the sun or were painted, ignoring the fact that biological family members have similar skin tones. Likewise, children's explanations for gender differences often focus on observable, but irrelevant, attributes, such as hair length or clothing. When talking about poor and rich people, preschoolers often assume that wealth depends on getting money from the bank or change back from store clerks. Disabilities may be erroneously associated with age (e.g., "He's just a baby and hasn't learned to walk yet.").

Against this developmental backdrop, some individuals may be more likely than others to develop and maintain stereotypes. For example, young children, who have rigid classification systems about the world in general, more frequently form and maintain stereotyped images of other groups than their more flexible peers (Bigler, Jones, & Lobliner, 1997; Bigler & Liben, 1993).

As they try to make sense of their world, young children may be wary of unfamiliar languages, appearances, or behaviors and draw conclusions that appear to be prejudiced and polarized. Children growing up in homogeneous settings are particularly at risk for developing negative attitudes about unfamiliar groups because they have no direct experience to challenge misinformation and fears (McGlothlin & Killen, 2005, 2006). Conversely, one study revealed that Anglo British children growing up in heterogeneous communities showed less own-group bias than their peers in predominantly white areas (Rutland, Cameron, Bennett, & Ferrell, 2005). Thus, creating programs that include children from a range of racial, cultural, and socioeconomic backgrounds is probably the most effective strategy for raising children with less bias. However, because of residential segregation, most schools and communities are highly racially and economically segregated.

When children encounter people who are different from them in some way, they often react negatively. They might reject a classmate with emotional disabilities because "He is always bad!" Pictures of same-sex couples or people wearing unfamiliar clothing may evoke laughter and ridicule. Boys and girls routinely find ways of demeaning and excluding each other. These sentiments, while disturbing, should not be equated with adult prejudice. Rather they reflect youthful efforts to make sense of human diversity and to develop identities, often in biased contexts. Children are absorbing and repeating assumptions, but, in many cases, they do not understand them. Moreover, when questioned, most are open to rethinking their ideas, unlike adults who often resist such efforts. However, these reactions need to be taken seriously because they can develop into full-blown prejudices if left unchallenged. As we describe later in this chapter, teachers can use these revelations as opportunities to probe children about their ideas and feelings and to develop activities to address them. Group norms that promote either exclusion or acceptance also influence children's attitudes toward unfamiliar groups (Nesdale, Griffith, Durkin, and Maass, 2005). Empathic children, in particular, develop accepting attitudes when they are in an environment that emphasizes positive out-group attitudes. Thus, as part of challenging children's negative comments, teachers can work with the children and their families to create an environment where acceptance and inclusion are the norms.

As they learn about differences and similarites among people, some children (especially those who are not part of the mainstream) experience discontinuity between their family and school lives, which may make them feel uncomfortable. Children also absorb and frequently enact messages about which groups have more power than others. As a result, some children become more reticent or passive in school while others may be overly assertive. In the next paragraphs we briefly describe how children's views about race, social class, gender, sexual orientation, culture, and abilities reflect societal attitudes and experiences of power differentials.

When considering children's awareness of race, many adults like to think that young children are "color blind" and that they do not notice racial differences. However, many studies have shown that children notice racial cues during infancy and that, by the age of 3 or 4, most children have a rudimentary concept of race (Katz, 1982; Katz & Kofkin, 1997; Van Ausdale & Feagin, 2001). After observing preschoolers' conversations and play in a racially diverse preschool for a year, Van Ausdale and Feagin concluded that:

> Young children quickly learn the racial-ethnic identities and role performances of the larger society . . . as white children grow up they learn, develop, and perform the meanings associated with the white identity-role. Black children and other children of color often must cope with the subordinating expectations imposed on them [by white children], expectations that they may accept or resist. (p. 182)

Van Ausdale and Feagin cite a number of incidents to support their conclusion that white preschool children do incorporate a sense of white superiority in their early identities. For example, one 4-year-old white child who noticed that she was darker than her two white companions asked worriedly, "Does that mean that I'm not white anymore?" and repeatedly asked for reassurance that she was still white, apparently concerned about the consequences of being seen as not white (Van Ausdale & Feagin, 2001, p. 48).

Social class often overlaps with race and and also influences children's perceptions of themselves, their peers, and the larger environment. In a recent study of second-graders in a racially and economically mixed urban classroom (Mednick & Ramsey, 2007), the children frequently divided themselves by gender, race, and social class and created a hierarchy that followed these lines. The white middle-class girls, in particular, exerted a great deal of social and academic authority over the children of color (who were mostly from low-income families), as seen in the following observation:

> *The children are finishing breakfast and the teacher has just announced to the entire class that they had 10 minutes to finish eating. Liza (a middle-SES, white female) turns to Ricki (a low-SES, African American male) who is sitting next to her, and, in a harsh tone she says, "All breakfasts must be thrown away before specials," as she rolls her eyes. The boy replies in a quiet voice, "I'm almost done." The girl then says in a stern tone, "You better be . . . Or I am getting the principal." The boy does not respond and looks around the room, then gets up and throws his cereal container away, leaving cereal in the bowl.*

The teachers often unconsciously supported these power differentials. They frequently bestowed authority on the white middle-class children (e.g., handing out and collecting papers), who then used these positions to reprimand or order around their classmates. In some cases, teachers punished children of color on the sole basis of a white girl's report.

> *Megan (a white, middle-SES, female) walks up to the teacher and says that Rosa (a low-SES, African American female) is talking, and the teacher immediately reprimands Rosa.*

Social-class differences also contributed to the divisions in the classroom because many interests and leisure and family activities were related to levels of affluence.

> *In a high-pitched voice, Megan (a middle-SES, white female) says to Amy (a middle-SES, white female), "Are you going skiing this weekend?" In a low voice Amy responds, "No." Cody (a low-SES, Latino male) then walks over and says in a slow voice with a small smile on his face, "I'm going ice-skating this weekend." Amy and Megan continued talking by themselves about skiing as they giggle. They do not respond to Cody.*

In this conversation Amy and Megan shared the common experience of skiing (an expensive sport that requires equipment and traveling). Cody seemed to be trying to enter the conversation by talking about ice-skating, which he probably associated with skiing since both are winter sports. However, Amy and Megan ignored him and kept talking about skiing.

Social-class differences and tensions are exacerbated by children's responses to our consumerist culture. Children often judge each other—and themselves—by the desirability and quantity of their possessions and by other measures of affluence, such as exotic vacations. Teachers bemoan how frequently their children enter the classroom talking exuberantly about their new shoes, videogames, or upcoming trip to Disney World. These announcements may then set off competitive discussions about who has what clothing item or game, which sometimes exclude children from less affluent families. In their media-induced desires for new toys, clothes, lessons, or experiences, children learn to pressure their families to purchase these items or, in some cases, get drawn into illegal activities in order to acquire highly desirable goods.

This frenzy to consume leads children to identify themselves as consumers and owners, rather than as creators or contributors, and poses a challenge for teaching them to care about the welfare of others. In the United States today, people who have adequate food, clothing, and shelter often "feel poor" because their lifestyles do not match the extravagant ones portrayed in media shows and advertising. Children are readily absorbing those messages and believe that being rich is better than being poor (Leahy, 1983) and that rich people are happier and more likeable than poor people (Naimark, 1983; Ramsey, 1991). As they get older, children also begin to blame poor people for their poverty by describing them as "lazy," whereas they view wealthy individuals as hardworking and deserving of their good fortune (Leahy, 1990).

In the classroom just described, it is interesting that the white middle-class girls had the most "authority," in contrast to the usual phenomenon of boys dominating girls. This pattern may have reflected the composition of the classroom, which included a larger cluster of white middle-class girls than boys. Most studies show that preschool girls more often adapt to boys' play preferences and concede to their wishes when engaged in mixed-gender interactions (Fabes, Martin, & Hanish, 2003).

A recent set of observations of a classroom of 3-and 4-year-olds showed how one girl shifted from drawing pictures of rainbows and flowers with other girls at the marker tables to whirling around as a "Power Ranger" when playing with a group of boys. The boys, in contrast, rarely approached the marker table and, if prodded to go there by a teacher, ended up noisily drawing pictures of weapons and fights. Boys' boisterous play often disrupted the conversation among the girls, who did not resist but often just left the table.

The gender split begins during the ages of 3 and 4 (Ramsey, 1995) and increases throughout the early elementary school years. Children find numerous ways to demarcate the gender divide. Boys refuse to use "girl" colors such as pink and purple; girls staunchly deny boys access to the "baby house." As with social class divisions, these antagonisms are also exacerbated by consumerism. Marketing strategies for young children often appeal to children with exaggerated sex stereotypes, such as highly feminized images and toys for girls (e.g., pink and purple stuffed animals and Barbie dolls) and hypermasculine ones for boys (e.g., muscular GI Joes, guns, and other war toys). As children go through preschool and enter elementary school, those with cross-gender friends or activity preferences (e.g., girls who like science and, particularly, boys who enjoy dressing up and playing with dolls) are increasingly rejected and ridiculed by both children and adults (MacNaughton, 2000; Sadker & Sadker, 1995). As children spend more time in gender-typed activities, they form gender-segregated groups that have their own cultures and rules, and the divisions become self-perpetuating and almost insurmountable (Maccoby, 1998). Breaking down the gender divide and equalizing power between the two groups, is difficult and requires active interventions (MacNaughton, 2000). Even when teachers implement strategies to reduce gender segregation, they are not always successful. Children may initially respond to rewards or new activities and play with more cross-sex peers. However, after the intervention ends, they usually revert back to their same-sex groups (Ramsey, 2004).

In addition to learning gender stereotypes, children are also absorbing assumptions about sexual preference and family composition. We have little formal research on children's views about sexual orientation because schools and families are reluctant to participate in studies on this topic. However, children frequently assign pretend roles that reflect prevailing societal messages (e.g., "No!! You canNOT have two moms!!"). However, if children learn about families with single-sex parents in a respectful way, their expectations may become more flexible. A preschool teacher recently talked about her classroom where, in the context of family visits to the classroom, two lesbian-headed families shared their stories with the children. They did not talk explicitly about being lesbian but rather showed pictures of their families doing activities together, many of which were familiar to the other children (e.g., going out for ice cream, visiting relatives, playing in the snow). The teacher reported that these visits and discussions seemed to allay children's concerns about family composition, and their "scripts" became more flexible and frequently included two mothers or two fathers along with other relatives.

In addition to gender roles, children are absorbing other cultural values and expectations from their families and the local community. Culture has a profound effect on all aspects of our lives. "[It] is a process which empowers people to function" (Phillips, 1990, p. 2). Through culture "children gain a sense of identity, a feeling of belonging, a notion of what is important in life, what is right and wrong, how to care for themselves and others, and what to celebrate, eat and wear" (Cortez, 1996, p. ix). They gain the power to influence their environment and to have an impact on the world (Phillips, 1988). At the same time, we cannot make sweeping assumptions about people based only on their cultural background. For one thing, cultures are not static; they are constantly evolving as groups come into contact with one another and with new technologies. For another, just as individuals within racial, social class, and gender groups vary widely, so do those within cultural groups.

Although most children are not consciously aware of culture per se, they do react when they see or hear something that violates their cultural expectations, as illustrated in the opening story of *Black Ants and Buddhists* (Cowhey, 2006). The arrival of black ants in the classroom set off a wave of stomping and killing on the part of the American children. However, one child, a Buddhist from Thailand, objected strenuously, "No! Do not kill them! They are living things!" (p. 2). This disagreement reflects how children have culturally defined world views, which often, as is the case here, reveal disparities in perceptions of the natural environment. The view that humans are meant to dominate the world and can use and abuse the environment at will has prevailed in the United States since the arrival of the European settlers, but it is not shared by all groups. In fact, with increased concerns about global warming and other environmental issues, this assumption is being challenged on many fronts.

Cultural differences can be particularly mystifying and difficult for children who are newcomers to this country or an unfamiliar community. They often have to adapt to new behavioral norms, which may lead to isolation and discomfort. A preschool teacher described a child whose family had recently come to the United States from Italy. Although she was fluent in English, the child was struggling in her efforts to connect with her classmates. Her entry strategies were ineffective and, on the rare occasions when she did engage with others, the interactions would fall apart quickly. She was angry and confused and was starting to be overtly rejected by other children. The teacher asked the child's mother to observe the classroom to see if she could help her develop a plan to support her daughter. The mother very quickly identified the probem: In their home community, children played in large groups, and everyone was included; there were no "best friends" and exclusive groups. Thus, her daughter had not learned how to "enter" groups or how to manage children's exclusionary behavior that was sometimes exacerbated by the classroom rules that limited the number of children allowed in specfic play areas (e.g., only three children allowed in blocks at one time). As this example shows, when children attend early childhood programs that are not culturally consistent with their home cultures, they are at risk. As Carol Brunson Phillips eloquently reminds us, "Remember what happened to E.T. when he got too far from home? He lost his power over the world. And so it is with our children when their school settings are so different from home that they represent an alien culture to them. They too lose their power" (Phillips, 1988, p. 47).

With the active influx of immigrant families, we need to be particularly aware of the effects of dislocation and cultural and linguistic discontinuities. Children of recent immigrants suffer from the anxiety and confusion that inevitably accompany leaving the familiar and coping with a whole new language and school structure. Igoa (1995) describes the initial confusion, exhaustion, and fear that immigrant children feel and the different stages that children go through as they become more comfortable with their new surroundings. As one child said, "When I first went to school in the U.S., I wanted to cry. . . . It was very confusing. I did not understand. . . . I did not know anyone" (p. 44).

These gaps and discomfort are exacerbated when children must also learn the language of the school in addition to adapting to new cultural norms. A nationwide study of 1,000 language-minority families (including Latin, Asian, Arab, and European immigrants and non-English-speaking Native Americans) whose children went to English-only preschool programs provides evidence that justifies this concern. The researchers found evidence of "serious disruptions of family relations occurring when young children learn English in school and lose the use of the home language" (National Association for Bilingual Education, 1990, p. 1). Lily Wong-Fillmore (1990, p. 7), director of the study, concludes:

> It is important to recognize the consequences that early education programs for language minority children can have on the family's ability to perform its socializing role. Admittedly, there are positive benefits to be had from an early immersion in the ways of speaking and learning that are the most highly valued in the school. The children will find it easier to make the transition to school eventually, but such programs achieve little if they contribute to a breakdown in parent and child relations. What is at stake is nothing less than the family's continued role in the socialization of its children.

In contrast, culturally and linguistically sensitive programs can help children develop their new cultural knowledge and language skills in a context that supports their home experiences and broaden children's experiences, rather than forcing them to choose between their home and school allegiances. As our example of the Italian child illustrates, teachers and family members can collaborate to build a mutual understanding of differences and to develop strategies to help children bridge those gaps.

Since the early 1970s bilingual education programs have been available to ease these transitions for many children by helping them maintain both of their languages and cultures and by making schools more hospitable for parents.

Many of these programs have been very successful, and, in some cases, parents and teachers have collaborated to create two-way bilingual/bilcultural programs (e.g., Vasquez, Pease-Alvarez, & Shannon, 1994). Unfortunately, as we discuss later in this chapter, bilingual education has been the target of a great deal of political opposition. As a result, in many states, bilingual programs have been curtailed or virtually eliminated and are no longer available to many families. Thus, the burden now falls more heavily on regular classroom teachers and parents to ease children's entry into new language environments.

If only one or two children speak a particular language, they may be particularly isolated from their peers, especially at the beginning of the year. A teacher recently described a 4-year-old girl whose family had recently arrived from Pakistan. Farah was outgoing and eager to play with peers and valiantly tried to participate in the ongoing fantasy play. The children were quite accepting at first, but when Farah was unable to understand and follow the themes and roles, she was increasingly left out. Children, reacting to the awkwardness of not having a shared language, may simply avoid each other unless teachers help them make connections.

As noted in the Wong-Fillmore quote (1990, p. 7), immigrant parents often have difficulty providing their children with support because they themselves are going through the same transition and are exhausted and confused. Ironically, because children usually learn new languages and customs more rapidly than their parents, they often have the additional stress of serving as translators, negotiators, and teachers for their parents. This role reversal enables children to learn to be responsible and to further develop their English language skills, but it can also undermine respect for parental authority. In some cases, children begin to refuse to speak their home language and may shift their allegiance to the language and culture of their peers. This communication gap also means that parents cannot teach their children their values, beliefs, and wisdom, and thus families become less intimate (Wong-Fillmore, 1991). Moreover, because language and culture are inextricably bound (Nieto, 2004), the loss of language also diminishes children's knowledge of their culture.

Parents and grandparents often feel threatened when values, learning goals, and social expectations differ between home and school. These disparities may lead to poor communication and working relationships between parents and teachers. Vasquez and colleagues (1994) describe how Mexican American parents feel undermined when teachers—speaking from their own cultural perspectives—tell children that individual achievement and rights are more important than family loyalty. A child who stays out of school to accompany his mother to the doctor or is absent for 2 weeks to go to a family funeral in Mexico may be criticized by the teacher and feel caught between two different sets of expectations (Valdés, 1996).

Differences in abilities is another dimension of diversity that can lead to confusion and isolation. Children as young as 3 years old have some awareness of sensory and orthopedic disabilities (Diamond & Innes, 2001), largely because of the visibility of the equipment that is associated with them, such as white canes or wheelchairs, but they have little knowledge and considerable misinformation about cognitive delays or emotional disabilities.

Unfortunately, in integrated classrooms, children with disabilities are often socially isolated and rejected and, in some cases, become more so over the school year, demonstrating that merely having contact does not break down the barriers between "typical" children and their peers. Acceptance or rejection of peers with disabilities is affected by the situation and nature of disability. For example, children are more likely to avoid peers with orthopedic limitations when they are doing physical activities. Children also are more accepting toward their peers who have disabilities that seem to be no fault of their own (e.g., specific physical disabilities, such as blindness) than they are toward peers perceived as having more responsibility for their disability (e.g., obesity, poor impulse control) (Diamond & Innes, 2001). Children with cognitive or emotional disabilities are particularly at risk because classmates are likely to be confused and even scared by their behavior (e.g., the inability of a child with cognitive delays to "keep up" with the fast-paced actions of fantasy play, the angry outbursts of a child with an emotional disorder). One teacher described Eric, a preschooler with Asperger syndrome, as usually standing alone in the playground physically and emotionally apart from his classmates who were racing around the yard engaged in various chasing games. Occasionally he would start to run after them but would stop after a few steps. Despite his vast knowldege in many areas (especially about machines) he could not "read" the children's feelings and purpose of the game well enough to participate. Unless a teacher deliberately orchestrated an activity with Eric and a classmate, the other children generally ignored him. Isolation, however, is not inevitable. A child may have one friend who serves as a social buffer and provides companionship or may find a niche in the classroom that provides some social visibility and peer contact. Eric's teacher excitedly reported that one day Eric was digging a hole in the sandbox when a couple of other children joined him and asked if they could help. Eric nodded quietly, and they all started to dig "the biggest hole in the world." This project became a classroom theme for the next few weeks, with Eric as the main organizer. Although still very reticent most of the time, Eric seemed to enjoy his role in this play and, during those times, was much more animated and connected with other children.

Across all dimensions of diversity, children absorb the images, stereotypes, and power differentials that are part of the fabric of their social milieu. They learn through direct and indirect instructions from parents, peers, and teachers and through contact with printed and electronic media. Some messages are subtle. Children may observe their parents' (possibly unconscious) reactions to different people or neighborhoods. Parents' or teachers' own discomfort with issues of diversity may lead them to avoid discussing these issues. When children ask questions, parents and teachers may worry that this curiosity is a sign of incipient prejudice and may dismiss children's queries about people's identities with statements such as "It's not polite to ask" or "I'll tell you later" or "It doesn't matter." This avoidance does not give children the help they need to form positive ideas about themselves or a prodiversity disposition toward others (Derman-Sparks & ABC Task Force, 1989).

The absorption of negative and inaccurate images of different groups impairs the development of all children. Over 50 years ago, Kenneth Clark identified serious consequences of racism to both African American and European American young children. (His research was one of the decisive factors in the 1954 Supreme Court desegregation decision.) In his chapter entitled "The White Child and Race Prejudice," Clark wrote:

> The social influences responsible for the development of racial prejudices in American children at the same time develop deep patterns of moral conflict, guilt, anxiety and distortion of reality in these children. The same institutions that teach children the democratic and religious doctrine of the brotherhood of man and the equality of all human beings—institutions such as the church and school—also teach them to violate these concepts through racial prejudice and undemocratic behavior toward others. (1955, p. 78)

The consequences of inequities for children who are the beneficiaries of unearned privileges because of their racial, economic, gender, or cultural backgrounds include distortions of reality, lack of intellectual skills and accurate information necessary for living in today's world, a false sense of identity based on superiority, tension and fears about people different from themselves, moral double standards, and conformity to undemocratic demands of silence (Clark, 1955; Dennis, 1981; Tatum, 1997).

The costs to children who are targets of prejudice affect every aspect of their lives. In addition to having fewer opportunities for decent health care, nutrition, education, and housing, they often internalize societal biases against their group. These beliefs can "profoundly affect self-concept, behavior, aspirations and confidence and inhibit a child before he or she has learned to define personal talents and objectives. They can evolve into self-fulfilling prophecies. Young people who are informed that they are going to be underachievers do underachieve with painful regularity" (Dorris, 1978, p. 2). Thus, it is in the interest of all children—those who are advantaged and those who are disadvantaged by discrimination—to develop and implement thoughtful and effective programs that challenge divisions and inequities.

EDUCATIONAL APPROACHES TO DIVERSITY: PAST AND PRESENT

This section discusses the five basic educational approaches to diversity and social injustice that emerged in U.S. society in the twentieth century and persists to the present. (For more detailed discussions about the sociopolitical contexts of these different movements, see Ramsey & Williams, 2003.) For each approach, we describe the underlying assumptions about diversity and society, educational goals and methods, and current criticisms. The first three approaches focus on populations that have historically been excluded from the mainstream in the United States, along with ways of explicitly or implicitly pressuring them to assimilate into the European American dominant culture. The last two approaches focus on all groups and reflect efforts to create more equitable social, cultural, economic, and political relationships among them.

Suppression of Cultural Diversity

The underlying assumption of the suppression of cultural diversity is that everyone needs to be

Nancy Sheehan Photography

Family members are integral to multicultural education during the early years.

assimilated into the European American culture to create a united nation. The justifications for this orientation rest on the racist assumptions that the European American culture is superior to others and that "it was here first." This approach further implies that the rights and privileges of the United States are only for those who choose to assimilate and therefore establishes a fundamentally unequal power relationship between European Americans and other racial/ethnic groups.

Early childhood curricula that reflect this orientation do not address diversity and discourage children and family members from bringing their own languages and cultural practices into the classroom. Schools that adhere to this view reflect only European American images, beliefs, and behaviors in their curricula, physical environments, and materials. Teachers who do so actively discourage children from retaining their own culture and language. For example, until the 1960s, schools run by the Bureau of Indian Affairs removed children from their home communities, and teachers and administrators sought to erase Native American children's culture and language and replace them with the language, values, and habits of middle-class white society. In many other schools, children were punished for speaking their native languages, and parents were urged to speak only English at home (e.g., Rodriguez, 1981). A statement made many years ago by Theodore Roosevelt exemplifies this attitude: "We have room for but one language here and that is the English language, for we intend to see that the crucible turns our people out as Americans, of American nationality, and not as dwellers in a polyglot boarding house" (quoted in Marquez, 1991, p. 6).

In the 1960s a new form of cultural suppression emerged under the rubrics of "cultural deprivation theory" and "compensatory education." This approach argued that "the inability of culturally different families to benefit from the opportunities for social equality in this country, and thus the inability of their children to benefit from school experience is, in part (if not totally), due to their culture" (Phillips, 1988, p. 43). Therefore, the educational solution was to institute special programs for both children and parents that would teach them to assimilate into the dominant European American culture. Although appearing to be more compassionate than programs in which children were physically punished for speaking in their native tongues, these programs have shared the same ultimate goals of making all children fit a single cultural mold. Consequently, these programs embodied a deficit orientation toward the children they are designed to assist (e.g., Baratz & Baratz, 1971).

This cultural deficit orientation violates what we recognize as good early childhood education practice. It is not based on current theories or empirical research about how children learn about themselves, about becoming competent individuals, and about diversity; and it hurts all children (Tatum, 1997). Schools with this approach cannot promote feelings of safety, security, and belonging for children. These conditions undermine children's social, emotional, and cognitive development and their relationships with their families. Although these settings may be less stressful for European American children, this approach ill prepares them for their future because, increasingly, white children will grow up to live and work in diverse communities and work sites. Because this perspective potentially condones or even encourages prejudice, it discourages children from learning about groups other than the identified mainstream (Derman-Sparks, 1992; Derman-Sparks & Ramsey, 2005, 2006).

Melting Pot

In the early part of the twentieth century, the national vision was one of a melting pot, an expectation that diverse groups would be fused in the crucible of the United States and emerge as common Americans. By obliterating differences, all Americans would gain equal access to the opportunities of U.S. society. Schools were expected to teach everyone the same "melted" culture. Although this ideal embodied an expectation that all cultures would contribute to the common mix, in actuality the "common culture" comprised the ethnic worldviews of western/northern Europe that were fused together to become the European American dominant culture. Even as the schools touted a "melting pot" approach, they were in fact pushing toward "Anglo conformity" (Ramsey & Williams, 2003; Vold, 1989). This one-way assimilation encouraged immigrants to renounce their ancestry, values, and language and become as similar to the dominant Anglo-Saxon group as possible.

Teachers who are oriented to the "melting pot" position often claim to be color blind. They may deny noticing whether their children are white, black, purple, or green and adhere to the position that "we are all Americans and share a common culture" and that "everyone is the same." With these pronouncements, teachers minimize differences, thereby ignoring the lifestyles and contributions of other groups as well as the effects of differential power and affluence on children's development.

This approach almost always results in teaching practices, environments, and materials that reflect European American culture and deny the realities of diversity and societal biases. Moreover, it confuses the concept of diversity with that of Anglo conformity and, thus, contradicts children's daily experiences and thwarts their efforts to understand their social worlds.

"Add-On" Multiculturalism

Criticisms of the cultural suppression approaches began to emerge as a result of the civil rights movement in the 1960s. Critics argued that recognizing cultural differences as strengths, rather than as problems, was necessary to create a more equitable society. A multicultural approach to education began to take shape in the 1960s with the underlying assumption that we are a society of many peoples and that we all need to learn to honor ourselves and one another. From this perspective, schools have a responsibility to support the cultures of all children, to teach children to respect themselves and others, and to get along with a wide range of people. The hope was that this approach would also reduce prejudice and discrimination.

Although advocates of multicultural education argue that the approach must be infused into all aspects of the education program, an insufficient version, critically termed *add-on multiculturalism,* has become the most frequently practiced approach. In this version of multicultural education, the existing classroom environment and curriculum continue to be based on the dominant European American culture, while other cultures (i.e., ethnic minority groups) are introduced into the curriculum from time to time through special activities. Thus, a classroom may have a special multicultural bulletin board, or may organize learning about diversity around special days or holidays, or may introduce week-long units about particular ethnic groups, but then the focus goes back to the regular curriculum.

Because add-on multiculturalism is organized around concrete and nonthreatening activities (e.g., foods, holidays, songs), many teachers find it easier to make these superficial gestures, or window-dressing changes, rather than to truly transform their curriculum. Many teacher education classes and in-service workshops continue to be influenced by the add-on approach. This response is abetted by the availability of (and heavily promoted) commercial curriculum materials and published curriculum guides that reflect an add-on version of multicultural education.

This form of multiculturalism has been strongly criticized as a "tourist" approach that stereotypes, trivializes, and misrepresents cultures different from the mainstream European American culture. It further perpetuates inequitable racial power relationships by keeping European American culture the center or norm and other cultures as satellites or occasional places to visit. An add-on or tourist approach to diversity does not adequately address diversity and cannot effectively support children's healthy development of identity or respectful attitudes toward others (Derman-Sparks et al., 1989).

Bilingualism/Biculturalism

The underlying assumption of the bilingual/bicultural approach is that children can and should learn to be effective members of both their own cultural group and of the wider, mainstream society. The prefix *bi* means *two:* two languages, two cultural ways of being. Biculturalism is based on the premise that the creation of a truly democratic society in which all groups have fair and equal access to opportunities requires that members of diverse ethnic, racial, and religious groups maintain an autonomous participation in their traditions, cultures, and special interests, while also becoming part of a shared nation (Appleton, 1983; Banks, 1988). For example, in the United States, this means people speak both English and their home, or "heritage," language (Krashen, Tse, & McQuillan, 1998). Early childhood programs that reflect this orientation foster children's ability to speak and learn in their home language and culture while learning the language and cultural rules of behavior of the dominant culture.

Bilingualism/biculturalism is not a new idea in American education. Heritage language programs have a long history in North America (Krashen et al., 1998). German-English schools were established in Ohio in the mid-nineteenth century (Grosjean, 1982), and many other communities formed their own language schools in Dutch, German, Swedish, Yiddish, and Italian (Dropkin, Tobier, & City University of New York, 1976; Fishman, 1966). However, powerful attempts to destroy the language of Native Americans, the enslaved Africans, and the conquered Mexican people also have a long tradition in U.S. history. In 1923 a total of 34 states had English-only educational policies affecting European immigrant languages as well as those of Mexican and the many Native American nations (Marquez, 1991).

In the 1960s self-determination and social-political rights movements fueled a renewed demand for education to support all people's cultural rights and to reverse the undermining of children's cultures, identities, and native languages that contributed to the disproportionately high school-dropout rates of non–European American children. The *Lau v. Nichols* decision in 1974 led many schools to start bilingual education programs (Crawford, 1999).

Early childhood education has a particularly salient and sensitive role in bilingual and bicultural education because the preschool years are key to all children's language and identity development. Knowing when to begin instruction in English for children whose home language is not English and the methods that best support continued growth in the child's home language while the child is also learning English are central to creating good programs. The National Association for the Education of Young Children (NAEYC) recognized this in its 1997 position statement entitled *Cultural and Linguistic Diversity,* which states that:

> As our nation becomes more linguistically and culturally diverse and as the issue of bilingual education becomes more politically charged, early childhood educators have a responsibility to understand how best to . . . provide effective early childhood education for all children. . . . Educators should encourage the use of home language learning while fostering the acquisition of English in order to strengthen ties between programs and families. (p. 1)

While some educators argue that maintaining the home language interferes with the acquisition of English (e.g., Porter, 1990), many studies demonstrate that young children can learn to be bilingual (e.g., Krashen et al., 1998; Sandoval-Martinez, 1982) and in the process benefit in other ways as well. Maintenance of home languages fosters earlier development of academic skills and eventually more proficient English (e.g., Crawford, 1991) and supports children's overall cognitive and emotional development and their ability to communicate with their families (Cummins, 1981, 1986; Wong-Fillmore, 1991). Collier and Thomas (1997) collected data on over 700,000 language minority students from 1982 to 1996 in schools that were using different kinds of well-implemented bilingual programs. They found that students in programs with the longest use of their home languages combined with strong content-based English as second-language instruction showed most academic success. Students who received only English instruction without any home-language instruction in the early years of schooling fared the worst academically. Several researchers have also found that children who have maintained their home language are more likely to develop positive self-identity because of the continuing connection with their cultural group. In addition, positive self and group concepts also foster more acceptance and respect for other ethnic and cultural groups (Tse, 1998).

Nevertheless, bilingual education is "the focus of a continuing debate over language choice in the society. The arguments against bilingual education carry . . . with them underlying political and social perspectives related to people's views of American society" (Wong-Fillmore, 1991, p. 2). Recently several states have virtually banned it from public schools, although families can still request that their children continue to receive bilingual education. Also early childhood programs that are outside of the public schools are allowed to offer bilingual education. Typically, opponents fear that bilingualism will lead to divisiveness and political unrest. However, there is no evidence that bilingualism or multilingualism causes political or economic problems in nations where people speak more than one language (Krashen et al., 1998). Civil harmony and strife occur in countries with one language and in those with many languages.

Despite the political opposition to bilingual education, schools will have increasing numbers of children who will need these services—even if they are delivered in other forms such as ESL or tutoring programs. To support these efforts, we need continued research to determine the most effective methods to implement bilingual/bicultural approaches in varying contexts and at different developmental periods. In particular, how might bilingual education be implemented in programs where many different languages are spoken or where only one or two children speak a language other than English? We also need to understand more precisely when and how to begin second-language English instruction and how to best support teachers to become fluent in languages other than English.

Based on the research to date, we agree with the United Nation's *Convention on the Rights of the Child* (1989) that becoming bilingual and bicultural is a basic right of the child. As Eugene Garcia (2005), a leading expert in early childhood bilingual development, stated, "Every strong tree has strong roots. If you transplant a young plant before its roots are strong enough, the plant does not thrive—it often withers and dies." Indeed, we believe that it is to the benefit of all children to become bilingual and bicultural—a necessity for effective work in our global society.

Antibias Multicultural Education

The goals of this approach are to ensure equitable individual participation in all aspects of society and to enable people to maintain their own culture while participating together to live in a common society. This approach embodies a profound acknowledgment and critique of the fundamental contradictions of the United States and a commitment to transform the inequitable power relationships in U.S. schools and society, while also including the initial goal of multicultural education of respect for oneself and others. The antibias multicultural approach has a pragmatic and an idealistic intent. The realities of changing demographics mean that we cannot afford as a society, to waste the human talent of an increasingly growing segment of the population and that white "majority" (soon to be the demographic "minority") children need to learn how to live effectively and be activists in a changing and diverse society. From this perspective, schools have a responsibility not only to teach children to respect themselves and create equitable relationships with a wide range of people but also to teach children how to work toward eliminating prejudice and discrimination.

The antibias multicultural education movement has several precursors and roots. One is the intergroup education movement of the late 1940s and early 1950s (Taba, Brady, & Robinson, 1952). During this period, some of the classic studies of young children's racial awareness and attitudes toward self and others were conducted (e.g., Clark, 1955; Trager & Radke-Yarrow, 1952). Unfortunately, information about the work of the intergroup movement, as well as of the pioneering research on children's development of attitudes, was subsequently ignored in mainstream child development and nursery school texts. However, it has reemerged in more recent work on early attitude development, and antibias multicultural education embodies many of the goals of the intergroup education movement. Another precursor is the ethnic studies movement of the 1970s, which argued for education that provided children of different groups with accurate information about their own cultures and histories. A third is the commitment to eliminate prejudice and discrimination that fueled the civil rights movement of the 1960s and ultimately led to the realization that white children and families must confront and unlearn their racism.

Multicultural education that began to develop during the late 1960s and 1970s initially focused on fostering respect within and across different racial and cultural groups. The antibias approach, which first appeared in written form in 1989 (Derman-Sparks & ABC Task Force 1989), argued that other aspects of identity such as gender, social class, religion, sexual orientation, and disabilities were also germane to the development of the children's positive identities and respect for others. By the 1990s, advocates of multiculturalism and of antibias education agreed that all educational programs should address the wider issue of underrepresentation and should incorporate all groups that have been excluded from the traditional curriculum (e.g., Derman-Sparks et al., 1989; Nieto, 1996; Ramsey, 1998). We choose to use the term *antibias multicultural education* to describe this perspective, although people in the field may use another term.

During the 1990s, antibias multicultural education more explicitly incorporated a social reconstructionist orientation that assumes that the creation of a just society requires a fundamental change in institutional structures, policies, and behaviors that inhibit the equitable participation of all racial and ethnic groups (Sleeter & Grant, 1987). As Enid Lee (1991) explained,

> It is a point of view that cuts across all subject areas, and addresses the histories and experiences of people who have been left out of the curriculum. Its purpose is to help us deal equitably with all the cultural and racial differences in the human family. It's also a perspective that allows us to get at explanations for why things are the way they are in terms of power relationships and equality issues. (p. 6)

Derman-Sparks and the ABC Task Force (1989) defined antibias education as

> An active/activist approach to challenging prejudices, stereotyping bias, and the "isms." In a society in which institutional structures create and maintain sexism, racism, handicapism, it is not sufficient to be nonbiased, nor is it sufficient to be an

observer. It is necessary for each individual to actively intervene, to challenge and counter the personal and institutional behaviors that perpetuate oppression. (p. 3)

In the 21st century, as the populations in the United States and in many other countries around the world become more racially, culturally, and linguistically diverse, educational movements advocating for multicultural, antibias, and bilingual/bicultural curriculum in early childhood care and education are active not only in the United States but also in countries such as Australia, Belgium, Canada, Denmark, Germany, The Netherlands, Sweden, South Africa, the United Kingdom, and New Zealand.

Over the past two decades, a number of books published in the United States provide resources to teachers wishing to use antibias multicultural approaches (Alvarado, Derman-Sparks, & Ramsey, 1999; Bisson, 1997; Derman-Sparks & Ramsey, 2006; Kendall, 1996; Pelo & Davidson, 2000; Ramsey, 2004; Ramsey & Williams, 2003; Tatum, 1997; Whitney, 1999; Wolpert, 1999; York, 1998). Recent articles have focused on specific ways to engage children in conversations about diversity and inequities using specific materials and activities (Lee, Ramsey, Sweeney, in press), short skits (Williams & Cooney, 2006), and children's literature (Chafel, Flint, Hammel, & Pomeroy, 2007).

Recently, some antibias multicultural writers have been pointing out connections between the marginalization and subjugation of particular groups of people and the exploitation of our natural resources and the competitive consumerism in our society (Cowhey, 2006; Ramsey, 2004). These latter themes relate to cultural and social class differences because how one views the natural world and consumption is influenced by one's culture and level of affluence. They also embody social justice issues because environmental degradation is concentrated in poor communities and countries (Fruchter, 1999), and global warming is already disproportionately affecting people who live in more vulnerable places, such as the polar regions and areas prone to flooding and drought.

Discussion about the nature of antibias multicultural work with white children and adults is another recent development. "What if all the kids are white?" has been one of the most frequently asked questions by white early childhood teachers over the past three decades. It echoes the misconception that antibias multicultural education is only about people who are "different than" whites. In the early days of multicultural education, teachers in predominantly white programs often assumed that education about diversity was not relevant to their children. More recently, however, many teachers of white children have become aware that a false sense of racial superiority is isolating and damaging and ill prepares white children to function in a diverse society. Such teachers also recognize that a society without racism will benefit *all* people and cannot be achieved unless *all* groups, especially those in power, join the struggle. Thus, many teachers today believe that antibias multicultural education *is* relevant to white children. However, they struggle with finding ways to engage children in learning about differences and social justice when teaching in relatively homogeneous settings. The authors of this chapter recently published a book, *What If All the Kids Are White?* (Derman-Sparks & Ramsey, 2006) that explores the many issues and possible strategies to address this question.

Critics who disagree with an antibias multicultural approach have raised several objections. One is the belief that learning about differences among people will make children become prejudiced. This assumption is based on a misconception, not on our knowledge about the early development of attitudes. As we have previously demonstrated, young children *do* absorb stereotypes but *not* because they are learning authentic information and having an opportunity to ask their questions about differences. Rather, children's misperceptions and biases reflect those that are expressed by family members, peers, television, movies, and books and become entrenched when they are left unchallenged. A second objection is that teachers are already overburdened and cannot add anything else to the curriculum. This assumption reflects a misunderstanding about the processes of antibias multicultural education. Teaching about diversity and justice is woven *into,* not added onto, the existing curriculum, so it is a change in perspective rather than an elaborate new curriculum.

Another criticism of antibias multicultural education rests on the belief that learning about diversity and discrimination diverts time from more important purposes of schooling. We argue that these critics are taking a myopic view of the purpose of education and not asking themselves the crucial question, "What world are we educating our children *for?*" Statistics about the changing demographics and the school failure and dropout rates of particular groups provide a powerful argument that multicultural education is essential to the health and success of society.

Another objection is that teaching the values of antibias multicultural education may conflict with the values of some children's families who either subscribe to biased thinking or may prefer to assimilate quietly into the society rather than challenge the system. These criticisms underscore the importance of involving families and community members in the process of designing and implementing curricula that reflect this approach. Finally, some critics have denounced multicultural antibias education for being too "political" because it presents a particular point of view. We argue that *all* education is political. Decisions about what to insert or omit in a storybook or textbook, selections of topics and activities for a classroom, and strategies for working with children and families all reflect our priorities and values. Thus, continuing to use material that focuses only on European Americans and supports assimilation and the status quo is as political as incorporating an antibias multicultural perspective.

Goals for Children in the Twenty-First Century

Children of the twenty-first century cannot function effectively if they are psychologically bound by outdated and limiting assumptions about their fellow inhabitants of their country and of the world. To thrive, even to survive, in this more complicated world, children need to learn how to function in many contexts and to recognize and respect different histories and perspectives. Moreover, as long as some groups are excluded and alienated from educational institutions and economic opportunities, the survival of the United States, as well as our world, is precarious.

Effective antibias multicultural education uses multifaceted approaches that engage the whole child, including cognitive, social, emotional, sensory, motor, and language modalities and skills. Not only does this approach appeal to a broader range of children, but it also encourages development in all of these areas. In the current climate of accountability testing that emphasizes literacy and math skills to the exclusion of other ones, this wholistic approach is ever more crucial. As experts in early development and education, teachers may find themselves taking on the challenges of resisting politically driven decisions to focus on narrow testable skills. Understanding the sociopolitical context of these pressures and how they affect children from different groups can help teachers be more effective advocates for developmentally appropriate, culturally sensitive, and inclusive early childhood education.

Quality early childhood education in the twenty-first century will integrate the goals, knowledge, and methods developed by the bilingual/bicultural, multicultural, and antibias movements. These approaches mutually support each other. Antibias multicultural curricula can enhance bilingual/bicultural education because they add another layer of skills for effectively managing and, where appropriate, resisting the structures and strictures of the dominant society. Conversely, creating an environment that

Barbara Schwartz/Merrill

Acknowledging someone for doing what is appropriate is often more effective than reacting to inappropriate behavior.

supports children's home cultures enables children to develop the confidence to become active players in the transformation of our society.

To develop creative solutions, early childhood educators, researchers, and family members need to talk with one another, try out ideas, evaluate the results, and then make modifications accordingly. Teachers and parents can collaboratively make decisions about prioritizing the many goals on the basis of the developmental levels and cultural and economic contexts of each group of children. For example, if the children come from European American backgrounds, they may be absorbing subtle messages that the European American culture is superior and desirable for everyone. In this case, the priority would be to challenge these assumptions by providing information about other groups and about local and global inequities. On the other hand, if the children's families are underrepresented in the curriculum and the media, then creating a bicultural and, if appropriate, bilingual environment would be the first priority. Then critical perspectives can be woven in as children become more comfortable and learn about the dominant social groups. Thus, the implementation of antibias multicultural education may vary from group to group. At the same time, the following underlying goals are consistent across groups: A few examples of activities are included with each goal to illustrate the range of potential strategies to meet them.

- Nurture each child's construction of a knowledgeable, confident self-concept and group identity by creating early childhood programs that encourage all children to deepen their ties with their families and communities and to know and appreciate their unique attributes.

Examples:
All the children in a program must be equally visible throughout that curriculum (including materials, songs, books). In many cases, this

will mean searching beyond the major commercial companies, which sell materials that primarily reflect dominant culture children and families. Photographs of all the children and their families can be displayed where children can readily see them. Through talking, singing, drawing, and writing, children can share information about themselves, including their interests, fears, pleasures, dreams, accomplishments, and family traditions. One cautionary note, however, is that some self-esteem oriented activities can take on a tone of "I am special" or "All about me" that is counterproductive, especially for children who may already be feeling superior to others. Rather, teachers can help children see how their attributes, capabilities, and challenges are similar and different from those of their peers (e.g., making graphs about hair color or their family's daily rituals). They can also support children's sense of belonging by creating ways that they can contribute to the group/society (e.g., cooperative activities in which everyone plays a significant role).

- Promote each child's comfortable, empathic interaction with people from diverse backgrounds by encouraging the cognitive awareness, emotional disposition, and behavioral skills needed to respect differences, to negotiate and adapt to differences effectively and comfortably, and to understand the common humanity that all people share.

  Examples:
  Teachers can encourage the children to explore the ways they agree and disagree and can use day-to-day conflicts and misunderstandings to help the children learn that their ways of seeing the world are not the only or the "right" ones. In diverse classrooms, teachers might encourage families to share their experiences in concrete ways by telling about family stories, traditions, or favorite foods. Teachers can read books and develop persona doll stories to enable all children to learn about and become comfortable with a wide range of experiences and to work through negative reactions to the unfamiliar (Whitney, 1999).

- Foster each child's critical thinking about bias by encouraging children to identify unfair and untrue images (stereotypes), comments (teasing, name calling), and behaviors directed at oneself or others (discrimination), *and* to develop the emotional empathy to know that bias hurts.

  Examples:
  Teachers can use books, persona doll stories, role plays, and skits to introduce concepts about fairness, to contrast particular stereotypes with accurate images and information, and to explore how stereotypes are hurtful. As children become more aware, they can look for stereotypes and bias in books (both who is omitted and who is misrepresented). As issues come up in the classroom, teachers can help children recognize biased language and behaviors.

- Cultivate children's abilities to act in the face of bias by helping them learn and practice a variety of responses to different situations, such as the following: when a peer acts in a biased manner toward them or another classmate, when an adult acts in a biased manner, and when they become aware of injustices in the neighborhood or larger community (Pelo & Davidson, 2000). Critical thinking and empathy are necessary components of acting for oneself or others in the face of bias.

  Examples:
  Teachers can use the same activities described in the previous paragraph to encourage children to talk about how they might confront bias and unfairness. They can also support children by "coaching" them to challenge a classmate or adult who is treating them in a biased way. When the children become concerned about a particular local or national issue, teachers might help them organize group projects such as letter-writing campaigns, petitions, or letters to the editor of the local newspaper to protest biased actions in the larger community (e.g., closing of summer programs that serve low-income families, inadequately maintaining a local park).

Preparing to Teach from an Antibias Multicultural Perspective

Teaching from this perspective requires careful scrutiny of one's own worldviews, experience with a wide variety of children and families, and in-depth knowledge about the current and past experiences of the particular children in their class. Unfortunately, however, teachers rarely receive this intensive and extensive experience. A recent large-scale study of teacher preparation programs (Ray et al., 2006) showed that they rarely prepare educators for working with a wide range of children. Ironically, most institutions "recognize the developmental and educational needs of children of color, children with special needs, low-income children, immigrants, and second language/dialect speakers as relevant [for] . . . early childhood teachers . . . [but] few hours of coursework and little practice [are] devoted to teaching early childhood teachers how to be effective educators of [diverse children] and [how to] work with their families and communities" (pp. vii–viii). The authors of this study suggest a number of reforms, including hiring new faculty, re-training current faculty, adding field work in diverse communities, and philosophically and structurally transforming programs. Clearly these reforms will take considerable time, and meanwhile, teachers need to develop the necessary skills. We hope that the following guidelines are useful, but we also recognize the need for more profound changes in preservice and inservice teacher programs.

The following guidelines are adapted from Derman-Sparks (1992), and specific activities and discussion questions related to each of these categories have been articulated by Bisson (1997), Ramsey (2004), Williams and De Gaetano (1985), and York (1998).

1. Teachers' history, knowledge, beliefs, values, and interests have a formative effect on the curriculum and on teaching practices. Teachers weave the curriculum together with threads that reflect their worldviews and their underlying goals for children and society. Which family and community concerns teachers notice and which ones they choose to act on or ignore are often influenced by their unexamined attitudes, discomforts, and prejudices. Therefore, an essential component of creating an antibias multicultural curriculum is the teacher's increasing self-awareness about his or her own identity, cultural beliefs and behaviors, and attitudes toward various aspects of other people's identities (Derman-Sparks & Phillips, 1997). Derman-Sparks and ABC Task Force (1989) and Ramsey (2004) suggest questions for becoming more aware of ways that stereotyped assumptions influence interactions between children and adults. If a teacher is truly comfortable with all facets of diversity and believes in the importance of creating an environment that promotes the goals of an antibias multicultural approach, children will absorb these values from everything the teacher says and does.
2. Children's needs, experiences, interests, questions, feelings, and behaviors reflect their culture and social and economic status. To be effective, curricula and teaching practices should embody a developmental perspective based on research about children's construction of identities and attitudes and a working knowledge of how children develop bilingually and biculturally. From the beginning and throughout the year, teachers can monitor children's ideas, feelings, and skills related to diversity and injustice and how they are changing. They can gain this information by observing children's peer interactions and noting their comments and questions when they are engaged with dolls, books, pictures, and other materials that portray different messages about diversity and

inequities. Another possibility is to informally interview children about their ideas and feelings (see Ramsey, 2004). Anecdotes from family members about their children's comments and questions in response to specific activities are also valuable sources of feedback.

3. Families' beliefs, concerns, and desires for their children reflect their histories and experiences and influence the interface between children and schools. Throughout the school year, teachers can provide opportunities for families to talk about how they and their children identify themselves and how their individual and group identities are changing; where family members fit on the bicultural/bilingual continuum; what experiences their children have had with diversity at home and in their community; what information they want their children to learn; what values they want their children to follow and how they try to teach them; how they want their children to handle bias directed against them or others; and what concerns or disagreements they have about antibias multicultural curriculum topics (see Ramsey, 2004). Teachers can gather this information in various ways, including informal conversations when family members bring or pick up their children, through written questionnaires for families who feel comfortable with this approach, and through discussions in individual conferences and larger meetings.
4. Societal events, messages, and expectations permeate children's environments. Children's ideas about themselves and others do not come just from their families—that is a misconception that many continue to hold. One important factor is how the groups in children's communities regard one another and are regarded by the larger society. To avoid being blindsided, teachers may want to closely observe the visual, verbal, and behavioral messages about human diversity, both positive and negative, that permeate the children's worlds. To keep tabs on local events and perspectives, teachers may want to read local newspapers and occasionally attend community meetings. Periodically watching children's television shows, movies, and videogames and visiting toy and clothing stores may help teachers stay current about broader fads and themes that may influence children's interests and play.

Planning Strategies

Ideally, all aspects of the classroom convey the message "This is a place that honors each of you, that recognizes diversity as a natural, key ingredient of life, and that models fairness to one another." Several planning strategies can help teachers achieve this goal. First, to set priorities and not feel overwhelmed, teachers should weigh the multiple goals of antibias multicultural and bilingual/bicultural education in relation to the needs of their specific group of children and families. After they decide what goals should have priority, they can identify what further knowledge and skills they need to implement in their program and, if appropriate, make plans for further staff development.

Second, teachers, preferably in collaboration with family members, can evaluate the physical environment. They can take a careful look at all the materials, books, images, and equipment in their classrooms to determine which ones to eliminate, which ones to keep, and which ones to modify. They can also decide what additional materials need to be purchased or made. (See Derman-Sparks & ABC Task Force, 1989; Kendall, 1996; and Ramsey, 2004, for guidelines and examples of how to make these changes.)

Third, antibias multiculturalism ideally is a natural part of everything a teacher does (see York, 1998). For example, many early childhood teachers do units about hospitals. Sometimes they are responding to children's interests in their bodies and worries about illness and injury or the hospitalization of a child or family member, or perhaps a number of family members work at the local hospital. Activities typically include a visit to a local hospital and/or classroom visits from health care workers. Often teachers set up a "hospital" in the classroom so that children can explore and enact their own understandings of health-related issues. Themes of diversity and social justice can be woven into all aspects of this curriculum. Teachers might provide stories and pictures that contradict children's assumptions about male doctors and female nurses and encourage children to enact different roles. Children's ideas about hospital-related jobs can be expanded by ensuring that the visit to the hospital or the classroom guest list includes meeting custodians, cooks, and technicians, as well as physicians and nurses, and that books about hospitals include these workers. They can encourage children to play these roles in the classroom "hospital." Honoring a wide range of workers in hospitals helps children see beyond the romanticized view of high-status doctors and to recognize and respect the contributions and dignity of all workers. To expand and challenge racial and gender stereotypes about who can do certain jobs, teachers should ensure that children meet (or at least see pictures of or read books about) members of different racial, gender, ability, and age groups doing a variety of jobs in the hospital. Teachers might introduce different cultural views of health and healing to help children see Western medicine in a broader perspective. They also can raise issues about the unfair distribution of health care and encourage children to share their experiences, which may include using public clinics and emergency rooms instead of private doctors. Children might decide to protest these inequities (e.g., writing letters to federal and local officials, hospitals, and the local newspaper).

Fourth, effective antibias multicultural teaching is constructed in the context of continuous interactions between adults and children. As teachers brainstorm, plan, and initiate activities, they can reflect on their children's interests and needs and talk over their ideas with family members. Careful attention to children's thinking and behavior and feedback from parents and colleagues can help teachers effectively modify their plans. A material and emotional environment that reflects children's needs and interests and conveys a clear message that diversity is valued encourages children to raise and explore issues. There is potential to make proactive decisions to support antibias multicultural work in all aspects of the curriculum and the setting: the material environment, physical layout, routines, curriculum themes, personnel decisions, relationships among staff, and relationships between staff and families, and of course between staff and children (York, 1998).

Collaborating with Parents, Colleagues, and Community Members

Antibias multicultural education is complex and potentially contentious. It requires authentic listening and collaboration. Because the mission and the material of antibias multicultural education are often very potent, fellow teachers, family members, and community people may be concerned about the implications of this approach and need to be involved in decisions and networks of support.

Engaging family members in all aspects of this work is critical. They can participate in planning, implementing, and evaluating curricular activities. They can serve on advisory or planning committees with staff members, provide information about their families' lifestyles and beliefs, participate in classroom activities, and serve as community liaisons. Frequent meetings, regular newsletters, and informal conversations can be used to share ongoing plans and classroom activities and elicit parent advice and resources.

Parent meetings on child-rearing and educational issues should incorporate culturally relevant perspectives and topics and be conducted in ways that honor and support family members' values and child-rearing styles and provide time for parents and teachers to learn from each other. Many schools now sponsor book groups during which family and school staff members read and discuss books related to diversity issues. Alternatively, groups could meet to watch and discuss films related to particular diversity and social justice issues.

When family members are involved in concrete ways, they can ask questions, express their concerns, and engage in discussions with teachers and one another that result in a deeper understanding of antibias multicultural issues and how this work potentially benefits all children. They also may gain a greater sense of their own responsibility to foster positive group identities and attitudes toward others. Ideally their participation in these decisions will make them feel validated and empowered (e.g., Neubert & Jones, 1998). When a family member disagrees with an aspect of the curriculum, teachers may initially feel defensive. However, if they understand their own backgrounds and philosophies, they can work through these feelings and listen carefully and sensitively to the issues underlying the disagreement. Recognizing and accepting the source of a family's concern can help teachers to be open minded and to problem solve with family members about how to meet their needs while also maintaining the goals of antibias multicultural education.

The techniques for working with family members on antibias multicultural issues are generally the same as those used for other child development and education topics. The difference, however, lies in teachers' level of comfort about addressing such topics with other adults. Working together with other staff members to explore their own feelings, beliefs, and behaviors in relation to diversity can help teachers become emotionally comfortable and prepared for these conversations. Many of the same strategies used with family members apply to discussions with fellow staff members, administrators, and community people (see Derman-Sparks & ABC Task Force, 1989, and Ramsey, 2004, for more specific suggestions).

Forming Support Groups and Networks

Antibias multicultural and bilingual/bicultural work is emotionally demanding. Moreover, as people change their perceptions and take risks, they often have to deal with the social consequences of conflict and isolation. For these reasons, developing a support system is essential for anyone engaged in this work (Alvarado et al., 1999; Derman-Sparks, 1998).

Many teachers engaged in antibias and bicultural work have formed networks with colleagues that have provided invaluable emotional support, wider access to resources, and practical suggestions for day-to-day teaching. Networks can also provide advice and examples for teachers who are having trouble convincing family members and colleagues of the positive aspects of these approaches. Support from parents and colleagues often translates into acceptance by administrators, who frequently need reassurance that changes are being implemented thoughtfully and with participation from all interested parties. By collaborating, sharing resources, generating strategies to overcome obstacles, and providing encouragement, teachers can maintain the joy and excitement of this work and continue to build curriculum and to develop and expand their practices.

Currently teachers can connect with like-minded colleagues through the Internet. Some of the current websites include the following:

Applied Research Center: http://www.arc.org
Educators for Social Responsibility:
 http://www.esrnational.org
National Women's History Project:
 http://www.nwhp.org

Rethinking Schools Online:
http://www.rethinkingschools.org
Social Justice Resources Center:
http://edpsychserver.ed.vt.edu/diversity
Teaching for Change:
http://www.teachingforchange.org
Teaching Tolerance (Southern Poverty Law Center): http://www.tolerance.org
National Association for Multicultural Education: http://www.nameorg.org

Although these long-distance connections do not offer the intimate support of a group that physically meets and stays connected by daily contact and phone calls, they do enable people from all over the world who are struggling to create more just schools for children to share their views, resources, and support. In addition, these Web sites post information about conferences where people can meet, hear about current work, and research and talk together. These networks also are wonderful tools for quickly organizing wide support for progressive national and international initiatives.

CONCLUSION

It is time to act on the premise that quality education for *all* children, from the earliest years onward, requires the implementation of bilingual/bicultural and antibias multicultural education in all of their dimensions. We need to move more energetically and systematically from good intentions to good practice. As our knowledge and practices continue to develop and improve, we will all learn more about the most effective ways to meet children's developmental needs. To move forward, we need to take advantage of the new models of action research in which teachers are involved directly in defining questions and conducting studies to understand the potential impact of this work on both children and adults.

As early childhood and other educators work with one another and with family members and community people to create programs that meet the developmental and educational needs of *all* young children, we may no longer need to use explicit terms such as *bilingual/bicultural* and *antibias multicultural education.* Perhaps in the 21st century we will come to understand that the terms *care* and *education* automatically mean fostering development in linguistically and culturally sensitive ways and teaching all children about diversity and how to confront and challenge bias in in its many forms. Early childhood educators will then be taking seriously Alice Walker's call to "Keep in mind always the present you are constructing. It should be the future you want" (Walker, 1989, p. 238).

REFERENCES

Alvarado, C., Derman-Sparks, L., & Ramsey, P. G. (1999). *In our own way: How antibias work shapes our lives.* St. Paul, MN: Readleaf Press.

Appleton, N. (1983). *Cultural pluralism in education.* New York: Longman.

Banks, J. (1988). *Multiethnic education: Theory and practice.* Boston: Allyn & Bacon.

Baratz, S., & Baratz, J. (1971). Early childhood intervention: The social science base of institutional racism. In R. H. Anderson & H. G. Shane (Eds.), *As the twig is bent* (pp. 34–52). New York: Houghton Mifflin.

Bigler, R. S., Jones, L. C., & Lobliner, D. B. (1997). Social categorization and the formation of intergroup attitudes in children. *Child Development, 68*(3), 530–543.

Bigler, R. S., & Liben, L. S. (1993). A cognitive-developmental approach to racial stereotyping and reconstructive memory in Euro-American children. *Child Development, 64,* 1507–1518.

Bisson, J. (1997). *Celebrate! Antibias guide to enjoying holidays in early childhood programs.* St. Paul, MN: Readleaf Press.

Chafel, J. A., Flint, A. S., Hammel, J., & Pomeroy, K. H. (2007). Young children, social issues, and critical literacy: Stories of teachers and researchers. *Young Children,* (January), 73–81.

Clark, K. (1955). *Prejudice and your child.* Boston: Beacon.

Collier, V., & Thomas, W. (1997). *General pattern of K–12 language minority student achievement on standardized tests in English reading compared across six program models.* Washington, DC: National Clearinghouse of Bilingual Education.

Cortez, J. (1996). Introduction. In J. Cortez & C. Young-Holt (Eds.), *Infant/toddler caregiving: A guide to culturally sensitive care* (pp. x–xii). San Francisco: Far West Laboratory for Educational Research and Development.

Cowhey, M. (2006). *Black ants and Buddhists: Thinking critically and teaching differently in the primary grades.* Portland, ME: Stenhouse.

Crawford, J. (1991). *Bilingual education: History, politics, theory, and practice.* Trenton, NJ: Crane.

Crawford, J. (1999). *Bilingual education: History, politics, theory, and practice* (4th ed.). Los Angeles: Bilingual Education Service Inc.

Cummins, J. (1981). The role of primary language development in promoting educational success for language minority students. In California State Department of Education, *Schooling and language minority students: A theoretical framework* (pp. 3–49). Los Angeles: Evaluation Dissemination and Assessment Center, California State University.

Cummins, J. (1986). Empowering minority students: A framework for intervention. *Harvard Educational Review, 56*(1), 18–36.

Dennis, R. (1981). Socialization and racism: The white experience. In B. Bowser & R. Hunt (Eds.), *Impacts of racism on white Americans* (pp. 71–85). Beverly Hills, CA: Sage.

Derman-Sparks, L. (1992). Anti-bias, multicultural curriculum: What is developmentally appropriate? In S. Bredekamp & T. Rosegrant (Eds.), *Reaching potentials: Appropriate curriculum and assessment for young children* (pp. 114–127). Washington, DC: National Association for the Education of Young Children.

Derman-Sparks, L. (1998). *Future vision, present work: Learning from the culturally relevant antibias leadership project.* St. Paul, MN: Redleaf Press.

Derman-Sparks, L., & ABC Task Force. (1989). *Anti-bias curriculum: Tools for empowering young children.* Washington, DC: National Association for the Education of Young Children.

Derman-Sparks, L., & Phillips, C. B. (1997). *Teaching/learning anti-racism: A developmental approach.* New York: Teachers College Press.

Derman-Sparks, L., & Ramsey, P. (2005). What if all of the children in my class are white? Anti-bias/multicultural education with white children. *Young Children, 47*(6), 20–27.

Derman-Sparks, L., & Ramsey, P. (2006). *What if all the kids are white? Engaging white children and teachers in multicultural education.* New York: Teachers College Press.

Diamond, K. E., & Innes, F. K. (2001). The origins of young children's attitudes toward peers with disabilities. In M. J. Guralnick (Ed.), *Early childhood inclusion: Focus on change.* Baltimore, MD: Paul Brookes.

Dorris, M. (1978). Why I'm not thankful for Thanksgiving. *Bulletin, 9*(7), 2–9.

Dropkin, R., Tobier, A., & City University of New York, City College Workshop Center for Open Education. (1976). *Roots of open education in America: Reminiscences and reflections.* New York: City College Workshop Center.

Fabes, R. A., Martin, C. L., & Hanish, L. D. (2003). Young Children's Play Qualities in Same-, Other-, and Mixed-Sex Peer Groups, *Child Development, 74*(3), 921–932.

Fishman, J. (1966). *Language loyalty in the United States.* The Hague, The Netherlands: Mouton.

Fruchter, J. (1999). Linking social justice concerns with environmental issues. *ZPG Recorder* (Special Issue on Kid-Friendly Cities), *31*(4), 10–11.

Garcia, E. (2005). Teaching and learning in two languages. New York: Teacher College Press.

Grosjean, F. (1982). *Life with two languages: An introduction to bilingualism.* Cambridge, MA: Harvard University Press.

Igoa, C. (1995). *The inner world of the immigrant child.* New York: St. Martin's Press.

Katz, P. (1982). Development of children's racial awareness and intergroup attitudes. In L. G. Katz (Ed.), *Current topics in early childhood education* (pp. 17–54). Norwood, NJ: Ablex.

Katz, P. A., & Kofkin, J. A. (1997). Race, gender, and the young child. In S. Luthar, J. Burack,

D. Cicchetti, & J. Weisz (Eds.), *Developmental perspectives on risk and pathology* (pp. 51–74). New York: Cambridge University Press.

Kendall, F. (1996). *Diversity in the classroom: A multicultural approach to the education of young children* (rev. ed.). New York: Teachers College Press.

Krashen, S. L., Tse, L., & McQuillan, J. (Eds.). (1998). *Heritage language development.* Culver City, CA: Language Education Associates.

Leahy, R. (1990). The development of concepts of economic and social inequality. *New Directions for Child Development, 46,* 107–120.

Leahy, R. L. (1983). The development of the conception of social class. In R. L. Leahy (Ed.), *The child's construction of inequality* (pp. 79–107). New York: Academic Press.

Lee, E. (1991). Taking multicultural, anti-racist education seriously. *Rethinking Schools, 6*(1), 6–7.

Lee, R., Ramsey, P. G., Sweeney, B. (in press). Engaging young children in conversations about race and social class. *Young Children.*

Maccoby, E. E. (1998). *The two sexes: Growing up apart: Coming together.* Cambridge, MA: Harvard University Press.

MacNaughton, G. (2000). *Rethinking gender in early childhood education.* London, England: Paul Chapman.

Marquez, N. (1991). *The language of learning: A framework for developing two languages in preschool education.* Unpublished manuscript, Administration for Children, Youth and Families, Washington, DC.

McGlothlin, H., & Killen, M. (2005). Children's perceptions of intergroup and intragroup similarity and the role of social experience. *Applied Developmental Psychology, 26,* 680–698.

McGlothlin, H., & Killen, M. (2006). Intergroup attitudes of European American children attending ethnically homogeneous schools. *Child Development, 77*(5), 1375–1386.

Mednick, L., & Ramsey, P. G. (2007, April). *Lessons in power and privilege: The effects of race and social class on peer relationships.* Annual meeting of the American Educational Research Association, Chicago.

Naimark, H. (1983). *Children's understanding of social class differences.* Paper presented at the biennial meeting of The Society for Research in Child Development, Detroit.

National Association for Bilingual Education. (1990, January). *The NABE No-Cost Study on Families* [press release]. Washington, DC.

National Association for the Education of Young Children. (1997). *Cultural and linguistic diversity* [brochure]. Washington, DC: National Association for the Education of Young Children.

Nesdale, D., Griffith, J., Durkin,K., & Maass, A. (2005). Empathy, group norms and children's ethnic attitudes. *Applied Developmental Psychology, 26,* 623–637.

Neubert, K., & Jones, E. (1998). Creating culturally relevant holiday curriculum: A negotiation. *Young Children, 53*(5), 14–19.

Nieto, S. (1996). *Affirming diversity: The sociopolitical context of multicultural education* (2nd ed.). White Plains, NY: Longman.

Nieto, S. (2004). *Affirming diversity: The sociopolitical context of multicultural education* (4th ed.). White Plains, NY: Longman.

Pelo A., & Davidson, F. (2000). *That's not fair! A teacher's guide to activism with young children.* St. Paul, MN: Redleaf.

Pfeifer, J. H., Brown, C. S., & Juvonen, J. (2007). Prejudice reduction in schools: Teaching tolerance in schools: Lessons learned since Brown v. Board of Education about the development and reduction of children's prejudice. *Social Policy Report, 21*(11). Washington, DC: Society for Research in Child Development.

Phillips, C. B. (1988). Nurturing diversity for today's children and tomorrow's leaders. *Young Children, 43*(2), 42–47.

Phillips, C. B. (1990). Culture: A process that empowers. In J. Cortez & C. Young-Holt (Eds.), *Infant/toddler caregiving: A guide to culturally sensitive care* (pp. 2–9). San Francisco: Far West Laboratory for Educational Research and Development.

Porter, R. P. (1990). *Forked tongue: The politics of bilingual education.* New York: Basic.

Ramsey, P. G. (1991). Young children's awareness and understanding of social class differences. *Journal of Genetic Psychology, 152,* 71–82.

Ramsey, P. G. (1995). Changing social dynamics of early childhood classrooms. *Child Development, 66,* 764–773.

Ramsey, P. G. (1998). *Teaching and learning in a diverse world: Multicultural education for young children* (2nd ed.). New York: Teachers College Press.

Ramsey, P. G. (2004). *Teaching and learning in a diverse world: Multicultural education for young children* (3rd ed.). New York: Teachers College Press.

Ramsey, P.G. (2006). Early childhood multicultural education. In B. Spodek & O. Saracho (Eds.), *Handbook of Research on the Education of Young Children* (2nd ed.) (pp. 279—301). Mahwah, NJ: Erlbaum.

Ramsey, P. G., & Williams, L. R., with Vold, E. B. (2003). *Multicultural education: A source book* (2nd ed.). New York: Routledge Falmer.

Ray, A., Bowman, B., and Robbins, J. (2006). *Preparing early childhood teachers to successfully educate all children.* New York: Foundation for Child Development.

Rodriguez, R. (1981). *Hunger of memory: The education of Richard Rodriguez.* Boston: Godine.

Rutland, A., Cameron, L., Bennett, L., & Ferrell, J. (2005). Interracial contact and racial constancy: A multi-site study of racial intergroup bias in 3–5 year old Anglo-British children. *Applied Developmental Psychology, 26,* 600–713.

Sadker, M., & Sadker, D. (1995). *Failing at fairness: How our schools cheat girls.* New York: Simon & Schuster.

Sandoval-Martinez, S. (1982). Findings from the Head Start bilingual curriculum development and evaluation effort. *NABE Journal, 7,* 1–12.

Sleeter, C., & Grant, C. (1987). An analysis of multicultural education in the United States. *Harvard Educational Review, 57,* 421–444.

Taba, H., Brady, E. H., & Robinson, J. T. (1952). *Intergroup education in public schools.* Washington, DC: American Council on Education.

Tatum, B. D. (1997). *"Why are all the black kids sitting together in the cafeteria?" and other conversations about race.* New York: Basic Books.

Trager, H., & Radke-Yarrow, M. (1952). *They learn what they live.* New York: Harper & Brothers.

Tse, L. (1998). Affecting affect: The impact of heritage language programs on student attitudes. In S. L. Krashen, L. Tse, & J. McQuillan (Eds.), *Heritage language development.* Culver City, CA: Language Education.

United Nations. (1989). *Proceedings of the Convention on the Rights of the Child,* New York: Author.

Valdés, G. (1996). *Con respeto: Bridging the distances between culturally diverse families and schools.* New York: Teachers College Press.

Van Ausdale, D., & Feagin, J. R. (2001). *The first R: How children learn race and racism.* Lanham, MD: Rowman & Littlefield.

Vasquez, O. A., Pease-Alvarez, L., & Shannon, S. M. (1994). *Pushing boundaries: Language and culture in a Mexican community.* Cambridge, England: Cambridge University Press.

Vold, E. B. (1989). The evolution of multicultural education: A socio-political perspective. In P. G. Ramsey, E. B. Vold, & L. R. Williams (Eds.), *Multicultural education: A source book* (pp. 3–42). New York: Garland.

Walker, A. (1989). *The temple of my familiar.* New York: Pocket Books.

Whitney, T. (1999). *Kids like us: Using persona dolls in the classroom.* St. Paul, MN: Redleaf.

Williams, K. C., & Cooney, M. H. (2006). Young children and social justice. *Young Children, vol. 61 (Spring),* 75–82.

Williams, L. R., & De Gaetano, Y. (1985). *ALERTA: A multicultural, bilingual approach to teaching young children.* Menlo Park, CA: Addison-Wesley.

Wolpert, E. (1999). *Start seeing diversity: The basic guide to anti-bias curriculum.* St. Paul, MN: Readleaf Press.

Wong-Fillmore, L. (1990). Latino families and the schools. In J. Cabello (Ed.), *California perspectives. Vol. I. An anthology from the immigrant students project* (pp. 1–8). San Francisco: California Tomorrow.

Wong-Fillmore, L. (1991). Language and cultural issues in early education. In S. L. Kagan (Ed.), *The care and education of America's young children: Obstacles and opportunities. The Ninetieth Yearbook of the National Society for the Study of Education* (pp. 30–49). Chicago: University of Chicago Press.

York, S. (1998). *The big as life: The everyday inclusion curriculum.* Vols. 1 & 2. St. Paul, MN: Readleaf Press.

Chapter 7
Early Prevention Initiatives

Karen L. Bierman, Celene Domitrovich, and Harriet Darling
The Pennsylvania State University

For some time, educators have known that children who grow up in poverty often experience delays in cognitive and social-emotional development (Lengua, 2002). Many start school unprepared for the academic and behavioral demands of the elementary classroom, causing an achievement gap that widens over time (Zill et al., 2003). Compared with national norms, rates of serious learning problems, underachievement, and school dropout are much higher among socioeconomically disadvantaged and ethnic minority students than among their more advantaged peers (Ryan, Fauth, & Brooks-Gunn, 2006). Because the number of children living in poverty in the United States over the last 7 years has grown by 11.3% to approach 13 million, or approximately 1 in 5 American children, the promotion of school readiness for at-risk children has become a national priority (Children's Defense Fund, 2005).

Head Start has been referred to as the nation's "premier" federally sponsored early childhood education program, developed to reduce socioeconomic disparities in educational attainment (U.S. Department of Health and Human Services [USDHHS], 2001). The national investment in Head Start programs was based upon research showing that high-quality preschool programs can substantially improve the school adaptation and life course of disadvantaged children, enhancing their academic achievement, high school graduation rates, and long-term employment opportunities (Barnett, 1995; Weikart & Schweinhart, 1997). Yet, significant delays in school readiness remain evident, even for children who participate in Head Start. The recent Head Start Impact Study, which compared children randomly assigned to receive Head Start with a similar group allowed to enroll in community non–Head Start services, demonstrated significant benefits, particularly on cognitive skills (U.S. Department of Health and Human Services, 2005). However, no effects were found on several important aspects of school readiness, including oral comprehension skills, phonological awareness, aggressive behaviors, or social skills.

In an effort to reduce the "achievement gap" associated with socioeconomic disadvantage, preventive interventions are being developed to strengthen the impact of Head Start and other pre-kindergarten programs on the school readiness of at-risk children. This chapter defines school readiness, explains the approach of preventive interventions, and provides specific examples of effective pre-kindergarten programs that foster school readiness among socioeconomically disadvantaged children. We focus primarily on interventions designed to promote social-emotional development to improve children's behavioral readiness for school. We also briefly discuss interventions designed to enhance language development and preliteracy skills, and we illustrate how these can be integrated with interventions targeting social-emotional development. The chapter concludes with a discussion of the implications for school programs and policies and for the professional development of early childhood educators and pre-kindergarten teachers.

Katelyn Metzger/Merrill
Interpersonal skills are needed for cooperative play.

DEFINING SCHOOL READINESS

Preventive interventions are most effective when they are based on developmental research (Coie et al., 1993). We define *school readiness* as the pre-kindergarten child characteristics and skills that have predicted positive academic and behavioral adjustment to school in longitudinal studies. These skills represent "protective factors" to be targeted in preventive intervention because they promote child resiliency in the face of disadvantageous life circumstances. A central focus of this chapter is on the social-emotional and self-regulatory skills that set the stage for learning at school, including the abilities to establish positive relationships with teachers and peers, cooperate and participate effectively in the classroom, and inhibit aggressive reactions.

Social-Emotional and Self-Regulatory Skills

As preschool children transition into kindergarten, they face heightened demands for self-regulation and social integration. They are expected to initiate and sustain positive relationships with teachers and peers, listen-and-learn on demand, follow classroom rules and routines, and, in general, show appropriate self-regulation, independence, and initiative in the classroom (Rimm-Kaufman, Pianta, & Cox, 2000). School readiness is enhanced by four interrelated social-emotional skills: (1) prosocial-cooperative skills, (2) emotional understanding and emotion regulation, (3) self-control, and (4) social problem-solving skills.

Prosocial-cooperative skills include the social skills that support friendships (e.g., being friendly and agreeable, sharing, helping) and the collaborative skills that support positive engagement in learning activities at school (e.g., following teacher directions, respecting classroom rules and routines, and working well in a group). Children who enter elementary school with higher levels of prosocial-cooperative skills learn more quickly at school and attain higher rates of achievement over the course of kindergarten than do students with lower levels of prosocial skill readiness (Ladd, Buhs, & Seid, 2000). Students with high levels of prosocial-cooperative skills also establish better relationships with both teachers and peers and enjoy rich, collaborative peer play experiences (Denham & Burton, 2004; Eisenberg & Fabes, 1992). Conversely, low rates of prosocial skill at school entry predict to social isolation, behavior problems, and peer difficulties in later school years (Bierman, 2004; Ladd & Profilet, 1996).

Emotional understanding includes knowledge about emotions and the abilities to accurately identify emotional expressions in someone else, to identify one's own emotional states, and to recognize events that are likely to elicit particular emotional reactions. Children with higher levels of emotional understanding show more empathy for others, and are more likely to behave altruistically

consequences of skill use. They also look for opportunities to cue and support the use of skillful strategies in "real life" situations that occur in the classroom throughout the day.

Teacher-led curriculum-based programs are termed *universal* when they are used by a classroom teacher to enhance the language skills and social-emotional competencies of all children in the classroom (Weissberg & Greenberg, 1998). During the preschool years, teacher-led classroom prevention programs may be particularly effective. Teacher-child relationships and interactions provide a primary context for social-emotional development and learning. Teachers are critical sources of support and socialization for young children and influence social-emotional learning in both formal and informal ways (Pianta, 1999). Teachers who are sensitive, warm, and responsive foster children's feelings of emotional security in the classroom. This security promotes children's comfort in exploring their physical and social worlds, and it enhances their ability to interact comfortably with other children and concentrate on learning tasks (Pianta, Rimm-Kaufman et al., 2002). Teachers who set up clear routines, establish appropriate classroom rules, and help children manage conflicts with discussion and problem solving foster the development of child self-regulation skills and their ability to inhibit aggressive reactions (Denham & Burton, 2004; Webster-Stratton et al., 2001). Training teachers to provide warm support and effective (nonpunitive) classroom management has positive effects on children's prosocial behavior and reduced aggression (Webster-Stratton, Reid, & Hammond, 2001).

In addition, teachers can foster social-emotional learning through the use of explicit curricula and teaching strategies. A rapidly growing research base suggests that social-emotional skill development can also be enhanced via the use of systematic instructional approaches in the classroom (Consortium on the School-Based Promotion of Social Competence, 1994; Elias et al., 1997).

I Can Problem Solve (ICPS) Program. One of the first universal social-emotional learning programs designed specifically for preschool children was the I Can Problem Solve, or ICPS, program (Shure, 1992; Shure & Spivack, 1982). This preschool curriculum includes skill presentation lessons and guided practice activities, which utilize pictures, role playing, puppets, and group interaction to teach social skills associated with understanding emotion and social problem solving. During the first 10 to 12 lessons, children learn word concepts to help them describe social sequences (e.g., some vs. all, if/then, same/different). The second unit (comprised of 20 lessons) focuses on identifying one's own feelings and recognizing the feelings of others. Students practice identifying people's feelings in problem situations and are shown how behaviors can affect others' feelings and responses. In the third set of 15 lessons, teachers utilize role-playing games and dialogue to promote social problem-solving skills. Teachers introduce hypothetical problem situations that commonly occur in preschool settings and ask children to generate and act out possible solutions as ways to encourage generative thinking and help children understand the consequences linked with various choices. A randomized, controlled trial showed that the ICPS program promoted gains in children's social problem-solving abilities and led to teacher-rated improvements in frustration tolerance, impulsivity, and task engagement (Shure, 1992; Shure & Spivack, 1982).

Al's Pals: Kids Making Healthy Choices. Another example of a universal social-emotional learning program designed for preschool children and carefully evaluated is Al's Pals: Kids Making Healthy Choices. Al's Pals includes 46 lessons designed for preschool, kindergarten, and first-grade children. A hand puppet named Al is a positive role model who, along with his puppet friends Keisha and Ty, demonstrates a set of social-emotional skills in puppet-led role plays, discussions, original songs, and books. Skill concepts are introduced during 20-minute lessons. Teachers are trained to then elicit and reinforce the skills throughout the day, as the opportunity arises.

In one study of Al's Pals, participating children who ranged in age from preschool to second grade showed improved social skills and problem-solving abilities, as assessed by teacher ratings, compared to children in randomly assigned control classrooms who did not receive the program (Dubas, Lynch, Gallano, Geller, & Hunt, 1998). Similarly, another randomized trial of this curriculum conducted in Head Start classrooms produced significant effects on teacher-rated behavior problems and independent functioning (Lynch, Geller, & Schmidt, 2004).

Preschool PATHS. The Preschool PATHS (Promoting Alternative Thinking Strategies) Curriculum (Domitrovich, Greenberg, Cortes, & Kusche, 1999) is a third example of a preschool social-emotional learning program, and it is one of the more comprehensive programs available that has undergone randomized trial evaluation. The PATHS Curriculum (Conduct Problems Prevention Research Group, 1999; Greenberg & Kusche, 1998; Kusche & Greenberg, 1995) was developed originally for elementary school students. In 1990, the developers began working with Head Start programs to develop a preschool version that represented a developmentally appropriate "downward extension" of the elementary program (Domitrovich et al., 1999; Domitrovich, Cortes, & Greenberg, 2007).

Preschool PATHS targets skills in five specific domains: (1) cooperative friendship skills (helping, sharing, taking turns, being a fun and friendly play partner), (2) emotional awareness and communication (being able to identify and label one's own and others' feelings, understanding the impact of common events and behaviors on feelings, listening skills), (3) self-control/emotion regulation (inhibition of impulsive reactivity when angry or upset, calming down), (4) self-esteem (complimenting oneself and others), and (5) social problem solving (being able to follow the sequence of calming down, identifying the problem, generating alternative solutions, and selecting a positive solution). The units are divided into 33 lessons that are delivered by teachers during circle time. In these lessons, teachers use modeling stories, illustrated with pictures, puppet demonstrations, and role plays to illustrate skill concepts. A set of puppet characters, including Twiggle the Turtle and Henrietta the Hedgehog, are central to the program and model the use of skills in everyday problem situations.

For example, in an initial modeling story, Twiggle the Turtle gets very upset, and a wise old turtle teaches him to stop himself from acting out when he feels that way. The wise turtle shows Twiggle how to pull into his shell and calm down first, so he is able to describe the problem, explain his feelings, listen to his friends, and find a way to solve the problem. Following Twiggle's example, children are taught to tell themselves to stop when they are very upset and to do "turtle" by placing their arms across their chest and taking a few moments to calm down. Once calm, they are encouraged to explain how they felt and what was bothering them, as the first step in effective self-regulation and social problem solving.

Twiggle has several puppet friends who are similarly involved in role plays and stories and serve to illustrate important friendship and social problem-solving skills. For example, Henrietta the Hedgehog is a friend of Twiggle. In one story that teaches friendship skills, Henrietta learns that she feels good when she is able to share things with her friend Twiggle, and it makes her happy when she sees her friend smile. During a PATHS lesson, Henrietta tells the children what she learned about "sharing" and how much fun it was for her and her friend when she shared with Twiggle: "Every time you share with someone, you are showing that you care about him or her. That will make the other person feel happy, and it will make you feel happy, too." Henrietta invites the children to think about their sharing experiences and ideas. In a follow-up practice activity on sharing, each child is given a small bag of stickers and asked to notice how he or she and classmates feel when they share the stickers with each other. In this way, the PATHS puppets become models and coaches in the preschool classroom, encouraging self-regulation and prosocial skills to build a supportive peer community.

Each lesson includes ideas for formal and informal extension activities that teaching staff can use throughout the day to generalize the key concepts of the curriculum. Teachers are encouraged to provide emotion coaching throughout the day, modeling feeling statements themselves when appropriate, helping children notice the feelings of peers, and prompting children to describe their own feelings. Teachers are also encouraged to watch for naturally occurring "teachable moments," such as peer disagreements or conflicts. At these times, teachers are taught to help children stop and calm down (using "turtle") and then talk through the problem-solving steps of defining the problem and their feelings, listening to their friend's feelings, and generating ideas for how to solve the problem. Such teaching goes far beyond "Use your words, please!"—an instruction often heard in early childhood classrooms, as it provides children with an explicit set of steps and guidelines to support emotion regulation, self-control, and effective conflict management.

A randomized trial compared the development of children in 10 Head Start classrooms that used the preschool PATHS program with children in 10 "usual practice" Head Start control classrooms; 287 children were followed for 1 year. Children who received PATHS showed higher levels of emotional understanding and were rated as more socially competent by both teachers and parents when compared to children in the control-comparison classrooms (Domitrovich, Cortes, & Greenberg, 2007).

Integrating Social-Emotional Interventions with Efforts to Foster Language Development

ICPS, Al's Pals, and PATHS were all developed as stand-alone universal social-emotional learning programs, designed for implementation in the context of any preschool setting. In all cases, the developers felt these programs would be particularly helpful to children who were experiencing delays in social-emotional development due to socioeconomic disadvantage. Meanwhile, parallel to the development of these preventive interventions, other developers were focusing on preventive interventions that targeted the delays in language and pre-literacy skills that also frequently accompany socioeconomic disadvantage.

In particular, language development is heavily affected by interactions with adults during early childhood, and it is frequently delayed among children growing up in poverty (Dickinson & Smith, 1994). For example, parents and teachers stimulate child language development when they use a rich and varied vocabulary in their talk with children and when they encourage and extend conversational exchanges between teacher and students. Talking about events and issues that are not represented concretely in the environment (e.g., "decontextualized" talk), such as talking about events that happened at another time, making future plans, or engaging in make-believe together all stretch and expand children's ability to use language more flexibly and extensively. In addition, adult responses that expand upon the child's utterances and model new grammatical forms build vocabulary and syntax skills. For example, a child might say "Dog eat," and an adult might expand "Yes, the dog ate the biscuit," providing a model that expands upon the child's statement and fosters new receptive and expressive skills. To enhance language development among children from low-socioeconomic backgrounds, preventive interventions were developed to increase the use of these types of language in the classroom (Dickinson & Brady, 2006; Dickinson & Smith, 1994). These preventive interventions utilize professional development activities to foster teachers' use of high-quality language and language expansions in the classroom, and several also focus explicitly on teacher language use during book-reading activities.

In interactive book reading (sometimes called *dialogic reading*), teachers engage children actively in discussions about the book as they read. These discussions go far beyond simple "yes or no" questions posed by the teacher and answered by the children. Teachers ask probing questions to help the children to reflect on the emotions felt by story characters, consider the story sequence and cause–effect links in the story, and identify key vocabulary. This book-reading method is designed to foster vocabulary growth, narrative understanding, and reading comprehension. The combination of curriculum-based interactive book-reading lessons and more general professional development activities that help teachers use language more effectively in the classroom has proven effective in promoting substantial gains in oral language skills (e.g., Dickinson & Sprague, 2001; Landry, Swank, Smith, Assel, & Guennewig, 2006; Wasik & Bond, 2001; Whitehurst, Arnold, et al., 1994; Whitehurst, Epstein, et al., 1994).

A good example is the recent study conducted by Wasik, Bond, and Hindman (2006). In this preventive intervention, an interactive reading program was implemented in 10 Head Start classrooms. During reading sessions, teachers were encouraged to ask questions, make connections, and build vocabulary by explicitly teaching target vocabulary words with props and extension activities. Teachers were also taught general strategies for expanding on children's utterances, extending conversations, and modeling rich language. The intervention was conducted over a 1-year period and included monthly workshops for teachers, combined with in-class coaching sessions in which a mentor modeled the strategy, observed the teacher using the strategy, and provided the teacher with written and oral feedback. The intervention succeeded in increasing the quality of language use in the classrooms, and children in intervention classrooms showed significant gains in vocabulary scores that exceeded those in the comparison classrooms (Wasik et al., 2006).

Given the developmental interplay between language skills and social-emotional skill development, it is likely that integrating preventive interventions that target these two domains will have mutually facilitative effects. Both language skills and social-emotional skills represent areas of development that are often delayed by socioeconomic disadvantage. Recognizing the importance of both types of skill, social-emotional learning programs are now evolving in order to integrate components that concurrently promote language and related pre-literacy skills. In the next section, we provide an in-depth description of one of these integrated programs.

Comprehensive Approaches to Preventive Intervention: Head Start REDI

The Head Start REDI (Research-based, Developmentally Informed) program was designed to provide an enrichment intervention that could be integrated into the existing framework of Head Start programs using High/Scope or Creative Curriculum (Bierman, Domitrovich, et al., 2007). The goal was to demonstrate that preventive interventions could successfully integrate social-emotional learning with other curricular components designed to promote language development and pre-literacy skills. Specifically, REDI was organized to promote teachers' capacities to utilize research-based practices in supporting both social-emotional learning and language/pre-literacy skill development. The

Adult support for teachers coaching.

intervention includes curriculum-based lessons, center-based extension activities, and training in "coaching strategies" for teachers to use throughout the day to support generalized skill development.

Social-Emotional Learning in REDI. In the REDI program, preschool PATHS provides the universal social-emotional learning program delivered by teachers in Head Start classrooms (Domitrovich et al., 2007). Each week, teachers implement one PATHS lesson and one PATHS extension activity. In addition, the PATHS themes are linked systematically with an interactive reading program. One of the interactive reading books used each week discusses the PATHS theme of the week, thereby serving as a second PATHS extension activity and tying together the reading and social-emotional learning programs. Teachers are also encouraged to use PATHS compliments daily and to support generalized skill development with ongoing emotion coaching and support for student use of the self-control ("turtle") technique and social problem solving.

Language and Pre-Literacy Skill Focus in REDI. REDI utilizes an interactive reading program, a "sound games" program, and print center activities to support concurrent language development and pre-literacy skills.

The interactive reading program is based upon the shared reading program developed by Wasik and Bond (2001; Wasik et al., 2006), which was, in turn, an adaptation of the dialogic reading program (Whitehurst, Arnold, et al., 1994). The REDI version includes two books per week (one focused on the PATHS theme of the week). On the first day of each week, teachers read the first book, which has scripted interactive questions. Teachers present props to demonstrate target vocabulary words and encourage children to comment on and discuss the story. On the second day of the week, teachers label and demonstrate the props that are provided to illustrate new vocabulary words in the story. Teachers also "walk through" the book, using scripted questions to encourage child recall and comprehension of the narrative. A book-related extension activity follows, to encourage language use and vocabulary practice.

On the third day of the week, the props and vocabulary words are reviewed, and a new book containing some of that week's targeted vocabulary is read, with scripted questions to encourage interactive discussion. On day four, target vocabulary is reinforced by asking children to identify the vocabulary illustrated in a "prop book," and another extension activity follows. In addition, teachers receive mentoring in the use of "language coaching" strategies, such as expansions and grammatical recasts, to provide a general scaffold for language development in the classroom during the normal daily routines, such as mealtimes, as well as during lesson presentation or small group times (Dickinson & Smith, 1994).

The REDI program also includes "Sound Games" to promote the pre-literacy skills associated with phonological sensitivity that support the initial decoding skills associated with learning to read (Adams, 1990). Phonological sensitivity refers to a child's ability to recognize and manipulate the smaller units of sound within spoken words, such as syllables and phonemes (Lonigan, Burgess, & Anthony, 2000). Children who are able to rhyme, blend sounds to form new words, and otherwise recognize and produce segmented words and syllables, not through print but through hearing and speaking, acquire initial reading skills more quickly than children without these phonological skills (Lonigan et al., 2000). A number of studies have demonstrated that phonological sensitivity can be taught by providing children with carefully sequenced learning activities that target discrete skills (Ball & Blachman, 1991; Hatcher, Hulme, & Ellis, 1994).

REDI provides teachers with a set of "Sound Games" to use with their students to promote phonological sensitivity skills. Building upon other programs, primarily the work of Lundberg and colleagues (Adams, Foorman, Lundberg, & Beeler, 1998), these games progress through six units, moving from easier to more difficult skills during the course of the year (e.g., listening, rhyming, alliteration, words and sentences, syllables, and phonemes). Teachers use a 10-to 15-minute small group Sound Game activity at least three times per week.

Finally, REDI also includes print center activities specifically designed to enhance children's letter recognition skills. These instructional activities are based on research that demonstrates that most children do not learn about letters in Head Start programs unless those programs are using an explicit curriculum and teaching strategies to provide intensive exposure to letters and letter names. Yet learning to recognize and identify letters of the alphabet is an important predictor of children's early success in decoding printed text and learning to read (Scarborough, 2001). By incorporating explicit and intensive exposure to letter names in the context of Head Start, the rate at which children learn letter names can be greatly accelerated (Ball & Blachman, 1991).

In REDI, teachers are provided with a developmentally sequenced set of activities to be used in their alphabet centers with individual children. They are asked to make sure that each pre-kindergarten child visits the alphabet center several times per week and are given materials to track the children's acquisition of letter names. Materials provided to support student learning include letter stickers, a letter bucket, materials to create a "Letter Wall," and craft materials for various letter-learning activities, such as letter collages, letter towers, and letter murals. During these activities, the teacher does not teach the "sound" of the letters. Rather, the focus is on identifying and naming the letters.

The preventive intervention components of the REDI program are designed for integration with a well-balanced and comprehensive preschool curriculum. For example, Table 7–1 illustrates how REDI is integrated with the Creative Curriculum (Dodge, Colker & Heroman, 2002), which is frequently used in Head Start.

The REDI Professional Development Model. The REDI professional development model for

TABLE 7–1
Typical Classroom Schedule: Head Start REDI with Creative Curriculum

	Tue	Wed	Thu	Fri
9:05–9:10	Arrival			
9:10–9:30	Whole Group "Meet & Greet" Circle (Calendar, Weather, *PATHS "Star of the day" & Compliments; Alphabet letter of the week introduced*)			
9:30–10:00	Breakfast			
10:00–10:15	Alphabet activities			
10:15–10:45	*PATHS Lesson*	*Sound Games*	*Sound Games*	*Sound Games*
small groups swap activities after 15 minutes	Math	Journal	*PATHS Extension*	Journal
10:45–11:15	Physical Development (Outside)			
11:15–11:25	Wash Hands/Free Book Time			
11:25–12:00	Lunch			
12:00–12:30	Music & Movement			
12:30–12:50	*Interactive Reading*	*Interactive Reading*	*Interactive Reading*	*Interactive Reading*
small groups swap activities after 10 minutes	Science	*Reading Extension*	Math	*Reading Extension*
12:50–1:50	Center Time *(Each child does 15 minutes REDI Alphabet Activity once during week)*			
1:50–2:05	Dismissal			

Note: Italicized entries indicate specific REDI curriculum components; REDI teaching strategies are encouraged throughout the day.

teachers includes initial training in the curriculum, as well as ongoing consultation and support provided by REDI consultants, designed to enhance integration of REDI concepts and techniques throughout the day. REDI consultants provide teachers with suggestions in the area of effective classroom management (e.g., establishing clear and appropriate rules and directions; providing positive and corrective feedback for appropriate behavior; applying natural response cost procedures to reduce problem behaviors; and strengthening positive relations with children and parents). In addition, REDI consultants coach teachers in the use of interactive reading and provide encouragement and ideas for the development of conversations that extend children's language skills throughout the day.

In a recent evaluation of the Head Start–REDI program, the progress of 356 four-year-old children was tracked over the course of the prekindergarten year. Classrooms were randomly assigned to use the REDI prevention curriculum or to continue with "usual practice." The REDI prevention program promoted significant gains in teachers' high-quality language use and social-emotional support for children (Domitrovich, Gest, et al., 2007). Children experienced important gains in multiple domains of school readiness—vocabulary, emergent literacy, emotional understanding, social problem solving, social behavior, and learning engagement (Bierman et al., 2007). Improvements in teaching quality played a critical role in promoting developmental gains in the students (Domitrovich, Gest, et al., 2007).

Strengthening the Impact of Universal, Classroom-Based Prevention Programs

Classroom curricula promote the school readiness skills of all children in the classroom and hence are called "universal" approaches. As illustrated by the Head Start REDI program, classroom programs that integrate research-based strategies in a comprehensive fashion to enhance oral language, emergent literacy, and social-emotional skills may be particularly valuable to children coming from low-socioeconomic backgrounds. Several additional prevention strategies are often used to strengthen the impact of classroom-based "universal" prevention programs.

Indicated Programs. Some children enter preschool with particularly large delays or special needs (such as developmental delays, language delays, or attention deficits) that put them at particular risk for school adjustment difficulties. These children often need services that are in addition to classroom-based programs and that provide more intensive instructional support, guided practice, and feedback (Odom & Brown, 1993). Prevention programs for children with delays or special needs are called "indicated".

For example, the *Incredible Years Dinosaur Social Skills and Problem Solving Curriculum* was developed specifically for preschool and early elementary children (ages 4 to 8) who show high levels of aggressive–disruptive conduct problems (Webster-Stratton & Hammond, 1997; Webster-Stratton, Reid, & Hammond, 2001). The *Incredible Years Dinosaur Social Skills and Problem Solving Curriculum* targets skills for positive peer interaction and friendship development, emotional understanding and expression, anger management, interpersonal problem solving, and appropriate classroom behavior. The program is delivered in weekly 2-hour sessions with small groups of five to six children for approximately 21 weeks.

Similarly, social skill coaching programs have also been developed for withdrawn and disliked preschool children (Guglielmo & Tyron, 2001; Mize & Ladd, 1990; Odom et al., 1999). In these programs, adult "coaches" work with children in small groups, focusing on participation and play skills, communication skills, and conflict management skills. Modeling stories and short puppet plays are used to model skill concepts, and children then have opportunities to practice the skills in play, guided and supported by the adult coach. Such materials and skill modeling may also be used in therapeutic interventions.

The randomized trial conducted by Odom and his colleagues (Odom et al., 1999) provides a good example of the value of social skills coaching for preschool children with special needs. In that study, an indicated intervention was provided to preschool children with mild to moderate developmental delays (e.g., mental retardation, behavior disorders, communication disorders) who were at risk for social and behavioral adjustment problems. In the child-focused coaching sessions, small groups (3 to 4) of developmentally delayed children met with teachers for 10 to 15 minutes per day for 25 days. These sessions targeted the play skills of initiating play, sharing, agreeing, leading a game, and trying a new way. In these groups, teachers introduced, demonstrated, and discussed the social skills concepts, and then had children role-play the social skills. The program also included peer partners who were "typically developing." Teachers provided prompts and praise to encourage positive play between the typically developing peer partners and the special needs preschoolers. Teachers specifically coached the typically developing peers to initiate social initiations. They also provided structured activities and supports in the classroom setting to enhance opportunities for peer play for the developmentally delayed students with their typically-developing peer partners. Odom et al. (1999) found that social skills coaching had a significant impact, increasing the quality of child social interactions (assessed with observer ratings) and social competence (assessed with teacher ratings).

The Resilient Peer Treatment (RPT) program (Fantuzzo, Manx, Atkins, & Meyers, 2005) provides another example of a program that operates at the *indicated* level, as it is designed to foster the social skills and social adjustment of socially withdrawn preschoolers who have a history of maltreatment. Classmates who show high levels of social competence are selected to be "Play Buddies" for the socially withdrawn children, and family volunteers provide the adult support needed to support therapeutic play opportunities for the withdrawn children and their Play Buddies in the classroom. In a randomized trial of the RPT program delivered in Head Start classrooms, observers recorded significant increases in positive play interactions and decreases in solitary play behavior for the socially withdrawn children. Teachers also reported higher levels of collaborative peer-play interactions in the treatment setting, and teacher ratings showed sustained gains in self-control and prosocial behavior and decreased levels of problem behaviors 2 months after the intervention.

Coordinated Parent-Focused Prevention Components. The impact of classroom-based prevention programs can also be strengthened by including coordinated parent-training programs. For example, in one trial of the *Incredible Years* program, families of 97 children with early-onset conduct problems were randomly assigned to receive the Dinosaur Curriculum, a parent-training program, the combination of Dinosaur Curriculum and parent training, or a wait-list control group (Webster-Stratton & Hammond, 1997). The Dinosaur Curriculum, used alone or in combination with parent training, produced significant improvements in social problem-solving skills (as measured in child interviews) and conflict-management skills (as measured by observations of play interactions with best friends). Parent training (used alone or in combination with Dinosaur Curriculum) produced greater effects on problem behaviors at home. The positive effects of the Dinosaur Curriculum and parent training were maintained at 1-year follow-up (Webster-Stratton & Hammond, 1997). This study suggests that comprehensive coaching programs for young children with aggressive behavior problems and concurrent social-emotional skill deficits can enhance their social competencies, especially when combined with training that helps parents understand and support the child's social-emotional growth.

CONCLUSION

In summary, prevention initiatives utilize developmental research to identify risk and protective factors associated with positive child outcomes. Preventive interventions are designed to foster the promotion of protective factors, and in that way to foster child resilience and positive outcomes. Although Head Start and other high-quality preschool programs have shown effectiveness in promoting school readiness (Barnett, 1995), research-based prevention initiatives can strengthen their effects, contributing to the school readiness of children at risk due to socioeconomic disadvantage. Critical skill domains associated empirically with school readiness and future school adjustment include social-emotional competencies (cooperative play skills, emotional understanding and regulation, self-control, and social problem-solving skills), and language skills. Comprehensive classroom-based prevention initiatives integrate a focus on skills in these two domains, fostering both the acquisition of specific knowledge and mature approaches to learning. Universal interventions are delivered by teachers and serve to promote the competencies and enhance resilience among all children in the classroom. They can be combined with indicated interventions, which provide more intensive therapeutic support to children with specific needs or developmental delays.

Implications for Education

The available empirical research provides a solid basis for guiding educational policy and practice. First, teachers should receive training in the developmental research that identifies risk and protective factors associated with school adjustment among children growing up in poverty, and the prevention approaches that promote those competences. Second, in addition to training, empirically supported emergent literacy and social-emotional curricula should be available to preschool teachers, enabling them to integrate these research-based educational strategies into their general preschool or pre-kindergarten curricula. In addition to access to these curricula, professional development and mentoring opportunities are critical. Teaching practices, including language use, emotion coaching, behavioral management strategies, and generalized support for student self-control and social problem-solving skills play an essential role in promoting gains in child social-emotional and language skills. Third, therapeutic support programs designed for children with special needs (e.g., developmental delays, learning difficulties, social withdrawal) should incorporate empirically supported social skill coaching procedures into intervention plans, and coordinated support should be provided to parents, particularly to remediate early problems with aggression.

Estimates suggest that, on average, 16% of children in the United States enter school with significant deficits in social-emotional readiness, with prevalence rates particularly high among socioeconomically disadvantaged children (Rimm-Kaufman, Pianta, & Cox, 2000). Research-based universal and indicated preventive interventions have been developed and proven effective in fostering school readiness and partially reducing the readiness "gap" associated with socioeconomic disadvantage. Ongoing efforts to further develop, evaluate, and widely disseminate effective preventive interventions should be a high priority in the education of preschool and pre-kindergarten teachers.

RECOMMENDED WEB SITES

http://www.excellence-earlychildhood.ca/home.asp?lang=EN

Centre of Excellence for Early Childhood Development

http://www.vanderbilt.edu/csefel

Center on the Social and Emotional Foundations for Early Learning

http://challengingbehavior.fmhi.usf.edu/about.html

Center for Evidence-Based Practice: Young Children with Challenging Behavior

http://www.casel.org

Collaborative for Academic, Social, and Emotional Learning

REFERENCES

Adams, M. J. (1990). *Beginning to read: Thinking and learning about print.* Cambridge, MA: MIT Press.

Adams, M. J., Foorman, B. R., Lundberg, I., & Beeler, T. (1998). *Phonological sensitivity in young children: A classroom curriculum.* Baltimore, MD: Brookes.

Ball, W. W., & Blachman, B. A. (1991). Does phoneme segmentation training in kindergarten make a difference in early word recognition and developmental spelling? *Reading Research Quarterly, 26,* 49–66.

Barnett, S. (1995). Long-term effects of early childhood programs on cognitive and school outcomes. *The Future of Children, 5,* 25–50.

Bierman, K. L. (2004). *Peer rejection: Developmental processes and intervention strategies.* New York: Guilford.

Bierman, K. L, Domitrovich, C. E., Nix, R. L., Gest, S. D., Welsh, J. A., Greenberg, M. T., et al. (2007). Promoting academic and social-emotional school readiness: The Head Start REDI Program. [Submitted for publication.]

Bierman, K. L., & Erath, S. A. (2006). Promoting social competence in early childhood: Classroom curricula and social skills coaching programs. In K. McCartney & D. Phillips (Eds.), *Blackwell handbook on early childhood development* (pp. 595–615). Malden, MA: Blackwell.

Bierman, K. L., Greenberg, M. T., & the Conduct Problems Prevention Research Group. (1996). Social skill training in the FAST Track program. In R. DeV. Peters & R. J. McMahon (Eds.), *Preventing childhood disorders, substance abuse, and delinquency* (pp. 65–89). Newbury Park, CA: Sage.

Blair, C. (2002). School readiness: Integrating cognition and emotion in a neurobiological conceptualization of child functioning at school entry. *American Psychologist, 57,* 111–127.

Children's Defense Fund (2005). *The state of America's children 2005.* Washington, DC: Author.

Coie, J. D., Watt, N. F., West, S. G., Hawkins, J. D., Asarnow, J. R., Markman, H. J., et al. (1993). The science of prevention: A conceptual framework and some directions for a national research program. *American Psychologist, 48,* 1013–1022.

Conduct Problems Prevention Research Group. (1999). Initial impact of the Fast Track prevention trial for conduct problems: II. Classroom effects. *Journal of Consulting and Clinical Psychology, 67,* 648–657.

Consortium on the School-Based Promotion of Social Competence (1994). The school-based promotion of social competence: Theory, research, practice, and policy. In R. J. Haggerty, L. R. Sherrod, N. Garmezy, & M. Rutter (Eds.), *Stress, risk, and resilience in children and adolescents: Processes, mechanisms, and interventions.* New York: Cambridge University Press, 268–316.

Denham, S. A., & Burton, R. (2004). *Social and emotional prevention and intervention programming for preschoolers.* New York: Kluwer Academic/Plenum Publishers.

Dickinson, D. K., & Brady, J. P. (2006). Toward effective support for language and literacy through professional development. In M. Zaslow & I. Martinez-Beck (Eds.), *Critical issues in early childhood professional development* (pp. 141–170). Baltimore, MD: Brookes.

Dickinson, D. K., & Smith, M. W. (1994). Long-term effects of preschool teachers' book readings on low-income children's vocabulary and story comprehension. *Reading Research Quarterly, 29,* 104–122.

Dickinson, D. K. & Sprague, K. (2001). The nature and impact of early childhood care environments on the language and early literacy development of children from low-income families. In S. Neuman & D. K. Dickinson (Eds.), *Handbook of early literacy* (pp. 263–292). New York: Guilford.

Dodge, D. T., Colker, L. J., & Heroman, C. (2002). *The Creative Curriculum for Preschool,* 4th ed. Washington, DC: Teaching Strategies, Inc.

Dodge, K. A., Bates, J. E., & Pettit, G. S. (1990). Mechanism in the cycle of violence. *Science, 250,* 1678–1683.

Domitrovich, C. E., Cortes, R., & Greenberg, M. T. (2007). Improving young children's social and emotional competence: A randomized trial of the preschool PATHS curriculum. *Journal of Primary Prevention, 28,* 67–91.

Domitrovich, C. E., Gest, S. D., Gill, S., Bierman, K. L., Welsh, J., & Jones, D. (2007). *Fostering high quality teaching in Head Start classrooms: Experimental evaluation of an integrated curriculum.* Manuscript submitted for publication.

Domitrovich, C. E., Greenberg, M. T., Cortes, R., & Kusche, C. (1999). *Manual for the Preschool PATHS Curriculum.* University Park: The Pennsylvania State University.

Dubas, J. S., Lynch, K. B., Gallano, J., Geller, S., & Hunt, D. (1998). Preliminary evaluation of a resiliency-based preschool substance abuse and violence prevention project. *Journal of Drug Education, 28,* 235–255.

Edwards, C. P. (1999). Development in the preschool years: The typical path. In E. V. Nuttall, I. Romero, & J. Kalesnik (Eds.), *Assessing and screening preschoolers: Psychological and educational dimensions,* 2nd ed. (pp. 9–24). Needham Heights, MA: Allyn & Bacon.

Eisenberg, N., & Fabes, R. A. (1992). Emotion, regulation, and the development of social competence. In M. S. Clark (Ed.), *Review of personality and social psychology. Vol. 14. Emotion and social behavior* (pp. 119–150). Newbury Park, CA: Sage.

Elias, M. J., Zins, J. E., Weissberg, R. P., Frey, K. S., Greenberg, M. T., Haynes, N. M., et al. (1997). *Promoting social and emotional learning: Guidelines for educators.* Alexandria, VA: Association for Supervision and Curriculum Development.

Fantuzzo, J., Manz, P., Atkins, M., & Meyers, R. (2005). Peer-mediated treatment of socially withdrawn maltreated preschool children: Cultivating natural community resources. *Journal of Clinical Child and Adolescent Psychology, 34,* 320–325.

Greenberg, M. T., & Kusche, C. A. (1998). Preventive intervention for school-aged deaf children: The PATHS Curriculum. *Journal of Deaf Studies and Deaf Education, 3,* 49–63.

Greenberg, M. T., Kusche, C. A., & Speltz, M. (1991). Emotional regulation, self control, and psychopathology: The role of relationships in early childhood. In D. Cicchetti & S. L. Toth (Eds.), *Internalizing and externalizing expressions of dysfunction: Rochester symposium on developmental psychopathology* (Vol. 2, pp. 21–66). Hillsdale, NJ: Erlbaum.

Guglielmo, H. M., & Tryon, G. S. (2001). Social skills training in an integrated preschool program. *School Psychology Quarterly, 16,* 158–175.

Hatcher, P. J., Hulme, C., & Ellis, A. W. (1994). Ameliorating early reading failure by integrating the teaching of reading and phonological skills: The phonological linkage hypothesis. *Child Development, 65,* 41–57.

Hughes, J. N., & Kwok, O. (2006). Classroom engagement mediates the effect of teacher-student support on elementary students' peer acceptance: A prospective analysis. *Journal of School Psychology, 43,* 465–480.

Izard, C. E., Fine, S., Schultz, D., Mostow, A., Ackerman, B., & Youngstrom, E. (2001). Emotion knowledge as a predictor of social behavior and academic competence in children at risk. *Psychological Science, 12,* 18–23.

Kusche, C. A., & Greenberg, M. T. (1995). *The PATHS Curriculum.* Seattle, WA: Developmental Research & Programs.

Ladd, G. W., Buhs, E. S., & Seid, M. (2000). Children's initial sentiments about kindergarten: Is school liking an antecedent of early childhood classroom participation and achievement? *Merrill-Palmer Quarterly, 46,* 255–279.

Ladd, G. W., & Mize, J. (1983). A cognitive-social learning model of social skill training. *Psychological Review, 90,* 127–157.

Ladd, G. W., & Profilet, S. M. (1996). The child behavior scale: A teacher measure of young children's aggressive, withdrawn, and prosocial behaviors. *Developmental Psychology, 32*(6), 1008–1024.

Landry, S. H., Swank, P. R., Smith, K. E., Assel, M. A., & Gunnewig, S. B. (2006). Enhancing early literacy skills for preschool children: Bringing a professional development model to scale. *Journal of Learning Disabilities, 39,* 306–324.

Lengua, L. J. (2002). The contribution of emotionality and self-regulation to the understanding of children's response to multiple risk. *Child Development, 73,* 144–161.

Lonigan, C. J., Burgess, S. R., & Anthony, J. L. (2000). Development of emergent literacy and early reading skills in preschool children: Evidence from a latent-variable longitudinal study. *Developmental Psychology, 36,* 596–613.

Lynch, K. B., Geller, S. R., & Schmidt, M. G. (2004). Multi-year evaluation of the effectiveness of a resilience-based prevention program for young children. *The Journal of Primary Prevention, 24,* 335–353.

McClelland, M. M., Acock, A. C., & Morrison, F. J. (2006). The impact of kindergarten learning-related skills on academic trajectories at the end of elementary school. *Early Childhood Research Quarterly, 21,* 471–490.

Mize, J., & Ladd, G. W. (1990). Toward the development of successful social skills training for preschool children. In S. R. Asher & J. D. Coie (Eds.), *Peer rejection in childhood* (pp. 274–308). New York: Cambridge University Press.

Odom, S. L., & Brown, W. H. (1993). Social interaction skills interventions for young children with disabilities in integrated settings. In C. Peck, S. Odom, & D. Bricker (Eds.), *Integrating young children with disabilities into community programs* (pp. 39–64). Baltimore, MD: Brookes.

Odom, S. L., McConnell, S. R., McEvoy, M. A., Peterson, C., Ostrosky, M., Chandler, L., et al. (1999). Relative effects of interventions supporting the social competence of young children with disabilities. *Topics in Early Childhood Special Education, 19,* 75–91.

Pianta, R. C. (1999). *Enhancing relationships between children and teachers.* Washington, DC: American Psychological Association.

Rimm-Kaufman, S., Pianta, R. C., & Cox, M. (2000). Teachers' judgments of problems in the transition to school. *Early Childhood Research Quarterly, 15,* 147–166.

Rimm-Kaufman, S. E., Early, D. M., Cox, M. J., Saluja, G., Pianta, R. C., Bradley, R. H., et al. (2002). Early behavioral attributes and teachers' sensitivity as predictors of competent behavior in the kindergarten classroom. *Journal of Applied Developmental Psychology, 23,* 451–470.

Ryan, R. M., Fauth, R. C., & Brooks-Gunn, J. (2006). Childhood poverty: Implications for school readiness and early childhood education. In B. Spodek & O. N. Saracho (Eds.), *Handbook of research on the education of children* (2nd ed.) (pp. 323–346). Mahwah, NJ: Erlbaum.

Scarborough, H. (2001). Connecting early language and literacy to later reading (dis)abilities: Evidence, theory and practice. In S. Neuman & D. Dickinson (Eds.), *Handbook of emergent literacy research* (pp. 97–110). New York: Guilford Press.

Shure, M. B. (1992). *I Can Problem Solve: An interpersonal cognitive problem-solving program: Kindergarten and primary grades.* Champaign, IL: Research Press.

Shure, M. B., & Spivack, G. (1982). Interpersonal problem-solving in young children: A cognitive approach to prevention. *American Journal of Community Psychology, 10*(3), 341–355.

Snow, K. L. (2007). Integrative views of the domains of child function: Unifying school readiness. In R. C. Pianta, M. J. Cox, & K. L. Snow (Eds.), *School readiness and the transition to kindergarten in the era of accountability* (pp. 197–216). Baltimore, MD: Brookes.

U.S. Department of Health and Human Services. (2001). *Third progress report on the Head Start program performance measures.* Washington, DC: U.S. Department of Health and Human Services.

U.S. Department of Health & Human Services. (2005). Head Start Impact Study: First Year Findings. Washington, DC. http://www.acf.hhs.gov/programs/opre/hs/impact_study/reports/

Wasik, B. A., & Bond, M. A. (2001). Beyond the pages of a book: Interactive book reading and language development in preschool classrooms. *Journal of Educational Psychology, 93,* 243–250.

Wasik, B. A., Bond, M. A., & Hindman, A. (2006). The effects of a language and literacy intervention on Head Start children and teachers. *Journal of Educational Psychology, 98,* 63–74.

Webster-Stratton, C., & Hammond, M. (1997). Treating children with early onset conduct problems: A comparison of child and parenting interventions. *Journal of Consulting and Clinical Psychology, 65,* 93–101.

Webster-Stratton, C., Mihalic, S., Fagan, A., Arnold, D., Taylor, T., & Tingley, C. (2001). *Blueprints for violence prevention, book eleven: The incredible years: Parent, teacher and child training series.* Boulder, CO: Center for the Study and Prevention of Violence.

Webster-Stratton, C., Reid, J., & Hammond, M. (2001). Social skills and problem-solving training for children with early-onset conduct problems: Who benefits? *Journal of Child Psychology and Psychiatry and Allied Disciplines, 42,* 943–952.

Weikart, D. P., & Schweinhart, L. J. (1997). *High/Scope Perry Preschool Program.* In G. W. Albee & T. P. Gullota (Eds.), *Primary prevention works: Issues in children's and families' lives.* Vol. 6. Thousand Oaks, CA: Sage.

Weissberg, R. P., & Greenberg, M. T. (1998). School and community competence-enhancement and prevention programs. In I. Siegel & A. Renninger (Eds.), *Handbook for child psychology* (5th ed.), Vol. 4: *Child psychology in practice.* New York: Wiley.

Whitehurst, G. J., Arnold, D., Epstein, J. N., Angell, A. L., Smith, M., & Fischel, J. E. (1994). A picture book reading intervention in daycare and home for children from low-income families. *Developmental Psychology, 30,* 679–689.

Whitehurst, G. J., Epstein, J. N., Angell, A. C., Payne, A. C., Crone, D. A., & Fischel, J. E. (1994). Outcomes of an emergent literacy intervention in Head Start. *Journal of Educational Psychology, 86,* 542–555.

Zill, N., Resnick, G., Kim, K., O'Donnell, K., Sorongon, A., McKey, R. H., et al. (2003). *Head Start FACES (2000): A whole child perspective on program performance—Fourth progress report.* Washington, DC: U.S. Department of Health and Human Services.

Chapter 8
Early Development and Education Programs in Public Schools

James E. Johnson and Jennifer L. Chestnut ⸺ *The Pennsylvania State University*

Early development and education (EDE) within public schools in the United States has roots that go back to the American kindergarten movement and precede the 20th century (International Kindergarten Union, 1919). From their origins, public school EDE programs have existed alongside many other forms of EDE programs found in society, such as private nursery schools and child life programs in hospitals. Over time U.S. public school EDE programs have expressed themselves in different ways and have served multiple functions.

For example, during the Great Depression and World War II, child-care centers were connected to public schools to assist in economic recovery and national security efforts, and many of the new federal Head Start programs located in the public schools were begun in the 1960s. During that decade, the three other federal initiatives enlisting the cooperation of the public schools were (1) the short-lived Project Developmental Continuity, begun in 1966, (2) Project Follow Through, implemented from 1968 to 1996, and (3) Title I of the Elementary and Secondary Education Act of 1965, which is now part of the No Child Left Behind (NCLB) Act of 2001 (P.L. 107-110) (Reynolds, 2006). Furthermore, the School of the 21st Century (21C) made its appearance before the end of the millennium. There are now over 1,300 such schools across at least 20 states, and a 21C National Network has been created (Finn-Stevenson, 2006). An important rationale for 21C is that public school buildings are ubiquitous and can be used as community hubs serving families and children from birth to 12 years of age with a variety of EDE programs.

We prefer the acronym EDE to ECE (early childhood education) because these programs in the public schools serve various developmental and educational needs of young children and their families. These programs require interdisciplinary teams, including family support, child service, and other professionals, in addition to schoolteachers. EDE captures the spirit of the movement toward more coordination and integration in early care and education. Moreover, EDE is a helpful label in that it reminds us that development comes before education and is the foundation for the design and the implementation of all appropriate school-related programs.

At the present time the growth of public school EDE has reached the point where it represents a major focus of policy discussion concerning the future of ECE. Widely accepted is the view that quality EDE programs are a necessary component in educational reform and improvement in public education. How young children should be educated there and the kinds of state-funded programs they should have are two very important questions being debated today. Another policy issue is the extent to which the institution of public education should determine how ECE is systematized and unified with respect to professional development and service delivery. The role of public education in the current trend toward more coordination and integration of early care and education—including early intervention, Head Start, and other comprehensive service programs—is a hot topic of discussion and debate. How far should we go in allowing the public schools to define our profession of ECE? The promise of solving the perennial three-way problem of supply or accessibility, quality, and teacher compensation that besets the field of early childhood care and education (ECCE), for instance, needs to be weighed against the risks of a downward extension of the academic model from the elementary grades into programs for younger children in pre-kindergarten (pre-K) programs rendering them developmentally inappropriate. Note here that the term *preschool* refers to general ECCE programs and the term *pre-K* refers to EDE and the *integration with* and *not mere transition into* kindergarten through third grade (pre-K to 3, or as it is sometimes listed, P–3).

The great amount of attention currently given to ECE by the public sector is certainly understandable. Advances in neuroscience research have led to a convincing picture of the very young child as a competent, intentional learner (Nelson & Bloom, 1997). Results from longitudinal studies, such as the Perry Preschool Program, the Abecedarian Project, and the Chicago Child-Parent Centers, have helped impress policy makers that ECE is a sound investment (Reynolds & Temple, 2006). And the perennial national (and global) problem of social inequities in school readiness begs still for some solution (Lee & Burkam, 2002; Malakoff, 2006). Accordingly, although always a presence in public education, EDE is now moving front and center at an accelerating rate in an increasing number of schools across the nation and abroad in the 21st century.

In this chapter we examine the increasing role that public education is playing within ECE. We first discuss the universal pre-kindergarten (pre-K) and the full-day kindergarten (K) movements as prime examples of recent trends within public education. We then move on to coverage of the pre-K to third-grade vision for public schools: the strong rationale that exists for this important development; characteristics and examples of this initiative; and advocacy and teacher education needs required to advance this new movement in EDE. Finally, we discuss the importance of teamwork and collaboration among teachers and teacher educators and other professionals with respect to creating and sustaining high-quality public school EDE—as well as bridging across public education EDE to other sectors of our overall vibrant and dynamic field of ECE.

PRE-K AND FULL-DAY KINDERGARTENS

As toddlers reach preschool age, the milestone of entering the formal school setting is realized and is a moment that families consider and remember. This transition produces certain emotions for the family who has prepared the child for this journey into the social structure of education.

Learning and growth begin at birth, and the years of early childhood are critical for building a solid foundation on which all further learning is placed. Throughout the early years an incredible amount of growth, development, and learning has occurred in all areas—social, emotional, cognitive, and physical. These preschool experiences have, hopefully, prepared the child to continue the school trek and master all the learning that will be expected during formal education.

The effectiveness and benefits of quality preschool programs are suggested by considerable and convincing research, with benefits affecting the child and his or her family and society. For example, gains made by children in the Perry

Preschool program (see Chapter 9) continued beyond their school years and affected lives well into adulthood. Among other social indicators, Perry Preschool graduates have been reported as more likely to complete high school, less likely to have a teenage pregnancy, and more likely to go to college and find a better-paying job, which suggests the effectiveness and benefits of this program. Through such studies, many assume that most children who attend quality preschool programs have advantages over others who do not have access to this critical component of development during the early childhood years.

In the United States, formal schooling typically begins at age 5 when the child is eligible to attend kindergarten. While this is generally the age children start school, many states have varying policies on compulsory school age. In Pennsylvania, for instance, the state mandates that at age 8 years children must attend formal school. The importance of pre-K and full-day kindergarten experiences should be examined in relation to any compulsory starting school age to foster greater understanding and cohesiveness in the early childhood community. Public School EDE programs, including pre-K, are important especially for those families who cannot afford high-quality preschools in the private sector. Not having pre-K in a community where the school district has an older starting age makes the absence of EDE services more of a disadvantage for these families than for others who can afford ECCE.

Public preschool originated, in part, in the federal government's War on Poverty that began in the 1960s. The Head Start (HS) project was implemented to help the poorest children begin school on an equal level with all other students, regardless of socioeconomic status. Head Start continues today and has touched the lives of more than 22 million children and their families as the program helps children prepare for school and thus narrows the achievement gap after school entry. Congress reauthorized HS for fiscal year 2008 with an estimated price tag of $7.4 billion (Goldfarb, 2007). With its emphasis on the whole child, HS can serve as a model for preschool education and for infant and toddler programming, special education, and comprehensive services as school districts and state-level government officials work to integrate EDE into the public educational system.

Public education for the 3- and 4-year-olds is definitely on the rise. State spending on pre-K programs nearly doubled between 2005 and 2007, from $2.4 billion to $4.2 billion. More than ever, this trend toward universal voluntary access to state-funded EDE programs, either housed within public school buildings or community centers, is growing across the nation. For example, pre-K programs are court ordered in New Jersey by the State Supreme Court *Abbot v. Burke* decision (Jacobson, 2007); voluntary preschool is voter mandated for all 4-year-olds in Florida (Wat, 2007); and free preschool is legislated for all in Georgia (Barnett & Hustedt, 2003). States that have taken significant steps toward adopting or expanding universal pre-K programs include Arizona, Illinois, Iowa, Kentucky, Maine, Maryland, New York, North Carolina, South Carolina, Tennessee, Texas, Oklahoma, Pennsylvania, Vermont, and Virginia (Association of Supervision and Curriculum Development, 2007).

Early childhood development and education are critical to learning and growth in the school setting and vital to lifelong success. As expectations increase and standards are expanded, young children are placed under growing curriculum strains. Children begin to learn before they enter the formal educational setting that is public school. Many school districts recognize the importance of early learning and the positive impact that pre-K and full-day kindergarten programs have on the development of literacy skills and social development for children. Research supports the idea that increased time in kindergarten produces students who are stronger readers and more confident learners (Ogens, 1990). In addition to the measurable academic gains, research also proves the promotion of social growth and development with the added advantage of serving children and families in one structured setting (Elicker & Mather, 1997). Pre-K and full-day kindergarten programs build a crucial block on which further learning can be firmly placed.

As of 2003, 55% of U.S. kindergarten students attended full-day programs. The idea of a full-day program is not a new one to the educational community. The first kindergarten programs implemented in the United States were an entire day in length. Kindergartens eventually changed to half-day programs due to financial issues. More children could be served at less cost in half-day settings. The educational needs and developmental aspects of children did not play into the decision of cutting back on the time allowed in the school setting. This decision to reduce the time for children was based on money and facility structure.

Originating with the work of Friedrich Froebel, the kindergarten movement began to develop during the late 1800s. These programs initially functioned as full-day settings serving children who were especially affected by urban poverty. Kindergarten was seen as a way to change the future and to have a positive impact on families. Kindergarten principles were based on the idea that an ounce of prevention was worth a pound of cure.

These historical ideas are supported by current research on the effects of full-day kindergarten and pre-K programming. Children who attend full-day programs have higher scores on standardized tests, fewer grade retentions, and fewer remediation classes (Clark & Kirk, 2000). Highly structured and teacher-directed early childhood programs, particularly those that are half-day, are known to depress motivation in children and to increase stress levels. Children can become less compliant in such educational settings (Shonkoff & Phillips, 2000). The time allowed in the full-day program offers increased opportunities for child-initiated learning activities. These opportunities promote higher levels of engagement, interest, and persistence. Teachers in full-day programs often report that children are less frustrated and stressed due to the fact that they have more time to engage in and to understand their work and play and that the schedule allows for more individually and developmentally appropriate challenges for children with varied backgrounds (Elicker & Mathur, 1997). The effects of full-day kindergarten on achievement include higher reading scores in second and third grade, higher scores on standardized tests, higher report card scores, and fewer grade retentions (Emery, Piche, & Rokavec, 1997). WestEd, which is a major research center in education, collated the results of seven studies and found that children in full-day kindergartens versus half-day programs had better attendance, higher academic achievement scores, and higher language and literacy scores through the primary grades (WestEd, 2005).

Pre-K and full-day kindergarten have positive effects on children in other developmental areas. Research has shown that full-day programs raise children's self-esteem, independence, and creativity (Emery et al., 1997). The unhurried day allows children to engage in activities of their choice in a more relaxed atmosphere compared to half-day alternatives. Children are able to feel a sense of community and belonging due to the increased time in the kindergarten group. They are offered a more encouraging environment. They tend to be less dependent and shy. Parents are also more committed to the full day, due in part to a belief that the program offers their children a better school experience. Research also indicates that full-day programs do not cause increased stress or fatigue for young children (Emery et al., 1997). In fact, side benefits of being full time in one setting include stress reduction resulting from both reduced transitions and travel for children between ECE settings and home and increased continuity in their relationships with other children and adults.

Research shows that pre-K and full-day kindergarten programs produce measurable results for young learners. The establishment of such programs has momentum throughout the United States and is receiving great interest all over the country. One major challenge is to ensure that, in the future, there will be ongoing integration of pre-K and kindergarten programs with the early elementary grades with respect to academic standards, curriculum, and assessment in order to maintain and extend the gains made by the children who attend the early childhood programs. Moreover, colleges and universities need to establish quality teacher-education programs—in particular, public school EDE and P–3 programming—to develop and support educators who understand child development and early education. The success of these ideas will be gauged in the early years by assessments but also by the lives of children as they become stronger students and more productive citizens.

Example Programs

Full-day programs around the country have been asked to prove their worth under the academic achievement model of education. Many school districts are working to implement their programs and to provide assessment data in areas that standards-based education deems important. To reach this goal, models of pre-K and full-day kindergarten need to provide children with challenging curriculum. However, these programs must also be developmentally and individually appropriate. Teachers must work toward having their programs reflect the developmental model and not just the academic achievement model (Armstrong, 2006).

In Montgomery County Public Schools in Maryland, a suburban community close to Washington, D.C., full-day kindergarten was implemented and researched prior to the state mandate of offering full-day kindergarten to all children in 2006. In this program, children who attended full-day programs showed higher achievement than those who attended half-day programs. This was especially true for students who were in a lower socioeconomic category and those who were English language learners. More than 80% of kindergarten students achieved at least foundational reading skills by the end of the school year, 69% were reading text, and 33% were reading at the first-grade level or beyond. Moreover, children who participated in free or reduced-price meal programs benefited the most from the full-day programming available in Montgomery County. Remarkably, 71% of these students reached foundational reading skills by the end of the school year, up from 5% at the initial time of testing. By contrast, only 54% of half-day kindergarten students from this low-income group were foundational readers at the end of the school year. Full-day programs that emphasize language were reported to be most effective in this study, especially for lower-income children and English language learners (Montgomery County Public Schools, 2001).

In Manheim Central School District in Pennsylvania, full-day programming was implemented as a pilot study in 2001. Data were collected comparing full-day kindergarten students with their half-day counterparts. Several assessment measures were utilized; data shown to school board members suggested measurable benefits for students. At the end of the year, using an evaluation tool to assess writing skills, 63% of full-day students reached the advanced level compared to 32% of half-day children. The district also used a high-frequency word recognition assessment and found that 89% of full-day children reached the advanced level, compared to 52% for the half-day children. In the Direct Reading Assessment (DRA) the comparison was notable as well. Of full-day students, 85% reached the advanced section, but only 45% of half-day children reached this level. The data are hard to ignore. Children in full-day kindergarten programs outperformed their counterparts in half-day kindergarten programs on all measures.

The results found in another setting, East Pennsboro Area School District in Enola, Pennsylvania, are strikingly similar. This school district implemented two full-day programs in each of two elementary buildings in 2004. Data were collected to compare the all-day classrooms with their half-day sections. Using the same writing evaluation tool as Manheim Central, 44% of full-day students reached the advanced level by mid-year while only 3% of half-day children met that same level. Using the Dynamic Indicators of Basic Early Literacy Skills (DIBELS), 42% of full-day students were shown to have low risk in the phonemic segmentation section, and 41% of half-day students scored in the at-risk category on this measure. On the initial sound fluency section of the DIBELS assessment tool, 27% of full-day students reached the established category at the mid-year evaluation point, while only 13% of half-day students were at the same level. These data were presented to the school board during the spring of the pilot year. The board members also were shown examples of the quality programming and educational structure that were developed by the teachers. In addition, the children and parents spoke to the board members and shared their enthusiasm and commitment to the idea of full-day kindergarten. At the meeting the discussion became more about the children and less about the data. The East Pennsboro School Board voted 9 to 1 to implement full-day kindergarten for all children in the district beginning in 2005.

Philosophy

The framing philosophy of pre-kindergarten and full-day kindergartens and public school EDE programs overall should be consistent and compatible with developmentally appropriate practices. Four key areas of growth should be nurtured: social, emotional, physical, and cognitive. All are interrelated and equally important in the classroom. Teachers must be prepared to match the curriculum and methods of instruction with each child's stage of development and individual needs. Differentiated instruction is a key component to any early childhood setting. Each child possesses different developmental needs and learning styles.

Children learn best when they are actively engaged in meaningful and appropriate activities that are child centered. Accordingly, the classroom should be a place full of inquiry, activity, questions, and excitement. The children can be involved in activities such as painting, planting, measuring, writing, dramatizing, listening, talking, cooperating, exploring, singing, dancing, moving, resting, and building, and all the while they are learning. All these activities need to be challenging, geared to abilities and interests, and responsive to individual differences in language use, cultural backgrounds, and special educational needs.

Design and Implementation

The design of pre-K and full-day kindergarten programs should take into account the needs and interests of the children, both developmentally and individually. The components of developmentally appropriate practices and the current standards employed by each state are intertwined to produce a child developmental model that is also based in academic integrity. In contrast, any form of an academic "push down" curriculum would be unacceptable for children at the pre-K, kindergarten, and primary-grade levels.

When kindergarten programs are based in these appropriate practices, a full day will increase the chance for long- and short-term gains for children (Fromberg, 1995; Herman, 1984; Naron, 1981). By having more time to spend with children, teachers are able to understand learning styles and needs of the children. This increased time also allows for a more complete and multifaceted program for all children (Emery et al., 1997; Morrow, Strickland & Woo, 1998). This provides more time for children to explore concepts and practice acquired skills, leading to more in-depth development of concepts and more skill development. In addition, full-day programs afford the opportunity for a greater variety of educational experiences.

An appropriate schedule for pre-K and full-day kindergarten should allow for extended blocks of uninterrupted time for activities that are play oriented and linked to learning standards from state mandates. This increased time provides flexibility in its use and thus more opportunities for student-initiated choices of activities during which they are motivated to try to do more literacy activities (Morrow et al., 1998). By providing this increased time for young children in appropriate early childhood settings, programs allow additional learning and growing time that can be a most effective and appropriate way to help young children master the information and skills needed to meet the high educational system standards in this era of accountability (Grant, 1998).

A typical day in a pre-K or full-day kindergarten program should allow for various activities and student choices. The daily schedule from the kindergarten classroom of one of the coauthors (Jennifer Chestnut) included the following:

Settling-In Time. As children arrive, they are allowed time to ease into their day, put their personal things away in their own spot, and have a choice of play-oriented activities. This time also allows the teacher to check in with each child, providing the important human interaction that helps to build and maintain the crucial relationships needed to increase learning opportunities and social/emotional development.

Morning Meeting or Circle Time. Children are called together in the community of learners to meet and greet each other and their teachers. Through the use of songs, language activities, and stories, teachers are able to incorporate literacy and other standards into this portion of the day and to do this in a developmentally appropriate way.

Learning Centers. These allow children to have a choice and to feel in control of the activities that they choose. The environment should be set up in a play-center-oriented structure that allows children to move freely between centers. A snack-time center is part of this section of the day, providing children with a nutritious snack to energize their bodies. Teachers work to promote learning opportunities for all children, guiding their choices and offering opportunities for activities that are appealing to children and match standards in the early childhood curriculum.

Outdoor Play. All children need to have time to move and play in the outdoors. This is a time for teachers to observe and offer new learning experiences for children in a different environment. The outdoor play area is considered an extension of the classroom, providing children with play experiences that are also linked to standards. Outdoor playtime also supports children's physical and motor development. Even the youngest children face health issues related to physical activity and nutrition in the early childhood settings.

Lunch. This provides opportunities for enrichment and additional learning for children across all developmental areas. Teachers in pre-K and kindergarten programs should begin the year by eating lunch with their children. Teachers can facilitate healthy eating habits, appropriate social interaction, and cognitive development through conversation and other symbolic expression. Children can practice language and communication skills with their peers and with the teacher in this less formal school setting.

Special-Area Classes. This time provides children with the opportunity to meet with music instructors, physical education teachers, computer guides, and art instructors in a different environment outside the usual classroom setting.

Closing Meeting. This provides time at the end of the day to review and share and to look ahead and make plans. Children may offer stories from their day experiences or share items they created during learning centers. This time allows the children to feel part of the classroom community and to have a sense of importance and belonging. Teachers work to include all children and also to continue to build relationships and to discuss future plans and events with the children.

Evaluation Issues

As the importance of quality early childhood experiences has come to the forefront of the work of educational leaders, researchers, and policy makers, the need has increased for research-based and other information associated with various aspects of such programming. Many early childhood and child development proponents are now examining the ways in which pre-K and pre-K–3 models can have positive effects on children's learning that are sustainable throughout the school years and beyond. Although the positive effects of pre-K experiences in the landmark studies such as the Perry Preschool Program intervention have been widely noted, enthusiasm over the results from these famous intervention studies have been tempered; other research has suggested the lack of long-term benefits sustained into the elementary years. For example, a child who participates in only one year of early education usually has not received enough preschool to reap sustaining benefits into the primary grades and beyond. Two years of intervention starting in the toddler or early preschool age range are needed for optimal impact.

Furthermore, program quality is very important. If pre-K and full-day kindergartens want to get the same positive effects as the landmark studies, then they have to do what these model programs did. Teachers have to be highly qualified specialists in ECE, and high adult–child ratios, family-based practices, and child-initiated curriculum are necessary. Moreover, attention must be given to what actually takes place in classrooms; it is insufficient to mandate a certain level of teacher education and a certain type of teacher specialization. A current and popular assessment for estimating classroom instruction, organization, and atmosphere is *Children's Learning Opportunities in Early Childhood and Elementary Classrooms (CLASS)* (Hamre & Pianta, 2006).

Third and fourth grades are important transitional years for children. Long-term success in later schooling is often at stake. Children must have the academic skills necessary to continue to progress and engage in school experiences by this time, or they risk school failure. Children are expected to demonstrate academic achievement to reflect the benefits of their earlier educational experiences. For example, third grade is the first point for testing under NCLB; teachers usually feel considerable pressure to prepare children for these standardized tests. This pressure is a main impetus behind the commonplace pushdown of testing and standards into the lower grades and even into pre-K and kindergarten programs.

The National Center for Education Statistics and the Northwest Evaluation Association have recently reported that most fourth-graders are not performing at proficiency levels and many are at the basic level on math and reading achievement standardized tests (Kingsbury, Olson, Cronin, Hauser, & Houser, 2003; National Center for Education Statistics, 2007). Only about 15% of low-income Hispanic and Black children are proficient readers, with about 40% of Asian and white fourth-graders scoring as proficient readers. In light of these results, a new model of education for children ages pre-K through third grade is clearly welcome; fortunately, one has been proposed to help reinforce the learning processes of the pre-K and K years and continue them throughout the elementary years.

Pre-K to Third-Grade Initiative

The PK–3 vision is developmental at its core and as such is a hopeful and humanistic one that can serve as tonic for hard-line school readiness discourse that is prevalent in the United States today. Externally, this vision encompasses universal availability of the full range of state-funded programs for 3- and 4-year olds (e.g., school- and community-based pre-K, Head Start, and family child care), all-day kindergarten, and high adult–child ratios in the primary grades. Saturday morning and summer enrichment activities, weekday wraparound child-service and educational programs, mixed-age and multi-grade classes, and flexible individual planning of academic programs for children—all are commonly seen in PK–3 schools. Furthermore, another distinctive feature is the inclusion of families in all communities as a resource for the academic development of their children, especially enlisting and empowering families in minority and immigrant communities toward this end. Noteworthy is that the PK–3 approach is compatible with the 21C movement launched in 1988. This national, comprehensive, school-based reform initiative clearly shows that our public schools can be used for preschool and nonacademic services (Zigler, Gilliam, & Jones, 2006).

Internally and more significantly, the PK–3 vision presumes that school readiness is a two-way street. Not only must the preschool years include developmentally enriching experiences to enable young children to gain the most from their first classroom-learning encounters and to be successful in school, but also schools must be responsive to the developmental variability that young students bring to the classroom. Teachers need to be sensitive and responsive to individual differences in the needs and interests of specific children in their class, as well as knowledgeable about differential rates of child development and about specific curriculum content (Graue, Kroeger, & Brown, 2003).

Another defining feature of the PK–3 initiative, as an educational reform to create a coordinated EDE system, is a major emphasis on the alignment of curriculum and learning, standards or educational goals, and assessment—horizontally, vertically, and temporally (Kauerz, 2006). Horizontal alignment refers to matching up standards, curriculum, and assessments within a single grade level; vertical alignment refers to the same across grade levels; and temporal alignment concerns the child's learning over the entire calendar year, which then also includes learning on weekends and in the summer between grade levels.

Continuity of learning experiences is needed for education to be developmentally sound. PK–3 aspires to provide such education for children and their families during the crucial formative years. The PK–3 initiative aims for a seamless system of standards, curriculum, assessment, and teacher preparation. This *pedagogical* alignment assumes that *structural* or *behavioral* or *functional* alignment in the form of orientation meetings, communication, and transfer of records exists and is well maintained (Kagan & Kauerz, 2007). Structural alignment is much more common in practice at the present time than is pedagogical alignment.

The PK–3 movement challenges EDE researchers, teacher educators, and practitioners to maintain a holistic and contextualized view of the young child. For example, as many experts in the field have suggested, no longer would anyone ask whether play and socializing goals *or* learning and academic goals should be included in programs for young children. EDE in the 21st century does not operate in such an either/or mode. Both play *and* learning are important, just as what happens to the child at home and at school are both important. Learnful play *and* playful learning are both critical factors for successful curricular planning and implementation from pre-K through third grade. Having this outlook on play and learning is especially important for successful realization of the PK–3 approach because play and learning have often been dichotomized in the past with play as something preschoolers do and learning as something school-age children do. Play and learning need to be combined for EDE to be developmentally appropriate, responsive, and engaging over the range of years represented by the PK–3 approach. In general, the PK–3 vision requires that we view learning as taking place in a dynamic system that includes multiple and interacting development–affective, cognitive, social, physical, and attitudinal or dispositional dimensions (i.e., approaches to learning).

The current PK–3 initiative affecting the United States at this time is in its infancy but is nevertheless an extremely important movement for the ECE field and for the public education institution. School reform based on an aligned and coordinated PK–3 educational system seems very promising, and it is based on research in early education and child development (Bogard & Takanishi, 2005; Kauerz, 2006; Maeroff, 2006). Since the year 2001 when the Foundation for Child Development began promoting the PK–3 initiative *Success by Third,* this movement has been gaining increasing attention in state departments of education across the United States (Boots, 2006). In addition, more and more school principals and others are now asking how to implement PK–3 rather than inquiring what it is all about or why one should do it (Foundation for Child Development, 2006).

FirstSchool. In North Carolina, an innovative idea in public education is being examined and structured into an actual school program. FirstSchool is a model program exemplifying the PK–3 vision of education reform and is funded by the Foundation for Child Development, which has "Success by Third" as a rallying cry. Many more children can be successful if they have a continuity of good learning experiences from pre-K through the third grade. FirstSchool is an effort to reexamine public education and the structure of the school setting. FirstSchool is being implemented to promote and support public school efforts to become more attuned to the needs and interests of the youngest learners. This effort to rethink public education offers new ideas, formats, and ways of thinking and problem solving about how we can better serve children at the youngest levels in the public school setting (Ritchie, Maxwell, & Clifford, 2007).

As state departments of education and school districts consider the importance of the early years, many leaders and policy makers are examining full-day kindergarten as well as pre-K programs. Currently, 40 states fund pre-K programs for at least some of their population of 4-year-olds; most are targeted to low-income families, and nationally only about 10% of preschoolers attend these programs (Zigler et al., 2006).

Public schools must be responsible to family needs and interests.

Krista Greco/Merrill

The idea of universal preschool is finding strength and backing throughout the United States, and these pre-K programs will likely continue to grow over the next few years so that public pre-K is available to more and more 3- and 4-year-olds and is a choice for all families as they work to enhance the lives of their children. As these programs are laid in place, it will be crucial to consider whether the pre-K classrooms should be added to the existing structure of public schools or whether early education and the structure of public primary and elementary schools should be reexamined (Foundation for Child Development, 2003). Should preschools be linked or integrated into the broader spectrum of formal education?

The vision of FirstSchool is grounded in the work of child development experts and aligned with standards and ideas put forth by the National Association for the Education of Young Children, the National Association of State Boards of Education, the National Education Association, and the National Education Goals Panel:

> FirstSchool is a learning community in which development and education of 3-to-8-year-old children [are] at the heart of everything we do. Every child has a right to a successful, enjoyable, high quality FirstSchool experience that fosters intellectual, physical, emotional, and social well-being, and optimizes learning and development. In partnership with families and communities, FirstSchool accepts responsibility for preparing each child for a lifetime of learning—in school and beyond. (FirstSchool, n.d.)

Educators must provide the highest quality of school experiences for the youngest learners; children need to develop in every domain—cognitive, physical, social, and emotional. Children must have a school where they are able to develop knowledge, skills, attitudes, and behaviors necessary to become productive citizens in our society. Our children deserve a school environment where they are able to acquire self-confidence, self-respect, and a lifelong love of learning. Children deserve to have a school where they learn to read and write and to problem solve in appropriate and stimulating contexts. Moreover, all children are better served in a school setting that understands the need to foster creativity, independence, a sense of wonder, and a love of school—all these characteristics of a good school lay the groundwork for all other learning opportunities children will have throughout their lives. FirstSchool aspires to become such a school. It hopes to become an example for others to follow so that all children can attend such schools in the 21st century.

The conceptual model of the FirstSchool is under construction at this time; its evolving and open structure and process are viewed as essential to progress in school planning and implementation in the future. FirstSchool proponents intend to integrate other existing models into the conceptual model to provide a more comprehensive theoretical framework to steer their efforts; they will not rely solely on their own conceptual model. The model of this innovative program will be based on common principles from many areas. Some important principles come from the systems change literature, developmental systems theory, and sociocultural and cognitive theories; also, the concepts of constructivism and social justice will find expression in this school (Ritchie et al., 2007).

FirstSchool also includes other key aspects on which the program under construction will be based. The first aspect is positive relationships. The formation of quality, positive relationships is considered crucial to every aspect of learning and life. From the planning to the implementation, formation, and evaluation of the program, positive relationships will be a guiding principle in the process leading to a successful result. A second key aspect is the social context of learning. Accordingly the work of Vygotsky is very relevant, as is the work of others from social constructivist or sociocultural traditions. A third key aspect is a prosocial emphasis. FirstSchool seeks to establish positive prosocial environments characterized by mutual respect and appreciation, reciprocity in relationships, and sharing, cooperation, and helping. FirstSchool in progress encourages a positive interaction process for adults and children involved in the development of this new program (Ritchie et al., 2007).

FirstSchool also recognizes the commitment to dialogue. Quality conversation with open-ended Socratic inquiry is seen as essential to planning for successful learning and development in children. Again, the importance of positive interpersonal relationships is seen as indispensable for these conversations to occur. As diverse groups continue their work in designing and implementing new programs, relationships based on trust and a shared commitment to a common goal are sought. Such relationships will enable diverse stakeholders to achieve quality communication in creating the infrastructure for FirstSchool. A diverse group of experts and citizens serves on planning committees; they represent the community, the university, and the school district and are currently working together to make FirstSchool a reality for the benefit of all the children to be served. FirstSchool is further seen as a vital component of change and is thus considered to be a future asset for young children everywhere.

FirstSchool works to blend evidence from research studies with innovation and creative thinking from practice. The best teaching practices and school and classroom policies for young children are informed by research in family involvement, child development, social sciences, and pedagogy. Policies and practices will follow developmentally appropriate guidelines in their implementation. FirstSchool exhibits a dramatic shift in thinking as it works to link evidence-based research to practice in the everyday settings of the school. Practitioners will work to identify, evaluate, and interpret the research to guide and apply better practices for educational reform.

Equity is another fundamental of FirstSchool. Equity in public education has been a much argued point throughout the history of schools. It also represents a multifaceted process that schools must consider if progress is to be made for children. In the planning stages of FirstSchool, equity is evident through the involvement of diverse groups of people, the encouragement of their participation in the dialogues, the recognition and questioning of assumptions, and the assurance that each child will receive the necessary components to contribute to his or her success in school. FirstSchool thinking follows social justice perspectives and recognizes inequalities in public education associated with race, social class, language differences, and gender. Democratic principles are used in the process of creating and launching FirstSchool—for the benefit of children, families, the school, the community, and society overall.

Another key component of FirstSchool is the contribution of context to content. The work begun by these dedicated educators can have far-reaching effects on the lives of children everywhere. Although FirstSchool is based in one local community, the context of their work may reach from a micro-level outlook to a more national approach to education. FirstSchool operates in this planning stage and will employ, in later implementation, a flexible conceptual framework that is mindful of a range of community contexts and specific concrete circumstances. FirstSchool anticipates variations in implementation that will depend largely on differences in individual contexts and community involvement in their work on educational reform for the benefit of society.

The idea of the PK–3 grade alignment of FirstSchool was broadened to include the local K–5 model already in place within an actual local community. The initial work includes aligning the curriculum along both horizontal and vertical paths and the integration of preschool children and their families into the local school structure. The alignment of instructional practices and environments between pre-K and kindergarten must constantly seek to improve and promote smooth transitions for all children. Currently, FirstSchool is working to partner with community officials, local school leaders, and families to negotiate the building of a modern physical facility in which the FirstSchool ideas will be placed. The completion date is set for 2010.

FirstSchool is only one working example of the PK–3 idea. There are many others, and the numbers of PK–3 schools and school districts are increasing. The National Association of Elementary School Principals is an advocate of linking early learning to the broader educational spectrum. Also, while PK–3 is a current trend and hope for school improvement, the idea has existed for years. For example, in Los Angeles, California, the Valerio Primary Center has been working to improve the delivery of education and services to the youngest learners since 1987.

Valerio contains pre-kindergarten, kindergarten, first grade, and second grade, and it is one of 11 schools devoted to early childhood initiatives in the Los Angeles Unified School District. It illustrates an important way quality schools can use best practices for young children. The communication among the teachers is strong across each level. All staff members are aware of each child's abilities, interests, needs, and progress in different domains such as language use, reading, mathematics, self-expression, and problem solving. The small learning communities generate a certain closeness or "family feel" that enables children to feel secure and important. The successes of Valerio children are recognized and celebrated as the kids reach higher achievement levels relative to their peers in the regular Valerio Elementary School. In addition, Valerio teachers are learners who keep current on their colleagues' work and participate in relevant professional development opportunities. Their commitment to learning plays a key role in the development of appropriate learning opportunities and pedagogy for their work with young children. Again, success is linked to the small learning community; the teachers know each other, the children, the families, and their own teacher needs at an intimate and important level (Maeroff, 2006).

Consider a second example of an older similar program. More than 10 years ago the central PK–3 idea of alignment came to the schools in Greece, New York. It came not as a new philosophy in ECE practices but as a means to solve a very practical problem: overcrowding. Families were moving to the suburbs of the Greece area and the K–5 and K–6 buildings could not accommodate this increasing population. So education officials redistricted the area and created K–2 schools that still operate today. The community has come to appreciate and value the concentrated effort that these schools offer to the youngest learners. A more aligned and coordinated program is operating. The focus on child development and early childhood practices has added to the success of the schools, which have achieved a coordinated and aligned continuum of learning experiences for the children enrolled and serve as small neighborhoods within the school district. This helps with family engagement in school activities and with children's learning and development. Each K–2 school is also linked and partnered with a nearby 3–5 school, which helps with the transitioning between the schools (Foundation for Child Development, 2007).

Advocacy: Research, Policies, and Practices

Three types of functions are associated with public school EDE programs: (1) service based, (2) teaching and guidance based, and (3) research and scholarship based.

Service. Developing public school EDE programs should improve the quality of basic services to children and families in public education and other settings as the United States inches toward a more comprehensive and better coordinated system of EDE in the new millennium. Quality personnel preparation and professional development are required to address social and individual needs and challenges relating to school readiness for young children on the one hand, and in connection with socialization and child-rearing support for parents or parent surrogates on the other hand.

Public school EDE programs can be especially responsive to current societal and familial needs when they put a concerted effort on balancing developmental enrichment with academic goals in basic EDE service delivery. Required will be their systematically addressing in a coordinated manner the needs of children and parents and the needs of EDE practitioners at various stages of their careers as they perform different functions in various job situations. In addition, public school EDE, across the various educational components, must give considerable attention to special education and inclusion, as well as to the particular needs and interests of English language learners and to education that is in general multicultural.

The most promising kinds of public school EDE programs are the ones that are responsive to family and community needs and interests. They are center based and have instructional supports and family services and community outreach (Reynolds, 2006). Respect and trust are built through communication and commitment to the "whole child" concept. Just as the child is viewed to be an integrated whole being living in particular real-world contexts, school-based programs providing a broad array of services must be designed and implemented in an integrated fashion (Pelletier & Corter, 2006; Perry, Kaufmann, & Knitzer, 2006). Though rare, the best public school EDE programs have deep integration of philosophy and goals, curriculum, staffing, governance, protocols, and funding sources. The same may be said about ECCE programs outside the public schools. Here, though, a key concern is the linkage between systems and the issue of transitioning children between ECCE programs and EDE programs in the public schools.

Teaching and Guidance. Public school EDE needs to provide curriculum, instruction, and assessment for children and parents. Moreover, resources must be available that can be used to foster and to scaffold EDE professional practitioners in the various stages of their career trajectories. Additional and more flexible professional and career opportunities can be generated and supported in the broad field of EDE—within and across public schools and other work settings. Those entering public school EDE without public school teaching certificates, for example, may be positioned to move into certified public school teaching at a later date in their careers with additional course work and practicum. Paraprofessionals in public-school EDE, for example, can have their work count toward fulfilling the requirements for bachelor's and master's degrees in ECE. Articulation of credits for degrees and certificates should be a central goal helping older students who are veterans in ECCE form unique or individualized careers in public education EDE. In addition, public education EDE programs are an ongoing resource for the consultation needs of other public school administrators and veteran teachers during periods of transition anticipated as more schools and school districts move into the design and implementation of EDE programs and systems.

Research. Public school EDE can also serve consultation and collaboration needs of researchers who seek to pose questions and to conduct studies relevant to the practices and policies of public school EDE programs. Public school EDE programs afford many opportunities to learn about a wide range of research problems, methods, analytic tools, concepts, and theories generated and encouraged by the interdisciplinary nature of the various endeavors. Researchers and practitioners can come to better understand the importance of a team approach to investigating and developing interventions for complex social and educational problems. They can come to appreciate and employ multiple and complementary modes of inquiry and analysis from different theoretical and disciplinary perspectives related to different domains of applicability in public school EDE.

Such undertakings can also benefit research and scholarship by creating new or additional opportunities for multidisciplinary conversations and investigations on problems or topics of shared concern. Professional development ensues from such collaborations, as well as from the spawning of ideas for cross-disciplinary projects. This communal scholarship should prove very beneficial for the advancement of "practice-embedded research," which includes not only practice-driven research and practice-oriented research, both currently now common in developmental science and prevention research, but also practice-inspired research now more common in educational and teacher action research especially.

For example, Selman and Dray (2006) recently urged balanced appreciation between research-informed practice and practice-informed research, introducing the three terms used in the preceding paragraph: (practice driven, practice oriented, and practice inspired) to replace the old adage "Link theory and research to practice." For this to happen, certain kinds of partnerships between researchers and practitioners are needed, characterized by mutual respect and a deeper understanding of each other's perspectives, backgrounds, work contexts, and work scopes. Significantly, public school EDE may help prepare practitioners and researchers for having such partnerships. In turn, this may favorably influence the climate of college and university faculties toward the realization of partnerships in academia to generate new collaborative programs to prepare personnel for public school EDE in the years to come.

In the context of public school EDE, teachers, child service workers, and other practitioners can become better informed about the benefits and limitations of research. In the future, teachers may be more astute judges of research quality, better able to recognize flaws in studies, and be less susceptible to incorrect uses of research. They may acquire a more balanced appreciation for the contributions of research investigations in relation to the value of learning from mentors who may or may not be the best examples of practice. For their part, researchers can grow in their understanding of the concrete realities facing classroom teachers and can acquire a more nuanced appreciation of teachers' values and beliefs. Partnerships between educators and researchers can lead to the formulations of important new research questions and can set the stage for more useful and ecologically valid investigations. This will improve public school EDE and ECCE together.

Years of research and theory construction and theory testing in developmental and prevention science and education science have created an excellent knowledge base that can inform the design and content of PK–3 and other EDE programs. Programs of professional preparation and development are needed to create and to support a high-quality EDE workforce. Public school EDE programs seek to help narrow the gulf that currently exists between theory and research knowledge on one side and actual policies and practices on the other.

Teacher Education

EDE is a cornerstone of American educational reform (Zigler et al., 2006), and the PK–3 movement in EDE is one of its central features. A new breed of teachers, administrators, and child-service workers are needed to help the PK–3 initiative succeed. Clearly, then, obtaining and maintaining the kind of high-quality work force that we need for PK–3 demands professional preparation and development in the special areas of child development and early education (Bowman, Donovan, & Burns, 2009; Shonkoff & Phillips, 2000), including positioning EDE and ECCE practitioners to work with all children—typically developing children, and children who are language learners and who come from diverse cultural backgrounds and with varying levels of acculturation, and children with special educational needs.

Achieving good preservice education and professional development programs to prepare and to support all personnel in their tasks of helping children get ready for school and learn for success in later grades, and assisting working families, are important goals. We must have these programs set to produce trained teachers and child-service workers to work in existing and future PK–3 educational settings throughout school districts. We must also serve ECCE programs that remain outside the public schools.

High-quality EDE and ECCE programs are characterized by a number of factors, such as developmentally responsive teaching, appropriate and engaging materials, curricular activities, and parent involvement. Having high-quality EDE and ECCE teachers is especially important. Good teachers are essential for helping children overcome pervasive and persistent educational shortcomings. Research shows that the professional development of teachers in the special areas of child development and ECE is the primary factor in ensuring the quality of EDE programs and positive child outcomes in the form of later academic success (Bowman et al., 2000; Shonkoff & Phillips, 2000).

Accordingly, for the United States or any nation to succeed in narrowing its achievement gap, good teacher-education programs must prepare high-quality EDE and ECCE teachers. In the United States, support for this mandate is provided by revised and improved standards for EDE and ECCE teacher preparation from the National Association for the Education of Young Children (NAEYC) and the National Council for Accreditation of Teacher Education (NCATE) (Hyson, 2003), by a position paper by the Association for Childhood Education International (ACEI, 2004), and by a white paper by the American Association of Colleges for Teacher Education (AACTE, 2004). These standards and papers are statements of the need to have good teachers to have good EDE and ECCE programs that can help bridge the achievement gap in our fast-moving times. These standards and recommendations recognize that new challenges and needs are facing the profession of EDE in a world marked by accelerated changes with respect to cultural and linguistic diversity and changing family structures, geographic locations, and values.

Programs that prepare new teachers are concerned about what knowledge, skills, and dispositions their graduates will have when they begin their teaching careers in EDE. Good EDE teachers should have at a minimum (1) knowledge of child development, (2) understanding of developmentally appropriate practices (DAP) and assessment, including the importance of play, (3) knowledge and understanding of the foundations for literacy and numeracy and effective methods to foster their development, and the development of knowledge in other areas, such as beginning science, social studies, art or music, and (4) understanding of the children and families with whom they work (AACTE, 2004; Hyson, 2003).

Preservice and in-service programs also need to help EDE and ECCE teachers and child service workers develop or further develop a personal philosophy and approach to the learning/teaching process consistent with research and theory (ACEI, 2004). To aspire to a more complete personal philosophy and a more comprehensive and thoughtful approach to EDE and ECCE, teachers should also become acquainted with curricular or program models in the field. A better sense of professional identity in the teacher and child-service worker can be achieved when programs include coverage of model EDE programs or curricula such as High/Scope, Bank Street, Montessori, Projects Approach, and many others. The present volume and its previous editions were written to help accomplish this teacher education goal.

An ECE graduate should also aim to become increasingly resourceful and knowledgeable about planning and carrying out research projects. Sometimes these projects are action-based in concrete practical settings and involve generating original empirical data to help answer research questions. Many times they are investigations of the literature to review a topic and to draw out implications for practice, using archival and translative methods. A considerable degree of computer literacy is needed.

Research ability also entails being able to read the literature critically, make sound judgments about the strengths and weaknesses of studies, and make correct inferences and recognize limitations or flaws in how research studies are designed or carried out, including understanding issues related to reliability and internal and external validity. EDE and ECCE preservice programs at a minimum must plant the seeds of competence in their students in this area of research and inquiry.

EDE and ECCE also require a sense of professionalism that includes knowledge, skills, and dispositions for collaboration with other human-service workers and an appreciation of the social ecology of the child, family, school, neighborhood, and community. *Social ecology* can refer to mental health issues, health, safety, moral well-being, family realities, vertical integration with later schooling, informal learning in public places, including faith-based public places, and the influence of media, popular culture, and technology. In addition, knowing and adhering to the professional code of ethics and being able to make sound ethical judgments are indispensable components of professionalism.

Finally, professionalism includes *political awareness and action* (e.g., concern about such issues as funding for programs, teacher salaries, other compensation, poverty, public health, consumer exploitation of children, and corporate interference with schools in the form of test and book publishing companies peddling developmentally inappropriate materials and technologies).

TRANSITIONS AND TEAMWORK

The transition from home, child care, or preschool to the formal public school is an important time in the lives of children and families. This beginning step into the educational system can influence later school success and set the stage for positive school experiences. This early schooling is considered a critical period that determines future school happiness and adjustment abilities (Belsky & MacKinnon, 1994; Pianta & McCoy, 1996). The success that young children feel at this time of their lives can affect how they view the school setting and the overall school experience.

Unfortunately, the transitional period between child care or preschool to kindergarten is often overlooked by educators and caregivers. Children face changes in the buildings where they spend time, teachers, schedule, and overall school experiences and these changes are seldom articulated and prepared for as children approach the formal school setting. These changes also affect the teachers and the families as they work to help children adjust to this sudden and unfamiliar alteration in their lives.

Frank Siteman

Technology can enhance learning in Pre-K classrooms.

Changing school policies affect children, parents, teachers, and administrators. Academic requirements are also new and unfamiliar to students and families. Children and their families are also unaccustomed to the school culture and the social environment of the public school setting. For all these reasons, it is clear this critical transition to public school is a period that warrants attention and work to assist families, schools, and teachers in preparing children.

This is not to say that the preparation for school is not an exciting and anticipated time in the lives of young children and their parents. Generally, the first day of kindergarten is prepared for by families by purchasing book bags, new clothes, and school items. Children sense the excitement, and families await the first day of school with mixed emotions. This is a positive experience in the lives of our youngest learners; however, it comes with the unfamiliar feelings, newness, and unaccustomed territory of the big school experience. Children and schools must be prepared and transitioned in a way to promote success and positive attitudes as the school journey begins. School readiness and transitions to school are major topics in many communities, with a focus on connecting public school EDE with ECCE outside the public schools.

Transition time can be improved by simple communication. Public schools and child-care centers should begin the conversation and the partnership long before children arrive at the front door of the kindergarten classroom. The critical period of development that occurs during the preschool and kindergarten years could be coordinated and followed up in EDE and ECCE by those responsible for the nurturance and education of the youngest learners. ECE partnerships forged between EDE and ECCE should be established, and work should start to join the valuable knowledge base and skill set that all ECE experts and practitioners should possess about children, programs, standards, models, curriculum and instruction, and assessment. Also, teachers and administrators must form and maintain transitional plans, which may include visits to the school, family-night programs prior to the start of school, parent meetings during which ECCE and EDE teachers and families can share and communicate about the transition time, and young childrens' abilities, interests, and needs. But such functional coordination is not enough. There must also be work toward greater pedagogical alignment in standards, curriculum, and assessment across ECCE and EDE.

As this time of change is considered, the child is the primary focus. The highlight of this entire process is the relationships that are formed between the school, the child, the child-care program, and the family (Pianta & Kraft-Sayre, 1999). Relationships are the key to progress in our field in both basic and higher education. Teacher education in ECE must be aligned to standards, curriculum, and assessment in basic EDE and ECCE.

CHILDHOOD STUDIES

The field of childhood studies includes disciplines such as the sociology of childhood, history of childhood, politics of childhood, anthropology, child lore, and other areas. Obviously childhood studies and these disciplines are important sources of information for informing public school EDE as well. They can help us better understand the contexts of public school EDE and the lives of young children and their families. They can help us to appreciate the importance of social, political, and economic realities and to try to see matters from the child's and parent's points of view. Both developmental and clinical concepts, as well as social and political concepts, are needed to comprehensively understand and serve all the stakeholders in this effort to better use the institution of public education in EDE. Yet child development is the primary lens for viewing the complex phenomena of public school EDE.

In addition, two conceptual lenses needed for public school EDE are *pedagogy* and *content.*

These derive more from the bailiwick of education than from the social sciences. Pedagogy is about the teaching and learning nexus and communication and instruction. Content is subject matter from academic areas, such as science, social studies, mathematics, reading and the language arts, music, dance and movement, and art education. Pedagogy and content interact with child development and childhood studies to bring into view hints and clues for guiding the design, implementation, and evaluation of the hodgepodge of programs, practices, and policies that comprise the complex world of public school EDE.

CONCLUSION

The season may be at hand when ECE as the banner for the profession in public schools should be replaced by EDE. This radical idea makes sense for successfully realizing the potential of public schools for serving young children and their families. Unlike ECCE, EDE makes explicit the developmental primacy of educational endeavors. No longer are debates about care versus education needed here, even as they may still be valid in ECCE, particularly with reference to infants and toddlers. The proper way for public schools to embrace EDE and PK–3 as mandates in educational reform is to recognize child development as the foundation or primary conceptual lens of the field of education. Teachers, family-support experts, child-service workers, and other professionals in public school EDE must have child development in their blood and bones. They are all applied developmental psychologists incarnate. Nurturing and caring for children this way are built into the equation of teaching them and supporting and scaffolding their growth and development. Child development first—and not academic achievement—must guide public education (Armstrong, 2006).

The field of ECE (i.e., ECCE and public school EDE) is at a crucial point in its history as it has achieved greater public acceptance, support, and scrutiny. Leadership from the field of early care and education is needed to define and articulate its identity, its purpose, and its responsibilities—and to know how it can ensure holding on to its identity and core values and principles in the face of strong and growing involvement by government state departments and public institutions across the nation (Goffin & Washington, 2007). Within public school EDE an inevitable trickle down will occur from elementary school models of policies and practices concerning goals or standards of education, curriculum, and assessment. However, ECE needs to provide trickle *up* to ensure that EDE in the public schools links together care and education and a concern with the child's well-being in the here and now, and not just the child's performance at the next grade level. ECE leadership in this era of public accountability and diversity is critically important. We must insist that public school EDE programs be effective not only in the academic achievement sense but also that they are developmentally and culturally appropriate and responsive to families and communities.

Teacher education is also at a crossroads. To prepare teachers for public school EDE and PK–3 systems of education, personnel preparation programs in colleges and universities must change in a most profound sense. The division and competition between human development and family studies departments and curriculum and instruction departments must be reduced. Also, the separation between elementary education and early education faculty must be relaxed. Interdisciplinary communication and collaboration are expected of those in basic education—in public school EDE and also in other forms of ECE. Likewise, faculty in higher education must seek to work together across disciplines to evaluate what must change and what can stay the same in courses and field experiences for their students who will one day be employed to serve children and their families in the changing realities of the public schools and social life.

RECOMMENDED WEB SITES

Build Initiative
www.buildinitiative.org

A multi-state partnership to build coordinated and comprehensive systems of programs, policies, and services for children from birth to 5 years.

FirstSchool
www.fpg.unc.edu/~firstschool

The FirstSchool at Chapel Hill, North Carolina, is a multidisciplinary university and community project that is designing a new public school based on the vision of PK–3.

Foundation for Child Development
www.fcd-us.org

Foundation for Child Development is a national private philanthropy devoted to fostering child development and well-being and promoting complementary learning and serving the disadvantaged. It is the major force and support behind the PK–3 vision and mission in the United States today.

Foundation for Child Development
Standardized Classroom Observations from Pre-K to Third Grade: A Mechanism for Improving Quality Classroom Experiences During the P–3 Years.
http://www.fcd-us.org/resources/resources_show.htm?doc_id=467485

This paper provides information about the Classroom Assessment Scoring System (CLASS), an observational tool for research and teacher and program development. Three categories of the classroom are addressed: instructional, socioemotional, and classroom organization aspects.

National Association of Elementary School Principals (NAESP)
www.naesp.org/ContentLoad.do?contentid=49

The NAESP has on its Web page information on the role of principals and teachers in PK–3 schools and PK–3 case studies.

Pre[k]now
http://preknow.org

Pre[k]now is an advocacy and informational organization for pre-K in relation to K–12 education. It provides up-to-date profiles on what states are doing in public education and comprehensive coverage of research and information about pre-K programs.

School of the 21st Century
www.yale.edu/21C/index2.html

The School of the 21st Century began in 1988 and comes from the Edward Zigler Center in Child Development and Social Policy at Yale University. This innovative educational reform movement develops, researches, networks, and supervises school programs that unite families, communities, and schools.

Society for Research in Child Development (SRCD)
***2005 Social Policy Report* (July 2005)**
http://srcd.org/documents/publications/SPR/spring19-3.pdf.

The Society for Research in Child Development is a professional organization composed of applied developmental researchers and developmental psychologists. This landmark social policy report endorses a PK–3 approach to education that takes into account the developmental characteristics and abilities of children and seeks to ensure continuity in learning experiences across this age range.

REFERENCES

American Association of Colleges for Teacher Education (AACTE). (2004). *The early childhood challenge: Preparing high-quality teachers for a changing society.* A White Paper of the American Association of Colleges for Teacher Education Focus Council on Early Childhood Education, Washington, DC: AACTE.

Association for Childhood Education International (ACEI). (2004). *Preparation of early childhood teachers.* Position Paper. Olney, MD: Author.

Association of Supervision and Curriculum Development (ASCD). (2007, August). Pre-K, In Play. *Education Update 49*(8). Retrieved September 20, 2007, from http://www.ascd.org/authors/ed_update/eu200708_online.html

Armstrong, T. (2006). *The best schools.* Alexandria, VA: Association for Supervision and Curriculum Development.

Barnett, S., & Hustedt, J. (2003). Preschool: The most important grade. *Educational Leadership, 60*(7). Retrieved May 23, 2007, from http://www.ascd.org/authors/ed_lead/el200304_barnett.html

Belsky, J., & MacKinnon, C. (1994). Transition to school: Developmental trajectories and school experiences. *Early Education and Development, 5*(2), 106–119.

Bogard, K., & Takanishi, R. (2005). PK–3: An aligned and coordinated approach to education for children 3 to 8 years old. *Social Policy Report: Giving Child and Youth Development Knowledge Away, 19*(3), 1–23, Society for Research in Child Development.

Boots, S. (2006, January). *Preparing quality teachers for PK–3.* FCD Meeting Summary, Foundation for Child Development.

Bowman, B., Donovan, M., & Burns, M. (Eds.) (2000). *Eager to learn: Educating our preschoolers.* Washington, DC: National Academy Press.

Clark, P., & Kirk, E. (2000). All day kindergarten: Review of research. *Childhood Education, 76*(4), 228–231.

Elicker, J., & Mathur, S. (1997). What do they do all day? Comprehensive evaluation of a full day kindergarten. *Early Childhood Research Quarterly, 12*(4), 459–480.

Emery, J., Piche, C., & Rokavec, C. (1997). Full versus half day kindergarten programs: A brief history and research synopsis. Bethesda, MD: National Association of School Psychologists.

Finn-Stevenson, M. (2006). What the school of the 21st century can teach us about universal preschool. In E. Zigler, W. Gilliam, & S. Jones (Eds.), *A vision for universal preschool education* (pp. 194–215). New York: Cambridge University Press.

FirstSchool. (n.d.) Vision. Retrieved April 8, 2008, at http://www.fpg.unc.edu/~firstschool/newvision.cfm

Foundation for Child Development. (2003). First things first: Prekindergarten is the starting point for education reform. New York: Author.

Foundation for Child Development. (2006, October). Ready to teach? Providing children with the teachers they deserve. A Report from the Foundation for Child Development. New York: Foundation for Child Development.

Fromberg, D. (1995). *The full day kindergarten: Planning and practicing a dynamic themes curriculum.* New York: Teachers College, Columbia University.

Goldfarb, Z. (2007, May 22). Clinton goes to bat for pre-K. *The Washington Post,* p. 84.

Goffin, S., & Washington, V. (2007). *Ready or not: Leadership choices in early care and education.* New York: Teachers College Press.

Grant, J. (1998). *Developmental education in an era of high standards.* Rosemont, NJ: Modern Learning Press.

Graue, M., Kroeger, J., & Brown, C. (2003, Spring). The gift of time: Enactments of developmental thought in early childhood practice. *Early Childhood Research & Practice, 5*(1). Retrieved April 8, 2008, at http://ecrp.uiuc.edu/v5n1/graue.html

Hamre, B., & Pianta, R. (2006). Learning opportunities in preschool and early elementary classrooms. In R. Pianta, M. Cox, & K. Snow (Eds.), *School readiness and the transition to kindergarten in the era of accountability* (pp. 49–83). Baltimore, MD: Brookes.

Herman, B. (1984). The case for the all-day kindergarten. Bloomington, IN: *Phi Delta Kappa.*

Hyson, M. (Ed.). (2003). *Preparing early childhood professionals: NAEYC's standards for programs.* Washington, DC: National Association for the Education of Young Children.

International Kindergarten Union (1919). *The kindergarten curriculum.* Washington, DC: Government Printing Office.

Jacobson, L. (2007, February). Community vs. school-based pre-K, *Education Reform.* Retrieved May 3, 2007, from www.ewa.org/library/site/prek%20reform.pdf

Kagan, S., & Kauerz, K. (2007). In R. Pianta., M. Cox., & K. Snow (Eds.), *School readiness and the transition to kindergarten in the era of accountability* (pp. 11–30). Baltimore, MD: Brookes.

Kauerz, K. (2006, January). Ladders of learning: Fighting fade-out by advancing PK–3 alignment. New America Foundation Early Education Initiative. Issue Brief #2.

Kingsbury, G., Olson, A., Cronin, J., Hauser, C., & Houser, R. (2003). *The state of state standards: Research investigating proficiency levels in fourteen states.* Portland, OR: Northwest Evaluation Association.

Lee, V., & Burkam, D. (2002). *Inequality at the starting gate: Social background differences as children begin school.* Washington, DC: Economic Policy Institute.

Maeroff, G. (2006). Building blocks: Making children successful in the early years of school. New York: Palgrave Macmillan.

Malakoff, M. (2006). The need for universal prekindergarten for children in poverty. In E. Zigler, W. Gilliam, & S. Jones (Eds.), *A vision for universal preschool education* (pp. 69–88). New York: Cambridge University Press.

Montgomery County Public Schools. (2001, September 10). *Study shows significant gains in literacy skills prior to first grade.* Retrieved April 17, 2008, at http://search.mcps.k12.md.us/cs.html?charset=utf−8+url=http%3A//

Morrow, L. M., Strickland, D. S., & Woo, D. G. (1998). *Literacy instruction in half and whole day kindergarten.* Chicago: International Reading Association.

Naron, N. K. (1981). The need for full day kindergarten. *Educational Leadership, 38,* 33–39.

National Center for Educational Statistics (NCES). (2007). *Mapping 2005 State Proficiency Standards onto the NAEP Scales.* Washington, DC: United States Department of Education, Institute for Educational Sciences, National Center for Educational Statistics, 2007-482.

Nelson, C., & Bloom, F. (1997). Child development and neuroscience. *Child Development, 68*(5), 970–987.

Ogens, E. M. (1990). Consider a full day kindergarten. *School Leader,* March/April.

Pelletier, J., & Corter, C. (2006). Integration, innovation, and evaluation in school-based early childhood services. In B. Spodek & O. N. Saracho (Eds.), *Handbook of research on the education of young children,* 2nd ed. (pp. 477–496). Mawhaw, NJ: Erlbaum.

Perry, D., Kaufmann, R., & Knitzer, J. (2006). Building bridges: Linking services, strategies, and systems for young children and their families. In D. Perry, R. Kaufmann, & J. Knitzer (Eds.), *Social and emotional health in early childhood: Building bridges between services and systems* (pp. 3–11). Baltimore, MD: Brookes.

Pianta, R. C., & McCoy, S. (1996). *High-risk children in schools: Creating sustaining relationships.* New York: Routledge & Kegan Paul.

Pianta, R. C., & Kraft-Sayre, M. E. (1999). Parents' observations about their children's transitions to kindergarten. *Young Children, 54*(3), 47–52.

Reynolds, A. (2006, January). *PK–3 education: Programs and practices that work in children's first decade* (Working Paper: Advancing PK–3 No. 6). New York: Foundation for Child Development.

Reynolds, A., & Temple, J. (2006). Economic returns of investments in preschool education. In E. Zigler, W. Gilliam, & S. Jones (Eds.), *A vision for universal preschool education* (pp. 37–68). New York: Cambridge University Press.

Ritchie, S., Maxwell, K., & Clifford, R. M. (2007). FirstSchool: A new vision for education. In R. Pianta, M. Cox, & K. Snow (Eds.), *School readiness and the transition to kindergarten in the era of accountability* (pp. 85–96). Baltimore, MD: Brookes.

Selman, R., & Dray, A. (2006). Risk and prevention. In K. Renninger & I. Sigel (Eds.), *Handbook of child psychology: Vol. 4. Child psychology in practice* (6th ed., pp. 378–419). New York: Wiley.

Shonkoff, J. P, & Phillips, D. A. (Eds.). (2000). *From neurons to neighborhoods: The science of early childhood development.* Committee on

Integrating the Science of Early Childhood Development. National Research Council and Institute of Medicine, Washington, DC: National Academy Press.

Wat, A. (2007, May). Dollars and sense: A review of economic analyses of pre-K. Retrieved April 7, 2008, from www.preknow.org/documents/DollarsandSense_May2007.pdf

WestEd. (2005, April). *Full-day kindergarten: Expanding learning opportunities.* San Francisco: WestEd.

Zigler, E., Gilliam, W., & Jones, S. (2006). *A vision for universal preschool education.* New York: Cambridge University Press.

Part III
Specific Approaches: United States

Chapter 9
The High/Scope Model of Early Childhood Education

David P. Weikart (deceased) and Lawrence J. Schweinhart ~ High/Scope Educational Research Foundation, Ypsilanti, Michigan

The High/Scope model of early childhood education provides teachers with an open framework of educational ideas and practices based on the development of young children. David P. Weikart and his colleagues developed the model in the 1960s for use in the High/Scope Perry Preschool program (Weikart, Rogers, Adcock, & McClelland, 1971). The High/Scope Educational Research Foundation continues to develop and apply the model today, incorporating new research findings regarding literacy, mathematics, science, social development, health and physical development, the arts and computer usage, and helping people apply the model to new circumstances and new populations of children around the world (Epstein, 2007; Hohmann, 2002; Hohmann & Weikart, 2002). Thousands of early childhood programs throughout the United States and in other countries now use the High/Scope model (Epstein, 1993).

Based on the child development theories of Jean Piaget (Piaget & Inhelder, 1969) and Lev Vygotsky (1934/1962), the progressive educational philosophy of John Dewey (1938/1973), and the more recent work of cognitive-developmental psychology (e.g., Clements, 2004; Gelman & Brenneman, 2004; National Research Council, 2005) and brain research (Bruer, 2004; Shore, 1997; Thompson & Nelson, 2001), the High/Scope model recognizes children as *active learners,* who learn best from activities that they themselves plan, carry out, and reflect on. Adults use complex language as they observe, support, and extend the work of the child as appropriate. Adults arrange interest areas in the learning environment; maintain a daily routine that permits children to plan, carry out, and reflect on their own activities; and join in children's activities, engaging in conversations that scaffold and extend children's plans and help them think things through. The adults encourage children to make choices, solve problems, and otherwise engage in curriculum activities that contribute to their learning on key developmental indicators that encompass all areas of intellectual, social, and physical development.

The High/Scope model does not require the purchase and use of special materials, such as the materials required for a Montessori classroom or the teacher and student workbooks required for an academic instructional classroom. The only cost involved is that of equipping the learning environment as would be typical of any good nursery school program. In less-developed countries or other settings with limited resources, material from nature, household discards, and other found materials are employed. Although often challenging for adults to learn initially, the methods implementing the model, once mastered, free staff for comfortable work with children, other classroom adults, parents, and supervisors. Rooted firmly in developmental theory and historical early childhood practice, the High/Scope model is an organized and transferable expression of what has worked well with children in many programs over time. The model is an example of culturally and developmentally appropriate practice as commonly defined today by the early childhood field (e.g., Ramsey, 2006), and it has been validated by longitudinal studies over 40 years (Oden, Schweinhart, & Weikart, 2000; Schweinhart et al., 2005; Schweinhart & Weikart, 1997). In addition, it lends itself to training, supervision, implementation, and assessment so that parents and administrators can rest assured that their children are receiving a high-quality, validated program. Delivery of high-quality programs is the most important task the early childhood field faces, as program ideas move into large-scale service to children, their families, and society at large.

HISTORY

The High/Scope model's development began in 1962 with the High/Scope Perry Preschool program, a program for 3- and 4-year-olds operated at the Perry Elementary School in Ypsilanti, Michigan. This program was one of the first in the 1960s designed to help children overcome the negative effects of poverty on schooling, an idea later embodied in Head Start programs. It was one of the first to achieve an exacting experimental design—children were randomly assigned to attend or not—permitting researchers to trace the program's effects throughout the subsequent lives of participants. This study showed that the preschool program provided participants with a striking variety of short- and long-term benefits: better preparation for school, greater success throughout schooling, and in adulthood, a lower arrest rate, higher employment rate, and lower welfare rate. The program was found to pay for itself many times over in economic returns to taxpayers and program participants: $16.14 returned for every dollar spent (Schweinhart et al., 2005).

In the late 1950s, Ypsilanti Public Schools Special Education Director David Weikart was concerned that easily identifiable children were failing in school—repeating grade levels, being placed in special education, and dropping out. Seeking changes in the schools to address these problems, he was frustrated that school administrators had few realistic alternatives. He turned to the preschool years as a way of reaching children before they fell into the traditional school patterns that spawned their failure.

Staffed by research psychologists and teachers, the preschool program Weikart designed established a creative tension between the psychologist's demand for explicit rationale and the trained preschool teacher's intuitive approach to dealing with children. The High/Scope model evolved from give-and-take among a team of people who had definite ideas about how to do things but were open to new ideas and could integrate them into their thinking and practice.

As the High/Scope Perry Preschool program entered its second year, the staff encountered and embraced the child development ideas of Jean Piaget (summarized by Piaget & Inhelder, 1969). Piaget offered a conceptual structure around which an early childhood education model could be built, an explicit rationale for the preschool activities. Piaget offered the idea of the child as an active learner, an idea not only with intuitive appeal but also with strong roots in early childhood tradition dating back at least to Friedrich Froebel (1887) in the nineteenth century. Later, the work of psychologist and educator Lev Vygotsky (1934/1962), particularly the notion that development occurs within sociocultural settings where adults scaffold children's learning, became the foundation for the High/Scope teaching model.

As the High/Scope model developed, the national enthusiasm for early childhood education models also emerged. The federal government

Scott Cunningham/Merrill

Planned activities foster learning with peers.

nurtured this enthusiasm by taking an active interest in early childhood education as a means of helping poor children avoid school failure and its tragic consequences. President Lyndon Johnson's War on Poverty and the Economic Opportunity Act of 1964 initiated the federal role in early childhood education through the national Head Start project, which has grown steadily over the years since.

Several projects permitted the High/Scope Foundation to develop the High/Scope model further and to extend it into the elementary school years. In 1968 the federal government initiated the Follow Through project to provide enrichment to children in the primary grades who had attended Head Start (Weikart, Hohmann, & Rhine, 1981). The Follow Through project was perhaps the largest funded effort ever offered for the development of early childhood educational models.

In the late 1970s, federal assistance permitted the High/Scope Foundation to develop and adapt its educational model to children with special needs and children in Spanish-speaking families (Hanes, Flores, Rosario, Weikart, & Sanchez, 1979). High/Scope today actively applies its model in other countries throughout the world. As of 2007, licensed national High/Scope training centers and institutes were in operation in Canada, Great Britain, Indonesia, Ireland, Korea, Mexico, Singapore, The Netherlands, and South Africa. The basic textbooks and assessment instruments are translated into Arabic, Chinese, Dutch, Finnish, French, Korean, Norwegian, Portuguese, Spanish, and Turkish. This work helps spread an educational model that is essentially democratic in operation, adaptable to local culture and language, and open to use by thoughtful adults everywhere.

ACTIVE LEARNING BY THE CHILD

Adults who use the High/Scope model must be fully committed to providing settings in which children learn actively and construct their own knowledge. Much of the child's knowledge comes from personal interaction with ideas, direct experience with physical objects and events, and application of logical thinking to these experiences. The adult's role is largely to supply the context for these experiences, to help the child think about them logically, and, through observation, to understand the progress the child is making and scaffold further learning based on the child's developmental level and interests. From an adult view, children are expected to learn basic tools of language and mathematics; apply the scientific method of hypothesis generation, experimentation, and inference; and demonstrate initiative and problem-solving skills in engaging with the world.

ROLE OF THE TEACHER

Even as children are active learners in the High/Scope model, so, too, are the teachers. By daily evaluation and planning using the High/Scope key developmental indicators as a framework, teachers assess children's experience and classroom activities and strive to achieve new insights into each child's unique tapestry of skills and interests. Teaching teams challenge themselves by observing one another's performance and interacting with one another in mutually supportive ways.

An important aspect of the High/Scope model is the role of the teacher in interacting with the child. Although broad developmental milestones are employed to monitor the youngster's progress, teachers do not have a precise script for teaching children. Instead, they listen closely to what children plan and actively work with them to extend their activities to more challenging levels as appropriate. Adult questioning style is important. The adult emphasizes questions that seek information from the youngster that will help the adult participate. Test questions such as those about color, number, or size are rarely used. Instead, the adult asks, "What happened?" "How did you make that?" "Can you show me?" "Can you help Talia?" and so on. Conversation is essential. The teacher is a participant rather than an imparter of knowledge. "Did you see that butterfly?" "May I touch the pizza, or is it too hot?" This questioning and conversation style permits free interaction between adult and child and models language for child-to-child interaction. This approach permits the teacher and the child to interact as thinkers and doers rather than in the traditional school roles of active teacher and passive pupil. All are sharing and learning as they work.

DAILY ROUTINE TO SUPPORT ACTIVE LEARNING

To create a setting in which children learn actively, a consistent daily classroom routine is maintained that varies only when children have fair warning that things will be different the next day. Field trips are not surprises, and special visits or events are not introduced to the classroom on the spur of the moment. This adherence to routine gives children the security and control necessary to develop a sense of responsibility and to enjoy the opportunity to be independent.

The High/Scope model's daily routine is made up of a *plan-do-review* sequence, group times and several additional elements. The plan-do-review sequence is the central device in the model that permits children opportunities to express intentions about their activities while keeping the teacher intimately involved in the whole process. The following subsections describe the elements in the daily routine.

Planning Time: Stating an Intention

Children make choices and decisions all the time, but most programs seldom have them think about these decisions in a systematic way or help them realize the possibilities and consequences of their choices. Planning time gives children a consistent, predictable opportunity to express their ideas and intentions to adults and to see themselves as individuals who act on decisions. They experience the power of independence and the joy of working with an attentive adult, as well as with peers. They can carry out their intentions.

The teacher talks over the plans with the children before they carry them out. This helps children form mental pictures of their ideas and get a notion of how to proceed. For adults, developing a plan with the children provides an opportunity to encourage and respond to the children's ideas, to suggest practical ways to strengthen the plans so they will be successful, and to understand and gauge the children's levels of development and thinking styles. But the teacher accepts the plans and their limits as determined by the children. Both children and adults receive benefits: children feel reinforced and ready to start their plans, while adults have ideas as to what to look for, what difficulties children might have, where help may be needed, and what levels of development children have achieved. In such a classroom, all are playing appropriate roles of equal importance. In this model, adult–child relationships involve shared control.

Work Time: Executing the Intention

The "do" part of the plan-do-review cycle is work time, the period after children have finished planning. The longest time period in the daily routine, it is an active period of play for both children and adults. While adults do not lead work-time activities—children execute their own plans of work—neither do they just sit back and watch passively. The adult's role during work time is first to observe children to see how they gather information, interact with peers, and solve problems, and then to enter into the children's activities and scaffold learning by encouraging, extending, setting up problem-solving situations, and engaging in conversation. Because the layout of the learning environment permits adults to see all the learning areas in the classroom, they can monitor, circulate, and support individuals and groups of children in a wide variety of activities.

Cleanup Time

Cleanup time is integrated into the plan-do-review cycle in the obvious place: after the doing. During this time, children return materials and equipment to their labeled places and store the incomplete projects, affixing a "work-in-progress" sign if they choose. This process restores order to the classroom and provides opportunities for the children to learn and use many basic cognitive skills, such as classifying and ordering objects. Of special importance is how the learning environment is organized to facilitate children's use of materials. All materials in the classroom available for children's use are on open shelves within reach. Clear labeling is essential, with a representation of the learning areas and objects on the shelves (such as actual items, drawings, photographs) and a simple written word. With this organizational plan, children can realistically return all work materials to their appropriate places. It also gives them a sense of confidence in their initiative by knowing where everything they need is located. Further, seeing labels in print helps to promote early literacy development.

Recall Time: Reflecting on Accomplishments

Recall time is the final phase of the plan-do-review sequence. It is the time when the children reflect on what they have accomplished or experienced. The children represent their work-time experience in a variety of developmentally appropriate ways. They might recall the names of the children they involved in carrying out their plan, dictate a story of their activity, or recount the problems they encountered. Other recall strategies include drawing pictures of what they did, making models, reviewing their plans, and verbally recalling the past events.

Recall time brings closure to their planning and work-time activities; it provides them opportunities to express insights on what they have experienced and thought about; and it often leads to follow-up ideas and plans for the next day. It provides opportunity to use language and illustrations to inform others. The teacher supports the linkage of the actual work to the original plan, including changes the child made in the course of solving problems. The use of complex language to discuss, describe, and predict outcomes is essential to this support process by the teacher.

Small-Group Time

The formal setting of small-group time is familiar to all preschool teachers: The teacher creates an activity in which children participate for a set period. These activities are drawn from the children's interests, their cultural backgrounds, field trips the group has taken, new materials available in the classroom, the seasons of the year, and age-appropriate group activities such as cooking and group art projects. Although teachers offer materials and structure for the activities, children are encouraged to contribute ideas and solve problems presented by the activities in their own ways. Activities have a beginning, middle, and end but are flexible in responding to each child's needs, abilities, interests, and cognitive levels. Once each child has had the opportunity for individual choice and problem solving, the teacher extends the child's ideas and actions by engaging in conversation, asking open-ended questions, and supporting additional problem-solving situations. In planning and implementing small-group time, active involvement by all children is important. Children move physically, use objects and materials, make choices, and solve problems. An active small-group time gives children the chance to explore materials and objects, use their bodies and their senses, and work with adults and other children.

Large-Group Time

At large-group time, the whole group meets together with the adults to play games, sing songs, do finger plays, perform basic movement activities, play musical instruments, act out a story they have read or imagined, or reenact a special event. This time provides an opportunity for each child to participate in a large group, share and demonstrate ideas, and imitate the ideas of others. Although the adult may initiate the activity, children provide some leadership and make as many individual choices as the activity allows. Large-group time is a good time to support the development of a steady beat through patting the floor or their bodies, marching, rocking, and moving to high-quality instrumental music (Weikart, 2003).

KEY DEVELOPMENTAL INDICATORS

Child progress in the High/Scope model is organized around a set of key developmental indicators developed from research findings and child development theory and designed to align with national, state, and local standards for early learning. As the plan-do-review sequence conducted within a consistent daily routine is the hallmark of the High/Scope model for the child, these key developmental indicators are the central feature for the teacher to implement the curriculum content. They are a way of helping the teacher understand, support, and extend the child's self-designed activity so that developmentally appropriate experiences and growth are constantly available to the child. These indicators guide the teacher in planning small- and large-group activities. They provide a way of thinking about curriculum that frees the teacher from total reliance on workbooks of activities and scope-and-sequence charts. They form the basis of the framework an adult uses to plan for and observe each child.

Dan Floss/Merrill

During small-group activities, children explore materials and objects, make choices, and solve problems.

The key developmental indicators are important to the growth of rational thought in children the world over, regardless of nation or culture. They are very simple and pragmatic. Preschool key developmental indicators have been identified in the following domains, which parallel the dimensions of school readiness identified by the National Education Goals Panel (Kagan, Moore, & Bredekamp, 1995):

- Approaches to learning
- Language, literacy, and communication
- Social and emotional development
- Physical development, health, and well-being
- Mathematics
- Science and technology
- Social studies
- The arts

Each of these categories is divided into specific types of experiences. For example, the following are the key developmental indicators in language, literacy, and communication:

- Talk with others about personally meaningful experiences
- Describe objects, events, and relations
- Have fun with language: listen to stories and poems, make up stories and rhymes
- Write in various ways: draw, scribble, and use letterlike forms, invented spelling, and conventional forms
- Read in various ways: storybooks, signs and symbols, one's own writing
- Dictate stories

The following are the key developmental indicators in social and emotional development:

- Take care of one's own needs
- Express feelings in words
- Build relationships with children and adults

- Create and experience collaborative play
- Deal with social conflict

Classroom learning experiences are not mutually exclusive, and any given activity will involve several types of key developmental indicators. This approach gives the adult a clear perspective from which to think about the program and observe the youngsters. In addition, the key developmental indicators give the model structure while maintaining its openness to child-generated experiences. Thus, High/Scope staff developing new curriculum domains have a vehicle for expanding the curriculum to include additional experiences. The key developmental indicators enable the High/Scope model to continue to evolve as an effective means of promoting children's healthy growth and development.

HIGH/SCOPE PRESCHOOL CHILD OBSERVATION RECORD

The High/Scope Preschool Child Observation Record (COR) (High/Scope Educational Research Foundation, 2003) measures the developmental status of young children 3 to 5 years old. The High/Scope Infant-Toddler Child Observation Record (High/Scope Educational Research Foundation, 2000) measures the developmental status of young children up to 3 years old. Originally developed to assess the outcomes of the High/Scope model, the COR was later expanded for use in all early childhood programs that engage in developmentally appropriate practice, whether they use the High/Scope model or not.

To use the High/Scope Preschool COR, the teacher writes brief notes over several months describing episodes of young children's behavior in six domains of development: (1) initiative, (2) social relations, (3) creative representation, (4) music and movement, (5) language and literacy, and (6) logic and mathematics. The teacher then uses these notes to classify the child's behavior on 32 five-level COR items in these domains. For example, the item on Making Choices and Plans has the following five levels, from lowest to highest:

1. Child indicates a choice by pointing or some other action.
2. Child expresses a choice in one or two words.
3. Child expresses a choice with a short sentence.
4. Child makes a plan with one or two details.
5. Child makes a plan with three or more details.

The statistical characteristics of the second edition of the Preschool COR (High/Scope Educational Research Foundation, 2003) were assessed with data collected by Head Start teaching staff in one grantee from 160 children in spring 2002 and 233 children in fall 2002. Children ranged in age from 3 years 0 months to 5 years 5 months. The average COR total scores were 2.49 in the fall study and 3.47 in the spring study. The alpha coefficients of internal consistency for all 32 COR items were .94 in the fall study and .91 in the spring study, with alpha coefficients for COR categories ranging from .75 to .88. The COR scores of 10 pairs of teachers and assistant teachers were correlated at .73 for the COR total scores and .69 to .79 for the category scores. A confirmatory factor analysis on data from the spring study affirmed the COR's internal validity and identified four factors that fit the COR categories rather well. The COR's external validity was supported by expected correlations of the COR total scores with the Cognitive Skills Assessment Battery (.46 to .62) (Boehm & Slater, 1981) and with children's ages (.31), with no significant association with gender.

ROLE OF PARENTS AND COMMUNITY

Parent participation has been a hallmark from the outset of development of the High/Scope model. In the initial period during the 1960s, teachers made home visits each week to each participating child and mother or other family member. Reflecting the movement of women into the workforce, parent participation now is more focused on group meetings and other means of contact. One component of High/Scope staff training provides teachers with strategies to involve parents in supporting their child's early learning in ways that are meaningful, developmentally appropriate, and feasible for the family.

The key to effective parent involvement is the primary focus on the child and the dual nature of information flow. Although the school and its staff have knowledge and training to provide to the family, the staff must also learn from the parents about the child, the family's culture, and their language and goals. For the program to be successful in various settings, teaching staff must respect the parents as the experts in their own domain.

TRAINING IN THE HIGH/SCOPE MODEL

Effective training in the High/Scope model has several key elements. It is on site and model-focused, with a growing number of distance learning options to supplement face-to-face contact with the foundation's trainers. It adapts to the actual work setting of the teacher physically and socially, adapts to the group of children involved (e.g., children with disabilities or learning English as a second language), relates to the culture of the children, and enables systematic parent involvement. Training sessions are scheduled about once a month because teachers need time to study training materials, think about the training experience, put new ideas into practice, see the gaps in their own thinking and in the program being presented, and make adaptations to their own setting. Consistent delivery to the individual teacher is maintained by observations and feedback.

The High/Scope model is flexible in various ways. It is open to all who understand its developmental principles. It is not so much a set of prescriptions as a methodological framework for education. The teachers and parents employing the framework arrange the context of the program and the general content; the child further specifies the content to some extent. In these ways, the program grows from the users rather than from the developers. This fact gives it extraordinary flexibility and usefulness as an effective framework for adults working with children.

The High/Scope Educational Research Foundation has trained early childhood teachers and teacher trainers throughout the United States and around the world. It has teacher training institutes and centers in Canada, Mexico, the United Kingdom, Ireland, The Netherlands, South Africa, Singapore, Indonesia, and Korea. Fledgling efforts in High/Scope training and use are taking place in many other countries as well. For example, the High/Scope Foundation is working with several organizations in the Caribbean to help shift their adult instruction from highly directive to more interactional—not a full adoption of the High/Scope model by any means but an effort to introduce its key principle of balanced interaction among people. While the initial communication of High/Scope ideas inevitably comes from its U.S. source, it is interpreted and adapted by indigenous peoples throughout the world.

RESEARCH SUPPORT FOR THE HIGH/SCOPE MODEL

The High/Scope model of preschool education has amassed a set of research studies that establish its value in a variety of ways. The High/Scope Perry Preschool Study found that the model has truly extraordinary long-term benefits when provided to young children living in poverty. The High/Scope Preschool

Curriculum Comparison Study shows that the model stands out from teacher-directed instruction in its contribution to young children's social development. The Training for Quality Study shows that systematic training in the High/Scope model helps teachers make greater contributions to children's development. The Preprimary Project of the International Association for the Evaluation of Educational Achievement shows that early childhood settings around the world contribute more to children's cognitive and language development if children are allowed to choose their own activities than if whole-group instruction is emphasized.

High/Scope Perry Preschool Study

Weikart and his staff of the High/Scope Perry Preschool program in the Ypsilanti Public Schools first developed and used the High/Scope model to assist economically disadvantaged children. By virtue of its experimental design (random assignment) and long-term duration (since 1962), the evaluation of the High/Scope Perry Preschool program is one of the most thorough examinations of program effects ever undertaken. The basic evaluation question is whether the High/Scope Perry Preschool program affected the lives of participating children. The study focused on 123 African American children born in poverty and at high risk of failing in school. In the early 1960s, at ages 3 and 4, these children were randomly divided into a program group who received a high-quality preschool program and a no-program group who received no preschool program. The two groups have been carefully studied over the years with only 6% of the data missing on average across all measures. At age 40, 91% of the original study participants were interviewed (7 of those not interviewed were deceased), with additional data gathered from their school, social services, and arrest records (Schweinhart et al., 2005). Post–preschool-program differences between the groups represent preschool program effects. Findings presented here are statistically significant (with a two-tailed probability of less than .05).

As shown in Figure 9–1, more of the program group than the no-program group graduated from high school or received a GED (77%

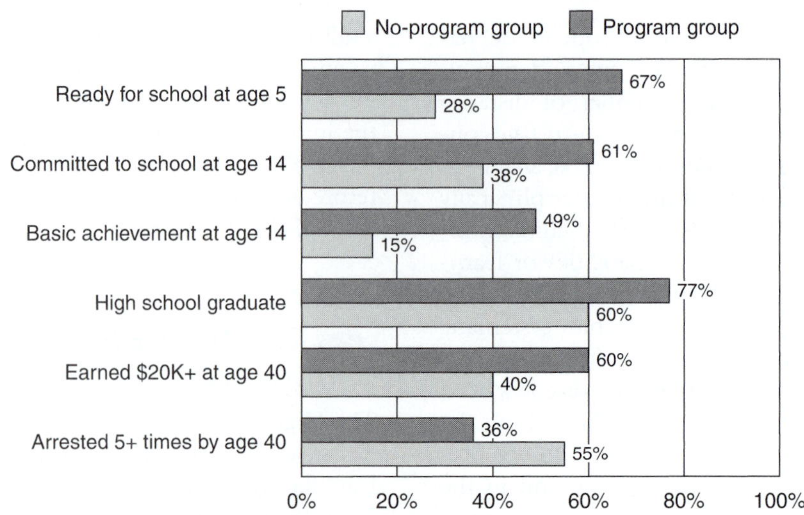

FIGURE 9–1 High/Scope Perry Preschool Study Major Findings Through Age 40
Source: From *Lifetime Effects: The High/Scope Perry Preschool Study Through Age 40* (p. xv) by L. J. Schweinhart, J. Montie, Z. Xiang, W. S. Barnett, C. R. Belfield, & M. Nores, 2005. Ypsilanti, MI: High/Scope Press. Copyright 2005 by High/Scope Educational Research Foundation. Adapted with permission.

vs. 60%). This difference was due to a 42-percentage-point difference between program and no-program females in high school graduation rate (88% vs. 46%). Earlier, program and no-program females had different rates of treatment for mental impairment (8% vs. 36%) and retention in grade (21% vs. 41%). However, the entire program group outperformed the no-program group on various intellectual and language tests from their preschool years up to age 7; school achievement tests at 7 to 14; and literacy tests at 19 and 27. The program group had better attitudes toward school than the no-program group as teens, and program-group parents had better attitudes toward their teen children's schooling than did no-program-group parents. The preschool program affected children's performance and attitudes, regardless of their gender, but this common effect seems to have led school staff to track girls but not boys.

More of the program group than the no-program group were employed at ages 27 (69% vs. 56%) and 40 (76% vs. 62%). The program group had higher median earnings than the no-program group, annually at ages 27 ($12,000 vs. $10,000) and 40 ($20,800 vs. $15,300), as well as monthly at both ages. More of the program group than the no-program group owned their own homes at ages 27 (27% vs. 5%) and 40 (37% vs. 28%). More of the program group than the no-program group had a car at ages 27 (73% vs. 59%) and 40 (82% vs. 60%). More program than no-program males raised their own children (57% vs. 30%).

Over their lifetimes, fewer in the program group than the no-program group were arrested 5 or more times (36% vs. 55%) or were arrested for violent, property, or drug crimes, particularly dangerous drugs, assault and/or battery, and larceny under $100. Fewer in the program group were sentenced to time in prison or jail by age 40 (28% vs. 52%).

As shown in Figure 9–2, in constant 2000 dollars discounted at 3%, the economic return

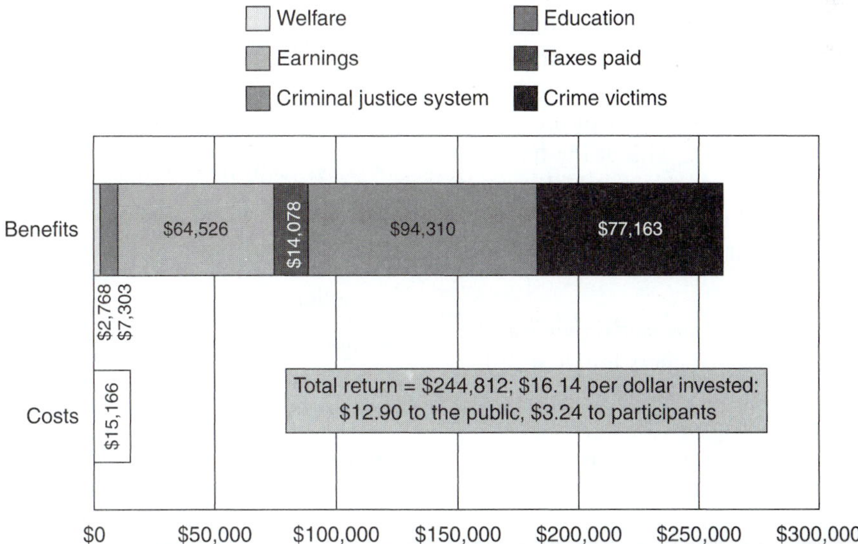

FIGURE 9–2 Large Return on Investment (Per participant in 2000 constant dollars discounted 3% annually)
Source: From *Lifetime Effects: The High/Scope Perry Preschool Study Through Age 40* (p. xvii) by L. J. Schweinhart, J. Montie, Z. Xiang, W. S. Barnett, C. R. Belfield, & M. Nores, 2005. Ypsilanti, MI: High/Scope Press. Copyright 2005 by High/Scope Educational Research Foundation. Adapted with permission.

to society for the program was $244,812 per participant on an investment of $15,166 per participant—$16.14 per dollar invested. Of that return, 80% went to the general public—$12.90 per dollar invested—and 20% went to each participant. Of the public return, 88% came from crime savings, and the rest came from education and welfare savings and increased taxes due to higher earnings. Males accounted for a full 93% of the public return because of the large program effect of reducing male crime. This finding for males stands in stark contrast to the large program effect on the high school graduation rates of females.

High/Scope Preschool Curriculum Comparison Study

In 1967, a second longitudinal study, the High/Scope Preschool Curriculum Comparison Study (Schweinhart & Weikart, 1997) was undertaken to explore possible effects of early education programs based on several major theoretical approaches. The question was whether the success of the High/Scope Perry Preschool program was to be expected only of preschool programs that used the High/Scope model or could be expected of other preschool programs with high standards as well. This study has followed the lives of 68 young people born in poverty who were randomly assigned at ages 3 and 4 to one of three groups, each experiencing a different model:

- In the *Direct Instruction model* that was current at the time, teachers initiated drill-and-practice activities, following a script with academic objectives, and rewarded children for responding correctly and following the teacher direction.
- In the *High/Scope model,* teachers and children both initiated actions. Teachers arranged the classroom and the daily routine so children could plan, do, and review their own activities and engage in the key developmental indicators described in this chapter.
- In the *traditional Nursery School model,* teachers responded to children's self-initiated play and introduced projects in a loosely structured, socially supportive setting.

Program staff implemented the model programs independently and to high standards, in $2\frac{1}{2}$-hour classes held 5 days a week and in $1\frac{1}{2}$-hour visits to children's homes every 2 weeks, when children were 3 and 4 years old.

Except for the educational model, all aspects of the programs were essentially identical. The three groups did not differ significantly on most background characteristics. The findings presented here are corrected for differences in gender makeup of the groups. Figure 9–3 portrays key findings.

By age 23 the High/Scope group had eight significant advantages over the Direct Instruction group:

- Fewer felony arrests
- Fewer arrests for property crimes
- Fewer years requiring treatment for emotional impairment or disturbance
- Fewer reporting that other people gave them a hard time
- Less teen misconduct
- A higher percentage living with a spouse
- More who ever did volunteer work
- More who planned to graduate from college

By age 23 the Nursery School group had four significant advantages over the Direction Instruction group.

- Fewer felony arrests at age 22 and over
- Fewer years requiring treatment for emotional impairment or disturbance
- More who did volunteer work
- Fewer suspensions from work (the only one not in common with the High/Scope curriculum group)

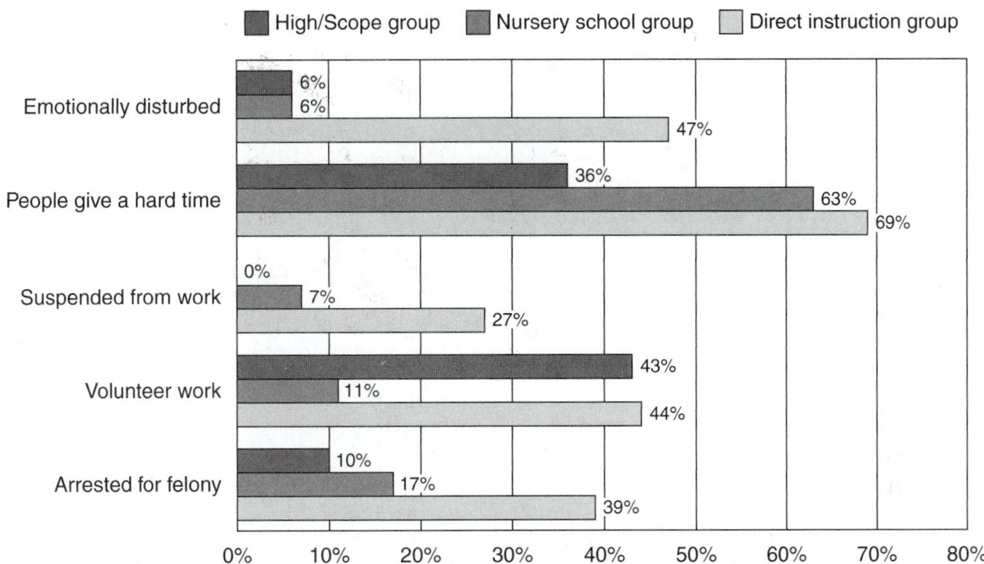

FIGURE 9–3 High/Scope Preschool Curriculum Comparison Study Major Findings at Age 23
Source: From *Lasting Differences* (pp. 40, 48, and 51), by L. J. Schweinhart, & D. P. Weikart, 1997. Ypsilanti, MI: High/Scope Press. Copyright 1997 by High/Scope Educational Research Foundation. Adapted with permission.

By age 23, the Direct Instruction group had no significant advantage on any outcome variable. By age 23, the High/Scope group and the Nursery School group did not differ significantly on any outcome variable.

Through age 10, the main finding of this study was that the overall average IQ of the three groups rose 27 points, from a borderline impairment level of 78 to a normal level of 105 after 1 year of their preschool program and subsequently settled in at an average of 95, still at the normal level. In spite of 2 years of academic training for the Direct Instruction group, throughout their school years to age 15, model groups did not differ significantly in school achievement. The conclusion at that time was that well-implemented preschool education, regardless of theoretical orientation, had similar effects on children's intellectual and academic performance. Time has proved otherwise.

The research supports the conclusion that, by age 23, scripted, teacher-directed instruction, touted by some as the surest path to school success, seems to purchase a modest extra improvement in academic performance at the cost of a missed opportunity for long-term improvement in important social behavior. Child-initiated learning activities, on the other hand, seem to help children develop their social responsibility and skills so that they less often need treatment for emotional impairment or disturbance and are less often arrested for felonies as young adults.

While the High/Scope and Nursery School groups did not differ significantly on any outcome variable at age 23, the High/Scope model is more readily replicated than the Nursery School approach because of its extensive documentation of practice, validated teacher training program, and well-developed program and child assessment systems. The Nursery School approach used in this study was the unique product of certain teachers trained in a general child development approach. It is unclear whether the results of this study apply to children who experience other versions of the Nursery School approach or an eclectic approach developed by their own teachers.

These findings constitute evidence that early childhood education works better to prevent problems when it focuses on child-initiated learning activities rather than scripted, teacher-directed academic instruction. Because biweekly visits to children's homes were part of each program, home visits by themselves do not account for these differences. These findings suggest that the goals of early childhood education should not be limited to academic preparation for school but should also include helping children learn to make decisions, solve problems, and get along with others—the goals of the High/Scope model of early childhood education.

The High/Scope Perry Preschool Study (Schweinhart et al., 2005) and the High/Scope Preschool Curriculum Comparison Study (Schweinhart & Weikart, 1997) suggest that the High/Scope early childhood model has significant, lasting benefits because it fosters the following:

- Empowers children by enabling them to initiate and carry out their own learning activities and make independent decisions
- Empowers parents by involving them in ongoing relationships as full partners with teachers in supporting their children's development
- Empowers teachers by providing them with an effective model supported by systematic, model-focused inservice training and supervision, and observational tools to assess children's development

Some might object that these programs are dated, passed over by time, never mind that it is only such programs that are in a position to demonstrate such long-term effects. But the programs are well documented, not only with descriptive narrative but also with both expert observations and systematic observation by trained observers (Weikart, Epstein, Schweinhart, & Bond, 1978); thus, they can be fully replicated today. Further, there is no reason to think that the relationships between the educational model and child outcomes found beginning in the 1960s are any different today.

Combined with similar findings from other independent investigators (Marcon, 1992; Nabuco & Sylva, 1997; Zill et al., 2003), these data have wide-ranging implications. They indicate that high-quality preschool programs for children living in poverty can have a positive long-term effect on their lives. Their early educational success leads to later school success, higher employment rates, and fewer social problems, such as crime and welfare dependence. Early childhood education can help individuals realize their potential, but the findings show more than good outcomes for individuals. They also indicate that citizens can expect substantial improvement in the quality of community life. An effective program can help reduce crime and improve participants' employment prospects. Further, an important improvement can be made in the available workforce because of better educational attainment and improved job-holding ability. However, such outcomes are not the results of all preschool programs but, rather, those programs that balance an emphasis on later academic success with an emphasis on social development and personal initiative.

The Training for Quality Study

The High/Scope Training for Quality Study (Epstein, 1993) offers evidence of the effectiveness of the High/Scope preschool education model as practiced throughout the United States today. In this multi-study evaluation, we analyzed participant reports of 40 training projects; surveyed 203 certified High/Scope teacher trainers; surveyed and systematically observed the classrooms of 244 High/Scope and 122 comparison teachers; and systematically observed and tested 97 High/Scope and 103 comparison children in these classrooms.

High/Scope trainers identified 244 High/Scope teachers in Michigan, New York, and California who had been employed at their agencies for at least 6 months, had attended at least four High/Scope workshops, and had received three classroom visits. We selected 122 comparison teachers from lists of licensed child-care centers and from agencies nominated by staff or trainers, with efforts to maintain proportions of agency types similar to those of the High/Scope teachers.

The 200 children in the child outcomes study attended preschool programs in 15 agencies in urban, suburban, and rural settings in southeastern Michigan and northwestern Ohio; 46% were in Head Start, 19% in public schools, and 35% in nonprofit centers. Children ranged in age from 2 to 6, average 4.3; 47% were male, 53% female; 43% were white, 32% were African American, 5% were Hispanic American, and 20% were of other ethnic groups. Their fathers and mothers averaged 13.7 years of schooling, identifying these parents as relatively well educated on the average. In both groups, according to Bureau of Labor Statistics codes, fathers' median occupational level was that of laborer, and mothers' median occupational level was that of service worker. Treatment groups did not significantly differ on any of these characteristics.

The Registry trainer survey found that half of High/Scope-certified trainers were in Head Start, 27% were in public schools, and 20% were in private child-care agencies. Eighty-eight percent had completed college, including 37% with advanced degrees; 70% majored in early childhood. They had a median of 15 years of experience in early childhood. Seventy-eight percent of them were still in the same agency they were in when they received High/Scope certification; 85% had teacher-training responsibility, although they only spent an average of 8 hours a week training teachers. On the average, they made a large-group presentation for 36 staff annually, a hands-on workshop for 15 staff monthly, an observation-and-feedback classroom visit monthly, and an informal classroom visit weekly. The average teacher had attended 1 presentation and 9 workshops and received 1 observation-and-feedback visit and 3 informal visits per month.

All the teachers trained had tried out the High/Scope model's room arrangement and daily routine; 91% had tried out the key experiences; 63% had tried out the child observation techniques. Eighty-nine percent were comfortable and effective with room arrangement; 80% with the daily routine; 56% with the key experiences; and 37% with the child observation techniques. Trainers said they would show visitors 45% of the classrooms of trained teachers as examples of the High/Scope preschool model, an average of 4 classrooms per trainer.

The High/Scope Registry listed 1,075 early childhood leaders in 34 states and 10 other countries who had successfully completed High/Scope's 7-week Trainer Certification Program in the past decade. The average trainer had trained 15 teaching teams, so an estimated 16,125 early childhood teaching teams, including 29% of all Head Start staff, had received High/Scope model training from these trainers. Since trainers regarded 45% of these classrooms as examples of the High/Scope model, they would nominate an estimated 7,256 early childhood classrooms throughout the United States and around the world as examples of the High/Scope model.

The teacher survey indicated that both High/Scope and comparison classrooms were of high quality. Both groups had at least 10 years of teaching experience. Majorities of both groups had college degrees and early childhood degrees. Both groups had over 40 hours of in-service training annually. In both groups, teachers' annual salaries averaged about $20,000 a year, considerably higher than the $9,400 national average for child-care teaching staff (Whitebook, Phillips, & Howes, 1993). The few group background differences seemed to compensate for each other: The High/Scope teachers had significantly more teaching experience than comparison teachers (12 vs. 10), but significantly fewer High/Scope teachers had college degrees (63% vs. 79%).

While High/Scope and comparison teachers did not differ significantly in their hours of in-service training per year, more High/Scope teachers received significantly more in-service training involving curriculum and teaching practices (91% vs. 71%), child assessment and evaluation (75% vs. 48%), and professional issues (48% vs. 34%). High/Scope teachers placed significantly more importance on the following topics than did comparison teachers: room arrangement, children choosing their own activities, adults participating in children's activities, ongoing training for adults, supervision and evaluation, multicultural awareness, and parent involvement.

High/Scope and comparison classrooms differed significantly in classroom environment, daily routine, adult–child interaction, and overall implementation, as assessed by the High/Scope Program Implementation Profile (High/Scope Educational Research Foundation, 1989) adapted for generic use. High/Scope advantages in classroom environment involved dividing the classroom into activity areas, providing adequate work space in each area, arranging and labeling materials, providing enough materials in each area, providing real household and work objects, making materials accessible to children, and providing materials to promote awareness of cultural differences. High/Scope advantages in daily routine involved implementing a consistent daily routine, encouraging children to plan and review activities, and providing opportunities for planning, doing, and reviewing. High/Scope advantages in adult–child interaction differences involved observing and asking questions, participating in children's play, and balancing child and adult talk. Comparison classrooms had no significant advantages over High/Scope classrooms on this instrument. These findings indicate that the High/Scope classrooms were implementing the High/Scope Preschool Curriculum to a significantly greater extent than were the comparison classrooms.

As shown in Figure 9–4, the children in High/Scope programs significantly outperformed the children in comparison programs in initiative, social relations, music and movement, and overall child development. High/Scope advantages in initiative involved complex play and

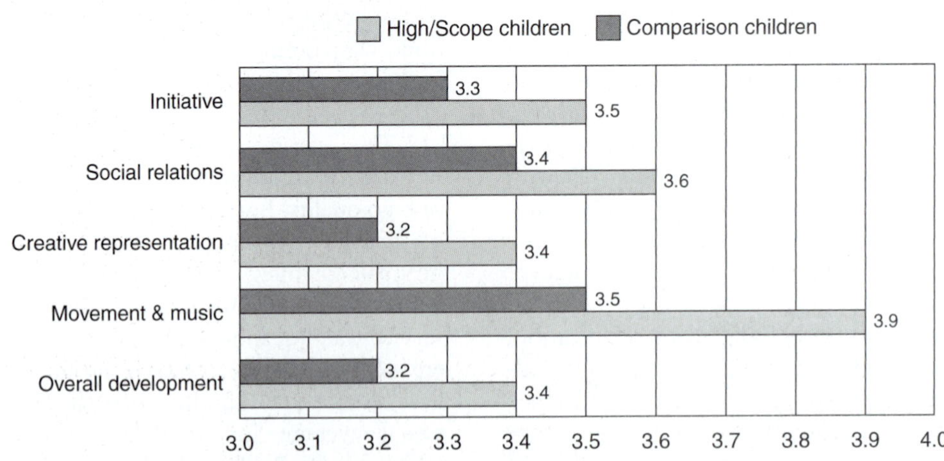

FIGURE 9–4 Findings: Training for Quality Children's Study

Source: Training for Quality: Improving Early Childhood Programs Through Systematic In-service Training by A. S. Epstein, 1997. Ypsilanti, MI: High/Scope Press. Copyright 2003 by High/Scope Education Research Foundation. Adapted with permission.

cooperating in program routines. High/Scope advantages in social relations involved relating to adults and social problem solving. High/Scope advantages in music and movement included imitating movements to a steady beat.

Significant positive correlations of .39 to .52 were found between classroom daily routine (measuring children's opportunities to plan activities, carry out their ideas, and review what they had done each day) and children's overall development, specifically their development of creative representation, initiative, music and movement abilities, and language and literacy.

The IEA Preprimary Project

The IEA Preprimary Project is a multi-nation study of preprimary care and education sponsored by the International Association for the Evaluation of Educational Achievement (IEA) (Montie, Xiang, & Schweinhart, 2006; Olmsted & Montie, 2001; Weikart, Olmsted, & Montie, 2003). High/Scope served as the international coordinating center. Working collaboratively with researchers in 15 countries, High/Scope staff were responsible for sampling, instrument development, data analysis, and the writing of five published reports and one in press. The purpose of the study is to identify how process and structural characteristics of community preprimary settings affect children's language and cognitive development at age 7. The study is unique because many diverse countries participated, using common instruments to measure family background, teachers' characteristics, setting structural characteristics, experiences of children, and children's developmental status.

The study is rooted theoretically in the ecological systems model of human development, which views children's behavior and developmental status as being influenced by multiple levels of the environment, some direct and proximal to the child, such as the child's actual experiences in an education or care setting, and some indirect and distal, such as national policy. The study findings focus on the influence of young children's experiences in community preprimary education and care settings on their language and cognitive development at age 7, controlling for family and cultural influences. Both proximal and distal variables are examined within that context.

The target population consisted of children in selected community settings who were approximately $4\frac{1}{2}$ years old. Data for the longitudinal project were collected in early childhood care and education settings in 10 countries: Finland, Greece, Hong Kong, Indonesia, Ireland, Italy, Poland, Spain, Thailand, and the United States. Each country's research team chose to sample settings that were used by large numbers of families in the community or were important for public policy reasons. With expert assistance, each country's research team developed a sampling plan, using probability proportional to size to select settings and systematic sampling procedures to select four children within each classroom. The age-4 sample included over 5,000 children in more than 1,800 settings in 15 countries. Ten of the initial 15 countries followed the children to age 7 to collect language and cognitive outcome measures. The median retention rate across countries was 86%, ranging from 41% to 99%. The number of children included in the longitudinal analyses varied from 1,300 to 1,897, depending on the particular analysis.

Working with High/Scope researchers, measures used in the study were developed collaboratively by members of the international team. At age 4, data were collected with three observation systems and three questionnaire/interviews. Children's cognitive and language performance was measured at age 4 and age 7. The observation systems collected time-sampled information about how teachers schedule and manage children's time, what children actually do with their time, the behaviors teachers use, and the nature of teacher involvement with children.

Interviews were conducted to collect family background information and gather information regarding teachers' and parents' expectations about what is important for preschool-age children to learn. A questionnaire that focused on the structural characteristics of the settings was administered to teachers and caregivers.

The children were followed until age 7, an age across countries when they had all entered primary school. At that time, cognitive and language measures developed by an international team were administered to assess developmental status.

Based on the structure of the data, with individual children nested within settings and settings nested within countries, a hierarchical linear modeling approach was used for the analysis. Accurate estimation of impacts for variables at different levels was especially important for this study because effects at two levels—settings and countries—were often confounded with one another. Although the relationship between setting variables and children's later development was of primary interest, any such findings would have been hard to interpret if country effects had not been accurately estimated and adjusted for. A three-level approach enabled decomposition of variation of child outcomes into three parts: variation among children within settings, among settings within countries, and among countries. As a result, relationships between care-setting variables and children's outcome scores are free of substantial influence from country-level effects.

Four findings emerged that are consistent across all the countries included in the data analysis:

- Children's language performance at age 7 improves as *the predominant types of children's activities that teachers propose are free rather than personal/social.* From greatest to least contribution, activity types were as follows:

  Free activities, which teachers let children choose

  Physical/expressive activities (gross- and fine-motor physical activity, dramatic play, arts, crafts, and music)

  Preacademic activities (reading, writing, numbers, mathematics, physical science, and social science)

  Personal/social activities (personal care, group social activities, and discipline)

- Children's language performance at age 7 improves as *teachers' years of schooling* increase.
- Children's cognitive performance at age 7 improves as they spend *less time in whole-group activities* (the teacher proposes the same activity for all children in the class: songs, games, listening to a story, working on a craft, or a preacademic activity).
- Children's language performance at age 7 improves as *the amount and variety of equipment and materials available to children in preschool settings* increase.

The wide range of environments throughout the world in which young children grow and learn creates challenging questions for everyone concerned with providing high-quality programs for preprimary children. What are the essential program elements that promote optimum child development? How are these elements delivered in various communities? The findings tell us that teaching practices matter; how teachers set up their classrooms and the activities they propose for children make a difference.

Across diverse countries, child-initiated activities and teachers' education appear to contribute to children's later language performance. And minimization of whole group activities and a greater number and variety of materials in preschool settings appear to contribute to their later cognitive performance.

Although more research is necessary in the various countries to establish a pattern of cause and effect and explore the learning mechanisms involved, early childhood educators and policy makers can use these findings to examine local policies and practices and consider if changes are advisable.

RELATIONSHIP OF RESEARCH TO THE HIGH/SCOPE MODEL

The High/Scope model defined the essential program elements in the day-to-day experience of children and teachers that were largely responsible for the program effects, that is, plan-do-review and key developmental indicators as a basis of planning and observation. Also among the key program elements were staffing, staff planning and development, class sessions for children, and a high level of parent involvement. The staff/child ratio was 1 to 5 or 6, with four teachers for 20 to 25 children in the High/Scope Perry Preschool program; and 1 to 8, with two teachers and 16 children for each class in the High/Scope Curriculum Comparison study. The teaching staff worked together in teams that planned, implemented, and evaluated each day's activities. Indeed, working in tandem with researchers and consultants, they developed and refined the High/Scope educational model. The preschool program had two components: daily $2\frac{1}{2}$-hour classroom sessions and weekly $1\frac{1}{2}$-hour home visits by the teacher to each child and mother or other caregiver. These program elements can be applied with some flexibility. Staffing could safely go as high as 20 children in a class with two trained adults. Teachers need to develop intellectual ownership of the model, preferably through daily planning, evaluation, and teamwork, and with the active support of the administration and the provision of inservice model training opportunities. Home visits are not the key to program effectiveness, as witnessed by the data from the Direct Instruction group (Schweinhart & Weikart, 1997), but parents and teachers do need to work together as real partners in the education of children, which means regular, substantive communication concerning the developmental status of the child and concrete strategies whereby families can extend the curriculum learning into the home. In short, the High/Scope Perry Preschool program group (Schweinhart et al., 2005) and the High/Scope group of the Curriculum Comparison Study (Schweinhart & Weikart, 1997) were successful because they implemented the essential elements of the High/Scope model and because they maintained consistent program policies that permitted the model to operate effectively.

To recapitulate, a high-quality preschool program observes these program policies:

- Teachers use and take ownership of a validated, child-development–oriented educational model through regular inservice training in the model.
- The teaching staff work as teams in planning, implementing, and evaluating each day's activities.
- The staffing ratio is no more than 10 children per staff member, and group sizes are no greater than 20.
- Parents join with teachers as partners in the education of the child and engage in substantive discussion and home extension of the learning topics.
- The administration provides model leadership, supervision, and assistance.

Many existing programs of early childhood care and education are not of adequate operational quality. Improving them is *the* major task of caregivers and educators. As with elementary and secondary school programs, early childhood programs must meet basic standards. These elements are neither easy to put into practice nor cheap to maintain. Yet the advantages of high-quality programs far outweigh the effort and cost of providing them.

What is it about young children's development that presents the opportunity for such effective programs? The preschool years are a watershed for several dimensions of child development. Physically, by age 3, young children have matured to the point that they have achieved both fine- and gross-motor coordination and are able to move about easily and freely. Mentally, they have developed basic language capabilities and can use objects for self-chosen purposes. In the terms of Jean Piaget, they have shifted from sensorimotor functioning to preoperational thinking. Socially, they are able to move away from familiar adults and social contexts to unfamiliar ones. The fear of strangers so common earlier is much reduced, and youngsters welcome relations with new peers and adults. What stands out among the basic accomplishments of early education is that children develop additional social, physical, and intellectual abilities. Armed with these acquired competencies, they learn to relate to new adults, who respond to their performance very differently from their families. In short, children learn to demonstrate abilities in novel settings and to trust new adults and peers enough to display these skills willingly. Children's willingness to try things and develop competencies is the seed that is transformed into later school and life success. Early success grows grade by grade, year by year, into adult success; each stage leads to a better performance at the next. These steps are documented by the research. The thrust is captured in the old folk adage "As the twig is bent, so grows the tree."

CONCLUSION

The High/Scope model of early childhood education is an open framework of developmental theory and educational practices based on the interactive development of young children. It is currently used in thousands of early childhood programs throughout the United States and in other countries. Based on Piaget's child development ideas (Piaget & Inhelder, 1969) and teaching practices derived from the social learning theory of Vygotsky (1934/1962), the High/Scope model views children as active learners who learn best from activities that they themselves plan, carry out, and reflect on. Adults arrange interest areas in the learning environment; maintain a daily routine that permits children to plan and pursue their own activities; join in children's activities and help them think things through; and provide language through conversations and observations. The adults encourage children to achieve key developmental indicators and help them learn to make choices, solve problems, and generally engage in activities that promote intellectual, social, and physical development. Decades of systematic empirical research indicate that the High/Scope model works to significantly improve the life chances of participating children.

High/Scope Educational Research Foundation
600 North River Street
Ypsilanti, Michigan 48198-2898
phone: (734) 485-2000
fax: (734) 485-0704
Web site: www.highscope.org

In addition, several High/Scope institutes in other countries have their own Web sites: Indonesia (www.highscope.or.id), Mexico (www.highscopemexico.org), The Netherlands (www.kaleidoscoop.org), and the United Kingdom (www.high-scope.org.uk).

REFERENCES

Boehm, A. E., & Slater, B. E. (1981). *Cognitive skills assessment battery* (2nd ed.). New York: Teachers College Press.

Bruer, J. T. (2004). The brain and child development: Time for some critical thinking. In E. Zigler & S. J. Styfco (Eds.), *The Head Start debates* (pp. 423–433). Baltimore, MD: Brookes.

Clements, D. H. (2004). Major themes and recommendations. In D. H. Clements, J. Samara, & A. M. DiBiase (Eds.), *Engaging young children in mathematics: Standards for early childhood mathematics education* (pp. 7–72). Mahwah, NJ: Erlbaum.

Dewey, J. (1938/1973). *Experience and education.* New York: Macmillan.

Epstein, A. S. (1993). *Training for quality: Improving early childhood programs through systematic inservice training.* Ypsilanti, MI: High/Scope Press.

Epstein, A. S. (2007). *Essentials of active learning in the preschool: Getting to know the High/Scope Curriculum.* Ypsilanti, MI: High/Scope Press.

Froebel, F. (1887). *The education of man* (W. N. Hailman, Trans.). New York: D. Appleton.

Gelman, R., & Brenneman, K. (2004). Science learning pathways for young children. *Early Childhood Research Quarterly, 19,* 150–158.

Hanes, M., Flores, L., Rosario, J., Weikart, D. P., & Sanchez, J. (1979). *Un marco abierto: A guide for teachers.* Ypsilanti, MI: High/Scope Press.

High/Scope Educational Research Foundation. (1989). *Program implementation profile.* Ypsilanti, MI: High/Scope Press.

High/Scope Educational Research Foundation. (2000). *The infant-toddler child observation record.* Ypsilanti, MI: High/Scope Press.

High/Scope Educational Research Foundation. (2003). *The preschool child observation record* (2nd ed.). Ypsilanti, MI: High/Scope Press.

Hohmann, M. (2002). *A study guide to educating young children: Exercises for adult learners* (2nd ed.). Ypsilanti, MI: High/Scope Press.

Hohmann, M., & Weikart, D. P. (2002). *Educating young children: Active learning practices for preschool and child care programs* (2nd ed.). Ypsilanti, MI: High/Scope Press.

Kagan, S. L., Moore, E., & Bredekamp, S. (Eds.) (1995, June). *Reconsidering children's early development and learning: Toward comment views and vocabulary.* (Goals 1 Technical Planning Group Report 95-03). Washington, DC: National Education Goals Panel.

Marcon, R. A. (1992). Differential effects of three preschool models on inner city four-year olds. *Early Childhood Research Quarterly, 7,* 517–530.

Montie, J. E., Xiang, Z., & Schweinhart, L. J. (2006). Preschool experience in 10 countries: cognitive and language performance at age 7. *Early Childhood Research Quarterly, 21,* 313–331.

Nabuco, M., & Sylva, K. (1997, September). *A study on the quality of three early childhood curricula in Portugal.* Paper presented at 7th European Conference on the Quality of Early Childhood Education, Munich, Germany.

National Research Council. (2005). *Mathematical and scientific development in early childhood.* Washington, DC: National Academy Press.

Oden, S., Schweinhart, L. J., & Weikart, D. P., with Marcus, S., & Xie, Y. (2000). *Into adulthood: A study of the effects of Head Start.* Ypsilanti, MI: High/Scope Press.

Olmsted, P., & Montie, J. (Eds.). (2001). *What do early childhood settings look like? Structural characteristics of early childhood settings in 15 countries.* Ypsilanti, MI: High/Scope Press.

Piaget, J., & Inhelder, B. (1969). *The psychology of the child.* New York: Basic Books.

Ramsey, P. G. (2006). Early childhood multicultural education. In B. Spodek & O. N. Saracho (Eds.), *Handbook of research on the education of young children* (pp. 279–301). Mahwah, NJ: Erlbaum.

Schweinhart, L. J., Montie, J., Xiang, Z., Barnett, W. S., Belfield, C. R., & Nores, M. (2005). *Lifetime effects: The High/Scope Perry Preschool Study through age 40.* Ypsilanti, MI: High/Scope Press

Schweinhart, L. J., & Weikart, D. P. (1997). *Lasting differences: The High/Scope preschool model comparison study through age 23.* Ypsilanti, MI: High/Scope Press.

Shore, R. (1997). *Rethinking the brain: New insights into early development.* New York: Families and Work Institute.

Thompson, R. A., & Nelson, C. A. (2001). Developmental science and media: Early brain development. *American Psychologist, 56*(1), 5–15.

Vygotsky, L. (1934/1962). *Thought and language.* Cambridge, MA: MIT Press.

Weikart, D. P., Epstein A. S., Schweinhart, L. J., & Bond, J. T. (1978). *The Ypsilanti Preschool Curriculum Demonstration Project: Preschool years and longitudinal results.* Ypsilanti, MI: High/Scope Press.

Weikart, D. P., Hohmann, C. F., & Rhine, W. R. (1981). High/Scope cognitively oriented model. In W. R. Rhine (Ed.), *Making schools more effective: New directions from Follow Through* (pp. 201–247). New York: Academic Press.

Weikart, D. P., Olmsted, P. P., & Montie, J. (Eds.). (2003). *A world of preschool experience: Observations in 15 countries.* Ypsilanti, MI: High/Scope Press.

Weikart, D. P., Rogers, L., Adcock, C., & McClelland, D. (1971). *The cognitively oriented model: A framework for preschool teachers.* Urbana: University of Illinois Press.

Weikart, P. S. (Producer). (2003). *Rhythmically moving series, recordings 1–9* [CD; 2nd ed.]. Ypsilanti, MI: High/Scope Press.

Whitebook, M., Phillips, D., & Howes, C. (1993). *National Child Care Staffing Study revisited: Four years in the life of center-based child care.* Oakland, CA: Child Care Employee Project. Retrieved April 8, 2008, at http://www.ccw.org/pubs/nccssrevisit.pdf

Zill, N., Resnick, G., Kim, K., O'Donnell, K., Sorongon, A., McKey, R. H., Pai-Samant, S., Clark, C., O'Brien, R., & D'Elio, M. A. (2003, May). *Head Start FACES (2000): A whole child perspective on program performance—Fourth progress report.* Prepared for the Administration for Children and Families, U.S. Department of Health and Human Services (DHHS) under contract HHS-105-96-1912, Head Start Quality Research Consortium's Performance Measures Center. Retrieved April 8, 2008, at http:// www.acf.hhs.gov/programs/opre/hs/faces/reports/faces00_4thprogress/faces00_4thprogress.pdf

Chapter 10

Tools of The Mind

The Vygotskian Approach to Early Childhood Education

Elena Bodrova ✤ *Mid-Continent Research for Education and Learning*
Deborah J. Leong ✤ *Metro State College*

THEORETICAL FOUNDATIONS OF THE VYGOTSKIAN APPROACH

Conceptual underpinnings for Tools of the Mind come primarily from Lev Vygotsky's theory of development. Three important concepts are the Cultural-Historical view of development, "tools," and lower and higher mental processes.

Cultural-Historical View of Development

To understand how Vygotskians view early childhood education, one must first understand the goal of education and the Cultural-Historical view of development that is its root. Vygotsky's approach is described by the Vygotskians themselves as the Cultural-Historical approach. It is important, however, that Vygotskians have their own and very specific definition of what the terms *culture* and *history* mean within this approach.

The *history* part refers to Vygotsky's idea that to truly understand psychological processes that are unique to humans, one has to study the history of the development of these processes. This history combines two distinct but interrelated aspects: an individual's history or *ontogeny* and the history of humankind or *phylogeny.* Fully developed psychological processes are difficult to study according to Vygotsky because they usually exist in an internalized and "folded"—or in Vygotsky's own words "fossilized"—form in which many of the component processes are not easily seen. Processes under development, on the other hand, still have an extensive external—and therefore accessible to observation—component, which may provide researchers with an insight into the nature of this particular process (Vygotsky, 1978). Think, for example, of the processes you engage in when reading this paragraph: as an experienced reader you probably carry out most of these processes automatically and cannot fully describe what is going on in your mind as you read. If you were a subject in a reading study, the researchers most likely would use some kind of indirect measure of your reading processes, such as giving you a comprehension test or perhaps scanning your brain as you read, because the processes themselves are not accessible to observation or measurement.

Now contrast this with the behaviors of a child for whom reading has not yet been automatized: most of the behaviors—pointing to the words, sounding words letter by letter, self-correcting, and so on—are external behaviors that a reading researcher can observe, measure, or manipulate. Thus, Vygotskians believe that studying reading from an individual's *historical* perspective allows for our better understanding of this process, its components, and the dynamics. In a similar way, the study of the history of literacy in humankind—from the knot writing of the ancient Incas to pictograms to hieroglyphs to alphabetic systems—reveals the relationships between the functions of written speech and the processes involved in the mastery of writing.

The Vygotskian definition of *culture* in *Cultural-Historical* is somewhat narrower than the meaning we commonly assign to this word. Vygotsky focuses mainly on one component of culture—various signs and symbols that serve as *cultural tools*—and their role in the development of uniquely human mental processes that he called *higher mental functions* (Vygotsky, 1997) Another place *culture* appears in the Cultural-Historical approach is when Vygotskians look at the specific *sociocultural context* of learning and development to see how specific cultural tools as well as culture-specific practices used to teach and learn these affect the development of higher mental functions in an individual or in a particular group.

The Concept of "Tools"

Vygotsky was in agreement with the view popular among his contemporaries that the difference between humans and lower animals is that humans use tools, make new tools, and teach others how to use them. These tools extend human abilities by enabling people to do things that they could not do without them. For example, although you can break smaller twigs and branches using your bare hands, you can cut larger pieces of wood only using an ax or a saw. In a sense, these physical tools act as an extension of human bodies; instead of having stronger hands you now have a "hand-ax" or a "hand-saw," making up for the fact that as a species we do not have bodies as strong as those of other animals.

Vygotsky applied the idea of humans beings as "tool-making animals" in a unique way different from his contemporaries and extended the idea to include a new kind of tool: *mental tools* or *Tools of the Mind*. Similar to the way that physical tools extend our physical abilities by acting as an extension of our body, mental tools extend our mental abilities by acting as an extension of our mind (Vygotsky, 1978). For example, quite often we find ourselves in a situation in which we need to remember too many things. It will not be a problem for the few individuals who have a phenomenal memory, but for the rest of us our memory store is limited in its capacity and we can benefit from some tool that would expand it. In fact, over the course of centuries, humankind has developed many tools that serve as "memory extensions." From a simple string tied around a finger to shopping lists to PDAs—these are all tools we use when we do not want to forget something important.

Like physical tools, mental tools make our life easier; however, unlike physical tools, they do so not by helping us change our environment but by helping us change ourselves. Without a tool we remain at the mercy of an environment that may or may not accidentally prompt our memory (think of all the times you walk into a grocery store only to realize that you forgot what you were supposed to buy and leave with something that has caught your eye!). On the other hand, with a tool, such as a shopping list, we take charge of our own behavior, deciding what we want to remember and when we need to recall this information. Our actions thus change as a result of tool use, from being "slaves to the environment" we become "masters of our own behavior."

Another similarity between physical and mental tools is that humans teach their young how to use both; in other words, children are not born knowing how to use existing tools or how to invent new ones. Therefore, for Vygotsky, one of the major goals of education—formal as well as informal—is to help children acquire the tools of their culture (Karpov, 1995). Teaching children how to use mental tools results in children mastering their own behavior, gaining independence, and reaching a higher developmental level. As children are taught and practice an increasing number of various mental tools, it transforms not only their external behaviors but their very minds, leading to the emergence of a new category of mental functions: *higher mental functions.*

Lower and Higher Mental Functions

Like many of his contemporaries, Vygotsky divided mental processes into lower mental functions and higher mental functions. In Vygotsky's time, it was common to describe lower mental functions as something that can be manifested in reflex, perceptual, and motor behaviors that are easy to observe and measure (think of Pavlov's experiments with dogs). Higher mental functions, on the other hand, were thought to be more complex processes to which objective methods of study were not applicable and which could only be accessed through a person's self-report. Unlike his contemporaries, Vygotsky did not consider lower and higher mental functions to be completely independent of each other, but he instead proposed a theory in which these two sets of functions interact (Vygotsky, 1997).

Vygotsky describes *lower mental functions* as common to human beings and higher animals. These functions are innate and depend primarily on maturation to develop. Examples of lower mental functions include sensations, spontaneous attention, associative memory, and sensorimotor intelligence.

Sensation refers to using any of the senses and is determined by the anatomy and physiology of a sensory system in a particular species. For example, diurnal animals typically possess color vision, while nocturnal animals are often color blind. Reactive attention refers to attention that is drawn to strong environmental stimuli, as when a dog suddenly reacts to the sound of a garage door opening or a baby starts crying at the sound of thunder. Associative memory is the ability to connect two stimuli together in memory after repeated presentation of the two together—one stimuli triggers the memory of its pair. Remembering someone's face or the phone number when hearing this person's name is an example of our use of associative memory. In a similar way, laboratory animals remember the shortest way to the food after having run the maze numerous times. Sensorimotor intelligence in the Vygotskian framework describes problem solving in situations that involve physical or motor manipulations and trial and error.

Unique to humans, *higher mental functions* are cognitive processes acquired through learning and teaching. The main difference between lower and higher mental functions is that the latter involve the use of mental tools. Higher mental functions include mediated perception, focused attention, deliberate memory, and logical thinking. When we distinguish different colors, placing lime green in a different category than olive green, we are using *mediated perception. Focused attention* describes the ability to concentrate on any stimulus, whether it stands out or blends with the background. Finding a particular word on a page filled with printed words calls for focused attention. *Deliberate memory* refers to the use of memory strategies to remember something. *Logical thinking* involves the ability to solve problems mentally using logic and other strategies.

All higher mental functions are acquired in a culturally specific way that affects their development via a system of practices common to a specific culture and mental tools this culture has developed to carry out these practices. Mediated perception, for example, is a higher mental function found in all humans, but different groups may develop better differentiation of certain colors, smells, or tastes.

Vygotsky describes higher mental functions as deliberate, mediated, and internalized behaviors (Vygotsky, 1997). By characterizing higher mental functions as *deliberate,* he means that they are controlled by the person and not by the environment and that their use is based on thought and choice. The behaviors guided by higher mental functions can be directed or focused on specific aspects of the environment, such as ideas, perceptions, and images, while ignoring other inputs. These deliberate behaviors become possible because they do not depend on the environment in an immediate and direct fashion but instead are *mediated* by the use of tools. Nondeliberate behaviors depend on external circumstances: for some students, for example, whether or not they can answer a question on a test depends on whether this piece of information was something they read most recently or something they heard most frequently. In contrast, students who use focused attention and deliberate memory go through an extra step of using tools: for example, they underline or highlight specific words and passages in the textbook—to make sure they will pay attention to these words later when studying for a test. By the time higher mental functions are fully developed, most of the tools used are not external but internal (such as mnemonics) and so are the processes involved in using these tools. Vygotsky describes this process as *internalization,* emphasizing that when external behaviors "grow into the mind," they maintain the same structure, focus, and function as their external precursors.

For Vygotsky, higher mental functions do not appear in children in their fully developed form. Instead, they undergo a long process of development in the course of which a fundamental reorganization of lower mental functions occurs (Vygotsky 1994). It means that as children start utilizing higher mental functions more frequently, their lower mental functions do not disappear completely but are used less and less. For example, as children acquire language, they continue to use their associative memory, but now they depend less and less on their ability to recollect things spontaneously and more and more on the use of various memory strategies.

Vygotsky described the mechanism of the development of higher mental functions as their gradual transformation from being shared by a child with two or more people to something that belongs to this child only. Vygotsky called this transition from shared to individual the *general law of cultural development* and emphasized the following:

> Every function in the child's cultural development appears twice: first, on the social level, and later, on the individual level; first between people (inter-psychological), and then inside the child (intra-psychological). This applies equally to voluntary attention, to logical memory, and to the formation of concepts. (Vygotsky, 1978, p. 57)

This view of higher mental functions differs significantly from other psychological theories that, while acknowledging other people's influences on a person's individual development, still ultimately place all mental processes in this individual's mind. For Vygotsky, in contrast, not only *what* a child knows but *how* this child thinks, remembers, or attends is shaped by the child's prior interactions with parents, teachers, and peers. For Vygotskians, early childhood education is the first step in a long process in which young children are engaged in the acquisition of "tools" and the development of higher mental functions that are learned from the people in the child's world.

VYGOTSKIAN VIEW OF LEARNING AND TEACHING

Teachers and young children can work and play together to co-construct knowledge and understanding, according to Vygotsky's view of learning and teaching.

Learning Can Lead Development

The Cultural-Historical approach holds that human development involves a complex interplay between the processes of natural development that are determined biologically and the processes of cultural development brought about by the interactions of the growing individuals with other people and cultural artifacts. In more practical terms, it means that although some learning cannot occur until the developmental prerequisites are in place—as in the case of children not being able to write until they reach a certain level of development of their fine motor skills—the opposite is also true: Certain developments in cognitive, social, or language areas cannot simply emerge as a result of maturation but rather depend on what a child learns. Based on research done on children of different ages raised in different cultures, Vygotsky concludes that some developments that were previously thought to be universally present in a certain age—such as the ability to use abstract reasoning—in reality are an outgrowth of a very specific kind of learning experience typically associated with formal schooling (Vygotsky, 1987). In the course of formal schooling, teachers teach—and students learn—a specific system of mental tools that brings these students' cognitive development to a qualitatively different level.

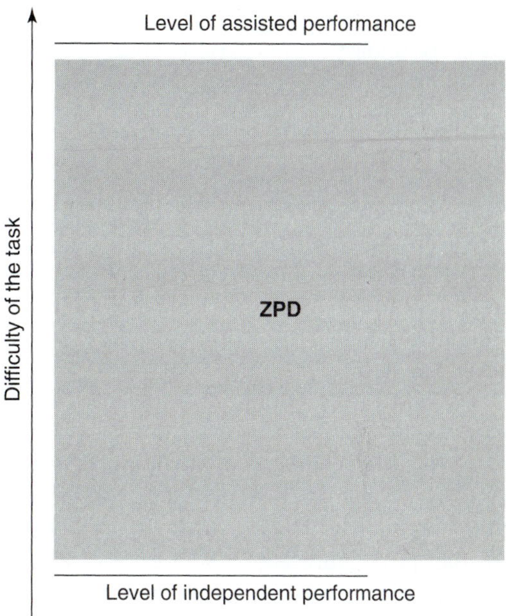

FIGURE 10–1 **The Zone of Proximal Development**

Zone of Proximal Development

Vygotsky's idea of the Zone of Proximal Development (ZPD) reflects both the complexity of the relationship between learning and development and the dynamics of the transitions from shared forms of mental processes to their individual forms (see Figure 10–1):

> [What] we call the Zone of Proximal Development . . . is a distance between the actual developmental level determined by individual problem solving and the level of development as determined through problem solving under guidance or in collaboration with more capable peers. (Vygotsky, 1978, p. 86)

The word *zone* is used because Vygotsky conceived children's development not as points on a scale but as a continuum of skills and competencies at different levels of mastery. By using the word *proximal,* he pointed out that the zone is limited to those skills and competencies that will develop in the near future. *Proximal* is meant to describe not all possible skills and competencies that will eventually emerge but only those that are closest to emergence at a specific time, or as Vygotsky put it, are "on the edge of emergence."

Two levels of performance define the boundaries of a child's ZPD:

- The lower boundary is defined by the child's level of independent performance. *Independent performance* is what the child is capable of doing alone, without any help from anyone else.
- The upper boundary is the most the child is capable of doing when given the help by a more knowledgeable person, such as the teacher. It is this child's level of *assisted performance.*

Between the levels of independent performance and assisted performance lie skills and competencies that require varying degrees of assistance to surface: those that are closer to the lower boundary require only little help, and those that are closer to the upper boundary cannot be displayed by the child without a great deal of assistance.

These skills and competencies do not determine children's developmental level but rather their learning potential. In the absence of guidance or collaboration with more competent others, this potential might not be realized and consequently a higher developmental level will be never attained.

A child's ZPD is fluid and changes as the child learns. What a child can only do with assistance today the same child will perform independently tomorrow. Then, as the child tackles more difficult tasks, a new level of assisted performance emerges (see Figure 10–2). This cycle is repeated again and again as the child acquires increasingly more complex skills and competencies.

Vygotsky used the idea of ZPD to demonstrate why methods of assessing children popular at his time cannot produce an accurate picture of child development. In the case of IQ testing, for example, these methods, which prohibited testers from providing any help to a child, did not discriminate between this child's low level of performance being a result of mental retardation or educational deprivation. Vygotsky suggested incorporating adults' assistance in the form of hints, prompts, or rephrasing the test questions into the very procedure of assessment. This modification allows for assessing not only children's existing skills and competencies but also the ones that have not yet surfaced due to the lack of adequate shared experiences but nonetheless have a potential to develop (Vygotsky, 1956). Vygotsky's insight later led to emergence of a new methodology of assessment called "dynamic assessment" that is currently used in such fields as clinical psychology and special education.

Vygotsky also defined ZPD as the area that should be targeted by instruction. He pointed

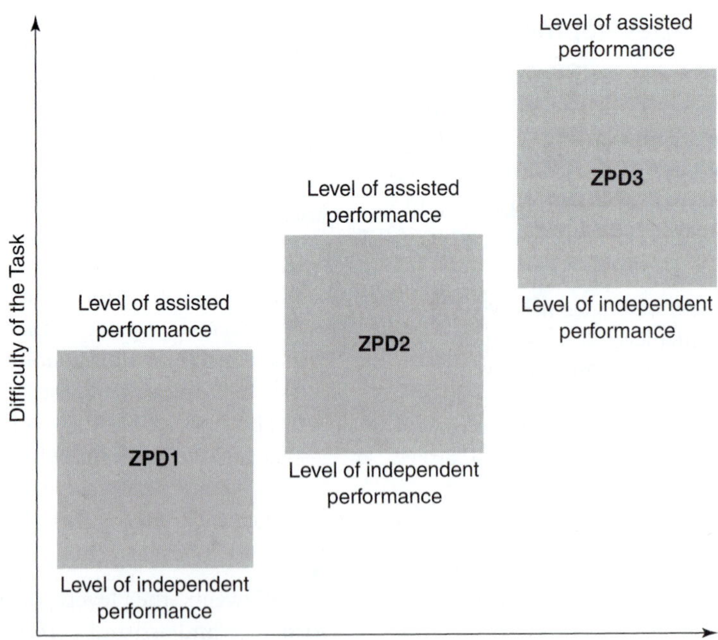

FIGURE 10–2 **Changes in a Child's ZPD Over Time**

out that to be maximally effective, instruction should be aimed at each child's individual ZPD (Vygotsky, 1978). Skills and competencies that are outside the child's zone cannot be affected by instruction either because the child has already mastered them completely or because they are so difficult that at this point in time the child is not yet ready to benefit from any assistance.

The Role of the Teacher in Children's Learning and Development

Consistent with his view of development as being culturally determined, Vygotsky believed that the role of the teacher is more than teaching facts and skills. Teachers, he noted, can actually shape children's development by helping them acquire the mental tools of their culture. This view is reflected in the following three main principles of Vygotskian-based education.

Teachers and Children Co-Construct Knowledge. Similar to other constructivists, Vygotsky believed that children construct their own understandings and do not passively reproduce what is presented to them. However, for Vygotsky, children's process of construction always takes place in a cultural context and is mediated—directly or indirectly—by other people (Karpov, 2005). In the classroom setting, a teacher can directly affect a child's construction of knowledge by focusing the child's attention on a specific object or by using specific words. The teacher can also affect the child's construction of knowledge in an indirect way by orchestrating the context for this child's interactions with other children or by providing certain instructional materials.

Scaffolding Helps Children Make a Transition from Assisted to Independent Performance. Even after children develop new skills and competencies sufficiently to perform a task with adult assistance, it may not mean that tomorrow they will be ready to perform this task independently. For most children, the transition from assisted to independent learning is a gradual process that involves moving from using a great deal of assistance to slowly taking over until eventually no assistance is needed (Wood, Bruner, & Ross, 1976). For a teacher, to facilitate this transition means that the teacher needs to *scaffold* student learning by first designing and then following a plan for providing and withdrawing appropriate amounts of assistance at appropriate times. Although not used by Vygotsky himself, the concept of scaffolding helps us understand how aiming instruction within a child's ZPD can promote this child's learning and development.

Instruction Should Amplify Child Development and Not Accelerate It. Vygotsky's idea of effective teaching being aimed at a child's ZPD was further extended by his students, namely Alexander Zaporozhets, who applied this idea to early childhood education. Emphasizing the need to teach skills and competencies within rather than outside young children's ZPD, Zaporozhets condemned the practice of *acceleration of development*—which intends to prematurely turn a toddler into a preschooler and a preschooler into a first-grader (Zaporozhets, 1986). An alternative to this unnecessary acceleration is *amplification of development*—using the child's ZPD to its fullest by making sure that all skills and competencies that have potential to emerge indeed emerge at the appropriate time.

VYGOTSKIAN VIEW OF CHILD DEVELOPMENT

For Vygotsky, child development during the early years leading to school readiness is driven by the types of interactions children have with the social environment centered on accomplishing important developmental tasks.

Social Situation of Development as the Main Mechanism of Development

Vygotsky believed that child development includes both qualitative and quantitative changes. When qualitative changes happen, the entire system of mental functions undergoes major restructuring, resulting in the emergence of new cognitive and social-emotional formations or developmental accomplishments. Likewise, there are periods when no new formations appear, but children still continue to develop their existing competencies. During these periods, growth occurs as a quantitative change in the number of things the child can remember and process. Though not strictly a "stage theory," Vygotsky's view of child development includes the concept of "age periods"—infancy, toddlerhood, preschool and kindergarten age, elementary school age, and adolescence—each building on the previous one and each defined by its unique set of developmental accomplishments (Karpov, 2005). Children's progress from one period to the next is determined by the interaction between children's existing and emerging competencies on one hand and their social situation of development on the other. *Social situation of development* comprises what society expects of children at a certain age, what kinds of activities and interactions become available to them, and what kinds of mental tools adults help them to acquire. For Vygotsky, social situation of development "represents the initial moment for all dynamic changes that occur in development during the given period. It determines wholly and completely the forms and the path along which the child will acquire ever newer personality characteristics, drawing them from the social reality as from the basic source of development, the path along which the social becomes the individual" (Vygotsky, 1998, p. 198). Vygotsky sees the changes in the social situation of development as the mechanism that propels development forward by providing new and more advanced mental tools that continue to shape children's growing competencies.

Developmental Accomplishments and Leading Activity

In the work of Vygotsky's students, his original view of age periods was refined and expanded to form the theory of child development that contains well-defined stages along with the explanation of the mechanisms underlying children' transition from one stage to the next (Karpov, 2005). One of the major innovations contributed by the post-Vygotskians to his theory of child development is the introduction of the idea of leading activity that replaced Vygotsky's original notion of social situation of development. *Leading activity* was defined as a type of interaction between children and the social environment that leads to the emergence of the developmental accomplishments in one period of life and that will prepare them for the next period (Leont'ev, 1981). *Developmental accomplishments,* in turn, were defined as competencies and skills that are not only new to a specific age period but are also critical for the child's ability to engage in a leading activity of the following period (Karpov). For example, the ability to think in images is a developmental accomplishment for toddlers because this ability is critical for the development of make-believe play, which is a leading activity of the preschool age. Table 10–1 summarizes the characteristics of the developmental periods of early childhood in the Vygotskian tradition.

The Vygotskian Approach to School Readiness

Vygotsky's view on school readiness stems from his idea of social situation of development as a main force propelling child development. The transition from preschool to school means major

TABLE 10–1
Leading Activities and Developmental Accomplishments in Early Childhood

Age Period	Leading Activity	Developmental Accomplishments
Infancy	Emotional interactions with caregivers	Attachment Object-oriented sensorimotor actions
Toddlerhood	Object-oriented joint activity with adults	Beginnings of symbolic thinking Beginnings of self-regulation Language Self-concept
Preschool and Kindergarten	Make-believe play	Ability to act on an internal mental plane Symbolic thought Self-regulation Imagination Integration of emotions and cognition
Elementary Grades	Learning activity	Theoretical reasoning Higher mental functions Motivation to learn

changes in the social situations that the child participates in—a change in the nature of the interactions involved in schooling and in the expectations associated with the role of "student." To gain awareness of society's expectations associated with the role of a student and to develop the abilities to meet these expectations, children have to actually participate in school activities and to enter specific social interactions with teachers and other students. In other words, for Vygotsky, school readiness was being formed *during* the first months of schooling and not prior to school entry. However, certain accomplishments of preschool age make it easier for children to develop this readiness. Among these accomplishments are mastery of some mental tools, development of self-regulation, and integration of emotions and cognition. With these prerequisites in place, a preschool-age child could make the necessary transition from learning that "follows child's own agenda" to the learning that "follows the school agenda" (Vygotsky, 1956).

APPLICATIONS OF THE VYGOTSKIAN THEORY IN THE EARLY CHILDHOOD CLASSROOM

Educational philosophy of teaching young children based on the Vygotskian theory can be summarized as follows:

- Teachers promote and foster development by engaging children in the activities that are the leading activities for their age, such as make-believe play.
- Teachers focus on promoting the development of higher mental functions and on children's acquisition of cultural tools and not on learning of discrete skills and concepts.
- Interventions for children with special needs are based on the idea of re-mediation: children are taught to compensate for the deficiencies in their lower mental functions by developing higher mental functions using specific mental tools.

Fostering Child Development by Engaging Children in the Leading Activities

Since make-believe play is the leading activity for preschool- and kindergarten-age children, supporting play is a priority in a Vygotsky-based early childhood classroom.

Vygotskian Definition of Play. As Vygotsky studied how play affects the young child's emerging higher mental functions, he concluded that play "is not the predominant form of activity, but is, in a certain sense, the leading source of development in preschool years" (1967, p. 6). This idea of play being the leading source of development for young children was later elaborated by Vygotsky's colleagues Alexei Leont'ev and Daniel Elkonin, who considered play the "leading activity" for preschool- and kindergarten-age children (Elkonin, 1972; Leont'ev, 1981). In their writings, however, Vygotsky and his colleagues limited their definition of play to the dramatic or make-believe play of preschoolers and children of primary-school age. The Vygotskian definition of play does not include such activities as object manipulations and explorations that are considered precursors to play and such activities as games and sports that are considered outgrowths of play. "Real" play, according to Vygotsky, has three components:

- Children create an imaginary situation.
- Children take on and act out roles.
- Children follow a set of rules determined by specific roles.

While imaginary situations and roles in make-believe play have been often mentioned by other researchers in their analysis of play, the idea that play is not totally spontaneous but is instead contingent on players abiding by a set of rules was first introduced by Vygotsky. At first, the notion of play being the most restrictive context for a child's actions may sound completely counterintuitive. However, Vygotsky argued that this rule-based nature is an essential characteristic of children's make-believe play:

> Whenever there is an imaginary situation in play, there are rules—not rules that are formulated in advance and change during the course of the game, but rules stemming from the imaginary situation. Therefore, to imagine that a child can behave in an imaginary situation without rules, i.e., as he behaves in a real situation, is simply impossible. If the child is playing the role of a mother, then she has rules of maternal behavior. The role the child plays, and her relationship to the object if the object has changed its meaning, will always stem from the rules, i.e., the imaginary situation will always contain rules. In play the child is free. But this is an illusory freedom. (Vygotsky, 1967, p. 10)

Make-Believe Play as a Source of Development. Vygotsky assigned play a special place in his theory, listing it specifically as one of the social contexts responsible for creating young children's ZPD:

> In play the child is always behaving beyond his age, above his usual everyday behavior; in play he is, as it were, a head above himself. Play contains in a concentrated form, as in the focus of a magnifying glass, all developmental tendencies; it is as if the child tries to jump above his usual level. The relationship of play to development should be compared to the relationship between instruction and development. . . . Play is a source of development and creates the zone of proximal development. (Vygotsky, 1978, p. 74).

Vygotsky's statement on play as a source of the ZPD means that young children's performance in play is higher than their performance in non-play contexts. This idea was confirmed in a series of experiments done by Vygotsky's students. For example, Manujlenko (Elkonin, 1978) and Istomina (Istomina, 1977) found that the young child's mental skills are at a higher level during play than during other activities, representing operating at what Vygotsky identified as the higher level of the ZPD. Manujlenko, in particular, found higher levels of self-regulation of children's physical behaviors in play than in non-play contexts. For example, when a boy was asked to be the lookout, he remained at his post and did not move for a longer period of time than he could when the experimenter asked him to stand still in a laboratory condition.

In another study, Istomina compared the number of words children could deliberately remember during a dramatic play session involving a grocery store with the number of words they could remember in a typical laboratory experiment. In both situations, children were given a list of unrelated words to remember. In the dramatic play situation, the words were presented as the items on a "shopping list" to use in a pretend grocery store. In the laboratory experiment, the instructions were simply to memorize the words. Istomina found that preschoolers remembered more items in the dramatic play condition, functioning at the level that older children could demonstrate in the non-play condition that was similar to a typical school task. These findings support Vygotsky's view of play as the "focus of a magnifying glass" (see preceding quotation), indicating that new developmental accomplishments do become apparent in play far earlier than they do in other activities.

Vygotsky maintained that for children of preschool and kindergarten age, their mastery of academic skills is not as good a predictor of their later scholastic abilities as the quality of their play. In a 4-year-old's play one can observe higher levels of such abilities as attention, symbolizing, and problem solving than in other situations—one can actually watch the child of tomorrow.

Implications of Vygotsky's Theory of Play for Early Childhood Educators. Vygotsky's theory underscores the value of make-believe play for child development, including the development of competencies that make children ready for formal schooling. First, play helps children develop the ability to self-regulate their physical, social, and cognitive behaviors: that is, to engage in these behaviors following some external or internalized rules rather than acting on impulse. Children who cannot pay attention or follow directions usually have a hard time mastering academic subjects, as do children who cannot control their emotions. Contrary to a typical adult's view of play as a time when children are free to do whatever they please, Vygotsky viewed play as the activity placing the *most* restraints on children's actions and thus forcing children to practice self-regulation far more often than in any other activity. These restraints come in the form of rules that a child has to follow: for example, once she agrees to play "baby" and not "mommy" (baby does not use a knife and needs to wait to be fed) or to use a paper plate to stand for a steering wheel and not for a pie (one can take a bite when holding a pie but not a steering wheel).

Not all play is equally beneficial for the development of self-regulation. Current studies of the relationship between play and self-regulation confirm Vygotsky's belief that make-believe play can improve self-regulation especially in highly impulsive, "hard to manage" children (Berk, Mann, & Ogan, 2006). However, it happens only when children are able to create a joint imaginary situation, take on the roles of various pretend characters, and act these out using imaginary props, language, and symbolic gestures.

Another important outgrowth of make-believe play is abstract thinking. Using various props to represent "the real things" in play, children learn to separate the meaning or idea of the object from the object itself. When a child pretends to "drive" a block on a carpet as if it were a truck, this child separates the idea of "truck-ness" from a truck and attaches it to the block. This ability to separate the meaning from the object is a precursor for the development of abstract thought when a child has to manipulate ideas that may not have an immediate connection with the tangible objects:

> A child learns to consciously recognize his own actions and becomes aware that every object has a meaning. From the point of view of development, the fact of creating an imaginary situation can be regarded as a means of developing abstract thought. (Vygotsky, 1967, p. 17)

As with self-regulation, not all make-believe play equally promotes the development of abstract thinking. The best kind of play is where children use props that are unstructured and multi-functional as opposed to function specific and realistic. With realistic toys, there is no need to separate meaning from the object since the real object and the pretend one look alike and can be used in a similar manner (see Figure 10–3). On the other hand, when children use non-realistic props they not only have to constantly change the meaning of these props but also have to use different words to describe these changes to their playmates (see Figure 10–4). For example, children can use the same cardboard box first for a garage, then for a gas station, and then for a grocery store. Since the box looks the same as it represents all three buildings, children will need to communicate the change in its function by naming it differently—otherwise a child playing "mechanic" will end up in the grocery store changing tires!

Elena Bodrova

FIGURE 10–3 Realistic Play Props: Plastic food is an example of a realistic prop.

Chris Gerding

FIGURE 10–4 Non-Realistic Play Props: A child uses a block as a telephone.

Table 10–2 shows the difference between the way a traditional early childhood classroom would support play and the way a classroom using a Vygotskian approach, such as a Tools of the Mind classroom, would support play.

Promoting Children's Acquisition of Mental Tools and Higher Mental Functions

For Vygotskians, the goal of education in general and early childhood education in particular is more than to equip children with a set of specific skills and knowledge. Instead, they see this goal as helping children acquire mental tools and higher mental functions (Bodrova & Leong, 2007). The examples of cultural tools that children begin mastering at a very young age include gaining control of their external behavior through the use of self-directed speech,

TABLE 10–2
Supporting Play as a Leading Activity of Young Children

Elements of Play	Most ECE Classrooms	Tools of the Mind Classrooms
Children engage in make-believe play	Mostly in the housekeeping/dramatic play area	In all centers
The duration of play	Remains unchanged throughout the year and depends on the duration of center time in the class schedule	• Will increase as children gain better control of their behaviors • By the end of the year, children have up to 50–60 minutes of uninterrupted play
Play time used by the teachers	• To provide additional one-on-one time to struggling students by taking them out of play centers *or* • To use play context for teaching content skills (e.g., working on numbers and shapes in the block area)	• To support children's use of play-related vocabulary • To support children's imaginary use of unstructured and multi-functional props • To support children's development of pretend scenarios
Play theme	• May remain unchanged for most part of the year (e.g., children play "family") • Often focuses on the objects • May change frequently (e.g., every week or every other week) as the teacher introduces a new unit (e.g., apples or insects)	• Lasts for 4 to 5 weeks to allow children to build background knowledge necessary for extended play • Focuses on people and the roles people play (e.g., the content of apples may be covered as children play Farm or Store)
Play props	• Often are heavily represented by store-bought toys and props or are made by the teacher • Often consist of very realistic replicas of objects	• Are largely multifunctional and/or unstructured • Can be made by children themselves or with minimal teacher's help
Teachers intervene when. . . .	Children argue or fight	Children need help to create, become involved in, maintain, or extend a play scenario

developing deliberate memory through the use of drawing and writing, and performing arithmetic computation by counting on fingers. In all these instances, tools help children solve problems that require engaging mental processes at the levels not yet available to them (e.g., when a task calls for deliberate memorization or for focused attention). In a typical early childhood classroom, we can see many cases of children using various tools to aid their learning, such as using alphabet charts to remind them of the associations between letter sounds and letter symbols or singing the ABC song to prompt their memory of the letter order in the alphabet. In the Vygotskian view, the use of these tools not only assists children with the task at hand but actually restructures their mind, supporting the development of higher mental functions.

Private Speech as a Mental Tool. For Vygotsky, many mental tools are language based and language itself is the most powerful mental tool. Major transformations in a child's mind associated with the development of higher mental functions depend on how well the child masters the use of speech—first oral and later written. According to Vygotsky, it is during preschool years that children start using their speech not only for communicating to others but also for communicating to themselves and a new form of speech—private speech—emerges (Vygotsky, 1987). When children use private speech they talk aloud, but many of their utterances are not addressed to anyone in particular and often cannot be understood by anyone but the child herself. Unlike Piaget who associated this phenomenon with children's egocentrism and considered it a sign of immature thinking, Vygotsky viewed private speech as a step on the continuum from public (social) speech to inner speech and eventually to verbal thinking (Vygotsky, 1987).* From this perspective, private speech becomes not a sign of immaturity but instead a sign of progressive development of cognitive processes.

Vygotsky described two major changes occurring in the use of private speech during preschool years. First, the function of private speech changes. Used initially to simply accompany children's practical actions, private speech eventually becomes exclusively self directed and changes its function to one of organizing children's own behaviors. At the same time, the syntax of private speech changes. From complete sentences typical for social speech, a child's utterances change into abbreviated phrases and single words unsuited for the purposes of communication to other people but sufficient for communicating to oneself. Eventually, private speech goes inside and evolves into verbal thought. Vygotsky uses these two metamorphoses of private speech to illustrate the universal path of the acquisition of cultural tools: They are first used externally in interactions with other people and then internalized and used by an individual to master his or her own mental functions. The onset of private speech signals an important development in self-regulation: Starting with regulating their practical actions, children expand their use of private speech to regulate a variety of their mental processes.

The use of private speech as an essential mental tool for young children should be encouraged in the early childhood classroom. Since for Vygotsky young children "think as they talk," teachers should not try to keep young children quiet when they engage in thinking and problem solving. On the contrary, current research supports Vygotsky's observations that children's use of private speech increases as children attempt to solve more challenging tasks. While it is natural for an adult to think quietly before speaking, for young children often the actual thought occurs in the process of expressing it, so a classroom full of very quiet kindergartners may be a sign that there is not much thinking going on!

Written Speech as a Mental Tool. The central part of Vygotsky's approach to early writing is the idea that children learn to employ the instrumental function of written speech to expand their mental capacities:

> The development of written language belongs to the . . . most obvious line of cultural development because it is connected with the mastery of an external system of means developed and created in the process of cultural development of humanity. (Vygotsky, 1997, p. 133)

Studies conducted by Vygotsky's colleague Alexander Luria, in connection with Vygotsky's general research program, demonstrated that even very young children do use written symbols as memory aids (Luria, 1998). Some of

---

*Vygotsky used the term "egocentric speech" to describe audible self-directed speech; however, in the Western literature, this phenomenon is commonly referred to as "private speech" (see, e.g., Berk & Winsler, 1995).

Luria's findings (such as the ability of 3-year old children to reliably "read" and "re-read" their own scribbles) made their way into Western literature and inspired researchers to study early forms of writing that appear prior to the onset of formal schooling (see, e.g., Ferreiro & Teberosky, 1982). Vygotsky traced the roots of children's writing to their early drawings, concluding that these drawings are used in the function similar to written words, both conveying only essential and constant characteristics of objects. From that, Vygotsky concludes that young children's drawings are "a unique graphic speech, a graphic story about something . . . more speech than representation" (Vygotsky, 1997, p. 138). It means that learning to write does not start from learning to form letters but instead starts from learning to use symbolic marks to represent a message. Learning letters supplies the final component to move the child from idiosyncratic forms of "drawing speech" to a conventional way of recording speech in written words (see Figure 10–5).

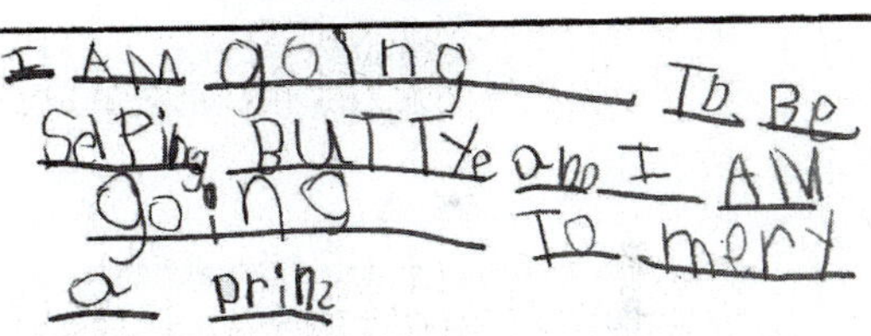

FIGURE 10–5 A Sample of Writing Done by a 5-Year-Old Child in the Context of Make-Believe Play

Discussing the methods of teaching writing, Vygotsky emphasizes that "teaching must be set up so that reading and writing satisfy the child's need" and that the goal of the instruction should be "to teach a child written language and not writing the alphabet" (Vygotsky, 1997). In the absence of play and self-initiated drawing, children who learn to write master merely the skills of letter formation: They do not use written language the way it is supposed to be used in the culture—as a means of communication with others and with oneself. Vygotsky uses an example of perfect handwriting produced by 4-year-olds attending Montessori schools: The content of their letters indicated that they did not use writing to express their own thoughts or feelings; they were writing what the teachers dictated to them, or they copied the teacher's messages (coincidentally, make-believe play has never been and still is not a part of the traditional Montessori curriculum).

At the same time, Vygotsky advocates early instruction in writing (at age 3 or 4) that emphasizes the communicative and instrumental function of written language and not the mechanics of its production (Vygotsky, 1997). True to his own belief that good instruction should lead development and not follow it, Vygotsky explains the value of learning to write early, not in the context of preparing children for formal schooling but in the broader context of using cultural tools for supporting the development of higher mental functions.

Table 10–3 summarizes the differences between how a traditional early childhood classroom and a Vygotskian-based classroom, such as in a Tools of the Mind classroom, would support the use of mental tools.

TABLE 10–3
Supporting Children's Use of "Mental Tools" Throughout the Day

Classroom Routines	Most ECE Classrooms	Tools of the Mind Classrooms
Large group	Teacher calls on an individual child to answer a question.	Children talk to each other as they answer the question.
Small group	Children work on individual projects or tasks.	Children work in pairs using visual aids to remind each partner of his or her role (see the picture of Buddy Reading, Figure 10–6).
Movement games	Children play movement games following music or teacher directions.	Children play movement games that require them to follow more complex rules or to switch from one set of rules to another. As they play these games, children are encouraged to talk to themselves to control their movements (see Figure 10–7, Pattern Movement Game).
Before center time	• Children are assigned centers by a teacher. *or* • Children choose a center and say to the teacher where they want to play.	Children make "play plans" (see Figure 10–8) representing what they want to do and with whom they want to play. They plan by engaging in talking, drawing, and writing
During center time	• Teacher monitors children's choice of centers, making sure children stay where they said they will. *or* • Children move between centers, often interrupting each other's play.	Children monitor their own and their friends' choice of centers by using visual reminders (e.g., colored clothespins or necklaces) that match the color of the center sign (Figure 10–8).
Cleanup time	The teacher signals when it is time to clean up by using a song or a timer.	Children use a specially selected song as a strategy to keep track of time left until the end of cleanup.

Re-mediation as the Core Principle of Special Education

Abnormal psychology and special education for Vygotsky were one of his passions and at the same time one of the main sources of his theoretical insights. Vygotsky's view of disabilities is consistent with his major principle of social determination of the human mind: For him a disability is a sociocultural and developmental phenomenon and not a biological one.

Social and Cultural Nature of Disabilities. Vygotsky believed that children with disabilities follow a different developmental path than their typically developing peers, with their disability affecting other areas of development in a complex and systemic way. To emphasize the complex and systemic nature of this relationship, Vygotsky used the terms *disontogenesis* or *distorted development,* emphasizing that distortions of development, as

Penny Farster-Narlesky

FIGURE 10–6 Buddy Reading

well as the normal path of development, are always culturally specific. The major components that determine the course of development for a child with a disability include the primary disability (e.g., visual impairment or restricted movements) and the social context in which the child develops (Vygotsky, 1993). This social context would determine the extent to which this child would be considered (and will consider himself) "disabled." For example, compare two children who experience similar problems in coordinating movements of their eyes while focusing on near objects. For a child living in a

Danielle Erickson

FIGURE 10–7 Pattern Movement

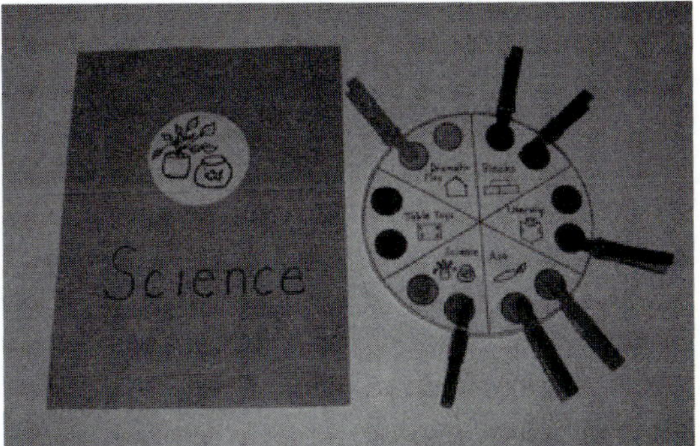

Jerry Hensen

FIGURE 10–8 Visual Reminder of Centers

Western industrialized country, this problem will interfere with her or his ability to track print when reading. On the other hand, a child living in a herding community might not even have a need for tracking small objects since most daily tasks will involve looking at larger objects at a distance. Evidently the same visual "deficit" may go virtually unnoticed in a society that does not rely on written texts for carrying out essential tasks but may put another child at risk of developing reading disability and, sometimes, even on the road to academic failure associated with the possibility of subsequent social and emotional complications.

As a result of the interaction between the primary disability and the social context, a secondary disability can develop. While the child's primary disabilities affect primarily lower mental functions, secondary disabilities are the distortions of higher mental functions. The reason that the secondary disabilities develop is that primary disabilities often prevent a child from mastering cultural tools critical for engaging in social interactions; in turn, limited social interactions prevent the child from acquiring even more cultural tools, which eventually leads to systemic distortions in this child's mental functioning. On the other hand, if the social context provides this child with an opportunity to learn an alternative set of cultural tools, this child may be able to participate in a wide range of social interactions and as a result may develop higher mental functions.

Vygotsky's Approach to Special Education. Unlike other approaches to special education that focus on restoring the very function that is affected, for Vygotsky the primary disability should not be the main focus of the remediation efforts (Vygotsky, 1993). He argues that, contrary to common wisdom, a primary disability is not the easiest one but the hardest one to remediate because it affects lower mental functions: Lower mental functions are biologically determined (in today's language, we would call them "hard-wired"), and it is exactly because of their biological nature that they cannot be changed by means other than radical medical intervention, such as inserting a hearing implant to improve hearing. On the other hand, higher mental functions are culturally and socially determined and as such can be successfully remediated in the course of specifically designed educational interventions. Vygotsky advocates focusing on higher and not lower mental functions in remediation, contending that "the developmental limitations in higher knowledge go beyond sensorimotor training which is possible in the elementary processes. *Thought is the highest form of compensation for the insufficiencies of visual perception*" (Vygotsky, 1993, p. 204).

For Vygotsky and his students, the way to engage higher mental functions to compensate for the deficiencies in lower mental functions is by using specific mental tools. Since all mental tools work as mediators, helping children gain control over their own mental functions—replacing a set of tools that do not work for a child with a disability with another set—can be called *re-mediation*. The best known example of such re-mediation is teaching visually impaired children to use Braille symbols instead of regular letters. Vygotsky's students extended this approach to many other disabilities, designing many disability-specific tools and strategies to teach these, thus creating the system of special education based on the ideas of re-mediation.

CONCLUSION

In this chapter we have discussed the Vygotskian approach to early childhood education, summarizing the major tenets of his theory and the application of these ideas to practical classroom interactions. The Vygotskian approach helps teachers to understand their role in the learning and teaching process with emphasis on process rather than product and on the importance of developing higher mental functions. In the section on applications to the classroom, it is clear that this theoretical view leads to specific recommendations for the development of make-believe play, the development of literacy, and the kinds of interventions that should be used when working with children with special needs.

RESOURCES

Web Sites on Vygotsky
http://en.wikipedia.org/wiki/Lev_Vygotsky

Classroom Applications/Curriculum
http://www.toolsofthemind.org

DVDs: http://www.davidsonfilmsstore.com

- *Vygotsky: An Introduction,* Davidson Films, 1994.
- *Play: The Vygotskian Approach,* Davidson Films, 1996.
- *Scaffolding Self-Regulated Learning in the Primary Grades,* Davidson Films, 1996.

Books on Vygotsky

Kozulin, A. (1990). *Vygotsky's psychology: A biography of ideas.* Cambridge, MA: Harvard University Press.

Kozulin, A., Gindis, B., Ageyev, V. & Miller, S. (Eds.). (2003). *Vygotsky's educational theory in cultural context.* Cambridge, MA: Cambridge University Press.

Moll, L. C. (Ed.). (1990). *Vygotsky and education: Instructional implications and applications of sociohistorical psychology.* New York: Cambridge University Press.

Van der Veer, R., & Valsiner, J. (1991). *Understanding Vygotsky: A quest for synthesis.* Oxford, England: Basil Blackwell.

Selected Readings from Vygotsky

Rieber, R., & Robinson, D. (Eds.). (2004). *The essential Vygotsky.* New York: Kluwer/Plenum.

Van der Veer, R., & Valsiner, J. (Eds.). (1994). *The Vygotsky reader.* Oxford, England: Blackwell.

REFERENCES

Berk, L. E., & Winsler, A. (1995). *Scaffolding children's learning: Vygotsky and early childhood education.* Washington, DC: National Association for the Education of Young Children.

Berk, L. E., Mann, T. D., & Ogan, A. T. (2006). Make-believe play: Wellspring for development of self-regulation. In D. G. Singer, R. M. Golinkoff, & K. A. Hirsh-Pasek (Eds.), *Play-learning: How play motivates and enhances cognitive and social-emotional growth* (pp. 74–100). New York: Oxford University Press.

Bodrova, E., & Leong, D. J. (2007). *Tools of the mind* (2nd ed.). Upper Saddle River, NJ: Merrill/Pearson.

Elkonin, D. (1972). Toward the problem of stages in the mental development of the child. *Soviet Psychology, 10,* 225–251.

Elkonin, D. (1978). *Psychologija igry* [The psychology of play]. Moscow, Russia: Pedagogika.

Ferreiro, E., & Teberosky, A. (1982). *Literacy before schooling.* Exeter, NH: Heinemann.

Istomina, Z. M. (1977). The development of voluntary memory in preschool-age children. In M. Cole (Ed.), *Soviet developmental psychology.* New York: M. E. Sharpe.

Karpov, Y. V. (1995). L. S. Vygotsky as the founder of a new approach to instruction. *School Psychology International, 16*(2), 131–142.

Karpov, Y. V. (2005). The neo-Vygotskian approach to child development. New York: Cambridge University Press.

Leont'ev, A. N. (1981). Problems of the development of mind. Moscow, Russia,: Progress Publishers.

Luria, A. (1998). The development of writing in the child. In M. K. de Oliveira & J. Valsiner (Eds.), *Literacy in human development* (pp. 15–56). Norwood, NJ: Ablex. [Original work published 1929.]

Vygotsky, L. S. (1956). *Izbrannye psychologicheskije trudy* [*Selected psychological studies*]. Moscow, Russia: RSFSR Academy of Pedagogical Sciences.

Vygotsky, L. S. (1967). Play and its role in the mental development of the child. *Soviet Psychology, 5,* 6–18. [Original work published in 1933.]

Vygotsky, L. (1978). *Mind in society: The development of higher mental processes.* Cambridge, MA: Harvard University Press.

Vygotsky, L. S. (1987). Thinking and speech. In R. W. Reiber & A. S. Carton (Eds.), *The collected works of L. S. Vygotsky: Vol. 1. Problems of general psychology* (N. Minick, Trans.) (pp. 39–285.) New York: Plenum Press. [Original work published 1934.]

Vygotsky, L. S. (1993). *The fundamentals of defectology (abnormal psychology and learning disabilities)* (Vol. 2) (J. E. Knox & C. B. Stevens, Trans.). New York: Plenum Press.

Vygotsky, L. (1994). The problem of the cultural development of the child. In R. v. d. Veer & J. Valsiner (Eds.), *The Vygotsky reader* (pp. 57–72). Cambridge, MA: Blackwell.

Vygotsky, L. (1997). *The history of the development of higher mental functions* (M. J. Hall, Trans.) (Vol. 4). New York: Plenum Press.

Vygotsky, L. S. (1998). *Child psychology* (Vol. 5). New York: Plenum Press.

Wood, D., Bruner, J. C., & Ross, G. (1976). The role of tutoring in problem solving. *Journal of Child Psychology and Psychiatry, 17,* 89–100.

Zaporozhets, A. (1986). *Izbrannye psychologicheskie trudy* [Selected works]. Moscow, Russia: Pedagogika.

Chapter 11
From Spectrum to Bridging
Approaches to Integrating Assessment with Curriculum and Instruction in Early Childhood Classrooms

Jie-Qi Chen and Gillian McNamee ⇝ *Erikson Institute*

Early childhood teachers enjoy teaching because they love to inspire young children to learn and grow. In contrast, few early childhood teachers would say they enjoy assessing or testing young children despite the fact that assessment is an integral part of effective teaching. James Popham, an educational psychologist at the University of California at Los Angeles, argues that "Teachers who can test well will be better teachers" (2008, p. 1). He means that when a teacher is a careful observer, she knows what children have mastered and what they are learning. This knowledge leads to curriculum planning that specifies in detail when and how to introduce new challenges that support and motivate children's learning.

Learning to teach is a complex journey. One of the most difficult and most important tasks is learning how to accurately assess individual children and effectively use the results to inform the development of learning activities. Assessment helps teachers to identify children's strengths and needs and to monitor their progress as they engage in learning activities. Teachers also use assessment to clarify goals and objectives for a particular group of children and to determine the effectiveness of teaching practices (Popham, 2008; Stiggins, Arter, Chappuis, & Chappuis, 2004). Early childhood teacher organizations, including the National Association for the Education of Young Children (NAEYC), agree that assessment is an integral part of the teaching and learning process. Understanding it and knowing how to use it appropriately are essential for effective teaching (National Association for the Education of Young Children & National Association of Early Chilhood Specialists in State Departments of Education, 2003).

Early childhood teachers have voiced a number of concerns about assessment and testing, including the following:

They take time away from teaching and children's play.

Numbers do not tell the whole story of a child's development.

Young children do not reliably perform well under the constraints of standardized testing.

One-time testing cannot accurately measure young children's learning because their development is sporadic.

Many tests do not produce information that is useful for curricular development and classroom teaching.

To improve classroom learning by informing teachers about each child's performance, assessment cannot be an add-on task that takes place

Nancy Sheehan Photography

Early childhood teachers foster learning across an array of developmental dimensions.

two or three times a year. It must become part of daily learning activities in the classroom. By the same token, assessment results cannot require expert interpretation. To be useful, assessment results must be transparent and directly related to curriculum planning and teaching.

In this chapter, we present two approaches to early childhood assessment. Both approaches strive for the integration of assessment with curriculum and teaching in early childhood classrooms. The first approach, *Spectrum Preschool Assessment* (hereafter referred to as SPA), was developed by staff at Project Spectrum, a research project at Harvard's Project Zero. Active from 1985 to 1994, Spectrum was dedicated to developing an innovative approach to the assessment and education of preschool children's strengths and talents in a wide range of areas (Chen, Krechevsky, & Viens, 1998). The second approach, *Bridging: Assessment for Teaching and Learning in Early Childhood Classrooms* (hereafter referred to as *Bridging*), grew out of the Bridging Project. Launched in 1999 at the Erikson Institute, the Bridging Project is an applied research program focused on developing tools that help PK-3 teachers to direct and engage in a seamless process of assessment, teaching, and learning that strengthens classroom practices and expands opportunities for children to experience school success (Chen & McNamee, 2007). The first author of the chapter was a member central to the Spectrum work until the end of the project, and the two authors have co-directed the Bridging Project since its inception. The chapter reflects the view of insiders in the development of the two approaches to integrating assessment with curriculum and instruction in early childhood classrooms.

To examine the two approaches in context, we first briefly review the history of child assessment practices. SPA is introduced in relation to the alternative assessment movement, which called for approaches that were more authentic and more relevant to the classroom than standardized testing. We describe SPA in terms of its theoretical foundations, distinguishing features, and contributions to strengthening assessment and curriculum integration. Next, we discuss trends in the field of early education since SPA's development and outline how these changes have affected the requirements of early assessment. With these needs in mind, we present work on the Bridging Project, including its theoretical underpinnings, its features to further advance the integration of assessment, and its achievements to date. Following the description of Bridging, we report on two empirical studies that demonstrate the important role that teachers play in sustaining assessment integration processes. These studies also show how an assessment tool such as Bridging can be used to affect teacher change in curriculum planning and classroom practice. The chapter concludes with a discussion of key considerations in developing integrated assessment that is sensitive to teachers' needs and responsive to emerging issues in the field.

THE HISTORY OF CHILD ASSESSMENT PRACTICES

The practice of assessing children's learning and development began with French psychologist Alfred Binet in 1904. Assessment was initially referred to as *testing*. Testing required the specialized training of psychologists who used standardized procedures and interpreted scores based on normative data. These tests were often used for diagnostic purposes. One of the most widely recognized was the IQ test, which measured decontextualized knowledge and skills that drew heavily on verbal and mathematical abilities. Test scores could be used to rank order children from superior to below average in intelligence (Wasserman & Tulsky, 2005). If a child's IQ were tested at the request of parents, a teacher was not necessarily informed of the score. If results were given to the teacher, they had little relevance to classroom teaching.

During the 1950s and 1960s, classroom teachers and psychologists involved with testing were trained differently, operated independently, and understood children from different perspectives (The Staff of Education Week, 2000). A teacher's job was to provide instruction that imparted knowledge and skills to students. Teaching was marked primarily by large group instruction and deskwork. Teachers did not collect or request assessment information. Although ability grouping was used in reading instruction, personalized teaching in response to individual students' developmental levels and prior knowledge was rare. Homework and paper-and-pencil tests were the primary means teachers used to judge students' progress in school learning. Schools were not designed to be responsive to children's needs. Teachers knew what to teach; it was up to children to meet the school's curriculum demands (The Staff of Education Week, 2000).

Outside of schools, in offices or testing clinics, the primary responsibilities of psychologists were to administer different kinds of standardized tests, examine children's learning potentials or problems, and score their performance based on normative data. It was not the concern of psychologists that these tests yielded little information relevant to classroom instruction. Not surprisingly, there was little dialogue or information exchange between teachers and psychologists. This lack of communication reinforced the separation of assessment from classroom teaching and learning (Wortham, 1996).

For purposes of this chapter, the most significant shift away from this early testing tradition occurred in the 1980s. Educators, politicians, parents, and concerned citizens began to speak of our country as a "nation at risk" (National Commission on Excellence in Education, 1983). One factor identified as contributing to this state of affairs was testing. More specifically, the lack of assessment information useful to teachers in planning daily learning experiences was seen as diminishing the power of education. These concerns spawned what has become known as the "alternative assessment movement" (Baker, O'Neil, & Linn, 1993; Hargreaves & Earl, 2002). Moving away from standardized testing, alternative assessment is typically performance based. Materials and activities are authentic. That is, they engage children in meaningful activities with goals and purposes that children subscribe to. Classroom observation, portfolio construction, and work sampling are among the most widely promoted alternative assessment tools. Many early childhood teachers have been trained in the use of one or more of these techniques.

The alternative assessment movement was welcomed by educators. It put assessment tools that allowed for more authentic information about each child in the hands of classroom teachers. The purposes of assessment were no longer diagnosing, labeling, or rank ordering children. Alternative assessments produced information about children that teachers could reflect on and use in the classroom. These tools held the promise that teachers could translate assessment results into appropriate and effective curriculum and instruction for children as individuals and in groups. This movement marked a significant advance in closing the gap between assessment and teaching (Bowman, Donovan, & Burns, 2001).

As teachers used these tools in the classroom, new challenges in integrating assessment became apparent (Baker, O'Neil, & Linn, 1993; Supovitz & Brennan, 1997). Performance-based assessment sometimes focuses on discrete behaviors. When behaviors are decontextualized, it can be difficult to determine their meaning for teaching in the classroom. Classroom observation generates large amounts of rich descriptive information; some of it may not be systematic, and some may not be comprehensive. Teachers may not know what to look for or understand how an observation relates to performance in other curricular areas. For similar reasons, it can be difficult to know what kinds of materials to collect for children's portfolios and what criteria to use to evaluate them (Chen & McNamee, 2006). Though advancing classroom use, the alternative assessments made available to early childhood teachers have not achieved the integration of learning and teaching processes. Project Spectrum entered the field of early education during the alternative assessment movement.

THE SPECTRUM APPROACH TO PRESCHOOL ASSESSMENT

Started in 1985, Project Spectrum was a 10-year research initiative based at Project Zero in Harvard's Graduate School of Education. Its goal was to develop an assessment and curriculum system that cultivated the variety of talents among the children present in every preschool and primary-age classroom. Spectrum holds that each child exhibits a distinctive profile of cognitive abilities. These abilities are not fixed; rather, they can be enhanced by educational opportunities, such as an environment rich with stimulating materials that support learning and self-expression (Chen, Krechevsky, & Viens, 1998). The launching of Project Spectrum marked a significant departure from traditional thinking about the nature of the human mind, its development, and the process of educating young children.

Theoretical Foundations

Spectrum is based on two theories: Howard Gardner's (1993, 1999) multiple intelligences theory and David Henry Feldman's (1994, 1998) theory of nonuniversal development. Although distinctive in significant ways, the theories of Feldman and Gardner share certain features in the conceptualization of human cognition, and it is these commonalities that provide the theoretical foundation for Project Spectrum. First, both theorists argue that cognitive ability is pluralistic. Feldman and Gardner recognize many different and discrete facets of knowing and doing, acknowledging that people have varied cognitive strengths, interests, and weaknesses (Feldman, 1998; Gardner 1999). It is in recognition of such a diversity of intellectual profiles that their joint project selected the name "Spectrum." More specifically, Project Spectrum's work, whether in assessment or in curriculum development, involves a range of domains including language, mathematics, movement, science, music, visual arts, and social understanding. Such a wide selection of domains is deliberate: Only by exposing children to a range of learning experiences in these various domains can we begin to identify and support the full complement of their diverse cognitive abilities (Adams & Feldman, 1993; Chen & Gardner, 2005).

Closely related to the notion of a pluralistic human intellect is Feldman and Gardner's mutual belief in domain-specific cognitive abilities. Their works suggest that cognitive abilities are more accurately described as specifically attuned to particular domains rather than seen as reflecting one general capacity, such as the traditional notion of IQ (Feldman, 1994; Gardner, 2006). This assertion entails a prediction that individuals often exhibit uneven profiles of ability when a wide range of domains is assessed.

In formulating the conceptual framework of Project Spectrum, both Feldman and Gardner maintained the need to recognize cognitive abilities as they are influenced by educational experiences and expressed in diverse cultures. Human culture actively constructs and significantly influences both the content of individual cognitive abilities and the course of their development. When we assess a child's cognitive abilities, we are assessing the child's intellectual proclivities, her past experience in the area, her familiarity with the assessment material, her opportunity to practice using the material, and the scaffolding offered by the assessor. Variability in intellectual proclivities reflects not only the individual child, but also educational practices, environmental factors, and cultural values (Feldman & Fowler, 1997a, 1997b; Gardner 2000).

Distinctive Features

Guided by the theories of Gardner and Feldman, the center of Project Spectrum's work was the development and implementation of the SPA. A performance-based assessment for 3- to 5-year-olds, the SPA includes 15 activities in seven domains of knowledge: language, math, music, art, sciences, movement, and social understanding (see Table 11–1). The assessments are embedded in meaningful, hands-on activities that utilize engaging materials to manipulate. Each activity focuses on key abilities to identify children's cognitive strengths (Krechevsky, 1998).

The first feature of this assessment system is that Spectrum assessment activities sample from multiple domains, rather than focusing only on narrowly defined academic areas such as language and mathematics. Spectrum assessment recognizes both those children who excel in linguistic and logical pursuits and those who have cognitive and personal strengths in other intelligences. By virtue of the wider range it measures, Spectrum assessment identifies more students,

TABLE 11–1
Spectrum Preschool Assessment Activities

Area	Measure	Activity
Movement	Creative movement Athletic movement	Biweekly movement curriculum Obstacle course
Language	Invented narrative Descriptive narrative	Storyboard activity Reporter activities
Mathematics	Counting/strategy Calculating/notation	Dinosaur game Bus game
Social Understanding	Social analysis Social roles	Classroom model Peer interaction checklist
Visual Arts	Art production	Year-long collection of children's artwork
Music	Music production Music perception	Singing activities Pitch matching games and song recognition
Science	Naturalist Logical inference Hypothesis testing Mechanical construction	Discovery area Treasure hunt game Sink and float activity Assembly activity

even *all* students, as "smart," albeit in different ways. At the same time, it also calls teachers' attention to domains of intellectual potential that require further attention and early intervention (Chen & Gardner, 2005).

Second, the Spectrum activities give children inviting materials to manipulate. To assess children's understanding of number concepts, for example, Spectrum responds to preschoolers' fascination with dinosaurs. While a board game motivates participation, the child's manipulation of dinosaur game pieces reveals her counting skills, ability to adhere to rules, and use of strategy. In a similar way, children's social understanding is assessed in Spectrum through a classroom model with small wooden figures. The figures have photos of the teacher and each child in the classroom. In the process of using the figures to act out, and react to, scenarios in their own classroom environment with their peers, children's abilities to observe, reflect on, and analyze familiar social events and experiences are examined. Because they are attractive and actively engage children in the assessment process, the Spectrum assessment materials are more likely to reveal children's cognitive strengths and to motivate their learning (Chen, 2004).

Third, the Spectrum activities are intelligence fair, using materials appropriate to particular domains, and providing children with opportunities to reveal their diverse talents in school. To assist teachers in domain-specific assessment, a set of key abilities was identified for each domain (Chen, Isberg, & Krechevsky, 1998). To illustrate how key abilities become visible, consider two Spectrum assessment activities. To measure mechanical abilities, a child is asked to disassemble and assemble a meat grinder, an oil pump, or some other common household gadget. In the process of dismantling and constructing these objects, the child's key abilities in the area of mechanical construction are observed and documented. These key abilities include understanding causal and functional relationships among parts, using a problem-solving approach with mechanical objects, visual-spatial abilities, and fine motor skills. In the domain of music, a child's music perception key abilities are assessed through a game with Montessori bells that look identical but produce distinctive sounds. To differentiate one pitch from another, the child cannot use her eyes; she must rely exclusively on her sense of hearing. In these Spectrum assessment activities, domain-specific cognitive abilities are measured through the use of domain-specific media to solve domain-specific problems (Gardner, 1999).

The result of the SPA process is a profile—a narrative report based on the information obtained from a child's engagement and performance in the 15 assessment activities (Krechevsky, 1998; Ramos-Ford & Gardner, 1991). Using nontechnical language, the report focuses on the range of cognitive abilities examined by the Spectrum assessment. It describes each child's relative strengths and weaknesses, and occasionally in relation to peers. Strengths and weaknesses are described in terms of the child's performance in relation to key abilities in different domains. For example, a child's unusual sensitivity to different kinds of music might be described in terms of facial expressions, movement, and attentiveness during and after listening to various music pieces. The conclusion of the profile typically includes specific recommendations to parents and teachers about ways to support identified strengths and improve weak areas (Adams & Feldman, 1993; Krechevsky, 1998). Reflecting a child's interests, capabilities, and experiences at a particular point in time, the profile changes over time through learning and development.

SPECTRUM'S CONTRIBUTIONS TO THE INTEGRATION OF ASSESSMENT AND CURRICULUM

Project Spectrum paved the way for educators to understand the diversity of children's learning potentials by creating methods that illuminate their strengths and talents in the classroom.

Spectrum also provides means for teachers to consider these talents in curricular decision making. In specific terms, Spectrum contributed to moving assessment closer to teaching by expanding the focus of assessment to include children's strengths as well as their less developed areas, by constructing profiles of ability rather than reducing a child's learning to a set of numerical scores, and by arguing that ongoing embedded assessment is more informative and more meaningful than infrequent formal assessment. We comment briefly on each contribution to underscore its significance and value.

Spectrum assessment that identifies children's strengths broke through the accepted focus of the testing tradition that looks primarily for deficits. Teachers are encouraged to use SPA for affirmative purposes that include helping a child recognize his or her strengths and planning learning experiences to build on those strengths. In this approach, instruction begins with the identification of a child's strengths from a wide range of areas, rather than the remediation of deficits in a very limited number of traditional academic disciplines, such as reading and math. Spectrum does not disregard the value of and need for remedial services in specific areas. Rather, it contends that while some students might benefit from this strategy, others might be more responsive to building on strengths (Chen, 2004). Observing their learning successes, teachers gather new information about children's knowledge and understanding. They extend and elaborate what engages a child's interest and curiosity in rigorous disciplinary learning (Gardner, 1999).

Preserving information about a child's strengths and less developed areas, the Spectrum profile report avoids the reduction of a child's wide range of interests and abilities to a set of scores or an average. A child's specific strengths are not assimilated and lost to a general descriptor such as "above average" or "below average." Nor is a child's need for instruction overlooked by scores that indicate she is "smart" or "dumb." Measuring a wide range of abilities and interests, the profile gives teachers a tool for systematically collecting and organizing this information. The Spectrum profile does not signify the end of an assessment process but, rather, marks new beginnings in teaching and learning. It is designed to be generative. Unlike a test score, the profile is not simply a record of performance that is filed away. It is a dynamic blueprint for building on children's achievements to develop new knowledge and skills.

When seen as separate from teaching and learning, assessment in the classroom occurs only two or three times a year. In high contrast, Spectrum argues that assessment is most meaningful and useful when it is ongoing (Krechevsky, 1998). The SPA materials are always available to children. Play with the materials gives children opportunities to explore and become familiar with them. This familiarity helps to ensure that assessment is accurate: The child's use of the material reflects his or her current development of the domain's key concepts and skills. The ongoing availability of materials supports a teacher's use of them for instruction as well as for assessment. SPA also supports ongoing assessment by encouraging teacher observations that are domain specific. Guided by key abilities in Spectrum domains, teachers learn to see children's multiple potentials and to begin planning related curriculum.

Complementing ongoing observation, SPA recommends that teachers collect evidence of what children do, such as children's artwork and dictated stories. It also involves tracing children's activity as a group and includes creating a classroom photo album and a video library of children's dramatization of favorite stories, often involving simple props and musical instruments. Children are actively involved in selecting what is recorded. The teacher regularly reviews this information to sharpen her awareness of children's ongoing development and learning. She also invites the children to comment on activities that they like and those that they believe they do well. These conversations often yield children's surprising insights into their own learning. By providing the means for teachers to make classroom assessment ongoing, Spectrum demonstrated that the integration of assessment, teaching, and learning is an achievable goal.

EMERGING ISSUES AND TRENDS IN EARLY EDUCATION

By the early 1990s, a number of trends in early childhood education had emerged, and they are setting new educational priorities that require the development of different approaches to child assessment (Bowman, Donovan, & Burns, 2001; Bredekamp & Rosegrant, 1995). To indicate how these trends affect early childhood assessment, we identify three and describe briefly the changes they call for in the design of assessment tools. The trends are (1) the development of early learning standards, (2) an increased emphasis on subject matter, and (3) the definition of early education as PK-3. Because these emerging issues are affecting the design of assessment, they are also changing what is entailed in the process of integrating assessment with curriculum planning and classroom teaching practices.

Early learning standards describe skills and knowledge that young children are expected to acquire during the initial years of formal schooling (Scott-Little, Kagan, & Frelow, 2005). Learning priorities established by the standards influence what is assessed and what is taught in early childhood classrooms. A major purpose of these standards is to provide a basis for teacher accountability. That is, teachers can be held accountable for children's progress toward meeting learning objectives that are included in the standards. Early learning standards help to ensure that children have equal opportunities to acquire the knowledge and skills needed for school success. To be useful to teachers, assessment must now be aligned with early learning standards (National Association for the Education of Young Children & National Association of Early Chilhood Specialists in State Departments of Education, 2003).

Accountability pressures have also led to greater emphasis on subject matter in early education. Increasingly, early childhood curricula are organized around content areas (Bowman, Donovan, & Burns, 2001). Corresponding to this shift, early childhood teachers are required to become more deliberate and conscious about addressing content knowledge and skills in their interactions with young children. This emphasis on content areas does not mean learning has become passive and rote. Early learning continues to uphold children's active engagement in the construction of knowledge while paying more attention to concepts and skills fundamental to the development of each subject area (Bredekamp & Rosegrant, 1992; Epstein, 2007). With greater emphasis on subject matter, teachers need assessment tools that are organized in terms of content areas found in most early education classrooms. These areas include arts, sciences, literacy, and mathematics.

A third shift is the trend toward defining early childhood education as preschool through third grade (PK-3). This differs from the traditional practice of defining early education primarily as the preschool years from 3 to 5 years old. Practical and developmental concerns have given rise to this new trend. On the practical side, kindergarten and now prekindergarten programs are offered through public schools. This means that some children start formal schooling at younger ages. From the developmental perspective, it is clear now that there is a wide range of variability in skill level, experience, and readiness to learn in the various content areas for a group of children 3 to 8 years of age. Limiting early education to the 3- to 5-year-old range does a disservice to meeting the uneven educational needs of individuals, as well as to a whole group of children.

Children start school at different ages, come with enormously different early experiences, and need time to adjust socially, emotionally, and intellectually to this new arena for development.

The PK-3 philosophy recognizes that early childhood teachers need to understand the development of concepts and skills across this wider age range to jump start learning for some while furthering the learning for those who are well on their way. In today's classrooms, there are children at different points of the developmental continuum. The teacher's knowledge and expertise must benefit the whole group, as well as each child. PK-3 curriculum has taken as its goal helping all children over a period of years to establish a strong start in all subject areas. Thus, to align with PK-3 curriculum goals, assessment must likewise move toward accommodating levels of development and learning that encompass this wider age range.

THE BRIDGING APPROACH TO ASSESSMENT IN EARLY CHILDHOOD CLASSROOMS

Bridging is the product of the Bridging Project, an applied educational research program launched in 1999 at the Erikson Institute. Its goal has been to create a framework and methodology for integrating child assessment, curriculum planning, and instructional practice into a seamless process (McNamee & Chen, 2005a). Each of the features and design elements of Bridging are responsive to the three shifts in the field of early childhood education: (1) articulated learning standards, (2) focus on content, and (3) attention to the PK-3 system. Building on the work of Project Spectrum, Bridging offers a classroom-based performance assessment process that includes a blueprint for teaching and learning processes for 3- to 8-year-olds in today's schools.

Theoretical Foundations

Bridging's conceptual framework draws on two theoretical sources: Gardner's theory of multiple intelligences (MI) and the activity theory of Leont'ev. Akin to the work of Project Spectrum, the content of Bridging assessment is based, in part, on MI theory. Gardner contends that human beings develop and use at least eight distinct, relatively autonomous intelligences over the course of a lifetime. Each of these eight intelligences is seen as valid and important in terms of opening pathways for individuals to achieve their human potential and contribute to society (Gardner, 2006).

Bridging reinterprets MI theory for classroom settings; it focuses on the opportunities to recognize multiple intelligences in diverse curricular areas, including language and literacy, mathematics, science, visual arts, and performing arts. The content of Bridging assessment is organized in terms of curricular areas rather than intelligences for several reasons:

1. Curricular areas reflect intellectual abilities valued in this society.
2. Curricular areas offer children points of entry for the pursuit of cultural activities.
3. Aligning assessment areas with curricular areas facilitates teachers' incorporation of Bridging assessment into ongoing curriculum planning.

The second source of Bridging's conceptual underpinning comes from the work of Russian psychologist Alexei Leont'ev. As a student of L. S. Vygotsky, Leont'ev (1978, 1981) proposed a small and yet radical departure from the traditional way of studying development—activity as the unit of analysis. In other words, he shifted attention away from the individual to instead focus on the individual in an activity in a particular social, cultural, and historical setting. By focusing on an individual's activity, it becomes possible to study a child's internal world of mental abilities, interests, and proclivities through observable behaviors, such as children's choice of activity, their degree of engagement, the level of their productivity, and the quality of their products. Activity also includes an analysis of both the expectations and support given to a child by peers and adults in the various settings of home, school, and the larger community. Each of these contexts and their participants hold expectations and opportunities for children to acquire knowledge, skills, and specific symbol systems important to the culture in which they live.

Guided by Leont'ev's activity theory, Bridging places child assessment in the context of ongoing regular classroom activities. Attending to activity and activity parameters in the assessment process enables teachers to examine children's learning and performance in greater detail. Beyond simply seeing a child's strengths and weaknesses, teachers can trace factors that might contribute to the child's varied levels of performance. For example, looking at the social parameters of activities, some children prefer to work independently while others are more comfortable in small groups. By focusing on activity in the assessment process, the results describe the child's performance as a function of the context in which it took place. Rather than attribute learning difficulties only to the child, such assessment yields information teachers can use to select activity parameters in classrooms that create optimal learning environments for children with diverse learning strengths and needs.

Distinguishing Features

Developed by the authors of this chapter and the staff of the Bridging Project, Bridging is an instructional assessment for use by teachers of children 3 to 8 years of age (Chen & McNamee, 2007). Using familiar curricular activities, Bridging provides teachers with a systematic approach to understanding individual children's learning within the classroom context. As an assessment tool, Bridging helps teachers determine each child's progress on developmental continua of key concepts and skills in a range of early childhood curricular areas. Key concepts and skills are deemed critical to the mastery of particular content knowledge. With the assessment results, teachers use Bridging to develop curriculum plans that cultivate children's diverse strengths while also targeting areas where individual children need experience, guidance, and practice (McNamee & Chen, 2005b).

Built upon previous work done by Project Spectrum, Bridging shares certain features with SPA, including sampling a range of learning areas, the identification of children's diverse cognitive strengths, the use of engaging activities, and a focus on guided observation and careful documentation. It also builds on the Spectrum assessment by further strengthening the integration of assessment and school learning. Bridging's distinguishing features (described in the following sections) include using familiar activities and easily accessible materials, identifying key concepts and skills in curricular areas, considering activity as a unit of analysis in child assessment, and offering curriculum ideas to align with assessment results (Chen & McNamee, 2006; 2007).

Using Familiar Activities and Accessible Materials. Bridging includes 15 activities, 3 in each of five curricular areas: language arts and literacy, mathematics, sciences, performing arts, and visual arts (see Table 11-2). Bridging activities are based on curriculum activities familiar to most early childhood teachers, including children reading books, story dictation, building a model car using recycled materials, using crayon to make a design, and using pattern blocks to solve a mathematical problem. The use of common classroom activities for the purposes of assessment is not a matter of coincidence or convenience. Use of these activities reflects the belief that assessment and curriculum are two sides of the same coin and that each is more effective when integrated

TABLE 11–2
Bridging Assessment Areas and Activities

Areas	Activities
Language Arts and Literature	1. Reading books (child's choice and teacher's choice) 2. Dictating a story 3. Acting out stories
Visual Arts	4. Experimenting with crayon techniques 5. Drawing a self-portrait 6. Making pattern block pictures
Mathematics	7. Creating pattern block pinwheels 8. Solving pattern block puzzles 9. Understanding number concepts
Sciences	10. Exploring shadows and light 11. Assembling a nature display 12. Building a model car
Performing Arts	13. Moving to music 14. Playing an instrument 15. Singing a song

to form a continuous teaching-learning process. In addition, materials used in the Bridging assessment process are commonly available in classrooms, such as picture books, pattern blocks, audiotapes, and other items easily obtained from a home and natural environment. This feature makes the Bridging assessment process more practical for teachers. It also contributes to the integration of assessment with teaching and learning; all of these processes make use of the same materials.

Identifying Key Concepts and Skills in Curricular Areas. Within each of the five curricular areas, Bridging assessment activities examine key concepts and skills identified in national standards set for early childhood education. Based on a developmental analysis of key concepts and skills, a 10-level, criterion-referenced rubric has been developed for each activity. The rubrics specify behavioral indicators of children's learning and mastery in each content area in relation to a developmental continuum for that area. The continua span the full range of early childhood from ages three to eight. Using the performance rubrics, teachers can pinpoint the skills that a child currently possesses as well as those she is in the process of developing in each curriculum area. The child's zone of proximal development, consisting of those skills and knowledge currently undergoing change in specific content areas, is revealed in the assessment process (Vygostky, 1978). By emphasizing key concepts and skills, Bridging calls teachers' attention to the progression in children's development of knowledge in each subject area. With in-depth understanding of key concepts and skills, teachers become more confident using them to plan learning experiences.

Considering Activity as the Unit of Analysis in Child Assessment. A third distinguishing characteristic of Bridging is the unit of analysis used in the assessment process. Rather than focusing on the individual child in isolation, which is the primary focus of most assessment instruments, Bridging views the "child engaged in activity" as the unit of analysis for learning and development. To understand children's development in the context of activities, Bridging examines how different activity parameters influence children's performance. These parameters include materials used in the assessment, the social dynamics of activity administration (e.g., individual, small, or large group setting), whether the child understands the goal of the activity, and the nature of the activity (e.g., open-ended versus structured). Teachers observe children's behavior and record their performance in relation to activity parameters. Teachers modify assessment activities in specific ways to become curriculum activities to promote optimal performance levels in children. As such, the assessment process naturally leads to intervention through carefully planned and positioned teaching activities.

Offering Curriculum Ideas in Alignment with Assessment Results. As the name indicates, Bridging begins with the assessment of children and leads to teaching based on knowledge gained from the assessment process. Guiding the transition from assessment to teaching are two Bridging curriculum components: reflection and planning. The *reflection* process asks teachers to look carefully at the assessment results as well as activity parameters that might affect children's performance. The *planning* section provides a set of curricular ideas for teachers to consider turning into learning experiences based on assessment results. These ideas help teachers build on children's skills to further their explorations and understanding of subject-area concepts and skills. The ideas do not prescribe a particular way to teach. Rather, they are suggestive, serving as guidelines for teachers' discovery and as a springboard for teachers' innovation. The goal of the planning section is clear: Bridging assessment does not end with knowing a child's developmental status. It uses that knowledge to plan curriculum and instruction that will help a child move forward based on what she or he knows and what she or he is ready to learn.

Contributions of Bridging to the Integration of Assessment and Curriculum

Bridging fundamentally changes the place and nature of assessment in early childhood classrooms. In traditional assessment, teachers follow instructions, carry out tasks, compute scores, and then read a test guide's interpretation for the meaning of sores. Settings and procedures are standardized. There is little flexibility in carrying out assessment protocols. Indeed, the goal of traditional assessments is to minimize any variance in implementation for the sake of standardization. Bridging is a very different sort of tool and process. It does not have a scripted procedure. There are many "right ways" to use it. The flexibility of its design enables teachers to determine its best use for gathering information to understand particular children and classroom groups and to plan for their learning in the days and weeks to come. Bridging has made specific contributions to advancing the integration of assessment with teaching and learning. These include giving teachers an active and central role in the assessment process; providing teachers with a tool to track present, past, and future learning; and supporting PK-3 education.

In Bridging, teachers play an active role in making decisions about assessment and apply their expertise at all stages of implementation. They decide which classroom areas to use for carrying out activities and how to integrate activities with daily classroom routines. They then observe children's performance in activities and also interpret the meaning of assessment findings. Teachers understand the content knowledge represented by each activity and what scores mean in relation to the child's current level of development. Moving seamlessly from assessment to curriculum, they translate assessment results into plans for future curricular activities with careful attention to the guidance and coaching they will provide as the children continue forward in their learning. Thus Bridging guides a teacher in connecting children's curiosity and interests with the intellectual demands of school and connecting a child's current developmental level with his or her future developmental path within and among curricular areas.

In Bridging, a child's activity score describes his or her current performance level and his or her position on a developmental continuum for the activity. In identifying each child's developmental status, Bridging assessment illuminates what the child is learning and helps teachers identify the kinds of knowledge and skills the child is working on to reach the next level of development. By indicating what a child is learning and ready to learn, the developmental level that Bridging identifies helps teachers establish short-term learning objectives in the context of longer-term development. In addition to locating a child's position on a developmental continuum, Bridging assists teachers in locating zones of proximal development by helping them examine the varied social interactions that elicit, encourage, and mediate children's performance and progress (McNamee & Chen, 2005b). In most instances, teachers can choose to carry out activities in small groups, with dyads, or in one-to-one interactions with children. Some activities may also be used with a large group. This differs from the typical approach to assessment that isolates a child before assessment begins. By carrying out assessment in different social groupings, Bridging offers teachers opportunities to gain a more complete understanding of what children are capable of doing independently, with teacher assistance, and through interaction with peers.

A third contribution Bridging has made to the integration of assessment is its demonstration that a single assessment tool can accommodate PK-3 education. As noted, the definition of early education as PK-3 is an emerging trend in the field. To be successful, teachers need assessment tools designed for the full age range, rather than having to rely on several instruments intended for use with children of a certain age. Complementing the set of assessment activities, Bridging can help PK-3 teachers to understand the unique characteristics and needs of young children during the early years of school, the progression of their development and learning in all content areas, and teaching methods that are likely to engage them in ways that are consistent with the active social nature of learning at this age. Traditionally, preschool focused on children's development, primary grades emphasized content. It is becoming clearer to child development and early childhood educators that children will have the strongest educational experience when developmental concerns and content issues are merged to form a continuous teaching-learning process across the PK-3 years. We are members of both groups of professionals and support this trend.

TEACHER DEVELOPMENT: KEY TO ASSESSMENT AND CURRICULUM INTEGRATION

Placing an effective tool in teachers' hands is undoubtedly a necessary step toward assessment and curriculum integration. Yet an effective tool does not necessarily lead to the actualization of integration. Teacher development must be facilitated to ensure that integration takes place. Using an analogy, computer technology is a great tool for student learning—but only when teachers understand its potential and know how to integrate it with subject areas to promote thinking and understanding. By the same token, an assessment instrument, regardless of how well it is designed, can never achieve its promised outcomes without the knowledge and preparation of teachers. Teacher development is as important as the development of tools.

What kinds of knowledge do teachers need to develop to use assessment effectively for teaching and learning processes? Can these kinds of knowledge be acquired while learning to implement a particular assessment tool? Our response to the first question is based on a conceptual framework. For the second, our answer is derived from the results of two empirical investigations.

To address the first question, we draw on the conceptual framework of pedagogical content knowledge (PCK). First introduced in 1985 by Lee Shulman, president of the Carnegie Foundation, the term *PCK* signifies the importance of the coalescence of three categories of knowledge for effective teaching: the what, who, and how of teaching. *What* refers to understanding the key concepts or ideas in a specific content area; *who* means knowing about learners and their background knowledge; and *how* represents the repertoire of methods that are appropriate to represent and present specific kinds of content to students of a particular age (Shulman, 2004).

Although primarily used to depict teaching effectiveness, the concept of PCK is just as powerful in describing the kinds of knowledge that teachers need to develop for the integration of assessment with curriculum and instruction. PCK requires the teacher to consider curricular content knowledge in relation to children's prior knowledge and their current developmental characteristics. It speaks about developmental sequences with attention to particular subject area knowledge. When referred to in the discourse of PCK, teaching methods are not a set of general instructional strategies. Rather, they are optimal ways to work with a specific group of children to construct a body of knowledge (see Figure 11–1). In this process, teachers observe, listen, and take stock of a child's progress in the course of classroom learning. Teachers use

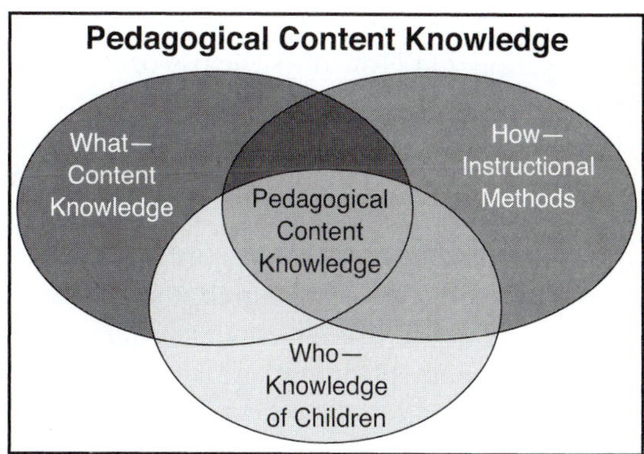

FIGURE 11–1

assessment information as the basis for effective curriculum planning and teaching. The process of acquiring and integrating the three PCK components mirrors the process of using assessment results to inform curriculum planning and instructional practice.

With regard to the second question—whether PCK can be obtained in the process of learning to implement an assessment instrument—our answer is an affirmative one based on two studies we have carried out. As teacher educators with strong human development backgrounds, we began the Bridging work with a keen awareness of teacher development as a critical component in the teaching-assessment integration process. As we have developed the Bridging assessment activities, we have worked with teachers at both preservice and in-service levels. We documented the process of their learning and implementing Bridging in their classrooms and studied their development of PCK knowledge in relation to the integration of assessment with curriculum and planning.

For preservice teacher development, we studied a total of 75 teacher candidates at the Erikson Institute who implemented the Bridging assessment process during their yearlong student teaching experience (see Chen & McNamee, 2006, for a detailed description of the study). Three research questions guided our investigation: (1) How does the use of Bridging facilitate student teachers' acquisition of new knowledge about individual children as diverse learners? (2) How does Bridging help student teachers gain a deeper understanding of content knowledge in a range of subject areas? (3) How does the use of Bridging strengthen student teachers' ability to use assessment results to inform curriculum planning and teaching? The three research questions reflect the three components of PCK.

The primary sources of data for the study were classroom observations and the reflection papers student teachers prepared at the end of the student teaching period. Positive results were found with regard to all three research questions. First, student teachers by and large indicated that they gained a new understanding of individual children as a result of using Bridging. This new knowledge included understanding the variability within each child's range of academic performance levels and being able to identify contextual factors that affect children's performance. The teacher candidates also showed increased content knowledge in a range of curricular areas at the end of their internship. Many of them credited such gains to the careful examination and study of performance rubrics for the Bridging activities. The process of applying these rubrics enabled them to develop a deeper understanding of the key concepts and skills in a range of curriculum areas. In terms of linking assessment to curriculum and instruction, student teachers reported that Bridging helped them think about curriculum through observation, documentation, and analysis of individual children's activity in specific content areas. Rubrics enabled them to understand the essentials of each curriculum area and to organize and sequence learning experiences. As they gained mastery over these fundamentals, they began to create learning experiences appropriate for their particular group of children.

For in-service teachers, we interviewed 53 teachers working in preschool and kindergarten classrooms in the Chicago Public Schools (see Melendez, 2007, for a detailed description of the study). Of the 53 teachers, 29 participated in a year-long professional development seminar designed to help teachers learn to use the Bridging assessment system in their classrooms and are, therefore, denoted as the intervention group. The remaining 24 were early childhood teachers on a waiting list for the Bridging professional development seminar. They comprised a comparison or control group. The two groups of teachers were similar in terms of years of teaching experience and level of education.

Trained researchers interviewed both groups of teachers twice: at the beginning and at the end of the school year. The analysis of the interviews was guided by the conceptual framework of PCK. The results indicated that at the beginning of the school year, the two groups of teachers were not significantly different in their mean scores in each of the three PCK categories, nor were they different in terms of the pattern of scores across the three categories. Specifically, teachers in both intervention and control groups showed moderate levels of knowledge in content areas, in understanding of individual children, and in considering useful teaching strategies to meet the needs of their students.

At the end of the school year, mean scores across the three areas of PCK increased for both groups. Although teachers in the intervention group earned higher mean scores than teachers in the control group in all three categories, differences between the groups were not statistically significant. However, we did note a finding of particular interest for intervention group teachers: the relationship among the scores of the three areas changed. Intervention group teachers' scores for the three components of PCK were significantly correlated. Similar correlations were not found in the control group.

This finding points to an often ignored fact in teacher development. Development entails more than quantitative increases in knowledge. It also involves the dynamic interaction of the elements essential to PCK. These results suggest the possibility that the more closely associated the three PCK components are, the more likely they will work together to support the integration of assessment with curriculum and instruction. Further empirical work is needed to test this hypothesis.

As revealed in the two studies, Bridging's integration of assessment and curriculum development is bi-directional. Assessment guides curriculum development; curriculum implementation is supported by assessment information to help teachers become more effective in their work. It is our conviction that assessment without conceptual connections to curriculum does not help teachers teach. On the other hand, curriculum implementation without accurate assessment information may or may not be appropriate for a particular group of children. In the integration process that we have developed in Bridging, the pattern is no longer limited to a linear sequence with assessment necessarily preceding curriculum development. Instead, the pattern is a spiral with each interacting to inform the other in a continuous process.

CONCLUSION

More than two decades have passed since the inception of Project Spectrum in 1985. The field of early childhood education has changed a great deal in the past 20 years. Today, accountability is the most pressing issue at all levels of the education system. The challenges are even greater for early childhood education, with the complex and varied developmental needs of young children. Accurately assessing individual children's knowledge and skills remains one of the most difficult, yet most important, tasks in teaching. To do so, teachers need reliable assessment systems to help identify students' strengths and areas in need of additional practice and guidance, monitor their progress, and decide on appropriate next steps in instructional practice (Popham, 2008). Understanding assessment and knowing how to use it appropriately is crucial to effective teaching (Shepard et al., 2005).

The path from the work of Project Spectrum to the development of Bridging indicates a concerted effort in the field to place effective assessment tools that are responsive to capturing the complex nature of young children's potential in teachers' hands. Many assessment instruments now available provide parents, educators, government officials, and the public with a wide range of information about how well students are doing in relation to goals and standards. SPA and Bridging stand out in the crowd of these assessment tools, in part because of their strong theoretical foundations. SPA and Bridging provide the field not only a "how-to tool" but also conceptual frameworks for understanding children's learning and development. Grounded in new ways of conceptualizing human development, SPA and Bridging bring teachers' attention to where children are at the moment for the purpose of planning for teaching and learning in the weeks and months ahead. As approaches to assessment, SPA and Bridging are conducive to the development of teachers as well as children.

Without impacting curriculum and instruction, assessment is only halfway to its destination. Project Spectrum worked to integrate assessment. Built on the work of Project Spectrum, Bridging has made further progress: It provides information on what young children know—but in a context and format that give teachers the ability to adjust their curriculum and instruction to improve children's learning opportunities. Improved learning is the putative goal of all accountability efforts. Bridging is designed to ensure that early childhood teachers have the knowledge and tools to reach that goal.

REFERENCES

Adams, M., & Feldman, D. H. (1993). Project Spectrum: A theory-based approach to early education. In R. Pasnak & M. L. Howe (Eds.), *Emerging themes in cognitive development: Vol. II. Competencies* (pp. 53–76). New York: Springer-Verlag.

Baker, E. L., O'Neil, H. F., & Linn, R. L. (1993). Policy and validity prospects for performance-based assessment. *American Psychologist, 48,* 1210–1218.

Bowman, B. T., Donovan, M. S., & Burns, M. S. (Eds.). (2001). *Eager to learn: Educating our preschoolers.* Washington, DC: National Academy Press.

Bredekamp, S., & Rosegrant, T. (Eds). (1995). *Reaching potentials. Vol. 2: Transforming early childhood curriculum and assessment.* Washington, DC: National Association for the Education of Young Children.

Chen, J. Q. (2004). The Project Spectrum approach to early education. In J. Johnson & J. Roopnarine (Eds.), *Approaches to early childhood education* (4th ed., 251–279). Upper Saddle River, NJ: Merill/Pearson.

Chen, J. Q., & Gardner, H. (2005). Assessment based on multiple intelligences theory. In D. P. Flanagan, J. L. Genshaft, & P. L. Harrison (Eds.), *Beyond traditional intellectual assessment: Contemporary and emerging theories, tests, and issues* (2nd ed., 77–102). New York: Guilford.

Chen, J. Q., Isberg, E., & Krechevsky, M. (Eds.). (1998). *Project Spectrum: Early learning activities.* New York: Teachers College Press.

Chen, J. Q., Krechevsky, M., & Viens, J. (1998). *Building on children's strengths: The experience of Project Spectrum.* New York: Teachers College Press.

Chen, J. Q., & McNamee, G. (2006). Strengthening early childhood teacher preparation: Integrating assessment, curriculum development, and instructional practice in student teaching. *Journal of Early Childhood Teacher Education, 27*(2), 109–127.

Chen, J. Q., & McNamee, G. (2007). *Bridging: Assessment for teaching and learning in early childhood classrooms.* Thousand Oaks, CA: Corwin Press.

Epstein, A. S. (2007). *The intentional teacher: Choosing the best strategies for young children's learning.* Washington, DC: National Association for the Education of Young Children.

Feldman, D. H. (1994). *Beyond universals in cognitive development* (2nd ed.). Norwood, NJ: Ablex.

Feldman, D. H. (1998). How Spectrum began. In J. Q. Chen, M. Krechevsky, & J. Veins, *Building on children's strengths: The experience of Project Spectrum* (pp. 1–17). New York: Teachers College Press.

Feldman, D. H., & Fowler, R. C. (1997a). The nature(s) of developmental change: Piaget, Vygotsky, and the transition process. *New Ideas in Psychology, 15*(3), 195–210.

Feldman, D. H., & Fowler, R. C. (1997b). Second thoughts: A response to the commentaries. *New Ideas in Psychology, 15*(3), 235–245.

Gardner, H. (1993). *Frames of mind: The theory of multiple intelligences* (10th anniversary ed.). New York: Basic Books.

Gardner, H (1999). *Intelligence reframed: Multiple intelligences for the 21st century.* New York: Basic Books.

Gardner, H. (2000). *The disciplined mind: Beyond facts and standardized tests, the K-12 education that every child deserves.* New York: Penguin Books.

Gardner, H. (2006). *Multiple intelligences: New horizons.* New York: Basic Books.

Hargreaves, A., & Earl, L. (2002). Perspectives on alternative assessment reform. *American Educational Research Journal, 39*(1), 69–95.

Krechevsky, M. (1998). *Project Spectrum preschool assessment handbook.* New York: Teachers College Press.

Leont'ev, A. N. (1978). *Activity, consciousness, and personality.* Upper Saddle River, NJ: Prentice Hall.

Leont'ev, A. N. (1981). The problem of activity in psychology. In J. W. Wertsch (Ed.), *The concept of activity in Soviet Psychology* (pp. 37–71). Armonk, NY: Sharpe.

McNamee, G., & Chen, J. Q. (2005a, December). *Assessment for teaching and learning in early childhood classrooms: Content, process, and learn-*

ing profiles. Paper presented at the annual conference of National Association for the Education of Young Children, Washington, DC.

McNamee, G., & Chen, J. Q. (2005b). Dissolving the line between assessment and teaching. *Educational Leadership, 63*(3), 72–77.

Melendez, L. (2007) *Pedagogical content knowledge in early childhood: A study of teachers knowledge.* Unpublished doctoral dissertation, Erikson Institute/Loyola University, Chicago.

National Association for the Education of Young Children & National Association of Early Childhood Specialists in State Departments of Education. (2003, November). *Joint position statement. Early childhood curriculum, assessment, and program evaluation: Building an effective, accountable system in programs for children birth through age 8.* Retrieved April 10, 2008 at http://www.naeyc.org/about/positions/pdf/pscape.pdf

National Commission on Excellence in Education. (1983). *A nation at risk: The imperative for educational reform.* Washington, DC: U.S. Government Printing Office.

Popham, W. J. (2008). *Classroom assessment: What teachers need to know* (5th ed.). Boston: Allyn & Bacon.

Ramos-Ford, V., & Gardner, H. (1991). Giftedness from a multiple intelligences perspective. In N. Colangelo & G. A. Davis (Eds.), *Handbook of gifted education* (pp. 55–64). Boston, Allyn & Bacon.

Scott-Little, C., Kagan, S. L., & Frelow, V. S. (2005, March). *Inside the content: The breadth and depth of early learning standards.* Greensboro University of North Carolina: SERVE (South Eastern Regional Vision for Education).

Shepard. L., Hammerness, K., Darling-Hammond, L., Rust, F., with Snowden, J. B., Gordon, E., Gutierez, C., & Pacheco, A. (2005). Assessment. In L. Darling-Hammond & J. Bransford, (Eds.), *Preparing teachers for a changing world: What teachers should learn and be able to do* (pp. 275–326). San Francisco, CA: Jossey-Bass.

Shulman, L. S. (2004). *The wisdom of practice: Essays on teaching, learning, and learning to teach.* San Francisco, CA: Jossey-Bass.

The Staff of Education Week. (2000). *Lessons of a century: A nation's schools come of age.* Bethesda, MD: Editorial Projects in Education.

Stiggins, R. J., Arter, J. A., Chappuis, J., & Chappuis, S. (2004). *Classroom assessment for student learning.* Portland, OR: Assessment Training Institute.

Shulman, L. S. (2004). *The wisdom of practice: Essays on teaching, learning, and learning to teach.* San Francisco, CA: Jossey-Bass.

Supovitz, J. A., & Brennan, R. T. (1997). Mirror, mirror on the wall, which is the fairest test of all? An examination of the equitability of portfolio assessment relative to standardized tests. *Harvard Educational Review, 5*(3), 472–506.

Vygotsky, L. (1978). *Mind in society.* Cambridge, MA: Harvard University.

Wasserman, J. D., & Tulsky, D. S. (2005). A history of intelligence assessment. In D. P. Flanagan, J. L. Genshaft, & P. L. Harrison (Eds.), *Beyond traditional intellectual assessment: Contemporary and emerging theories, tests, and issues* (2nd ed., 3–22). New York: Guilford.

Wortham, S. C. (1996). *The integrated classroom: The assessment-curriculum link in early childhood education.* Upper Saddle River, NJ: Merill/Pearson Education.

Chapter 12
The Developmental-Interaction Approach at Bank Street College of Education

Harriet K. Cuffaro and Nancy Nager ~ *Bank Street College of Education*

Although some use the term the *Bank Street approach* to describe this method of early childhood education, many practitioners and proponents prefer the term the *developmental-interaction approach.* Although admittedly more cumbersome, developmental-interaction specifies key features of the approach and also removes it from its geographically specific site of origin. Many early childhood and elementary schools, as well as individual classroom teachers, consider themselves exemplars of this approach to teaching, although Bank Street College of Education claims the longest consistent association with this way of thinking about and practicing education.

The term *developmental-interaction* calls immediate attention to the centrality of the concept of development, the ways in which children's (and adults') modes of apprehending, understanding, and responding to the world change and grow as a consequence of their continuing experience of living. The term *interaction* refers to the tenet that thinking and emotion are interconnected, interacting spheres of development; and it also highlights the importance of engagement with the environment of people and the material world. The term has been in use since 1971 (see, e.g., Biber, Shapiro, & Wickens, 1971; Goffin, 1994; Nager & Shapiro, 2000; Shapiro & Biber, 1972; Shapiro & Weber, 1981), but the basic ideas have a much longer history. We begin with the origins of these principles and practices both to indicate the forerunners of several of the key educational ideas and also to demonstrate that programs for young children have a more extensive history than is often recognized.

HISTORY AND EVOLUTION

One notable aspect of the early days of the 20th century, a period now known as the Progressive era, was that many women were rebelling against conventional restrictions on women's lives. Social reformers were exposing social inequities and working to show ways toward a more democratic, egalitarian society. For example, Jane Addams and Lillian Wald were pioneering social workers; Susan B. Anthony, Lucretia Mott, and Elizabeth Cady Stanton fought for women's suffrage. In New York City alone, there were innovative educators such as Caroline Pratt, who founded the Play School, later known as the City and Country School; Elisabeth Irwin, who founded the Little Red School House; and Margaret Naumberg, who began the Walden School.

Among the small, independent educational enterprises designed to model new ways of teaching and new social arrangements was the Bureau of Educational Experiments. Founded in 1916 by Lucy Sprague Mitchell, it later became Bank Street College of Education. Mitchell was strongly influenced by the work of John Dewey, a philosopher, psychologist, educator, and prolific writer, whose ideas still inform thinking about education. Dewey's belief in the importance of education for the development of a democratic society was crucial. Central too was the proposition that school learning should be connected to children's lives in meaningful ways. The school that Dewey founded at the University of Chicago in 1896 was a laboratory, synthesizing the study of human development and the creation of curriculum. The school was an experiment in guiding children's development toward greater collaboration and living out democratic ideals (see, e.g., Cahan, 1992; Dewey, 1991a, 1991b; Tanner, 1997).

Mrs. Mitchell founded the Bureau as a research organization; Harriet Johnson, who had been working for the Public Education Association, became the founding director of the Bureau's nursery school in 1919. The school was designed to be an arena for studying children and for devising teaching practices that fostered growth and development. When Bureau staff—teachers and researchers—spoke of development or of schooling, they did not refer only to cognitive gains. They saw children's growth as encompassing physical, social, emotional, aesthetic, and intellectual domains. The concept of "the whole child" captures a salient aspect of this approach to education (see Biber, 1972). The Bureau was part of an informal network of experimental schools that shared a commitment to progressive pedagogy and a spirit of inquiry (see Winsor, 1973, for a compilation of bulletins from these schools).

Mitchell combined a full-scale career with an active family life; she was a pioneer of what her biographer, Joyce Antler (1981, 1987), calls "feminism as life process." Like Dewey, she was a strong believer in the then remarkable idea that schools that would enhance and support children's growth should be based on knowing more about how children learn, how to build on their interests, and how to introduce concepts and knowledge in ways that made sense to children. In *Two Lives,* a book that combines her autobiography and a biography of her husband, the economist Wesley Clair Mitchell, she wrote, "It seemed to me that knowledge gained through all the kinds of work I had seen . . . was relevant to a study of children, and surely one had to understand children in order to plan a school that was right for their development" (Mitchell, 1953, p. 273).

Over time interest grew in making this kind of education available to more children of preschool age and extending it into the elementary years. In 1930 the Cooperative School for Teachers was initiated to prepare teachers to work in these new kinds of ways and to help teachers learn as the children did: by active experimentation. This approach is compatible with what is now known as *constructivism.*

Subsequently, Mrs. Mitchell and the Bureau (later, College) staff worked in public school classrooms where teachers volunteered to have staff members bring curriculum ideas and materials to their classrooms and model teaching techniques. The Public School Workshops, as they were called, continued for many years in New York City and neighboring communities. The staff introduced progressive educational ideas to many schools that followed basically traditional teaching methods. In turn, staff had the opportunity to work with a more diverse student and teacher population. In this sense, the workshops laid the groundwork for Bank Street's leadership and participation in national educational programs such as Head Start and Follow Through (Shapiro, 2003). More recently, Bank Street has been engaged in a notably successful collaboration with the public schools of Newark, New Jersey, in a multi-year restructuring of early childhood education (Silin and Lippman, 2003).

Mrs. Mitchell was joined by dedicated colleagues who made important contributions to clarifying and expanding the fundamental philosophy of the developmental-interaction approach. Many deserve mention, but Barbara Biber stands out. A volume of her collected papers represents 50 years of thoughtful attention to the blending of psychological and educational insights (Biber, 1984; see also, Zimiles, 1997). Her work demonstrated psychological depth, a keen understanding of children's development, and a pervasive faith in the potential power of schooling to provide a context for living democratic ideals.

Two concepts of broad scope were central to the evolving developmental-interaction approach: progressivism and mental health. Although the term *mental health* is no longer in common use, its meaning has been incorporated into generally accepted views of the potential of schooling for fostering healthy development. The school was seen as a vehicle for promoting mental health by providing opportunities for creative and satisfying work; by cultivating cooperation rather than competitiveness; by offering children meaningful and stimulating rather than rote and fragmented learning; by nurturing individuality; and by furthering values of social democracy. The school was, and is, seen as much more than simply a place to learn basic cognitive skills. Certainly, the developmental-interaction approach does not fit what Freire (1970) described as a "banking model" of education, one in which the expert teacher deposits knowledge into the passive child recipient.

BASIC PRINCIPLES

As noted, the roots of the developmental-interaction approach are found in two major areas: educational theorists and practitioners—primarily John Dewey and early progressive pioneers such as Lucy Sprague Mitchell, Harriet Johnson, Caroline Pratt, and Susan Isaacs—and developmental theorists, especially those who viewed development in dynamic terms and in social context—such as Anna Freud (1974), Erik Erikson (1963), Heinz Werner (1961), Jean Piaget (1952), and Kurt Lewin (1935).

Several general principles about development and children's interactions with the social and physical environment are basic to understanding the developmental-interaction approach. A fundamental tenet has already been mentioned in the definition but bears repeating be-

The utility of the Bank Street approach has been demonstrated in the public school system as well.

Scott Cunningham/Merrill

cause it is a distinctive feature of the approach: "that the growth of cognitive function . . . cannot be separated from the growth of interpersonal processes" (Shapiro & Biber, 1972, p. 61). This guiding principle governs the theory and practice of the developmental-interaction approach. The concept of development is dynamic. It is not a simple maturational unfolding but, rather, involves shifts in the way individuals organize and respond to experiences. True to the constructivist paradigm, the child is viewed as an active maker of meaning; the school must provide opportunities for authentic problem solving.

Another basic principle is that engaging actively with the environment is intrinsic to human motivation. Further, as children grow, they construct more and more complex ways of making sense of the world. In general, the direction of growth involves movement from simpler to more complex and integrated modes.

When thinking about developmental sequences, one must remember that individuals are never at a fixed point on a straight line but operate within a range of possibilities. Earlier ways of organizing experience are not eradicated but become integrated into more advanced systems. While the concept of stages was invoked in the past to describe sequential patterns of developmental organization, recent research has raised serious questions about the invariance and universality of stage concepts.

A central idea shared with numerous other educational approaches is the importance of development of a sense of self as a unique and independent being. The idea of self described in developmental-interaction is informed by the thinking of George Herbert Mead:

> [T]he self is both image and instrument. It emerges as the result of a maturing process in which differentiation of objects and other people becomes progressively more refined and self-knowledge is built up from repeated awareness and assessment of the powers of the self in the course of mastering the environment. The shape and quality of the self reflect the images of important people in the growing child's life. (Biber & Franklin, 1967, pp. 13–14; Mead, 1934)

Growth and maturing involve conflict. Conflict is necessary for development—sometimes within the self, sometimes with others. The nature of interaction with significant figures in the child's life and the demands of the culture will determine the way conflicts are resolved.

In recent years, the work of the Russian psychologist and educator Lev Vygotsky has had a major impact on our conceptualization of interaction. We cannot claim that his work influenced earlier formulations, because the relevant writings were not translated into English until 1978. However, his work and that of his followers is now providing an important perspective that highlights the social context for children's learning and development and emphasizes the interactive nature of learning (see, e.g., Moll, 1990; Rogoff, 1990; Vygotsky, 1978; Wertsch, 1985).

From these general principles of development and interaction, a picture emerges of the learner and future citizen. School becomes a place to promote the development of competence in all areas of children's lives and helps them attain a sense of autonomy and personal and group identity. The development of social relatedness is equally stressed.[1] The school empowers children to deal effectively with their environments. It is an active community, connected to the social world of which it is a part,

---

[1]In an analysis of the evolution of the Bank Street approach, Nager and Shapiro (2000) point out that in earlier formulations the development of an autonomous and independent sense of self was seen as a goal. Until relatively recently, the concept of individuality was so deeply embedded in developmental theory that its assumptions were seldom noticed or questioned. Today, however, we have become more aware that different cultural groups place quite different values on independence as opposed to community or collectivity. We are more sensitized to the depth and scope of the formative impact of culture on growth and development. Learning is extended beyond the classroom setting to other sources of knowledge.

rather than an isolated place for learning lessons. This means that the school shares responsibility with children's families and neighborhood institutions. Sharing responsibility means sharing power and actively seeking engagement. In a time of increased immigration and greater diversity in school populations, these points take on enhanced meanings.

CURRICULUM

Explicitly or implicitly, any theory or philosophy of education holds within it a view of the learner, consideration of the relationship between learning and teaching, and a statement of what knowledge is deemed most worthy of knowing. As evident throughout this volume, approaches to early childhood education differ in the degree of exactness and specificity required in the relationship between theory or philosophy and practice. Some educational programs translate theory into explicit goals and strategies and the teacher is seen as a skilled implementer of a delivered curriculum. In contrast, in educational programs like developmental-interaction, the underlying philosophy generates principles that guide, rather than determine, practice. In such programs, teachers are expected to develop curriculum content and practices within a stated framework of valued aims and beliefs (Schoonmaker & Ryan, 1996). From the history, philosophy, and developmental theory of Bank Street, how are ideas and expectations realized in and through practice? How does this approach to education respond to the fundamental *how, what, when, where,* and *why* questions of curriculum? What choices are made concerning knowledge? How are the teacher and learner portrayed?

The Learner

From birth, children are seen as curious beings who are actively engaged in interaction with their social and physical environment and who, through sensorial exploration and experimentation, work eagerly to make sense of the world in which they live. Each child has a history of experiences in a world shaped and influenced by the social forces of family, community, and culture. In their encounters with the social and physical environment, children respond with a wholeness of self. As Lucy Sprague Mitchell (1951) noted,

> [A] child is not to be regarded as a sum of special faculties to be trained or developed separately; [the child] is to be regarded as a person, an organism, reacting to experiences as a whole . . . for purposes of discussion a child may be divided into a physical body; an intelligence with certain capacities and limitations; a social being reacting to others—either adults or his peers; a creature capable of definite social responses. But no one has ever met such split-off division of a child all by itself." (p. 189)

The concept of a democratic society guides the development and education of the learner in the developmental-interaction approach, influencing curricular decisions about content, practices, and the quality of the social and physical environment. This all-permeating concept reflects Bank Street's historical roots in the Progressive movement and the influence of Dewey's educational philosophy in which school and society, democracy and education, are intrinsically connected. The communication, participation, and associated living essential to a democratic society become a way of life to be experienced in the community of the classroom (Cuffaro, 1995; Dewey, 1991b). "If we really want to know what democracy is like, we have to have firsthand contacts with it—that is, we have to live democratically. This holds true for teachers and children alike" (Mitchell, 1942, p. 1). What might democracy look like in a classroom of three- or five- or eight-year-olds?

Knowledge and Experience

In the Bank Street approach, social studies is the core or center of the curriculum. Social studies is about the relationships between and among people and their environment, the world in which we live and our place in it. It concerns the near and far and past and present. Fundamental to this approach is that the school provides consistent opportunities for children to experience democratic living.

> [T]he responsibility of the social studies program is to give children a sense of man's use of his environment and the role which technology plays in the development of that environment, and understanding of the meaning and structure of society and appreciation of man's striving toward the beautiful, the attainment of his goals. (Winsor, 1957, p. 397)

It is essential that the *what* and *how* of learning are interconnected. *What* one learns about the world is not separated from *how* that knowledge is gained and used. From its inception, fundamental to this approach to education is the concept of learning from experience.

To "learn from experience" is to make a backward and forward connection between what we do to things and what we enjoy and suffer from things in consequence. Under such conditions, doing becomes a trying, an experiment with the world to find out what it is like; the undergoing becomes an instruction—the discovery of the connection of things (Dewey, 1966, p. 140).

To learn from experience, children must engage directly and actively with the social and physical environment and be offered varied opportunities to see, hear, touch, smell, and taste their world. Thinking, sensing, feeling children make connections and discover relationships. To make what is learned and discovered their own, children also need opportunities to give form to and express the connections they are making. Mitchell (1951) named this process *intake* and *outgo*—having an experience as children "take in" the world and the necessary "outgo" as children express, through art, writing, block building and discussion, their view of the world they are creatively constructing.

For experience to be educative there must also be continuity—where "every experience both takes up something from those which have gone before and modifies in some way the quality of those which come after" (Dewey, 1963, p. 35). *Experience, community, communication, connections, relationships, experiment, continuity,* and *problem solving* are key terms in the developmental-interaction approach.

The Teacher

The classroom is a learning situation in which the teacher becomes the link between the child's personal world of interests and experiences and the objective, ordered world of the fields of study (Dewey, 1959). Teaching is complex and demanding, requiring knowledge, skills, and dispositions. Firmly grounded in knowledge of development, coupled with understanding each child's individuality, and with deep knowledge of the curriculum content, the teacher's task is to consider, analyze, and integrate meaningfully the *what, how, when,* and *where* of daily classroom life. Teachers must be knowledgeable in the content of the social study not for giving children information but as a guide to asking meaningful questions; to planning opportunities for their experiencing (trips, books, activities); to knowing available resources; and to assessing the development of the study. Academic and practical skills are embedded throughout the curriculum. Guiding the teacher's consideration of these many factors is the *why* of education, the principles of a democratic community. Consequently, attention is given to creating a social atmosphere in the classroom that will invite discussion and the presence of varied perspectives while also encouraging and supporting a common purpose in working together.

The Learning Environment

What does a developmental-interaction classroom look like? It is a dynamic environment that welcomes active participation, cooperation and independence, and variety in expression and communication. There are unit and hollow blocks, clay, paint, water, sand, paper, crayons, and wood, materials whose lack of structure invites activity, experimentation, imagination, and transformation. There are also more structured materials, such as puzzles, manipulatives, Cuisenaire rods, Dienes blocks, teacher-made materials, paper and pencils for writing, and a wide range of books. Also included are activities such as cooking, planting, weaving, and computer use in the primary grades. The inclusion of materials and activities is determined on the basis of the richness of the opportunities they provide for exploration, discovery, and further learning. The allocation of space provides ample room for dramatic play, block building, and group meetings, as well as space to work alone or in a small group. Flexibility in the schedule provides extended periods of time for children to actively explore the potential of materials, to take trips, to become involved in expanding ideas and interests, and to work together. Flexibility exists within the familiar context of the expected routines of snack, lunch, story, rest, specials, and outdoor periods.

A consistent part of daily classroom life is creating an environment that stimulates literacy with many and varied opportunities for speaking and listening, conversations and discussions, listening to and writing stories, reading, singing, and rhyming. Developments in the fields of anthropology, social theory, and linguistics have influenced our understanding of literacy. Ever-growing developments in technology also influence our thinking about literacy. To speaking, listening, reading, and writing, now we add viewing—what children do—as they respond to and interact with the increasing presence of computers, videos, and television in their lives. Printed and written words now include movement, action, sound, and images. As we enlarge and integrate our understanding of literacy, a range of strategies is necessary to respond to the individuality of children, including features from whole language and the earlier language experience approach, as well as phonetic understanding.

Understanding that words, printed or spoken, may be insufficient for young children to communicate their complex questions and concerns, other opportunities for communication are offered through art materials. It is with paint, clay, crayons, paper, and wood that children have varied opportunities to give form to and express their thoughts and feelings. From beginning colorful crayon strokes of "rain" on paper, to paintings that tell a story, to murals and models that integrate the trips and information gathered about their social studies, children construct and communicate their understanding of the world (Gwathmey & Mott, 2000; Levinger & Mott, 1992).

Experiencing and Integrating Knowledge

In social studies, the history and story of people's lives—their struggles, aspirations, accomplishments, hopes—are viewed from the perspective of different fields of knowledge. The centrality of the *social* in social studies brings questions and ideas back to people. As Dewey noted in a discussion of geography, one of the disciplines within social studies, "the ultimate significance of lake, river, mountain, and plain is not physical but social; it is the part it plays in modifying and directing human relationships" (Dewey, 1975, pp. 34–35). Lucy Sprague Mitchell (1934) adds further detail to this perspective in her discussion of "human geography":

> For human geography deals with the interrelations between the needs of human beings and the outside environment in which they must satisfy their needs. One half of human geography is what people do to modify the earth's surface; the other half is what the phenomena of the earth's surface do to condition men's activities, most of which are concerned with their work. (p. 100)

In social studies multiple opportunities are offered for questioning, problem solving, and making sense of the social and physical environment of our interactions. In such studies there is an ever-widening spiral of learning and understanding of self and the world, for example, 3-year-olds' interest and exploration of themselves and their families; 5-year-olds' study of community services and jobs; 8-year-olds' research on the history of the original settlers of the area in which they live.

The Family

It is essential that the teacher is aware of the multiple meanings of *family* for the children in the class and makes no assumptions about the composition of the family or the values it holds. It seems safe to assume that all families want the best for their children, but it does not necessarily follow that we know what a particular family considers best. In many instances family values may conflict with the values of the school and the larger culture (see, e.g., Delpit, 2006; Ramsey, 2004; Wasow, 2000).

Self and family are topics of abiding interest for children and a familiar place from which to branch out into the larger world. In a classroom of 3-year-olds, the study of family might be evident in photographs of children's families posted at the children's eye level. Conversations are stimulated between and among children as they make comparisons and find similarities and differences. Diversity among family structures is discussed at group meetings, and ideas and conversations are extended through books and stories that include the many ways in which families are constituted—traditional and extended families, gay and lesbian–headed families, single parents (see, e.g., Casper, Cuffaro, Schultz, Silin, & Wickens, 1996; Casper & Schultz, 1999). From each family in the group there are songs and stories to hear, favorite foods to be tasted, and holidays and traditions to learn about. Trips within the school and in the immediate neighborhood begin to expand the children's worlds. And in their dramatic play, children reconstruct their experiences and experiment with their increasing understanding of their immediate world. Within such multiple sharing of interests and stories, of self and family, a sense of community begins to grow.

The Community

Gradually, children's interest in the world outside the family broadens. Making sense of the world now includes unraveling the mysteries of a highly technological and complex world where origins are often hidden. "How does that work?" "Who's the boss?" "Why?" are the questions of 5-year-olds. When the teacher adds a simple question, "What is a neighborhood?" a foundation can be laid for focusing, organizing, and directing children's curiosities and interests and beginning a study of community life. In the discussions that follow, children have the opportunity to think about and express their ideas, their information, and misinformation. Extending the scope of the initial question, a new question can be posed: "What do families need?" This may lead to investigating different types of food and housing; the services provided in the community; the variety of neighborhood stores; available means of transportation; and people's work. In researching and exploring these varied questions through interviews and observations, children come to know the details of people's lives and work, the world in which they live.

Through trips and discussions, one question leads to another, increasing both the scope and depth of children's learning. Children seek not only facts and information but also an understanding of relationships. As knowledge is constructed through many neighborhood trips, it is recorded through trip sheets, graphs, charts, children's written stories and drawings, and murals. Trips and discussions are essential to developing a dynamic social studies program at all ages. Connections are extended and strengthened in daily group meetings and in the children's imaginative dramatic play with blocks as they symbolically create the social and physical world of a neighborhood. In the interactions of their dramatic play, children test hypotheses using the data they have collected, and in the process they experience and reconstruct their knowledge. The perspectives of both scientist and artist are encouraged in the work of the classroom. And, in the reality of the world the children have constructed in play, new questions surface, interrelationships are discovered, and the need for further information becomes evident.

For example, on a Monday morning during the 5-year-olds' group meeting, the children choose what they will build. Painted on the floor are two blue lines for the river that will wind through the block scheme. The structures the children have chosen to build are a hospital, a pizza store, a school, a fire station, a house, a zoo, a bus company, and a doctor's office. During the morning discussion, the "bus drivers" state that they will build a bridge so that they can go back and forth between both parts of the town. This leads to children asking where the bus stops will be. An animated discussion follows with questions such as: Will you stop at every building? Should there be a bus stop in front of the fire station? What will happen if the fire engines have to rush out and there's a bus there? Should the fire station be next to the hospital (because sick people have to sleep and rest and siren noises would disturb them)? If there's a fire in the hospital how will the sick people get out?

By midweek there is much activity. The "teacher" at the school is gathering the wooden block figures to go on a trip to the zoo and asks, "Did everyone go to the bathroom?" Using the information they learned on a recent trip to a fire station, the "fire fighters" are inspecting the hospital to check that it is safe. A sign is posted at the pizza store: "GD PIZA $5 NO SMCNG." Beside the house, a child is holding a block figure and waiting impatiently for the bus. Then, with obvious irritation, the child says to the teacher, "They don't come! I just wait and wait. We need a meeting! It's not fair." And an argument is breaking out at the doctor's office. "No, they don't." "Yes, they do." "I'm going to ask." The building partners go to the teacher and ask, "Do doctors give shots or give lollipops?" Nearby, a child comments, "My doctor gives me a shot *and* a lollipop."

Interactions continue and multiply. Observing individual children and the group dynamics, the teacher notes possible trips to take and questions to ask at the next group meeting.

While the type of trip taken depends on the age of children, going out into the world often may include unexpected encounters with societal problems and issues. For example, on a trip to a local railroad station by a group of 6-year-olds studying transportation, besides gaining information about train tracks and workers, schedules and waiting rooms, the children also see several people who are homeless sitting on benches. Does the unexpected—homelessness—become part of the curriculum? In the partnership between children and teachers in the development of curriculum, how is this question answered? Does the teacher wait to see if the children include homelessness in their discussion, wait to see what appears as the children include the train station in their block scheme? If homelessness does not appear in the children's conversations or buildings, does the teacher introduce the topic?

These questions are fundamental to curriculum planning and are connected intrinsically to the *why* of what is worth knowing. Such questions go beyond the happenings of a specific trip because the world with all its complexities and problems always *is* in the classroom. Children are in and part of the world. They hear adults talk. They watch television. They feel adult tensions and anxieties. They hear words they do not understand. They have questions. Children encounter and are affected by societal issues and attitudes, whether directly or indirectly.

Robert Harbison

Learning is extended beyond the classroom setting to other sources of knowledge.

For children to truly make sense of the world, the social atmosphere of the classroom should create opportunities for children to express their thoughts and feelings. A democratic community invites rather than silences questioning and discussion. The questions teachers ask, or choose not to ask, extend or narrow children's view of the world. At times, adults may believe that they must protect children from disturbing aspects of the world. In our protective caring, we may neglect that what we present to children shapes their vision of the world and their place in it. As Dewey noted, "the crucial question is the extent to which the material of the social studies . . . is taught simply as information about present society or is taught in connection with things that are done, that need to be done, and how to do them" (1991a, p. 185). Raising questions offers children varied opportunities to reflect on their experiences and to extend their thinking. As children reveal their thoughts, feelings, and questions in their play, drawings and paintings, stories and conversations, adults have the opportunity to clarify, to support, to share concerns and feelings. And, it is in associated living, in the daily interactions and work of classroom life that children experience what is valued and the community we strive to achieve.

Communities of the Past

In the primary grades, children's curiosities gradually turn from interest in the here and now to the lives of people in the past. To be relevant and meaningful to children, and mindful of the still-emerging development of children's understanding of historical time, the teacher might select for study immigration or the early settlers of their community.

"What do people need?" remains a primary question, but it is now viewed from a different perspective as children must imagine and research change in the physical environment over time. Human geography comes explicitly to the forefront as children take local trips noting physical changes and the geographic features that have influenced the possibilities and direction of an area's growth. As Mitchell (1934) noted, "Everywhere people have been conditioned by the earth forces around them; and everywhere they have to a greater or lesser extent changed the earth they live in" (pp. 14–15). Questions such as "How have people worked together to solve ever-present human problems?" come to the forefront, as do the concepts of change and interdependence. Trips in the area are supplemented with research in libraries and with museum trips during which children may study artifacts from the past. Times are also regularly scheduled for learning and practicing the skills necessary to read, write, and compute at increasingly complex levels—skills essential to recording their research.

To integrate and communicate their growing knowledge and research, children become deeply involved in refining their mathematical and mapping skills. They learn to work in scale. They create relief maps and models as ways of expressing and consolidating knowledge. Writing becomes an increasingly important tool as children write reports about researched information, such as family stories of immigration, or create imaginative reconstructions of what it might have been like to be a child in their community in the past. Science experiments help children to understand how food was kept and preserved in the past, how herbs and plants were used to create simple remedies. Play appears again but in a more organized, planned manner as the children bring together what they have learned over months of study and create a play. They work on story development and dialogue, simple scenery, and props. The social studies may also culminate in an extensive exhibit created by the children in which they display their work—murals, science experiments, books, maps, dioramas, charts. In whatever form the culminating activities may appear, they are shared with other groups and parents.

Curriculum becomes integrated and whole as various skills and subjects are used as means or tools to organize and understand social studies content. At the same time, art, science, math, music, movement, and language all represent ways of knowing the world. These ways of knowing and expressing are explored in their own time within the days and weeks of classroom life. Further, independent of the social studies, there are animals to observe and care for; processes and changes in cooking to be investigated; seeds to be planted; simple machines to construct that illustrate basic laws of physics. Together, these activities encourage the development of a scientific attitude that requires observation, investigation, hypothesizing, and experimentation.

The educator's aim is to create a dynamic learning environment offering multiple opportunities for the expansion and realization of children's potential and capacity. Guided by the philosophical principles of the developmental-interaction approach, the teacher's choice of content will expand and deepen the children's view of the world and their place in it, while encouraging questioning, reflection, responsibility, shared work, and community. These attitudes and activities are necessary to experiencing democratic living.

Assessment

Multiple curriculum-embedded assessments provide the teacher an essential means with which to know how children are learning and growing and therefore how to guide curricular decisions in a seamless dynamic cycle, consistent with what is referred to as authentic assessment or a learner-centered approach (Cenedella, 1992; McCombs & Whisler, 1997; Meier, 2000; Perrone, 1991). Bank Street has long advocated a broad approach to assessment, based on understanding how the growing child makes sense of his or her world and providing a range of opportunities for the student to represent that understanding. Competence in basic skills, the development of an analytic capacity, and a wide range of knowledge in subject areas are fundamental to children's learning in school. Of equal importance are attitudes and characteristics of the learner in interaction with the physical and social environment, such as the interrelated abilities to work both independently and collaboratively, to exercise initiative, to communicate effectively, and to be a socially responsible member of the community. This emphasis on social and emotional dimensions of learning is consistent with national polling findings that indicate Americans say the single most important purpose of public schooling is to prepare children and youth to become responsible citizens (Cohen, 2006).

In contrast, current federal policy primarily defines desirable outcomes for students in terms of test scores, particularly literacy and mathematical competencies, driving school reform movements to place assessment at the forefront of educational change to achieve higher standards of academic achievement. Many schools have responded to this emphasis by teaching to the test at the expense of complex curriculum. In our view this indicates an oversimplified and narrow view of teaching and learning. In addition, the use of test scores as a high-stakes barrier to passing a grade or completing a program of study reflects a fundamentally undemocratic approach to the education of children (Cuffaro, 2000; Perrone, 1989).

In a test-driven educational environment, the desired outcomes in social, emotional, and cognitive domains stressed in the developmental-interaction approach are often relegated to secondary status. This is compounded by the fact that no readily administered assessments adequately measure these attributes of the learner, a point made by Zimiles (1987) some twenty years ago. Recognizing these realities, classroom teachers are urged to advocate for children in two important ways: First, by examining the quality of assessment tools and raising appropriate questions about implementation; second, by preparing children for test taking without sacrificing rich curriculum with opportunities for academic, social, emotional, and physical learning.

The developmental-interaction approach has long stressed rigorous and systematic assessment of children's learning and development. A central tool for assessment is reflective observation and recording of children's behavior over time (see Cohen, Stern, & Balaban, 1997). Haberman (2000) provides a vivid example of how a student teacher observes, analyzes her observation, and achieves an important insight about the use of materials, curricular goals, and the range of conceptual development in the group:

> Most of the other kindergartners also had difficulty with this problem. I definitely think it was too big a chunk to give them . . . the problem was not necessarily too *complex* for Molly—I think she understood the underlying concept: that if you add up all the reds, yellows, blues and greens and then add all *those* together, you get the total number of tiles. I do think, however, that there were too many tiles. When the numbers get that high it is so easy to lose track and get confused. . . . The underlying concept would have struck her more consciously with a smaller number of tiles. Instead she got lost in the crazy mechanics of counting. (p. 211)

This student teacher's careful observation and analysis deepened her understanding of children's learning. Informed by strong subject matter knowledge and content-specific pedagogy, teachers analyze children's responses to understand each child's characteristic strengths and needs, what a child knows and can do, as well as what he or she needs to know. Equally important, the teacher shares insights and raises questions to help children learn to self-assess and guide their own learning. Data for this analysis include the full range of daily classroom activities, interactions, and work products (e.g., playing, reading, solving mathematical problems, working with materials, and interacting with others). In addition, close examination and assessment of portfolios of children's work over time provide an important story of growth through artwork, writing, computations, and constructions. For older children, teacher-designed techniques for checking the quality of student learning can take the form of reading and writing logs, lab reports, and inventories and culminating projects at the end of a unit of study.

This approach to assessment illustrates Dewey's (1963) scientific method, as well as the experimental approach that permeates Bank Street. Articulating the goals of teacher preparation at the Bureau of Educational Experiments (Bank Street's original name), Mitchell (1931) described, "Our aim is to turn out teachers whose attitude toward their work and toward life is scientific. To us, this means an attitude of eager, alert observation; a constant questioning of old procedure in the light of new observations; a use of the world, as well as of books, as source material; an experimental open-mindedness, and an effort to keep as reliable records as the situation permits, in order to base the future upon accurate knowledge of what has been done" (p. 251).

Assessment and instruction mutually inform each other in a constructivist, dynamic manner (see Shepard, 2000, for discussion of paradigms of assessment). Assessment data also provide a meaningful basis for parent–teacher conferences during which parents and teachers can share their differentiated knowledge of a child. In this way, assessment, learning, and the curriculum are integrated, a basic premise of the experimental attitude of progressive education.

IMPLICATIONS FOR TEACHER EDUCATION

Bank Street's conceptualization of teaching applies equally to the education of children and adults, although its theoretical underpinnings and practical applications have been elaborated more fully in relation to young children. Responding to this gap, Nager and Shapiro (2007) identified five interrelated principles for the education of teachers that emerge from Bank Street's history and practice.

1. Education is a vehicle for creating and promoting social justice and encouraging participation in democratic processes.
2. The teacher has a deep knowledge of subject matter areas and is actively engaged in learning through formal study, direct observation, and participation.
3. Understanding children's learning and development in the context of family, community, and culture is needed for teaching.
4. The teacher continues to grow as a person and as a professional.
5. Teaching requires a philosophy of education—a view of learning and the learner, knowledge and knowing—that informs all elements of teaching.

While enactment of these principles can and must vary in response to changing times and needs, the principles provide a coherent framework with which to evaluate and adopt new practices, thus ensuring their consonance, validity, and legitimacy. These principles are interrelated and overlapping, each having equal power. Thus for example, a curriculum designed to further social justice must be based on a view of learning and the learner; deep knowledge of subject matter; and a sound knowledge of children, their families, and the sociocultural context of the school. Each principle is enriched by its necessary connection with the others. In this sense, the principles form an integrative whole that is greater than the sum of its parts.

These principles provide a vision of good teaching that infuses the preparation of teachers and comes to life in schools for children, as well as in the classrooms of the adults who are learning to teach. Informed by Lucy Sprague Mitchell's conviction that learning processes for adults and children are fundamentally similar, the teacher education program attempts "in all fields to give firsthand experiences (in studio, laboratory, and field work) to supplement 'book learning'" (Mitchell, 1953, p. 471). The developmental assumption is that becoming a competent teacher is tied not only to information but also to the ways in which teachers experience, internalize, and construct their growing knowledge and sense of self as a maker of meaning. It is a process of epistemological development in which teachers come to value their own voice, self, and mind, enabling them to create opportunities for children to achieve similar processes of discovery and invention (Nager, 1987). Active participation in real problems provides a basis for both child and adult learning. Therefore, the set of opportunities for teaching and learning that comprises supervised field work is vital to the teacher's personal and professional development.

A system of advisement encompasses the graduate student's entire academic program at Bank Street and thereby serves an integrative function. Advisement incorporates fieldwork, conference group, and course work. Guiding the student's work is the advisor, a member of the graduate school faculty. The term *advisor* rather than *supervisor* is noteworthy and indicates a process of guiding learning and thinking and modeling communication and interpersonal relations. The student has a biweekly individual conference with the advisor. One of these meetings follows an observation of the student's teaching and entails shared reflection on that work. Each student also participates in a yearlong weekly conference group with the advisor and a small group of students with whom the advisor is also working. This group provides an opportunity for peer learning and support, as well as an opportunity to participate in the broader and deeper project of democratic culture building (Pignatelli, 2000).

The content of group discussion is open ended. Students bring issues of personal and professional importance to the group, learning and gaining support from the advisor and the peer interaction. Considerable personal growth is required for faculty to assimilate and practice this approach to education (Shapiro, 1991). In attending to individual learning needs, advisement affords the kind of nurturing and stimulating environment that teachers are encouraged to provide for children. Again, the parallel process of attending to the complex interrelationships between children's cognitive and affective development is made explicit.

"The image in advisement is . . . setting individual goals, solving specific problems, attaining mutual insights, evaluating approaches and outcomes, defining and refining values. It combines approaches of the artist, the philosopher, and the scientist" (Bloomfield, 1991, p. 86). Pignatelli (2000) notes that this model challenges "an understanding of professional development defined largely as a matter of enlarging skill level and technical knowledge base" (p. 23). Knowledge is valued as a process of inquiry, reflection, and construction. Teachers are helped to achieve a sense of competence that is both cognitive and affective.

Not surprisingly, knowledge of development constitutes a core foundation of the teacher education curriculum. Teachers learn to think about education in terms of children's developmental needs and characteristics; their knowledge and approach to learning; and the values their families and cultures have emphasized. Academic study of child development is combined with learning to observe and record children's behavior as a critical tool for understanding children and planning curriculum (see previous section, "Assessment").

In all areas of curriculum, candidates in teacher education are immersed in principles and theory and the opportunity to experience them in practice. In curriculum courses, students explore questions about content—what is worth knowing—and consider how to enact the assumptions behind these choices through, for example, their room arrangements, scheduling, and curricular choices. Adult students take trips connected to social studies, and participate in block workshops. In addition, they have opportunities to paint, sculpt, and create; they visit schools to observe what different philosophies of education look like in practice; and they work with math manipulatives to reconstruct their understanding of number and mathematical problem solving. Writing logs and research essays, as well as creating portfolios, provide opportunities to use their growing knowledge to reflect on self, children, and curriculum.

CONCLUSION

In this chapter, we briefly summarize the developmental-interaction approach, long associated with the Bank Street College of Education. Its roots are in the Progressive era and the educational philosophy of John Dewey and Bank Street's founder, Lucy Sprague Mitchell. Concepts found in the dynamic psychologies of Erik Erikson, Anna Freud, and more recently Lev Vygotsky contribute a developmental understanding of teaching and learning.

Principles of the approach serve as a context for the teacher's decision making concerning choice of content, methodology, and the physical and social environment of the classroom. The developmental-interaction approach is not a codified set of procedures. Rather, the teacher has the complex task of using these values and principles to guide planning, implementation, and assessment of curriculum and children's growth.

These same principles apply to the education of teachers. Through direct experience, children and adults engage actively with the environment, expand their knowledge base, and strengthen their sense of competence and mastery. Teachers educated at Bank Street are expected to have a broad understanding of children's learning and developmental needs and the ability to create caring, intellectually challenging, and democratic classrooms.

WEB SITES OF INTEREST

http://www.bankstreet.edu
http://streetcat.bankstreet.edu/essays/main.html

REFERENCES

Antler, J. (1981). Feminism as life process: The life and career of Lucy Sprague Mitchell. *Feminist Studies, 7,* 134–157.

Antler, J. (1987). *Lucy Sprague Mitchell: The making of a modern woman.* New Haven, CT: Yale University Press.

Biber, B. (1972). The "whole child," individuality and values in education. In J. R. Squire (Ed.), A new look at progressive education. *ASCD Yearbook* (pp. 44–87). Washington, DC: Association for Supervision and Curriculum Development.

Biber, B. (1984). *Early education and psychological development.* New Haven, CT: Yale University Press.

Biber, B., & Franklin, M. (1967). The relevance of developmental and psychodynamic concepts to the education of the preschool child. *Journal of the American Academy of Child Psychiatry, 6,* 5–24.

Biber, B., Shapiro, E., & Wickens, D. (1971). *Promoting cognitive growth: A developmental-interaction point of view.* Washington, DC: National Association for the Education of Young Children.

Bloomfield, D. (1991). A theoretical framework for advisement. *Thought and Practice, 3,* 85–93.

Cahan, E. D. (1992). John Dewey and human development. *Developmental Psychology, 28,* 205–214.

Casper, V., Cuffaro, H. K., Schultz, S., Silin, J. G., & Wickens, E. (1996). Toward a most thorough understanding of the world: Sexual orientation and early childhood education. *Harvard Educational Review, 66,* 271–293.

Casper, V. & Schultz, S. (1999). *Gay parents, straight schools: Building communication and trust.* New York: Teachers College Press.

Cenedella, J. (1992). Assessment through the curriculum. In A. Mitchell & J. David (Eds.), *Explorations with young children: A curriculum guide from The Bank Street College of Education* (pp. 273–282). Mount Rainier, MD: Gryphon House.

Cohen, D., Stern, V., & Balaban, N. (1997). *Observing and recording the behavior of young children* (4th ed.). New York: Teachers College Press.

Cohen, J. (2006). Social, emotional, ethical, and academic education: Creating a climate for learning, participation in democracy, and well-being. *Harvard Educational Review, 76,* 201–239.

Cuffaro, H. K. (1995). *Experimenting with the world: John Dewey and the early childhood classroom.* New York: Teachers College Press.

Cuffaro, H. K. (2000). *Educational standards in a democracy: Questioning process and consequences.* Occasional Paper #4, Child Development Institute, Sarah Lawrence College.

Delpit, L. (2006). *Other people's children: Cultural conflict in the classroom* (2nd ed). New York: The New Press.

Dewey, J. (1959). The child and the curriculum. In M. S. Dworkin (Ed.), *Dewey on education* (pp. 91–111). New York: Teachers College Press. [Original work published 1902]

Dewey, J. (1963). *Experience and education.* New York: Collier Books. [Original work published 1938]

Dewey, J. (1966). *Democracy and education.* New York: Free Press. [Original work published 1916]

Dewey, J. (1975). *Moral principles in education.* Carbondale: Southern Illinois University Press. [Original work published 1909]

Dewey, J. (1991a). The challenge of democracy to education. In J. A. Boydston (Ed.), *The later works of John Dewey, 1935–1937* (Vol. 11, pp. 181–190). Carbondale, IL: Southern Illinois University Press. [Original work published 1937]

Dewey, J. (1991b). The Dewey School: The theory of the Chicago experiment. In J. A. Boydston (Ed.), *The later works of John Dewey, 1925–1953* (Vol. 11, pp. 202–216). Carbondale, IL: Southern Illinois University Press. [Original work published 1936]

Erikson, E. (1963). *Childhood and society.* New York: Norton.

Freire, P. (1970). *Pedagogy of the oppressed.* New York: Seabury.

Freud, A. (1974). *The writings of Anna Freud* (5 Vol.). New York: International Universities Press.

Goffin, S. G. (1994). *Curriculum models and early childhood education: Appraising the relationship.* Upper Saddle River, NJ: Merrill/Prentice Hall.

Gwathmey, E., & Mott, A. M. (2000). Visualizing experience. In N. Nager & E. Shapiro (Eds.), *Revisiting progressive pedagogy: The developmental interaction approach.* Albany, NY: SUNY Press.

Haberman, E. (2000). Learning to look closely at children: A necessary tool for teachers. In N. Nager & E. Shapiro (Eds.), *Revisiting progressive pedagogy: The developmental interaction approach.* Albany, NY: SUNY Press.

Levinger, L., & Mott, A. M. (1992). Art in early childhood. In A. Mitchell & J. David (Eds.), *Explorations with young children: A curriculum guide from the Bank Street College of Education* (pp. 199–214). Mount Rainier, MD: Gryphon House.

Lewin, K. (1935). *A dynamic theory of personality.* New York: McGraw-Hill.

Mead, G. H. (1934). *Mind, self, and society: From the standpoint of a social behaviorist.* Chicago: University of Chicago Press.

McCombs, B., & Whisler, J. (1997). The *learner-centered classroom and school.* San Francisco: Jossey-Bass.

Meier, D. (2000). Educating a democracy. In J. Cohen, & J. Rogers (Eds.), *Will standards save public education?* Boston: Beacon Press.

Mitchell, L. S. (1931). A cooperative school for student teachers. *Progressive Education, 8,* 251–255.

Mitchell, L. S. (1934). Social studies and geography. *Progressive Education, 11,* 97–105.

Mitchell, L. S., with Johanna Boetz and others (1942). *The people of the U.S.A.: Their place in the school curriculum.* New York: Progressive Education Association.

Mitchell, L. S. (1951). *Our children and our schools.* New York: Simon & Schuster.

Mitchell, L. S. (1953). *Two lives: The story of Wesley Clair Mitchell and myself.* New York: Simon & Schuster.

Mitchell, L. S. (1934/1991). *Young geographers: How they explore the world and how they map the world.* New York: Bank Street College of Education.

Moll, L. C. (Ed.). (1990). *Vygotsky and education: Instructional implications and applications of socio-historical psychology.* New York: Cambridge University Press.

Nager, N. (1987). Becoming a teacher: The development of thinking about knowledge, learning, and the self. *Thought and Practice, 1,* 27–32.

Nager, N,. & Shapiro, E. (Eds.). (2000). *Revisiting a progressive pedagogy: The developmental interaction approach.* Albany, NY: SUNY Press.

Nager, N., & Shapiro, E. (2007). *Some principles for teacher education. Occasional Paper #18.* New York: Bank Street College of Education.

Perrone, V. (1989). *Working papers: Reflections on teachers, schools, and communities.* New York: Teachers College Press.

Perrone, V. (1991). *A letter to teachers: Reflections on schooling and the art of teaching.* San Francisco: Jossey-Bass.

Piaget, J. (1952). *The origins of intelligence in children.* New York: International Universities Press.

Pignatelli, F. (2000). Furthering a progressive educational agenda: Advisement and the development of educators. In N. Nager & E. Shapiro (Eds.), *Revisiting a progressive pedagogy: The developmental interaction approach.* Albany, NY: SUNY Press.

Ramsey, P. G. (2004). *Teaching and learning in a diverse world: Multicultural education for young children* (3rd ed.). New York: Teachers College Press.

Rogoff, B. (1990). *Apprenticeship in thinking: Cognitive development in social context.* New York: Oxford University Press.

Schoonmaker, F., & Ryan, S. (1996). Does theory lead to practice? Teachers' constructs about teaching: Top-down perspectives. In S. Reifel & J. A. Chafel (Eds.), *Advances in early education and day care* (Vol. 8, 117–152). Greenwich, CT: JAI Press.

Shapiro, E. K. (2003). Precedents and precautions. In J. Silin & C. Lippman (Eds.), *Putting the children first: The changing face of Newark's public schools.* New York: Teachers College Press.

Shapiro, E. (1991). Teacher: Being and becoming. *Thought and Practice, 3,* 5–24.

Shapiro, E., & Biber, B. (1972). The education of young children: A developmental-interaction point of view. *Teachers College Record, 74,* 55–79.

Shapiro, E., & Weber, E. (Eds.). (1981). *Cognitive and affective growth: Developmental-interaction.* Hillsdale, NJ: Lawrence Erlbaum.

Shepard, L. (2000). The role of assessment in a learning culture. *Educational Researcher, 29,* 4–14.

Silin, J., & Lippman, C. (Eds.). (2003). *Putting the children first: The changing face of Newark's public schools.* New York: Teachers College Press.

Tanner, L. N. (1997). *Dewey's laboratory school: Lessons for today.* New York: Teachers College Press.

Vygotsky, L. (1978). *Mind in society: The development of higher psychological processes* (M. Cole, V. John-Steiner, S. Scribner, & E. Souberman, Eds.). Cambridge, MA: Harvard University Press. [Original work published 1922–1935]

Wasow, E. (2000). Families and schools: New lenses, new landscapes. In N. Nager & E. Shapiro (Eds.), *Revisiting a progressive pedagogy: The developmental-interaction approach.* Albany, NY: SUNY Press.

Werner, H. (1961). *Comparative psychology of mental development.* New York: Science Editions.

Wertsch, J. V. (1985). *Vygotsky and the social formation of mind.* Cambridge, MA: Harvard University Press.

Winsor, C. B. (1957). *What are we doing in social studies?* Forty-fifth Annual School Men's Week proceedings. Philadelphia: University of Pennsylvania Press. Reprinted by Bank Street College.

Winsor, C. B. (Ed.). (1973). *Experimental schools revisited: Bulletins of the Bureau of Educational Experiments.* New York: Agathon Press.

Zimiles, H. (1987). Progressive education: On the limits of evaluation and the development of empowerment. *Teachers College Record, 89,* 201–217.

Zimiles, H. (1997). Viewing education through a psychological lens: The contributions of Barbara Biber. *Child Psychiatry and Human Development, 28,* 23–31.

ACKNOWLEDGMENTS

We dedicate this chapter to the memory of our friend and colleague, Edna K. Shapiro, whose keen intellect and warm spirit continue to inform this chapter.

We thank the editors and Herbert Zimiles for permission to use material from his chapter "The Bank Street Approach," which appeared in previous editions of this volume.

Chapter 13
The Project Approach
An Overview

Lilian G. Katz ⇝ *University of Illinois*
Sylvia C. Chard ⇝ *University of Alberta, Canada*

The inclusion of in-depth investigations in the early childhood and primary school curriculum has a long history. First inspired by the ideas of John Dewey during the Progressive era, it was promoted by William H. Kilpatrick, who referred to it as the "project method." The project method was also used in Dewey's Laboratory School at the University of Chicago at the turn of the twentieth century (Tanner, 1997).

More recently, project work was a central part of preschool and primary education in Britain during the so-called "Plowden Years" in the 1960s and 1970s, which inspired many U.S. educators to adopt the project method using the term *open education* (cf. Smith, 1997). A highly creative variation of the project method can now be seen as part of the curriculum in preprimary schools in the small northern Italian city of Reggio Emilia (Edwards, Gandini, & Forman, 1998). A contemporary extension and elaboration of earlier practices, currently referred to as the Project Approach, has been adopted in preschool and primary classes in many parts of North America and is being widely adopted in many other countries as well (see Katz & Chard, 2000). We have worked with teachers in Korea, China, Poland, The Philippines, Costa Rica, Mexico, and many other countries. In general, teachers in these countries adopt the project approach as a significant part of the early childhood curriculum, as is common in North America.

We use the term *project approach,* rather than *method* or *model,* to suggest that children's investigations (i.e., project work), constitute one of many important elements of an early childhood or primary curriculum. As a *part* of the curriculum for children from the ages of about 3 to 8 years, project work functions in a *complementary* relationship to other aspects of the curriculum, rather than as a total pedagogical method or curriculum model, and thus does not require the abandonment of a wide variety of other curriculum elements that support children's development and learning.

We begin this overview with a definition of a project, followed by a summary of the theoretical rationale for its inclusion in the curriculum (discussed in greater detail in Helm & Katz, 2001; Katz, 1991; Katz & Chard, 2000). In addition, we offer some guidelines for project topic selection and outline the phases of project work. This is followed by a brief description of how the project approach can be implemented at the kindergarten level.

WHAT IS A PROJECT?

A project is an extended in-depth investigation of a topic, ideally one worthy of the children's attention, time, and energy. Projects are usually

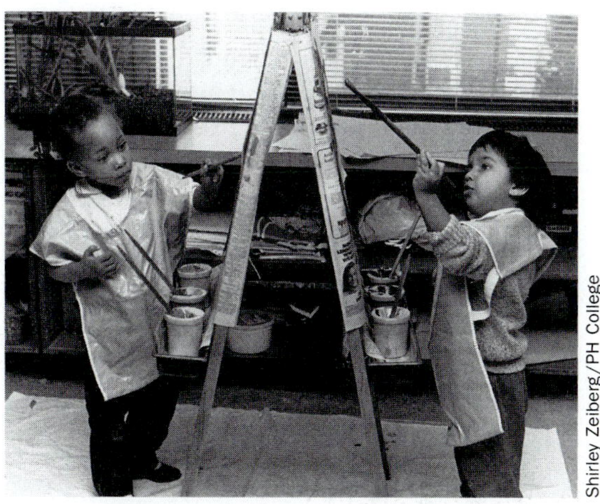

Shirley Zeiberg/PH College

These children work on an art project they planned.

undertaken by a whole class, sometimes by small groups within a class, and occasionally by an individual child. Even when a project is undertaken by the whole class, children typically work in small groups and often individually on specific subtopics related to the larger one under investigation. In discussions with their teacher, children generate a set of questions about specific aspects of the topic that the investigation will attempt to answer.

The investigation undertaken in a project involves the enactment of a variety of intellectual and social dispositions, as well as academic skills. Depending on the range of skills already available to the participating children, the work ideally includes the following elements:

- Sharing and discussing previous experiences and knowledge related to the topic in the first phase of the work
- Gathering and recording new data
- Sketching and drawing
- Painting, model making, creating stories, planning and engaging in dramatic play
- Interviewing experts on the topic
- Reading, writing, taking measurements, developing and distributing surveys and questionnaires
- Looking things up in a library and on the Internet

A project ideally also involves the acquisition of worthwhile knowledge, understandings, and concepts in a variety of disciplines, such as the sciences, social studies, language arts and literature, and all the fine arts. In addition, the activities usually employed in project work at all ages include collecting information through direct observations, conducting experiments related to subtopics of interest, making collections of related artifacts, and preparing visual and verbal reports of the findings.

Furthermore, in project work the children are encouraged to identify subtopics of special interest to them and to accept responsibility for particular types of tasks that will contribute to the overall investigation. In addition to the value of the new knowledge and understandings acquired, and the skills applied, the feelings of mastery of a topic resulting from such sustained effort can lay the foundation for a lifelong disposition to persist in reaching for in-depth understanding of worthwhile topics.

The main features of project work that distinguish it from the traditional didactic way of introducing children to new knowledge are these:

1. The children's role in generating the questions to be answered by their investigation
2. Openness to possible shifts in the direction of the inquiry as it proceeds
3. The children's acceptance of responsibility for the work accomplished and for the kinds of representations of findings that are prepared, documented, and reported

PROJECT WORK AND OTHER PARTS OF THE CURRICULUM

The project approach is advocated on the assumption that during the primary years project work is the informal part of the curriculum that complements and supports its more formal components, such as systematic instruction in basic literacy and numeracy skills. *Systematic instruction* refers to formal instruction of an individual or of small groups of children—and in the case of older children, the whole class—who require adult assistance with learning the specific skills and subskills involved in becoming literate and numerate. By comparison, in the case of preschool children—for whom spontaneous play, informal activities, music, story reading, and so on are more typical and appropriate than formal instruction—project work constitutes the more formal part of the curriculum.

In the early primary years, project work and formal instruction can be seen as complementary to each other in several ways:

1. Formal instruction aids children with the acquisition of basic skills, while project work gives them opportunity to apply the skills in meaningful contexts.
2. In formal instruction, the teacher addresses children's deficiencies, while project work gives children opportunities to apply and strengthen their proficiencies.
3. In formal instruction, the teacher directs the instructional sequences and organizes the work on the basis of expert knowledge of how the skills are best learned by individual children with particular learning characteristics. In project work, children are encouraged to choose the tasks and the level of task difficulty most appropriate for themselves.
4. During systematic instruction, learners are in a passive and receptive posture as the teachers provide them with information and instructions. In project work, children are actively engaged in planning and conducting the investigation, applying knowledge and skills, and making decisions and choices on all aspects of the work.
5. While children are usually intrinsically motivated to remain engaged in their project work, in systematic instruction the teacher takes advantage of children's motivation to please him or her and to meet his or her expectations. Furthermore, in project work the usefulness, relevance, and purposes of basic literacy and numeracy skills typically become self-evident. The experience of relevance tends to strengthen children's motivation to improve such skills and increases their receptivity to the teacher's help in mastering them through systematic instruction.

In project work, the teacher's role is more consultative than instructional. The teacher facilitates the progress of the work by guiding and monitoring the children's progress. The teacher uses observation of the children at work during the project to identify cues concerning the kinds of instructional activities that might be needed by individual children and notes the readiness of individuals or groups of children for the introduction of new knowledge and skills.

In the case of preschool children, the teacher's role includes both consultation and leadership in helping to organize the progress of the investigation, encouraging in-depth and extended attention to the work of answering the questions raised in discussion. The teacher arranges the time schedule so that the project can proceed. The teacher also makes suggestions for how children can represent their findings. At both the preschool and primary levels, the teacher plays an important role in documenting the experiences of the children as the work proceeds (Helm, Beneke, & Steinheimer, 2007; Katz & Chard, 1996).

In summary, we suggest that young children's development and learning are best served when they have frequent opportunity to be involved in investigations about worthwhile topics, especially during the primary years, when the teacher's formal instruction in basic skills is also available for those who cannot achieve mastery without such assistance. Teachers are encouraged to balance these two important provisions for learning in the early years.

In addition, children can learn to make increasingly sophisticated use of computers in the course of project work. With increasing age and experience, children can use computers for writing, preparing graphs, compiling posters, producing visual essays, designing simple games, and other forms of representation. They can also have access to a wide variety of types of information via selected Internet sites as they seek answers to the questions that represent the main thrust of their investigation.

THEORETICAL RATIONALE FOR THE PROJECT APPROACH

The recommendation for including project work in the early childhood curriculum is based partly on our conception of the goals of education and partly on our view of a developmental approach to implementing those goals. In addition, we find support for the value of project work in recent research on children's motivation and interactive abilities. Schidt, Burts, Durham, Charlesworth, and Hart (2007) compared the effects of developmentally appropriate versus developmentally inappropriate teaching practices on the development of kindergarteners' social competence, indicating that the former provided genuine contexts for children to develop skills involved in working together and coordinating their efforts, a major element of project work. We begin by defining the goals and follow with the principles of practice based on combining the goals and our understanding of how young children develop and learn. A fuller discussion of these points can be found in Katz and Chard (2000).

Four Types of Learning Goals

We suggest that at every level of education four types of learning goals must be addressed: knowledge, skills, dispositions, and feelings. At the early childhood level, they can be broadly defined as follows:

1. *Knowledge* During the preschool and early primary school period, knowledge and understanding can consist of ideas, concepts, schemas, facts, information, stories, myths, legends, songs, and other such contents of the mind. The experience of involving young children in projects leads us to emphasize the importance of helping young children to achieve deeper and more accurate understanding of their own experiences.

Principles Related to the Acquisition of Knowledge

Recent insights into children's development suggest that, in principle, the younger the child, the more readily knowledge is constructed and acquired through active and interactive processes rather than passive, receptive, and reactive ones. With increasing age, children become more able to profit from passive reception of instruction. This developmental principle suggests that, in practice, young children in the preschool and early primary years best construct and master knowledge and understanding from their own firsthand, direct experiences and from interaction with primary sources of knowledge.

The interactive experiences from which knowledge and understandings can be constructed and acquired must have content that is meaningful to the children—perhaps more meaningful to some of them than others, at least at first. We suggest that, in principle, the content of interaction should be related to matters of actual or potential interest to the children involved. However, because not all of children's interests are equally deserving of attention, and because adults can and should help children acquire new interests, some selection by the teacher of what content is most worthy of attention is required. We suggest that the interests most worthy of strengthening in young children are those likely to extend, deepen, and improve their understandings of their own environments and experiences (Dresden & Lee, 2007).

We suggest furthermore that, in principle, the younger the learner, the more integrated the curriculum should be; conversely, as children increase in age and experience, their capacity to profit from subject- or discipline-based study increases. Young children do not differentiate their ideas, thoughts, and interests into categories such as science, language, and mathematics; they are more likely to gain knowledge and understanding by pursuing a topic to which scientific, linguistic, mathematical, and other discipline-related concepts can be applied.

2. *Skills* are defined as small, discrete, and relatively brief actions that are fairly easily observed or inferred from behavior (e.g., cutting, drawing, counting a group of objects, coordinating activities with peers, fine and gross motor skills).
3. *Dispositions* are relatively enduring habits of mind, or characteristic ways of responding to experience across types of situations (e.g., persistence at tasks, curiosity, generosity or avarice, the disposition to be a reader, to look things up, or to solve problems, etc.). For example, curiosity can best be defined as a disposition or habit of mind. Unlike an item of knowledge or a skill, a disposition is not an end-state to be mastered once and for all. It is a trend or consistent pattern of behavior, and its possession is established only by its increasingly repeated manifestation in the appropriate context.

Some of the most important dispositions included in the goals of education are inborn. All children are born with the disposition to learn, to observe, to investigate, to make sense of experience, to play, and to develop attachments to others—granted, any of these dispositions may be stronger in some children than in others.

Anne Vega/Merrill

Collaboration on connected curricular activities is commonplace.

Thus, experiences should be provided to young children that support and strengthen these inborn dispositions. Other dispositions, however—desirable and undesirable—are likely to be learned from being around and interacting with adults who have them and in whose behavior such dispositions can be observed fairly frequently by the children.

Strengthening Desirable Dispositions. Parents, teachers, and school officials invariably include many dispositions in their lists of the desired effects of education. Among them are the desire to learn, to be cooperative and creative, and to be eager to approach and solve problems. The underlying assumption is that mastery of knowledge, understandings, and skills ideally should be accompanied by robust dispositions to employ them.

4. *Feelings* are subjective emotional or affective states, such as feelings of belonging, self-esteem, confidence,

adequacy and inadequacy, competence and incompetence, anxiety, and so forth. Feelings about significant phenomena may vary from being transitory to enduring, intense to weak, or ambivalent.

Feelings related to schooling are likely to be learned as by-products of experience, rather than from instruction or exhortation. Both dispositions and feelings can be thought of as incidental learnings in that they are incidental to the processes by which knowledge and understandings are constructed and acquired and by which skills are learned. However, to label feelings as incidental is not to belittle them or to devalue the role of the teacher or the curriculum in their development; rather, it is to emphasize that feelings cannot be taught didactically. Children cannot be instructed in what feelings to have or not to have!

Feelings Related to School Experiences. Like dispositions, feelings cannot be taught directly; they are experienced and strengthened or weakened in the context of the interactions and activities that give rise to them. However, when a curriculum is focused on a narrow range of academic tasks (e.g., drill and practice in workbooks, lessons in phonics), it is likely that a substantial proportion of the learners will be unable to work effectively and thus will be unlikely to develop feelings of competence (Marchand & Skinner, 2007). Indeed, when a single instructional approach is employed with any group of children who are diverse in background, ability, and development, and many other ways, some feel left out and are prone to develop feelings of incompetence or inadequacy (Slavin, et al., 1996). The inclusion of project work increases the variety of types of tasks and levels of difficulty available, such that all members of the class are likely to find meaningful work that can enhance feelings of competence, of belonging, and of being a contributor to the group effort.

Implications for Practice

Learning in all four goal categories—knowledge/understanding, skills, dispositions, and feelings—is facilitated in different ways. In the case of knowledge and skills, learning can be aided by active research, observation, a wide variety of types of data gathering, appropriate instruction, and many other processes. However, dispositions and feelings cannot be learned from study or from direct or systematic instruction. Furthermore, for dispositions to be strengthened, they must be enacted, and their enactment must be associated with some satisfaction.

As already suggested, dispositions cannot be taught directly. We recommend that, in principle, if dispositions are to be strengthened, ample opportunity for their enactment must be available. For example, the disposition to be problem solvers can be strengthened only if children have frequent real and meaningful problems to solve in the course of their daily activities. In similar fashion, the disposition to be responsible can be strengthened only when children have appropriate responsibilities. The findings of the research in this area suggest that a curriculum that emphasizes child-initiated meaningful learning tasks is more likely to strengthen such dispositions as to seek mastery, to exert real effort in the face of difficulties, and to persist at challenging tasks—as well as many others usually alluded to in lists of goals and desirable educational outcomes.

In summary, all four categories of learning goals are worthy of the teacher's continuing attention and concern. The inclusion of project work in the curriculum helps to ensure that the construction and acquisition of worthwhile knowledge and the mastery of basic skills can occur in such a way that the *dispositions* to use them are also strengthened (Katz, 1994). Our assumption is that if knowledge, understandings, and skills are acquired in meaningful contexts with ample opportunity to apply them, then the dispositions to seek and deepen knowledge and understanding, and to use the skills in the processes of doing so, can be acquired and can be strengthened; conversely, without such meaningful application, the dispositions to use knowledge and skills may not be developed or may even be weakened. In addition, our experience is that children's involvement in project work is typically accompanied by feelings of self-confidence, engagement, enthusiasm, and often of pleasure and satisfaction with what is accomplished, including satisfaction in overcoming setbacks encountered during the work.

In principle, then, the incorporation of project work in the curriculum helps to ensure that all four categories of learning goals are addressed concurrently.

The Development of Social Competence

Current research on young children's social development strongly indicates that the first 6 or 7 years of life constitute a critical period for the achievement of social competence and that failure to do so during the early years can have serious long-term negative consequences (Flook, Repetti, & Ullman, 2005; Katz & McClellan, 1997). In principle, a curriculum for young children is best when it provides frequent activities and experiences in which cooperation, collaboration, coordination of effort, and resolution of conflicts among the children are functional, consequential, and satisfying to them. The project approach provides frequent and real contexts in which children can be supported in developing a wide range of social knowledge, social skills, social dispositions and feelings of an interpersonal nature. One such feature is that in the conduct of project work on a topic shared by the whole class, children usually work in small subgroups investigating subtopics that will contribute to the larger findings of the investigation. In such a context, each subgroup can solicit suggestions from classmates, make suggestions to other subgroups, prepare reports to give to them about their findings, and in many other ways participate in real contexts in which they anticipate others' responses to, interests in, and feelings about their reports. Anticipation of the possible responses of peers, parents, and others with whom they will share their work is an important component of social competence.

In summary, the incorporation of project work into the curriculum of early childhood and primary education addresses all four main categories of learning goals and makes possible the application of the principles of practice derived from current knowledge of many important aspects of young children's development and learning.

IMPLEMENTING THE PROJECT APPROACH

To a very large extent, the benefits of project work are related to the topic being investigated. The sheer number of possible topics is so large that some kind of selection process is advisable. Teachers have the ultimate responsibility for judging whether the topic is worthy of children's time and energy and of the preschool's or school's resources. Furthermore, to support good project work, teachers must often undertake extensive preparation, study, and exploration. Thus, topic selection warrants serious consideration by the teacher and by those who define the curriculum (see Chard, 1998a, 1998b, http://www.projectapproach.org).

Selecting Topics for Projects

Many factors contribute to the appropriateness of a topic. Much depends on characteristics of the particular group of children, the teacher's knowledge and experience related to the topic and his or her own interest in it, the local resources available, the larger context of the school and community, and various mixes of all these factors. Furthermore, it is important to keep in mind that many topics of importance are not suitable for projects. It can also be difficult to predict which topics will work well with any given group of children.

Responding to Children's Interests

Teachers sometimes select project topics on the basis of the children's expressed or assumed interest in them. However, the interest of an individual, a group, or a whole class presents a number of potential pitfalls in topic selection. On a practical level, in a class of 25 children, the number of possible interests is potentially too large to be able to address in a single year. Thus, teachers need some criteria to determine which of the interests is worthy of being addressed. Furthermore, it is not clear what children mean when they say that they are interested in a topic. Interests can be of relatively low value to the child's total learning (e.g., interest in pirates or in the *Titanic* stimulated by exposure to a movie). Some interests might be passing thoughts or fancies, fleeting concerns, phobias, fetishes, or topics nominated by a child who wants to please the teacher.

In addition, the fact that an individual or group expresses interest in a given topic (e.g., dinosaurs) does not necessarily mean that the teacher should support and strengthen interest in it. Children's enthusiastic response to a Disney movie about pirates, for example, does not mean that the topic is worthy of a project. The children can be given opportunity for spontaneous dramatic play involving pirates if the teacher agrees to it; they can be encouraged to discuss their reactions to the film and their understanding of its implication in a discussion setting, and so forth. But such interest does not imply that an in-depth study of the topic of pirates is in their best developmental, educational, or even moral interests. We suggest that it is useful to *distinguish between providing opportunity for child-initiated spontaneous play* around a topic of interest to them and what may not be worthy of the kind of effort and energy required for conducting an in-depth investigation of it. The topic of a project should be part of the general commitment of the teacher and the school to taking children and their intellectual powers seriously, and to treating them as young investigators of phenomena worth understanding more fully.

We suggest that adults have substantial responsibility to educate children's interests and to alert them to events and phenomena around them worthy of their attention and understanding. This does not mean that the teacher indicates disrespect or disdain for the children's own expressed interests. However, children's awareness of the teacher's real and deep interest in a topic (e.g., the changes in the natural environment over a 6-week period) is likely to engender some level of interest in the topic among the children who respect and look up to the teacher. In this way, adults take responsibility for educating children's interests.

Sometimes teachers select exotic and glamorous topics in the hope of exciting the attention of children who are sometimes reluctant or uninvolved members of the group. For example, projects revolving around the rain forest in a kindergarten in a U.S. Midwest location may entice young children into participation and certainly do no harm. However, our experience of working with many teachers all over the world indicates that young children can be no less fascinated and intrigued by the experience of close observation and study of their own immediate natural environments, whether cornfields, apple orchards, or a nearby bicycle shop. Furthermore, if the topic is an exotic and therefore remote one, it is difficult for the children to contribute to the direction and design of the project investigation. The less firsthand experience the children have in relation to the topic, the more dependent they are on the teacher for the ideas, information, questions, hypotheses, and so forth that constitute the essence of good project work.

Young children are indeed dependent on adults for many important aspects of their lives. However, project work is that part of the curriculum in which children are encouraged to take the initiative in setting the questions to be answered and the direction of the study; it is also where they are prompted to accept responsibility for gathering the data and to define the work to be accomplished.

Along similar lines, topics are sometimes chosen because they are expected to amuse or even entertain the children. Such topics are thought by teachers to stimulate children's imaginations (e.g., the Little Mermaid, teddy bears). However, these topics are more fanciful than imaginative. In good project work, children have ample opportunity to use and strengthen their imaginations when they make predictions about what they will find before taking a field trip, when they predict the answers to their questions that a visiting expert might give, or when they argue with each other about possible causes and effects related to the phenomenon under investigation. Project work stimulates and strengthens young children's imaginations in many other ways as well; for example, during the early phases of a project, they are encouraged to report their actual experiences and memories related to the topic but also to make up their own stories related to it (e.g., stories of actual experiences of riding a tricycle and imaginary and fictional stories of bike rides).

Diversity of Experiences. In some classes, the diversity of the incoming pupils' experiences might be so great that it would be beneficial to *begin* the year with a topic that the teacher is reasonably certain is familiar to all children. At the beginning of the life of the classroom group, it is probably best to ensure that all the children have sufficient experience related to the topic to be able to recognize and share their own experience and participate in discussion with some confidence. As the school year progresses and children become adept at project work, they can more readily appreciate that classmates have different interests and prefer to work on different subtopics. In this way, children's appreciation of differences in experiences, interests, and abilities among their peers can be deepened.

Diversity of Culture and Background. The project approach is highly responsive to diversity of cultures and backgrounds within the group of children being served. One consideration to be made when selecting topics for diverse groups is that some topics may be considered delicate in some cultures and not others. Furthermore, some topics might embarrass children of some backgrounds. However, we find it useful to make a distinction between a child's culture and a child's heritage. *Culture* refers to the current day-to-day experiences and environment of the children; *heritage* refers to historic and ancestral characteristics and past experiences associated with their origins. From a developmental perspective, young children can deepen their understanding of their culture through good project work; deepening their knowledge of their heritage is more appropriately accomplished through other parts of the curriculum, especially as children get older.

Preparation for Participation in a Democratic Society

An important consideration in the selection of the topics of projects is a commitment to building children's abilities to be able, ultimately, to participate competently in a democratic society. In the service of this goal, good topics are those that deepen children's understanding, knowledge, and appreciation of the contribution of others to the well-being of all. In addition, one of the many potential benefits of good project work is that it provides a wide range of experiences within the classroom that constitute participation in democratic processes: collaboration, listening and responding to each others' ideas, coordinating efforts and diverse contributions of members of the whole and of subgroups, negotiating disagreements, reaching consensus on how to solve problems and accomplish tasks, and so forth. All these processes help to lay the foundation for competence in democratic living.

Furthermore, in the interests of the goal of preparing for participation in democracy, we ask, "Will the study of this topic strengthen and/or deepen the disposition to examine closely the real world and its complexities?" Thus, we suggest avoiding topics that are frivolous, banal, or of trivial consequence. Instead, we recommend choosing topics that involve children in unpacking the familiar, deepening their understanding of what goes on behind the scenes and of how various people's efforts contribute to daily community life; these topics can contribute to children's growing capacity to appreciate the diverse ways that others contribute to their well-being, which is basic to a democratic community.

Criteria for Selecting Topics

Based on the preceding discussion, we offer the following list of criteria for selecting topics: *A topic is likely to be a good one if. . . .*

1. Relevant phenomena are directly observable in the children's own environments.
2. It is within children's experiences.
3. Firsthand direct investigation is feasible (and involves no potential dangers).
4. Local resources are favorable and readily accessible.
5. It has good potential for a variety of representational media (role play, construction, multidimensional representaton, graphic organizers, etc.).
6. Parental participation and contributions are likely; parents can become involved in the investigation with little difficulty.
7. It is sensitive to local culture as well as culturally appropriate in general.
8. It is potentially interesting to many of the children or is an interest that adults consider worthy of developing in children.
9. It is related to curriculum goals of the school and district.
10. It provides ample opportunity to apply basic skills appropriate to the ages of the children.
11. The topic is *optimally* specific—not too narrow and not too broad (e.g., a study of the teacher's own dog at one end and the topic of "music" at the other).

PHASES OF PROJECT WORK

Once the topic of a project has been agreed upon by the children and their teachers, a central feature of project work is the children's involvement in identifying which aspects of it to explore, formulating the research questions, planning the work, and defining the kinds of representations of findings and reports to be prepared. In other words, project investigations can be thought of as having the same kind of *narrative* or *sequential* quality as any other scientific endeavor: The investigators develop a set of questions, predict where they are most likely to get useful answers, proceed to collect the data they predict will yield answers, analyze and summarize their findings, and report them to others who might also have some interest in them. Projects can be planned and conducted in three approximate sequential phases (see Chard, 1998a, 1998b).

Phase 1: Getting Started on a Project

In the first phase of a project, the teacher encourages the children to share their own personal experiences and recollections related to the topic and to review their knowledge of it, using representational and expressive competencies such as dramatic play, drawing, reporting their experiences, and writing about them. During these initial activities, the teacher can learn of the special interests of individual children and their parents; this sharing also helps establish a baseline of understanding for the whole group involved in the project. Parents may be able to contribute to the project in a variety of ways, such as arranging places to visit, lending items for display, being interviewed by the children, and providing access to information.

In the process of reviewing their current understanding of the topic during the first phase of a project, children raise questions about the topic. Often the questions reveal gaps in knowledge or even misunderstandings, which can form the basis for planning the second phase of the project. In the role of consultant, the teacher is not too quick to correct misconceptions that emerge during phase 1; these can be excellent resources for learning as the children investigate and test their predictions and theories (Table 13–1).

We suggest that an important part of question table development is to ask children who offer predictions (in a positive and encouraging tone) questions such as "What makes you think so?" By asking such questions from time to time, the teacher is supporting children's development of the disposition to reflect on the bases of their predictions, ideas, opinions, and assumptions that should serve them well throughout life. The question table can remain visible throughout the life of the project, and when appropriate during group discussions more questions and recent findings, as well as indications of their sources, can be added to the table.

Phase 2: Developing a Project

The main thrust of the second phase is gaining new information, especially by means of firsthand, direct, real-world experience. The sources of information used can be primary as well as secondary, depending upon the ages of the children involved.

Primary sources include field trips to real settings and events, such as an actual construction site to be observed, the working of a machine, or the goods-delivery section of a supermarket. Interviewing people who have direct experiences related to the topic also provides firsthand information. All occasions for interviews should be carefully prepared in advance so that the children appreciate the activity's usefulness and spend the time productively. Developing and distributing surveys and questionnaires can also be included in the data-gathering process at all ages. Secondary sources of information, such as books, relevant educational films, videotapes, brochures, and pamphlets can be examined at this time also.

Fieldwork. During phase 2, a field site visit can be planned by the children and teacher together. Field site visits do not have to be elaborate, involving expensive transportation to distant places. They can involve going to places close to

TABLE 13–1
The Question Table

Questions	Predictions	Findings	Sources
How many shoes are sold in a day?	1. 100 2. 50 3. 10		
What do you do with the money?	1. Put it in a box 2. Take it home		

the schools—shops, the town hall, stores, parks, construction sites, walks in the neighborhood and such—taking note of the variety of buildings, types of windows and doors, and so on. With teacher aides and volunteer parent helpers, the children can go to these sites in small groups, enjoying the opportunity of having an adult to talk with about what they are observing.

Preparing for fieldwork includes identifying questions to be answered and deciding on people to talk to who can be good sources of information about their topic or subtopic. To help them record their observations, children can carry simple clipboards and can sketch or write things of special interest to be reviewed on return to the classroom. During the visit, children can also be encouraged to count, note shapes and colors, learn any special words, figure out how things work, and use all their senses to deepen their knowledge of the phenomena studied. Many projects are enriched by the children sketching and drawing what they observe. The focus for these experiences is not on the elements of art but on how best to represent what has been observed and to make it available for futher inspection on return to the class.

In the classroom after fieldwork and site visits, the children can recall many details and review the information collected from interviews. The children can represent their findings in increasingly elaborate ways as they learn more about the topic. At this time, the children apply the skills of talking, drawing, dramatic play, writing, making simple mathematical notations, taking measurements, making charts and histograms, diagramming sequences of events, and so on. If a field site is nearby, such as a construction site in the vicinity of the school, it can be visited on several occasions and comparisons can be made between what was observed on one visit and on subsequent ones.

The children's work can be accumulated in individual project folders, in wall displays, and in group record books in which work is shared with others. Children can be fully involved in discussing and planning what will be displayed and how. The work can also be stimulated and enriched by a variety of secondary source materials, books, charts, leaflets, maps, pamphlets, and pictures.

As the work progresses in phase 2, the children often develop a strong concern for realism and logic about the topic, and drawing real objects becomes an increasingly absorbing activity. In their observational drawing, young children can look closely at the plants and animals, see how the parts of a bicycle interconnect within the whole, or note how the pattern inside a carrot dissected different ways indicates the way water and other nutrients contribute to its growth. Interest is stimulated by frequent recognition, review, and discussion of the progress in the development of the project.

Phase 3: Concluding a Project

The main thrust of the last phase of a project is the completion of the individual and group work and summary and review of what has been learned. For older children, this last phase can include preparing documentation of the story of the project and sharing the findings. For the youngest children, it may be taken up with dramatic play in their project constructions. Thus, if they have built a store or a hospital, they will be enacting roles associated with those settings.

At the beginning of this final phase, at all ages, the teacher can engage the children in a discussion about what aspects of the project they think should be shared with others, as well as what they think might be of most interest to their parents about the project. This process should be initiated before their interest in the topic wanes. It is possible that a project can go on too long; almost any topic can be run into the ground.

The third phase of the project can include inviting visitors to see the work at an open house, or other classes in the school could be invited to see some of the displays of the children's work. It is also satisfying for the children to share their ideas with the principal and other interested teachers; this offers a good debriefing experience for the class following the investment of considerable effort. Preparation for such occasions provides real purpose for a review of the work achieved. At this time, the children can also be encouraged to evaluate their own work, to compare what has been discovered with the questions they generated during phase 1. During this phase the children can discuss what should be included in the completed question table shown in Table 13–1. The children and teacher can come to agreement concerning what has been learned, their new understandings of the topic, and what more they might want to learn about the topic in the future.

Evaluation of Projects. To date no systematic formal evaluations of the project approach have been reported. However, several criteria may be used by teachers to evaluate their own implementation of the approach. Among them are the appropriateness of the topic under investigation and what was accomplished during each of the three phases. One important critierion for evaluating a project is the extent to which the children did the essential work. Carefully developed documentation and displays telling the story of the children's experiences and work can also help to evaluate the strengths and weaknesses of what was accomplished.

We next present a brief outline of how a whole-class project on the topic of shoes might proceed.

A KINDERGARTEN PROJECT ON SHOES

The following account describes a project on shoes that was undertaken by a kindergarten class. The teacher was having a discussion with the children about footwear, provoked by the fact that several of them had new shoes at the beginning of the school year. The shoes had many interesting features: Some lit up, some made noises, and some had laces with different patterns and colors. The teacher thought of several possible lines of inquiry the children might pursue in a study of shoes. She brainstormed ideas and represented them in a topic web.

Getting Started on the Project (Phase 1)

The children in the class talked about their shoes and their experiences of buying shoes. The children began to wonder about shoes and to raise questions. The teacher helped the children make a list of questions and added to it throughout the first week of the project. The children drew and painted pictures of shoes and of their experiences of buying shoes. The children were encouraged to ask their parents, friends, and neighbors for shoes they might have to contribute to the class shoe collection for the study. The teacher brought in some shoes from her 16-year-old daughter's closet and added these to the dramatic play area. They set up a simple shoe store and tried on the different shoes there. The parents were informed of the topic of study and were invited to discuss shoes with their children. They were also invited to share with the class any special knowledge they might have about footwear of many kinds. At the end of the first week, the teacher arranged for a child in the class to bring in his baby brother to show the class his first pair of walking shoes.

Developing the Project (Phase 2)

The teacher and the children talked about what they could do to find answers to their questions about shoes. The questions included "What are shoes made of?" "Where are shoes made?" "How much do they cost?" "How do you know what size you wear?"

As the children began to discuss money, they talked about what the storekeepers did with the money people paid when they bought shoes. Some thought the salespersons gave it to poor people, others thought they took it home for their pay, and some thought the boss kept it all. The children predicted a variety of answers to their questions, which heightened their curiosity and desire to find out more details about what goes on in the shoe store. The teacher arranged a field site visit to a family shoe store in their city. The children worked for a whole week to prepare for the visit. They decided which parts of the store needed to be investigated, who would take responsibility for drawing which parts of the store, and who would ask which questions of the manager and of the salespersons. The fieldwork was planned to get the information needed to make a more elaborate shoe store in the classroom on their return.

Five groups formed around the children's special interests. They were interested in the following:

1. The cash register, how many shoes are sold in a day, and the amount of money collected each day
2. The storeroom, how the shoe boxes are arranged (e.g., men/women/children, sizes, dress/sport, etc.)
3. The shoe salesperson's responsibilities, activities
4. Different kinds of footwear available and the sizes, colors, and number of shoes in stock
5. Where the shoes came from, where they were delivered, and the frequency of deliveries

The teacher discussed with each group the questions they wanted to ask and what they wanted to find out from the people at the store. The teachers helped the children think about ways to record the information to be gathered at the field site.

The teacher contacted the personnel in the shoe store in advance to prepare them for the visit. She explained the expectations she had for the field experience. She outlined the questions the children wanted to ask and described the field sketches planned, the observations the children wanted to make of the salespersons at work, and the items in the store that the children wanted to examine closely.

When the big day arrived, the three personnel at the shoe store spent a few minutes with each group of children. The students returned to school with much to think about. The teacher led discussions in large and small groups to debrief the children about what happened during the visit.

Each subgroup told the others in the class about their experience and the information they had acquired. Then they set out to build a shoe store in their classroom. Throughout the next 3 weeks, the teacher talked to each group about their progress, and the children listened to each other's ideas and made suggestions to each other.

Some children worked on making cars to get to the store. Others made a bird in a cage like the one they had seen in the store and a television set like the one they had seen there. They made catalogs for the shoes in their own store. They marked the shoe boxes they had collected to indicate which kinds of shoes were in them and added price labels. Some children made money for the little cash register the teacher provided. They worked on a book to tell new shop workers how to sell shoes. They made a wooden bench for children to sit on while waiting to be served by salespersons. In some cases, several versions of these items were made because children wanted to be involved personally in particular contributions to the store. For example, they made many shoe catalogs.

During this period of investigating and representing the items the children wanted to put in their shoe store, the teacher invited several visitors to the classroom. Another teacher in the school was a dancer and showed her tap dancing shoes and her special jazz dancing shoes. A Chinese parent helped the two children from China to produce a Chinese version of a shoe catalog and to post advertising and directional signs in Mandarin. One father was a member of the police force and helped the children understand the importance of the evidence of shoe prints at the site of a crime for finding criminals. Another parent visitor showed her special shoes for bicycle racing. A grandfather of one of the children had repaired shoes in his work and was able to tell the children about how and of what shoes are made; with this knowledgeable man's help, the children were able to examine the materials used in a shoe's construction: the leather, thread, tacks, and glue. Various other kinds of sports shoes were shown to the children by older siblings and their special features were discussed: ice skates, inline skates, ski boots, fishing waders, soccer shoes with and without cleats, wooden clogs from The Netherlands, ballet slippers, and cowboy boots and spurs.

During the field visit, the children had watched the process of selling a pair of shoes to a customer. They had followed the sale and purchase, noting the steps in the process from the salesman's and customer's points of view. They were able to use four steps in the dramatization of the sale and purchase of shoes in their own shoe store: (1) Interviewing prospective buyers as to the kind of shoe they wanted, the color, and the price they wanted to pay; (2) measuring customers' feet; (3) taking pride in and showing several pairs of shoes to them; and (4) concluding the sale and put the unsold shoes back in their boxes and back on the storage shelves after the sale had been concluded.

The children who made the money for the cash register also set up a bank so the money could be used to purchase shoes in the store. A dollar amount was provided to help those children who wished to use it to count out an appropriate amount of money they wanted to spend.

Concluding the Project (Phase 3)

The teacher arranged an opportunity for the parents to come to the school to visit the children's shoe store and see what had been learned in the process of developing the children's interests in shoe store construction and play. The parents had the opportunity to buy the shoes in the store and be served by their children.

And after several weeks, the children became interested in new kinds of play. They wanted to explore the bus travel that had begun during the shoe project as some customers "came to town" to buy shoes using the local transit system. Meanwhile, the parents were able to look at the children's drawings and paintings. They were able to read the documentation of the project. They read the word labels and captions written by children and the teacher on the representational work and the photographs taken throughout the project to record the high points and various aspects of the children's learning. Among the skills applied by the children were counting and measuring; using technical vocabulary; developing color, shape, and size recognition; interviewing; collaborating; and other social skills. The parents were able to appreciate the knowledge the children had gained concerning the processes of designing, manufacturing, and selling a wide variety of footwear and the information about the variety of materials used in making their different parts. The children also demonstrated their understanding of how a store worked and the interdependence of the number of different people involved in enabling people to wear something as basic as shoes. The parents who had participated in the final sharing of the children's work were left in no doubt that a wide range of valuable in-depth learning had taken place over the 8 weeks of the project.

Commentary. This project is described as fairly typical for a class of kindergarten children.

However, it is difficult to describe projects as typical because much of the work of any project with any teacher or group of children is related to the availability of local resources for firsthand investigation and to the interests expressed by the particular participants.

The availability of parent experts willing to help the children made a crucial contribution to the quality of what was accomplished. The parents of any class group might include a number of people involved in house construction, vehicle driving and maintenance, food services, farming, the health services, and so on. Teachers can find out about the particular expertise of the parents of the children in the class and can plan some of the project work to enrich the children's experience with their special knowledge. Bilingual parents can help to sensitize the children to words that are used in different cultures to describe the same objects and processes. This can help to ensure that all children in a group or class are involved in the investigation and that an awareness of different languages can begin early in children's lives.

The age of the children affects the extent to which project work can involve a class of children for an extended period of time. Younger children would probably not have benefited from quite such elaborate dramatic play, and the project probably would not have continued to develop over so many weeks. Older children, on the other hand, might have seen a DVD of a shoe factory, built an assembly line on one side of the classroom, focused on their understanding of the process of shoe design and production, studied the workings of a shoe store, and included a variety of mathematical studies involving average sizes, costs, and surveys of classmates' shoes and preferences.

CONCLUSION

The inclusion of project work in the curriculum for young children addresses the four major learning goals of all education: the construction and acquisition of worthwhile knowledge; development of a wide variety of basic intellectual, academic, motor, and social skills; strengthening of desirable dispositions; and engendering of positive feelings about self as a learner and participant in group endeavors. Because project work is complementary to formal instruction, children have the opportunity to apply their basic skills in the course of studying meaningful topics. In this way, school experience becomes interesting not only to the children but to the teacher as well.

REFERENCES

Bransford, J. D., Brown, A. L., & Cocking, R. R. (Eds.). (1999). *How people learn. Brain, mind, experience, and school.* Washington, DC: National Academy Press.

Brown, J. S., Collins, A., & Duguid, P. (1989). Situated cognition and the culture of learning. *Educational Researcher, 18,* 32–42.

Chard, S. C. (1998a). *The project approach. Practical guide 1. Developing the basic framework.* New York: Scholastic.

Chard, S. C. (1998b). *The project approach. Practical guide 2. Developing curriculum with children.* New York: Scholastic.

Dresden, J., & Lee, K. (2007). The effects of project work in a first grade classroom. A little goes a long way. *Early Childhood Research & Practice.* http://www.ecrp/uiuc/edi/v9n1/dresden.html

Edwards, C., Gandini, L., & Forman, G. (Eds.). (1998). *The hundred languages of children: The Reggio Emilia approach to early childhood education* (2nd ed.). Norwood, NJ: Ablex.

Flook, L., Repetti, R. L., & Ullman, J. B. (2005). Classroom social experiences as predictors of academic performance. *Developmental Psychology, 41*(2), 319–327.

Helm, J. H., Beneke, S., & Steinheimer, K. (2007). *Windows on learning. Documenting young children's work,* 2nd ed. New York: Teachers College Press.

Helm, J. H., & Katz, L. G. (2001). *Young investigators: The Project Approach in the early years.* New York: Teachers College Press.

Katz, L. G. (1991). Pedagogical issues in early childhood education. In S. L. Kagan (Ed.), *The care and education of America's young children: Obstacles and opportunities. Ninetieth Yearbook of the National Society for the Study of Education.* Chicago: University of Chicago Press.

Katz, L. G. (1994). *The project approach. ERIC Digest.* Champaign, IL: ERIC Clearinghouse on Elementary and Early Childhood Education.

Katz, L. G., & Chard, S. C. (1996). *The contribution of documentation to the quality of early childhood education.* Champaign, IL: ERIC Clearinghouse on Elementary and Early Childhood Education.

Katz, L. G., & Chard, S. C. (2000). *Engaging children's minds: The project approach* (2nd ed.). Stamford, CT: Ablex.

Katz, L. G., & McClellan, D. (1997). *Fostering social competence: The teacher's role.* Washington, DC: National Association for the Education of Young Children.

Marchand, G., & Skinner, E. (2007). Motivational dynamics of children's academic help-seeking and concealment. *Journal of Educational Psychology, 99*(1), 65–82.

Schidt, H., Burts, D. C., Durham, S., Charlesworth, R., & Hart, C. (2007, Spring). Impact of developmental appropriateness of teacher guidance strategies on kindergarten children's interpersonal relations. *Journal of Research on Childhood Education,* (*21*)3, 290–301.

Slavin, R. E., Madden, N. A., Dolan, L. J., & Wasik, B. A. (1996). *Every child, every school: Success for all.* Thousand Oaks, CA: Corwin.

Smith, L. S. (1997). Open education revisited. *Teachers College Record, 99*(2), 371–415.

Tanner, L. N. (1997). *Dewey's laboratory school: Lessons for today.* New York: Teachers College Press.

Part IV

Specific Approaches: Europe

Chapter 14

Reggio Emilia's Approach to Early Care and Education

Creating Contexts for Discussione

Rebecca S. New ⇝ *University of North Carolina, Chapel Hill*
Rebecca Kantor ⇝ *The Ohio State University*

As visitors enter one of the *nidi* (infant/toddler centers) or *scuole del'infanzia* (the preprimary schools) in Reggio Emilia, Italy, the first thought they are likely to have is that the environments designed for young children are, in a word, beautiful. The strong and colorful Italian aesthetic as observed in the arrangement of red and yellow peppers at the market, rainbows of gelato cones, or dignified rows of cypress trees on the hillside is made explicit in Reggio Emilia classrooms through purposeful arrays of toy irons on shelves, bottles of colored water lining bathroom windows, and the careful and colorful way in which art supplies have been arranged. Mobiles with light-catching materials, simple arrangements of fragile shells, puddle-shaped mirrors on the floor, expansive leaf-laden latticework serving as room dividers, and large colorful cushions—these features and others contribute to a space that conveys not only a concern with appearance but also a welcoming message of respect and possibilities for children and their families. The Reggio Emilia early childhood environments are also highly personal and purposeful. Few, if any, mass-produced images or furniture are found in the classrooms; rather, images are of the children and their parents, together and separately, who make up the school's population. Number charts and other forms of instructional aids, if they exist at all, have been created by the children. Messages to parents are displayed on carefully arranged panels that include samples of children's work. The artifacts that are displayed come from the children's experiences at home, at school, or in the community. None have been ordered from a catalog. Each infant/toddler center, each pre-primary school is, as Lella Gandini (1984) has described, "not just anywhere." Rather, teachers and parents have worked hard to make their early childhood centers into "particular" places that are both caring and supportive of children's early learning (Gandini, 1998).

With a bit more intentional viewing, the visitors come to know that the early childhood environments in Reggio Emilia's municipal schools are not just visually pleasing and personally relevant reminders of the larger community culture. They are also explicitly designed to foster social activity, elicit curiosity and exploration, and promote an awareness of the history of the school community. These goals are in evidence in the messages to read, displays to contemplate, invitations to linger. The entranceway is filled with photographic images of children working on their projects, of parents engaged in discussions at council meetings, of teachers and staff in humorous poses. Throughout are carefully tended plants, cozy arrangements of adult-size furniture, and more displays of children's work, some from previous years. The centrally located piazza includes natural light whenever possible. There is usually some form of enticing play apparatus that parents designed and built for the children and that has now become part of the center's physical history. The qualities of the materials displayed, sometimes fragile and delicate, acknowledge children's capacities to notice and take care of their environment.

In 1988, at the annual conference of the National Association for the Education of Young Children (NAEYC), less than two dozen people attended a small session dedicated to Italian perspectives on early care and education. At that session, Lella Gandini and Baji Rankin shared slides and stories about a small northern Italian city that had developed its own particular approach to providing early care and educational services to its youngest citizens, beginning in the first year of life and continuing through the kindergarten year. At about the same time, a traveling exhibition from this same Italian city was making its way through New England, having already made several stops in New York and Massachusetts. Two years later, the city of Reggio Emilia was featured on the cover of *Young Children* (New, 1990). A few months later, at the 1990 NAEYC conference in Washington, D.C., crowds spilled out into the halls trying to see and hear more from the Italian educators (e.g., Filippini, 1990) who were sharing some provocative new ways of thinking about and teaching young children. Today, Reggio Emilia's municipal early care and educational program is a major reference point for early childhood educators in the United States and around the world.[1]

This chapter describes this city's interpretation of early care and education, with particular attention to its Italian origins and, more recently, its 20 years of impact upon the field of early childhood education in the United States. Against this backdrop, the discussion highlights key features of Reggio Emilia's municipal program for young children that have become synonymous with the city's name—that is, those elements that are now part of the constellation of what is referred to as "the Reggio Emilia approach" (REA).[2] This description of Reggio Emilia's municipal program for children includes its interpretations of the physical environment, curriculum as extended projects or *progettazione,* teachers as researchers, documentation as a tool for collaborative inquiry, and parents as essential partners in children's early education. The chapter then illustrates some of the ways in which U.S. educators have applied these principles to their own work in American early childhood settings and the challenges they have encountered. In particular, the work of policy makers, teachers, and higher educators in the state of Ohio provides a case study of the potentials and complexities of learning about Reggio Emilia's pedagogy and learning about ourselves in the process. But first—what and where is Reggio Emilia, and why is it so special?

[1]The Reggio Children network of international relations now includes Canada, Greenland, Mexico, Costa Rica, Guatemala, Cuba, Puerto Rico, Trinidad, Brazil, Bolivia, Paraguay, Chile, Norway, Sweden, Denmark, Finland, Iceland, Spain, United Kingdom, The Netherlands, Germany, Belgium, Israel, Switzerland, France, Portugal, Tanzania, Senegal, India, Nepal, China, Korea, Japan, Taiwan, Hong Kong, Thailand, Malaysia, Phillipines, Singapore, Australia, New Zealand, and the United States.

[2]REA is the acronym frequently used to refer to the Reggio Emilia Approach.

UNDERSTANDING REGGIO EMILIA'S HISTORY: A KEY TO UNDERSTANDING ITS ROLE IN U.S. EARLY CHILDHOOD EDUCATION

Few would deny the role of history in making sense of contemporary cultural phenomena, and the case of Reggio Emilia aptly illustrates this premise. Examining Reggio Emilia's place in two distinct cultural settings—its Italian home and the United States, where it has become a frequent and familiar visitor—helps to explain Reggio Emilia's cultural bases as well as its current status in the United States and worldwide. The most essential key to understanding how Reggio Emilia has come to have such influence on early childhood education is, of course, its own particular story within the Italian culture.

Reggio Emilia, Italy: A Particular Response to Cultural Values and Traditions

Reggio Emilia is a small city of 150,000 inhabitants in northern Italy. Many early admirers assumed that the city is either like all Italian cities, or like none other, in its interpretation of high-quality early care and educational services. In fact, Reggio Emilia is both. As a contemporary of other Italian cities, large and small, Reggio Emilia citizens share many of the same cultural values that characterize the Italian culture writ large, including a centrality of the family in community life, an image of children as a shared social responsibility, and a keen appreciation of local dialects and interpretations of quality—whether of wine, cheese, or early childhood services (New, 1993b).

Beyond this shared membership with the Italian culture, Reggio Emilia has an identity that is linked to its regional address.[3] One of several small, wealthy, and progressively minded cities in the region of Emilia Romagna, Reggio Emilia has much in common with its neighbors Parma and Modena, including a jointly produced and world-famous cheese (Parmigiano-Reggiano), as well as the local wine, Lambrusco. Reggio Emilia also shares a cultural and political history with the region, including a commitment to the arts and industrial innovation, a tradition of collaboration and civic engagement, and a leading role in the resistance movement of World War II. Equally important to note is the common history, not only within the region of Emilia Romagna but much of north and central Italy, of well-financed public early childhood services for young children and their families.

As is now the case in most Italian communities,[4] Reggio Emilia has three forms of early childhood services for young children: private (*scuola materna*) services typically provided by the Catholic Church; state-funded preschools;[5] and a municipal program (which is the focus of this chapter). Much of what is regarded as particular to Reggio Emilia's early childhood services (for example, the continuity of children's class membership and teachers from one year to the next) is also common to other high-quality Italian early childhood programs. Where Reggio Emilia has distinguished itself is in its persistent efforts to reconceptualize early care and educational services—and to share its discoveries with the world.

While some Italians will argue that Reggio Emilia cannot be considered "the best" in a culture where local innovations and standards

[3]Indeed, the city's official name, Reggio nel Emilia, distinguishes it from another Reggio city in Italy, that of Reggio nel Calabria.

[4]Readers who are interested in contemporary Italian child care and early educational services and the history of their development are urged to see other more extensive descriptions: e.g., Corsaro & Emiliani, 1992; Mantovani & Musatti, 1996; New, 1993b; as well as the recent Organization for Economic Cooperation and Development review (2001), *Starting Strong*.

[5]The term *state* when used in this context refers to the national Italian government.

must prevail, few would disagree with Reggio Emilia's leading role in exploring the potentials of (1) children's multiple symbolic languages in their learning; (2) teachers as active classroom researchers; and (3) parents as willing and able partners in designing and evaluating early care and educational services. These features have roots that extend deep into the city's political history, including its reputation for resisting the status quo, particularly when those norms limit the possibilities for active engagement of all citizens in the life of the community.

Several historic events are routinely highlighted in depictions of Reggio Emilia's early history of services for *infanzia* [early childhood],[6] including the fact that the current city-wide program was begun by a small group of parents following World War II, who were soon joined by a philosopher-journalist by the name of Loris Malaguzzi (Malaguzzi, 1998). The Reggio Emilia parents wanted a different sort of child care for their children—not the custodial model as developed by the Catholic Church but, rather, one that would allow parents to play an active role in a preschool setting where children could learn how to live in and contribute to a free and democratic society. Under Malaguzzi's leadership, these new goals for early education expanded to include the promotion of children's multiple symbolic languages, not just those associated with traditional language and literacy development. Thus Vea Vecchi was hired—the city's first *atelierista*—with expertise in the arts, not in child development. Early accounts also point to Reggio Emilia's leadership with respect to the professional development of teachers. Responding to Italy's lack of provisions for pre-service teacher education,[7] Reggio Emilia's early childhood programs were conceptualized from the very beginning as learning environments for teachers as well as for young children. These early initiatives soon became hallmarks of the "Reggio Emilia approach." This attitude of resistance to more traditional Italian interpretations of children's early learning potentials and the roles of adults in those processes continued to characterize Reggio Emilia's work locally and nationally over the next several decades.

Throughout the 1960s and 1970s, as the city of Reggio Emilia continued to develop its own services for children, leaders of the municipal program participated in a series of national campaigns drawing attention to the benefits of early childhood services for children, families, and the larger society. Reggio Emilia's own municipally funded early childhood services preceded by several years the 1968 national law proclaiming the rights of all Italian children to pre-primary schools. As state-run services were soon added to the hundreds of municipal ones already in place, Reggio Emilia's solidarity with leaders of other cities' services helped to ensure a continued role for local innovation and experimentation (New, 2001) More modest laws for increased provision of infant/toddler care were eventually passed in 1971. By the late 1970s, city leaders demonstrated another feature of Reggio Emilia—one that distinguishes it from other cities both inside and outside Italy—and that is its eagerness to share, on a global scale, its compelling interpretation of "a new culture of childhood." Again under the charismatic leadership of Loris Malaguzzi, city leaders collected, organized, and displayed their observations and new understandings of children's

[6]Cf., both editions of *The Hundred Languages of Children* (Edwards, Gandini, & Forman, 1993; 1998) and a video dedicated to the story of Reggio Emilia's infant/ toddler centers and pre-primary schools (*Not Just Anywhere*, Washington, DC: Reggio Children, 2002).

[7]In 1998 a law was passed making university training mandatory for newly hired preschool and elementary teachers in Italy. Prior to that time, a vocational high school degree and course work in child development were the only prerequisites to applying for a teaching position in early and elementary education.

learning in a traveling exhibition that soon attracted attention from educators in countries as diverse as Sweden and Germany, Portugal and Denmark. It was a full decade later, in 1987, that an English-language version arrived in the United States.

What Americans saw in the exhibit were beautifully arranged graphic displays and photographs of children accompanied by their drawings and constructions, translated texts of their conversations, hypotheses, and explorations of the natural world (rain clouds, shadows, reflections) and their sense of self in relation to others (emotions as expressed through hands and voices, gender roles), as well as fantastical constructions (a dinosaur, a horse, clouds). The exhibition was overwhelming in its size, its complexity, its beauty, and its message: that children have social and intellectual and creative potentials not fully realized in traditional early care and education programs, even those that espouse a play-based and child-initiated curriculum, and that children could, and adults should, do much better.

Reggio Emilia's Early History Within the United States

Reggio Emilia's arrival in the United States by way of the exhibit was timely, coinciding with a growing debate between early childhood and elementary educators regarding the "developmental appropriateness" of direct instruction in early academics versus child-initiated and play-based approaches to learning. The first widely distributed document outlining these differences—NAEYC's *Developmentally Appropriate Practice in Early Childhood Programs Serving Children from Birth Through Age Eight* (Bredekamp, 1987)—was seen as a watershed moment for early childhood educators who were eager to use the document's child development research base to defend their preferred early educational practices. Within this same time period, the early childhood community began to actively debate the merits of Reggio Emilia's examples of children's long-term projects in contrast to stage-based interpretations of children's developmental limitations in determining curriculum possibilities. By 1991, one of Reggio Emilia's preschools had been proclaimed by *Newsweek* magazine (1991) as "the best in the world." As news of this Italian city spread, parents, policy makers, and the larger educational community began to take note. As Reggio Emilia was being hailed as an "inspiration to U.S. educators" (Cohen, 1992),[8] new concerns were raised regarding NAEYC's developmentally appropriate practice (DAP) guidelines.

Challenges to DAP guidelines and especially the identification of practices labeled as "inappropriate" continued to come from elementary educators as well as some parents who wanted young children to enter school already acquainted with basic numeracy and literacy skills and understandings. Other criticisms came from those engaged in the reconceptualist movement (e.g., Kessler, 1991). Still other critiques were from advocates for children with special needs (Mallory, 1992) and those from cultural and linguistically diverse families (New, 1993a). These and other criticisms converged in their focus on the outdated theoretical premises, highly individualistic orientation, and American middle-class values embedded in the guidelines (Mallory & New, 1994). Eventually, Reggio Emilia became an illustrative example in support of many of these critiques, including the false dichotomy of teacher-directed versus child-initiated learning, as well as the positioning of the teacher as recipient of someone else's "knowledge base" (New, 1994).

Throughout the 1990s, early childhood educators in the United States continued to study and visit Reggio Emilia, and a growing number of national leaders were explicit about

---

[8]Two versions of the exhibition (including an updated version of the original) continue to travel from city to city in the United States, while other versions of the exhibition have recently toured Asia and South America.

their admiration for the city's efforts and understandings regarding children's early learning potentials (cf., Bredekamp, 1993; Katz & Cesarone, 1994). Accompanying these and other pronouncements of support was a voluminous and growing body of literature (including two lengthy edited volumes with contributions from Italian educators: Edwards et al., 1993; Edwards et al., 1998) that had a powerful effect on U.S. early childhood educators locally and nationally, including those in national positions of authority (e.g., Child Development Associates, NAEYC). It came as no surprise, therefore, when references to Reggio Emilia—once used as a counterexample—were used to illustrate NAEYC's revised interpretations of developmentally appropriate practices (Bredekamp & Copple, 1997). By the end of the 20th century, the "Reggio Emilia approach" was a dominant theme in discussions among U.S. classroom teachers, program directors, early childhood teacher educators, local and state policy makers, and members of national organizations concerned with early care and education.

But what was it about Reggio Emilia that attracted so much attention?

PRINCIPLES AND PRACTICES OF THE REGGIO-EMILIA APPROACH: OLD AND NEW COMBINED

The philosophy of education behind Reggio Emilia's municipal program has been described in various ways by Italian educators (cf., chapters by Malaguzzi in both the 1993 and 1998 edited volumes by Edwards, Gandini, & Forman), each time with reference to several key principles:

- Children have numerous creative, intellectual, and communicative potentials; and they also have the fundamental right for these potentials to be respected and nurtured. Adult interactions with children reflect an underlying "image of the child" that can be powerful or impoverished.
- Schools are systems of relations, such that the well-being of children is dependent on the well-being of teachers and families.
- Teachers must learn about children as they try to teach them, and the incentive of uncertainty is central to processes of collaborative inquiry.
- Educational spaces must serve the needs of all who utilize them, such that early childhood centers are conceptualized as centers of exchange and relationship building among and between children, teachers, and families.

Although these principles do not strike early childhood educators in the United States as particularly new or problematic, as "students" of Reggio Emilia got closer and more deeply engaged in exploring the principles and practices found in the Italian classrooms, they discovered elements that are distinctively *Reggiano* and clearly challenging to beliefs and practices in many U.S. early childhood settings. This discussion describes Reggio Emilia's translation of their philosophical foundation as they appear in practices and features common to the town's municipal *asili nido* and *scuola del'infanzia,* including the following:

- Use of the environment to promote learning and relationships
- Curriculum projects based on inquiry and the "hundred languages" of children
- Documentation as a means of observation, research, and advocacy
- Partnerships with parents that exceed current notions of parent education

1. An Environment That Welcomes, Nurtures, and Inspires

The feature most visible to those who come to observe Reggio Emilia's municipal program is also regarded as central to those who work

Rebecca S. New

Even the bathroom becomes a space for play and contemplation. Parents and teachers designed this tube arrangement through which colored water flows when children turn on the faucets.

inside the city's infant–toddler centers (*asili nido*) and pre-primary schools (*scuole dell'infanzia*). Functioning as what anthropologists would call a "developmental niche" (Super & Harkness, 1986), the Reggio Emilia schools are characterized by a number of environmental features purposefully designed to create a school culture that reflects and promotes the values and goals of the larger community. For example, the communal ethos maintained by the central piazza found in every Italian city and town is echoed in the large central space through which children, parents, and teachers must traverse as they move about the school.

The potential of school spaces to serve as another "teacher" of young children is especially apparent upon entering the classrooms, each of which is filled with what Reggio Emilia educators describe as "messages and possibilities" (Filippini, 1990). As might be expected, classrooms are divided into spaces for group gatherings, dramatic play, and large and small construction activities. Spaces for small-group and teacher-led activities are available at child-size tables dispersed throughout the classroom. Other features are more particular to Reggio Emilia, including a mini-atelier or small work space adjacent to the classroom, where teachers and children can pursue long-term projects without distraction. Reflecting Italian beliefs regarding the importance of one's sense of self in relation to others, mirrors and other reflective surfaces are situated throughout the classroom space as well as in the bathrooms and hallways. A keen appreciation for the pleasure and possibilities of light is also apparent in the frequent use of light boxes and light tables to display collections of leaves or other found objects, or an array of tissue paper just waiting to be composed. In most classrooms large windows open up to the outside, allowing shadows and sunshine, as well as the sounds of the neighborhood, to enter into the classroom.

The environment also serves as an essential source for the development of relationships among and between adults and children, such that the physical space is arranged and furnished in a manner that brings children and adults together. Children are invited to connect with each other within and outside their classrooms by way of "talking tubes" and transparent openings that allow them to call, speak, and gesture to one another from opposite sides of the classroom. Even the dress-up clothes are arranged in ways that invite the development of new relationships, stored as they often are in a central location outside the classroom. Children often visit each others' classrooms, and their project work often spills out into the large open spaces beyond their classroom doors. Everywhere one looks is evidence of the thought given to the potential interface between children, spaces, and relations (Ceppi & Zini, 1998). Adult relations—with each other, with teachers, and with the children—are also promoted through the careful arrangement of adult-size furniture in the central space and in classrooms, including the occasional rocking chair that invites the visiting parent or grandparent to linger.

Within this adult-friendly environment, teachers create occasions that purposefully foster the development of relationships among parents. As is the case in most early childhood programs in Italy, parents are invited to stay at the center during the child's initial transition period.[9] In Reggio Emilia, the goal is not only to support the child's transition to the new environment but also to support the development of adult friendships among parents. Thus mothers and fathers are encouraged to share coffee together in a small room adjacent to the classroom, where they may also make some materials for use in the classroom. The environment continues to support adult relationships throughout the school year, and not only between parents and teachers. The kitchen, typically surrounded by glass divides or open windows, is often frequented by children and their parents upon arrival, when the cooks share tastes of the menu for the noontime *pranzo*. Evening gatherings of parents sometimes take place in the kitchen, where recipes are shared and the cooks again provide samples of food that they are serving to their children. The relationships with teaching and non-teaching staff are also supported during the daily meals, when teachers take turns enjoying a leisurely lunch with the cooks who have prepared it for them. Teacher work spaces are also designed as comfortable, attractive, and engaging environments so that teachers will enjoy their time working together while children nap or after they have gone home for the day. Such relationships are not only valued; they are essential, given the lack of a principal or head teacher in charge of the school and, thus, the need for group decision making.

Reggio Emilia's early childhood environments are fascinating to visitors accustomed to settings filled with manufactured cartoons, look-a-like furniture, and primary colors, and yet the implications are straightforward and compelling—classrooms can, with purposeful and creative planning, become inviting, stimulating, and highly personalized places for adults as well as children. Combined, these features of the environment support the philosophical premise of schools as systems of relations and create a sense of place for children and their families (Bruner, 1998) that is not captured by the use of terms such as *programs* or *services*. This sense of place, in turn, makes possible some of the other features that make Reggio Emilia's municipal program so compelling, including its conception of an early childhood curriculum.

2. Curriculum as Collaborative Explorations through Symbolic Representations

For most observers of and visitors to Reggio Emilia, the most essential and perplexing aspect of the Reggio Emilia curriculum is the long-term projects known as *progettazione*, many of which are represented in the traveling exhibitions.[10]

---

[9]The initial period of home–school transition is treated with a great deal of attention and respect in Italy. Many communities have devised distinct ways of ensuring that children, families, and teachers have ample opportunity to get to know one another. See Bove (1999) and New (1999) for further discussion of Italian approaches to the period of *inserimento* or *transizione*.

[10]Reggio Emilian educators, under the guidance of Loris Malaguzzi, created two elaborate traveling exhibitions on their work. *L'Occhio se Salta il Muro* (When the Eye Jumps Over the Wall) was the first to open in Europe in 1981 and continues to travel to nations outside of Italy, most recently to Latin America. Another exhibition was created for Japan, and yet a third exhibition has recently traveled across Australia. These exhibitions are in addition to the English-language version (The Hundred Languages of Children) that has been traveling through the United States since 1987. For information about the exhibition schedule, contact exhibit curator Pam Houk at the Dayton Art Institute in Ohio.

The complexities of children's projects, sometimes spanning periods of weeks if not months; the quality of their drawings and other forms of representation of their ideas, designs, and understandings; and the extensive and collaborative nature of what appears to be constructive play all suggest that the children in Reggio Emilia schools are either gifted or specially trained. And yet these examples of what Reggiani children are challenged and invited to do are also part of the normal course of a day's events in a Reggio Emilia classroom—they represent the results of purposeful and carefully designed early learning opportunities—in other words, an early childhood curriculum.

But educators in Reggio Emilia rarely talk about curriculum issues in terms familiar to American educators. That is, there are no specified goals and objectives as they might pertain to specific developmental or learning potentials, such as developing fine motor skills or learning how to tell a story in sequence. Rather, goals are discussed in broad culturally valued aims such as (1) developing relationships, (2) learning how to collaborate, and (3) appreciating diversity in ideas and their expression. These aims are then pursued through the exploration of concepts that have already captured the attention of the children and/or the adults—for example: Where do shadows come from? Can an enemy become a friend? What makes it rain? As such, the curriculum in Reggio Emilia emerges from the shared experiences of children, teachers, and families (Rinaldi, 1993).

Reggio Emilia teachers use children's questions and curiosities to promote their exploration of materials, to experiment with various ways of communicating and then to test out hypotheses, to debate and negotiate their multiple points of view. In such explorations, embedded within a pedagogical process described as *progettazione*, Reggio Emilia teachers create conditions by which children are supported in their efforts to participate in the world that is around them, making sense of and adding their own interpretations to the events of the day. A trip to the market can become the first step in a long exploration of the city boundaries, leading to map making and the development of new relationships as children discover side streets, buildings, and merchants previously unknown. Teachers do not necessarily wait for children to convey a curiosity or interest; rather, they carefully observe and document children at play, paying close attention to their conversations, and then talk with colleagues in other classes and with parents as part of the decision-making process regarding how best to prepare for the next day's learning encounters, which may involve one of the two classroom teachers with a small group of children (four or five) or perhaps the entire class. It is not by accident that numerous such *progettazione* involve the use of developing numeracy and mathematical skills, but those are generally regarded as the means rather than the aims of the children's collaborative efforts.[11]

Although it is difficult to identify the starting point of such a problem-based curriculum, the aims are always to understand, first, the directions that children wish to take in pursuing their own questions; and then to support children's ongoing inquiry and problem-solving efforts as responses to initial hypotheses lead to the articulation of new ideas and possibilities. Such curriculum practices reflect a fundamental Reggio Emilia principle of curriculum as something that should "enable children to utilize their own skills and competence" (Rinaldi, 2003, p. 1). Such an interpretation of curriculum is in direct response to a fundamental principle of the Reggio Emilia approach, which is the underlying image of the child. Within a context in which children are seen as unique,

[11]See, for example, a project involving children's exploration of mathematics as they attempt to re-create a much beloved table in their classroom that was carefully documented and eventually published as *Scarpe e metro* (*The Shoe and the Meter*) by Reggio Children. This small publication and those of other projects are available for purchase through Reggio Children, Washington, DC 20005-3105.

powerful, full of potential and born with the right to be protagonists of their own narratives, caring adults utilize these qualities as starting points for their work with children. Such a pedagogy has recently been described by Reggio Emilia educators as a "pedagogy of listening." If this image includes the belief that children have limited attention spans, are in preschools to get ready for later school, or are vessels to be filled by caring adults, then the likelihood is low that we are listening and observing them for these starting points.

One of the most obvious distinguishing characteristics of Reggio Emilia's *progettazione* is the level of creative exploration and symbolic representation associated with children's collaborative work. Beyond an emphasis on group learning to promote children's social relations, Reggio Emilia educators are purposeful in creating conditions by which children will find it necessary to share their understandings. Thus teachers ask children to explain their ideas through drawings, to create visual hypotheses through the creation of models or designs to help others envision the essential steps of a problem-solving agenda. As children share their understandings with one another, they are often challenged to revisit and revise their own ideas. This sequence of representation and exploration, regarded as central to children's processes of knowledge construction, has been described by others in both text form (c.f., Forman & Fyfe, 1998) and on videotape:[12]

No way. The hundred *is* there.

The child
is made of one hundred.
The child has
a hundred languages
a hundred hands
a hundred thoughts
a hundred ways of thinking
of playing, of speaking.
A hundred always a hundred
ways of listening
of marveling of loving
a hundred joys
for singing and understanding
a hundred worlds
to discover
a hundred worlds
to invent
a hundred worlds
to dream.
The child has
a hundred languages
(and a hundred hundred hundred more)
but they steal ninety-nine.
The school and the culture
separate the head from the body.
They tell the child:
to think without hands
to do without head
to listen and not to speak
to understand without joy
to love and to marvel
only at Easter and Christmas.
They tell the child:
to discover the world already there
and of the hundred
they steal ninety-nine.
They tell the child:
that work and play
reality and fantasy
science and imagination
sky and earth
reason and dream
are things
that do not belong together.
And thus they tell the child
that the hundred is not there.
The child says:
No way. The hundred *is* there.

*Loris Malaguzzi**

[12]A listing of available videos of Reggio Emilia *progettazione* can be obtained by writing to Reggio Children, 2460 16th St. NW., Washington, DC 20005-3105.

**Note.* From "No Way. The Hundred Is There" by L. Malaguzzi, translated by L. Gandini, in *The Hundred Languages of Children: The Reggio Emilia Approach—Advanced Reflections* (p. 3), edited by C. Edwards, L. Gandini, and G. Forman, 1998, Greenwich, CT: Ablex.

Teachers frequently reference Malaguzzi's hypothetical "hundred languages of children" as the rationale for providing multiple means by which children can explore and share and reflect on their understandings. Thus, pairs of children may be invited to represent their understandings of trees blowing in the wind, one with clay and another with a fine-tipped felt pen. As they compare the details afforded by their diverse materials, they can also compare their experiences and their understandings, eventually co-constructing new understandings as supported by their diverse representations that reveal the best of what each has learned. While some observers consider this element of children's project work to be an art activity, Malaguzzi was explicit about his belief that creativity is not a separate mental faculty but rather a characteristic "way of thinking, knowing, and making choices." As such, he regarded the development of children's creative potentials as inseparable from other curriculum goals and activities. The practical consequences of his theory of the relationship between creativity and intelligence include the hiring of an *atelierista* (art educator) who works closely with teachers to discover and promote children's developing symbolic languages and to provide daily opportunities for children to explore multiple types of media and symbolic representation through the use of clay, drawings, painting, shadow play, and large and small constructive activities that far exceed the typical and brief periods of block play found in U.S. early childhood settings. These activities are further supported through the use of a separate atelier or studio space (Gandini, Hill, Cadwell, & Schwall, 2005), where children can work together in small groups on projects over longer periods of time with support from the *atelierista*.

Taking Risks with a Reality-Based Curriculum. Another distinguishing feature of Reggio Emilia's *progettazione* is likely linked to cultural differences in the roles of adults in protecting children from certain realities of the world in which they live. In the Italian culture at large, for example, in contrast to middle-class U.S. norms, young children are more often included in adult activities and conversations, have fewer restrictions placed on nudity, have relatively easy access to sexually explicit language and information, and are more likely to understand that before one eats chicken for dinner, someone must kill and pluck the chicken. Thus, while many of the *progettazione* found in Reggio Emilia's municipal schools are based on children's curiosities about the physical and social worlds (What is the nature of a shadow? Why are there so many crowds?) or practical propositions (Why don't we build an amusement park for the birds? Let's have an athletic event!) that might also be pursued in U.S. early childhood settings, other topics of potential exploration are much less likely to be pursued by U.S. early childhood educators. Such topics as found in Reggio Emilia classrooms include children's philosophical dilemmas (Can an enemy become a friend? What is love? Who is God?), as well as their anxieties or insights about the world around them, including their views of sexuality, their conceptions of children's rights, and their fears for themselves and the soldiers during the ongoing conflicts in the Middle East. Not only are such projects as common in Italy as they are rare in the United States, they are also highly engaging and unlikely to bore the children and teachers who participate in their collaborative explorations.[13]

This description of *progettazione* is not meant to imply that the children in Reggio Emilia classrooms spend most of their time engaged in long-term collaborative explorations of

[13]Reggio Emilia is not alone in this use of the surrounding sociocultural context for curriculum content. A wine-making project was observed in a Naples preschool, where parents and grandparents worked together with the teacher to ensure that children were well acquainted with the traditions indigenous to the community (New, 1999).

physics or philosophy. In fact, much of the child's day at the center is spent doing the sorts of things that children do elsewhere, including engaging in socio-dramatic and constructive play, as well as fine and gross motor activities. Classrooms are filled with blocks of various sizes, puzzles, clay, and other manipulative materials, as well as dolls, housekeeping supplies, and other play materials frequently found in high-quality early childhood settings. What is different about the use of these materials is not how the children are engaged; rather, it is how teachers use this time to observe, listen to, and record children's conversations and activities and then subsequently link these insights to their planning for long-term projects. This role of the teacher is linked to a third distinguishing feature of Reggio Emilia's work with young children, which is that it is not only focused on the children.

3. Documentation as a Tool for Research, Reflection, and Relationships

The Reggio Emilians have often stated publicly that the critical piece to understanding their work is the process of documentation. Under the guidance of Loris Malaguzzi, Reggio Emilia teachers have consciously adopted a Deweyian approach to scientific inquiry, posing hypotheses about children's social and intellectual capacities, creating experimental conditions to test those hypotheses, and then systematically collecting artifacts of children's activities and transcripts of children's and adults' conversations. Together, sometimes with parents and teachers from other schools, often with the *atelierista,* teachers analyze their data and frame new hypotheses. They move through the *progettazione* in a process remarkably similar to the one that characterizes the children's learning. Where the children's contemplative and communicative efforts associated with their projects are captured under the rubric of symbolic languages, for the teachers this process is facilitated through documentation.

Documentation as a Support for Teacher Research. The administrators, teachers, and parents in Reggio Emilia have engaged in a form of collaborative action research for the past 35 years—research as they have defined it within their own classrooms and community. The primary aim of this research has been to better understand children in order to design learning experiences and environments that foster the development of multiple forms of communication and cognition. Within this context, teachers in Reggio Emilia have fine-tuned the art and science of careful observation and documentation of children's behaviors and understandings in both the social and physical realms. As children are learning through their active engagement with each other and through long- and short-term projects, the teachers are learning about the children as individuals and as members of groups. Teachers routinely debate the significance of these observations and develop their own questions and hypotheses about children's existing understandings, as well as the processes associated with their meaning making. As explained previously, many of the questions or proposals associated with *progettazione* come from the children's own activities; teachers may also initiate an exploration based on a proposition that they present to the children. This role of teacher as provocateur builds upon teacher observations and documentation of what is (or is not) happening in the classroom or the community (New, 1990). This use of documentation also helps teachers to address questions that the teachers or parents themselves may have about children's development and learning. Each of the previously mentioned types of Reggio Emilia curriculum projects (practical ideas, questions about the world, or philosophical inquiries) are also based, in some way, on adults' hypotheses regarding children's developing theories about the world around them. Thus documentation serves as an essential tool for a "projecting curriculum" for teachers to learn from (Rinaldi, 1998).

Documentation as a Form of Reflection for Children. Teachers are not the only ones to benefit from their ongoing documentation efforts. Reggio Emilia classroom walls are filled with evidence of the processes and high-quality products associated with children's school experiences, especially their participation in long-term projects. The frequent use of photographic images of children at work, coupled with samples of their finished products and their conversations, has been described previously. Such displays provide children with the opportunity to reflect upon their prior abilities and understandings even as they develop more elaborate and sophisticated skills and knowledge. Such displays are not only of ongoing and recently completed activities but also from previous years, often eliciting questions from the children about a particular event or child. In this way, documentation serves both to represent and promote an interest in the history of the school itself, with images of families, teachers, children, and their work from previous years making explicit the community that new classes of children will join. Also implicit in the documentation products displayed throughout the early childhood environment is an advocacy for both the work being done by the children and their teachers and for the rights of parents to be informed about and involved in these experiences.

Documentation as a Means of Connecting with Families and Communities and Advocating for Young Children. Early childhood educators in Reggio Emilia, as well as those in Pistoia and San Miniato, have spent several decades exploring the possibilities of documentation as a means of promoting parent relationships as well as fostering a better understanding and greater interest among the community at large in children's early childhood education. Everywhere, it seems, there is testimony to children's work and the respect it garners from their teachers. Photographs, transcriptions of conversations, and teacher descriptions of the aims and outcomes of various short- and long-term projects supplement elegant displays of the products of children's collaborative activities. Combined, these features of the environment convey messages of welcome, as well as an invitation to learn more about the activities that characterize this learning environment. They also direct attention to the qualities of children's competencies and the context that supports and inspires their development. By reading teacher explanations regarding children's processes of knowledge construction and viewing the numerous visual images of their activities, parents and community leaders alike can learn about children's development as it is supported within the school environment. In this sense these documentation displays serve as a form of advocacy for children and for the program. The recent project *Reggio Tutta,* which entailed children's explorations throughout the city, exemplifies the role of documentation in helping children to connect with their city and ensuring that the city stays mindful of the children in its midst (Bruner, 2002). This pedagogical documentation is both formative (during projects) as a support to careful and intentional planning and decision making and summative (at the end of projects) as a communicative tool for displaying the story of a project and making visible what children and teachers learned by being engaged together in that project (Rinaldi, 2006).

Documentation efforts also support parental understanding of their individual child's learning and developmental progress. Rather than provide assessment results typical of many U.S. early childhood programs, parents in Reggio Emilia and other like-minded communities "receive extensive descriptive information about their children's daily life and progress and share in culminating productions or performances" (Carolyn Edwards, personal communication, April 2002). Documentation strategies provide the materials to use in creating these descriptions as well as more elaborate "portfolios or other products of children's individual and group work, some of which are displayed and others sent home at key intervals and transitions" (Edwards, 2002). As do teachers in a number of other municipal programs in Italy (Gandini & Edwards, 2001), teachers prepare *diarios* (memory books) with samples and stories from children's experiences in the *nido* and *scuola del'infanzia*. This use of documentation to promote shared understandings between parents and teachers is one element in a larger component that is likely the key to the success of Reggio Emilia's municipal program—the notion of *partecipazione* (participation, or civic engagement) as essential to the design and maintenance of the city's early childhood services.

4. Parent Engagement, Not Parent Education

Of all the elements associated with Reggio Emilia's work with children and their families, the concept of parental engagement is probably the least visible to outsiders and yet most central to its philosophy, practices, and 30-year success story. Grounded in cultural values regarding the importance of adult collaboration and fine-tuned in a region distinguished by high levels of *partecipazione* (Putnam, 1993), Reggio Emilia played a leading role in establishing national guidelines and implementing practices that support community involvement and parent engagement in early childhood settings.

The concept of *gestione sociale* (social management), originally developed for the labor market, is premised on the essential right of parents to be directly involved in the running of local child-care centers. In most Italian cities with municipal early childhood programs, the concept of *gestione sociale* is represented in various forms of parent–teacher–citizen advisory councils (New & Mallory, 2005). Reggio Emilia has further elaborated upon the general principle of an advisory council to create specific practices that promote the collaborative engagement of families in the early childhood services (New, Mallory, & Mantovani, 2000).

This importance of family participation is directly linked to the philosophical premise of schools as "systems of relations," but Reggio Emilia's interpretation goes beyond ensuring that parents feel welcome and included in the school environment. As interpreted in Reggio Emilia, *partecipazione* requires that parents and citizens become intimately involved with the processes and aims of the educational enterprise. The intent is to offer "the possibility of the citizens (most of all the parents) to contribute actively to the conducting of educational services, refusing to delegate their potentials and their responsibility" (Spaggiari, 1991, p. 112 [translated from Italian]).

The concept of participation is more than a set of ideals; it also has multiple practical interpretations aimed at developing trusting and reciprocal relations with parents. In addition to the formal advisory councils (which include both citizen and parent representation), numerous other strategies have been designed to ensure that parents and citizens have opportunities to play what the Italians refer to as "co-protagonist" roles (Spaggiari, 1998). For example, each class has regular individual and full-class meetings regarding events particular to their group; there are also small-group meetings of parents and teachers for discussion of particular topics of interest. Groups of parents and sometimes grandparents are invited to come together in the evenings to have cooking lessons with the cook or to get together on weekends to make something for the school. Schoolwide meetings may focus on educational issues (i.e., the role of technology), or a topic on child development (i.e., the changing role of grandparents), or issues associated with budgetary matters. While many such meetings involve the sharing of teacher documentation to inform the discussion, other meetings may include a guest speaker. All meetings with parents and the larger community are documented to validate their importance and to ensure that those who were not present can share in the learning that took place.

In addition to meetings where parents, teachers, and other citizens talk about their own understandings of and responsibilities for children's learning, other occasions serve as culminating events to children's long-term project work. Although not the case with every project, every Reggio Emilia school finds occasions during the year to share and celebrate children's work to which families and members of the larger community are invited. These and many other strategies have been designed to promote the development of reciprocal home–school relationships and community involvement. The success of these strategies is apparent in the high levels of participation that characterize these events. It is also apparent in the quality and sustainability of Reggio Emilia's highly successful and municipally funded program of early educational services over the past 40 years (New, 2007).

Reggio Emilia's creation of a school environment that nurtures adult as well as child relations, interpretation of curriculum as a catalyst for children's and teacher's collaborative investigations, and commitment to ensuring ongoing communication and exchanges with families and community members represent much more than an approach to early childhood education. Rather, this collection of principles and their related practices reflect an attitude that draws upon political, philosophical, and cultural views of what it means to live and contribute to a democratic community (New, 1998). The particulars of Reggio Emilia's history, culture, and politics make it risky to blithely assume that U.S. early childhood educators might incorporate various features of Reggio Emilia's municipal program for use in their own work with young children. And yet, thousands of teachers and teacher-educators across the United States have done just that. The following discussion suggests that the REA in the United States has taken on a life of its own, in a context of its own.

REGGIO EMILIA'S INFLUENCE IN THE UNITED STATES: OHIO AS CASE STUDY

It is difficult to adequately describe the current and potential influences of REA-inspired conversations and collaboration that are taking place in the United States. Once considered an exotic point of reference for those fortunate enough to have traveled to Italy, Reggio Emilia is now regarded as a major curriculum approach in the professional literature, as evidenced by its inclusion in this volume and its many references found in contemporary early childhood texts in the United States and abroad.[14] Reggio Emilia has its own track of sessions at NAEYC's national conference, multiple Listservs and study groups, a newsletter, annual U.S. delegations, and dozens of Internet reference sites. As a result of this widespread exposure, tens of thousands of teachers and teacher-educators are now striving to understand and apply the REA to U.S. education, including, in a few instances, elementary (New, 2003) and middle school (Hill, 2002) settings. Thirty-seven of the 50 states have contacts who help teachers connect with others who are interested in exploring the premises of Reggio Emilia's work with young children. Teachers in early childhood programs in Chicago, St. Paul, Boulder, St. Louis, Columbus, Santa Monica, Miami, Atlanta, and San Francisco are currently collaborating directly with Reggio Emilia educators, as is the World Bank

[14]C.f. Abbott & Nutbrown, 2001, for a discussion of Reggio Emilia's growing influence in the United Kingdom.

Children's Center in Washington, DC (New, 2002). Besides generating this large-scale interest and enthusiasm, what influence has Reggio Emilia had on U.S. early childhood education? What have been the complexities and challenges to interpreting and appropriating these pedagogical principles in American settings?

As American visitors moved beyond amazement at what they saw in Reggio Emilia, many began to grapple with how they should make sense of the pedagogy. For some, this has evolved into a quest to understand the pedagogy deeply enough to replicate it with fidelity in their own settings. These programs have become "referent points" in the United States and have received much in-country consultation with the Reggio Emilians and indeed their "blessing" to advertise themselves as Reggio programs (e.g., the Columbus School for Girls in Columbus, Ohio, and the St. Michael's School in St. Louis, Missouri). Other educators have chosen to self-consciously avoid the goal of direct replication of pedagogy and instead have chosen to speak of "Reggio-inspired" pedagogy. This group has decided to explore the principles and apply them in ways that make sense in their local settings (e.g., Virginia Tech University, The Ohio State University). Early childhood teacher educators in the United States have begun to talk with each other about how to incorporate the principles of the REA into their teacher education work in various U.S. institutions. In fact, a group of higher educators (e.g., University of Vermont) have come together under the name "Reggio Inspired Teacher Educators" (RITE).

The Teaching Potential of Amiable Space

Immediately following an initial study tour of the classrooms in Reggio Emilia, American visitors often try to redesign their physical environments to look more like those they saw in Italy. However, the Italian educators are quick to point out that while each of their classrooms is designed with similar principles of transparency, intimacy, and light in mind, for example, and each classroom is designed to invite exploration, it is also true that across the system each classroom has a unique design, an identity that reflects the people who live there and the more local context of the building. For example, the school in the heart of the city park reflects its busy, more urban environment while the more rural school reflects its wide-open green spaces. American students of the Reggio Emilia environments are urged to start with a reflection upon their identities and how they want them reflected in their room designs before moving a table or purchasing a new one. Classrooms need not include bottles of olive oil and terra cotta palettes but rather the authentic cultural artifacts of those who live within them. The Italian educators start always with questions: "Why this table?" "Why placed here?"

Revealing Children's Thinking and Learning

As outlined in the introduction, Reggio Emilia played a central role in expanding U.S. conceptions of children's capacities and therefore notions of developmentally appropriate practices. This influence was in great part due to the exhibition's success in illustrating children's theorizing, meaning making, and use of semiotic tools that went way beyond what we were expecting children to do and show us, thus challenging our understanding of contemporary theories of children's learning and development. Already under criticism for a too-heavy reliance on Piagetian theories and associated interpretations of an activity-based and child-centered early childhood curriculum, early childhood teacher educators and many among the NAEYC leadership welcomed Reggio Emilia's ability to demonstrate more advanced conceptual understandings of children's learning. Many of Reggio

Emilia's principles about how children learn are embedded within the theoretical construct of the zone of proximal development, a Vygotskian construct central to the theoretical framework of sociocultural theory and one that has major implications for how we conceptualize and experience educational change (New, 1998). Reggio Emilia's *progettazione,* for example, provided numerous and compelling illustrations of the interplay between social and intellectual processes. It was not just academics who experienced paradigm shifts in their theoretical interpretations of children's learning. Classroom teachers also became fascinated with the question of how children learn as a result of seeing and learning about Reggio Emilian teaching strategies.

The practical examples of Reggio Emilia were seen by many as "a helpful way for the field to understand that Piagetian theories did not explain everything" (John Nimmo, personal communication, 2002). In particular, the intensity of engagement over periods of weeks and months by Italian children as young as 3 and 4 years, in projects that they co-constructed with their teachers, served as a powerful provocation for early childhood educators to rethink their dichotomous distinctions between teacher-directed and child-initiated learning. Because they were illustrated with fascinating photographs and vignettes rather than in strictly academic terms, these theoretical insights led many classroom teachers and teacher-educators to more carefully explore contemporary Vygotskian and neo-Vygotskian literature (e.g., Rogoff, 1990) as it could inform and improve educational practice. Seeing and reading about teachers who carefully attend to children's questions as they up the ante in presenting new problems to ponder helped U.S. educators to rethink the instructional implications of readiness in the new terms of "zoped" or zones of proximal development, a state that is characterized by a dynamic tension between what is known and what is being sought (Brown & Ferrera, 1985). Numerous publications have since utilized Reggio Emilia as an example of theory into practice, linking Reggio Emilia to theories of constructivism and social constructivism (New, 1998) for typically developing children as well as those with special needs (Mallory & New, 1994).

Reggio Emilia's influence on theoretical understandings has not been limited to views on cognitive development. Its work also "draws attention to children's need for comfort and security" as essential to their successful engagement in Reggio Emilia projects (Carolyn Edwards, personal communication, 2002). This relationship between children's emotional well-being and cognitive development "resonates with what we are learning about attachment as well as the new brain research" (Carolyn Edwards, personal communication, April 2002). And beyond the theoretical abstractions of the processes of children's learning, Reggio Emilia has also challenged our understandings and expectations of the content and consequences of children's learning. As revealed through the documentation of children's conversations and constructions, Reggio Emilia educators have demonstrated beyond doubt that the limits in our theoretical understandings have been accompanied by vast underestimations of the potentials that children bring with them to early childhood settings (Katz, 1998). American students of the REA have struggled to reveal the interactional and material mediators the Italian educators provide to engage with children in such rich, extended project work. Indeed the Italian educators have struggled to articulate their decision making for us. Recent collaborations with the Project Zero group at Harvard have tried to "make [teaching] and learning visible" (Project Zero, 2003; Project Zero and Reggio Children, 2001).

From Traditional Scripts to Purposeful and Collaborative Teaching

It is one thing to have a foreign experience provide a new way of understanding, of theorizing, and of planning for children's learning processes and potentials. It is altogether different to begin to change the day-to-day practices that might be linked with these abstractions. For some classroom teachers the changes to practice came first. Beginning with increased attention to the physical environment (such that bottles of colored water began appearing in bathrooms across the country), teachers became emboldened to think more critically about their classroom work with young children. Taking advantage of supports provided by the growing number of study groups and Reggio Emilia dedicated Listservs, teachers began to more actively explore ways to use what they were learning about young children as they planned more purposeful but also open-ended learning encounters. Some of these teacher explorations took place in isolated settings, others in places that dedicated their entire program to exploring ways to re-create relevant principles and practices from Reggio Emilia in new contexts. Two examples are worth mentioning here: the St. Louis schools (three private preschool settings) and the Chicago Commons project (a consortium of federal, state, and locally funded early childhood and parent–child centers for low-income families). As described by program directors of these two communities, each of whom has been exploring implications from Reggio Emilia for the past decade, the challenge has been to figure out what and how to "bring Reggio Emilia home" (Cadwell, 1997). Over the slow and deliberate process, teachers in each setting—as distinct from each other as they are from Reggio Emilia—embarked on a study of and debate about the principles of Reggio Emilia as they might pertain to and improve their services for young children. Thus, for example, in St. Louis teachers have focused on pedagogical documentation as a link to the creation of an investigative framework that guides teachers' work with children (Cadwell, 2002). In Chicago, African American parents who have recently assumed roles as Head Start teachers have visited Reggio Emilia, returning to initiate schoolwide discussions on what it really means to involve parents in children's learning. And these are only two of the hundreds of early childhood settings where teachers, individually and together, continue to use their experiences and understandings from Reggio Emilia to promote their ongoing reflection about their own work with young children and families (see, for example, the 2002 issue of *Innovations* for discussions with directors of three different American schools). Reggio Emilia educators have worked closely with many of these teachers and program directors, illustrating through their international partnerships the benefits of "collaboration in all its meanings" (Bredekamp, 2002).

New Forms and Functions of Parent–Teacher Relationships

The REA has also influenced teachers' thinking with respect to how they relate to and work with parents, although the translation of these ideas into actual practices has been somewhat less widespread. Traditional interpretations of professional responsibilities have often placed parents in a consumer rather than in a partner role with educators. The demands of contemporary family life make the idea of 3-hour classroom meetings a rarity rather than a reality in most U.S. settings. And the diversity of perspectives likely found among a group of parents in a pluralistic society such as the United States makes some teachers hesitant to even inquire as to what parents actually want for their children. Nonetheless, some U.S. teachers have creatively found ways to minimize the assumed hierarchy of teachers over parents and to seek more active and reciprocal relationships. Thus two kindergarten teachers invited a group of parents to help them with a problem—a real problem, not one that they had manufactured for the occasion—having to do with the need for a "birthday policy" that would acknowledge and respect the diverse cultural and religious perspectives represented in their classroom. Subsequent to that decision, the teachers described a slow but significant change in parents' relationships to each other as they came to understand that their hopes and preferences for their own children did not always coincide with the goals for other people's children. In a similar vein, after several years of exploring principles from Reggio Emilia and other Italian early childhood programs, one Early Head Start teacher invited teenage parents to take on the role of documenting children's learning, trusting them with the videocameras, and, eventually, with selecting, arranging, and writing about the images on bulletin board displays. These parents came to increasingly value their roles in helping the teacher to identify and promote children's learning and development. Each of these examples illustrates a Reggio Emilia principle that has been appropriated for a particularly American controversy or context.

Documentation as a Tool for Professional Development

One of the most visible consequences of Reggio Emilia's influence on U.S. early childhood practices is the growing use of documentation—not only as a means of observing and assessing young children but also as a vehicle for teacher

Bruce Mallory

As as example of the nature and focus of *partecipazione* in Reggio Emilia, parents, teachers, grandparents, and citizens engage in series of meetings addressed to questions of education today.

development. Described in terms of its potentials for sharing and reflecting, classroom teachers (e.g., Oken-Wright, 2001) describe with detail the importance of more carefully listening to and observing the children with whom they work so that these insights can guide their ongoing curriculum decisions. U.S. educators are also increasingly utilizing documentation strategies as a means for systematically following and studying the ways that individuals as well as groups of children develop ideas, theories, and understandings (Project Zero & Reggio Children, 2001; Turner & Krechevsky, 2003). More recent advocates of documentation highlight its usefulness in illuminating the processes of *teaching* (Project Zero, 2003) as well as learning; others have focused on its potentials for self-reflection and as a means of gaining insights into one's own teaching goals and practices (Fleet, Robertson, & Patterson, 2006). These potentials of documentation have not been lost on early childhood teacher educators who advocate for the potentials of documentation to help preservice teachers learn how to observe, record, and understand child development (Goldhaber, Smith, & Sortino, 1997; Moran & Tegano, 2005). The summative story panels that dominated the first attempts of Americans to bring Reggio home have more recently given way to more purposeful inquiry with the use of documentation to inform and sustain teacher research which, in turn, informs and sustains their work with young children.

Increasingly, Reggio Emilia–inspired teacher education programs now incorporate the practices of teacher research (Rinaldi, 2003) through collaborative documentation into their university-based teacher professional development programs (Gandini & Goldhaber, 2001; Moran, Desrochers, & Cavicchi, 2007). Together with other Reggio Emilia principles, documentation has helped to provoke and sustain a paradigm shift among an increasing number of university laboratory schools (Stremmel, Hill, & Fu, in press) and early childhood teacher education programs (Fu, Stremmel, & Hill, 2002).

Ohio as Case Study

Ohio represents a setting in which state and local representatives from various professional perspectives have joined together to explore principles of Reggio Emilia's work as they might inform U.S. early childhood education. As has been the case in many settings—including Reggio Emilia—there was a convergence of timing and the leadership of particular people. In Ohio, Sandy Miller used her new position at the state department to speak to the wider early childhood community across the state. In 1993, she sponsored the traveling exhibit from Reggio Emilia in Ohio. This spectacular exhibit of documentation of the children's and teachers' work sparked much interest and curiosity. Leveraging funds from a private foundation, Miller invited small groups of educators to form and receive funds to create study groups—small discussion groups with the purpose of exploring Reggio Emilia pedagogical principles, experimenting with them in their classrooms, and providing critique and friendly support for each other. She also organized state-wide all-day professional development events that often included a speaker who infused the network with new information and models to inspire them. At the time when Miller initiated this system of support, there were 8 groups and 150 participants. Today there are 42 groups and over 500 participants coming from private and public early childhood and primary programs from all over the state. The study groups have flourished and sustained themselves long after the funding stopped—in fact, some of them have been in progress for over 12 years. For these groups, a paradigm shift has occurred where it would be hard to turn the clock back to outline what they were like before they were introduced to Reggio and who they are now. They no longer talk about the Reggio Emilia approach per se, but one can definitely see the inspiration reflected in their work as they debate, for example, how to collaborate more effectively with parents in the promotion of children's early learning. Of equal importance to these changes in understanding the potentials of teaching and learning, study group participants have learned to "go public" with their work and to offer and receive critique and discussion of their teaching. This is a new experience for Ohio teachers—and American teachers in general—who have traditionally crafted a very individualistic stance to teaching.

More recently, Ohio teachers' commitment to these pedagogical ideas has been challenged by the standards-based education related to the accountability movement in America. Teachers who have spent years in study groups and have embraced a new way of thinking about their work with young children are struggling once again to align the more open inquiry work of REA with the more structured presentation of the disciplinary standards. It remains to be seen how teachers inspired by Reggio Emilia will respond to the increasing performance-based evaluations of their work and children's learning.

CONCLUSION

The story of Reggio Emilia is only one of many such stories in contemporary Italy (Gandini & Edwards, 2001; Mantovani & Musatti, 1996), each characterized by a respect for cultural traditions as well as innovation (Mantovani, 2001). One of the aims of this discussion has been to distinguish between what happens in the classrooms of one particular Italian city and what has come to be known, in the United States, as the Reggio Emilia approach. The point here is that any educational innovation becomes transformed as others attempt to understand and make use of it. Some transformation is unintentional or unavoidable. There are a number of practical and policy-related challenges of interpreting Reggio Emilia in the United States beyond the challenges of implementation, including the trivializing of Reggio Emilia principles and practices, the American tendency to seek out quick fixes for complex educational challenges, the lack of infrastructures at the local and state levels to support teacher collaboration, and the difficulties of retaining poorly paid teachers over time, not to mention the lack of a nationwide commitment to the provision of early childhood services. This is not to say that Reggio Emilia has nothing to offer to U.S. early childhood education. The previous discussion has highlighted some of the ways in which Reggio Emilia has already changed at least some U.S. educators' ways of thinking about and working with young children and their families.

A second aim of this discussion has been to reveal the wealth of possibilities that exist when teachers and others involved in education don't try to imitate but, rather, try to learn from such international examples. Such possibilities are conveyed in the sincerity of Sergio Spaggiari's message: "If you want to be like us, don't copy us. We have never copied anyone. If you want to be like us, be original" (cited in Cadwell, 2002, p. 163). Thus a growing number of U.S. educators are attempting to "reinvent" the promise of Reggio Emilia as it might be realized elsewhere (Fu, 2002; Strong-Wilson, 2007), keeping in mind the particular facts and circumstances of that Italian city itself—what Peter Moss (2001) refers to as the "otherness" of Reggio Emilia—as a means of keeping in the forefront the inextricable relationship between culture and education (Bruner, 1996).

What Reggio Emilia has been most successful at doing is setting an example of a commitment to hard work and collaborative inquiry on behalf of young children. What is really exotic about Reggio Emilia is not the beautiful images on the walls or the carefully rendered drawings by children of their ideas and understandings. What has inspired American educators to rethink, collaboratively and over time, their images of children, parents, and their own professional identities is the *fact* of Reggio

Emilia (New, 2002). It is difficult to imagine a city in the United States that dedicates 10% of its annual budget to the care and education of its young children, that continues to do so for 30-plus years no matter what is happening in other parts of the nation, and that does so in a way that involves families, engages teachers, and promotes children's skills and understandings beyond imaginable levels. Indeed, the United States remains far behind most other industrialized nations in developing any sort of system, national or otherwise, for the early care and education of its children (Organization for Economic Cooperation and Development, 2001). That Reggio Emilia has done these things, and successfully, in the face of its own challenges (Piccini, as quoted in Gambetti, 2002) gives educators around the world the message that, in their settings as well, things could change. If nothing else from Reggio Emilia makes a lasting impression, the city and her citizens have demonstrated what might happen when parents, teachers, and other citizens refuse to accept the status quo and come to collectively imagine that there might be another way to care for and educate young children.

REFERENCES

Abbott, L., & Nutbrown, C. (Eds.). (2001). *Experiencing Reggio Emilia: Implications for pre-school provision*. Buckingham, England: Open University Press.

Bove, C. (1999). *L'inserimento del bambino al nido* [Welcoming the child into child care]: Perspectives from Italy. *Young Children, 54*(2), 32–34.

Bredekamp, S. (1987). *Developmentally appropriate practice in early childhood programs serving children from birth through age eight*. Washington, DC: National Association for the Education of Young Children.

Bredekamp, S. (1993). Reflections on Reggio Emilia. *Young Children, 49*(1), 13–17.

Bredekamp, S. (2002, Winter). Developmentally appropriate practice meets Reggio Emilia: A story of collaboration in all its meanings. *Innovations, 9*(1), 11–15.

Bredekamp, S., & Copple, C. (Eds.) (1997). *Developmentally appropriate practice for early childhood programs serving children from birth through age eight* (Rev. ed.). Washington, DC: National Association for the Education of Young Children.

Brown, A., & Ferrara, R. (1985). Diagnosing zones of proximal development. In J. V. Wertsch (Ed.), *Culture, communication, and cognition: Vygotskian perspectives* (pp. 273–305). New York: Cambridge University Press.

Bruner, J. (1996). *The culture of education.* Cambridge, MA: Harvard University Press.

Bruner, J. (1998). Some specifications for a space to house a Reggio pre-school. In G. Ceppi and M. Zini (Eds.), *Children, space, and relations—A metaproject for an environment for young children.* Reggio Emilia, Italy: Reggio Children; and Modena, Italy: Domus Academy Research Center.

Bruner, J. (2002). Commentary. In *Reggio Tutta: A guide to the city by the children.* Reggio Emilia, Italy: Reggio Children.

Cadwell, L. B. (1997). *Bringing Reggio Emilia home.* New York: Teachers College Press.

Cadwell, L. B. (2002). *Bringing learning to life: The Reggio approach to early childhood education.* New York: Teachers College Press.

Ceppi, G., & Zini, M. (Eds.). (1998). *Children, spaces, relations: Metaproject for an environment for young children.* Modena, Italy: Reggio Children and Domus Academy Research Center.

Cohen, D. L. (1992, November 20). Preschools in Italian town inspiration to U.S. educators. *Education Week, 12,* 12–13.

Corsaro, W., & Emiliani, F. (1992). Child care, early education, and children's peer culture in Italy. In M. E. Lamb, K. J. Sternberg, C. P. Hwang, & A. G. Broberg (Eds.), *Child care in context* (pp. 81–115). Hillsdale, NJ: Erlbaum.

Edwards, C. (2002). Three approaches from Europe: Waldorf, Montessori, and Reggio Emilia. *Early Childhood Research and Practice, 4*(1). Retrieved April 11, 2008, at http://ecrp.uiuc.edu/V4n1/edwards.html

Edwards, C., Gandini, L., & Forman, G. (Eds.). (1993). *The hundred languages of children: The Reggio Emilia approach.* Norwood, NJ: Ablex.

Edwards, C., Gandini, L., & Forman, G. (Eds.). (1998). *The hundred languages of children: The Reggio Emilia approach—Advanced reflections* (2nd ed.). Greenwich, CT: Ablex.

Filippini, T. (1990, November). *Introduction to the Reggio approach.* Paper presented at the annual conference of the National Association for the Education of Young Children, Washington, DC.

Fleet, A., Robertson, J., & Patterson, C. (Eds.). (2006). *Insights.* Sydney, Australia: Castle Hill, New South Wales: Pademelon Press.

Forman, G., & Fyfe, B. (1998). Negotiated learning through design, documentation, and discourse. In C. Edwards, L. Gandini, & G. Forman (Eds.), *The hundred languages of children: The Reggio Emilia approach—Advanced reflections* (2nd ed., pp. 239–260). Greenwich, CT: Ablex.

Fu, V. R. (2002). The challenge to reinvent the Reggio Emilia Approach: A pedagogy of hope and possibilities. In V. Fu, A. Stremmel, & L. Hill (Eds.), *Teaching and learning: Collaborative exploration of the Reggio Emilia approach* (pp. 23–35). Upper Saddle River, NJ: Merrill/Prentice Hall.

Fu, V. R., Stremmel, A. J., & Hill, L. T. (2002). An invitation to join in a growing community for learning and change. In V. Fu, A. Stremmel, & L. Hill (Eds.), *Teaching and learning: Collaborative exploration of the Reggio Emilia approach* (pp. 5–11). Upper Saddle River, NJ: Merrill/Prentice Hall.

Gambetti, A. (2002). The evolution of the municipality of Reggio Emilia: An interview with Sandra Piccini. *Innovations in Early Education: The International Reggio Exchange, 9*(3), 1–3.

Gandini, L. (1984). Not just anywhere: Making child care centers into "particular" places. *Beginnings, 1,* 17–20.

Gandini, L. (1998). Educational and caring spaces. In C. Edwards, L. Gandini, & G. Forman (Eds.), *The hundred languages of children: The Reggio Emilia approach: Advanced reflections* (2nd ed., pp. 161–178). Greenwich, CT: Ablex.

Gandini, L., & Edwards, C. (Eds.). (2001). *Bambini: The Italian approach to infant/toddler care.* New York: Teachers College Press.

Gandini, L., & Goldhaber, J. (2001). Two reflections about documentation. In L. Gandini & C. Edwards (Eds.), *Bambini: The Italian approach to infant/toddler care* (pp. 124–145). New York: Teachers College Press.

Gandini, L., Hill, L., Cadwell, L., & Schwall, C. (2005). *In the spirit of the studio: Learning from the atelier of Reggio Emilia.* New York: Teachers College Press.

Goldhaber, J., Smith, D., & Sortino, S. (1997). Observing, recording and understanding: The role of documentation in early childhood teacher education. In J. Hendrick (Ed.), *First steps in teaching the Reggio way.* Upper Saddle River, NJ: Merrill/Prentice Hall.

Hill, L. T. (2002). A journey to recast the Reggio Emilia approach for a middle school: A pedagogy of relationships and hope. In V. Fu, A. Stremmel, & L. Hill (Eds.), *Teaching and learning: A collaborative exploration of the Reggio Emilia approach.* Upper Saddle River, NJ: Merrill/Prentice Hall.

Jones, E., & Nimmo, J. (1994). *Emergent curriculum.* Washington, DC: NAEYC.

Katz, L. (1998). What can we learn from Reggio Emilia? In C. Edwards, L. Gandini, & G. Forman (Eds.), *The hundred languages of children: The Reggio Emilia approach—Advanced reflections* (2nd ed., pp. 27–45). Greenwich, CT: Ablex.

Katz, L., & Cesarone, B. (Eds.). (1994). *Reflections on the Reggio Emilia Approach.* ERIC/EECE, University of Illinois, Urbana and Edizioni Junior, Bergamo, Italy. (Available from Reggio Children USA and ERIC/ECE.)

Kessler, S. (1991). Alternative perspectives on early childhood education. *Early Childhood Research Quarterly, 6,* 183–197.

Malaguzzi, L. (1998). History, ideas, and basic philosophy: An interview with Lella Gandini. In

C. Edwards, L. Gandini, & G. Forman (Eds.), *The hundred languages of children: The Reggio Emilia approach—Advanced reflections* (2nd ed., pp. 49–97). Greenwich, CT: Ablex.

Mallory, B. (1992). Is it always appropriate to be developmental? Convergent models for early intervention practice. *Topics in Early Childhood Special Education, 11*(4), 1–12.

Mallory, B., & New, R. (1994). *Diversity and developmentally appropriate practices: Challenges for early childhood education.* New York: Teachers College Press.

Mantovani, S. (2001). Infant-toddler centers in Italy today: Tradition and innovation. In L. Gandini & C. P. Edwards (Eds.), *Bambini: The Italian approach to infant/toddler care* (pp. 23–37). New York: Teachers College Press.

Mantovani, S., & Musatti, T. (1996). New educational provisions for young children in Italy. *European Journal of Educational Psychology, XI*(2), 119–128.

Moran, M. J., & Tegano, D. W. (2005, June). Moving toward visual literacy: Photography as a language of teacher inquiry. *Journal of Early Childhood Research and Practice, 7*(1).

Moran, M. J., Desrochers, L., & Cavicchi, N. (2007). *Progettazione* and documentation as sociocultural activities: Changing communities of practice. *The Journal of Theory into Practice, 46*(1), 81–90.

Moss, P. (2001). The otherness of Reggio. In L. Abbott & C. Nutbrown (Eds.), *Experiencing Reggio Emilia: Implications for pre-school provision.* Buckingham, England: Open University Press.

New, R. (1990). Excellent early education: A city in Italy has it! *Young Children, 45*(6), 4–6.

New, R. (1993a). Cultural variations on developmentally appropriate practice: Challenges to theory and practice. In C. Edwards, L. Gandini, & G. Forman (Eds.), *The hundred languages of children: The Reggio Emilia approach to early childhood education* (pp. 215–231). Norwood, NJ: Ablex.

New, R. (1993b). Italy. In M. Cochran (Ed.), *International handbook on child care policies and programs* (pp. 291–311). Westport, CT: Greenwood Press.

New, R. (1994). Reggio Emilia: Its vision and its challenges for educators in the United States. In L. G. Katz, & B. Cesarone (Eds.), *Reflections on the Reggio Emilia approach.* Urbana, IL: ERIC/EECE Monograph Series, No. 6.

New, R. (1998). Theory and praxis in Reggio Emilia: They know what they are doing, and why. In C. Edwards, L. Gandini, & G. Forman (Eds.), *The hundred languages of children: The Reggio Emilia approach—Advanced reflections* (2nd ed., pp. 261–284). Greenwich, CT: Ablex.

New, R. (1999). What should children learn? *Early Childhood Research & Practice, 1*(2), 1–19.

New, R. (2001). Reggio Emilia: Catalyst for change and conversation. Washington, DC: Office of Educational Research and Improvement. (ERIC Document Reproduction Service No. ED4748081.)

New, R. (2002). *The impact of the Reggio Emilia model on early childhood education in the U.S.* Unpublished paper, commissioned by the Board of International Comparative Studies in Education's Committee on a Framework and Long-term Research Agenda for International Comparative Education Studies, Washington, DC.

New, R. (2003). Reggio Emilia: New ways to think about schooling. *Educational Leadership, 60*(7), 30–37.

New, R. (2007). Reggio Emilia as cultural activity theory in practice. *Theory into Practice, 46*(1), 5–13.

New, R., & Mallory, B. (2005). Children as catalysts for adult relations: New perspectives from Italian early childhood education. In O. Saracho & B. Spodek (Eds.), *Contemporary perspective on families and communities and schools in early childhood education* (pp. 163–179). Greenwich, CT: Information Age Publisher.

New, R., Mallory, B., & Mantovani, S. (2000). Cultural images of children, parents, and teachers: Italian interpretations of home-school relations. *Early Education and Development, 11*(5), 597–616.

Newsweek. (1991, December 2). The 10 best schools in the world and what we can learn from them. *Newsweek,* 50–59.

Oken-Wright, P. (2001). Documentation: Both mirror and light. *Innovations in Early Education: The International Reggio Exchange, 10*(2), 1–4.

Organization for Economic Cooperation and Development. (2001). *Starting strong, early childhood education and care.* Paris: Organization for Economic Cooperation and Development.

Project Zero. (2003). *Making teaching visible: Documenting group learning as professional development.* Cambridge, MA: Project Zero.

Project Zero & Reggio Children. (2001). *Making learning visible: Children as individual and group learners.* Reggio Emilia, Italy: Reggio Children.

Putnam, R. (1993). *Making democracy work: Civic traditions in modern Italy.* Princeton, NJ: Princeton University Press.

Rinaldi, C. (1993). The emergent curriculum and social constructivism. In C. Edwards, L. Gandini, & G. Forman (Eds.), *The hundred languages of children: The Reggio Emilia approach* (pp. 101–111). Norwood, NJ: Ablex.

Rinaldi, C. (1998). Projected curriculum constructed through documentation—*Progettazione:* An interview with Lella Gandini. In C. Edwards, L. Gandini, & G. Forman (Eds.), *The hundred languages of children: The Reggio Emilia approach—Advanced reflections* (2nd ed., pp. 113–125). Greenwich, CT: Ablex.

Rinaldi, C. (2003). The teacher as researcher. *Innovations in early education: The International Reggio Exchange, 10*(2), 1–4.

Rinaldi, C. (2006). *In dialogue with Reggio Emilia: Listening, researching, and learning (Contesting Early Childhood Series).* New York: Routledge.

Rogoff, B. (1990). *Apprenticeship in thinking: Cognitive development in social context.* New York: Oxford University Press.

Spaggiari, S. (1991). *Considerazioni critiche ed esperienze di gestione sociale.* [*Critical considerations and experiences of social management*]. In A. Bondidi & S. Mantovani (Eds.), *Manuale critico dell'asilo nido* [*Critical manual of day care*] (pp. 111–134). Milan, Italy: Franco Angeli.

Spaggiari, S. (1998). The community-teacher partnership in the governance of the schools: An interview with Lella Gandini. In C. Edwards, L. Gandini, & G. Forman (Eds.), *The hundred languages of children: The Reggio Emilia approach—Advanced reflections* (2nd. ed., pp. 99–112). Greenwich, CT: Ablex.

Stremmel, A. J., Hill, L. T., & Fu, V. R. (2003). An inside perspective of paradigm shifts in child development laboratory programs: Bridging theory and professional preparation. In S. Reifel (Series ed.), *Advances in Early Education and Day Care, 12,* 89–111.

Strong-Wilson, T. (Ed.). (2007). Reggio Emilia [Special issue]. *Theory into Practice, 46*(1).

Super, C., & Harkness, S. (1986). The developmental niche. A conceptualization at the interface of child and culture. *International Journal of Behavioral Development, 9,* 545–569.

Turner, T., & Krechevsky, M. (2003). Who are the teachers? Who are the learners? *Educational Leadership, 60*(7), 40–43.

Chapter 15
The Waldorf Approach to Early Childhood Education

Christy L. Williams ⁓ *Fairbrook First Steps Christian Preschool*
James E. Johnson ⁓ *The Pennsylvania State University*

Today increasing numbers of teachers and parents are becoming aware of Waldorf education. Like Montessori and Reggio, Waldorf has its roots in Europe and has been spreading worldwide. Many are drawn to this approach because they see it as an alternative to traditional education and as an inspiration for improving education (Edwards, 2002). The Waldorf model of education is relevant to early childhood education because it seeks to promote a healthy, unhurried, developmentally appropriate learning environment for young children. Waldorf early childhood education (ECE) has been applied in a variety of service delivery settings including home- and center-based child care, parent and child groups, parent support programs, and kindergarten and mixed-age programs for children from 3 to 7 years of age (Oldfield, 2001). Lesser known in the United States, this approach founded by Rudolf Steiner (1861–1925) was first implemented in Germany.

RUDOLF STEINER AND ANTHROPOSOPHY

Any overview of Steiner's philosophical beliefs would have to begin with *anthroposophy* (from the Greek: *anthropo* = man + *sophia* = wisdom). Most simply stated, anthroposophy is the exploration of humanity in combination with the spiritual. The goal of anthroposophy is to bring about truths or new knowledge not wedded to any particular tenets or dogma that would make it an orthodoxy. Central is the quest to hear the truth about spiritual things (Wilkinson, 1996).

Anthroposophy is a spiritual-science movement with its roots in Christianity. Begun by Steiner, it has grown to be widely recognized and has followers all over the world. Two important components of anthroposophy are *oneness with the world* and *search for self.* Oneness with the world encompasses the idea that everything is interconnected, from the cycles of the moon and planets, including Earth, to the cycles of the seasons, to the cycles of human life and death. Each choice that we make will impact others in ways that we may not foresee.

An example that comes to mind is the current situation with the planet's rain forests. As we continue to destroy the trees that make up the rain forests, not only are we destroying the plant and animal life there but our actions are having many other far-reaching consequences. Because trees serve to "clean" our air by using CO_2 and producing oxygen, we are seeing an abundance of air pollution that was previously at least partially filtered by the vast acreage of forest. We are also seeing the effects of global warming, caused in part by abundant amounts of carbon dioxide in the atmosphere. Destruction of rare species of plants and animals in short periods of time also seriously disrupts the food chain, affecting other species that depend upon those that are disappearing. These effects, not even considered when the choice was made to harvest the rain forests, demonstrate the interconnectedness of every facet of our world. Anthroposophy sees the value in being aware of those connections, suggesting that life can be much more fulfilling and meaningful when we recognize and act upon them.

A second important component of anthroposophy is the search for self. Steiner stressed the importance for each individual to develop his or her own faculties in a variety of areas, in order to obtain a "wholeness." Through the study and exploration of intellectual subjects, artistic endeavors, craft and skilled labor, and spiritual meditation, a person can strengthen his or her spirit and sense of self. "The human being cannot escape—indeed, should not seek to escape—worldly experiences, but he must be in a position to discriminate and not be dominated by them" (Wilkinson, 1996, p. 53). Steiner felt that through the philosophy of anthroposophy, the value of preparing the body, mind, and spirit for a life of continued learning and growth could be realized.

Steiner's Theory of Child Development

Consistent with his anthroposophical beliefs, Steiner created his own theory of child development. He proposed 7-year cycles that incorporate both physical and spiritual development. In the first 7 years of life, Steiner said, children's development is focused on their physical body. They imitate the adults around them to learn about their world. They practice "real" work through their play and through craft projects. Simultaneously, spiritual development is occurring as well: Steiner's concept of "Will," which is also nurtured through imitative play. Important in this time period is the exploration of fantasy and imagination. At this stage, Steiner taught that formal academic instruction is inappropriate.

The next 7-year cycle encompasses the ages of 7 to 14 and is marked by the growth of the child's permanent teeth. In this stage of development the child is becoming more aware of the surrounding world and is thus ready to begin academic instruction. The spiritual concept of "Feeling" is being realized at this time, and therefore the child is intrigued by imagery and pictorial stimulation that evoke emotions. Personal relationships are important at this stage as well.

The third 7-year cycle ranges from ages 14 to 21 and begins with the onset of puberty. Then young people are ready to combine their intellect with more abstract thoughts and applications, hence the spiritual development of "Thinking." A sense of independence takes root in this stage and propels the student to seek individually relevant explorations and connections. Steiner outlines 7-year cycles and their corresponding characteristics throughout the life span until the age of 85 years (Wilkinson, 1996).

Closely connected to Steiner's theories of development are his beliefs about education. Steiner observed that schooling should stress the child's all-around development of body, mind, and spirit. The focus should be on educating the "whole" child because developing a child's faculties is more important than teaching subjects. This can be interpreted to mean that it is more important to teach children to learn and think for themselves than to teach children facts and book knowledge. Steiner also believed that specific types of learning were appropriate primarily at certain ages and stages. These basic tenets later served as Steiner's guidelines when he was given the chance to open a school in Germany to put his ideas into practice.

Context of Waldorf Education

Some Waldorf schools only provide kindergarten education, while others provide schooling from kindergarten through the 12th or 13th grade.

Waldorf Kindergarten. The kindergarten in Waldorf schools is very different from the other levels of schooling, as well as being different from most typical kindergartens with which we are familiar. A Waldorf kindergarten serves children between the ages of 3 to 6 years, consistent with the first 7-year cycle in Steiner's theory of development. The curriculum consists of imaginative play, fairy tales, fables, folklore, imitation, art activities, "real" work such as knitting and baking bread, musical instruments, dance, drama, and awareness of nature, cycles, and seasons. This curriculum is based upon Steiner's ideas about the child at this stage. Since Steiner felt that young children are working to develop their physical body and their will, the activities are not academic in nature, but hands on. Many opportunities exist for creativity and make-believe, traits that Steiner believed enhance the development of the will. The toys at school are simple and open ended to encourage imaginative uses. Many objects found in the classroom are natural materials, such as gourds, pinecones, branches, and pebbles. The purpose of these materials is to foster connections with nature and the concept of "oneness with the world."

Going into this kind of classroom environment has been compared to "stepping back into the 19th century" in the sense that the toys are simple and natural, the teachers are often busy mending clothes or baking bread, and the children are actively engaged in imaginative play or imitative work. The Waldorf kindergarten is designed to be an extension of the home. There is no formal academic instruction, educational toys and even books are rarely found in the classroom; this is based directly on Steiner's theory that academic instruction at this first developmental stage is inappropriate. A rich and stimulating environment is required with teachers providing language and literacy experiences through stories, poems, and songs. Mathematical experiences occur naturally through cooking and imaginative play. Likewise art, music, drama, and science experiences have a place—but not in the overt manner so prevalent in the typical public school setting.

In the Waldorf kindergarten children are expected to be children first and foremost. The stage of development they are in is well understood and appreciated by the teacher. Waldorf in this way contrasts with the reality today in which children are often rushed through their childhood in an attempt to help them become the best and the brightest; unfortunately, many children thereby miss the opportunity to simply be, to have the childhood to which they are entitled.

Waldorf education respects the child holistically the stages that a child goes through, and supports the belief that there is a right time for everything. Take the Waldorf approach to reading, for example. It is not unusual for a Waldorf student to begin to read in Grade 3 or 4, much later than the typical public school student. Waldorf preparation will allow the child to be much better prepared for the reading experience when he or she reaches that point, even if it takes a bit longer. The essential matter is not how soon reading can occur. Short-term results are not that important. What is important is to build a solid developmental foundation that will contribute in the long term to a happier, healthier, and more well-rounded and competent child.

Waldorf Grade School. At 7 years of age the child enters the next stage of development and schooling, corresponding to grades two through eight. During this period the child remains with the same teacher and class of students for the entire cycle. This serves to sustain important relationships (a key part of the second 7-year cycle) and to create more consistency in the child's schooling. This also is a way to keep the teacher from becoming stagnant, as he or she will have to grow with the students over the 7-year period.

According to Steiner's theories, children at this second stage are now ready to learn academic subjects. They have a strong foundation from proper kindergarten experiences and can build upon it. Their awareness of the outer world is steadily growing. They are also developing their spiritual sense of "Feeling," so subjects, images, and pictures that evoke emotion are very effective learning tools. The main academic areas covered at this point are typically reading, writing, language skills, math, geography, history, and the sciences. It is the teacher's challenge to present these materials in such a way that the students can explore and master the content to the fullest extent possible.

A typical daily schedule in a Waldorf Grades 1 to 8 class would proceed as follows. Each morning, the teacher greets students individually as they arrive, assessing their mood and state of being in an attempt to be sensitive to their needs. Then the class gathers to recite the morning verse. This is usually an inspirational passage that the class adopts for the entire year. Next, the main lesson begins and its study lasts for 2 hours. This block is used to approach the subject in a number of ways—not simply lecture but also various related activities. The same subject is usually explored during this time for 3 to 4 weeks, and then a new subject is chosen for study. Two more lessons follow, of approximately 45 minutes each, with lunch perhaps in between. Then the afternoon is spent on less intellectual topics, such as art, music, and practical activities, which would include craft and skilled work. Time periods and activities are adjusted according to the developmental level of the class.

Waldorf Teacher Training. Because the Waldorf philosophy is well organized and contains so many interlocking components, Waldorf teachers must be trained in the philosophy and theories behind their craft, as well as in proper ways to incorporate these ideals into the classroom. Currently, there are over 50 full-time training schools worldwide, at least eight of those are in the United States. The Rudolf Steiner College in California is one of these. The college offers a wide variety of programs and courses that train teachers, teacher educators, followers of the anthroposophy movement, and others who are interested in Steiner and his applications. Programs are available full time, part time, during the summer, and through weekend seminars. Teacher training in Waldrof education focuses on the lectures and writings of Rudolf Steiner; a solid understanding of his theory of child development is required to guide ECE practice. Based on a thorough understanding of Steiner's theory of child development, a teacher can better recognize the needs of individual children.

Diversity. Waldorf education originated in Germany and has been adapted to other cultures worldwide. In the United States, adaptations have taken several forms. In public schools, in order to comply with separation of church and state regulations, Waldorf has been stripped of all religious and spiritual exploration. Even with such profound changes, Waldorf programs have been very successful, especially in inner-city public schools, by changing heavily Eurocentric readings and history to include American literature, history, and diversity perspectives. Moreover, multicultural perspectives and interests have been added. Private schools have been better able to keep the spiritual side intact while also adding U.S. and multicultural perspectives. Overall, and especially in private schools, the basic tenets of Steiner's original educational philosophy have remained at the heart of Waldorf education.

Waldorf education has been successfully adapted to numerous other cultures as well, such as those in Europe, Africa, the Middle East, Japan, and Australia. Waldorf schools in these cultures all profess the same original ideas, concepts, and philosophy of the very first Waldorf school in Germany. The curriculum is similar in subject matter and materials, although modified to incorporate the literature and culture of each particular country. Waldorf education is mostly found in countries that accept Christianity, given anthroposophy's connection to this religion, even though Waldorf does not require the students to be of any particular faith. Each school is different because curriculum and administration are not fixed, leaving room for innovations. Waldorf curriculum is easily modified to accommodate multicultural points of view without compromising the basic philosophy.

Many embrace the ideals of Waldorf education because of its simplicity. In this time of technology, busy schedules, competition, and fast food, there is a growing sense of disconnectedness, a feeling that something is missing. Waldorf education strives to eliminate the rush, allowing us to focus on what is really important, to remember where we came from and what life is all about. Waldorf helps children to learn how nature supports us and how we must support nature, to be aware of its rhythms and cycles, and to become one with the world. Waldorf education is about learning who we are as individuals, learning what we can do and what we know, "finding ourselves," so to speak, and recognizing the spirit within us. It is about taking time to "smell the roses" and to appreciate where they came from, an ideal that transcends cultural boundaries.

PROGRAM CHARACTERISTICS

Creating a Caring Community of Learners

The Waldorf approach ECE incorporates certain community elements into its design. The importance of the physical environment, age groupings, planned activities, schedules, and social relationships were all discussed in great detail by Rudolf Steiner, and each element is an integral part of the Waldorf kindergarten.

Children's Sensitivity to the Environment. Steiner begins with the environment, which includes the layout and design of the classroom as well as the outdoor area used by the children. As it will set the stage for future learning, the environment is an important place to begin. The aesthetics of the room play a key role in the general feel of the learning space and, as such, are tailored to the developmental needs and interests of the children who are served. The Waldorf early childhood environment nourishes the child's senses with beauty and order (Trostli, 1998).

Wooden stands draped with cotton or silk cloth invite child-centered imaginative play.

James E. Johnson

Steiner felt that young children are extremely sensitive to their environment, absorbing information through all five senses and experiencing it throughout their entire body. For this reason, Steiner specifically addressed issues such as the paint color on the walls, classroom materials, and furniture. He suggested that the walls of the early childhood classroom be "plain light colors without wallpaper designs" (Grunelius, 1991). Colors play a very important role—for example, loud, bright colors can be overly stimulating, grays and browns can be dreary, plain light colors will promote a light airy feeling, reminiscent of cherry blossoms or spring leaves. This aesthetic beauty stimulates the child's imagination and is at the same time also calming. The simplistic charm of the classroom is achieved by incorporating natural materials, such as solid wood furniture polished with beeswax, curtains made of natural fibers and colored with plant dyes, and toys handcrafted from natural materials.

The Waldorf early childhood classroom is seen as an extension of the home, in both design and function. The prevailing atmosphere is that of the traditional home, where daily chores provided the rhythm of family and community life. In these hurried times, when the pace of life dictates processed foods, synthetic products, entertainment in a box, and gadgets and machines that perform much of the chores that once provided satisfaction, Waldorf provides a sanctuary for children.

The Importance of Imitation and Play. Steiner emphasizes two valuable ways in which young children develop a sense of community. One is imitation, the other is play. Young children are innately curious about the work of adults and instinctively imitate what they see to deepen their own understanding. Waldorf teachers find it very important to give children something valuable to imitate. Therefore, they engage in the work of the home/classroom, such as mending classroom materials, preparing food for snacks, polishing tables, washing floors, and caring for the plants that adorn the windowsills. Each of these tasks is rooted in meaningful, day-to-day necessity. The children are never forced to do this work alongside the teacher and are always welcomed when they choose to imitate the teacher's actions. Through this self-initiated imitation, children learn not only to do their part for the classroom community but also to rely on others.

Play is another crucial method through which children develop a sense of community. Play provides "safe" opportunities to practice social interactions. Children can try out different roles, work through conflicts, and attempt various methods of communication, all under the pretense of play. In terms of social development, play is an opportunity for children to practice their social skills and to learn how to function within a group. Lengthy periods of time designated for true imaginative play in the Waldorf classroom allow children to *experience* community in a nonthreatening manner, while developing their emotional maturity.

Benefits of Mixed-Age Grouping. Another factor that contributes to Waldorf's caring community of learners is the mixed-age grouping of children. Children in a Waldorf kindergarten range in age from 3 to 6 years old, meaning that they have the continuity of building a relationship with one another and with the teacher for up to 3 years. This design also promotes a family atmosphere in the sense that the class replicates siblings with a stratification of ages, which is much more natural than a class of children all the same age. This diversity in ages offers the younger children role models, with older children to look up to and learn from their example. The youngest children's learning is scaffolded by the nurturing assistance that they receive from the older children. The older children benefit from this design as well. They gain an attitude of caring and responsibility and improve social cognitive skills. There is much beauty in watching a child begin as the youngest, attempting to imitate the actions of the older children, and progress over 3 years to become one of the oldest, looking out for and nurturing the younger children.

Establishing Rhythm and Routine. The rhythm and routine that are an integral part of the Waldorf kindergarten also serve to foster a sense of community. Teachers take it upon themselves to establish routines that are repeated daily, weekly, seasonally and yearly. There is a rhythm to each day that involves a balance of time spent "breathing in" and "breathing out." These times offer children experience with both self-expression and communal moments. There is a rhythm to each week, with Monday designated as "bread-baking day" and Tuesday as "vegetable soup day" and each other day of the week with its own identity that the children come to recognize and depend upon. It is this predictability that lifts children's anxieties and builds their trust in their social worlds and trust in the teachers. Children feel safe and secure in the community of their classroom—they know they can trust in what they will find there.

Teaching to Enhance Development and Learning

Underlying the very premise of Waldorf education is a profound respect for childhood. Sally Jenkinson, a former Waldorf kindergarten teacher, expresses Steiner's beliefs beautifully: "[W]hat remains constant (in Waldorf education) is a deeply held belief that childhood matters; that the early years are not a phase of life to be rushed through, but constitute a stage of tremendous importance needing to be experienced fully in its own right" (Oldfield, 2001, p. xvii). There are three feelings regarding early childhood education that Waldorf teachers espouse: reverence, enthusiasm, and protection. These three words demonstrate how Waldorf teachers respect and value the children that they work with daily.

Reverence, Enthusiasm, and Protection. *Reverence* can be described as the attitude of a teacher toward a child. Steiner speaks of the first 7 years of a child's life as critical. The child is very impressionable, absorbing stimuli from the environment through all senses and experiencing it with the whole body, making it vital for the teacher to provide beneficial stimuli. When a teacher approaches a child with reverence, caution should be taken to speak clearly so as not to confuse the child, to be worthy of imitation, and to allow the child to proceed at his or her own pace, recognizing that it is the quality of development, not the speed, that is important.

Recognizing that the art of teaching presents many challenges, Steiner urges that those persons called to teach must accept their role with *enthusiasm*. Not every person's nature includes being a teacher, but those who choose this career should be truly dedicated and enthusiastic about the responsibility that they are undertaking. This will translate to the child, who senses a teacher's enthusiasm and cannot help but to get caught up in it. It is that true spirit of childhood—the sense of wonder, the inquisitive nature, the naivete—that affords a child the ability to explore the world with such excitement and awe.

The third duty of the teacher is *protection* of all children in their care, physically, emotionally, socially, and psychologically. The Waldorf early childhood classroom is a sanctuary from all that works against the healthy development of young children. The teacher provides a stress-free environment with a slow, calming pace that allows children to take the time to build the foundation that will support their future learning. Children do not feel the pressure of standards, testing, or the necessity to read but enjoy rich literacy experiences that call on their imagination to take them to fairy-tale lands of elves and gnomes. They are protected from the fast-paced, overstimulating bombardment of images from television and computer games. Instead, they dig in the earth under a tree fragrant with apple blossoms and discover the purpose in a worm's slow deliberate movement. In addition, the food that children in a Waldorf kindergarten eat is free from processing, free from pesticides and insecticides, and free from genetic alteration. It is natural and pure, promoting a healthy physical constitution.

Providing an Engaging and Responsive Environment. Teaching to enhance development and learning requires that teachers create an engaging and responsive environment. In a Waldorf classroom this takes many forms. The aesthetic beauty and welcoming feeling of warmth discussed previously is one important component. Another is the toys and materials that teachers make available to children. Waldorf kindergartens are full of materials that invite young hands and minds to touch, manipulate, create, and imagine. Baskets of natural items, such as sticks, seashells, and moss, are arranged in areas where children will incorporate them into their play. Wooden stands will be pulled out and draped with play cloths made of natural fibers, such as cotton or silk. These may be arranged in a variety of formations by the children, creating houses, stores, spaceships, or stages. Toys are handcrafted from wood in various forms that inspire creativity, unlike commercial toys marketed today for young children that have but one purpose and are often so realistic that they leave nothing for the child to add to the experience. Such commercial toys will not be found in a Waldorf classroom. Instead, you find children having a particular wooden toy for a phone one day, and then upon desire or necessity it will be transformed into an airplane on another. This perspective on toys affords children the luxury of open-ended thinking. They learn that the possibilities are endless, rather than learning that there is one correct way to do something.

Children's Connection with Sensory Experiences. Another aspect of the environment of the classroom concerns Steiner's belief that young children are "wholly sense organs," meaning that young children are inextricably connected with their sensory experiences. A child is "united with sensation, and therefore deeply affected by what it conveys, and her psychological development is influenced by the immediate surroundings" (Oldfield, 2001, pp. 101–102). The natural materials in a Waldorf classroom—the lightly colored walls, the soft play cloths, the rich watercolor paints, the smell of the bread baking and the rhythm of hands clapping in ring time—all provide sensory stimulation without creating sensory overload. Due to children's vulnerability to the environment and all that takes place within it, Waldorf educators take great responsibility in providing worthy sensory experiences.

Also important to consider is the quantity of sensory experiences that children encounter daily. Waldorf again seeks to protect its children from the bombardment of images, smells, sounds, tastes, and touches afforded by our fast-paced, thrill-seeking society. Children can become overstimulated by factors in their environment, and their body reacts by shutting down. They may withdraw, manifesting a zombie-like trance, such as fixating on the stimulus or looking off into space (Healy, 1999). The child also may react by losing self-control and acting out in socially unacceptable ways. Waldorf education with its calming natural environment is an antidote to the excitability that children so easily internalize.

Collaborating with Peers. Collaborating with peers is another essential part of healthy development and learning that Waldorf teachers foster in the kindergarten. Teachers provide many opportunities for children to work and play together. When children choose to imitate a teacher's work, perhaps kneading dough for the morning bread baking, they often join together with peers in this united purpose. From the youngest ages, children are working side by side kneading their own piece of dough while enjoying the comfort of a common activity. Older children learn the give and take of working together, perhaps taking turns or assigning

Waldorf green spaces and gardens nurture serenity, free thinkers, and the creative impulse.

"jobs." These events and opportunities widen and deepen children's social and emotional experiences, thereby enriching their development.

Learning Through Doing. Waldorf teachers do not employ direct instruction as a teaching method in the kindergarten classroom, as they find it counterproductive to require this form of child participation. Rather, Waldorf teachers encourage the children in self-discovery. When children choose to engage in imitation or play, they will do it wholeheartedly and gain much more than if they had been coerced. Steiner promotes the idea that children learn from doing, and whether they do it correctly or incorrectly, they still receive valuable information. The teacher's role, then, is to ensure that there are plenty of opportunities throughout the day for children to *do*.

Natural environments and materials are valued highly in Waldorf programs.

Responsibility and Self-Regulation. One of the foremost goals of the Waldorf early childhood curriculum is to help children develop a sense of responsibility and self-regulation. Steiner gives much attention to this topic in his lectures and writings. Again, this is one reason why children are not forced to participate in any activity but are given the freedom to choose their own activities. By having choices to make, young children can begin to exercise their own self-control.

An important part of this approach is recognizing that this development of responsibility and self-regulation is a process. For this to happen, children need sufficient time, space, and opportunity to practice making choices and exerting independence and interdependence under careful adult supervision and guidance. Because young children have limited self-control, teachers set goals that are reasonable for their level of development and allow for approximation of meeting these goals. Moreover, with imitation as a valuable teaching tool, Waldorf teachers can gradually guide their young children through this transformation. A sense of self-regulation, as well as group-regulation, "involves the development of self control of movement, *i.e.* also knowing when *not* to move—for example, holding back inappropriate behavior" (Oldfield, 2001, p. 56). Lynne Oldfield also offers a beautiful vignette to illustrate this concept:

One morning at snack-time, a mixed age group (3–6 years) was gathered around a table. On one side was seated a group of three and four year olds. One boy accidentally fell off his chair and then began to hit his chair, saying "Silly, silly, chair!" Immediately, all the other three and four year olds threw themselves on the floor and began banging their chairs, with a great deal of laughter. Across the table, seated next to the teacher (their favorite spot since they had turned six) were two girls. One said "I want to fall off my chair, but I won't," and her friend replied, "So do I. But I won't either!" (2001, p. 57)

Constructing Appropriate Curriculum

The Waldorf early childhood curriculum is designed to educate the whole child: "the head, the heart and the hands" (Easton, 1997). It speaks to the development of the social, emotional, spiritual, moral, physical, and intellectual aspects of each individual child. It nurtures these important elements of the human being through a curriculum that seems very simple on the surface, yet in reality is amazingly complex.

Nurturing the Whole Child—"Head, Heart and Hands." The curriculum can be described by just a few activities, but the depth that they reach requires lengthy discourse. A typical kindergarten day is marked by the rhythm of familiar activities, alternating between "breathing out" (a time of self-expression) and "breathing in" (a time of quieter, teacher-led reflection).

The morning begins with a full hour of uninterrupted time in which children are free to choose their activities. They can be found caught up in artistic endeavors, imitating the teacher as they prepare the snack, or swept away in a playful adventure that is only bounded by their own imaginations. This time allows for all manner of developmental growth, from practicing social skills in a "restaurant" to learning the fundamentals of engineering by making a suspension bridge with the blocks. Yet the freedom of play alleviates any pressure for performance and gives wings to children's sense of self-direction. And, singing a familiar song or verse, the teacher gently signals the transition from this activity to the next, which is ring time.

Transition periods themselves are important parts of the curriculum. As the teacher carefully and deliberately places the art supplies back in their rightful spots and washes the bowls and spoons used to prepare the snack, for instance, the children can absorb the teacher's sense of reverence and imitate the teacher's purposefulness. With the room returned to order, all gather together in a circle or ring.

Children knit stockings to hold flutes they play in school orchestra and music class.

James E. Johnson

Ring time is one part of the daily schedule when the children participate as a large group with the teacher directing their activity. They often begin with a morning verse, repeated daily to allow even the youngest children to pick up the language and rhythm with which it is recited. Ring time may involve movement, songs, poems, or finger plays and is a dynamic, yet predictable, time of the morning when the children direct their learning inward as they enjoy the sense of community that comes from participating in a group.

Next the teacher leads the group outside, where the children are free to explore the natural world. They revel in the changing seasons, comfortable with the pleasures each one affords. Out of doors their senses are stimulated—the colors of the changing fall leaves, the smell of fresh-cut grass, the feel of mud between their toes, and the taste of sweet snowflakes on their tongues. Again they will play and imitate as they busy themselves.

When children return to the classroom, they will wash themselves and settle at the small tables and chairs for a snack. The teacher will light a candle, and they will join together in a poem of gratitude. The snack that they helped to prepare will be served, and they will enjoy each other's company as they nourish their bodies. They transition easily from snack to the circle again for the culmination of their morning together. It is at this time that they engage their fullest mental capacities as they visualize the story that the teacher presents to them. The teacher does not read from a book, but tells the story, being careful to include a rich vocabulary of imagery, assisting the young children in painting pictures in their minds. At the end of the story, the children will gather their things and leave the kindergarten with fairytale creatures dancing in their minds. This seemingly simple curriculum incorporates much content.

Enhancing Holistic Development. Waldorf strives to develop the whole child—not just intellectual capacities but a balance among all faculties.

Social development is stimulated and practiced through imaginative play. Conflicts arise and children must work through them and find a solution. The give and take of social discourse is learned also during snack time, as the children converse with one another.

Emotional development is supported in the close personal relationship that each child develops with the teacher, and through friendships that the child builds with peers. The child learns to gain greater control of emotions with development as it occurs in an environment that is safe, secure and free of stress. The child plays out situations and role plays various emotions, internalizing appropriate actions to accompany feelings. It is also through the arts that the child cultivates knowledge of feelings. The entire Waldorf early childhood curriculum is infused with an artistic element. From the design and decoration of the classroom to the art experiences offered, the child learns to feel the colors and shapes. The child learns that art is a form of expressing what is inside.

Spiritual development is fostered through imitation of the teacher's reverence for childhood, nature, the materials in the classroom, and the food eaten for snack. It is also learned through the sense of gratitude that permeates each aspect of the day. "Indeed, fortunate is the child who can thus imitate the very gestures and language of gratitude, thereby learning from early years to turn his attention to the source of the many and varied gifts of life, instead of concentrating on his own wants" (Pusch, 1993, p. 28). Steiner wrote often of the spiritual nature of children and the responsibility that adults have to respect and nurture this element of the child's development. Spiritual development manifests itself as social responsibility and concern for the world; the foundation for both of these concepts is laid in the community of the Waldorf kindergarten classroom.

The importance of self-regulation has been discussed previously: Children need to learn how to control their behavior and to make good decisions. Waldorf education is designed to lay these foundations for *moral development*. "If the goal is responsibility, inner discipline, the willingness to do one's share, and eventually the ability to give oneself direction and purpose in life, the soil for this blossoming will have to be prepared early in life" (Pusch, 1993, p. 27).

Physical development is nurtured through movement. Waldorf teachers recognize that young children learn through movement about spatial relationships, and they internalize the essence of whatever they touch and move. Children are very active, and Waldorf teachers support this high level of activity throughout the morning. Significant amounts of time spent outdoors encourage large muscle movement and development, while the many artistic projects encourage fine motor skills.

Intellectual development comes not from direct instruction but through self-regulated discovery and imitation. Young children should be building a love of learning that will inspire them to continue to seek knowledge throughout their lives. Best accomplished by respecting a child's own pace and in anticipation of subsequent stages of development and education, teachers provide an enriching, stimulating environment that offers many opportunities for children to build a strong foundation.

Incorporating a Wide Variety of Disciplines. Through the Waldorf curriculum of play, imitation, art, and stories, children also gain experience in a wide variety of disciplines. Many schools are struggling today to develop integrated curricula. Often teachers identify with their disciplines. Waldorf teachers, on the other hand, have always taught math, science, literature, the arts, and so on as part of an organized whole. The foundations for literacy and numeracy, for instance, are laid through everyday experiences such as puppet shows and setting the table for snack time. Science-related concepts are an inherent part of many activities, including cooking, with the tasks of chopping, measuring, pouring, and weighing. Problem-solving skills and divergent thinking are instilled through the use of simple open-framework toys that leave much to the imagination.

Maintaining Intellectual Integrity. A key component of the curriculum is intellectual integrity, which Steiner considered very important. Because young children imitate the actions of those around them, the teacher must provide actions that are worthy of imitation. The teacher models everyday tasks necessary for the care of the school and home, including mending and cleaning, cooking and washing. These are all valuable, purposeful tasks worthy of imitation. With the decline of family farms and the trends of city living, fewer children have quality model behaviors to imitate. They need real-life experiences, activities that foster a sense of satisfaction for a job well done.

Embracing Diversity. Waldorf education can be viewed as a model multicultural program since it easily adapts to the cultures and heritage of the children and community that it serves. Persons not familiar with Waldorf often have a difficult time understanding this, especially when they confuse Waldorf education with its Christian roots. In fact, the worldview or philosophy of anthroposophy, which guides Waldorf education, is not a religion at all. Anthroposophy promotes the idea that all human beings have a spiritual core, and it maintains harmony with many world religions and philosophies, while eschewing the tenets of a religion. Anthroposophy per se is not taught in Waldorf education, but its influence can be seen in the curriculum and festivals. Many of the festivals are based around religious holidays—but not just Christian ones. Waldorf teachers are careful to delve "into diverse world cultures with as much reverence and depth as possible" (Ward, 2001, p. 3). The purpose of Waldorf education is to provide children with an "education toward freedom," which is why the goal is to help children develop strong independent judgment. Rudolf Steiner believed that the best way to accomplish this is to expose children to a wide variety of world religions and the values and traditions that they espouse. So the answer to the question "Is Waldorf education Christian?" is "no." This answer is based on the understanding that although stories from both the Old and New Testaments are introduced to children, and some plays and festivals are centered around biblical events, such experiences form only one set of influences in their studies of world cultures and religious traditions:

> A more relevant and revealing approach is to ask: What image of the human being do the Waldorf schools seek to bring to the children as a model and inspiration? Here the answer is unequivocal. It is an image of the human being as loving, compassionate, reverent, respectful, engaged, tolerant, peaceful, joyful, patient, good, upright, wise, balanced, in harmony with the cosmos, nature and humanity. No religion or code of ethics can arrogate these fundamental and universal values as its unique possession. (Ward, 2001, p. 3)

Numerous Waldorf schools are in countries all over the world. Each one is unique in its culture, language, and materials, but each one upholds Rudolf Steiner's ideals. Tina Bruinsma, a teacher from Amsterdam supporting the Sloka, India, initiative, writes:

> The Waldorf curriculum brings meaning to education. In an Indian context it can de-Anglicize the curriculum and promote the dignity of labour. Teachers and children come to the school with thirteen different mother tongues and seven different religions, and yet this form of education can embrace this diversity. In a country where education has come to mean merely performance, memory and competition bordering on rivalry, a Waldorf school brings with it the deeper meaning behind education. (Oldfield, 2001, p. 28)

Ann Sharfmann, teacher trainer, Centre for Creative Education, Cape Town, South Africa, writes:

> Our work is to prove that Waldorf education can happen in less affluent circumstances, such as the South African township environment. And it does, and it works! Definitely not at all like the European Waldorf kindergarten model, and definitely not yet at all as we want it to be. But we are making a difference in our own small way and we are being noticed. (Oldfield, 2001, p. 21)

Introducing play kits of dolls, puppets, blocks and other materials gradually allowed the children to enter different play worlds and experience their childhood in a new way. Ann Sharfmann continues:

> In some classes, where the children have a daily ring time, stories, puppets and the opportunity to draw, model, paint, the difference is astonishing. (Oldfield, 2001, p. 21)

The Waldorf curriculum, by its very nature, embraces diversity and creates a caring community.

ASSESSING CHILDREN'S LEARNING

The purpose of the Waldorf ECE curriculum is neither to teach basic academics and test-taking skills nor to help prepare students to meet government-declared "standards" for various ages and stages or grade levels. In fact, standardized testing is not part of Waldorf education at any grade level. It is interesting to note, however, that many Waldorf graduates do pursue a college education and have performed well enough on the Scholastic Aptitude Test (SAT) to gain acceptance at such highly esteemed universities as Harvard and Yale (Oppenheimer, 1999). In fact, a recent survey based on the responses of about 550 Waldorf high school graduates in the United States and Canada and published by the Research Institute for Waldorf Education discovered that "94% of the graduates taking part in this survey reported having attended college" (Gerwin & Mitchell, 2007).

Assessment is necessary even in the kindergarten to ensure that students are meeting the objectives of the curriculum. Waldorf teachers are very aware of the developmental progress of each of their individual students. So why and how do they achieve this without using conventional methods of assessment? The answer follows.

The purpose of Waldorf education is to foster in children a sense of individuality, self-esteem, and wholeness. Each day includes rich opportunities to develop all aspects of growth and learning—social, emotional, spiritual, psychological, physical, and cognitive. Children learn through art and music and movement and exploration and experience, through rhythm and routine and gratitude and beauty. Children learn to respect one another and to find their strength in community, not competition. Traditional methods of assessment pit one child against another and create stress and feelings of self-doubt. Steiner wrote that each child is filled with potential, it is simply a matter of giving every child a nurturing environment and the freedom to unfold at one's own pace. This is what is meant by respecting childhood. Waldorf teachers exhibit the patience of gardeners, taking a long view of education. They believe that when the seeds of learning are sown in fertile soil and tender shoots emerge, there will be a rich harvest when all bears fruit at the end of a long growing season (Petrash, 2002).

So many early childhood programs do not appreciate this process and rush children into learning for which they are not ready. Steiner warned against this:

> Even though it is necessary in modern civilization for people to be completely awake or "heads up" later in life, it is just as necessary to allow children to live in their gently dreamy experiences as long as possible so that they grow slowly into adult life. They need to remain in their imaginations, in their pictorial capacities without intellectualism, for as long as possible. The assumption is that if you allow the child to be strengthened without intellectualism, children will later grow into the necessary intellectualism in the proper way. If you do not you may ruin the person's soul for the remainder of life. (Trostli, 1998)

Waldorf education is based on the understanding that it is important for a child to develop a strong foundation and a love of learning as a prerequisite to developing necessary academic skills, which will come later when a child is ready.

In light of this perspective, assessment of young children is approached very differently by Waldorf teachers. Rather than pressure students to meet predetermined standards of learning, teachers use Steiner's theory of child development as a guideline and adjust curriculum and instruction to the pace of each individual child. They focus on the whole child, on individual areas of strength and weakness, with the purpose of helping the child to develop into a well-balanced human being with a love of learning that will act as a motivator and guide throughout life. Waldorf kindergarten teachers gather information about each student's development and learning, but discreetly so as not to pressure the child. Teachers begin with perhaps their most valuable resource—parents. Parents are employed to give insight into the child's home life and experiences; the teacher will visit the child at home before the first day of kindergarten.

Classroom observation is perhaps the most frequently used tool to keep track of children's growth. ECE teachers are especially concerned with all areas of development and can learn much by simply observing a child during imaginative play. Insights into social development are apparent through interactions with other children. Play offers information about cognitive development and socioemotional well-being. In fact, it could be argued that true imaginative play is a window into the child's developmental state and well-being.

Once gathered from many sources and many situations, teachers utilize *assessment data* not to grade or scale the students but simply to develop a deeper understanding of the child so as to best facilitate development and learning in the classroom. Even in the upper grades, most Waldorf schools hold off giving letter grades as long as possible. Teachers take a more holistic, formative, and interpersonal approach to assessment. One teacher was observed to write a poem and draw a picture about each of her students at least once a year as part of her strategy of assessment. This method allowed the teacher to express creatively some of the traits that she was observing in her students and to encourage the development of other aspects of their characters. This type of assessment serves to provide important educational information in a meaningful manner while encouraging a personal intimacy between the teacher and student (Uhrmacher, 2007).

ESTABLISHING RELATIONSHIPS WITH FAMILIES

Waldorf education is so integrally entwined with the family that the two cannot be separated. Waldorf educators place great value on the role that parents play in their children's lives. Parental involvement and support have primary influence on a child's success, and when combined with a school's influence that promotes this dynamic, potential is tremendous. Teachers need the support of the parents; the parents need the support of the teachers. Education is seen as a partnership, with both parties working together to further the natural and holistic development of the child.

Developing a sense of community is an important goal of Waldorf education. For this reason many Waldorf schools offer informational sessions for prospective parents. Parents are encouraged to learn how Waldorf schools approach education. They learn some fundamentals, receive applications, and then are invited to ask questions. This is often the beginning of a relationship of mutual respect between teachers and parents.

Given the deep reverence that Waldorf holds for the parental role, teachers naturally make every effort to further their connection with parents, to work together with them to develop goals for each individual child's learning, to share a sense of responsibility for the child's growth and development, and to strive for consistency between the home and school environments. This can only truly be accomplished through the continual communication between parent and teacher that is fostered by the welcoming nature of the Waldorf kindergarten. Frequent seasonal celebrations, parent education opportunities, and other events allow ample opportunity for parents and teachers to build their relationships and to share ideas and information within the community of the Waldorf school (Oldfield, 2001).

Waldorf education holds high standards for parents, the reason being that much of a young child's learning occurs in the context of the home environment. With only part of the day spent in the kindergarten, parents are responsible to see that the important aspects of development are encouraged at home. Taking care to acknowledge parents' goals and choices for their children, Waldorf teachers also find themselves educating parents about Waldorf's goals for their students. An example that lends itself well to this topic is the issue of television. In the first stage of child development, from birth to 7 years of age, children learn best by doing, so they need ample time to move—run, jump, dig, climb, and explore. Critical also is protection from potentially harmful environmental influences. For these reasons, Waldorf educators encourage parents to limit their child's time spent in front of the television in favor of more appropriate activities that promote healthy development. Teachers also find that observing the parents and child at home is helpful, and this usually can be arranged.

As a matter of policy, Waldorf teachers make home visits before the first day of school to gain a sense of the environment that had been provided for the child as an infant, toddler, and preschooler and to learn what sources of imitation were made available to the child; this can provide much insight into the child's development. Being aware of the child's home life is considered just as important to teaching as being aware about what is done in the classroom (Trostli, 1998).

WALDORF AND OTHER APPROACHES

The Waldorf approach to early education seems to possess certain distinct appeals and, arguably, compares very favorably with other well-known models. Certainly Waldorf has a great deal in common with developmentally appropriate practices (DAP) as set forth by the National Association for the Education of Young Children (NAEYC) (Bredekamp & Copple, 1997). In Table 15–1 we compare in summary form the DAP guidelines with Waldorf early childhood education. Waldorf's approach contains features that qualify it as falling under the DAP orientation to the education of young children in all five categories: (1) creating a caring community of learners; (2) teaching to enhance development and learning; (3) constructing appropriate curriculum; (4) assessing children's learning and development; and (5) establishing reciprocal relationships with families.

Although in general correspondence is good between DAP and Waldorf under the five categories of program characteristics discussed in this chapter, DAP guidelines would appear to recommend a more differentiated approach to assessment than what is offered in Waldorf's nontraditional approach to assessment. An even more glaring discrepancy is found within the dimension of constructing appropriate curriculum, where DAP recommends or at least acknowledges the use of technology and urges its integration into a program. Indeed, mainstream ECE today recognizes the need to prepare future techno-citizens of the 21st century and has computers in programs for young children. Waldorf bucks this trend. Computers, to be sure, are part of Waldorf education but only with children and adolescents well past the early childhood years.

TABLE 15–1
Comparison of DAP Guidelines and Waldorf Education

DAP Guidelines	Waldorf Education
1. Creating a Caring Community of Learners • The setting functions as a community of learners. • Consistent, positive relationships with adults and children further healthy development. • Social relationships are an important context for learning. • A safe and stress-free environment promotes community. • Children thrive on organization and routine.	**Waldorf Aspects of Community** • Children's sensitivity to the environment • The importance of imitation and play • Benefits of mixed-age grouping • Establishing rhythm and routine
2. Teaching to Enhance Development and Learning • Teachers respect and value children. • Teachers make it a priority to know each child well. • Teachers create an intellectually engaging, responsive environment. • Teachers foster collaboration with peers. • Teachers use a wide variety of teaching strategies. • Teachers facilitate the development of responsibility and self-regulation.	**Teaching to Enhance Development and Learning in Waldorf** • Reverence, enthusiasm, and protection • Respecting and valuing children • Providing an engaging and responsive environment • Children's connection with sensory experiences • Collaborating with peers • Children learning through doing • Responsibility and self-regulation
3. Constructing Appropriate Curriculum • Curriculum provides for all areas of development. • Curriculum includes a broad range of content across disciplines. • Curriculum builds upon what children already know and are able to do. • Curriculum integrates across subjects briefly. • Curriculum promotes the development of knowledge, understanding, processes, and skills. • Curriculum content has intellectual integrity. • Curriculum provides opportunities to support children's home culture and language. • The curriculum goals are realistic and attainable. • Technology is physically and philosophically integrated, when utilized.	**Constructing Appropriate Curriculum in Waldorf** • Nurtures the whole child: head, heart, hands 1. Emotional 2. Spiritual 3. Moral 4. Physical 5. Intellectual • Incorporates a wide variety of disciplines • Maintains intellectual integrity • Embraces diversity

DAP Guidelines	Waldorf Education
4. Assessing Children's Learning and Development • Assessment is ongoing, strategic, and purposeful. • The content of assessments reflects progress toward important learning goals. • Methods of assessment are appropriate to the age and experience of young children. • Assessment is tailored to a specific purpose. • Decisions are never made based on a single assessment device. • Developmental assessments are used to identify needs and plan accordingly. • Assessment recognizes individual variation and allows for differences.	**Assessing Children's Learning and Development in Waldorf** • Nontraditional approach to assessment • Freedom to unfold at own pace • Assessment of each child as an individual • Observation to gain insights into child's development
5. Establishing Reciprocal Relationships with Families • Reciprocal relationships require mutual respect. • It is important to establish and maintain regular, frequent, two-way communication. • Parents are welcome in the program and participate in decisions about their child. • Teachers acknowledge parents' choices and goals for their children. • Teachers and parents share knowledge of the child. • The program involves families in assessing and planning for individual children. • The program links families with a range of services. • Developmental information about a child is shared among all with educational responsibility for that child.	**Establishing Reciprocal Relationships with Families in Waldorf** • Parents welcomed at school from the beginning • Communication as a key element • Parents' role in child's development seen as critical • Promotes a community of families

Nevertheless, Waldorf early childhood education has many redeeming virtues. The case can be made that Waldorf contributes to cognitive and social competence, even school readiness. Of course, school readiness would not be a priority in Waldorf ECE given its devotion to the integrity of childhood and the fact that children tend to stay in Waldorf throughout their school careers. Especially commendable, it would appear, is Waldorf's use of projects similar to Reggio

Emilia and the Project Approach (see Chapters 13 and 14). Children in Waldorf ECE have a full hour of indoor and outdoor freedom to engage in fruitful learning encounters that usually take the form of long-term investigative activity. Moreover, like the Spectrum Approach (see Chapter 11), a multitude of diverse activities available in the curriculum stimulate various budding talent areas in young children, consistent with the notion of multiple intelligences. These program features can serve to enrich intellectual and social-emotional development in children by providing an engaging learning environment that fosters positive dispositions and work habits.

How Does Waldorf Approach Special Education?

With respect to the area of special education, you may be curious about the way in which Waldorf education approaches this sensitive, but increasingly important, topic. Intriguingly, Rudolf Steiner called it by a different name altogether: *curative education.* The very name suggests a novel way of thinking about the education of children with special needs. The attitude toward these children is one of respect with the recognition that each person, whatever the disability, has something to contribute to society.

> In curative education, an essential view is that a child's spiritual integrity remains intact regardless of the nature and severity of a disability that may be physical, sensory, mental, emotional or social, or a combination of any of these. The special child is viewed as in need of special soul care and the children are helped to cope with and overcome their disabilities in a carefully designed therapeutic setting in which their diverse and unique developmental, educational, and therapeutic needs can be met. (Juul & Maier, 1992, p. 212)

Teachers work with these children "in need of special care" in residential schools or villages designed to create a humanistic and holistic environment. These communities cater to the needs of their members, in an attempt to reach the whole child: head, heart, and hands. Teachers teach children in an integrated setting, working to achieve a balance within each child that will enable them to develop their abilities and work to overcome their disabilities. The curriculum is similar to that of a traditional Waldorf school but also includes therapeutic art activities, adaptive physical procedures, vocational training, and occupational experiences (Juul & Maier, 1992).

Waldorf ECE has been popular in the United States for affluent families with children with disabilities, as well as for children born into deprived circumstances worldwide. Waldorf ECE is nondenominational, holistic, and based on a deep respect for children as people and a profound understanding of human development and worth. There would appear to be something *intrinsically therapeutic* about Waldorf ECE, with its homelike physical features (curtains, carpets, subdued lights and colors, simple and natural furniture, etc.), its emphasis on creative play and artistic expression, with its delicate order and reassuring rhythmical nature. Accordingly, Waldorf seems ideally suited for children experiencing anxiety and stress-related symptoms, such as refugee children who have lived in refugee camps, grown up in slums and poverty, or lived through conflicts rife with violence or war. Waldorf ECE reaches out to these children (Oldfield, 2001).

Criticisms of Waldorf Education

So far, we have highlighted the strengths and benefits of Waldorf education, but all models of education have critics. Thus we ask, what is being criticized about Waldorf? Certainly one can criticize Waldorf ECE for its neglect of technology. Others may see limitations in the way Waldorf views early literacy learning goals, or its laid-back approach to reading, or its nonchalant stance concerning assessment. These are valid concerns. However, other valid or less-than-valid objections to Waldorf have also been advanced.

An organization named People for Legal and Nonsectarian Schools (PLANS) has created a Web site (http://www.waldorfcritics.org) that offers critics and "survivors" (of Waldorf schools) a forum to voice their opposition to Waldorf education. From the information available on this Web site, it is apparent that this group has very strong opinions about the Waldorf approach and that it is very outspoken in its concerns. Three major criticisms of Waldorf education seem to continually surface on the PLANS Web site: (1) Waldorf schools are religious schools, (2) Waldorf curriculum is based on Steiner's anthroposophical theories, and (3) Waldorf schools do not inform parents of their philosophy or ties to anthroposophy.

The first complaint relates to the recent movement of Waldorf schools into the public school sector. "Waldorf-inspired" public and charter schools in the United States, critics feel, are a violation of the separation of church and state laws. PLANS members argue that the religion of anthroposophy and Rudolf Steiner's spiritual beliefs are inseparable from Waldorf education and that any re-creation of Waldorf methodology in the public sector retains its anthroposophic roots and therefore is not acceptable. One example noted that changes being made to festivals celebrated in public Waldorf-inspired schools in an attempt to remove the religious nature are only acting on the surface, leading them to believe that the same "spiritually-based" rituals are being performed under different names.

Another issue is the influence of anthroposophy on the curriculum as children are introduced to theories of history and science. Anthroposophy promotes some nontraditional ideas about the functions of the body's organs, reincarnation, karma, and historical events, to name a few. PLANS claims that this is "pseudoscience" in Waldorf education: "crazy" anthroposophical ideas infiltrating the classroom. Proponents of Waldorf, however, hold the position that teachers study anthroposophy but do not teach it in the classroom.

Still another concern is that some parents are generally unaware of the philosophical beliefs surrounding Waldorf education, even intentionally kept in the dark by teachers who were unwilling to offer clear answers to their questions. The PLANS Web site (2008) also contends the following:

> A huge amount of literature about Waldorf education has been produced within the closed system of Anthroposophy. Much of the available information fails to describe the spiritual mission of the Waldorf school system honestly. We have found that even experienced parents of Waldorf students usually know little about the Anthroposophical principles that determine the teaching methods and the Anthroposophical doctrine that permeates the curriculum.

As a rejoinder, parents who choose not to send their child to a public school have the responsibility of educating themselves about the philosophy of the school that they decide upon for their child. Being informed about what a chosen school believes and how and what it teaches is the parents' responsibility. Parents can research on the Web and find a great deal of information, observe in the classrooms, and talk with numerous teachers before the child is enrolled, limiting the chance of surprises later.

Can Waldorf Education Be Replicated in Public Schools?

This question is an important one to address with the popularity of this movement currently on the rise. With increasing attention on Waldorf education in the United States, many new initiatives have been undertaken for Waldorf-inspired elementary school programs. Bruce Uhrmacher, an education professor at the University of Denver, has written a very informative article on the topic of borrowing ideas from alternative education. He offers two important factors to consider when making a decision about using an idea from another model or approach to education: recognizing where ideas come from and reflecting on where ideas go (Uhrmacher, 1993, 1997).

First, the teacher must consider the context or framework from which to borrow and how that idea fits within that context. An example from Waldorf early childhood education might be the idea of providing a full hour of imaginative playtime at the beginning of the day. A teacher wishing to borrow this strategy and implement it in the classroom must understand the philosophy behind its use in the Waldorf approach. The teacher must understand that Waldorf values childhood and sees imaginative play as one of the most important expressions of childhood. True play to Waldorf teachers means giving children the freedom to be self-directed, allowing their inner thoughts and ideas to manifest in truly creative ways. A teacher who does not recognize this may apply this concept in an inappropriate manner, perhaps by interrupting the children's play in an attempt to encourage teacher-directed learning, such as asking children to explain what they are doing or to describe the colors they are using when building with the blocks. In the eyes of a Waldorf teacher, this draws the children out of their play experiences and undermines the importance of what they are doing.

According to Uhrmacher (1997), it is also important for a teacher who is considering borrowing an idea to anticipate how the application of this new idea will affect the current curriculum. With any change to an established routine, disruptions may certainly be experienced. The teacher must carefully reflect upon how this new idea will fit with personal philosophy, and even the administration under which the program functions. Will the teacher have to compensate elsewhere to balance this new addition? These are all important considerations and must be thoroughly addressed in advance. There is much debate about taking ideas from a particular approach to education and transplanting them in other programs. Some people feel that borrowing, when done properly, can be helpful and beneficial. Others feel that borrowing will always remove ideas from their intended context and cause inappropriate application.

In terms of Waldorf education, even Waldorf teachers are divided on this issue. Many feel that a Waldorf education has much to offer. If their particular methods of teaching are working for children, then why not encourage the widespread use of those methods, even if it means taking them outside of the Waldorf schools. On the other hand, many other Waldorf educators feel that these ideas will lose their meaning, and therefore their inherent value, when taken out of the context of the Waldorf schools. Teaching ideas based on Steiner's principles of child development are closely tied to the tenets of anthroposophy. Teachers fear that without this contextual framework the ideas will not hold the same purpose or benefit to students. The strong spiritual aspect of Waldorf makes the transition to public schools nearly impossible because of the separation of church and state. Is Steinerian education without the spiritual aspect? Waldorf educators take varying stances on this hotly debated issue.

Nevertheless, many success stories exist regarding Waldorf-inspired public school programs in the United States. One is the Urban Waldorf School of Milwaukee, Wisconsin, opened in 1991 as the first public school to attempt to adapt Waldorf pedagogy as an effective model. Three years after it began, the program was evaluated by seven non-Waldorf affiliated educational researchers (Easton, 1997). The researchers found the school to be successful in providing a safe, warm educational environment for the inner-city children who were attending. Standardized test scores had risen dramatically, and there was relatively little evidence of aggression, considering the violent neighborhood, or other negative social behaviors. Teachers working with the children were able to develop meaningful relationships with them, were able to consistently negotiate misbehavior, and were able to help the students develop character and cognitive learning in preparation for good citizenship (Easton). Although this evidence suggests that this school was successful in meeting the needs of its students, questions remain. How well did it apply the Waldorf pedagogy? Was it the Waldorf influence that was responsible for the students' success or were there other factors? Perhaps a Hawthorne effect—a temporary and usually positive change to behavior or performance due to a change in environmental conditions—was operating.

CONCLUSION

Despite its humble beginnings in war-torn Germany, Waldorf has remained timeless in its philosophy and is every bit as dynamic and progressive today as it was in 1919. Waldorf ECE and best practices in ECE as epitomized in the DAP guidelines (Bredekamp & Copple, 1997) are closely aligned. Both seek an appropriate approach to ECE based upon an understanding of child development. Both value the child as an individual and respect the importance of childhood.

Furthermore, we feel that in many ways Waldorf may have even exceeded the standards set forth by the NAEYC, taking basic concepts to new heights through both application and attitude. For instance, while NAEYC addresses the whole child as physical, social, emotional, linguistic, aesthetic, and cognitive, Waldorf takes this wholeness to a deeper level by also considering a child's spiritual and moral development.

Currently, there are more Waldorf kindergartens than Waldorf grade schools in the United States, even though much of the published information tends to focus on Grades 1–12. While having more information on the education of younger children from the Waldorfian perspective would be helpful, having research data from third parties is even more important for a comprehensive and fair analysis of the philosophy and developmental and educational ideas of Waldorf to our field of early childhood care and education. Certainly research needs to be done in this area, and although we do not pretend to cover this topic here, it appears that a new interest is beginning to emerge in the area of empirical research (Gerwin and Mitchell, 2006). Much remains to be learned about Waldorf pedagogy in the early years. It seems an especially promising approach to educating young children, particularly in these troubled times and with the accelerating pace of our lives.

WEB SITES OF INTEREST

Alliance for Childhood
http://www.allianceforchildhood.net

Anthroposophical Society in America
http://www.anthroposophy.org

Association of Waldorf Schools in North America
http://www.awsna.org

European Council for Steiner Education
http://www.steinerwaldorfeurope.org

People for Legal and Nonsectarian Schools (PLANS): Our Concerns About Waldorf Schools
http://www.waldorfcritics.org/active/concerns.html

Rudolf Steiner Archive
http://www.elib.com/Steiner/

Rudolf Steiner College
http://www.steinercollege.org

The Online Waldorf Library
http://www.waldorflibrary.org

The Steiner Books Spiritual Research Center
http://www.steinerbooks.org/research

Waldorf Early Childhood Association of North America
http://www.waldorfearlychildhood.org

Waldorf Homeschooling Sites
http://www.waldorffamilynetwork.com
http://www.waldorfwithoutwalls.com

Waldorf Materials Shopping Sites
http://www.naturalplay.com
http://www.waldorfshop.net

Waldorf World: Waldorf Education on the Web
http://www.waldorfworld.net

Why Waldorf Works: Everything You Need to Know About Waldorf Education
http://www.whywaldorfworks.org

INTERNATIONAL WALDORF SCHOOLS ON THE INTERNET

Federation of Waldorf Schools in Southern Africa (language: English)
http://www.waldorf.org.za

Nairobi Waldorf Schools in Kenya (language: English)
http://www.nairobiwaldorfschool.org

Steiner Schools in Australia (language: English)
http://www.mrss.com.au

Steiner School in Italy (language: Italian)
http://www.rudolfsteiner.it

Steiner Waldorf Schools Fellowship in the United Kingdom and Ireland (language: English)
http://www.steinerwaldorf.org.uk

Swedish Waldorf Schools (language: Swedish)
http://www.waldorf.se

BOOKS RELATED TO WALDORF EDUCATION

Berger, T. (1992). *The harvest craft book.* Edinburgh: Floris Books.

Berger, T., & Berger, P. (1999). *Gnome craft book.* Edinburgh: Floris Books.

Jenkinson, S. (2001). *Genius of play.* Gloucestershire, England: Hawthorn Press.

Leeuwen, M. V., & Moeskops, J. (1990). *Nature corner.* Edinburgh: Floris Books.

Masters, B. (1984). *Waldorf songbook.* Edinburgh: Floris Books.

Nobel, A. (1996). *Educating through art: The Steiner school approach.* Edinburgh: Floris Books.

REFERENCES

Bredekamp, S., & Copple, C. (1997). *Developmentally appropriate practice in early childhood programs* (Rev. ed.). Washington, DC: National Association for the Education of Young Children.

Easton, F. (1997). Educating the whole child, "Head, Heart and Hands": Learning from the Waldorf experience. *Theory into Practice, 36*(2), 87–94.

Edwards, C. (2002). Three approaches from Europe: Waldorf, Montessori, and Reggio Emilia. *Early Childhood Research & Practice, 4*(1). Retrieved April 8, 2008, at http://ecrp.uiuc.edu/v4n1/edwards.html

Gerwin, D., & Mitchell, D. (2006). Report from the co-directors. *Research Bulletin, 11*(2), 3.

Gerwin, D., & Mitchell, D. (2007). Standing out without standing alone: Profile of Waldorf school graduates. *Research Bulletin, 12*(2), 7–16.

Grunelius, E. M. (1991). *Early childhood education and the Waldorf school plan.* Fair Oaks, CA: Rudolf Steiner College Publications.

Healy, J. (1999). *Endangered minds: Why our children can't think and what we can do about it.* New York: Touchstone Books.

Juul, K. D., & Maier, M. (1992). Teacher training in curative education. *Teacher Education and Special Education, 15*(2), 211–218.

Oldfield, L. (2001). *Free to learn: Introducing Steiner Waldorf early childhood education.* Gloucestershire, England: Hawthorn Press.

Oppenheimer, T. (1999). Schooling the imagination. *Atlantic Monthly, 284*(3), 71–83.

People for Legal and Nonsectarian Schools. (2008). Our concerns about Waldorf Schools. Retrieved April 12, 2008, at http://www.waldorfcritics.org/active/concerns.html

Petrash, J. (2002). *Understanding Waldorf education: Teaching from the inside out.* Beltsville, MD: Gryphon House, Inc.

Pusch, R. (Ed.). (1993). *Waldorf schools: Vol. I. Kindergarten and early grades.* Spring Valley, NY: Mercury Press.

Trostli, R. (1998). *Rhythms of learning: Selected lectures by Rudolf Steiner.* New York: Anthroposophic Press.

Uhrmacher, B. P. (1993). Coming to know the world through Waldorf education. *Journal of Curriculum and Supervision, 9*(1), 87–104.

Uhrmacher, B. P. (1997). Evaluating change: Strategies for borrowing from alternative education. *Theory into Practice, 36*(2), 71–78.

Uhrmacher, B. P. (2007). Artful curriculum, evaluation, and instructions: Lessons learned from Rudolf Steiner's spiritually based Waldorf education. In D. Hansen (Ed.), *Ethical visions of education: Philosophies in practice* (pp. 141–156). New York: Teachers College Press.

Ward, W. (2001). Is Waldorf education Christian? *Renewal, 10*(1).

Wilkinson, R. (1996). *The spiritual basis of Steiner education.* London: Steiner Press.

Chapter 16
Montessori Education Today

Martha Torrence ⟿ *Cambridge Montessori School*
John Chattin-McNichols ⟿ *Seattle University*

Maria Montessori (1870–1952) was an extraordinary person by any standard who overcame great difficulties to become one of Italy's first female physicians. Her gift of observation was sharpened by her studies in anthropology, resulting in her first book, *Pedagogical Anthropology* (Montessori, 1913). She also worked with what were then called "defective children" at the state Orthophrenic School in Rome. In her work with this very diverse population, she drew from the work of Jean Itard and Edouard Seguin, French physicians and educators of developmentally disabled children (Loeffler, 1992). In 1907, she was asked to create a program to care for the children of families in a housing project in Rome serving a lower-income population of 4- to 7-year-olds; this was the first Casa dei Bambini, or Children's House.

In the United States, there was a great deal of interest in her methods from 1910 to 1920 (Montessori's program was demonstrated with a model classroom in San Francisco at the 1916 World's Fair), but then Montessori education was all but forgotten in the United States until the late 1950s. Perhaps this happned because parents at the time viewed young children as best cared for at home and because educators had a poor understanding of Montessori.

In the late 1950s, the contemporary American Montessori movement began as a set of private schools serving an almost entirely middle-class population. Many of these early schools were founded by parents. In 1959 the American Montessori Society (AMS) was established. Its founder, Nancy McCormick Rambusch, asserted that not only adoption but also adaptation of Montessori's method were necessary in order for it to be both translated and "naturalized" into the diverse American cultural setting (Rambusch, cited in Loeffler, 1992). A teacher shortage, predicated by the mushrooming number of schools, resulted in the opening of private Montessori teacher training centers, typically freestanding and not associated with a college or university.

The word *Montessori* has been used in the public domain in the United States, and so both schools and teacher education programs proliferated and were licensed without name-brand regulation or restriction. Some schools (then and now) used the name *Montessori* when referring to programs that have little relation to the schools Rambusch described. The AMS, the Association Montessori Internationale (AMI), and a number of other organizations have established criteria as to what constitutes a quality Montessori school. Membership in these organizations is voluntary, and organizational criteria do not apply to state licensing standards.

Beginning in the late 1960s, parents in several school districts, many of whom had graduated from private Montessori preschools, began to advocate for public schools to offer the Montessori model for their children. This push was given a strong boost by the availability of federal funds for magnet programs. Today, more than 350 schools in 150 districts nationwide (Kahn, 1990; Schapiro & Hellen, 2007) offer some form of public Montessori program. These programs serve children from age 3 through high school. The combined total of public and private Montessori schools in the United States is just under 4,000 (Schapiro & Hellen).

KEY TENETS AND BACKGROUND INFORMATION

What are some of the characteristics of a Montessori classroom, then, that differentiate it from a traditional early childhood classroom? What might a visitor to a contemporary Montessori classroom expect to see?

The first thing that an observer might notice is the mixed-age grouping: typically, 3-, 4-, and 5-year-olds are together, as are 6-, 7-, and 8-year-olds, and so on. Another difference is the arrangement of the room, with low, open shelves holding many carefully arranged materials from which the children can choose. Tables and desks are grouped to facilitate individual or small-group work, rather than an arrangement in which furniture is oriented in one direction to facilitate whole-group instruction. Open floor space allows for work on the floor. The amount of shelving needed to hold the required Montessori materials is more than is generally seen in other educational models, with all walls of the classroom typically containing some shelving and shelving extending into the classroom at several points to create bays, or focus areas. The Montessori manipulative materials are designed for use by individual students or small groups, rather than as teacher presentation aids. For example, small globes are provided for children to handle and explore, rather than one big globe provided at the front of the room for teacher-centered instruction.

The single most important criteria for judging a program to be a good implementation of Montessori is the activity of the students. For major portions of their school day—from 3 to 4 hours per day for children attending full-day programs—students should be engaged in individual and small-group work of their own choosing.

Another important aspect of Montessori classrooms is an attitude of cooperation rather than competition in completing work. Students complete work independently and then check responses with the "control" material or ask other children for help. Here students are not perceiving the teacher as the sole source of information in the room.

This availability of a correct answer accompanies a reduced emphasis on conventional forms of testing. There is instead an emphasis on authentic assessment methods, which include portfolios and performance-based assessment and extensive teacher observation. During individual and small-group presentations, students are asked to practice the relevant activities, giving the teacher an immediate opportunity for assessment of the success of that lesson. Ongoing teacher observation of children's work adds to the teacher's cumulative knowledge of their progress. Individual instruction with a given skill or concept is always an option as a result of such observation. Whenever called for, teacher intervention is given in the form of a suggestion, redirecting activity to a different use of the material or toward another material. Even when teachers seem too quick to intervene and redirect, it is appropriate to keep in mind that the richness of the Montessori environment makes it likely that the child will be able to find another activity meeting his or her needs and interests.

Finally, development of individual responsibility is strongly emphasized. For example, children return materials to their place after use, they clean and maintain the classroom, at least in part, and they participate in the development of classroom rules.

Children working together using Montessori materials inventively.

James E. Johnson

The following vignette, taken from an observation of a Montessori environment for 3- to 6-year-olds, offers a glimpse of what a visitor might see on a "typical" day:

9:05 a.m.: Several children are already engaged in individual activities. One is beating soapsuds with an eggbeater, another is placing pegged wooden pieces into a puzzle map of North America, a third is polishing a piece of silver. The teacher stands near the door, quietly greeting new arrivals. As each child enters the room, the teacher gets on his or her eye level and shakes his or her hand, welcoming each by name. Brief conversations with individual children ensue; for example, one child describes in detail the skunk that was in her family's garage the previous evening. The teacher listens and responds, asking detail-provoking questions.

The assistant teacher moves through the room, helping children to initiate individual activities, making suggestions to the hesitant or undecided. Two girls stand near the guinea pig's cage, observing as he nibbles at a fresh carrot. The girls chat about the guinea pig; one then gets a lap board, art paper, and colored pencils and begins to sketch this classroom pet. When finished she labels her picture "ginee pig" and places it in her cubbie.

By 9:15 all the children have arrived, a total of 24. A fairly even mix of 3-, 4-, and 5-year-olds comprises the group. The children move about the room, some engaging in individual pursuits, others uniting in interest groups of twos and threes. One 3-year-old boy has chosen a stack of five sandpaper letters to trace; he asks the teacher to watch as he traces each and pronounces the letter's sound. He spontaneoulsy repeats this activity five times with each letter!

A 4-year-old girl paints on large paper at the easel. She uses the paintbrush to apply paint, then tracks with a roller over the original paint, spreading it and adding texture. A 3-year-old chooses a basket of wooden zoo animals from the language shelf. She says, "This is animal matching," and proceeds to match each animal to its pair. She then names the animals. She accurately names the elephant and rhinoceros, calls the wolf a fox, but later renames it "wolf" when she gets to the actual fox, which she calls an "ant killer."

Two 5-year-olds collaboratively set up the "bank," a large collection of thousand cubes, hundred squares, ten bars, and unit beads, on a mat. Later they will use these quantities to build large numbers in the thousands, which they will match with corresponding numeral cards. One child will be the "banker," the other the "customer."

Two children decide to snack together. They don aprons, which are stored on each of two chairs at the small snack table. Each washes her hands at the nearby child-size sink, then proceeds to serve herself a muffin from a basket on the serving table (a sign says "1," indicating the number each child may have). Each pours her own juice into a small glass, carries it to the table, and sits down. The two chat as they eat. When finished, each child places her napkin in the trash and her glass in the dish basin, then sponges her placemat.

A range of such activities ensues until, at 11:00 a.m. the teacher gathers the children for circle using a rhythmic call and response. With the support of the assistant, children put their respective activities back on the shelves. A few are in the midst of lengthy activities that cannot be completed prior to the group gathering. These children get their name cards from a collective basket; each places his or her name card on the work, marking his or her spot to return to it later.

The teacher shows and names the contents of a "c" object basket that a child has brought from home. She then leads the children in a group "I Spy" game, giving descriptive clues about each object as the children take turns guessing. The children are dismissed one at a time to line up at the door in preparation for playground time.

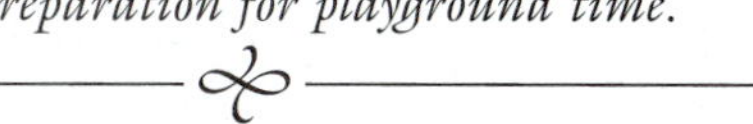

MONTESSORI'S VIEW OF HUMAN DEVELOPMENT

Montessori viewed education as a vehicle for "giving help to the child's life . . . helping the mind in its process of development" (Montessori, 1949/1967a, p. 28). Her oft-cited phrase "follow the child" is meant to infer that by following the child's development, the educator can make the most helpful match between instructional methods, curriculum, and child. A discussion of Montessori's educational philosophy, then, must begin with her view of human development.

In Montessori's view, development does not progress in one continuous inclined plane (the implication of that model being that the child is simply a small adult) or in a linear or constant fashion from birth to maturity. A further implication of the inclined plane model is that mental activity on the more elevated end of the scale—representing an older, more developed person—is inherently more valuable than that of a very young child. On the contrary, Montessori viewed the first period of life to be the most developmentally dynamic and of the highest importance.

Montessori's developmental paradigm depicts a series of four related triangles, which she termed "the constructive rhythm of life" (see Table 16–1). Each triangle represents a 6-year period (or plane) of development: birth to 6 years of age (infancy); 6 to 12 years of age (childhood); 12 to 18 years (adolescence); and 18 to 24 years (maturity). The first and third planes are described as particularly volatile and active with respect to physical and psychological changes; the other two are seen as relatively stable periods of strengthening and integration (Grazzini, 1996).

TABLE 16–1
Planes of Development

Planes	Characteristics/Sensitive Periods
0–6	***The child is constructing himself from experiences.*** • Need for order in the environment • Exploration of the environment through use of hands and tongue (leads to language development) • Movement • Fascination with minute and detailed objects • Interest in the social aspects of life
6–12	***The child has constructed tools to explore the world, now wants to move outside the classroom.*** • Exploration of culture • The imagination • Morality • Social relationships
12–18	***Child reconstructs himself now as a social being, in relationship with adults, peers, and society. This important social task means less attention is available for academic work, especially work with no obvious connection to the real world.*** • Humanistic explorers • Interest in justice • Need for work in the real world
18–24	***The young adult, having done the needed social reconstruction, now is able to make full use of available educational resources.*** • Self-motivation in learning, application of knowledge to real-world problems • Moral and spiritual development noticeable, have influence on choices

Based on Grazzini (1996).

Each plane is distinct unto itself, having its own particular characteristics; at the same time, each prepares the child for the one that follows. Montessori described the key characteristics or mental tendencies that distinguish each plane as "sensitive periods." "These periods . . . are transitory, and confined to the acquisition of a determined characteristic. Once the characteristic has evolved the corresponding sensibility disappears" (Montessori, 1966, p. 38). Montessori viewed the sensitive periods as the most opportune time in life for an individual to develop key characteristics or abilities.

According to Grazzini, Montessori viewed development as a series of "births," or periods of heightened sensitivity, each sensitivity giving rise to new interests and skills. Although these sensitivities heighten to a crescendo, then fall away, the acquired abilities remain for the whole of the individual's life (Grazzini, 1996). For example, Montessori noted that beginning at birth, but peaking in the 2- to 4-year-old, a sensitive period for order is manifested. During this period, young children exhibit an almost ritualized interest in putting or finding things in their exact place in the environment. This sensitivity manifests itself in many ways, including children becoming upset when events occur out of their usual order or then delighting in hearing the same story told in the same way, many times over.

Montessori viewed this love of order as the outward manifestation of the child's inner need for a precise and predictable environment. The child's drive for external order generally diminishes by about age 5 to 6, according to Montessori. By this time, the needs of this sensitive period will have been met, given time and experience in an appropriate environment. The child will have formed an "inner conceptual framework," which will serve her in the next plane of development as she moves toward more abstract thinking, reasoning, and complex problem solving.

This example demonstrates two essential qualities of the sensitive periods: They are by nature both transitory and retained in the form of lasting mental capacities. One primary goal of the educator, then, is to maintain awareness of the natural drive of these sensitive periods and to prepare an educational environment that responds accordingly.

The Absorbent Mind

Montessori noted, with great respect, the unique capacity of the very young child to assimilate one's surroundings. She observed that from infancy this capacity enables the child to absorb each experience in a powerful and direct way. Through the process of such absorption, the mind itself is formed. Thus, the child directly assimilates the physical and social environment in which he or she is immersed, simultaneously developing his or her innate mental powers. As Montessori phrased it, "Impressions do not merely enter his mind; they form it. They incarnate themselves in him. The child creates his own 'mental muscles,' using for this what he finds in the world about him. We have named this type of mentality, *The Absorbent Mind*" (Montessori, 1949/1967a, pp. 25–26; emphasis in original).

According to Montessori, this powerful mental construction occurs between birth and the age of 6 years and consists of two distinct phases: From birth until about 3 years of age, the child is in the phase of the unconscious absorbent mind, during which time the child explores the environment through the senses and through movement, also absorbing the language of the surrounding culture. The child retains memories of these experiences, but they are not conscious; that is, they cannot be called upon at will for the child's use. Montessori asserted, "If we call our adult mentality conscious, then we must call the child (of under 3 years) unconscious, but the unconscious mind is not necessarily inferior. An unconscious mind can be most intelligent" (Montessori, 1949/1967a, p. 23).

As an example, Montessori cited the very young child's powerful absorption of the sounds, rhythms, and structures of language. An infant hears a multitude of environmental sounds but is naturally and unconsciously cued in to the sound of the human voice. Gradually, but without conscious effort by the child or direct teaching by the adult, the child absorbs the sounds and rhythms of his or her native language, as well as its vocabulary, semantics, and syntax. The child, at least during the early stages of this process, does not have a conscious memory but must construct such memory through experience, absorbing the patterns of human language powerfully and directly (Montessori, 1949/1967a).

At about the age of 3 years, according to Montessori, the child's capacity for such powerful absorption shifts to a more conscious, purposeful type. The child becomes a factual, as well as a sensory, explorer, noting relationships between things and making comparisons. The child begins to classify and refine sensory experiences, bringing to consciousness many impressions that were previously absorbed. In so doing, "he constructs his mind step by step till it becomes possessed of memory, the power to understand, the ability to think" (Montessori, 1949/1967a, p. 27). This process evolves throughout the period of the "conscious absorbent mind," approximately between the ages of 3 and 6 years. It is worth noting that Montessori's period of the unconscious absorbent mind correlates closely with Piaget's sensorimotor period of birth to 2 years; the period of the conscious absorbent mind correlates closely with Piaget's preoperational stage (ages 2 to 7 years).

Discipline: The Development of the Will

In Montessori's view, children actively construct not only their own understanding of the world but also their own sense of inner discipline, or ability to control and direct their focus and actions. Thus, "discipline" in a good Montessori classroom arises not from the teacher's superimposition of will over the child, but from each child's gradual development of a sense of inner purpose, originating in focused activity.

As children enter the learning environment, they are unaccustomed to its materials, social expectations, and ground rules. They can be impulsive and seem to lack focus, but when they discover something that is of deep interest, they begin to act on it. According to Montessori, such purposeful engagement deepens the experience and deepens children's ability to concentrate and direct actions in other situations as well. Through such a series of actions on the environment, the children's will, or ability to direct their own actions, begins to develop. Although "the school must give the child's spirit space and opportunity for expansion" (Montessori, 1949/1967a, p. 264), this is not a permissive method in which anything goes. If this were the case, chaos would reign, and only the teacher's direct imposition of control would restore harmony. Rather, behavioral limits are designed and implemented so that all may work in peace.

In other words, within Montessori classrooms an atmosphere of freedom within limits is maintained—freedom to choose and use materials with purpose and care, to direct one's own learning, to interact with others, to move about the space freely. Limits are imposed to offer children guidelines for peer consortium and bounds of appropriate use of materials and to maintain a sense of social dignity and peace. Ground rules are often described as being in place to ensure respect for oneself, for others, and for the environment. The peace that can arise through such a balance between freedom and limits is not to be mistaken for inaction or immobility. Rather, "a form of active peace" (Montessori, 1949/1967a, p. 254) is said to prevail in a disciplined Montessori classroom.

Given the unique capacities of the young child's mind, and the tenet that education should be a "help to life," what type of educational environment, materials, and methods match the task?

PROGRAM CHARACTERISTICS

The Prepared Environment

The child, in Montessori's view, is a constant inquirer who "absorbs his environment, takes everything from it, and incarnates it in himself" (Montessori, 1949/1967a, p. 66). Not a passive recipient of experience, the child ideally interacts purposefully and freely with a specifically designed, learner-sensitive environment for optimal development to occur.

The Montessori-prepared learning environment is both physical and psychological. The physical environment is designed to be ordered, proportioned to the child's size, aesthetically pleasing, and visually harmonious. Although the environment is carefully prepared before the entry of the children, it is constantly refined and adjusted to keep pace with the ongoing needs and interests of each particular group. In other words, it is orderly but not rigid, prepared but not fixed. The teacher constantly re-prepares or fine-tunes the environment based on observations of the children's interests and needs.

The preparation and subsequent refinement of the environment are central tasks of the Montessori teacher. Though not the central figure in the class, the teacher in a Montessori classroom is far from passive: The teacher supports the child's engagement with the environment by initiating a psychological tone of calm and focused activity; by responding genuinely, warmly, and with dignity to each child and his or her needs; and by helping to make the "good match" between child and material. Much of the success of the prepared environment will depend "on the teacher's ability to participate with the children in a life of becoming" (Lillard, 1972, p. 61).

Lillard (1972) outlined six essential components of the Montessori learning environment: (1) freedom, (2) structure and order, (3) reality and nature, (4) beauty and an atmosphere that encourages a positive and spontaneous response to life, (5) Montessori learning materials, and (6) the development of community life. Another characteristic that distinguishes a Montessori learning environment is its provision of extended, uninterrupted blocks of time for child-centered activity. These blocks of time enable children to repeat activities as often as they wish, extend their concentration spans, and socialize, rest, reflect, and engage in a wide range of possible work choices within each routine day.

Freedom

In Montessori's view, the natural thrust of the child is toward independence of the "I can do it myself" variety. In addition, the child internally possesses the blueprint for his or her own development, which will unfold quite naturally given an appropriate environment and the freedom to act on the directive thrust of this inner guide.

Freedom is necessary so that the child can choose those that are of most use and interest at any point from among the materials and experiences offered. The adult in turn observes the child's interest and activity, gaining insight into the child's personality and development, and fine-tunes or modifies the environment to meet the child's needs. It is only in an atmosphere of freedom, according to Montessori, that true discipline can begin.

When a child undertakes a purposeful task that satisfies an inner developmental need, attention is fixed on this task in a manner that lengthens the focus, attunes the "will" toward a purpose or object, and thereby begins growth toward self-discipline. The quality of freedom in a Montessori classroom is dependent on this internal development of focus and self-discipline. According to Montessori, one cannot logically occur without the other.

Structure and Order

"The child, left at liberty to exercise his activities, ought to find in his surroundings something organized in direct relation to his internal organization which is developing itself by natural laws" (Montessori, 1965, p. 70). The external organization of the environment, in other words, should both mimic and promote the internal order unfolding within the child. Given the young child's acute sensitivity to order (see Table 16–1), it makes sense that the rhythms and routines of the classroom should be predictable, the learning materials should be organized in a logical fashion, and the delivery of lessons as guides to action should be exact and concise.

The word *rigid,* however, does not apply. Such appropriate structure manifests in many forms in a Montessori classroom, from a routine cycle of activities each day, to finding a material in an expected location, to the carefully designed symmetry of the learning materials, to the predictability of the basic ground rules or limits that govern the behavior of all.

Reality and Nature

Because of the absorbent quality of the young child's mind, Montessori felt that the material placed in a child's hands should be of authentic quality and should tangibly represent the real world. She shunned the practices of offering materials of inferior quality to the young child and of presenting fantasy-based images.

Children are provided with real, workable, child-size tools of everyday living in the Montessori environment. Objects such as child-proportioned brooms, dustpans, and glassware are commonplace. The Montessori didactic materials are generally made of sturdy hardwoods, glass, and (in this age) high-quality plastics. Quality and authentic materials are advocated in teacher education programs.

Montessori felt strongly that young children should be immersed in a world of reality, not fantasy. Her position was that the child's imagination develops from a sensory base and a foundation in real-world experiences, rather than from an immersion in adult-created fantasy (Montessori, 1965). Lillian Katz seemed to concur on this point, applying it to the modern era of media and mass marketing: "I believe the majority of our young children suffer from a surplus of adult-generated fantasy. We have reached a stage that I call the abuses of enchantment; it is another aspect of treating children like silly empty-headed pets that have to be amused and titillated" (Katz, quoted in Loeffler, 1992, p. 193).

Because the child is inherently drawn to the natural world—to its cycles, rhythms, and inherent order—Montessori felt that nature should be part of the learning environment. Plants, animals, and small gardens cared for by the children are standard in many Montessori classrooms.

Beauty and Atmosphere

Montessori advocated not only that aesthetic qualities be built into learning materials but also that the environment itself convey a sense of overall harmony. The environment should be clean, attractive, and well cared for. It should be colorful to attract the child, yet uncluttered so as not to overstimulate. In addition to the aesthetic qualities of beauty, Montessori advocated an overall environment of peace, nurturance, and, in a sense, spiritual beauty in which to immerse the developing child. Anita Rui Olds, in an essay entitled "Places of Beauty" (quoted in Bergen, 1988, p. 185), echoed this sentiment: "Japanese architecture features an arch called a 'torre' to signal the transition from profane to sacred territory, from that which is spontaneous and ordinary to that which is spiritually and aesthetically integrated. I have often thought that every child space should be framed by such an arch, and that the space should be designed to fulfill its meaning. Passage beyond the torre would then surround each child with beauty, wholeness, and care."

Montessori Learning Materials

"The 'prepared environment' is designed to help the child achieve a sense of himself, self-mastery and mastery of his environment through the successful execution and repetition of apparently simple tasks which are nonetheless linked to the cultural expectations the child faces in the context of his development" (Rambusch, 1962, p. 71). These "apparently simple tasks" refer to the Montessori didactic materials, generally associated with the Montessori method. To some, the sheer presence of these materials distinguishes a learning environment as Montessori in practice. However, it is not the materials themselves but, rather, their design principles that make them necessary, but not sufficient, components of a Montessori setting.

These inherent design principles isolate a particular concept or difficulty and contain a built-in control of error (i.e., auto-educational). They involve movement or activity by the child. They begin as relatively simple activities but add complexity as the child gains experience and judgment. Moreover, Montessori materials are designed to prepare the child both directly and indirectly for other subsequent learning.

They have visual appeal and are aesthetically pleasing.

The isolation of a single difficulty is intended to induce clarity in the child's learning experience and to focus attention on a key concept. For example, the tower of cubes (or pink tower) is a series of 10 cubes, graded in size at exact increments. Each cube is exactly identical except for the single variable of size. This draws the child's attention to that quality, allowing the exploration of the size relationships among the cubes without unnecessary distraction. In contrast, many contemporary commercially made materials are designed with the notion that "more is better." In the commercial version, similarly sized cubes might be adorned with a variety of colors, letters, numerals, or textures. In Montessori's view, the child may be entertained by using such multifaceted cubes but also may be unnecessarily distracted by the extraneous stimuli offered.

The notion of control of error is often misunderstood to mean that children should be ushered by the materials through drill toward a sort of methodical perfection. Montessori was a scientist and viewed error to be an inherent and constructive component of all learning. She considered errors to be essential tools for cognitive self-construction in that the perception of "errors" stimulates the child's careful observation and analysis of the learning experience at hand. Montessori designed controls of error (or design cues) into her materials to offer feedback that children can read and interpret, liberating them from dependency on adult approval or disapproval. Montessori assessed that "The control of error through the material makes a child use his reason, critical faculty, and his ever increasing capacity for drawing distinctions" (Montessori, 1948/1967b, p. 103).

The most frequently cited example of this design principle lies in the Montessori cylinder blocks, which are blocks of solid wood containing 10 knobbed cylinders of graduated dimension, each of which exactly corresponds to an equally sized socket. In general, children quite naturally match cylinder with socket; any "error" in the match becomes apparent due to a cylinder not fitting into a socket, wobbling through having been placed in a socket too large, or remaining socketless due to a prior mismatch. The child detects "errors" through the process of observation and experimentation and thereby engages in a cognitive dialogue with the material. As the child gains such experience and, therefore, judgment, the external and obvious control of error in subsequent materials is diminished. For example, the knobless cylinders (a more advanced material) duplicate this initial experience without blocks or sockets into which to place the cylinders. The child grades the series without the benefit of a preset form to follow, replacing the guiding construct of the material with independent judgment.

Appreciative of the neuromuscular connection between physical movement and cognitive development, Montessori intended that child activity or movement be part of all of her didactic materials. Children in Montessori classrooms lift, carry, balance, stack, pour, sweep, assemble, and grade various objects as they actively engage and manipulate the learning environment.

Such motor activity serves to sustain the child's interest in the learning experience. Montessori claimed that "The ability of a thing to attract the interest of a child does not depend so much upon the quality of the thing itself as upon the opportunity that it affords the child for action" (Montessori, 1948/1967b, p. 104). Integrating movement with perceptual learning helps embed the activity or concept into the child's "muscle memory" and affords the child the opportunity to develop control of movement. The child adapts physical movements to the demands of a given activity, developing coordination, balance, and overall motor refinement.

Montessori didactic materials generally progress from simple to complex, adding one degree of difficulty as the child progresses to the next experience. This enables a child to reach a sense of internal mastery of a skill, material, or concept before moving on to something that has more steps or requires increased judgment. Since the curriculum is child driven rather than teacher driven, there is no one blueprint for progression through the didactic materials. Materials are presented to each child according to interest and the requisite preparatory skills—the goal being child success and independence, not completion of a preset curriculum or a preset timetable.

In addition to progressing from simple to complex, Montessori materials are generally designed as scaffolding or indirect preparation for other, subsequent learning. For example, by grading sets of size-related materials, such as the pink tower or red rods, children indirectly prepare themselves for comprehension of the base-10 number system, as all of these graded series contain 10 elements. By using a three-finger grasp to handle the knobbed cylinders, children indirectly prepare their fingers for handwriting. By pouring liquids from one larger container into three equally sized smaller containers, children indirectly prepare themselves for fractions and division.

Overall, materials are evaluated in their composite, not in terms of one exclusive set of materials. The greatest hallmark of good Montessori classrooms is the teacher as scientific pedagogue; under the guidance of this type of teacher, the Montessori materials become a well-designed set of possibilities, not a complete instructional package.

The Development of Community Life

It would be a mistake to take the thrust toward independence and individual development in Montessori classrooms as an indicator that little socialization occurs. In fact, some might say that nothing could be further from the truth. "To the question 'what provision is made for socialization?' one could reply that the very condition of learning in this Montessori environment depends on socialization as an atmospheric element" (Rambusch, 1962, p. 79). Liberated from spending long periods of time in teacher-led large-group instruction, children routinely interact with each other, sharing work, watching another's activity, offering or seeking peer help with a material, or sharing snack and conversation. Productive sociability, not mere togetherness, should be a prominent feature of a good Montessori class (Rambusch).

Although many activities are designed with an individual learner in mind, many others, such as language activities, are specifically intended for two or more children. Teachers are subtle but key community builders who spend time moving about the room, offering lessons to individuals and small groups, making conversation, and helping children to resolve conflicts mutually.

Grouping together children of three different age groups, spanning 3 years (which is common to most Montessori environments), supports the development of community life as well. Older children are actively encouraged to support younger learners and to serve as leaders and role models. Children are free to choose friends from a wide range of possibilities and to discover and explore qualities in others unlike themselves. Cooperation and respect for others are foundational concepts in a Montessori classroom community.

CURRICULUM AREAS

The Montessori learning environment for 3- to 6-year-olds is generally divided into four basic areas: practical life (everyday living), sensorial (materials focusing on one or more of the senses), language, and mathematics. In addition, music, art, movement, and drama are included in the curriculum (American Montessori Society, 1994).

Practical Life

The curricular area called *practical life* is generally seen as the sine qua non of the Montessori curriculum because, through involvement with practical experiences in everyday living, the child begins to develop these skills and tendencies that will support focused learning in all other classroom endeavors. Through involvement with familiar, home-based experiences such as sweeping, sewing, and gardening, the child begins to focus attention on a single activity and learns to follow a sequence from beginning to end, learns to coordinate movements toward a particular goal, and learns to organize each step of a given task, thereby attaining independence through self-directed activity. Thus, while the direct or practical aim of an activity such as carrot cutting may be the peeling, cutting, and serving of a carrot, the underlying or indirect aims include the development of independence, order, concentration, hand–eye coordination, community life (through serving the carrot to others), and realistic self-esteem (through accomplishment). Practical life activities invite the child's participation in the surrounding culture through offering child-size versions of activities commonly done in the home—reinforcing for the child a fluent transition from home to classroom. Specific activities involve self-care (e.g., tooth brushing, dressing frames for practice with various types of fasteners, nose blowing, hair combing); care of the environment (flower arranging, shoe polishing, table scrubbing, gardening); life skills (sewing, food preparation); fine motor development (transferring activities, e.g., pouring and basting); and community living (setting a table, saying "excuse me" or "thank you," etc.).

Since few practical life activities are standardized, teachers create most materials for this curricular area. Great diversity exists from one classroom to the next as each teacher responds to the needs, interests, and cultural makeup of the class. For example, in a Montessori school in Hawaii, teacher adaptations are made to reflect Hawaiian culture and the surrounding natural environment: Stringing is done with flowers, seeds, or leaves; pouring and scooping are done with small shells and seeds—large shells are often used as pouring vessels; dressing frames are made with Hawaiian tapa-cloth designs; food activities include preparing rice sushi, pounding poi, and drying fruits and seeds Chinese style (Bogart, 1992).

As children mature, practical life involves more complex cooking activities, first aid, bicycle repair, telephone manners, computer skills, and knowledge of simple machines (Chattin-McNichols, 1992).

Sensorial

From birth, children are immersed in a stimulus-rich environment and unconsciously use all their senses to absorb sensory impressions in the absorbent mind (Montessori, 1973). In the third year of life, according to Montessori, the child can begin to order and classify impressions through hands-on examination of specifically prepared materials. Sensorial materials were designed with this purpose in mind; they originate from Montessori's own designs and are adapted from the work of Jean Itard and Edouard Seguin (Montessori 1948/1967b).

The sensorial materials are a series of sequenced exercises, aesthetically pleasing and seemingly simple in design, which are offered so that the child can "catalog and classify" (Montessori, 1948/1967b) sensory impressions. These activities refine and sharpen the senses and create a sensory foundation for further intellectual development. "The training and sharpening of the senses, has the obvious advantage of enlarging the field of perception and of offering an ever more solid foundation for intellectual growth" (Montessori, 1948/1967b, p. 99).

Materials appealing to the visual, muscular–tactile, auditory, gustatory, and olfactory senses are presented, serially, each isolating one specific concept or sensory perception. Examples are the long rods (which isolate length), the color tablets (which isolate color), the touch tablets (which isolate rough and smooth textures), the sound cylinders (which isolate sound volume), and the smelling jars (which isolate particular scents).

Each series proceeds from simple to complex. For example, in using the first color box, the child matches only the primary colors: red, yellow, and blue. In the final work of this series, the child grades seven shades of each of nine colors, from darkest to lightest. As the child progresses through the series, increased judgment and refined perception gained from prior lessons serve as inner guides.

These exercises also advance from an immediate and concrete experience to the child's more abstract awareness of the relevant concept or quality. For example, when using the geometric cabinet, an early activity that introduces geometric figures, the child handles a blue-knobbed wooden triangle and places it into a corresponding inset (like handling a piece of a simple knobbed puzzle). The term *triangle* is introduced by the teacher at some judicious point. Through subsequent activity, the child eventually recognizes a thin blue outline on a card as *triangle* and later locates other triangles in the environment ("I see a triangle on your shirt!"). By doing this, the child has internalized the image and identity of *triangle*, and knowledge has reached the conceptual stage. Later, the child will construct a definition of *triangle* as well as of the various types of triangles explored earlier in this hands-on way.

When using sensorial materials, the child is initially encouraged to follow a pattern of comparison or gradation modeled by the teacher but is later urged to experiment with other possibilities to discover variations (alternative arrangements of a material) and extensions (discovery of the relatedness of two different materials or the extension of the activity into the environment) (Torrence, 1993). Many of the sensorial materials are open-ended sets and can be used to generate a variety of child-initiated designs, thus allowing for exploration and creativity.

Language

> [Language] is not a material; it is a process. If we consider the Montessori legacy for "language as process," the language area . . . expands to include much more—the whole learning environment and, in fact, the whole world. The language curriculum becomes a context rather than a content, a smorgasbord rather than a carefully prescribed diet; and the key to the pantry is the child's own spoken language. (Turner, 1995, p. 26)

Language development in a Montessori classroom is fostered throughout the environment: the social environment of community and free exchange between children; the exact terminology offered by the teacher through specific lessons; the songs, rhymes, and conversation shared during whole-group gatherings; the selection of quality books found in the library corner; and the specific didactic materials developed to promote language and literacy development. The Montessori classroom provides a rich context for oral language development, which lays the groundwork for the child's eventual conquest of the mechanics of written language.

Montessori would concur with current whole language theorists that spoken and written language are corollaries as means of self-expression (Montessori, 1964). According to Montessori, for the child to learn to write (which is seen as social activity), he or she must first acquire the mechanics of writing. This is accomplished in part through use of didactic material called the "metal insets," which are a variety of metal geometric templates that allow for a large number of different tracing and drawing activities, appropriate to a wide range of pencil skills (Chattin-McNichols, 1992). The child's hand is prepared for these activities in the previous handling of practical life and sensorial materials.

Development of the mechanics of writing is also accomplished through the child's handling of individual wooden letters, as well as tracing sandpaper letter forms, which have been glued to Masonite plaques (the sandpaper letters) (Montessori, 1964). Through the activation and association of visual, muscular–tactile, kinesthetic, and auditory modalities (the teacher makes the letter's sound as the child handles the letter), the child, with practice, retains a mental image of each letter as well as its related sound. Eventually, the child, with a storehouse of symbols and their sounds embedded in memory, begins to investigate printed language through "writing" (sound-spelling) words and messages, at first using a large box of wooden letters (the movable alphabet) and later forming such words with a pencil or some other writing utensil.

Montessori's method of acquainting very young children with alphabetic symbols may appear to some to be "pushing" early reading. But her intentions, on the contrary, were to acquaint children with the tools of written language at a key period of sensitivity, so that later, the child's "explosion" into written language would be experienced as spontaneous, rather than as an uninspired product of so much abide-by-the-rules drudgery and rote practice.

Most contemporary Montessori teachers consider the metal insets, the sandpaper letters, and the movable alphabet as core language materials that are expanded upon by a great variety of teacher-generated materials, all designed to meet the needs and interests of specific children. Additional activities commonly found include nomenclature cards, rhyming objects and pictures, sequence story cards, go-togethers, boxes of objects grouped by phonetic commonality, picture–label matching sets, dictation games, command games (which use both pictures and words to offer instructions), and grammar games.

The Montessori language sequence assumes that writing (or encoding) generally precedes reading (or decoding) and that the two are highly interrelated. Many specific activities supporting the skills of beginning readers (labeling activities, sight word cards, as well as a wide array of phonetic and predictable texts) are included in most classrooms.

Mathematics

Mathematical thinking originates in many other seemingly unrelated activities that happen prior to experiences in the math area proper. Montessori felt that the order, precision, attention to detail, and sense of sequence fostered through use of the practical life and sensorial materials lay the foundation for what she termed the "mathematical mind." "Prerequisite activities prepare a child for the exactness and logical order required for mathematics" (Scott, 1995, p. 26).

The concept of one-to-one correspondence, for instance, is embedded in the use of dressing frames (one button for each hole), the knobbed cylinders (one cylinder for each socket), and all matching activities. The child explores and compares similarities and differences through all grading and sorting activities, explores spatial relations through making relational patterns with sensorial materials, and explores temporal relations through experiencing the predictable pattern of daily routines. The child is indirectly introduced to the base-10 system through grading sensorial series that contain 10 objects (tower of cubes, broad stair). Moreover, grading various series (e.g., long rods, knobbed cylinders) acquaints the child with the concepts of *greater than* and *less than.*

The math sequence proper begins as a logical extension of a familiar sensorial experience. The child who previously graded the 10 red rods according to length is now introduced to identical rods on which red and blue segments, denoting quantity, are included. The child orders these rods from shortest to longest, counting each segment. Later, following a visual and tactile introduction to numerical symbols (sandpaper numerals), the child returns to the rod activity, relating numerical symbol to quantity.

In similar fashion, all of the Montessori mathematical materials progress gradually from the concrete and known to the abstract and unknown, targeting one difficulty at a time; math materials are the physical manifestations of abstract concepts, or "materialized abstractions" (Montessori 1948/1967b, p. 174).

Montessori math materials are grouped into four categories: (1) 0 to 10 numeration and quantification, (2) linear counting (systematic number-line counting of increasingly large numbers), (3) the decimal system (using the classic golden bead material to represent place value–unit beads, 10 bars, 100 squares, and 1,000 cubes), and (4) operations (addition, subtraction, etc.). As is generally the case with the use of Montessori materials, presentations of the math materials are brief and are always offered to a willing and interested child; materials are chosen by the child, not assigned by the teacher. The purpose for their availability and use is not to push early academics, artificial abstraction, or memorization of math facts. Rather, Montessori believed mathematics to be a natural and satisfying function of the human mind. Systematic discovery of the relationships between numbers lead children to become mathematical thinkers and problem solvers. "Abstraction is a creative process undertaken by the child to construct knowledge" (Chattin-McNichols, 1992, p. 97). As stated in the American Montessori Society's "Position Statement on Mathematics Education" (American Montessori Society, 1996), "[M]athematics arose as a way of solving problems associated with daily life—involving space, size, and quantity." Children are urged to think clearly and to use concepts learned in new and imaginative ways. The ability to understand and use concepts in problem solving is considered the purpose of all education, not just mathematics education.

Artistic Expression

"Concurrent with emphasis on the developing cognitive skills must go attention to the child's affective life, inner thoughts and feelings, and modes of self-expression" (American Montessori Society, n.d.). It is to these ends that contemporary American Montessori programs emphasize child self-expression through the visual arts, music, dance, and drama (American Montessori Society, 1994).

Montessori was a pioneer in environmental aesthetics in education and saw the profound effect that aesthetic quality and overall balance in the environment can have on the young child's development. She favored an indirect environmental approach to aesthetic education during the early years, feeling it important to include beautiful and carefully selected works of art in the early childhood environment (Montessori, 1964). A wide, rich array of sensory experiences, both through classroom materials and from the natural world (Montessori, 1964, 1965) provide an ample palette for the child's later blossoming of creative expression.

Today's Montessori classrooms reflect this focus on aesthetics and rich sensory experience, as well as an awareness of the importance of the visual arts in child self-expression and symbolic meaning making. A wide range of expressive art media, such as paints, clay, collage materials, various drawing and coloring media, and papier-mâché, are generally included in contemporary Montessori environments. American Montessori training courses offer core instruction in modes of child artistic expression (Montessori Accreditation Council for Teacher Education, 1996) and many professional development workshops (AMS and North American Montessori Teachers Association [NAMTA]) are offered to deepen teachers' awareness and skill level in this important area of child development.

Music

Musical awareness and expression and training in the basic elements of music are inherent in Montessori programs (American Montessori

Society, n.d.). Exercises that prepare the ear for the distinction of sounds, such as the "silence game," the sound cylinders, and the Montessori bells (for distinction of pitch), are considered core curriculum in Montessori early childhood programs (Montessori, 1948/1967b). Rhythmic activities (movement on the line to various rhythms), listening to classical and other types of music, group singing, experimentation with simple musical instruments, and simple music notation (using movable wooden notes on a large staff) are music activities additionally described by Montessori and found in contemporary settings (Montessori 1948/1967b).

Montessori programs in elementary schools typically offer children the opportunity to study various instruments, as well as to read and write music and to engage in group musical experiences. For example, two schools, one located in Albuquerque, New Mexico, and one in Cincinnati, Ohio, boast elementary and high school steel drum bands, respectively (Leto, 1996).

The Cultural Subjects: Geography and Science

Embedded in Montessori's philosophical frame is a cosmic view of the systematic interrelatedness of all living and nonliving things (Montessori, 1973). This view is based on assumptions that the universe is an organizing force and that in order for the child to reach understanding of individual facts and phenomena, he or she must also gain an appreciation of the interdependent nature of all life forms and elements (Duffy & Duffy, 2002). This philosophical view underlies the Montessori approach to the life and physical sciences, as well as to what Montessori calls "physical and cultural geography."

Montessori viewed the needs of humans as universal, and the study of the diverse cultures of earth as an investigation of the ways in which humans interact with nature to meet such needs (Montessori, 1965). Cultural celebrations, unit studies of a particular culture, or the use of objects or vessels from a varied range of cultural contexts—all are ways in which the child may absorb an awareness and knowledge of different cultures within a Montessori classroom. The child is invited to choose freely from a range of areas and activities that are provided to grant many possibilities in an integrated curriculum.

For example, in the first author's classroom during a study of Japan, the children transferred objects with chopsticks and rolled sushi with rice and seaweed in the practical life area; young children matched lovely flowered fabric patterns and tasted green tea in the sensorial area; they learned Japanese expressions of routine daily communication (*hello, excuse me, thank you*) in the language area; they counted polished stones on an enameled tray in math; they assembled the puzzle map of Asia (locating Japan) in geography; they created a Japanese rock garden (raking sand and arranging rocks in pleasing patterns) in art; finally, they constructed a Japanese tea house, and two at a time, they donned kimonos, entered, and served each other green tea (after observing a tea ceremony presented by a visitor) as a combination practical life and dramatic play activity.

In most Montessori classrooms, children are offered physical models of land forms (e.g., an island to surround with water, a lake to fill with water) and puzzle maps of the continents and other areas of Earth.

Scientific exploration, for preschoolers, involves "direct observation (which provides the basis for generating and testing informal hypotheses). The role of the senses in direct observation of nature provides the experimental base for later abstract thought" (American Montessori Society, n.d.). For the young child, this means direct daily contact with the natural world; the opportunity to experience, label, and begin to categorize natural phenomenon; the opportunity to ask "What?" and "How?" questions; and routine interaction with an adult who is willing to serve as mentor to the child's inborn sense of wonder.

THE ROLE OF THE TEACHER

Montessori's goal was nothing less than to re-create the world into a more peaceful, compassionate, and purposeful place by focusing on both the nature and development of the child. Within this scheme, the teacher's role is to regard the child respectfully, appreciate the unfolding of each child's development, and protect the child's natural impulse or drive to create her own personality (Cossentino & Whitcomb, 2003).

This being the goal, Montessori realized that a new paradigm or model of the role of the teacher would have to be created (Montessori, 1964). The school and the teacher must permit freedom within a prepared environment if the goals of this new type of education are to be reached. According to Montessori, the child who is given such freedom in a carefully prepared environment will develop according to the child's own natural timetable and tendencies. Therefore, the teacher's job is not to artificially "teach in" what the child lacks but rather to be a careful observer of each child's development, providing learner-responsive materials as well as guidance in the form of instruction, consistent structure, and appropriate encouragement.

The role of teacher as observer differed most radically in Montessori's day (as it still does today) from the common notion of the teacher as the controlling, central force in the classroom. Misunderstood by some as a laissez-faire or passive stance, the observation of a trained Montessori teacher is, on the contrary, the studied observation of a scientist. "The book for the teacher, the book which inspires her own actions, and the only one in which she can read and study if she is to become an expert, is the constant observance of the children as they pass from their first disordered movements to those that are spontaneously regulated" (Montessori, 1948/1967b, p. 55). As the teacher first observes these "disordered movements" exhibited (even today) by children new to the environment and unfamiliar with the routines and materials therein, he or she sets in motion active imagination; the teacher begins to imagine a child "who is not yet there." The teacher trusts in the eventual appearance of a focused and calm child who will reveal himself or herself through the purposeful activity referred to as "work" (Montessori, 1963).

The teacher's primary roles beyond this central one of keen observer (or in today's vernacular, "kid watcher") are to carefully prepare and maintain the learning environment, to deal with disorderly children through redirection and attention to their perceived difficulty, and to present lessons with didactic materials to those children who show interest. Teachers are also responsible for conducting large group meeting times and for maintaining careful records on each child. They are generally expected to maintain close contact with each child's family through periodic communication, such as conferencing.

Montessori's method is often confused with a standard set of didactic materials, many of which were designed by Maria Montessori and bear her name. It is true that she developed and routinely trained teachers in the specific use of these materials and that Montessori teacher trainees today spend much time and effort consumed in mastering presentations of the same. But Montessori apparently did not intend for these materials and their use to define her work. As stated in *The Montessori Method*, "This book of methods compiled by one person alone, must be followed by many others. It is my hope that, starting from the individual study of the child educated within our method, other educators will set forth the results of their experiments. These are the pedagogical books which await us in the future" (Montessori, 1964, p. 373). Accordingly, in Montessori's view, the new relationship between teacher and child, based on observation, was to be noted as the hallmark of her method, much more so than a particular set of didactic materials.

Nevertheless, the classic Montessori didactic materials, along with teacher-generated materials, do play a vital role in the child's activity in a Montessori classroom. The teacher plays an active role in establishing the initial connection between child and materials and, as such, invites the child to investigate materials and provides specific lessons on their use (Montessori, 1948/1967b). These lessons should be brief, simple, and exact. They are offered to clearly demonstrate the purpose of an activity—blueprints for subsequent investigation by the child but not standards of perfection to be exactly emulated.

Paradoxically, although the teacher is expected to have worked each lesson to mastery, this same standard is not to be imposed on the child. The offering of each lesson is intended "to stir up life, but leave it free to develop" (Montessori, 1948/1967b, p. 111).

Upon the child's purposeful involvement, the teacher should take a back seat to the child's active interaction with the material. The primary learning is seen to reside in the child's doing, not the adult's teaching. "It is the child who uses the objects; it is the child who is active, and not the teacher" (Montessori, 1948/1967b, p. 149). The trained Montessori teacher must, in fact, specialize in observing the delicate balance between intervention and nonintervention in a child's activity. The control of error, designed into the material, is intended to assist the child in successfully investigating the material. But how does this work in practice? One survey (N = 422) examined teachers' reported intervention in cases when children were making errors in seriating and classifying tasks. Teachers from four countries with a wide range of experience and from seven different Montessori teacher education backgrounds were quite consistent in reporting that they would be unlikely to intervene in these situations; however, their responses were much less consistent when asked about intervening in math and language errors or in fantasy play (Chattin-McNichols, 1991).

The teacher's role is to intervene and actively redirect whenever children exhibit roughness, rudeness, or disruptive behavior, but to sensitively observe and remove herself from interference with the child's spontaneous interest and involvement whenever the child's behavior corresponds with the intended purposes of the material (Montessori, 1948/1967b). The teacher observes, records, and thereby comes to know the needs and interests of the children, preparing and maintaining an attractive, ordered learning environment that contains both traditional Montessori learning materials and those originally developed. The teacher seeks the good match between children and materials through observation, serving as a potent but subtle catalyst for child activity. The teacher offers polished, streamlined, and concise lessons, demonstrating a clear set of impressions as to the purpose and direction of a given material. The teacher redirects in cases of inappropriate or abusive acts and maintains a watcher's stance when the child is engaged in purposeful, focused activity.

RESEARCH ON MONTESSORI

The research base on Montessori education is small, especially considering the approximately 5,000 schools in the United States alone (Schapiro & Hellen, 2007). Although well over a hundred studies have been published, the numerous problems that beset the research literature make it impossible to draw other than very tentative conclusions (Boehnlein, 1988; Chattin-McNichols, 1981, 1992). Methodological problems include the difficulty of separating the effects of parents who have chosen Montessori from the effects of the model itself. Another common weakness is the use of a single or small number of teachers in a classroom or school that is assumed (rather than demonstrated) to be representative of best Montessori practices. The short-term nature of most studies also is incompatible with the Montessori idea of 3 years in a single classroom with the same teacher. A further difficulty lies in the lack of specification of the Montessori model in some study samples. Evaluations of programs that may do only a partial implementation of a Montessori program do not advance our knowledge significantly.

Nevertheless, research examining Montessori classrooms suggests the following:

- Students spend relatively little time in whole-group instruction. Rather, they move about the classroom, choose activities, work individually or in small groups, and talk with each other. This behavior set has been described as characteristic of independence (Feltin, 1987; Miller & Dyer, 1975; Wirtz, 1976).
- Work with manipulatives is more frequent than in other preschool programs (Feltin, 1987; Schmid & Black, 1977; Stodolsky & Karlson, 1972).
- Children spend significant time conversing, and a relatively high portion of this is either related to school work or actual peer teaching. Lack of similarity in observation instruments obscures the extent to which this is true at different ages (Baines & Snortum, 1973; Feltin, 1987; Wirtz, 1976).
- Montessori children do engage in fantasy and role-playing activities, although the typical program lacks a designated role-play/dress-up area (Black, 1977; Chattin-McNichols, 1991; Feltin, 1987; Miller & Dyer, 1975; Reuter & Yunik, 1973; Schmid & Black, 1977; Stodolsky & Karlson, 1972; Torrence, 1992; Wirtz, 1976). Bear in mind that some of these findings are stronger than others, in terms of sample size, recency of data collection, and so on.

Perhaps the single most important recent works are two publications by Angeline Lillard (Lillard, 2005; Lillard & Else-Quest, 2006). The book *Montessori: The Science Behind the Genius* (Lillard, 2005) is a major contribution to the scholarly work written on Montessori, and is especially important as a "bridge" book, one that will help increase understanding between Montessori educators and the educational mainstream. Lillard, a developmental psychologist, gathered research intended to show which parts of the Montessori approach are supported by current research findings and which are not. She found that, except for the devaluation of pretend play for children under 6 years of age, all of Montessori's major ideas *that have been studied* have been validated by research on human learning and development. The book is organized around the following eight core Montessori principles, each of which is contemporized and critiqued through the lens of relevant research studies:

- The impact of movement on learning and cognition
- Choice and its impact on learning
- Interest and its role in human learning (i.e., how we learn better when the topic or method of learning is one in which we are interested)
- Extrinsic rewards and their negative impact on motivation
- Collaborative arrangements and their impact on learning
- Meaningful contexts for learning
- Adult interaction styles and optimal child outcomes
- Order in the environment: its impact on learning process and outcomes.

One point that Dr. Lillard makes very well is a response to a criticism of Montessori that has been frequently voiced. That criticism is, "Yes, Montessori is fine but *our* program has X," where X is one of Montessori's innovations (for example, use of some manipulative materials, mixed-age groupings, cooperative learning, and so on). Dr. Lillard accentuates the difference between a traditional school setting with one or two innovations, but with the basic assumptions about children and learning (Lockean model of the child, factory model of curriculum division and delivery; Bennett & LeCompte, 1990) still strongly in place, and a designed-from-scratch program such as Montessori that integrates *all* of these changes at once.

One problem is that Lillard, whose Montessori background and training are with the Association Montessori Internationale (AMI) has written the book from the standpoint that only AMI schools and teacher education programs can be considered authentic Montessori models. At first, this may seem like a minor point; surely the author can decide for herself what is and what is not Montessori. And many authors, including the coauthors of this chapter, are concerned about the negative effects of programs that do not adhere to Montessori principles but call themselves Montessori. But Lillard's distinction is in fact a very important one, which may have serious negative consequences for the book. First, using Lillard's standard, the number of Montessori schools in the United States is effectively reduced from over 5,000 to approximately 300 schools, based on the number of AMI schools listed on the AMI-USA Web site (http://www.montessori-ami.org). It seems possible that this reduction in numbers may decrease the interest of non-Montessori educators in Montessori.

There are other, more serious consequences. If one believes that only AMI schools are truly Montessori, then virtually 100% of the research done in Montessori schools is not worth mentioning, since so little of it has been done exclusively in AMI schools. I would argue that the proper way to make use of the studies that have taken place in Montessori classrooms of unknown quality is to be extra cautious about the strength of the conclusions, not to ignore the research base entirely.

Overall, Lillard's excellent review of mainstream educational and developmental research shows strong support of a number of Montessori's basic concepts.

Finally, Lillard and Else-Quest (2006) report on a well designed study comparing Montessori students in the Milwaukee, Wisconsin, public Montessori program with students who had applied for entry but had not won the lottery to be accepted. This clever strategy helps to alleviate the usual difficulty with effects of parent choice, social economic standing (SES), family pattern, values such as educational aspirations, ethnicity, and so on. Included in the study were 53 control students and 59 Montessori students. Comparisons were made between 5-year-olds and 12-year-olds in both the Montessori and control groups, which makes this a relatively small sample for each age group. The study is exemplary in that it used a variety of measures at each of the two ages studied. The 5-year-old Montessori children were statistically significantly better on three of seven scales in the Woodcock-Johnson Test Battery: Letter-Word Identification, Word Attack, and Applied Problems (math). There were also statistically significant findings favoring the Montessori 5-year-olds on executive function, which is "thought to be important for success in school" (Lillard & Else-Quest, 2006). On social/behavioral measures, the Montessori 5-year-olds were significantly more likely to "use a higher level of reasoning by referring to justice or fairness" (Lillard & Else-Quest, 2006) on a test in which they were given stories and asked how to resolve the problems presented. Two measures of social behavior observed during playground time also favored Montessori children at age five. Finally, a False Belief task examined children's understanding of the mind; 80% of Montessori five year olds vs. 50% of controls passed this test.

There were fewer statistically significant differences at age twelve. Stories written by the Montessori children were judged as more creative and used more sophisticated sentence structure. On social/behavioral measures, Montessori children were more likely to choose the "positive assertive response" to social problems. On a questionnaire about feelings toward school, Montessori 12-year-olds reported a greater sense of community.

Critics of this research study have noted that the results are all from a single Montessori school, that the Montessori sample had a higher percentage of girls than the control group, and that the study did not take into account the influence of peers in the Montessori setting, compared to the control setting.

Other researchers examining outcome effects or the impact of Montessori schooling have tentatively suggested the following:

- Early studies generally showed some initial gains from Montessori preschool experience with great difficulty establishing long-term gains. In perhaps the best-controlled study, Montessori children showed the highest IQs compared to other programs and controls (Miller & Bizzell, 1983, 1985; see also Dawson, 1988; Dreyer & Rigler, 1969; Duax, 1989; Karnes, Shwedel, & Williams, 1983; Miller & Dyer, 1975; Takacs & Clifford, 1988).
- With respect to academic achievement outcomes, Montessori preschools are seen as strong as any program studied. Duax (1989) examined the performance of children in a Milwaukee, Wisconsin, public Montessori program and found that only one student did not score at or above the national mean. Parent selection bias may well be a factor. Still, Duax's teacher survey data showed that Montessori graduates in middle school had higher scores on the following five items:
    1. Uses basic skills necessary to survive in middle school
    2. Is responsible and can be counted on
    3. Shows enthusiasm for class topics
    4. Is individualistic and not afraid to be different
    5. Exhibits multicultural awareness

As far as more recent studies of achievement test results and other typical measures of learning, there are only a few to report. Duax (1995) examined a private Montessori elementary school in a diverse suburb and found high levels of achievement. Glenn (1993, 1996, 1999) employed a minilongitudinal approach in accessing achievement in a private Montessori school. At 10 years, his admittedly small sample scored above the average on achievement test scores as compared to the general population. Results of perhaps greater interest came from Glenn's online survey administered to these same students during their high school and college years. Forty-five students completed the online survey, which focused on psychological, social, and vocational issues. The study postulated two hypotheses: (1) the number of Montessori Education Years (MEY) would positively relate to qualities emphasized in Montessori education and (2) participants with any Montessori education would be at least as successful as the general population. Although tempered by drop out sample bias, findings provided considerable support for the first hypothesis on lifelong learning and self-development. The personal value of lifelong learning was identified as most prevalent among students with 10 to 15 MEY. The striving for self-development was manifested by a strong desire for self-understanding, general personality development, self-direction and discipline, and a strong positive attitude toward social-interactive activities.

Rathunde and Csikszentmihalyi (2005) reported on the motivation and quality of the experience in middle-school children in a Montessori and a traditional school environment. Their sample of 290 children was a matched sample; five well-established Montessori schools were selected, and middle schools matching these Montessori schools in demographic variables such as SES and ethnicity were chosen from a larger study. The authors described this study as exploratory. The multivariate analyses show Montessori middle-school children with greater affect, potency (i.e., feeling energetic), intrinsic motivation, flow experience, and undivided interest relative to controls.

Positive results have been found for mathematics achievement (see Baker, 1988; Bausch & Hsu, 1988; Dawson, 1988; Fero, 1997; Glenn, 1989; Miller & Bizzell, 1985; Takacs & Clifford, 1988). In one longitudinal study, mathematics achievement for boys enrolled in Montessori was statistically significantly different from children enrolled in other preschool programs and control groups at that grade level (Miller & Bizzell, 1983, 1985; Miller & Dyer, 1975). In another study, the achievement test data from public Montessori school students in the Houston, Texas schools were examined by ethnicity to discern how Montessori served children from different ethnic backgrounds. All grade and ethnicity groups scored at least one half of a grade equivalent above their actual grade. Some fifth-graders had a grade equivalent of mid-tenth grade in the area of math (Dawson, 1988). Reed (2000), who studied Montessori first- through third-graders' procedural and conceptual abilities on place value tasks, found that these students did well in the following areas: identifying the value of digits in a number, using standard addition algorithms for multidigit numbers, solving two-digit addition and missing addend questions with and without materials, and solving word problems involving three- and four-digit numbers. Her study separated conceptual knowledge from procedural knowledge. She found no differences in procedural knowledge but significant differences in a Chi-square analysis for the first-graders and the overall group in conceptual knowledge. This study calls out for replication and further research to those of us who have seen how badly a lack of understanding of place value can cripple a child's later progress in math.

In summary, increasing support exists for the benefits of a Montessori education, particularly during the early years. However, better designed research projects that include larger numbers of subjects are needed to resolve questions about the Montessori method's outcomes, strengths, and weaknesses. A recent review (Lillard, 2005) of key Montessori practices in light of relevant research from the developmental psychology literature supports the use of these practices for learners throughout the lifespan.

MONTESSORI EDUCATION IN THE ELEMENTARY YEARS

Montessori programs for children from ages 6 through 12 have been a part of the Montessori movement since Dr. Montessori's years of internment (as an Italian citizen) in India during World War II. It was during this time that she created the model for Montessori elementary education (Standing, 1962). Montessori elementary programs are increasingly common in both the private and public sectors in the United States.

The elementary-age child is moving from an understanding of the world through movement and physical examination to an understanding of abstract concepts. A traditional framework for the Montessori elementary curriculum is a series of "Great Lessons" (the story of the universe, the coming of life, the coming of humans, the story of communications in sign, and the story of numbers) (North American Montessori Teachers' Association, 1995) designed to capture the child's imagination and inspire a keen interest in the disciplines related to each question. From the core of the story frameworks, which offer the big picture of an epoch to the child, come the details of the related disciplines: mathematics (including arithmetic, geometry, and algebra); language (including speaking, writing, reading, and grammar); science (including botany, zoology, chemistry, and geology); and geography (including physical and cultural geography). Because of the unifying picture offered through the Great Lessons, no subject stands independent from the others.

Many of the same curricular and instructional innovations found in the early childhood program are also a part of Montessori elementary classrooms. Such innovations as mixed age groupings, use of manipulative materials to support the child's thinking and advancement toward abstract concepts, integrated curriculum, and cooperative learning have become more common in a variety of educational settings in recent years, but Montessori elementary classrooms are the only places where these innovations are united in an integrated whole, informed by more than 50 years of practice (Lillard, 2005). A number of features foster the integration:

- Elementary classrooms are usually organized around the same 3-year age spans found in the early childhood programs: 6- to 9-year-old and 9- to 12-year-old groupings are typical. The children stay with the same teacher for 3 years; at the start of the year, only one third of the children in a class are new to the teacher.
- The attitude is one of cooperation, rather than competition. Of course, Montessori education is not magical, and an observer would certainly find examples of competition among children in a typical American classroom. But a number of practices serve to reduce this, for example:

  The cooperative nature of many of the tasks, rather than a focus on who finishes first, or who gets the best grade

  The availability of the answers in many of the activities (this focuses the attention on understanding rather than "Who got the right answer"?)

  An explicit commitment, as well as materials and curriculum, in the areas of conflict resolution and peace education.
- A large number of manipulative materials, in every subject area, are available for the students to work with. It's important to understand the difference between occasional use of manipulatives, for example, to demonstrate math operations in a traditional classroom, and what happens in a good Montessori elementary classroom. In the Montessori elementary classroom, the most common form of instruction is a short introduction to a material, which is typically given to an individual or small group, followed by the child or children working with the material. The Montessori principle of *Control of Error* finds expression in the elementary classroom through having most answers (to math problems, for example) available to the child. And finally, the range of the curriculum is truly impressive. Math work for the 9- to 12-year-olds includes volumes of objects such as cylinders and pyramids, areas of regular polygons, square and cube root, and quite a bit of work with other number bases. Work in grammar and in life and physical sciences is also available in areas most of us did not work in until high school or college. But the number of manipulatives and the more advanced content are only part of the picture. Two of these differences are these:

1. Manipulatives can be used in a variety of ways to support children's learning. In Montessori classrooms, math, materials are used to give the child a "big picture" of a concept, such as addition or long division, angles, perimeters, and so on. There are other materials and presentations that aid children in their memorization of facts. But perhaps the most impressive materials are those which allow the child to discover the algorithm, the pencil-and-paper method for doing this math task, on his or her own. This is true discovery learning, and it is not limited to children who are gifted in mathematics. The math material and

the work that the child does with it are guided by the teacher's presentations and her observations of the work of the child.

This chapter's co-author has seen in his own classroom, again and again, children of average abilities "discover" the algorithm for long division, division by fractions, square root, the area of any regular polygon, the volume of a pyramid, and so on. This tight linkage between the physical material and its layout on the table or floor and the algorithm—giving the child a chance to discover a step that can be done on paper as a shortcut—is perhaps unique to Montessori materials. And, of course, steps discovered in this way make sense to the child and come with the pleasure (perhaps even a sense of having found a secret shortcut) that will help in remembering the process.

2. The relationship between the curriculum, the materials, and the goals for instruction differ between Montessori and traditional elementary instruction. While there is increasing discussion of differentiated instruction in traditional education, most observers would see a strong continuation of the idea that a good teacher will "cover" the content (often laid out in a textbook) for all the children in her class. That is, in science the goal is that all the children will get through the lessons, readings, and activities in the science textbook so that all the children can then advance to next year's science curriculum. While the instruction might be differentiated, the goal may be the same for each child. In a Montessori elementary classroom, the goal is to maximize a child's learning in each subject area. So, a child with an uneven learning profile—ahead in reading but only at grade level in another area—is typical rather than unusual for Montessori children. The upper third of the curriculum in a Montessori elementary classroom is to support the child who takes off in a particular area, what traditional teachers might describe as "enrichment material."

One further noteworthy difference between Montessori and more traditional elementary approaches can be seen by comparing Montessori's Cosmic Education versus the "expanding horizons" curriculum still widely in use in traditional classrooms. In the expanding horizons model, children in kindergarten might study their own neighborhood, including trips to the post office, fire station, and so on. In first grade, the focus is expanded to the city or region. In second grade, the state might be studied, followed by the region or country, and so on. After this, however, the units of social studies are not necessarily grouped in any way that has meaning for the child; countries in Europe, Asia, and South America, for example, coexist with history units (e.g. the Revolutionary War, the Middle Ages, etc).

In contrast to the notion of starting the child out with his or her own neighborhood, Montessori starts with the world. Preschoolers are introduced to a softball-size globe, painted blue for the oceans, and with tan sandpaper for the continents. Through a series of presentations followed by periods of active, hands-on work, the children work with the puzzle maps to learn the names, shapes, and locations of countries on each continent. Later, generally in the elementary years, maps add the names of capital cities, flags, rivers, and so on. While this political geography strand is going on, the children are also learning physical geography. Starting with clay and water models of island and lake, isthmus and strait, they soon move on to locating these features on the planet: bays of the world, rivers of the world, and so on.

In addition to this strong focus on geography, the children are learning history through a variety of materials, many of which are timelines. Montessori saw the timeline as a good way to allow children to get a concrete understanding of the years, centuries, and millennia involved in history, to offer them a "big picture" view of the development of Earth and various achievements of humans (such as writing and mathematics).

Montessori elementary social studies makes use of a series of lessons entitled the "Fundamental Needs of People." A variety of presentations, discussions, and work by the children leads each class to its own ideas about what needs of humans are fundamental. Typical needs are food, clothing, shelter, heat and light, defense, transportation, and so on. These needs, studied first in the children's own culture, allow interdisciplinary tie-ins in life science, cooking, architecture, physics (simple machines, for example), and other areas.

These four strands (physical geography, political geography, history, with extensive use of timelines, and fundamental needs work) can be viewed from the expanding horizons framework to contrast Montessori's vision. First, we should acknowledge that the Montessori approach delays social studies work until the intermediate grades because of all the foundational content work. Second, this approach is at odds with some constructivist ideas on curriculum, which argue that the starting point should be the child's own neighborhood, based on the direct experience of the child. But imagine how a Montessori upper elementary (9- to 12-year-olds) teacher would approach a unit on Japan. The lesson might start with a review of fundamental needs applied to the new area of study. Imagine how the teacher might decide to focus on foods: What sort of protein might be available in Japan? Who will like to check prices for beef and tuna in Tokyo? Who will like to look at the physical geography of Japan to determine how much grazing land and how much coastline is available? Who will like to look at the timeline of civilizations to see the cultural heritage of the Japanese people? Now, what about their grains? Wheat, corn, rice? Similarly, clothing and housing can be studied as a logical consequence of what the students know (geography and history) based on the very same fundamental needs we all share. So the rice and sushi, the kanji and the shoji screens, silk clothes, and so on are all understandable choices and actually serve to show similarities among humans, rather than highlighting their differences.

PUBLIC MONTESSORI PROGRAMS

Approximately 150 to 160 public school districts in the United States currently operate some kind of Montessori program (D. Schapiro, personal communication, April 2008). About 50 of these districts operate multi-site implementations, examples being Cincinnati, Ohio, with 7 sites; Arlington, Virginia, with 10; Houston, Texas, with 7; and Denver, Colorado, with 5. Most other districts offer Montessori in just one site. The multi-site districts tend to be larger urban districts, the single-site districts tend to be smaller, suburban, or rural.

Perhaps the biggest problem in starting and maintaining a high-quality public program is the scarcity of good Montessori elementary teachers. To teach in a public program, the teacher must have both state teaching certification and Montessori elementary teacher training. Practically, this means that either a state-certified teacher must become so enamored of Montessori to take either a year or at least a summer to study Montessori or that a Montessori elementary teacher takes a year off to enroll in a program to become a state-certified teacher. In either case, the teacher is paying tuition twice and is certainly having to sit through at least some of the same content twice. Even with the higher public school salaries and benefit packages (compared to private schools), public programs often have a hard time filling positions. This usually results in teachers working in Montessori programs without the combination of full elementary Montessori certification or state credentials.

Montessori programs usually are successful magnets in both attracting and retaining students and in educating them well, as shown by the achievement test data (Dawson, 1988; Duax, 1989; Takacs & Clifford, 1988; Villegas & Biwer, 1987). Duax (1995) looked at attrition patterns at a nonselective Montessori magnet school in Milwaukee, Wisconsin, and found that children were retained at a rate approximately twice that of the district average and that there was no significant difference in retention of African American versus Anglo American students.

Montessori programs are a continuous and steady presence in public schools today, and up-to-date information on public Montessori schools is available. Descriptions of current public Montessori programs are available from a new resource group, the Montessori Public Schools Consortium, representing AMI, AMS, and NAMTA. This consortium can be reached at the NAMTA address given at the end of this chapter. There is also a newsletter, *Public School Montessorian*, that is circulated free to all public programs and provides a forum for discussion of the issues that impact public Montessori programs. The newsletter is published by Jola Publications, Box 8354, Minneapolis, MN 55408.

In general, public school Montessori continues to grow. The decline in federal support for magnet programs (especially start-up money) seems to have reduced only slightly the launching of Montessori public school programs. Those public programs started through persistent parent advocacy seem to be continuing, perhaps in part because of Montessori's continued success in the private sector. The charter school movement has led to additional publicly funded Montessori programs in 19 states (Schapiro & Hellen, 2007).

Current difficulties continue to be the training of public Montessori school teachers and the tendency for the last years in the Montessori school (typically fourth and fifth grades) to become much more traditional, as concerns increase about the transfer to non-Montessori school settings. Also, the increased push for standardized achievement testing has emerged as an issue about which traditional education and Montessori education have sharply differing views.

Montessori in Developing Countries

Montessori has been a global movement almost since its inception. Many schools were developed throughout Europe and India through

James E. Johnson

Developmentally appropriate ways to teach academic content with specialized tools of learning—a major Montessorian contribution to early childhood education today.

direct inspiration from Dr. Montessori's lectures and teacher training courses. Over time, the Montessori movement has spread to every habitable continent, to include schools and teacher education programs in Europe, North America, Asia, South America, Australia, and Africa (American Montessori Society, 2007; Association Montessori Internationale, 2007). AMS currently accredits teacher education programs in 8 countries plus Puerto Rico and has member schools in 21 countries. AMI lists teacher education programs in 21 countries.

In seeking to study the spread of Montessori worldwide we can also examine the role of the Montessori Accreditation Commission for Teacher Education (MACTE) in providing recognition for programs outside the United States. Up until the formation of MACTE in 1992, the AMS was the only international organization with Montessori teacher education programs. Although designed primarily to provide an accrediting agency for U.S. programs that would be accepted by the Department of Education, MACTE was seen by international programs as a way to gain recognition. When AMS joined with a consortium of other organizations and independent teacher education programs to form MACTE, there were two AMS teacher education programs in Mexico. In 2007–2008, MACTE lists nine programs in Canada, three in Korea, two in China, and one each in England, Taiwan, Ireland, Mexico, Dominican Republic, Israel, and South Africa.

Beyond this type of membership and accreditation data, the spread of Montessori worldwide is very difficult to document without a worldwide network of researchers. A few observations can be made, however.

International schools and teacher education programs that choose to take on the rigorous standards required for membership and/or accreditation with a recognized organization may not (and likely *do* not) represent the majority of international Montessori education programs. Anecdotal reports from teachers and teacher educators in China offer examples of "teacher training courses" being set up by material vendors grant certificates after a mere 1- or 2-week training period. Under relatively unregulated conditions, standards of quality can vary widely, with some schools offering an authentic model of Montessori and others offering a poor representation. Without models of quality to emulate, it is difficult for parents in areas where Montessori is relatively new to judge whether the model being implemented is a good example of Montessori education or not.

Middle-class families in countries such as Brazil, China, and Korea are often eager to educate their children in the best way possible and seize upon the name "Montessori" as meaning high-quality education. However, in many cases, these same parents (not unlike some in the United States) make demands on schools that compromise core Montessori principles—for example, insisting on a 1- or 2-year age span, rather than 3 years or emphasizing academics and paperwork at the expense of extensive use of hands-on materials.

Both authors of this chapter have been involved in Montessori teacher education programs in diverse areas, including Puerto Rico, China, Korea, and Brazil. Our anecdotal experiences vary but include examples of beautiful implementations of Montessori despite very little in the way of material resources (Puerto Rico), examples of extremely hard-working and dedicated teacher trainees producing their own materials (Korea, Puerto Rico, and Brazil), and of gorgeous implementation of Montessori being available to only the very elite among the local population (China). Consistency of implementation of the Montessori model is difficult in areas remote from other schools and teacher education programs. With fewer schools in an area there are fewer opportunities for support, and with trainers and recognized organizations at such a distance, it is very difficult to enforce standards that are not internally generated and accepted.

With increasing demand for Montessori schools and therefore for trained Montessori teachers in developing countries, there will be increasing demand on organizations such as AMS and AMI not only to offer support, training, and standards to fledgling Montessori communities but also to offer encouragement toward development of a local Montessori infrastructure (local training courses and trainers, national or regional organizations) within each region.

CONCLUSION

The core Montessori curriculum continues to be developed and expanded by innovative teachers worldwide applying Montessori principles to new situations and to meet the interests and needs of diverse individual learners. Over the past two decades, Montessori programs have been incorporated into many public school systems as an experimental model, expanding the availability of this largely private school movement to a wider base of socioeconomic, racial, and cultural groupings.

Research continues to try to keep up with the results of the Montessori public school venture, as well as the long-term results of Montessori education in general. Hopefully, a range of longitudinal, experimental, and naturalistic studies can be undertaken to further document current practice and to seek answers to far-reaching questions regarding the nature and effects of the Montessori school experience both in the United States and abroad.

MONTESSORI RESOURCES

Who Was Maria Montessori?
www.montessori-namta.org/NAMTA/geninfo/mmbio.html

This site includes an introduction to Maria Montessori, a bit of history, and an introduction to her ideas.

All About Montessori Schools
American Montessori Society. http://www.amshq.org

Association Montessori Internationale. http://www.montessori-ami.org

www.montessori.org/schools/search.php

This URL will let you search a database of Montessori schools by location, name, or other keywords.

All About the American Montessori Society
http://www.amshq.org

This is the American Montessori Society's site, including a database of schools, position papers, upcoming conferences, teacher education program listings, award winners for the best research thesis and dissertation on Montessori, and more.

All You Need to Know About NAMTA or NAMTO
http://www.montessori-namta.org

This is the site for the North American Montessori Teachers' Organization, with information on its activities, including upcoming conferences.

What You Need to Know About the Toronto Montessori School
http://www.toronto-montessori.ca

The Toronto Montessori School's Web site has a long list of other resources on Montessori.

Major U.S. Montessori Organizations
American Montessori Society (AMS)
281 Park Ave. South, 6th Floor
New York, NY 10011
212-358-1250

Association Montessori Internationale (AMI/USA)
410 Alexander St.
Rochester, NY 14607–1028
716-461-5920

Montessori Accreditation Council for Teacher Education (MACTE)
17583 Oak Street
Fountain Valley, CA 92708
888-446-2283

North American Montessori Teachers Association (NAMTA)
11424 Bellflower Rd. NE
Cleveland, OH 44106
216-421-1905

REFERENCES

American Montessori Society. (1994). *Montessori education*. New York: Author.

American Montessori Society. (2007). http://www.amshq.org

American Montessori Society. (n.d.). *American Montessori Society position papers*. New York: Author. Retrieved April 13, 2008, at http://www.amshq.org/member_positionPapers.htm

Baines, M., & Snortum, J. (1973). A time-sampling analysis of Montessori versus traditional classroom interaction. *Journal of Educational Research, 66*, 313–316.

Baker, K. (1988). *The interpretation of subtraction held by children in the Association Montessori Internationale curriculum*. Unpublished master's thesis, University of Maryland.

Bausch, J., & Hsu, H. (1988). Montessori: Right or wrong about number concepts? *Arithmetic Teacher, 35*(6), 8–11.

Bennett, K. P., & LeCompte, M. D. (1990). How schools work: A sociological analysis of education. New York: Longman. In A. S. Lillard (2007). *Montessori: The science behind the genius*. New York: Oxford University Press.

Bergen, D. (Ed.). (1988). *Play as a medium for learning and development*. Portsmouth, NH: Heinemann.

Black, S. (1977). *A comparison of cognitive and social development in British infant and Montessori preschools*. Unpublished doctoral dissertation, Temple University.

Boehnlein, M. (1988). Montessori research: Analysis in retrospect. *Special Edition of the North American Montessori Teachers' Association Journal, 13*(3).

Bogart, L. (1992). Transmitting the tools of a culture. *Montessori Life, 4*(3), 27–28.

Chattin-McNichols, J. (1981). The effects of Montessori school experience. *Young Children, 36*, 49–66.

Chattin-McNichols, J. (1991). *Montessori teachers' intervention: Preliminary findings from an international study*. Urbana-Champaign, IL. (ERIC Document Reproduction Service No. ED 341499)

Chattin-McNichols, J. (1992). *The Montessori controversy*. Albany, NY: Delmar.

Cisneros, M. (1994). *Multiple measures of the effectiveness of public school Montessori education in the third grade*. Unpublished doctoral dissertation. University of North Texas.

Cossentino, J., & Whitcomb, J. (2003, April). *Culture, coherence, and craft-oriented teacher education and the case of Montessori teacher training*. Paper presented at the Annual Meeting of American Educational Research Association, Chicago, IL.

Dawson, M. A. (1988). *Comparative analysis of the standardized test scores of students enrolled in HISD Montessori magnet and traditional elementary classrooms*. Unpublished master's thesis, Texas Southern University.

Dreyer, A. S., & Rigler, D. (1969). Cognitive performance in Montessori and nursery school children. *Journal of Educational Research, 67*, 411–416.

Duax, T. (1989). Preliminary report on the educational effectiveness of a Montessori school in the public sector. *North American Montessori Teachers' Association Quarterly, 14*, 2.

Duax, T. (1995). Report on academic achievement in a private Montessori school. *NAMTA Journal, 20*(2), 145–147.

Duffy, M., & Duffy, D. (2002). *Children of the universe*. Hollidaysburg, PA: Parent Child Press.

Feltin, P. (1987). *Independent learning in four Montessori elementary classrooms*. Unpublished doctoral dissertation, Seattle University.

Fero, J. R. (1997). *A comparison of academic achievement of students taught by the Montessori method and by traditional methods of instruction in the elementary grades.* Unpublished doctoral dissertation, Montana State University, Bozeman.

Glenn, C. (1989). A comparison of lower and upper elementary Montessori students with a public school sample. *North American Montessori Teachers' Association Quarterly, 14,* 263–268.

Glenn, C. (1993). *The longitudinal assessment study: Cycle 3* (seven year) follow up. (ERIC Document Reproduction Service, No. ED 370679)

Glenn, C. (1996). *The longitudinal assessment study: Cycle 4 (ten year) follow up.* (ERIC Document Reproduction Service No. ED 403013)

Glenn, C. (1999). The longitudinal assessment study: Thirteen year follow up. (ERIC Document Reproduction Service No. ED 431543)

Grazzini, C. (1996). The four planes of development. *The NAMTA Journal, 21*(2), 208–241.

Kahn, D. (Ed.). (1990). *Implementing Montessori education in the public sector.* Cleveland, OH: North American Montessori Teachers' Association.

Karnes, M., Shwedel, A., & Williams, M. (1983). A comparison of five approaches for educating young children from low-income homes. In The Consortium for Longitudinal Studies (Ed.), *As the twig is bent: Lasting effects of preschool programs* (pp. 133–169). Hillsdale, NJ: Erlbaum.

Leto, F. (1996). Let the music flow: A conversation with Frank Leto. *Montessori Life, 8*(5), 22–26.

Lillard, A. (2005). *Montessori: The science behind the genius.* New York: Oxford University Press.

Lillard, A., & Else-Quest, N. (2006). Evaluating Montessori education. *Science, 313,* 1893–1894.

Lillard, P. (1972). *Montessori: A modern approach.* New York: Schocken.

Loeffler, M. H. (1992). Montessori and constructivism. In M. H. Loeffler (Ed.), *Montessori in contemporary American culture* (pp. 101–113). Portsmouth, NH: Heinemann.

Miller, L., & Bizzell, R. (1983). Long-term effects of four preschool programs: Sixth, seventh, and eighth grades. *Child Development, 54*(3), 727–741.

Miller, L., & Bizzell, R. (1985). Long-term effects of four preschool programs: Ninth- and tenth-grade results. *Child Development, 55*(4), 1570–1587.

Miller, L., & Dyer, L. (1975). Four preschool programs: Their dimensions and effects. *Monographs of the Society for Research in Child Development, 40* (Serial No. 162).

Montessori Accreditation Council for Teacher Education. (1996). *Montessori accreditation council for teacher education standards for teacher education programs.* Pasadena, CA: Author.

Montessori, M. (1913). *Pedagogical anthropology.* New York: Stokes.

Montessori, M. (1963). *Education for a new world.* Madras, India: Vasanta Press.

Montessori, M. (1964). *The Montessori method.* New York: Schocken.

Montessori, M. (1965). *Spontaneous activity in education.* New York: Schocken.

Montessori, M. (1966). *The secret of childhood.* Notre Dame, IN: Fides.

Montessori, M. (1967a). *The absorbent mind.* New York: Dell. (Original work published 1949)

Montessori, M. (1967b). *The discovery of the child.* Notre Dame, IN: Fides. (Original work published 1948)

Montessori, M. (1973). *From childhood to adolescence.* New York: Schocken.

North American Montessori Teachers' Association (D. Kahn, Ed.) (1995). *What is Montessori elementary?* Cleveland, OH: NAMTA.

Rambusch, N. M. (1962). *Learning how to learn.* Baltimore, MD: Helicon.

Rathunde, K., & Csikszentmihalyi, M. (2005, May). Middle school students' motivation and quality of experience: A comparison of Montessori and traditional school environments. *American Journal of Education, 111,* 341–371.

Reed, M. (2000). A comparison of the place value understanding of Montessori and non-Montessori elementary school students. *Dissertation Abstracts International, 61,* No. 05A.

Reuter, J., & Yunik, G. (1973). Social interaction in nursery schools. *Developmental Psychology, 9,* 319–325.

Schapiro, D., & Hellen, B. (2007). *Montessori community resource.* Minneapolis, MN: Jola.

Schmid, J., & Black, K. (1977). An observational study of the choice and use of toys by Montessori and non-Montessori preschoolers. In S. Makhick & J. Henne (Eds.), *Evaluations of educational outcomes: Proceedings of the national conference on the evaluation of Montessori and open classrooms* (pp. 79–92). New York: American Montessori Society.

Scott, J. (1995). The development of the mathematical mind. *Montessori Life, 7*(2), 25.

Standing, E. M. (1962). *Maria Montessori: Her life and work.* New York: New American Library.

Standing, E. M. (1964). *The child in the church.* Notre Dame, IN: Fides.

Stodolsky, S., & Karlson, A. (1972). Differential outcomes of a Montessori curriculum. *Elementary School Journal, 72,* 419–433.

Takacs, C., & Clifford, A. (1988). Performance of Montessori graduates in public school classrooms. *North American Montessori Teachers' Association Quarterly, 14*(1), 2–9.

Torrence, M. (1992). Montessori and play: Theory vs. practice. *Montessori Life, 7*(3), 35–38.

Torrence, M. (1993). From percept to concept: The sensorial path to knowledge. *Montessori Life, 5*(3), 28–30.

Turner, J. (1995). How do you teach reading? *Montessori Life, 7*(3), 25–34.

Villegas, A., & Biwer, P. (1987). Parent involvement in a Montessori program: The Denver public school experience. *North American Montessori Teachers' Association Quarterly, 13*(1), 13–24.

Wirtz, P. (1976). *Social behavior related to material settings in the Montessori preschool environment.* Unpublished doctoral dissertation, George Peabody College for Teachers.

Chapter 17
The Pyramid Method

Jef J. van Kuyk ~ CITO Corporation, Arnhem, The Netherlands

BASIC CONCEPTS

Pyramid is an educational method for all children between the ages of $2\frac{1}{2}$ and 7 years of age (in this chapter we describe Pyramid up to the age of 6). The method has a number of special features for children who need extra support. These include extra language stimulation, interactive storytelling, extra play and initiative learning activities, activities for gifted children, and tutoring (van Kuyk, 2003).

Education in the Pyramid Method means starting with the vulnerable child who cannot yet manage daily tasks without help and support, while at the same time stimulating children to distance themselves from us so they can learn to manage on their own.

Pyramid is based on a new theory: a synthesis of the theories of Piaget and of Vygotsky that moves beyond their work, the Dynamic Systems Theory (Fischer & Bidell, 2006; van Geert, 1998). This theory opens new perspectives for the education of young children (van Kuyk, 2006). In contrast to the theory of Piaget, which has fixed developmental stages, the Dynamic Systems Theory consists of a series of dynamic long-term and short-term cycles in the early part of the life span. During these growth cycles the child learns and relearns new skills through self-regulation and through scaffolding by adults. Scaffolding provides assistance on an as-needed basis, with fading out of assistance as competence increases (Pressley, Hogan, Wharton-McDonald, & Mistretta, 1996). There is a great difference between development through self-regulation and development through scaffolding. Through self-regulation, the child can reach a normal (lower) level of development; through scaffolding by the teacher the child can reach an optimal (higher) level of development (Fischer & Bidell, 2006). Is it desirable to try to bring children to an optimal level at all times? Child and teacher: each has limits. The teacher has to spread his or her energy and time among all the children. The child has to switch between tension and relaxation and needs time for both self-regulation and scaffolding.

In this chapter, we clarify how we constructed the Pyramid curriculum to create physical and psychological space to offer children the possibility for self-regulation through play and initiative learning. We also explain how the teacher can scaffold, on the one hand, the improvement of play and initiative learning and, on the other hand, take the initiative to optimize the growth cycles through projects in which children learn to take initiative to move from the here and now to more distant and abstract representations (Sigel, 1993) and through sequential activities. We explain play and initiative learning as forms of self-regulation, as well as the short-term and long-term cycles of Dynamic Systems Theory as forms of scaffolding (12 projects in a year) and translate them into practice. Short-term cycles, found in every project, involve the four steps of distancing: Orientation, Demonstration, Broadening, and Deepening, also known as ODBD. The long-term cycles are the year plans in which the short-term cycles are nested. We also describe the sequential activities another way for teachers to take initiative.

This curriculum is set up with a relational component the way in which the teacher treats the children. Derived from attachment theory, this includes safety and well-being, emotional support, care and understanding, loving relationships, respect for autonomy, structure and rules, and opening perspectives to explore the world. Complementing the relative component is the educational component or the way in which the teacher stimulates the development of the children, challenges their curiosity, and works to understand what motivates them internally and externally. This component is derived from Dynamic Systems Theory (Fischer & Rose, 1998) and from Distancing Theory (Sigel, 1993). Within these two components, four concepts are brought together: initiative of the child, initiative of the teacher, nearness, and distance.

The Child's Initiative

The question raised here is, to what extent can children optimize their development on their own? According to Piaget (1970), children possess enough cognitive power to direct their own development. This is done through confrontation with objects from their physical and social environment. The child's initiative is the beginning and end of the educational process. The human being is oriented towards self-regulation (Fischer & Bidell, 2006; van Geert, 1998). As soon as a child is born we see that he or she wants to discover the world. At a very early age children begin to grasp objects, listen to sounds, and follow movements. They pay attention to things that interest them and lose interest when things are known. They learn to make choices by themselves. The first objective of the Pyramid Method is to support and optimize the child's capacity to take initiative. It is also the ultimate objective, as later the child must be able to manage his or her everyday life. For this a child's own initiative is essential.

The Teacher's Initiative

The question asked regarding the teacher's initiative is, what form of teacher initiative secures optimum development? The initiative of the teacher is essential to the education process (Fischer & Bidell, 2006; van Geert, 1998). The role of the teacher is to scaffold children in their development, which cannot be achieved without support (Bowman, 2000). The teacher can support the child during play and initiative learning by stimulating him or her to take the initiative. However, the teacher also takes initiatives that encourage optimal development. He or she does this during group activities or when children are carrying out tasks on their own. The teacher has a broad spectrum of educational skills. The teacher creates possibilities, offers support, motivates, sets a good example, gives instructions, and guides children in learning to think about and solve problems.

Nearness

When educating children, it is important that the attachment between the child and the educator is a solid one (Ainsworth, Blehar, & Waters, 1978; Bowlby, 1969; Erickson, Sroufe, & Egeland, 1985). It is important that the child has the feeling that the educator is close by. This allows the child to feel safe, secure, and free enough to go forward and explore the world. The educator gives the child this freedom but, at the same time, creates a clear structure and establishes rules. These rules are not to restrict the child but to indicate where there is space for playing and learning. Structure and rules also give the child a sense of safety. In a safe environment, children take the initiative and explore the world. The task of the educator is to pick up signals and to help the child find the answers that will allow the child to be him- or herself. The educator gives emotional support when needed while respecting the autonomy of the child. A child may, for example, show signs that he or she is not yet ready to take part in group activities. Such signals should be respected. If a child is playing intensively, the educator should remain in the background. If a child reaches an impasse, then a teacher can offer more intensive guidance. We refer to this as *sensitive response attitude.*

Distance

The distancing concept is embedded in Sigel's conceptual framework (Cocking & Renninger, 1993; Sigel, 1993). Distancing can serve as instructions within Vygotsky's zone of proximal development (Vygotsky, 1962). Under the condition of nearness, the teacher removes distance from the here and now. He or she must begin close to the child, in here-and-now situations, using what can be directly observed with the senses involving concrete material. At the same time, the teacher must help the child take more and more distance. The teacher asks here-and-now questions but also asks questions and talks about subjects that are not in the here and now. In this way, a child can learn that the world existed before being born and that mothers and fathers were also once small children. A child can learn to think about places never seen before, things that happened long ago or have not yet happened. For example, "We are going on holiday. What will the place we are going to look like?" "What did you do yesterday?" "What are you going to do tomorrow or next week?"

In this way, children learn to create representations that can be recalled later. Research has shown that children who have parents who engage them in diverse activities outside the here and now develop well but those with parents who remain in the here-and-now are less developed or may even display signs of underdeveloped skills (Sigel, 1993). The basic principle is this: Begin close with concrete situations and materials and then help the child represent things and events not in the here-and-now by using symbolized mediators and questions that make the nonpresent mentally present (more abstract concepts comprehensible/accessible to the child).

THE RELATIONSHIPS AMONG THE BASIC CONCEPTS

The four basic concepts (cornerstones) we identify in the Pyramid Method are closely related (Figure 17–1). If the child takes initiative, the

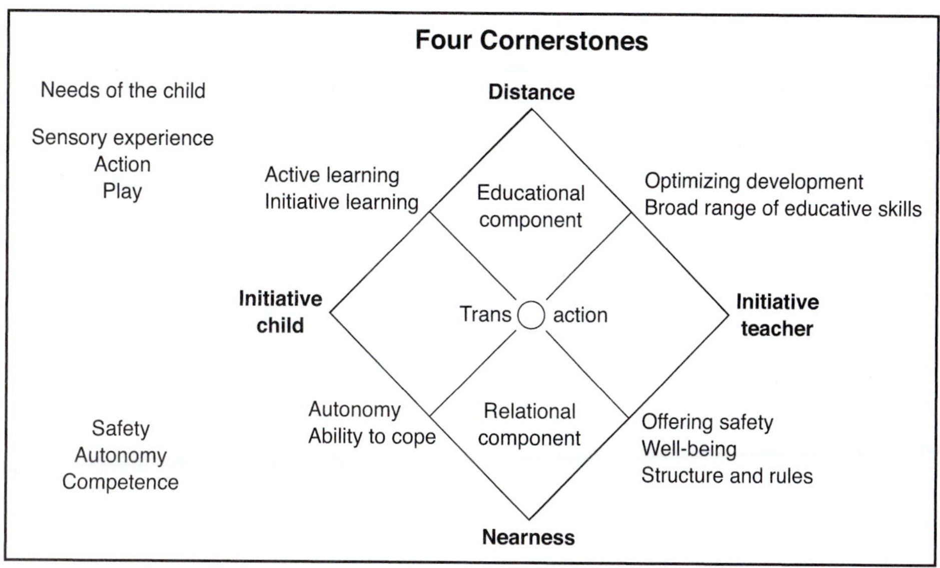

FIGURE 17–1 Relational and Educational Components

educator can remain in the background. If the child shows little initiative, the teacher must provide support. There is a transactional relationship between teacher and child; they influence each other.

Nearness and distance are also strongly related to each other. Nearness makes possible distance: if children feel safe they can explore; they can take distance from the here-and-now.

The relationship between the concepts is important, but the teacher must also consider the relational needs of the child—the need for safety, the need to be oneself (autonomy), the need to master things (competency)—as well as the educational needs of the young child—the need for sensory experience, the desire to do things in an active way, and the need to play. This strategy strengthens freedom, well-being, motivation, and curiosity in children: the engine for optimal development.

OPTIMIZING

Research has shown that it is not true that children always function at the same level, but they *can* function at many different levels of action and thought (Figure 17–2). The level at which they will function depends on the circumstances (Fischer & Bidell, 2006). If the relational component is optimal, child can act at a normal level. If circumstances are less favorable—for example, if there is unrest or stress—then the child can function at a minimal level. If children are disturbed by lack of structure and rules, they will not be able to function at a normal level.

Through education, we can stimulate children to rise above the normal level to reach self-regulation. Research shows that education helps children reach an optimal level of development (Fischer & Bidell, 2006; Sigel, 1993). This can be achieved, for example, by supporting children in their play and by stimulating initiative learning. During individual activity, the teacher can enrich play by introducing a new role or material, or he or she can support the writing of a word. In group activities, he or she can provide clear examples, describe the main features of a situation, or guide the process of understanding a phenomenon. To help children learn in an active way scaffolding can support if given only to the extent that it does not impinge on the capacity of children to take the initiative (Vygotsky's zone of proximal development). Expert scaffolding provided by a teacher

FIGURE 17–2 **Levels of Action and Thought and Social Support**

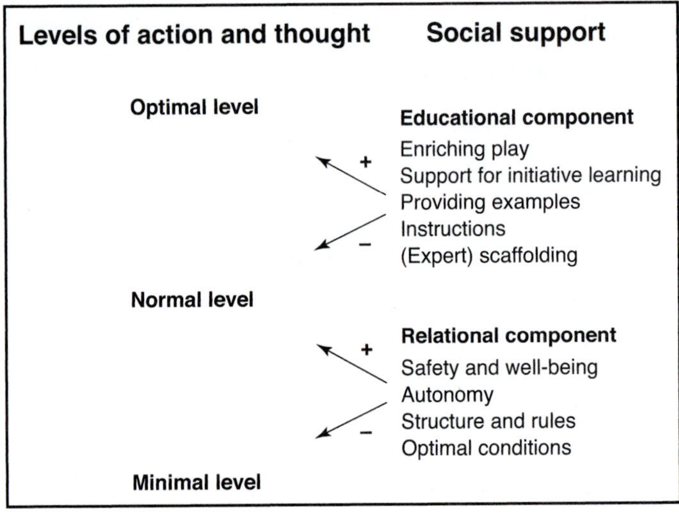

with considerable knowledge and experience is the best form of support. For this reason, we attach special importance to stimulating the development of children via the Pyramid Method. By stimulating children at an early age, and encouraging them to deal with everyday task by themselves, we lay the basis for their success at school and encourage them to deal with everyday tasks by themselves.

During early childhood, the teacher should ensure that the relational component is such that children can function in a normal way. The educational component can then take effect so that children can reach their optimal level. This requires considerable professionalism, as a teacher is not just concerned with optimizing the development of one child but rather the whole group. This demands a broad repertoire of educational skills. The teacher has to provide for a large group of children between 12 and 15 in the case of young children and sometimes between 20 and 25 in the case of older ones. It is impossible to give all children individual attention at all times. It is important that the teacher find a balance between what children themselves can learn and what the teacher must teach. The teacher offers relational and educational supports necessary for active learning given at children's levels of development and independence.

CONTENT

In the introduction we indicated how we work with children to optimize their development. This is the basis of the Pyramid Method. The questions we now pose are: what is the focus of our efforts to optimize development and what development is being fostered? In searching for answers we have been inspired by the Theory of Emotional Intelligence (Salovay & Mayer, 1990) and by Gardner's Multiple Intelligence Theory (Gardner, 1993).

We can describe the content of the Pyramid Method in terms of three intelligences (van Kuyk, 2003) and indicate which developmental areas are involved in these intelligences. In the Pyramid Method, we work by balancing these three intelligences equally (Figure 17–3).

THREE INTELLIGNECES

In the Pyramid Method we proceed from three intelligences. In daily life we often speak of the gift of the head: cognitive intelligence; the gift of the heart: emotional intelligence; and the gift of the hand: physical intelligence. Children possess these gifts or intelligences in varying degrees. We have differentiated them in this way as we want to offer children a balanced development paths that involves all three intelligences, and not because we wish to focus learning on intelligences where the most capacity exists. Due to the fact that the intelligences are abstract and general, we have concretized them in developmental areas that are recognizable worldwide to all those involved in teaching young children.

Cognitive Intelligence

Cognitive intelligence is the capacity to control language and thought and to work with them. Here we see the development of perception, language, and thinking and orientation of space and time. All perception, language, and thought take place in space and time. Children learn to get a grip on their everyday world by developing these areas. They learn to distance themselves from the here and now. Language has a double function. Language is the means whereby children can communicate and learn from the teacher. Language enrichment is also an important educational objective.

Emotional Intelligence

Emotional intelligence refers to the capacity to sense one's own emotions, the emotions of

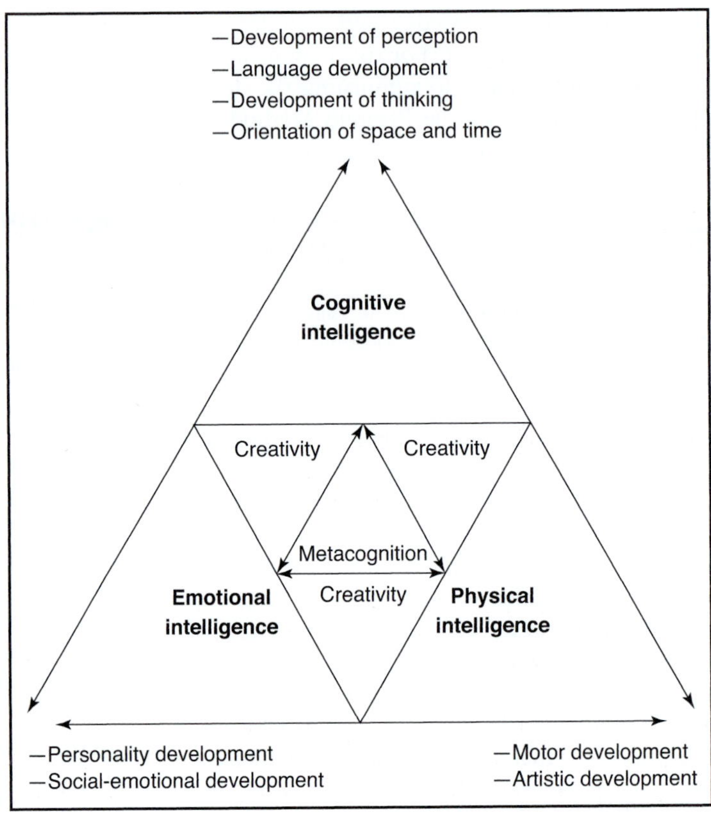

FIGURE 17–3 Intelligences and Developmental Areas in the Pyramid Method

others, and to conduct oneself socially. This intelligence area includes personal development and social-emotional development. Children learn to develop confidence, perseverance, and self-regulation. In addition, they learn to recognize their own feelings and those of others and to show respect for these in the way they behave and conduct themselves (moral development).

Physical Intelligence

Physical intelligence is the capacity to initiate movement, to control it, and to express oneself creatively. Here we make a distinction between motor development and artistic (music and art) development. Within these areas children learn to move, to act, to control their body, and to know their boundaries. They learn to be creative in relation to their own body, how to develop their body language, and how to work with materials, tools, and instruments in the process of artistic development. They learn with their bodies and with the help of appropriate materials and instruments come able to create new things and to express themselves in art and music. This is, for the most part, a total experience.

LEVELS OF ACTION AND THINKING

Here we identify three levels of action and thinking reflecting an increasingly individualized more flexible and conscious use of what is being learned.

Basic Level

The basic level is the level of basic knowledge and basic skills. This is what the child copies and learns from others through imitation and example. Children learn this in the first steps of the projects and in the sequential activities.

Creative Level

The second level is the level of creativity. By this we refer to the capacity to create or think of something that is new and worthwhile. At this level, children use their basic knowledge in a creative way. They play with what they have learned and begin to follow new paths. In play and initiative learning and in the project steps, especially broadening and deepening, in which active learning is indicated, children learn to use knowledge and skills in a creative way.

Metacognitive Level

At the highest level of knowledge and skills we speak of metacognition. This level is attained when children are aware of their knowledge and skills and consciously change their own behavior. Under the direction of cognitive intelligence, children can become conscious of their physical, emotional, and cognitive actions and work with them in a flexible and creative way. During reflections on play and initiative learning ("What is important? Can you find the solution?") and during the active learning of projects, the child is stimulated to learn and think on a metacognitive level.

FOUR PROGRAMS

In the Pyramid Method we have four programs to work out the relational and educational components from the initiative of the child and the initiative of the teacher, to enable us to optimize the development of the children. Two programs are initiated by the child: play and initiative learning. *Initiative learning* is a new term that we use to express that children take the initiative to learn. Two other programs are initiated by the teacher: the projects, in which the teacher explores the outside world with the children, and sequenced activities (Figure 17–4), in which a hierarchy of activities is offered for the children to learn.

Initiative Child	**Initiative Teacher**
Play	Project
Initiative learning	Sequenced activities

FIGURE 17–4 Various Initiatives Expressed

In the Pyramid Method we focus strongly on the fact that children should regulate themselves. Children are stimulated by a rich and stimulating play and learning environment to take the initiative to make choices for themselves in both play and learning activities.

We know, however, that children cannot learn everything by themselves. In fact they learn a great deal from other children and especially from their teachers. The teacher's initiative is important in teaching children new things. This can be done on an individual basis through tutoring (Slavin, Madden, & Karweit, 1994), for example, when a teacher gives guidance to individual children who need extra support or more learning time. But individual tutoring is expensive. It can be done better and more efficiently by tackling subjects and exploring them in groups with the help of projects and sequential programs. The teacher sets an example, instructs the children, and supports them in active learning. He or she motivates the children and teaches them what they should know and be able to do.

THREE LEVELS OF INTERVENTION

We differentiate the co-construction process of children and teacher into three levels of intervention (Figure 17–5). We do this to ensure that

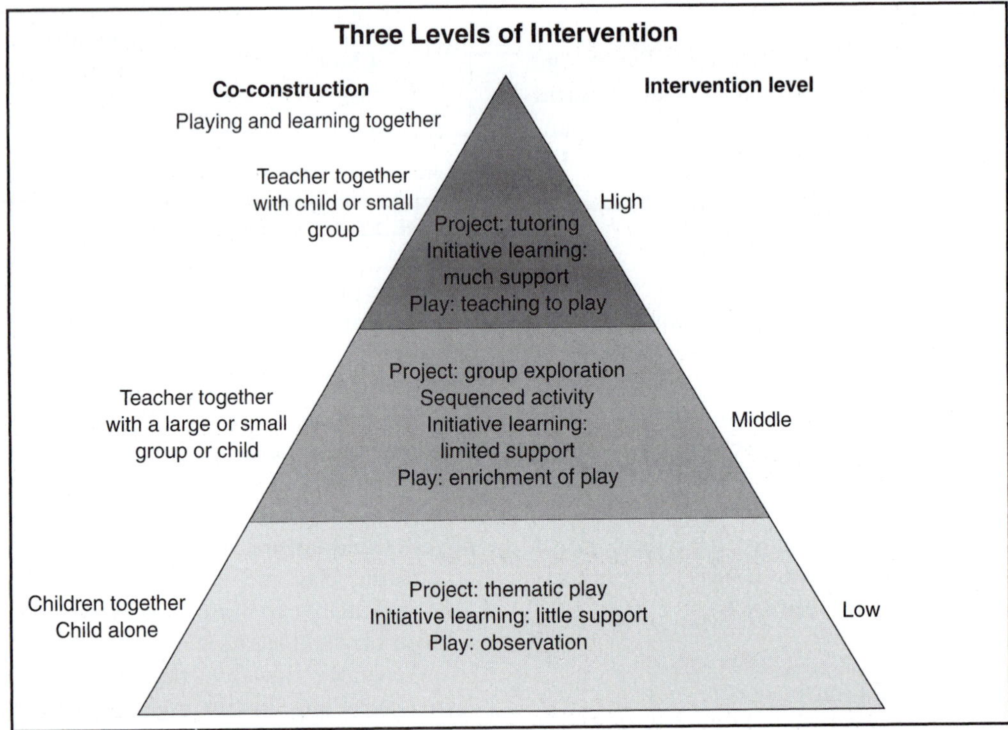

FIGURE 17–5 Three Levels of Intervention

the support children need when they decide to take the initiative and what they must learn—as individuals or in a group when supported by the teacher's initiative—are in balance and attuned to each other.

Low Level

Children play and learn independently without intervention from their teacher. The teacher gives little or no support. If support is necessary, the teacher will adjust it to the development level of the child and the degree of independence displayed.

Middle Level

Children play, explore, and learn together with the teacher. A middle level of support is given either in large or small groups. During the projects, the teacher initially gives more than the average amount of support to help get the process started. The teacher then slowly tries to hand over activities, bit by bit, to the children. The amount of help offered depends on the level of development and the degree of independence the children display.

High Level

The teacher or tutor (individual support given by a special teacher) plays with or teaches individual children or smaller groups requiring extra help. The teacher or tutor, therefore, gives considerable support. In general, the developmental levels of the children will be low and their degrees of independence limited. The intensity of help is in proportion to what is needed to bring children to a higher level of development and to make them more independent.

ELABORATION OF THE PROGRAMS

The practical basis for the programs is planning and furnishing of the play and learning environment.

Play and Learning Environment

From brain research we know that "the brain takes what the environment offers" (Shonkoff & Philips, 2000). While in the womb the fetus is already responding differently to speech sounds and other (less structured) sound or noises. What teachers need to do is offer children a rich and high-level structured environment to give children the possibility for self-regulation in which they can find new structures for learning.

High-level Structure. The environment offers new challenges to play and to explore, in which children can find materials and situations that fit their level of development and challenge them to reach a higher level. The child has opportunities to make his or her own choices and can make his or her own, flexible decisions.

In this environment we need centers in which children can play, as well as cupboards and other storage areas containing different levels of materials, and discovery tables offering structures for learning and play. To practice a project the teacher changes centers to challenge children to experience new materials and new ideas. He or she offers open cupboards so children may choose educational materials for assignments.

The teacher has to provide physical and psychological space to create an environment that stimulates the child to take initiative.

Physical Space. The teacher offers every child enough room to play and opportunities to take initiative for initiative learning. In the centers, the teacher offers enough materials for each child to choose activities that represent the different developmental areas. Children can do this alone or together with other children. Vygotsky proved that through communication with other children, the child has to react to the ideas, actions, and language of other children. Each child has to constantly change his or her mind. This stimulates flexible and resilient thinking.

Psychological Space. The teacher allows, or even stimulates, the children to take initiatives that promote the feeling that what they are doing is received well. Children do not have to ask for confirmation within the bounds of structure and rules. The teacher creates psychological space and affirms what the child is doing.

1. PLAY PROGRAM

Play is an activity that is initiated by the child. Children make choices and explore freely in a rich play environment. This is also possible in the projects discussed later in this chapter. In the Pyramid Method, there are three ways in which involvement in play is optimized.

Creating Rich Play Situations

We identify different types of play. Each type of play places different demands on the play environment. In the Pyramid Method we distinguish between five sorts of play: material play, motor play, pretend play, imaginary play, and rule play.

In addition to creating play situations in the material environment, we also stimulate children toward rich play. If there is not enough rich play, then we move to the second level.

Play Enrichment

In the past, teachers often thought they should not disturb children when they were playing,

Toos van Kuyk

Pyramid teachers expect learning in specific sequences in large or small groups.

and this is certainly still the case when children are playing richly and deeply. In the Pyramid Method we proceed from the idea that adults can and should play an active role in enriching play. Children like to play with adults; however, what is more important and what scientific research has confirmed, is that children will act and think at a higher level if an adult guides them in their play (Fischer & Bidell, 2006). The process of enrichment can take two forms.

Joining in the Play. By playing together with the child or a group of children, the teacher shows that he or she values and enjoys the play in which the child is engaged. The child feels valued, and from this position the teacher can "enter into the play" of the children and work to enrich the play. However, when the teacher starts instructing, for example, "Take the cups," he or she is an instructing teacher and not a playing teacher. Once the teacher is involved as a participant in the child's play or the group's play, he or she can even offer suggestions, but only if this fits into his or her role!

Enriching Play. Each day the children play at drinking tea in the home center. The teacher comes to visit them and drinks tea with them.

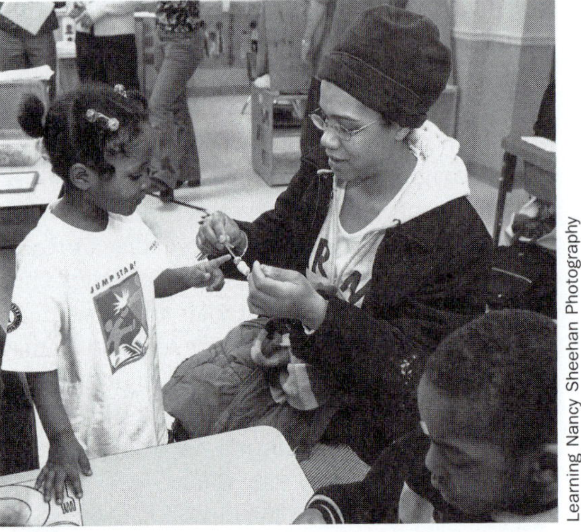

Learning Nancy Sheehan Photography

Parents are critical for learning throughout the early years.

After this ritual has been completed, the children "clean up" after themselves. The teacher can observe their play and assess the degree of involvement.

Do the children take the initiative? Do they make their own rules? Is the play still exciting enough? Are the roles becoming too stereotyped? Is fantasy being used?

The things that show that the play is not rich enough—for example, lack of persistence in play, limited use of imagination, and impoverished scripts can often be a source of inspiration for enriching play. In this way, the teacher can introduce a new role into play: "What do I hear? Is that a bell? Who can that be? Who is coming to visit us?"

Learning to Play

Sometimes there are children in a group who do not play. They may feel ill, worried, or afraid. Some children may not have a good command of the language and feel left out. There are also children who are not used to play: Their play has never been appreciated, has been forbidden, or has been rejected. How can we get these children to play?

In the Pyramid Method we teach children to play in three stages: by showing them how to play, by encouraging the children to play by themselves, and by allowing them to play independently (van Kuyk, 2003).

In connection with the play activities we offer the Pyramid Play Book, in which the teacher

Toos van Kuyk

Children need to feel they are in control of what is being done. Pyramid Method materials are used to encourage this imitative learning.

can find different kinds of play activities, as well as the 10 golden rules for imaginary play and how to challenge children to play individually and in groups. The book also includes ideas on how to enrich play and how to teach play.

2. INITIATIVE LEARNING

Children do not only want to play—they also want to find out how things work and are motivated to understand the world around them. They set goals for themselves. We see this very clearly in the area of beginning literacy, beginning numeracy, and exploring the world. In the Pyramid Method, it is exactly this motivation and curiosity to act out the adult world and to come to know and master it that we stimulate. We must give the child the opportunity to take initiative, and the teacher must adjust his or her approach accordingly. In the Pyramid Method centers are designed (for example, the language center, discovery center, and math center) and developmentally appropriate materials are introduced to encourage initiative learning.

Inspiring Initiative Learning

A Good Example. In general, the initiative for initiative learning will come directly from the child; however, we can also inspire children and challenge them to learn on their own. The best way to do this is to give children a good example. In the beginning, the emphasis is put on developing interest, not on skill. The teacher can achieve this by allowing children to see many examples of reading, writing, math, and experimenting. For example, the teacher makes notes on the board, writes notes using text and numbers, studies the water to see how the tadpoles are getting on in spring, and checks to see if the seeds are germinating.

Talking About What Is Important. Talking to children about what we are doing is yet another source of inspiration. We can talk about the value of writing and math and their usefulness later in life. The teacher gives the children meaningful examples of where communication is necessary (e.g., shopping). The children must look for ways to formulate what they want (e.g., in the shop, you need a shopping list) and how to pay for what they buy in the supermarket (e.g., the grocer receives money for what he or she sells). With young children it is necessary to make links with their experiences: Begin close and slowly foster more distance.

Offering Support with Initiative Learning

It is clear that knowledge and skills are needed to support young children. The most important condition is that the children themselves retain the initiative and a feeling of competency. That is to say they feel they have achieved the best possible result. It is, therefore, necessary to offer strategic help, but only as much as children need to complete their chosen task. We already referred to this strategic help as scaffolding. Before the teacher provides support and determines a strategy, he or she observes the level of development, the degree of independence, and the amount of motivation the child has.

In connection with initiative learning, the teacher can find suggestions in the Pyramid Learning Book about how to furnish centers for children to experience reading, writing, and math and to experiment. The book includes materials that can be used and information about how to order them from simple to difficult. The teacher also will find suggestions on how to work with educational materials and how to support initiative learning with little, limited, or much involvement.

3. PROJECTS

A project is a well-balanced body of activities. These activities are closely linked to each other and built around a particular focus that fits the experiences and interests of young children.

Each year there are 12 projects. The subjects are chosen by designers on the basis of child interests (house, safeguard) and child experience (water in the summer). During the year there is an increase of difficulty in the projects. A suquential framework is used to design a holistic approach. A network of concepts, based on the sequential framework forms the basis of each project. In the Pyramid Method the teacher brings the outside world inside the classroom. He or she integrates each new project in the play-learning environment, where he or she explores each focus together with the children.

A project is a body of programs set out in a Project Book, containing some 40 pages. Each project begins with a Play Program. On the basis of a project focus, children can make play choices for themselves and carry out initiative learning activities within the context of a rich play-learning environment. This Play Program can be compared to free play, with one difference: The teacher introduces new elements into the play-learning environment during each project to give the children new challenges to play and learn.

At the core of each project is the Group Program, during which children investigate a topic introduced or encouraged by the teacher. In addition, each project contains a number of sequenced activities in the context of the project focus that can be carried out in the circle. The teacher differentiates the activities in the Group Program: Activities are made easier or more difficult, and the teacher presents them in an interactive way in which the children are active learners. A separate manual helps teachers deal with the differences present in heterogeneous groups. After the Group Program activities have been completed, the skills learned can be implemented during individual and group work (cooperative learning) in the centers.

Two programs within the project books are not carried out by the teacher: The Tutor Program is carried out by the tutor, and the Parent Program is carried out by the parents in cooperation with the teachers. What is important that all the activities are connected to the same project focus.

Projects have a double function in the Pyramid Method. First, children learn about important things in the world as they experience them. They learn to recognize an integrated body of concepts that—in a particular context—belong together. In the second place, the projects provide the children with examples of how they can learn a variety of things on their own using their own initiative. The projects provide examples of initiative play and learning. A segment in the project supports the development of language.

Learning to Take Distance

One of the basic concepts in the Pyramid Method is taking distance. As stated (Sigel, 1993), we have seen that children whose parents or teachers go beyond the here (other places, close by and far off) and now (what has happened previously and what will happen) appear to develop well.

Here is an example (Figure 17–6): Imagine a picture of an elephant against a green background. When the picture is shown to the children we ask a few "nearby" questions (the answers can be found on the picture) and a few "distance" questions (the answer must be thought up, creatively found, fantasized, or found by using existing knowledge).

We should not ask only "distance" questions. "Nearby" questions are also important: They are closer to the children, give them something to hold on to, help to make things more lucid, provide them with a feeling of safety, and give them a stable basic knowledge. However, we

"Nearby" Questions	"Distance" Questions
What color is the elephant? Where is his trunk? How many ears does the elephant have? Where is the elephant standing?	Where is the elephant going? What does an elephant eat? Why is his trunk so long? Where does an elephant live?

FIGURE 17–6 Question Types and Illustrations

must not be satisfied simply with asking "nearby" questions. In fact, we should ensure we ask *many* "distance" questions. These are much more difficult to prepare, but they also are more effective, as we know from research (Sigel, 1993).

Learning to take distance occurs in two ways: in the short-term cycle and in the long-term cycle.

Short-Term Cycle. A number of steps are taken in the group exploration of each project. We begin close to the world as the child experiences it, and then, bit by bit, we take distance from it. The child must learn to make representations: mental images that begin to develop from the age of 2 and enable the child to think (Fischer & Rose, 1998). At first these representations are very concrete, but they slowly become more abstract: first simple representations and later more complex ones. The period between 2 and 6 years is a particularly sensitive one, during which children begin to make representations on their own. This process takes place in four stages: orientation, demonstration, broadening, and deepening.

1. Orientation. This first step is not a learning step but is intended to help children orient to the context of the project focus. This takes place mainly by linking into children's experience and what they already know about the focus. This gives them a sense of safety and the feeling that they can trust the coming activity. It puts children in a good mood.

In every step the teacher can choose from five activities.

ACTIVITY FROM ORIENTATION

MAKE LEMONADE
Read the book *Amanda Pig and the Very Hot Day* by Jean van Leeuwen.
Talk about how hot the day is (Amanda is as droopy as the plants in her father's garden).
Ask the children how Amanda cools off (a cool shower with a hose and lemonade).
Let the children talk about what makes them thirsty and what they like to drink when they are thirsty.
How do they know when they are thirsty?
What signs do their body give them?
Next, give each child their own cup and plastic spoon.
Let each child pour water from a pitcher into their cup.
Give each child a wedge of lemon and let them smell and lick it.
Talk about how it smells and how it tastes.
Ask them if they can think of any other food that is sour.
Now let the children squeeze the lemons into their cups of water.
Tell the children to take a sip and see how it tastes.
Pass around a bowl of sugar cubes and let children sweeten their lemonade.
Ask how it tastes.
Which way do they like it best, sour or sweet?
Then ask "How can we make it colder?"
Have ice in a cooler ready to let each child scoop out an ice cube with a spoon.
Ask them to stir the ice around and then taste again.
How does it feel now? Do you like it better warm or cold?
What drinks do you like to drink when they are warm and what drinks do you like to drink when they are cold?"
*Intent: Understand various uses of water * Compare sour and sweet tastes * Observe sugar dissolving in water * Compare temperature of water * Follow sequence of story*

ACTIVITY FROM DEMONSTRATION

HAULING WATER UP AND DOWN
Ahead of time tie a long rope to a plastic bucket handle.
Gather the children on the playground. Throw the rope over a beam to create a pulley.
Show the children a picture of a well with a bucket attached to a rope *(can be found in Project Resources)*.
Ask them if they know how to get the water from the well.
Sing the song *Jack and Jill Went Up the Hill* and talk about the fact that they are going up the hill to the well to get some water to take home.
Show the children the rope and bucket.
Ask a child to pull the empty bucket up using the rope.
Let each child take a quick turn.
Now challenge them with the question "What could we use to make the bucket really heavy?"
Let them fill the bucket with whatever they think will make it the heaviest.
Ask children what they hear as they put the different things in the bucket.
Now let each child try to pull the bucket up with the rope.
What do they notice? Let them help each other if necessary.
Fill the bucket with different amounts of water and let children experience the change in weight.
Leave the bucket outside on the playground for the remainder of the project so children can continue to experiment with it.
(Note: This will relate to the book *Tikki Tikki Tembo* that is introduced in the Broadening step.)
*Intent: Demonstrate use of rope and pulley * Solve problems collaboratively * Observe changes in weight * Describe differences in weight*

2. Demonstration. This first learning step begins close to the world as the children experience it. The teacher presents clear examples. In this first step a great deal of work is done with the senses, as in this way children gain multifaceted experiences. The teacher points out the most important aspects to the children. Concepts are discussed and named. The teacher simultaneously shows (displays) and tells the children what he or she is doing. The teacher makes use of concrete situations and concrete materials, and on the basis of this, children build up a great deal of sensory experience. The teacher provides clear examples to help children understand. The teacher also uses pictures to illustrate his or her points. Children learn concrete representation in this way.

3. Broadening. This refers to the broadening of concepts. Relevant characteristics are sought in various examples, comparisons are made (What are the similarities, and what are the differences?), and more difficult examples are introduced. Language plays an important role in comparison. The teacher draws heavily on the children's own experience in the comparisons and helps the children take more and more distance. The teacher begins to ask distance questions. He or she reminds them about things that have happened previously and refers to things that are not actually present or that have not yet happened.

4. Deepening. This last step aims to encourage the child to use what he or she has learned by demonstration and broadening in new and often more difficult situations. Some of these situations will be familiar and some will not. Children must learn to solve problems by themselves. The business of thinking things out plays an important role alongside sensory experience and language. By going into more depth,

ACTIVITY FROM BROADENING

CLEAN AND DIRTY WATER

Put out three tubs of clean water on a large plastic sheet.

Ask the children if the water in the tubs is clean or dirty.

Ask what we can use clean water for (washing, drinking, cooking, etc.).

Then ask them how water can get dirty (bathing in it, washing dishes, pollution).

Break the children into three groups, one for each tub of water.

Give each group ingredients to make their water dirty.

The first group will wash some dirty dishes with soap.

The second group will clean off some paintbrushes.

The third group will add dirt, small stones, and leaves.

Let the children look in all three containers and talk about what they notice.

Next ask the children how we might be able to make the water clean again.

Try pouring some of the water from each tub through coffee filters or cheesecloth and ask the children what they observe.

Do it several times and see what happens to the water the more times it gets filtered.

Put the jars of filtered water in the Discovery Center with magnifying glasses so children can look more closely at the water.

Finish by reading *Harry the Dirty Dog* by Gene Zion.

*Intent: Observe and compare clean and dirty water * Work collaboratively with others * Demonstrate understanding of filtering water * Follow story sequence * Expand vocabulary*

children learn to be flexible in using what they have learned and experienced. They learn to switch between different senses and between different types of representations. "Distance" questions become the main type of question asked. The teacher allows the children to anticipate new situations. He or she encourages them to reflect on what they have learned and to draw

ACTIVITY FROM DEEPENING

HOW DOES WATER CHANGE THINGS?

On a large plastic sheet in the middle of the circle place an assortment of items such as a piece of dark cotton cloth, a sheet of aluminum foil, a piece of tissue paper, a coffee filter, a plastic container lid, a piece of waxed paper, several sugar cubes, a facial tissue, a piece of paper towel, and a small bowl of cooking oil.

Talk with the children about each item and ask what they know about it.

Tell them you are going to experiment to see how water affects each of the items.

Let one child use an eyedropper to wet the first item.

Observe and discuss any changes that occur.

Before each of the next experiments, ask children to predict what they think will happen.

When you have experimented with all of the items, ask the children to help you put them in order from things the water affected least to things the water affected most.

*Intent: Predict the effect of water on various substances * Test predictions through hands-on experimentation * Observe the effects of water on various substances * Discuss the ways water affects things * Expand knowledge of properties of water*

conclusions from what they have experienced (metacognition). In this way representations become more complex and abstract. These representations are necessary for future learning. To go more deeply into a subject, a certain amount of knowledge is necessary to ask the most appropriate "distance" questions and to provide the most suitable answers.

In taking the initiative the teacher is supported by a wide range of educational tools designed to motivate children each step of the way. During the first step, the teacher assumes that the group does not have much information about the subject. He or she gives examples and instructions. During subsequent steps the teacher motivates the children to use what has been learned by providing (expert) scaffolding. This enables the children to make use of their deeper knowledge and reflection in other learning activities and helps them to think independently.

In connection with the projects we offer the picture book *Interactive Storytelling*. From research (Stoep & van Elsäcker, 2005) it became clear that "reading" picture books more than once in a structured manner is more effective than reading them only once. In the Pyramid Method we use a picture book along with each project book that is related to the project focus. Together with the proficiencies needed for interactive storytelling (psychological space), we use the four project steps to elaborate the storytelling in an interactive way. The same is true for activities for gifted children. Gifted children mostly need steps such as broadening and deepening on a high level. They are also connected to the project. These activities are enrichments of the projects. For practicing projects on an individual level, we make use of many digital materials. Children work with one or two computers in the classroom.

Long-Term Cycle. For children between the ages of $2\frac{1}{2}$ and $6\frac{1}{2}$ years—the period of representation (Fischer & Rose, 1998)—a 3-year plan is implemented. Each year Pyramid begins with a welcome program followed by 12 projects that are carried out every 2 or 3 weeks. The youngest group ($2\frac{1}{2}$ to 4 years), the middle

Toos van Kuyk

The Pyramid Method includes an emphasis on emotional learning; the capacity to sense one's own emotions and the emotions of others and to conduct oneself in a social way.

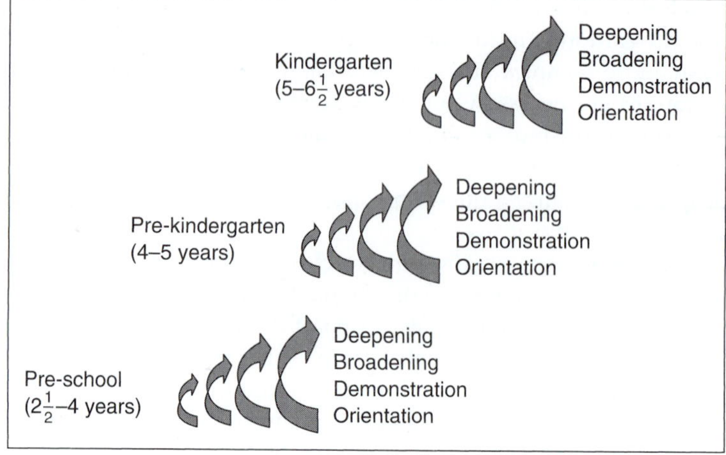

FIGURE 17–7 Short-Term and Long-Term Cycle in the Pyramid Projects
(See also Fischer & Rose, 1998)

groups (4 to 5 years), and the older groups (5 to $6\frac{1}{2}$ years and 6 to 7 years) explore the same focus. Each year the teacher and children expand on the level of distancing (Figure 17–7): In the beginning it is closely connected to the child's world of experience and his or her needs; later he or she has to imagine more distance from the here and now. The children learn and relearn to make representations at an increasingly higher level and with greater complexity and abstraction.

4. SEQUENTIAL PROGRAMS

In a sequential program, the teacher finds activities that the children learn in particular developmental areas, ranging from easy to difficult. This takes place in the context of either a large or a small group and requires a great deal of concentration. The teacher takes the initiative to give children tasks from the projects and sequential programs.

Sequenced Activities

The sequenced activities in the projects are designed for children between the ages of 4 and 6 years. The activities are related to these areas:

- Fine motor development, drawing, and writing skills
- Language development and preparation for reading and writing
- Thinking and math development
- Orientation of space and time and discovering the world

These activities are derived from sequential programs. In the projects, they are organized according to degree of difficulty and are placed in the context of the project focus. Sequenced activities are mainly carried out in the sequential circle. In this circle, which usually does not last long, sequenced activities are learned, practiced, and repeated.

The Sequential Programs

Sequential programs have been developed (or are being developed) for each developmental area. The programs include activities of increasing levels of difficulty. They are not tied to specific projects and can, in fact, be used in all contexts or used independently of context. The hierarchical structure provides a reference point for those project activities in which all developmental areas are connected. As we have indicated, sequenced activities are also built into the projects. These activities follow the order given in the year program. This makes it possible to include sequenced activities in the projects using the criterion as degrees of difficulty. Sequenced activities are rooted in the sequential programs. In the projects designed for the youngest children ($2\frac{1}{2}$ to 4 years), no separate sequenced activities are included. The sequential activities of all developmental areas are built in the project books. In fact, the sequential programs deliver a sequential framework for the projects in which all the developmental areas are connected (van Kuyk, 2006).

5. THE TUTOR PROGRAM

The tutor program is a mirror of the group exploration in the project book. Slavin et al. (1994) have shown that tutoring is effective, and that the best tutoring is directly connected to the daily program and is preventive. In the Pyramid Method we use tutoring not only in primary school for learning to read but also in the youngest groups (3 to 6 years) on a broader basis. The same four steps as in the group exploration are used to challenge the tutored children. Prior to group exploration, a special teacher tutors children, mostly individually, creating a positive spiral so that the children feel more involved in the group activities. They receive extra and more intensive learning time. The activities are performed informally with play, a lot of action, and intensive use of the senses. Children who do not receive enough preventive tutoring and have yet to master the basic concepts in that project will then receive remedial tutoring after each project.

6. THE PARENT PROGRAM

The parent program provides strong support for the Pyramid Model and runs parallel with the yearly projects. Parent involvement is important. This has been shown in the metastudy conducted by Royce, Darlington, and Murray (1983). The educational task is shared by school and parents (Gestwicki, 1987). Parent activities are important: They are the manifestations of the cooperation between education at home and at school. Parents can help to extend the child's play and learning time, which can have an important effect on child development, showing that effective educational aspects support each other to create optimum development.

Parents can be involved in the following ways:

- The teacher makes an annual parent plan outlining the various interrelated parent activities.
- Every morning during "open-house play" parents are free to play with their children in the classroom. This links the education at home with the education in the preschool, pre-kindergarten, and kindergarten.
- At the beginning of each year, a parent week is held, during which parents work with their own child in the group after the teacher has demonstrated an activity: for example, interactive reading aloud (storytelling) or explaining an assignment. These activities may be continued in the home environment.
- In the welcome program, offered at the beginning of the year and for all projects, parents take home play and learning activities to extend the children's play and learning time at home. These activities enhance the project activities in the group or classroom. If necessary, instruction is given in the parents' own language. Parents are also encouraged to provide their children with theme-related materials, including materials that are part of their specific culture, to take to school with them.

The involvement of parents in the project activities creates a special "binding agent." Children benefit frequently and permanently from activities that can be carried out in the home environment. Open-house play and the discovery table, which accompany each project theme, introduce parents to the project theme in a very visible way.

EVALUATION

In the Pyramid Method we work toward optimizing the child's development. It seems obvious, therefore, that we should follow the development of each child over the whole Pyramid period and, where possible, improve the education process. In doing so, we take note of the children's behavior (Can the child work independently?) and the results achieved (e.g., vocabulary expansion). We study both the individual child and the whole group. We refer to this as *child assessment.* We also approach the evaluation process from the perspective of the teacher. How does the teacher interact with the children (Is he or she available for each child? Is he or she capable of organizing the process in such a way that the children are able to achieve good results?). We refer to this as *teacher evaluation.* We then ask ourselves whether the Pyramid Method is a valid method and worth using in practice (Is it as good as or better than other methods when compared with control or reference groups?). We refer to this as *program evaluation.* We describe the procedures we use to perform these necessary evaluations. Assessment is integrated into the entire Pyramid Method as it affects children between the ages of 3 and 6 years.

CHILD ASSESSMENT

Child assessment is the most important of the three evaluation processes and helps us support the child's learning process. We perform this in a balanced way. In the Pyramid Method, children develop through play and learn both from taking initiatives themselves and through the initiatives undertaken by their teacher. A balanced assessment is sought to reveal how development takes place in each developmental area and how well the objectives or teacher aims are achieved. Development steps, described for each developmental area, provide a good reference point in evaluating play and initiative learning. The objectives described in the program aims are used to evaluate the learning process initiated by the teacher. We have selected evaluation procedures that best suit these two processes.

Authentic and Individual Assessment

To come as close as possible to what the child does, we use reliable procedures that focus on the individual child. These are procedures that fit into the child's natural play-learning environment. We examine the child's actual behavior: How does the child behave, and what are the child's achievements (Figure 17–8)? In this way we are able to come close to the uniqueness of the individual child, the child's creativity, and the child's own "learning power," as formulated by Piaget (1970).

Systematic and Communal Assessment

To ascertain the extent to which the children have realized the objectives set for them, we use systematic, standardized procedures that relate to all children to the same degree. We look at their behavior and achievements to measure how they use their own initiative and how much they rely on the initiative of their teacher.

Instruments

In conducting the various evaluations we make use of several different instruments, since no single instrument is suitable for all goals. Each instrument has advantages and disadvantages. We also look at the quality of the instruments, the importance of the decisions reached, the period to which they apply,

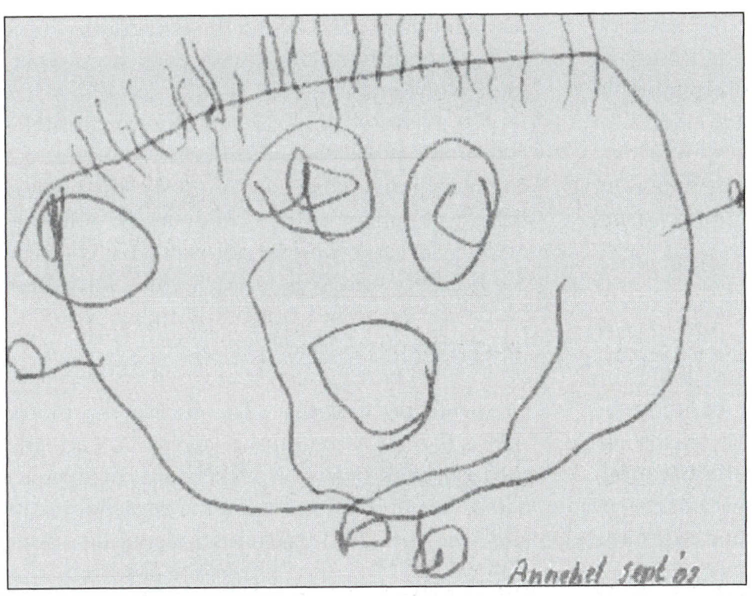

FIGURE 17–8 Portfolio: Child's Drawing

and the consequences they have. The quality criteria are reliability (each teacher comes to the same result), validity (to measure what should be measured), and practicality (easy collection of information over a short period of time). More than 2,000 teachers have tested the practicality of these instruments and the Cito (International Institute for Educational Assessment, based in The Netherlands, also established in the United States as Cito USA) has studied their reliability and validity using Item Response Theory (Eggen & Sanders, 1993). We use observation scales and tests that require decisions made over a longer period of time. These instruments are used to support both relational and educational decision making. The three types of evaluation—daily evaluation, half-yearly evaluation, and diagnostic evaluation—use different procedures. These are tailored to specific functions and involve as few disadvantages as possible (subjectivity is maintained in observation by making observation scales and using computer-assisted testing to prevent subjectivity in data collection).

Daily Evaluation

Daily evaluation takes place in the everyday, natural environment of the group. In the Pyramid Method, both the child's behavior and the results he or she has achieved are assessed.

Observation. As he or she works, the teacher uses his or her relational and educational knowledge to observe the child. As far as the relational component is concerned, the focus falls on safety, autonomy, emotional support, structure, and rules. In the educative component, the activities that the child undertakes on his or her own initiative, such as playing and initiative learning, are emphasized. The teacher also observes the child during group exploration sessions as he or she carries out tasks.

Recordkeeping and Portfolio. The teacher keeps a register of what each child has done. To maintain an overview of work the child produces, the teacher keeps a portfolio and collects examples of the work made on the child's own initiative. This can be anything related to art development, such as drawings and three-dimensional objects (digital photographs are useful here), as well as written pieces or products related to beginning literacy, numeracy, and discovery. Each half year the most important pieces of work are taken out of the portfolio and saved in the archive portfolio.

Half-Yearly Evaluation

Twice a year the teacher takes time off from everyday duties and assesses the children by using observation scales and performing some digital tests with the children in a student monitoring system (Figure 17–9). This assessment focuses on each child's behavior and what the child has learned from the initiatives undertaken by the teacher, for example, from the projects and sequenced activities. The objective of this evaluation is to find out what the child has learned, or whether the program that the child has followed during the last 6 months should be adjusted. The teacher will also note the children should receive tutoring in the coming 6 months (25% lowest-scoring children). Assessment takes place over a longer period of time and has important consequences as far as tutoring is concerned.

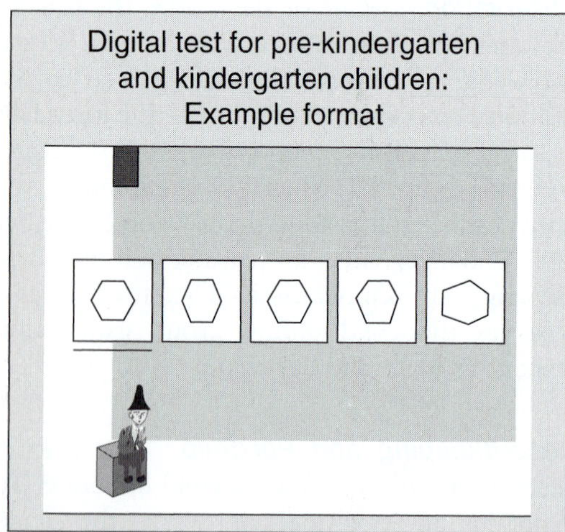

FIGURE 17–9 Digital Test for Pre-Kindergarten and Kindergarten Children

In assessing physical and emotional intelligence, we make use of observation scales; for cognitive intelligence, we use tests. In this way the development of the child can be followed every half year. Using set norms we can compare the behavior and skills of each child with those he or she possessed 6 months earlier and with the norms of reference group.

Observation Scales. To observe the motor skills, the social-emotional development, and the play-work behavior of the child, the teacher uses two observation scales: the preschool scale and the pre-kindergarten/kindergarten scale (Figure 17–10). All children are observed.

Digital Tests. The three digital tests for cognitive intelligence are language development and the development of reading, the development of thinking and numeracy, and orientation of space and time.

Data gathered from the tests allow us to follow the development of each individual child and of the group as a whole in the same way, and to identify which children require tutoring according to set procedures. This is a long-term computerized monitoring system.

Adaptive Tests. After extensive research into whether it was actually possible for children to take a digital test, computer tests for young children were developed. Children like working with the computer as they can concentrate on the tasks. The tests are adaptive, so the children only do those assignments that are appropriate to their skill level; they are not given tasks that are either too difficult or too easy for them. In addition, the computer ensures that the procedure is objective and the same for each child and not influenced by differences in interpretation on the part of the teachers. Extensive research has shown that young

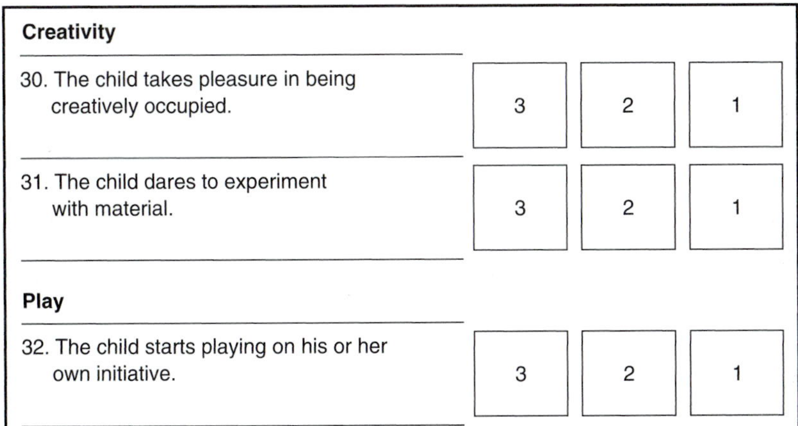

Creativity			
30. The child takes pleasure in being creatively occupied.	3	2	1
31. The child dares to experiment with material.	3	2	1
Play			
32. The child starts playing on his or her own initiative.	3	2	1

FIGURE 17–10 Example from the Preschool Observation Scale

children can work easily with a computer mouse and that, after practicing with a mouse module and with the help of a funny figure that keeps motivating and supporting them (a virtual coach called Primo), they can easily complete the test themselves. Registration and the making of graphs and tables can be automatically generated when the computer program developed by Cito is used. According to the Netherlands Institute for Psychology (NIP), these tests conform to a high standard.

Information from the preschool scale illustrated in Figure 17–10 is another tool to enable the teacher to follow the development of each child in the same way.

Diagnostic Evaluation

Although in general the procedures we have mentioned appear to be satisfactory and allow us to follow the child's development and make decisions, other diagnostic instruments are available for exceptional cases and difficult problems. These are useful when a teacher is not certain how to proceed with a particular child.

Diagnostic Interview. A diagnostic interview is used to develop a picture of the child's behavior.

Observation Programs. The teacher can use any or all of three observation programs to establish how far the child has come in the cognitive domain: language development (language fun), development of thinking (ordering), and orientation of space (orientation of space).

The observation programs are criterion (not norm) referenced: What has the child mastered, and what has he or she yet to master? On the basis of this diagnosis, the teacher draws up a plan of action.

TEACHER EVALUATION

The teacher evaluation focuses on the way the teacher deals with each child (relational component) and the extent to which she optimizes the development of each child (educational component). Teachers working with the Pyramid Method receive a professional training from a certified Pyramid trainer. The training takes 18 days and is spread over a period of 2 years.

During the Training

During the training the teacher is coached on the "work floor." In order to carry out the training in an effective way the trainer makes use of the Pyramid Implementation Assessment (PIA). This instrument covers all the relevant objectives of the Pyramid Method and is presented in an easily recognizable way. Trainer and trainee can decide together how they will work to optimize the skills that the trainer can observe.

After the Training

After the training has been completed, it is necessary to keep these skills up to date. Pyramid has developed a Web-based competence "mirror," known as the Pyramid Competence Mirror (PCM), for this purpose. This instrument in based on the PIA. All trained teachers can check the status of their skills on the basis of eight competencies. Teachers are confronted with a number of questions that address both the desired behavior, as well as the actual behavior, displayed by the children. The instrument is available from the Cito Web site: http://www.cito.com.

PROGRAM EVALUATION

Evaluation is an important dimension of the Pyramid Method and is done internally, as well as externally.

Internal Evaluation

Within the school system, internal evaluation is an acceptable procedure. Schools can evaluate their own teaching with the help of the Pyramid instruments (curriculum independent) developed by Cito. At a higher level of aggregation, the standardized tests can be used to establish results from a school; groups of schools; a municipality; or a random, national sample of schools. In this way a child's development can be followed over a period of 3 years. Using the computer program from Cito, available data can be aggregated to a higher level. It is, therefore, easy for each school and municipality to use the computer to discover the effectiveness of the Pyramid Method for themselves.

Figure 17–11 illustrates a scale used to establish the results of an internal evaluation. From the scale we can read not only average results but also the distribution of results set against a national reference group whose norms are already established.

Based on the graph in Figure 17–11, it appears that at pre-test 75% of children who started the Pyramid Method when they were 3 years old were at the E or D level compared with a national reference group. At the end of the experiment, following a period of 3 years, this percentage had been reduced to 25%. This is a decrease of 50% of at-risk children. In a period of 3 years, children in a Pyramid program achieve a result that is roughly the average level of the reference group. Children who started later—when they were age 4 or 5—also scored D or E level initially but went on to achieve good results, although to a more limited extent than the group that followed the Pyramid program for 3 years. It is clear that children who follow the whole program from beginning to end have the best results. The same conclusions can be reached when examining performance on ordering and the space and time tests.

Conclusion. Children should begin at age 3 and remain with the Pyramid Method over the whole period of 3 years. In this way, children accelerate in development leading to better opportunities for a successful primary school education. This does not mean that only low-scoring children profit. Comparing the children at the beginning of the experiment who scored D and E (lowest 25% in the reference group) less likely to be successful and A, B, and C (highest 75% in the reference group) best chance to be successful on mathematics, 60% of children were at D and E levels and 40% of A, B, and C levels. After 3 years the percentage of D and E children was 21% (lower than in the

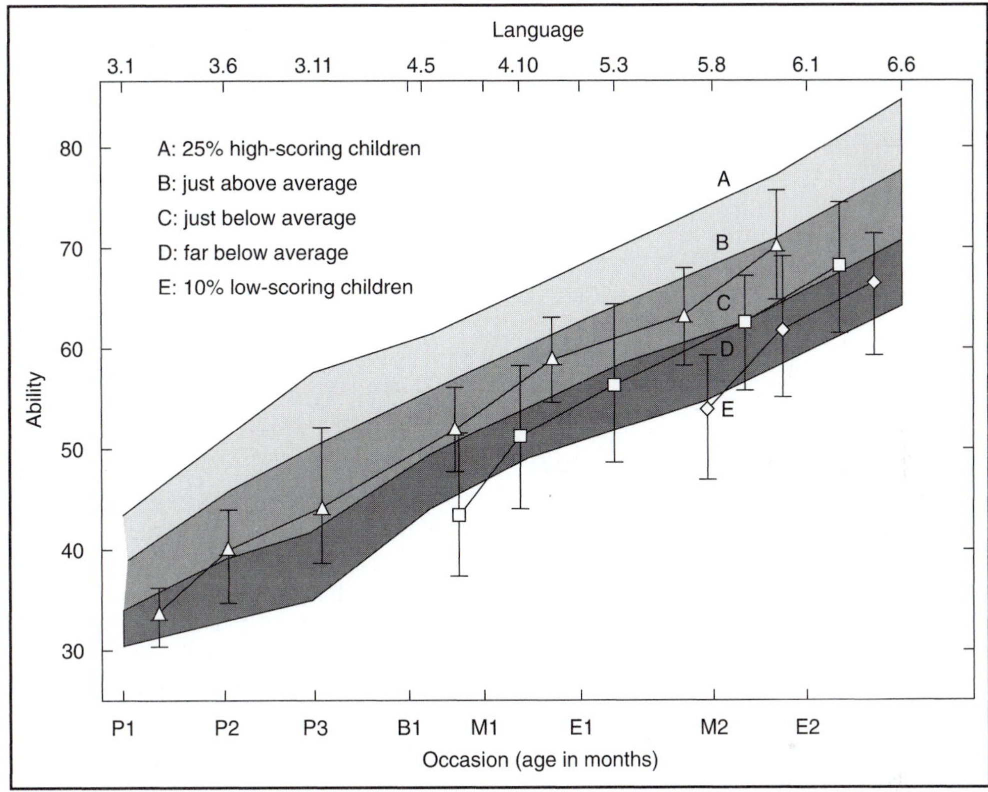

FIGURE 17–11 Language Results, Means, and Variations

reference group) and the percentage of A, B, and C children was 79%, higher than in the reference group. More children than in the reference group have chances to be successful. Thus we conclude that the Pyramid program works for at-risk children and for successful children.

Tutor Evaluation

Important questions to ask are, Is the program efficacious, and what role does tutoring play in ameroliating risk? To examine the effectiveness of tutoring, an assessment designed with a pre-test and post-test design was selected. We looked at all the children who took part in the Pyramid Method for a half year. For all these children, the ability scores (language, thinking, and space and time) are known. These scores are the pre-test. Part of this group was given tutoring in the period following this pre-test (experimental group); another part was not (control group). A half year later the children were tested again (the post-test). If tutoring is effective, then in the experimental group, the percentage of at-risk children (E and D scores) should be considerably lower in the post-test than in the pre-test. In the control group the percentages should be about equal. If the percentages decrease only in the experimental group, we can conclude that the effect is caused by tutoring (Figure 17–12).

FIGURE 17–12 Pre-Test and Post-Test Percentages of Risk Children (Tutored and Not Tutored)

	No Tutoring (n = 855)		Tutoring (n = 219)	
	Pre-test	Post-test	Pre-test	Post-test
Thinking	43.2	41.6	74.4	53.4
Language	48.1	48.4	88.1	73.5
Space and time	51.2	48.9	84.4	74.0

It is clear that the percentage of children at risk in the experimental group dropped considerably. There is no such drop in the control group. We can therefore conclude that tutoring is indeed effective.

External Evaluation

1. National Experiment To be able to present acceptable research findings, it is better to have an external evaluation carried out by independent researchers. The University of Amsterdam and the University of Groningen have made a study of the Pyramid Method at the request of the Ministry of Health and the Ministry of Education. The university researchers carried out their study in preschools (3–4 years), prekindergarten groups (4–5 years), and kindergartens (5–6 years) with a relatively high proportion of children from disadvantaged backgrounds, which included a significant number of migrant children. The researchers studied the level of implementation (Groningen) and effectiveness (Amsterdam) of the Pyramid Method and an American method adapted to the situation in The Netherlands: the High Scope (Kaleidoscope) Method (Homann & Weikart, 1995). Children who needed extra support were given an extra teacher for four sessions a week (Kaleidoscope) or a tutor (Pyramid). The research was carried out between 1996 and 1999. The results were compared to those of a control group.

From the results it appears that the level of implementation of both approaches was high and that the level of involvement of the children in educational activities was very high (85%). However, the researchers did have a number of critical comments. In the Pyramid Method, it was concluded that language development—given its focus in children from disadvantaged backgrounds—was not emphasized enough in the programs available. The steps in group exploration, designed to increase breadth and depth, were insufficient and not sufficiently clear.

The Pyramid Method—as did of learning the Kaleidoscope Method—has weak to strong positive effect in reducing educational risk in young children. In terms of effect sizes, using criteria suggested by Cohen (.20 = weak; .50 = moderate, .80 = strong), it appeared that language and reading development, when compared to the control group, was weak to moderate. Kaleidoscope had a somewhat better effect. In the areas of thought and numeracy, development outcomes were better for the Pyramid Method than for the Kaleidoscope Method. Perhaps in both the Pyramid and the Kaleidoscope Programs intervention should begin earlier in the child's development and continue for longer periods.

2. Amsterdam Assessments—Preschool and Kindergarten. Between 1998 and 2000, after the National Experiment, a similar study was carried out in Amsterdam by the University

Pre-school Experiment Amsterdam University Groningen			
Cohen effect: .20 = weak; .50 = moderate; .80 = strong			
Pyramid		Kaleidoscope (Highscope)	
From pre-school		From preschool	
Language		Language	
Language test 3–6 years	.81	Language test 3–6 years	.38
Thinking		Thinking	
Ordering 3–6 years	.72	Ordering 3–6 years	.35

FIGURE 17–13 Preschool—Kindergarten Experiment, Amsterdam

of Groningen. The necessary improvements had been introduced into the Pyramid Method: A new language approach had been incorporated into the projects with a specific structure for vocabulary development, and the steps toward broadening and deepening in group exploration in the project books had been made more explicit. Children who needed extra support were given an extra teacher or provided tutoring. This study involved preschool (3–4 years), pre-kindergarten (4–5 years), and kindergarten children (5–6 years) with a high proportion of disadvantaged children (Figure 17–13).

Based on the study it seemed that children enrolled in the Pyramid Method had better language development than their comparisons. The effect sizes for the Kaleidoscope Method was weak to moderate. As for the development of thinking, the effect size for the Pyramid Method was good and for the Kaleidoscope Method was weak to moderate. From observational data, it appeared that neither the extra teachers (Kaleidoscope) nor the extra tutors (Pyramid) had been able to function effectively. Pyramid appeared to be a robust method that can be effectively used in less favorable circumstances.

3. Prima Cohort Study. In a study searching for best practices, the Amsterdam local authorities and the University of Amsterdam used the findings from the Prima Cohort study (Veen, Roeleveld, & van Daalen, 2005) and selected 30 Amsterdam schools that work with a concept to support at-risk children, most of them were children of immigrants. The majority of these Amsterdam schools work with the Pyramid Method, a smaller number with High Scope, and one with Reggio Emilia and other approaches. In the investigation, the results of the Amsterdam schools were compared with the National Cohort sample. From the 30 Amsterdam schools that participated in the Prima Cohort Study, 10 schools had data from 3-year-old children (primary school starts at 4 years). In the study the results of the Amsterdam schools were compared with the National Cohort Study of the 6-year-old children. All children participated in language and math assessments and three observation sessions focusing on behaviour, work attitude, and self-confidence.

The achievements of the Amsterdam schools with large numbers of at-risk children were lower than the national reference group; however, when the data were examined in a multi-level model, the results of the Amsterdam schools were even higher than the national average. The 10 schools that worked with an intensive program, such as the Pyramid Method or High Scope, scored $\frac{1}{3}$ standard deviation higher than the national average (see Figure 17–14).

Test	Uncontrolled	Controlled	Intensive
Language	−6	+0.1	+2.8
Thinking	−2.5	+1.5	+.2

FIGURE 17–14 Results in Uncontrolled, Controlled, and Intensive Programs in a National Cohort Study

On average, children in the experimental group had better work attitude than children in the reference group. The six best-achieving Amsterdam schools were selected as "best-practice schools," to be investigated on "best-practice" characteristics. The key question was, how can we explain the results of those best-achieving schools (the qualitative part of the investigation)? Invariably, the "best-practice schools" were overwhelmingly viewed in a positive light on 26 "best-practice characteristics" (60% of the questions as positive, only 4% as negative). Of the six best-scoring schools with best practices, five were Pyramid Schools and one was a High Scope school. It was concluded that most of the Pyramid schools proved to have "best practices."

CONCLUSION

In all four studies the Pyramid Method was shown to have positive effects on developmental outcome measures. We see these effects (in the same positive direction) in the local studies also. The Pyramid Method, therefore, appears to be an effective and practical method that aids teachers in implementing successful preschool and kindergarten education. Pyramid is a robust method that can be applied in favorable and less favorable situations. The method is more effective when tutoring is applied.

Pyramid is a balanced method offering optimal opportunities for children to develop themselves: balance in initiative of the child and initiative of the teacher; in the relational and educational components; in content (three intelligences are developed in a holistic concept); in the possibilities of children (at-risk children are reached as well as bright children); and, last but not least, balance in evaluation procedures (authentic enough for teachers to assess their own characteristics and the creativity of the children and systematic enough to see if the aims of the teacher are realized).

RESOURCES

The Power of Pyramid Principles:
http://www.pyramidprinciples.com

Cito:
http://www.cito.com

For educationally appropriate materials:
http://www.nienhuis.com

Cito USA Inc.
931 Monroe Dr. NE, Ste.A-102-315
Atlanta, GA 30308
Phone: 1-801-815-9247
Fax: 1-404-601-6853
E-mail: support.usa@cito.com

van Kuyk, Jef. J., 2003. *Pyramid: The Method for Young Children*, Arnhem, The Netherlands: Cito.

REFERENCES

Ainsworth, M. D. S., Blehar, M. C., & Waters, E. (1978). *Patterns of attachment: A psychological study of the strange situation.* Hillsdale, NJ: Erlbaum.

Bowlby, J. (1969). *Attachment and loss. Vol. 1.* London, England: Hogarth Press.

Bowman, B. T., Donovan, M. S., & Burns, M. S. (2001). *Eager to learn: Educating our preschoolers.* Washington, DC: National Academy Press.

Cocking, R. R., & Renninger, K. A. (Eds.). (1993). *The development and meaning of psychological distance.* Hillsdale, NJ: Erlbaum.

Eggen, T. J. H. M., & Sanders, P. F. (ed.), (1993). *Psychometrie in de praktijk* [Psychometrics in practice]. Arnhem, The Netherlands: Cito.

Erickson, M. F., Sroufe, L. A., & Egeland, B. (1985). The relationship between quality of attachment and behavior problems in preschool in a high-risk sample. In I. Bretherton & E. Waters (Eds.), *Growing points of attachement theory and research.* Monographs of the society for research in child development, *50,* 147–166.

Fischer, K. W., & Bidell, T. R. (2006). *Dynamic development in action and thought.* In W. Damon & R. M. Lerner (Eds.), *Handbook of child psychology.* New York: Wiley, chapter 7.

Fischer, K. W., & Rose, S. P. (1998). Growth cycles of brain and mind. In *Educational Leadership, 56*(3), 56–60.

Gardner, H. (1993). *Multiple intelligences: The theory in practice.* New York: Basic Books.

Gestwicki, C. (1987). *Home, school, and community relations: A guide to working with parents.* Albony, NY: Delmar.

Homann, M., & Weikart, D. P. (1995). *Educating young children.* Ypsilanti, MI: High/Scope Educational Research Foundation.

Piaget, J. (1970). *Genetic epistemology.* New York: Columbia University Press.

Pressley, M., Hogan, K., Wharton-McDonald, R., & Mistretta, J. (1996). The challenges of instructional scaffolding: The challenges of instruction that supports student thinking. *Learning Disabilities Research & Practices, 11,* 138–146.

Royce, J. M., Darlington, R. B., & Murray, H. W. (1983). Pooled analyses: Findings across studies. In *The Consortium for Longitudinal Studies. As the Twig is bent . . . Lasting Effects of preschool programs.* Hillsdale, NJ: Erlbaum.

Salovay, P., & Mayer, J. D. (1990). Emotional intelligence. *Imagination, Cognition, and Personality, 9,* 185–211.

Shonkoff, J. P., & Philips, D. A. (Eds.). (2000). *From neurons to neighborhoods: The science of early childhood development.* Washington, DC: National Academy Press.

Sigel, I. E. (1993). The centrality of a distancing model for the development of representational competence. In R. R. Cocking & K. A. Renninger (Eds.), *The development and meaning of psychological distance.* Hillsdale, NJ: Erlbaum, 141–158.

Slavin, R. E., Madden, N. A., & Karweit, N. L., (1994). Success for all: A comprehensive approach to prevention and early intervention. In R. E. Slavin, N. L. Karweit, & B. A. Wasik (Eds.), *Preventing early school failure: Research, policy and practice.* Boston: Allyn & Bacon.

Stoep, J., & van Elsäcker, W. (2005). *Peuters interactief met taal. De taallijn VVE: Taalstimulering voor jonge kinderen* [Preschool children, interactive with language. The Language Line]. Nijmegen: Expertisecentrum Nederlands.

van Geert, P. (1998). *A dynamic systems model of basic developmental mechanisms: Piaget, Vygotsky, and beyond.* In *Psychological Review, 105*(4), 634–677.

van Kuyk, J. J. (2003). *Pyramid: The method for young children* (English version). Arnhem, The Netherlands: Cito.

van Kuyk, J. J. (2006). *Holistic or sequential approach to curriculum: what works best for young children?* In J. J. van Kuyk. *The quality of early childhood education.* Arnhem, The Netherlands: Cito.

Veen, A., Roeleveld, J., & van Daalen, M. (2005). *Op zoek naar 'Best Practice': Opbrengsten van de Amsterdamse Voorscholen.* [In search for 'Best Practice': Results of Amsterdam preschools and kindergartens]. Amsterdam: SCO-Kohnstamm Instituut.

Vygotsky, L. (1962). *Thought and language.* Cambridge, MA: MIT Press.

Author Index

Subject Index